End-User Information Systems

Implementing Individual and Work Group Technologies

End-User Information Systems

Implementing Individual and Work Group Technologies

SECOND EDITION

Elizabeth A. Regan, Ph.D.
Morehead State University

Bridget N. O'Connor, Ph.D.
New York University

Prentice Hall

Upper Saddle River, NJ 07458

Regan, Elizabeth Ann.
    End-user information systems : implementing individual and work group technologies /
Elizabeth A. Regan, Bridget N. O'Connor.—2nd ed.
      p. cm.
Includes bibliographical references and index.
ISBN 0-13-018264-8
    1. Management information systems.   2. End-user computing.   I. O'Connor, Bridget N.,
    1952- II. Title.
HD30.213.R44 2001
658.4'038'011—dc21

00-044607

Acquisitions Editors: *Robert Horan and David Alexander*
Editor-in-Chief: *Mickey Cox*
Associate Editor: *Lori Cerreto*
Editorial Assistant: *Erika Rusnak*
Media Project Manager: *Nancy Welcher*
Senior Marketing Manager: *Sharon Turkovich*
Marketing Assistant: *Jason Smith*
Production Manager: *Gail Steier de Acevedo*
Production Coordinator: *Kelly Warsak*
Permissions Coordinator: *Suzanne Grappi*
Associate Director, Manufacturing: *Vincent Scelta*
Manufacturing Buyer: *Natacha St. Hill Moore*
Cover Design: *Majory Dressler*
Cover Illustration: *Majory Dressler*
Composition: *BookMasters, Inc.*
Full-Service Project Management: *BookMasters, Inc.*
Printer/Binder: *Hamilton Printing Company*
Cover Printer: *Coral Graphics*

10 9 8 7 6 5 4 3 2 1
ISBN 0-13-018264-8

Dedication

To my husband Charles, my children Keith, Meredith, and Deanne,
and my family, friends, and associates who have encouraged
me throughout this endeavor.

Elizabeth A. Regan

To my husband Michael Bronner, my sounding board and greatest
supporter, who has enriched my life so very much.

Bridget N. O'Connor

CONTENTS

PART III   END-USER INFORMATION SYSTEMS: IMPLEMENTATION AND SUPPORT   205

Contents

Contents

Contents

Preface

In this second edition of *End-User Information Systems: Implementing Individual and Work Group Technologies,* we continue our examination into how technologies are impacting not only organizations, but also the individuals and groups who integrate technologies to support the work they do. What does the information systems professional or manager who is responsible for planning and implementing new information systems-based work tools need to know about this dynamic field? What are these new tools? How can they support specific business objectives? What people-related issues are involved and how do managers address them? How can information technology improve individual and group performance? How can it be used to streamline work flow and improve business processes? What do you need to know to ensure that the right technologies are used in the right way by the right people?

Throughout the text, we emphasize the need to *improve business performance,* not merely to automate existing procedures. We believe that the successful implementation of technology is a management issue. Toward this end, end-user information systems (EUIS) is viewed as a catalyst for innovative problem solving. We bring to bear a wealth of experience on improving performance in the workplace. Thus, this text is designed to develop an understanding of business applications and organizational development as well as technology. It is intended to bring the impact of high-level talk about communications tools and business process redesign to the practical level of implementation at the desktop where it counts most.

As both practitioners and academics, we bring together the best of two worlds: a strong conceptual framework and good, practical know-how. Our combined years of experience and study of the field have resulted in a unique textbook that addresses the need for effective planning, use, and management of information technologies at all levels of the organization. Our goal here is not only to describe the *what* and *how* of EUIS but also the *why.*

Thus, the purpose of this book is to provide a balanced discussion of the technological and managerial issues related to integrating information systems into the workplace. Using information technology is not the same thing as integrating it into work processes. Integrating means changing the way work is done to improve workplace performance. It is not a one-shot solution but an evolving, continuous process. This text acknowledges that process and identifies not only the technology but also the need for systems professionals, managers, and end users to work together to understand their corporate culture and business requirements. This is the only way to ensure effective solutions. *End-User Information Systems: Implementing Individual and Work Group Technologies* is appropriate for information systems courses related to end-user information systems, systems analysis and design, business process design, the management of information technology, or technology and change management. It meets the requirements for *IS'97.3 Information Systems Theory and Practice* in the IS'97 model undergraduate curriculum co-sponsored by the Association for Computing Machinery (ACM) and the Association of Information Technology Professionals (AITP; formerly DPMA) and *OEIS-1 Organizational and End-user Information Systems Concepts,* and *OEIS-3 & 4 Organizational and End-user Information Systems Planning and Design/ Implementation and Evaluation* in the *Organizational and End-user Information Systems Model Curriculum* sponsored by the Organizational Systems Research Association.

ABOUT THIS BOOK

The book is divided into five parts and sixteen chapters. The parts and chapters are presented in a logical conceptual order, but each unit can be used alone as needed to meet specific instructional objectives. Adopters of this textbook will also have access to an auxiliary chapter, "Trends and Future Directions," which will be available through the Prentice Hall Web site. This online chapter will examine organizational "shifts" and their implications for the future management of information systems.

Part I, "End-User Information Systems: Organizational and Technical Foundations," presents an overview of managerial issues and technologies for end-user information systems. It introduces the concept of using information technology to improve workplace performance. Part I also includes perspectives on understanding the way today's networked organizations operate, thus setting the stage for subsequent chapters.

Part II, "End-User Information Systems: Business Solutions," begins by describing how specific technologies are used by various information or knowledge workers. Software applications appropriate for managers, professional and technical workers, sales and marketing personnel, and administrative support staff are discussed in detail. This second edition also devotes a chapter to work group computing, describing the technologies and the planning required for their successful implementation. The part concludes with a discussion of how Knowledge Management (KM) is permeating all aspects of our work lives and ways in which end users make significant contributions to KM development, implementation, and use.

Part III, "End-User Information Systems: Implementation and Support," covers the theory and practice vital to understanding the impact of information technologies on individuals, groups, and the organization. In this section we examine formal and informal strategies individuals use to apply technologies to their work and communications tasks. We also describe trends and directions related to the management of the Help Desk. This section concludes with an overview of the myriad of technology-related issues facing line managers and end users, including virus protection, encryption systems, and physical security of hardware and software.

Part IV, "Workplace Performance: The Impact of Information Technology on Individuals, Groups, and Organizations," begins by defining productivity, and summarizes strategies for putting hard dollar values on end-user productivity. Human factors of information technologies—hardware, software, and workplace design issues are also overviewed. Theoretical and practical aspects of managing change are examined in regard to the introduction of new technology tools. This part concludes with a discussion of the importance of business process and job design issues and strategies.

Part V, "End-User Information Systems Project Management," describes EUIS project management, a process that is unique to this text. It provides a practical methodology for linking technology implementation to workplace performance. Part V addresses both the theory and practice related to designing and implementing effective EUIS. This part emphasizes issues involved in planning and implementing information technologies and offers practical solutions to problems encountered in the systems analysis process.

FEATURES OF THE BOOK

End-User Information Systems: Implementing Individual and Work Group Technologies includes a wide range of features to facilitate coverage of important topics and ensure readers' understanding.

1. *Objectives.* Each chapter begins by identifying specific behavioral objectives to help the reader focus on key information presented in the chapter.
2. *Discussion Questions.* Each chapter concludes with questions appropriate for generating classroom discussion. The questions require readers to integrate and apply the knowledge gained in each chapter.
3. *Application Exercises.* Each chapter also concludes with enrichment exercises that ask the reader to interview a vendor or end user, investigate an identified problem, or develop a solution to a specific problem. Such activities suggest appropriate field work or library research.
4. *Suggested Readings and Web Sites.* To build on or expand the concepts presented in the chapter, each chapter concludes with a list of readings and Web sites that the reader may pursue for additional information or study.
5. *Spotlight on Solutions.* Interspersed throughout each chapter are illustrations of ways in which the concepts being discussed are applied in organizational settings. These are stories about real people and real organizations.
6. *Practical Approach.* Throughout the text, we've attempted to offer realistic approaches to designing and implementing effective end-user information systems. The text combines practical experience with the latest research findings on EUIS to present a realistic, informed approach to understanding what works and what does not in organizational settings.
7. *Attractive Format.* An attractive format and extensive charts, diagrams, photographs, and illustrations enhance the readability of the text and promote readers' understanding of the material.
8. *New Chapters.* The text includes new chapters on work group computing, Knowledge Management, Help Desk management, and organizational change, topics seldom covered in information systems or computer systems introductory texts. Additionally, chapter 14, "EUIS Project Management: Foundations and Overview," offers the theoretical foundation for a newly expanded and comprehensive project management method that is covered in detail in the following two chapters. New topics mean a new definition of what the systems professional and the line manager should know!
9. *Case Studies.* Case studies are provided at the end of selected chapters and parts. Additional cases will be available on the text Web site.

An instructor's manual with test item file is available to adopters, including a lecture outline, chapter overview, teaching suggestions, and suggested answers to the end-of-chapter questions. Please contact your local Prentice Hall representative to obtain a printed copy. The instructor's manual, without the test item file, is also available for download from the text Web site at www.prenticehall.com/regan. The Web site also features the online chapter, "Trends and Future Directions," PowerPoint slides, additional cases, and links to related Web sites as referenced in the text.

End-User Information Systems: Implementing Individual and Work Group Technologies offers a comprehensive overview of end-user information systems in organizations and emphasizes the evolving roles of the systems analyst, the line manager, and the end user. The text describes technology in a style and format that make the opportunities and risks it presents understandable to the reader. At the same time, the text challenges readers to learn more about this dynamic field and the many career opportunities it provides.

Elizabeth A. Regan
Bridget N. O'Connor

Acknowledgments

We wish to thank the following individuals for reviewing the manuscript, making useful suggestions, or providing other assistance for the development and production of the text: Joel D. Levy, Senior Vice President/CIO, The Segal Company, New York City and Mark Bell, graduate student and instructor at University of Kentucky, Lexington Community College.

In addition, thank you to the following reviewers: Sherri Harms, Lincoln University; Steven Hunt, Morehead State University; Roberto Mejias, The University of Oklahoma; Carol Okolica, Dowling College; and Donald Robertson, Florida Community College.

We also thank the dedicated staff at Prentice Hall: Mickey Cox, Editor-in-Chief; David Alexander, Senior Editor; Bob Horan, Executive Editor; Gail Steier de Acevedo, Production Manager; Kelly Warsak, Production Coordinator; Natacha St. Hill Moore, Manufacturing Buyer; Lori Cerreto, Associate Editor; Sharon Turkovich, Senior Marketing Manager; Nancy Welcher, Media Project Manager; and Erika Rusnak, Editorial Assistant.

The Authors

Elizabeth A. Regan is associate professor and chair of the Department of Information Systems, College of Business, Morehead State University. She holds a Ph.D. from the University of Connecticut. Prior to coming to Morehead 2 years ago, Dr. Regan spent 16 years as a senior consultant and project manager in the Information Systems Division at MassMutual Financial Group. She has a wide range of experience in systems design, implementation, and organizational restructuring. Dr. Regan also taught for 7 years in the University of Connecticut School of Business and as an adjunct professor at New York University. Her research interest are primarily in the area of information technology, strategy, innovation, and change. She is author of numerous articles, publications, and grants related to these topics. She has served as president of the Organizational Systems Research Association and other elected and appointed civic and professional positions. Dr. Regan is a trustee of Andover-Newton Theological School and listed in *Who's Who Among American Women.*

Bridget N. O'Connor is associate professor and director of the Program in Business Education at New York University. Her research and writing activities have focused on the effective application of technologies to support a wide range of individual and group processes both in the workplace and in adult educational programs. She is also co-author of *Training for Organizations* (South-Western Educational Publishing Company, 2nd edition, 2001). She is editor of the *Information Technology, Learning, and Performance Journal* (www.osra.org). She has served as president of the Organizational Systems Research Association and as chair of the Special Interest Group, Workplace Learning, of the American Educational Research Association. She is active in the New York Metropolitan Chapter of the American Society for Training and Development, serving on its newsletter advisory committee. She serves on the board of trustees for American Skandia University. In 1997, she was named "Professor of the Year" for the New York University School of Education.

Part

End-User Information Systems: Organizational and Technical Foundations

Information systems are integral to most contemporary business operations. Personal computers (PCs) have become standard desktop tools in the workplace, whether the location is a traditional office building, a room at home, an automobile, a hotel, or a plane over the Pacific. For many workers, PCs are no longer optional; they have become essential tools. Moreover, the explosive growth of the Internet has changed expectations about what information technologies can and should do for us.

Many young people today take PCs on the desktop for granted. The latest statistics show that more than half of the U.S. population now has a PC at home. It has been barely two short decades, however, since computer systems first started to move out of secluded backroom technical environments and into the workplace. The movement started with word processing, expanded to end-user computing tools, such as query and reporting systems, and exploded in the early 1980s with the introduction of end-user PC software, such as spreadsheets and graphics packages. The Internet is poised to have an even more far-reaching impact.

In many organizations, end users are taking a much larger role in planning and developing information systems. A growing percentage of computing is being done by end users with little or no formal assistance from technical information systems specialists. This practice, called end-user computing, is made possible by the increasingly powerful fourth-generation software tools. With fourth-generation programming languages, graphic languages, PC tools, and Web software, end users can access data, create reports, design Web pages, and create entire information systems on their own, with little or no help from technical systems analysts or programmers.

The area of IS that involves implementing, managing, and supporting computing in the workplace by non-IS technical specialists is called *end-user information systems (EUIS)*. EUIS can be defined as "the application of information technologies to support business processes and individual performance with the objective of improving overall organizational effectiveness in direct support of business goals and strategies."

Some IS texts use the terms *knowledge work systems* (KWS) and *office automation systems* (OAS). However, in our view, the distinctions these terms suggest are no longer valid for the twenty-first-century workplace in which almost everyone has a PC on their desktop. In the typical contemporary enterprise, most routine tasks are automated, job roles have been expanded, and workers at all levels are empowered to make decisions within their scope of responsibility. Most importantly, workers at all levels of the organizational hierarchy, which is a lot flatter than it used to be, have powerful PC platforms on their desktops and are increasingly savvy about using them.

Another term that has emerged recently is *knowledge management* (KM)—the concept of managing organizational knowledge. Not yet well defined, the concept represents a convergence of several previously separate areas such as information resource management, document production, work-flow management, document imaging systems, performance support, training, artificial intelligence, group collaboration systems, and the like. A growing number of new requirements also have emerged in recent years, such as Help Desk, Web site development and maintenance, Intranets, and network administration. EUIS today encompasses this broad spectrum of individual and work group information technologies for knowledge workers at all levels. All of these areas share in common the need for a combination of organizational savvy, business knowledge, and technical competence, but not necessarily computer programming languages. EUIS is the area of IS that addresses the direct connection between technology and its application at the desktop—how end users apply computing skills to do their work and achieve their business results.

Although enterprise computing and transaction processing systems still form the backbone of information systems in most large enterprises, end-user information systems have made their way into the mainstream. EUIS puts business decision makers in the driver's seat instead of technical systems professionals. Although end-user computing has created many benefits, it also poses organizational risks because it occurs largely outside of traditional mechanisms for information systems management and control. The value of end-user information systems and desktop technologies has not been accepted universally among business personnel either, despite their rapid growth. Some detractors argue that the claimed benefits and productivity improvements from the billions invested in end-user technologies are yet to be proved.

Moving computers into the front office next to rubber tree plants and onto desktops has brought with it a unique set of requirements apart from technical considerations. These include the need for greater customization, flexibility, and usability than typical centralized transaction processing systems. Moreover, sociological, organizational, and business factors play a larger role than originally recognized. These and other issues are addressed by end-user information systems.

An understanding of this specialized area of information systems is important for individuals considering careers in management, computer science, management information systems, administrative services, and business education, as well as those preparing for careers in end-user information systems. Individuals charged with responsibility for end-user systems must have broad technical skills combined with an understanding of organizational dynamics, management practice, and business process.

Part I of the text is divided into two chapters. Chapter 1, "Introduction to End-User Information Systems," provides an overview of this specialized area of information systems and discusses the impact of information technology on workplace environments. It offers historical perspective and provides a foundation for understanding work environments. Chapter 1 also explains where EUIS fits into the typical enterprise's information systems organization. Finally, it offers perspectives on career opportunities in this emerging field.

Chapter 2, "Life in Networked Organizations," examines the rapidly expanding impact of information technologies and digital networks on workplace environments—people, processes, and organizational structures. It also looks at implications of the economic environment, the digital divide, and the Next Generation Internet.

Case Study   The Globally Wired Organization

The Facts

PricewaterhouseCoopers was created in 1998 by the merger of two firms—Price Waterhouse and Coopers & Lybrand—each with historical roots going back some 150 years. The firm had worldwide revenues of $17.3 billion in 1999. The company has roughly 9,000 partners and 160,000 total partners and staff. The geographic coverage of the firm is 150 countries and territories.

PricewaterhouseCoopers is one of the leading organizations in the utilization of technology including the use of many types of networks and mobile computing.

At PricewaterhouseCoopers, the network isn't just the computer—it is what runs the business. That's because the primary asset of this global consulting and accounting firm is the brainpower of its employees. Increasingly, those professionals rely on PricewaterhouseCoopers's enterprise networks to share ideas with one another and, more importantly, with clients.

They're doing a lot of sharing. Thanks to an explosion of new collaborative Web-based applications, traffic on PricewaterhouseCoopers's networks is growing by two to three times per year. The demand for network bandwidth, said Karl Wagner, the New York-based company's director of global networking, is almost insatiable.

"Everyone wants it there all the time, and they always want more of it," Wagner said. "Data networks are just like the telephone today. They want to plug in their PCs and just get their stuff."

To deal with that kind of growth, PricewaterhouseCoopers has aggressively turned to newer technologies, such as virtual private networks (VPNs), and tried-and-true standards such as Synchronous Optical Network (SONET) rings. Those technologies have helped the company keep networking costs under control while increasing flexibility, reliability, and responsiveness.

Not surprisingly, the world's biggest network—the Internet—has created much of the new demand on Price-

waterhouseCoopers's global network. The number of external partners and customers that want to use the Internet to plug directly into PricewaterhouseCoopers's intellectual capital has skyrocketed. To accommodate customers, the company has begun developing a series of secure Extranets that can be used to share research and collaborate with clients.

The company's six main practice areas—tax, audit, management consulting, human resources, business process outsourcing, and financial advisory services—determine the types of Extranets it is developing. The first such Extranet, launched in the fall of 1996 by PricewaterhouseCoopers's global tax services practice, is called the Tax News Network. About 5,000 corporate tax professionals at large companies now use the tax network to stay up to date on tax laws and PricewaterhouseCoopers's research, said Susan O'Neill, a partner in the company's global knowledge management group.

Other PricewaterhouseCoopers Extranets allow customers and consultants to link up on secure sites to collaborate on projects.

While Extranet development has been strong for about two years, "it's been exponential in growth and discussion within the organization" over the past year, O'Neill said. "We think that e-business is business, and we certainly think being connected to our clients through virtual communities and secure Web sites has to be part of the way we do business."

However, external customers are not the only ones driving up PricewaterhouseCoopers's network traffic. Internally, employees are relying increasingly on the company's 5-year-old Intranet to administer their benefits, stay abreast of company news, and search for technical information. They also browse the Web to conduct research.

In addition to PricewaterhouseCoopers's traditional desktop users, about 80,000 of the employees are mobile and typically work at hotel rooms or reserve space at the firm's offices worldwide. PricewaterhouseCoopers plans to implement a virtual private network—a private network configured within a public network—to provide notebook users with secure access to its data. The firm is testing this VPN at offices in North America and is preparing to roll out the network to 70,000 workers in North America and Great Britain at the rate of 3,000 per week.

PricewaterhouseCoopers also is staffing its offices with IT workers who speak multiple languages, so visiting notebook users are more likely to find someone they can talk to for technical support. That's been a problem for employees with notebook support needs that arise outside the business hours of their home offices. "If you're in a hotel room in Taiwan, you're not going to call your office in Oklahoma," says Michael Schoenholtz, a partner who oversees global IT support strategies.

The Payoff

The VPN is paying off so far. In the United States, the cost of a remote dial-up connection is between $4.20 and $6.10 per hour. Through the VPN, the same connection averages about $1.40 per hour for the Internet access provided by an Internet service provider (ISP).

Along with lowering remote access costs, the VPN provides a secure tunnel over the Internet, allowing encrypted data to travel from behind PricewaterhouseCoopers's firewall to a user who has accessed the Internet through a dial-up connection, another company's LAN, or a broadband connection at home.

Several thousand PricewaterhouseCoopers employees are using digital subscriber line and cable modem services in conjunction with the VPN to conduct business from their homes. Later this year, PricewaterhouseCoopers will connect three major European offices through a VPN service managed by an ISP. The corporate locations—in Paris; London; and Frankfurt, Germany—represent about 20,000 employees.

PricewaterhouseCoopers is at the forefront of global companies realizing that site-to-site VPNs can help bring the costs of their European networks more in line with those in the United States, experts say. In general, the cost of private telecommunications services in Europe is about five times what it costs in the United States.

Accommodating all those new global users and applications, however, means a lot more traffic on PricewaterhouseCoopers's LANs and WANs. To help manage it all, the company has begun turning to SONET technology.

SONET technology involves the use of fiber optics to connect networks. These networks are sometimes called T1 or T3 lines. These networks offer high-speed connections that can transport huge amounts of data quickly.

PricewaterhouseCoopers started using SONET in the spring of 1998 at its data centers in Floral Park, New York, and Tampa, Florida. The company had started consolidating its servers for enterprisewide applications, such as Lotus Development Corp.'s Notes and enterprise resource planning (ERP) software, into the data centers as a way to cut costs and better manage the applications.

"Once some change happens, either a new application or a change in business, or, heaven forbid, they combine three offices and forget to tell you, then you've got to be able to respond to that quickly," Wagner said.

PricewaterhouseCoopers officials expect that the company's need for networking bandwidth and flexibility will only increase. The next wave of demand could well come from the trend toward hosted applications. In addition to beginning to provide hosting services to clients through its business process outsourcing practice, Pricewaterhouse-Coopers has begun using application service providers.

Currently, in fact, the company is discussing an arrangement with its ERP vendors and expects to have the application hosted by the end of the year, said Rowan Snyder, the company's deputy CIO.

With the use of these present technologies and other advancements on the horizon, PricewaterhouseCoopers truly is becoming a networked organization both digitally and collaboratively.

Sources: Hicks, Matt, "Keeping Ideas Flowing—Pricewaterhouse-Coopers turns to VPN, SONET to Plug Global Users into Its Intellectual Capital," *eWeek* (May 8, 2000): 105; Vitiello, Jill, "Road Rage; Companies Are Going after Remote and Mobile Computing with a Vengeance, Creating Lots of Opportunities for IT Pros with the Right Skills," *Computerworld* (March 27, 2000): 88; Davey, Tom, and Amy K. Larsen, "The Mobile Infrastructure—As Use of Notebooks Increases, So Does the Demand for Security and Support," *InformationWeek* (June 23, 1999): 20.

CASE STUDY QUESTIONS

1. What are some of the ways in which digital networks are changing the way PricewaterhouseCoopers employees work? How have these changes increased their effectiveness? What disadvantages/negatives do you see?

2. What are some of the ways in which digital networks are changing PricewaterhouseCooper's relationship with partners and clients? What do you think might be some of the results?

CASE STUDY CLASS PROJECTS

1. Check out the PricewaterhouseCoopers Web site. How has PWC implemented some of the changes discussed in this case?
2. Imagine that you or your assigned group are (an) employee(s) at PricewaterhouseCoopers. Using this case, information in chapter 2, the PricewaterhouseCoopers Web site, and other references regarding the changing digital workplace, create a one- to two-page scenario of a typical day of work on a consulting assignment at PricewaterhouseCoopers. Make up any details you wish within the context established by the PWC case.
3. Share stories with classmates. Summarize the results by listing and discussing how digital networks are enhancing performance of individuals and groups.

Chapter 1

Introduction to End-User Information Systems

Learning Objectives

Upon completing this chapter, you should be able to:

➤ Define end-user information systems (EUIS) and explain how it relates to other areas of information systems.

➤ Explain how EUIS fits into an overall enterprise information systems architecture.

➤ Identify the benefits of end-user information systems.

➤ Understand how end-user information systems relate to changing roles and expectations in the workplace.

➤ Explain how business processes addressed by end-user information systems differ from those handled by large data centers and transaction processing systems.

➤ Describe the changing requirements (characteristics) of work in the Information Age.

➤ Describe the impact of end-user information systems on workplace environments.

➤ Understand the relationship between workplace performance and technology.

➤ Explain the concept of Help Desk and assistance centers.

➤ Identify career opportunities in the area of end-user information systems.

1.1　INTRODUCTION

Information technology is transforming how business and government enterprises operate and, as a result, how people work. Information is the critical raw material for decision making and the foundation for producing products and providing services. People create information; people use information; people control information. The growing economic importance of information in modern society led sociologists such as Alvin Toffler and John Naisbitt to characterize our society as the *Information Age.* In fact, more than half of today's workforce is employed in information-related jobs, compared to less than 20 percent 30 years ago. Most of those people spend a significant portion of their workday *"in the office,"* which might be at home, in a hotel room, at the airport, in a car, in a plane, or at some other remote location, as well as in a traditional office building.

In an information age, knowledge and core competencies (the two or three things that an enterprise does best) are key organizational assets. Only recently, the value of a company was thought to reside primarily in its tangible assets: machinery, buildings, inventory, and real estate. This Industrial Age notion that an enterprise should be measured mainly in terms of its goods and property no longer holds. In today's global economy, producing unique or lower-cost products and services requires superior knowledge of design, business processes, and distribution. Knowing how to do things effectively and efficiently in ways that other enterprises cannot duplicate easily is a primary source of profit. As knowledge becomes a critical asset, the success of the enterprise increasingly depends on its ability to gather, produce, maintain, and disseminate information and knowledge. Information technology and digital networks are transforming how this is accomplished.

More and more information today is stored, processed, and distributed in digital format. The Internet is having a profound influence, and The Next Generation Internet will provide greatly expanded capabilities for transmitting and displaying information in all formats. E-commerce and e-business are fundamentally changing the dynamics of the marketplace, opening many new possibilities for communicating, collaborating, and transacting business. The anticipated impact is so revolutionary that the pundits already are calling the twenty-first century the *Digital Age*.

A PC on the desktop is an expectation for the typical knowledge worker today. Most likely, the PC is connected to the company network, which provides access to e-mail, proprietary systems, and the Internet. In addition to individual productivity tools—such as word processing, spreadsheets, graphics, and presentation software—the PC probably provides access to work group support such as Outlook or Lotus Notes. The desktop PC also is likely to be the gateway to a wide variety of company information, such as personnel directories, human resource information, procedure manuals, and other reference information available online on a company Intranet. The company network provides connections to other offices nationwide or worldwide. If workers travel, in all likelihood, they carry a notebook and can dial in to company systems from anywhere in the world. Many workers also carry pagers and personal digital assistants (PDAs), such as the Palm Pilot. They may be assigned to work teams that are disbursed in several locations worldwide so that tasks must be coordinated with minimum face-to-face contact.

Through the application of information technologies, organizations continually are finding more effective ways for people to manage information and capture knowledge. One area of IS that has changed significantly and grown in importance in recent years is end-user information systems (EUIS). End-user technologies, also called *knowledge work systems*—especially in the form of desktop productivity tools, collaborative work group tools, knowledge management, Intranets, desktop publishing, multimedia, and online learning—are the fastest-growing applications in business today.

The digital revolution has put millions of personal computers on the desks of employees who have little experience using them, connecting them to powerful communication networks, rearranging social relations in the office, changing reporting patterns, changing business processes, and redefining business goals. Planning, designing, implementing, and supporting the technology with all its challenges is only half the picture. The challenges of transforming and managing the end-user environment have turned out to be equally as great. More often than not, the technology is successful, but projects still fall short on delivering promised benefits. These and other challenges of using technology to improve individual, work group, and organizational performance are the province of end-user information systems and the subject of this text.

Chapter 1 provides an overview of end-user information systems and discusses the impact of information technology on individual and work group performance. It sets the stage for topics that are discussed in more detail throughout the text. In the next section, you will learn more about the field of EUIS and how it differs from other areas of IS.

End-user information systems (EUIS) is such a rapidly evolving field that defining it has been somewhat challenging. The field has changed noticeably in just 4 to 5 short years. This section offers a current definition of EUIS and explains what distinguishes it from other areas of IS and where it fits into the total IS field.

1.2.1   What Is End-User Information Systems?

End-user information systems can be thought of as the application of information technology to support workplace performance. The focus is on providing systems that directly support individual, group, and departmental needs. It involves implementing, managing, and supporting computing in the workplace by non-IS technical specialists. The term *end user* emerged in the early days of computing and refers to the nontechnical personnel who use systems, as opposed to technical IS personnel who design them. When fourth-generation languages and PC application packages were first introduced to nontechnical workers, it was referred to as "end-user computing" or programming done by non-IS technical specialists. EUIS is the area of IS that addresses the direct connection between technology and its application at the desktop—how end users apply computing skills to do their work and accomplish their business results.

This is a field of growing importance as workers at all levels of the organizational hierarchy have powerful PC platforms on their desktop and are increasingly savvy about using them—a trend that has been greatly accelerated by the Internet. As tools continue to become more powerful and easier to use, end-user computing represents a growing proportion of all enterprise computing. Although originally the exception to the rule, end-user computing now has become part of the mainstream information systems environment. Many organizations have not yet developed strategies and policies to capitalize on the benefits while ensuring that end-user-developed applications meet organizational objectives or meet quality-assurance standards appropriate to their function.

The study of end-user information systems is a multidisciplinary field, demanding a combination of organizational savvy, business knowledge, and technical competence, but not necessarily computer programming skills. EUIS encompasses the following broad areas:

1. Productivity tools for knowledge workers
2. Work group computing
3. End-user development
4. End-user training
5. End-user support—Help Desk, information center
6. Knowledge management/performance support
7. Human factors and ergonomics
8. Business process and job (re)design
9. Change management
10. Project management

The Organizational Systems Research Association (OSRA) has defined EUIS as the application of information technologies to support business processes and individual performance with the objective of improving overall organizational effectiveness in direct support of business goals and strategies. Other sources define *end-user computing* simply as "the use of computers by knowledge workers without the direct intervention of professional systems analysts and programmers."[1] EUIS, as a field of study, can be distinguished by its emphasis on the use of information technology to meet the needs of individuals, groups, and departments. One of the primary areas addressed by EUIS is the organizational issues involved in designing and implementing information systems. You can think about EUIS as a marriage between the disciplines of IS and organizational development.

Information technologies generally associated with EUIS are listed in Figure 1-1. However, EUIS is more than special types of computer systems or software programs. EUIS, as a field of specialization, offers methods and models for conceptualizing the complex dynamics of work environments—which are increasingly anytime, anyplace—and applying them to information system design and implementation. It encompasses problem analysis, needs definition, selection or development, and implementation of computer systems to support work groups and individual performance. It is concerned with the diffusion and assimilation of information technology at all levels of the enterprise. EUIS methods draw on basic systems analysis concepts and organizational design principles for applying information technology to restructure work flows, procedures, and information access to improve overall effectiveness and productivity. It places a heavy emphasis on understanding how people work. How does the user view the work? What are the critical success factors for performing the job? At what point in the work process is information required? Where in the

Figure 1-1
Some EUIS tools

Category	Software and Hardware Examples
Text handling/document management	Word processing, desktop publishing, work-flow management systems, integrated document management systems, scanners, printers, copiers
Data handling tools	Spreadsheets, databases, statistical packages, project management, decision support systems
Multimedia/graphic and design	Computer graphics, presentation software, computer-aided design, Web-publishing software (Dreamweaver, Adobe Acrobat, PageMaker, Illustrator, Front-Page, Shockwave, Flash)
Communication tools	Local area networks, electronic mail, voice mail, teleconferencing, compressed video, facsimile, cellular telephones, pagers, Web casting
Group systems/collaborative technologies	Group support systems, C-U/C-Me, netmeeting, distance learning software
Time management	Electronic calendars, electronic notebooks and tracking systems, electronic "to do" lists, project management software, directories, personal digital assistants
Knowledge management/performance support	Electronic sales support, sales force automation, expert systems, artificial intelligence, data warehouses, data mining, knowledge repositories, online help, performance support, online reference, help desk, GrapeVINE, Lotus Notes, Intraspect, Red Tools, search and retrieval engines, intelligent agents, Web-based tools such as Vignette Story Server

work flow can information technology best be applied? The answers to questions of this nature are critical to improving individual and work group performance.

1.2.2 Where Does EUIS Fit into Enterprise Information Systems?

Information systems are classified generally based on types of systems and intended users. Although you may find variance in the terms used by textbooks or other literature to describe them, the five classifications most commonly used are:

1. Transaction processing systems (TPS)
2. Management information systems (MIS)
3. Decision support systems (DSS)
4. Executive information systems (EIS)
5. End-user information systems (EUIS), or Knowledge work systems (KWS)

Although this classification may be useful for studying the design of information systems, it generally does not coincide with the way a typical information systems (IS) organization assigns roles and responsibilities. Typical IS organizations are divided along lines of responsibility for managing and operating computer data centers and services versus applications development and support, as depicted in Figure 1-2. Computer data centers typically are responsible for managing communication networks, defining enterprise-wide information systems architectures and data repositories, and providing technical support for application developers. Applications development departments generally are responsible for designing, implementing, and supporting transaction processing and other business application systems. In large enterprises, application development areas may be decentralized by region or product line.

Until fairly recently, EUIS—most likely under titles of office information systems and office automation—were operated as separate departments. They may have been autonomous departments under the IS organization, but more likely they were a separate department or under some administrative services group. The trend has been to integrate EUIS into mainstream IS operations. The reasons for this will become clearer as you read on.

To better understand EUIS, let's briefly consider typical activities and contrast them with those handled by traditional IS operations in corporate organizations.

Typical assignments for EUIS specialists may range from selecting a single software package to designing a complex local area network with customized software

Figure 1-2
Typical IS organization structure

ENTERPRISE OPERATIONS AND NETWORKS	IS APPLICATIONS DEVELOPMENT
Computer center operations	Enterprise applications
Networks	Transaction processing systems (TPS)
IS planning and architectures	Management reporting systems
Data repositories	End-user information systems
Technical support	Internet, Intranet, Extranet

Typical IS organizations are divided along lines of responsibility for managing and operating computer data centers and services versus applications development and maintenance.

and special applications to support dozens of users. An EUIS specialist may be expected to analyze work flows and assess opportunities for restructuring business processes and implementing organizational changes. EUIS specialists train business personnel in the use of software, answer questions, resolve technical problems, staff hot lines and Help Desks, create user documentation, evaluate software packages, design PC applications, and perform dozens of other tasks. They also provide access to mainframe data for download to PCs and assist users with specialized packages and fourth-generation reporting and query languages, such as SQL and SAS. Typical software applications include word processing, spreadsheets, desktop publishing, micro databases, graphics, and project management. Other primary applications include online help and reference, quality printing, copying, facsimile transmission, image processing, forms design, and document management. The recent explosion of Internet technologies has created a demand for new competencies in Web-page design, Intranet development and support, and knowledge management. Typical EUIS projects run from a few days or weeks to several months.

In contrast, typical IS responsibilities include designing and maintaining transaction processing systems, installing and operating complex national and international communication networks, operating large computer data centers, defining technical architectures, and designing and maintaining complex enterprise databases. These tasks require highly specialized technical skills and structured methodologies (systems development life cycles). Typical development cycles run from 6 months to 2 to 3 years. A large transaction processing system may process millions of transactions each day. The American Airlines SABRE reservation system, for example, processes more than 2,000 transactions per second. In such systems, technical efficiency and data security and integrity often override issues of usability or flexibility. Typical IS positions include application programmers, systems analysts, technical specialists, computer operators, and systems programmers. Until recently, most business systems were programmed in COBOL, and to a lesser extent FORTRAN, BASIC, RPG, Assembler, and fourth-generation languages. Now traditional programming methods are being enhanced with the use of CASE (computer-aid software engineering) tools, database technology, and client/server architectures. New systems design methods include visual programming, object-oriented design, and Internet-based systems development. Networking has become a more integral part of systems operations, and information systems development and management has become more strategic in nature.

IS traditionally has addressed well-defined, stable processes, such as those in accounting and manufacturing. Applications include transaction-oriented, numerical applications such as payroll, inventory, order entry, and accounts receivable and payable. Processing volumes must warrant the high cost of developing systems. Changes are expensive to implement, and systems are not always interactive. Some IS applications lend themselves to batch processing (hold and process together at one time). In contrast, EUIS applications are always highly interactive. They have evolved primarily in response to loosely structured text, data analysis, and communications requirements. EUIS addresses applications that require flexibility for handling exceptions and making changes. EUIS is appropriate for individual and departmental processing. It meets a need for quick response and offers cost-effective solutions for applications that do not have volumes high enough to warrant the expense of developing mainframe or other large-scale systems. Some of the key distinctions between IS and EUIS are summarized in Figure 1-3. However, the dividing lines are fuzzy, and the distinctions are often more a matter of emphasis and orientation than specific technologies.

EUIS ANALYST	MIS ANALYST
Focus on individual and work group productivity	Focus on enterprise information systems, networks and online transaction processing systems
Quick response	Formal development cycle
Analyzes user requirements and work flows, evaluates hardware and software packages, recommends solutions	Analyzes user requirements and translates them into programming design specifications
Develops applications with software packages (Lotus 1-2-3, Excel, Access, etc.) or fourth-generation languages (FOCUS, SAS, etc.)	Develops (codes) complex business systems using computer languages (COBOL, C++, Java, FORTRAN) or CASE tools
Integrates tools into the work environment	Ignores work flow/job issues
Assists people in using computers to perform their jobs	Develops solutions (writes programs) for people
Business tasks, people-oriented	Technical, production oriented
Flexible, less well-defined activities	Repetitive, well-defined processes
Nonprocedural	Transaction oriented
Emphasis on ad hoc requirements	Emphasis on well-defined process
User responsible for control and security procedures	Formal control and security procedures
Practical for small applications	Practical for high-volume applications
Optimizes human productivity	Optimizing processing speed/machine efficiency
Deals with hardware and software solutions	Usually concerned about writing (coding) software (hardware environment is a given; the responsibility of a separate computer operations department)
Web page development	Web-based programming and network configuration

Figure 1-3
Contrast of EUIS and MIS environments

An additional area of critical importance to EUIS and IS is networking. Networking refers to the electronic transfer of data between computer devices. Networking might be accomplished through direct coaxial wiring, leased lines, modem devices, local area networks (LANs), wide area networks (WANs), or some combination of transmission devices. Enterprises can link their LANs and WANs to create networks that connect entire enterprises. These enterprise networks put more computer power on the desktop and can connect them to other organizations outside the firm and to the Internet. Moreover, the Internet has opened up exciting new possibilities for doing business that are transforming organizations and the use of information systems in everyday life. It is creating a universal platform for connectivity.

EUIS has grown in importance as an integral part of the total IS architecture as technologies have become increasingly integrated (see Figure 1-4). At the same time, information systems have come to play an ever-widening role in contemporary organizations. Interdependence is growing among business strategy, rules, and processes on the one hand, and information systems hardware, software, databases, and networking on the other. As information systems have become more central to business operations, managers and knowledge workers have become more savvy about their use and more involved in their design, implementation, and management. The field of EUIS provides strategies and methodologies to encourage and support EUIS while ensuring adequate controls and fit with overall IS architecture.

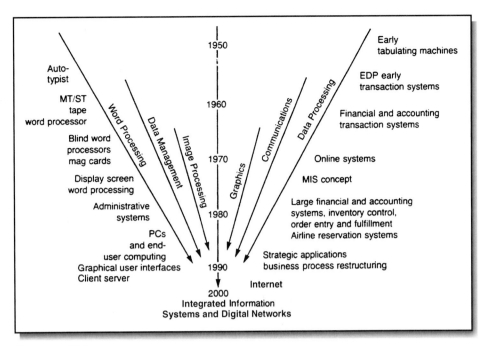

Figure 1-4
Converging information technologies

1.3 WORKPLACE ENVIRONMENTS IN AN INFORMATION AGE

EUIS specialists address the diverse information needs of knowledge workers in the changing workplace. Who are knowledge workers? What is the nature of knowledge work? How are workplaces changing? What is the role of the organization? What are the important issues that differentiate end-user applications from enterprise applications? These and other questions are addressed in this section.

1.3.1 Who Are Knowledge Workers?

According to the U.S. Bureau of Labor Statistics, the white-collar workforce constitutes 60 percent of adult employees in the United States (see Figure 1-5). About 70 percent of salaries and wages are paid to this white-collar workforce. The white-collar workforce generally is defined to include the following employment categories:

1. Executive and managerial personnel
2. Professional and technical knowledge workers
3. Sales and marketing personnel
4. Administrative support, including clerical

Some sources are using the terms *knowledge workers* or *information workers* to describe these employment categories. Other sources define knowledge workers much more narrowly to include only the second category of professional and technical knowledge workers. In this text, knowledge worker is used in the broader

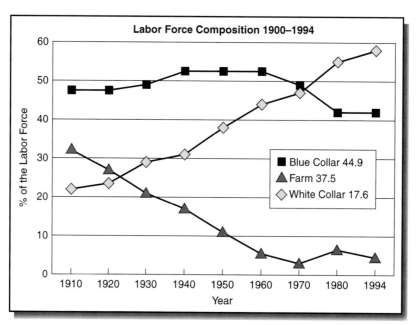

Figure 1-5
Labor force composition 1900–2000

Source: Adapted from U.S. Department of Commerce, Bureau of the Census, Statistical Abstract of the United States, 1994, Table 644, and Historical Statistics of the United States, Colonial Times to 1970 Vol 1, Series D, 182-232.

sense to include all four categories. Whatever terms are preferred, these workers are the target population for EUIS and productivity-improvement efforts.

1.3.2 The Role of Organization

Whenever two or more people work together to accomplish specific objectives, some form of organization is necessary. Organization is required to coordinate the efforts of the various people so that each individual and each group contributes to the overall goals. To be purposeful and personally satisfying, work must contribute to an enterprise's goals. Organization also brings other necessary resources such as materials, equipment, capital, and markets together in a practical format to accomplish enterprise goals.

Through organization, people can accomplish more work than individuals working alone can. Activities are organized into manageable units in which the work can be planned and controlled effectively. Group goals are defined, and individuals are assigned specific responsibilities. Through team effort to accomplish defined organizational goals, the value of each member's contribution is increased. Confusion about who is to do what work is minimized. A supportive work environment is provided. A good organizational structure creates synergy: 2 + 2 produces 5, not just 4.

In any work environment, people, tasks, and technology are organized to facilitate the accomplishment of specific objectives. Generally, these objectives are directed toward producing some type of marketable product or service. Information is central to the operation and coordination of required activities. Information may take the form of decisions, directives, or documents. The way in which work is organized into the functions or business processes people perform depends primarily on three factors:

1. The nature of the tasks.
2. The knowledge and skills of the staff.
3. The technology and resources available to accomplish those tasks.

The role of *technology* is to help accomplish required tasks. In performing that role, the technology influences how people and tasks are organized. Each organization is not only unique, it is also dynamic. The ways in which technology, tasks, and people are organized into specific functions or processes change over time in response to changing business requirements.

The organizational framework, as reflected in a formal organization chart, defines who does what in an enterprise. How are responsibilities divided, coordinated, and linked together? Who should report to whom? Who should make what decisions? Which members should be in which groups? What amounts of what basic resources should be used, and by whom? What work environment should be provided? An effective organization should facilitate the exchange of information and minimize duplication of effort.

Generally, enterprises are organized into two main categories: *primary functions,* such as product research and development, production, and marketing; and *support functions,* such as human resources, public relations, and information systems. The primary functions constitute those activities directly involved in producing and marketing the enterprise's products or services. Support functions provide essential ancillary services. The nature of the enterprise is defined by its primary functions. EUIS specialists must have a good understanding of these primary and support functions.

1.3.3 Changing Organizational Structures

Coordination and control of an organization are responsibilities of management. In many enterprises, management is becoming less authoritarian and more participative. Traditionally, planning and decision making were done at the top of the organization structure. Today, however, authority is frequently accorded by expertise as well as by position. Information technologies allow managers to oversee and control more workers spread over greater distances, which has led to pushing responsibility down the organizational hierarchy, empowering workers.

As more responsibility is "pushed down" in the organization, offices are experiencing an increase in technical/professional positions and a decline in clerical positions. Until 1980, clerical jobs increased at a rate faster than the national employment growth rate. Since then, however, the growth rate in clerical positions has eased to 2 percent below the national employment growth rate. According to one study, the number of jobs for secretaries, stenographers, and typists has declined by 100,000 since 1980. Researchers attribute this decline to EUIS, job loss in industrial areas resulting from the shift away from manufacturing toward a service-based economy, and drops in government employment levels.

Joseph V. Brophy, former Senior Vice-President of Data Processing, Travelers Insurance Company, says that the microcomputer is instrumental to a "fundamental demographic transformation in our company." In 1970, two-thirds of Travelers'

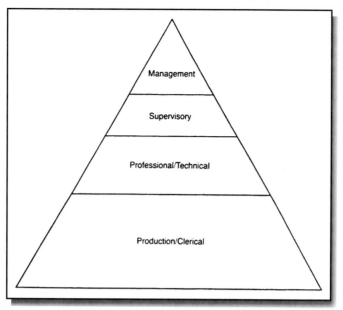

Figure 1-6
Historical organizational hierarchy. Historically, organizational hierarchy has been represented by a triangle with a broad base of low-level employees and a much smaller number of professional, technical, supervisory, and managerial personnel.

30,000 employees were clerical and one-third were professional. Today, that ratio is reversed.

The typical representation of an organizational hierarchy is shaped like a pyramid, as shown in Figure 1-6. The purpose of the hierarchical structure is *control*. Computers are diminishing the need for this hierarchical structure by providing direct access to information and greater control of business processes. In view of the recent statistics on the white-collar workforce, a truer characterization of the organizational hierarchy today would be diamond-shaped (see Figure 1-7).

1.3.4   The Changing Nature of Knowledge Work

Much more is known about what kinds of tasks are performed by knowledge workers than is known about *how* workers perform these tasks. Yet the questions about how work is performed are crucial to efforts to improve productivity. When systems analysts deliver a tool, it quickly falls into disuse when it does not match the task that needs to be performed. For example, a follow-up or tracking system that does not allow staff to look up information in all the ways needed would lead them to keep and use their old manual system as a cross-reference. In all likelihood, maintaining two separate systems soon would become cumbersome, and the new, automated tracking system would fall into disuse. It has become apparent that the developers of EUIS must understand more about the nature of work performed at all levels of an organization if technology is to serve information-processing needs at those levels effectively.

Part I   EUIS: Organizational and Technical Foundations

Figure 1-7
Organizational hierarchy in the Information Age. Today, the typical organizational hierarchy is more accurately represented as a diamond than as the traditional triangle of the past.

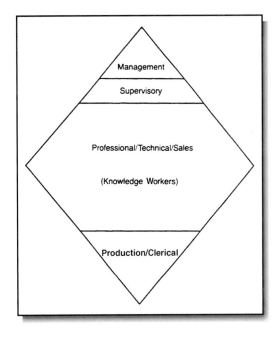

Although identifying lists of tasks is easy, little is known about the nature of knowledge work from the standpoint of *information processing;* that is, how people interact with their work. How do they identify information that is critical to their tasks or decision making? How do they go about locating or researching this information? How do they organize it, use it, store it, and assimilate it? How do they interact and interface with other information-processing functions? What information-processing tasks do professional, technical, sales, supervisory, and managerial personnel do themselves, and what do they delegate to support personnel? To what extent are these tasks based on the nature of the work and to what extent on personal preference? What aspects are performed individually and what aspects involve collaboration?

Workflow analysis is an industrial engineering technique that has been applied frequently to job design for clerical personnel and factory production workers. At higher levels, however, work-flow techniques are seldom applied. In fact, until fairly recently few people were concerned about the productivity of professionals and managers. The transition in the United States to an information-based economy and the opportunities afforded by EUIS are changing that attitude.

The nature of information processing performed by professional, technical, and managerial knowledge workers is aligned closely to the functional areas in which they work. Primary functions such as finance, marketing, production, and research and development, as well as support functions such as legal services and personnel administration, have information requirements unique to their operations. Information may be used for planning, maintaining operations, evaluating results, reporting to executive management, and complying with government regulations. Typical functional divisions in large organizations and examples of information relating to their operations are depicted in Figure 1-8.

Descriptions of office work often depict clerical support personnel as processors of information for managers who use the information for decision making. The

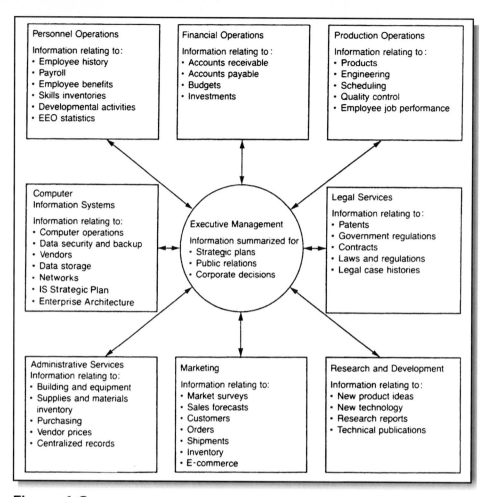

Figure 1-8

Typical functional divisions and related information requirements in a large enterprise

tendency is to think of the office as an information factory that produces correspondence, reports, and other information products. These descriptions are misleading, however, and conceptualizing the office in these ways poses several risks for designing effective information systems.

First, professional, technical, sales, supervisory, and managerial personnel process a great deal of information themselves in addition to the information that is processed by clerical staff. Determining how technology can provide support for these professional information-processing tasks is a prime challenge for EUIS.

Second, the focus on highly visible products of the office such as reports, correspondence, transactions, and decisions leads analysts to focus on product *quantity* rather than *quality*. Computer systems tend to be based on the inherent structure of these products instead of on the processes people use to create them.

Third, the true objective of information processing activities generally is to *filter* information rather than *produce* information. The office serves to capture information and reduce it to a form that is useful for decision making. In this sense, the filtering process of the office resembles the filtering process of the human mind. The office also serves as a collective memory for the organization, documenting results of past actions and maintaining resources that may be useful for future actions.

The best source of information about how end users perform their jobs and the tools they need is the end users themselves. Thus, information systems professionals, working alone, never will be able to devise systems that truly meet individual needs. New tools and procedures, if they are to evolve, will evolve out of a joint effort. EUIS, therefore, must be driven by business needs—not by technology. Solutions must focus on enhancing the capacity of end users to perform their jobs. In order for EUIS to serve information processing needs effectively at all levels, it is crucial to understand more about the nature of work performed at those levels. Chapter 3 discusses characteristics of the knowledge work environment and provides approaches for understanding end-user needs and matching those needs to software solutions.

1.3.5 A Shift in Focus to Business Process and Work Group Support

Much of the focus of EUIS has shifted recently from individuals to departmental and work group computing. In the 1980s, the major application of information technology in the office environment was to support the automation of clerical tasks. As PCs grew more powerful and easier to use, the emphasis shifted to supporting knowledge workers and managers at all levels of responsibility. However, the emphasis was still primarily on individual performance. Today, information technology is being used increasingly to support group processes and to coordinate activities in addition to individual tasks.

Improving individual performance does not necessarily add up to increased effectiveness, reduced cost, or improved performance for the organization as a whole. Saved time, for example, may not necessarily be spent on more productive activities. Bottlenecks may be shifted. Incremental improvements do not necessarily lead to significant productivity improvements in an overall process. Eliminating inefficiencies in one part of a process may even compound problems somewhere else. To bring gains to the bottom line, enterprises must address individual productivity within the larger picture of the work group and the overall business process.

Consequently, emphasis in 2001 and beyond is expected to be on work flow or business process reengineering to take advantage of digital networks. Because of the need for workers to work together to solve problems, acceptance of groupware tools is expected to grow dramatically. The area of departmental and work-group computing holds much promise but is fraught with challenges. It is hard to predict what the future will bring in this area. Chapter 4, "Work Group Computing," addresses the rapidly growing area of work group support.

1.3.6 Characteristics of the Knowledge Work Environment

Tailoring information systems for work groups or individuals involves a different set of considerations than designing systems on an enterprise level. User interface issues and flexibility, for example, become much more important, and security and

Table 1-1
Characteristics of the knowledge work environment

1.3.7.1 *Variability*

The EUIS specialist will find that work varies considerably from one department to the next. Even for similar functions, procedures for doing work may vary considerably.

1.3.7.2 *Work styles*

Personal work styles are an important influence on the acceptance and use of hardware and software. End users may demand workstations that are customized to their needs.

1.3.7.3 *Departmentalization*

Although all business units and departments contribute to organizational objectives, not all activities are corporate in nature. Much of the work that goes on in separate departments is unique to their particular operation, with only specific products or services that move to other departments or up the organizational hierarchy. EUIS specialists are likely to find that different departments operate fairly autonomously. Even the culture may vary from department to department in large enterprises, depending on the management style of the unit head.

1.3.7.4 *Dispersed*

Today's anytime/anyplace office may be a hotel room, a car, a plane, a room at home, a temporary site at another company or in another country, or almost anywhere. Even within the office operations per se, people may be scattered in various buildings and locations.

1.3.7.5 *Specializations*

The work of professional, managerial, and technical knowledge workers varies considerably depending upon the business function in which they work. The workdays for accountants, engineers, actuaries, human resource personnel, and salespeople, for example, all differ significantly, even though they work for the same company and are located in the same office building.

1.3.7.6 *Nonproductive activities*

A significant percentage of office work activities could be termed *nonproductive*. These activities may include incomplete telephone calls, waiting time, poorly run meetings, false starts, misunderstood assignments, searching for information, following up on activities or requests, rework, work scrapped due to changing priorities, duplication of effort, and moving from location to location due to restructuring, among others. These areas represent opportunities for significant productivity improvement with information technology.

1.3.7.7 *Soft information*

Much of the information dealt with in the office environment might be termed *soft information*. It is loosely structured, anecdotal, variable, and specific to the task at hand. This is in sharp contrast to the type of information handled by typical TPS, which can be precisely defined, calculated, and coded. For example, consider names, ID numbers, addresses, product names, prices, and quantities in contrast to telephone inquires from clients, complaints, problems, tax laws, government regulations, special requests, and analyses of marketing data.

1.3.7.8 *Deadline pressures*

The business of end users is business, not computers. When pressured by deadlines, end users have little tolerance for learning complex software or putting up with hardware problems.

1.3.7.9 *Project versus production environments*

Needs and solutions vary based on whether the business environment is production or project oriented. A production environment (underwriting, accounting, sales, claims processing) is characterized by structured work flow, repetitive or cyclical work, procedural orientation, and little discretionary time. In contrast, professional or project environments (legal services, research and development, engineering, information systems) have less structured work flows. They tend to be deadline oriented; involve analysis, research, and creative-type activities; and allow personnel more discretion in allocating time to tasks.

control issues become less overriding. Table 1-1 identifies important characteristics of the knowledge work environment, which will be elaborated in more detail in part II. EUIS analysts must keep these characteristics in mind when designing and supporting systems.

1.4 WORKPLACE PERFORMANCE: THE IMPACT OF EUIS ON WORK

Workplace performance, discussed in part IV, is a measure of the *quantity and quality of work.* The idea of using technology to improve performance is far from new, of course. In fact, history shows that people constantly strive to improve their ability to get things done by using technology. They strive to do more work faster and better with less effort; in short, to be more productive.

New technologies are not always welcomed, however. The individuals on whom technological improvements are imposed frequently resist the changes that technology brings. An interesting example of resistance to technology was the Luddites' protest against industrialization in the weaving mills of England during the early 1800s. Organized bands of masked English handicraft workers rioted and tried to destroy the textile machinery that was displacing them from their traditional jobs (see Figure 1-9). This example also illustrates how advances in one area

Figure 1-9
Luddites rioting in weaving mills

of technology often lead to breakthroughs in other areas. Ironically, the same Jacquard weaving looms that the Luddites opposed later inspired Hollerith's invention of punched cards, the original computer storage medium.

As one might expect, knowledge workers have not always welcomed new technologies either. When typewriters were introduced in the mid-1800s, businessmen rejected typed correspondence as too impersonal. Thus, many eighteenth-century businessmen continued to handwrite their letters long after typewriters became available. Typewriters often were used to create drafts of documents, and the final copy was then carefully handwritten. Gradually, the need for efficiency forced businesses to change.

Typing machines precipitated other rather revolutionary changes in the nineteenth-century business world. They brought women into the business world in large numbers for the first time. In 1881, the New York City YWCA began teaching typing to its first class of eight young women. Those who were trained to operate typing machines were called *typewriters.* These typing-course graduates were in high demand. Eager to gain employment, thousands of women soon discovered that being a typewriter provided entry into the business world. Proprietary business schools sprang up to train eager students. The secretarial and clerical jobs previously held by men became dominated by women. Jobs multiplied rapidly as the size and number of industrial organizations exploded during the Industrial Revolution.

As many enterprises race to implement IS technologies, others are proceeding more slowly with decidedly less enthusiasm. So while some firms are transforming their businesses into new age global networked enterprises and dot.coms have become Wall Street's hottest commodities, many firms and institutions struggle with making the necessary changes. The power of computer technology has grown much more rapidly than the ability of most organizations to apply and use it. This is a major challenge faced by today's EUIS specialists.

Some authorities still question whether use of EUIS technologies has resulted in any significant gains in white-collar productivity. Even organizations that have been aggressive in implementing new technology sometimes report less-than-dramatic results. The disappointing results have received increasing attention in the past few years as enterprises seek ways to assess the value of information technologies. Recognition is growing that it is not sufficient merely to throw technology at problems. Significant productivity improvements require attention to human factors and thoughtful restructuring of business operations. Payoffs are achieved through business process redesign and careful management of change.

As we just discussed, efforts to introduce change are not always welcome. Resistance to change may manifest itself in both overt and subtle ways. The impact of change in the workplace is an important consideration in the implementation of EUIS. The potential of EUIS can be realized only when technology is implemented as part of a carefully planned program for performance improvement. Such a program requires a systems approach that gives adequate attention to business requirements, business process, job design, and technology. *People* make technology work; the inverse cannot be taken for granted. In and of itself, technology does not make people more productive.

1.4.1 EUIS and Business Value

Assessing the value of information technology has drawn increased attention in recent years. As budgets for information systems have skyrocketed, executives have demanded better justification and more accountability for results. The value of information technology usually is assessed in relation to its ability to reduce costs or increase revenues. The ratio of costs to revenues generally is defined as productivity. In order to assess the value of information technology, an EUIS specialist must understand how to improve productivity and measure results.

For several years, economists have been modifying the idea that capital investment produces gains in national wealth. They have been moving toward a theory of human capital, recognizing that people and human behavior also affect productivity. These ideas are reflected in the growing emphasis on productivity-improvement programs such as self-managed work groups, empowerment, total quality management (TQM), continuous quality improvement (CQI), and other worker-centered efforts to improve productivity. Technology plays an important role in most restructuring (reengineering) efforts.

Technology is important to these efforts because it extends what people can do and offers new alternatives for structuring business processes. The EUIS specialist who understands workplace performance and how technology can facilitate performance can bring much relevant experience to work-improvement efforts. Chapter 9, "Assessing the Value of Information Technology," addresses the issues and complexities of quantifying and measuring the results of EUIS.

1.4.2 EUIS and Human Factors

Concern about productivity as well as the health, safety, and comfort of workers in the workplace has led to increased interest in human factors—the application of information about physical and psychological characteristics to the design of devices and systems for human use. The term *human factors* generally is used synonymously with the term *ergonomics*, which is the study of the natural laws of work. Ideally, knowledge workers should be in an environment that fosters good work habits, combining design and usability principles that balance technology, procedures, and human needs.

Software, hardware, and workspace design can impact productivity. Applications of human factor principles already known, and still being developed, can have a positive outcome for the organization and the individual. Chapter 10, "Human Factors: Software, Hardware, and Workplace Design," offers an overview of principles related to software design, hardware design, and workplace design.

1.4.3 EUIS and Job/Business Process Design

In reality, worker performance is a result of the interdynamics of several factors. These factors include management practices, skill variety, task significance, task identity, autonomy, and feedback on the job. Understanding the nature of job performance is important to successful implementation of EUIS. If one is to improve performance, which is the prime objective, one must first understand what factors contribute to performance.

The past decade has witnessed a renewed emphasis on quality and service. Enterprises facing the demands of a more diverse workforce are implementing more flexible work arrangements. Technology alone cannot achieve the productivity increases needed to keep American industry competitive. Old work processes and practices need to be revamped to take advantage of new technologies. Restructuring, or reengineering, has become the watch word. Enterprises are capitalizing on information technologies by pushing decision making down the organization structure, empowering workers and reducing the levels of middle management.

The importance of leadership and teamwork is being emphasized at all levels of the enterprise. Empowered workers are expected to take more initiative in solving problems and identifying opportunities to make concepts such as continuous quality improvement the way of doing business. Expertise and performance may be more important determinants of recognition and reward than rank or time at the job. All of these trends are bound to influence the implementation of EUIS.

Topics related to business process reengineering and job design for individuals and work groups are addressed in detail in chapter 12, "Business Process and Job (Re)Design."

1.4.4   EUIS and Organizational Change

The organizational learning curve for assimilating new technology often is underestimated. The typical pattern can be characterized by a series of stages. Attempts to solve a problem often lead to invention or application of technology in new ways. However, the technology tends to be adapted to old ways of doing things and is often slow to catch on. As technology is used, it slowly generates new ideas or insights, which, in turn, lead to improvements, modifications, or new technologies. This can be a slow process when left to chance. Progression through the stages of technological innovation is not automatic. Organizations can accelerate the assimilation process with intervention strategies.

Moreover, business process redesign requires changes in the work behavior of people; managers, professionals, salespeople, and secretaries may need to change their habits, thinking, and values. To effect permanent changes in work behavior requires more than training in the use of a system. Patterns in the flow of work may need to be altered. Reporting relationships may shift. New standards and procedures may need to be established. Jobs may have to be redesigned and performance criteria revamped. Experience indicates that innovation often comes from those who know the job best. This factor is one reason why empowerment and self-managed work teams can be highly effective when appropriately implemented. Before managers rush out to buy the latest in information technology, they must take a long, hard look at organizational and work changes that will be required to achieve intended results with the new technology.

Change must be supported by an educational process that enables individuals to assimilate new technologies. Implementing new technologies requires new procedures and new problem-solving skills. It disturbs the way people work and disrupts accustomed patterns of handling and using information. New opportunities associated with the technology may not always be evident immediately. A detailed discussion of organizational change is provided in chapter 11.

In summary, EUIS, like all information systems, must be aligned closely to enterprise goals and workplace performance. Indeed, the greatest challenges EUIS professionals face lie in helping their enterprises harness technology in ways that improve business processes and bring benefits to the bottom line. These are all topics that will be explored in greater depth in part IV, "Workplace Performance: The Impact of Information Technology on Individuals, Groups, and Organizations."

1.5   PLANNING AND IMPLEMENTING EUIS

The complexity of introducing EUIS increases with the size and complexity of the organization. Just attempting to stay informed about technological changes and the wide range of available alternatives is almost overwhelming. To be manageable, EUIS solutions must address specific needs and solve specific business problems. Questions such as which technology is best, which software should be used, and what capabilities are most important can be answered only in relation to the specific objectives one wants to accomplish.

This section provides a brief overview of EUIS planning and implementation. These topics are covered in detail in part V, "End-User Information Systems Project Management."

1.5.1   Strategic Planning: Linking EUIS to Business Needs

To achieve maximum benefit from EUIS, organizations need to link their systems planning to business plans. All too often, acquisition and implementation of technologies are disjointed and unmanaged. In such cases, the potential for substantial benefits is unrealized. While specific applications may be effective, the overall impact of EUIS in the organization may be short changed. Achieving substantial gains in productivity, as well as information processing support, requires more than simply building and installing computer-based systems.

Organizations need a business framework to prioritize projects and guide selection among the dizzying array of hardware and software. Addressing requirements on an application-by-application basis will not necessarily add up to information systems that produce significant business benefits. To be confident that their firm is addressing the appropriate applications and spending technology dollars effectively, management must develop a strategy based on business objectives.

An effective Information Systems Strategic Plan directly supports the business plan and establishes the enterprise systems architecture within which EUIS are planned and implemented. Ideally, this enterprise IS plan allows for flexibility while ensuring compatibility, expandability, and security. A comprehensive discussion of planning and innovation is provided in chapter 13, "Innovation and Strategic Planning."

1.5.2   Overview of EUIS Project Management

The steps for EUIS project management are described briefly in this section. It involves a number of specific steps and procedures (See Figure 1-10) that are generally followed to initiate and carry out projects. If you are familiar already with traditional IS systems development life cycle (SDLC) methodologies, you will notice many parallels, although significant differences also can be found. In general, EUIS project management is less rigid and less formal because of the variability in types of projects. The formality of the project management process depends on a number of factors, including organizational culture and policies, scope of project, resources, and time frames, among others. Even the smallest project requires some level of planning. With experience, the EUIS analyst learns to make these kinds of value judgments. Part V of the text provides a detailed discussion of steps, methods, and alternatives for planning and implementing EUIS projects.

1.5.2.1   Defining Project Scope

The first step is to define the project scope. This step involves defining the business problem or opportunity and identifying the business objectives, issues to be addressed, and project deliverables. The description of project scope basically becomes the "contract" between the business sponsor and the EUIS specialist or team.

Step	Deliverables
1. Define the project's scope	Business objectives
	Expected results
	Time frames
	Budget
2. Plan the project	
3. Assess the requirements	Economic, technical and operational issues
	Evaluate alternatives
	Identify impact/interface with other systems
	Prototype
4. Design: Describe the solution in detail	Requirements, costs, user input, outside assistance
5. Select or develop the solution	Purchase externally
	Buy and customize, build, document, user interface, programming
6. Convert and implement the solution	Detailed plan identifies tasks, dates, responsibilities
	Phased, parallel, or direct conversion
	Trial/pilot period
	Train users
	Modify work flow
	Redesign jobs
7. Evaluate the results	Measure results against defined objectives
	Incorporate insights from new learning
	Correct problems; modify to improve results
8. Institutionalize the results	Reinforce and reward desired behaviors
	Provide advanced training
	Align other organizational operations with new system

Figure 1-10
EUIS project management

1.5.2.2 Plan the Project

Generally, a project will have a project sponsor, usually a senior business manager of a business unit, and an EUIS project manager who is responsible for planning and carrying out all project activities.

1.5.2.3 Assess Requirements

The requirements study involves investigating the economic, technical, and operational issues. EUIS analysts must determine who will be affected by the proposed system, including the primary users and anyone who will be impacted. To start, it is important to understand the basic purpose and structure of the current system or proposed new system. Analysts identify basic business requirements for a new system and identify possible alternatives for achieving them. A rough estimate is then made of the costs and benefits of the various alternatives.

1.5.2.4 Describe the Solution in Detail

If approval is granted to proceed with the project, analysts then begin the detailed analysis stage. This stage begins with documenting the structure and purpose of the current system. Then, system requirements for the new system are defined in detail. This step may involve significant process redesign. Next, analysts evaluate alternative solutions and develop a detailed proposal for the recommended solution. The proposed development plan, budget, and hardware and software to be acquired are submitted to management for approval.

1.5.2.5 Select or Develop Proposed Solution

If the project budget is approved, analysts proceed to evaluate and select application software that is to be acquired, evaluate and select hardware and system software, develop application software or customize purchased software, and develop business applications.

1.5.2.6 Convert and Implement Solution

The conversion from existing systems must be planned and managed carefully. Detailed plans must be developed to identify tasks, dates, and responsibilities. Analysts must develop and deliver documentation, implementation procedures, and training materials and programs.

1.5.2.7 Evaluate Results

After a new system has been implemented and all users have been fully trained, results of the new system are measured against defined business objectives. Problems are corrected. Modifications and follow-up training are provided to improve results. Strategies are needed to take advantage of insights from new learning.

1.5.2.8 Institutionalize Results

The final stage is critical to achieving benefits of information technology. Specific strategies are needed to align business processes and sustain workplace changes.

A project plan, whether brief or detailed, is critical to ensure that there is agreement on objectives, the process for achieving them, and who will be responsible for what by when. The plan serves to keep everyone informed about what is going on and what is expected of them.

1.6 HOW ENTERPRISES STAFF AND MANAGE EUIS

Every enterprise must staff and manage the activities required to plan, implement, operate, and support information systems needed to produce and deliver their products and services. This is generally the role of an IS organization. This section describes typical approaches and explains how EUIS fit into the picture.

1.6.1 Who Is Responsible for EUIS?

Who is responsible for EUIS in enterprises? The answer to this questions depends on the enterprise. EUIS can be found with many names, roles, and responsibilities.

Most enterprises have integrated EUIS with IS to varying degrees. Integration may range from fairly autonomous departments within IS to almost total merger with other IS operations. For example, a large insurance company in the Northeast assigns EUIS analysts, called business analysts, to the IS teams that support each business unit. PC/LAN, minicomputer, and mainframe technical support all operate as specializations within the same support department. A "Professional Computing Services" department provides EUIS support as part of the overall IS technical consulting area. PC training is offered by the corporate training department. Hotline and Help Desk services are coordinated under one IS centralized area.

1.6.2 IS Organizations

The increased integration of computer and communications technologies seems to be driving most enterprises toward merging IS, EUIS, and Networking (or Telecommunications) under one IS organization. As indicated in the previous section, the degree of integration varies considerably. It may occur only at a high level, creating a sort of IS umbrella over all systems-related activities, or the integration may go deep into the IS organization. Clearly, enterprises are struggling to find the most effective ways to meet the demands for information technologies in a constantly changing world.

The IS organization generally is responsible for overall management of the enterprise's information architecture and information technology (IT) infrastructure (discussed in more detail in the next section). The IS organization typically is managed and operated by technical personnel. However, information technologies usually are viewed as shared resources available to all of a firm's units and applications, and ultimate responsibility for allocating resources and making decisions regarding investment in IT resources belongs to general management.

Management and organization of IS resources in all likelihood will continue to evolve with the network revolution and growing role of computers in business operations. EUIS professionals must be aware of the overall IS management structure and how EUIS fits into the picture.

1.6.3 Information Technology Architecture

Information technology architecture refers to the specific design that information technology (IT) takes in a specific organization to achieve selected goals or functions.[2] It encompasses the IT infrastructure or platform and the *business system applications* they support. The IT infrastructure consists of hardware; software; data storage; digital networks; and the technical specialists to build, operate, and maintain them. The business system applications include the wide range of solutions for which computers are used, including end-user information systems.

Currently, many enterprises seem to be moving toward a concept of enterprisewide information architecture. It is unclear, however, exactly what shape such an organization should take. In fact, definitions of enterprisewide computing even vary. Some firms have a vision of retaining strong, centralized control over all enterprise information systems. Others envision centralized coordination and operation of corporate data centers with distributed departmental networks and PCs under the control of business units. Yet another group envisions decentralized computing with each business unit responsible for all of its own information systems, both IS and EUIS. Clearly, there are tradeoffs, and clearly the direction taken is likely to have a major impact on EUIS.

AN ALTERNATIVE VIEW OF THE IS ORGANIZATION

An organizational design works only if the people at all levels of the IS function understand the model, their role, and their relationship to others within and outside the department. Without such a shared vision, it is unreasonable to expect people to evolve toward excellence in their assigned function. A prominent EUIS consultant, N. Dean Meyer, believes that many IS departments are organized less than optimally to meet today's demands to provide a far broader variety of technologies and disciplines. Most IS organizations have evolved under numerous top executives. Structural adjustments were made to accommodate new technologies and services, special projects, and occasionally to handle personal career issues. Periodically, charters and working relationships were changed as cyclic pressures for centralization and decentralization were felt. As new IS functions spring up, such as new technology groups or a strategic systems implementation team, new organizational issues arise. Whether by word or action, these groups' initial activities will specify their charters and relationships to other IS groups. Simply patching the old organization to accommodate new functions and technologies will no longer work.

To address these problems, N. Dean Meyer and Associates (NDMA) applies the principles of structural cybernetics. Cybernetics is the study of the control of complex systems. The NDMA approach to structural cybernetics is comprised of three parts: principles of healthy organizational design, a straightforward model of the discrete functions in an IS department, and a practical process of organizational change.

NDMA suggests this alternative view of an IS structure that advocates dividing responsibilities along the lines of functions rather than technologies. NDMA suggests the following roles:

- An architecture function that addresses requirements such as computing platforms, technical strategies, planning for hardware and software, and standards.

- Service bureaus that are responsible for operating the data centers and networks.

- Technologists who specialize in business applications development (IS), process applications development (computer-integrated manufacturing or CIM), and end-user information systems (EUIS).

- Consultants who are business specialists and technology generalists. Consultants provide the interface for linking business strategy and information technologies. Two types of consultants are needed: those who work proactively with business leadership to link technology planning with business strategies, and those who provide the needed services and support for the effective use of information technologies in the workplace.[4]

Although it is too early to point to any definite trends, many enterprises are struggling to find more effective ways to organize the IS function. NDMA's alternative is consistent with the growing need to link technology more closely with business operations.

Source: N. Dean Meyer, *Structural Cybernetics* (Ridgefield, Conn.: N. Dean Meyer and Associates, Inc., 1995).

These organizational questions are control issues. IS executives argue that a centralized "service center" operation is the most economical from a corporate perspective. They also view it as essential to providing integrated global networks. Such an organization can provide a challenging technical environment that attracts highly qualified personnel. It is in a better position to provide ongoing technical training, plus it can provide cross training, rotate assignments, and shift personnel to meet changing needs. Strong, centralized coordination is essential to maintain any semblance of standardization and interoperability among the jungle of technical alternatives.

Business unit executives, on the other hand, argue that if they are to be held accountable for bottom line results, they must have more control over their IS expenditures, which constitute a major chunk of most budgets. Executives may not understand the long lead times for systems development and concerns for standardization. They believe that under their control, systems development and support could be more flexible and responsive to changing business needs.

The future is unclear. Some firms that have highly centralized IS functions are moving toward decentralization. Other firms that tried decentralization, such as Aetna Life and Casualty Insurance Company and General Motors, are now moving back toward more centralized control. Sometimes these shifts are driven by changes in philosophy as executive management changes hands. Others are driven by business requirements. A firm with decentralized IS that needs to provide interconnectivity may find itself faced with an impossible mix of incompatible equipment. Moreover, the costs of supporting a highly complex environment with multiple hardware and software platforms may spiral out of control.

Some leaders are advocating a middle ground—the centralization of data center operations and architecture planning with some degree of decentralization for TPS application development and EUIS. In this vision, computer services are seen to operate as a utility, much like the telephone company or electric company, where users can select from an array of services and "plug in" their own equipment as necessary.

For the near future, EUIS specialists are likely to find the IS environment highly variable depending on the enterprise. There is no right approach for everyone. EUIS specialists will need to understand the IS environment within their enterprise and operate accordingly.

1.6.4   Help Desks and Information Centers

A rapidly growing area of end-user support is the *Help Desk.* Formerly called an information center, this user support function has evolved with the rapid growth of computers at the desktop. Originally, information centers provided training, consulting, and user assistance. Through these information centers, users obtained the necessary skills and guidance to manipulate and analyze mainframe data, create and modify their own reports, produce graphs, and make ad hoc inquiries. Originally limited to use of mainframe tools, information centers evolved to support PCs as well, and often played a key role in managing end-user information systems. In fact, in some firms, information centers assumed accountability for guiding and supporting acquisition of PCs throughout the organization. Common information center services included hot lines and user support groups.

Over time, the support functions were decentralized, and as demand grew, hot lines evolved into today's Help Desk. Most modern Help Desks are high-volume call centers that use sophisticated technology and are staffed with trained specialists to assist users with technical problems. Help Desks are discussed in detail in chapter 7, "Support and Help Desk Management."

1.6.5   The Role of the Chief Information Officer (CIO)

The concept of a chief information officer (CIO) has caught on in recent years. The CIO is defined as "the highest ranking executive at the corporate, business unit, or functional division level with primary responsibility for information systems."[3] Perspectives on what has led to the emergence of this new executive role vary. John P. Imlay, Jr., chairman and CEO of Management Science America, Inc., writing in *FE: The Magazine for Financial Executives,* linked the rise of the CIO to the growing importance of information technology:

> All of this implies a changing role for the information manager. He or she will now aspire to being CEO, because in automating administration, in

automating mail, in automating the standard computing functions, and tying in communication, he becomes the heartbeat of the company. And the computer is his tool. Do you doubt a new title is forthcoming? You've seen him or her go from data processing manager to MIS director. Now you're going to see all this coming together as he becomes a new officer in the firm and is called the chief information officer.[5]

The *role* of the CIO (but not necessarily the title) is emerging in response to the increased importance of information technologies:

> By centralizing information management in the hands of a CIO, business can coherently manage increased office automation, the proliferation of PCs, and the expanding use of communications technology. . . . Furthermore, the CIO offers a focal point for determining how to control access to data, what types of end-user support are needed most, how to integrate data and telecommunications systems effectively, and what impact the implementation of new technologies will have on corporate culture. The CIO can also be a leader in strengthening his or her company's current and future competitive position by using technology wisely.[6]

An annual IS survey of executives sponsored by Coopers & Lybrand and *CIO* magazine revealed that CIOs have continued their ascent into the ranks of senior management. The survey sampled 201 non-IS executives ranging from CEOs to vice presidents from a broad spectrum of industries about the role of IS in their organizations and their perceptions of their CIO (used generically to describe the organization's top IS manager). Three-quarters of those surveyed called the CIO a key part of the executive decision-making process. Ninety percent said that their CIO is at least somewhat involved in the formulation of overall business strategy and plans, and just over half stated that the CIO is "very" or "extremely" involved, up from 45 percent the previous year. In addition, 72 percent said that "ideally," the CIO should be very or extremely involved, compared to 62 percent the prior year. Three quarters of the respondents said IS is a significant component of business strategy in achieving a competitive advantage, 82 percent said the same of management effectiveness, and 87 percent of improving productivity. Even more significant, the numbers citing IS influence in facilitating organizational change and restructuring the business shot up to 59 percent and 78 percent, respectively, which is an increase of almost 20 percent from the previous year.[7]

1.6.6 Career Opportunities in EUIS

The job market for individuals with a high level of computer competency, but not necessarily programming languages, is growing rapidly. Skills in Web development, knowledge management, desktop publishing, multimedia, and Help Desk operations, for example, are in high demand. Moreover, as the networking revolution continues to transform the business environment, the demand for business leaders who know how to transform work processes and manage change is growing rapidly.

Career steps for specialists in EUIS are not as clearly defined as the more traditional IS roles. A rapidly changing field, EUIS offers many opportunities, but risks also exist. Both IS and EUIS are still dependent upon technology development. Major new developments could alter the current directions quickly. Tugs-of-war between decentralized EUIS and centralized IS create politics and frustrations. The

Figure 1-11
Sampling of job titles
for individuals with
EUIS skills

High-Level Positions
1. Chief Information Officer (CIO)
2. Vice-President, Information Systems
3. Chief Knowledge Officer (CKO)
4. Web Master
5. Director of End-User Systems
6. Professor of Information Systems
7. President, Knowledge Management Consulting Firm
8. Training Director for Information Systems
9. Director, Reengineering
10. Help Desk Manager
11. Information Systems/Library Administrator

Mid- and Entry-Level Positions
1. Project Manager
2. EUIS Systems Analyst
3. Director, Desktop Systems
4. LAN Administrator
5. PC Software Application Developer
6. Web-Page Designer
7. Web Master
8. EUIS Programmer/Analyst
9. System Trainer/Instructional Designer
10. Computer-Based Training Author
11. Information Center Consultant
12. Office Environment Specialist
13. EUIS Business Analyst
14. EUIS Business Consultant
15. Product Support Manager
16. PC Support Specialist
17. PC Training Specialist
18. Desktop Publishing Manager
19. End-User Support Specialist
20. Vendor Sales Representative

organizational structure and management practices of enterprises also influence how end-user services are handled. Because of the similarity in technologies, lines between EUIS and other IS careers are fluid. Individuals who have strong technical skills and strong human relations skills commonly move back and forth between these two fields. A career path that has combined experience in both EUIS and IS provides especially strong preparation for higher-level IS positions. The resulting breadth of experience provides the broad perspective required for high-level information systems management.

Careers in EUIS include PC application developers, systems analysts or business analysts, network administrators, Help Desk managers, EUIS project managers, Web developers, and a variety of others. Careers in EUIS require a combination of training and experience in computer skills, systems analysis, organizational development, and business knowledge. Courses appropriate for the student pursuing a career in EUIS include the following:

- PC productivity tools (spreadsheets, graphics, database, project management, word processing)
- Multimedia software
- Web development tools such as HTML, scripting, etc.
- Introduction to information systems
- Programming languages such as Visual Basic, C++, and Java
- Fourth-generation languages, such as FOCUS, Statistical Analysis System (SAS), APL, SQL, RPG-III, Nomad2, and others
- Telecommunications and networking
- Systems analysis
- Project management
- Business management
- Organizational development and change management
- Business communications
- End-user information systems
- Ergonomics or human factors (including user interface design)
- Training and instructional design

Figure 1-11 presents a sampling of technical job titles for individuals with EUIS skills.

1.7 SUMMARY

Chapter 1 provides an introduction to the field of end-user information systems (EUIS) and sets the stage for the rest of the text. Information is crucial to the operation of business and government enterprises. The hub of the enterprise that processes and provides that essential information is the business office. EUIS provide new ways to manage information and support business processes. Without these advanced systems, enterprises could not provide the diversity of products and services today's complex society demands.

As computers have become more powerful, less expensive, and easier to use, they have moved out of backroom technical environments into the workplace and onto desktops. The evolution of end-user information systems provides an excellent example of how technology evolves in response to specific needs to resolve problems. At the same time, people and organizations adapt and change in response to new technology.

To take full advantage of new information technologies, organizations must change old ways of doing things. Change must be a learning process that enables individuals to assimilate new technologies. Change disturbs the way people work and disrupts accustomed behavior patterns. New opportunities associated with technology often are not immediately evident.

EUIS is defined as the application of information technologies that support business processes and individual performance with the objective of improving overall organizational effectiveness in direct support of business goals and objectives. Today's end-user information systems make it possible to eliminate or integrate routine tasks, formerly delegated to support personnel, with other business activities. It introduces many new possibilities for helping individuals and groups effectively manage and use information.

End-user, or knowledge work, environments are characterized by variability, specialization, deadline pressures, widely dispersed operations, autonomy, customization, and loosely structured activities. The nature of information processing performed by professional, technical, and managerial personnel is aligned closely to the functional areas in which they work.

EUIS technologies should not be viewed as a magic answer to improving productivity. The potential offered by these tools may be realized only when EUIS technologies are implemented as part of a carefully planned program for increased productivity. Adequate attention must be given to business requirements, work processes, and job design in addition to technology. In and of itself, technology does not make people more productive.

The EUIS project management, introduced here and explained later in the text, provides a framework for managing both the technical and organizational aspects of EUIS projects. Roles and responsibilities for EUIS within an enterprise depend on how the IS function is organized. Although EUIS and IS originated as separate functions, most enterprises appear to be merging them under a single IS organization. The EUIS field provides many challenges for individuals interested in this specialized area of information systems.

The next chapter provides a more in-depth look at the changing nature of today's networked organizations. It presents key technology trends important to EUIS professionals with an emphasis on the implications for individual, group, and organizational performance.

KEY TERMS

- Applications
- Business process (re)design
- Business system
- Chief information officer (CIO)
- Digital Age
- End users
- End-user computing (EUC)
- End-user information systems (EUIS)
- Executive information systems (EIS)
- Help Desk
- Information Age
- Information technology infrastructure
- Information processing
- Knowledge workers
- Knowledge worksystems (KWS)
- Management information systems (MIS)
- Primary functions
- Support functions
- Transaction processing systems (TPS)
- Work flow analysis

DISCUSSION QUESTIONS

1. What are EUIS? How are EUIS different from IS?
2. Who is the end user? How have developments in EUIS been directed to the end user?
3. List six categories of EUIS tools used in offices today.
4. What is the focus of EUIS? How do EUIS facilitate knowledge work?
5. Summarize the relationship between productivity and EUIS.
6. How has the introduction of PCs changed jobs in the knowledge work environment?
7. List characteristics of the end-user environment. How do these characteristics affect the design and implementation of EUIS?
8. What is an office? What role do offices fulfill in the organizational structure of an enterprise?

9. What is work group computing? Why has some of the focus of end-user information systems shifted from individuals to work groups?
10. How do EUIS fit into the overall IS organizational structure?
11. What is a Help Desk? What purpose do Help Desks serve? How do they fit into the typical IS organization?

APPLICATION EXERCISES

1. Pretent that you have just been appointed as manager of an information systems department in a medium-size enterprise. The department is now organized into just two groups: data center operations and IS applications development. However, the department has been growing rapidly and has outgrown its current organization chart. Desktop systems, local area networks, group tools, and the Internet require a growing proportion of time and effort. Using the information in this chapter, draw a new organization chart for the department showing how you would reorganize responsibility for all the major imformation systems functions. Compare your chart with others in the class and discuss some of the different approaches.
2. Task workflow restructure activity. Take a manual document preparation task—restructure w/networked PC's with outlook or lotus notes.
3. Visit an information systems department in a large enterprise or interview someone who is responsible for EUIS. How are responsibilities for EUIS organized? Where does it fit into the IS organization? How many staff support EUIS? What are their titles? What responsibilities do they have? Who are their clients? How many devices are distributed on office desktops? What technologies and services are provided? What is (are) the name(s) of the department(s) that supports EUIS? Share your findings with others in the class.

SUGGESTED READINGS

Drucker, Peter F. *Innovation and Entrepreneurship.* (New York: Perennial Library, Harper & Row Publishers, 1985).

Freedman, David, "The Call for Leadership," *CIO* 5 (February 1992): 17-21.

Meyer, N. Dean. *Structural Cybernetics.* (Ridgefield, CT: N. Dean Meyer and Associates, Inc., 1995).

Naisbitt, John, and Patricia Aburdene. *Megatrends 2000: Ten New Directions for the 1990s.* (New York: William Morrow & Company, Inc., 1990).

Panko, Raymond R., "The Office Workforce: A Structural Analysis," *Office Systems Research Journal* 10 (Spring 1992): 3–20.

Toffler, Alvin. *The Third Wave.* (New York: Bantam Books, 1980).

ENDNOTES

1. D. L. Davis and M. H. Olson, *Management Information Systems: Conceptual Foundations, Structure and Development* (New York: Mc-Graw-Hill, 1995).
2. Kenneth C. Laudon and Jane P. Laudon, *Management Information Systems, 6th* ed. (Upper Saddle River, N.J.: Prentice Hall, 2000), 27.
3. International Business Machines Corporation, "The Chief Information Officer," *IBM Information Processing* (Summer 1985): 33.
4. N. Dean Meyer, *Structural Cybernetics* (Ridgefield, Conn.: N. Dean Meyer and Associates, Inc.,1995).
5. International Business Machines Corporation, "The Chief Information Officer," *IBM Information Processing* (Summer 1985): 33.
6. Ibid.
7. David Freeman. "The Call for Leadership," *CIO* 5 (February 1992): 17–21.

Chapter 2

Life in Networked Organizations

Learning Objectives

Upon completing this chapter, you should be able to:

➤ Describe the impact of digital networks on business and other organizations worldwide.

➤ Explain how information technology, especially the growth in digital networks, is changing the way people work in organizational environments.

➤ Identify key trends that are driving change and their implications for people, technology, business process, and organizational structure.

➤ Differentiate among Internets, Intranets, and Extranets and the types of applications supported by each of them.

➤ Identify key trends in networking hardware and software.

➤ Describe the expanded capabilities and benefits of the Next Generation Internet.

➤ Identify major opportunities and challenges for EUIS in networked organizations.

➤ Analyze a business setting and recommend changes needed to reinvent it for the digital economy.

2.1 INTRODUCTION

With the explosion of the Internet and phenomena such as e-commerce, e-business, and globalization, the pace of change has become relentless. Enterprises that survive and thrive into the twenty-first century will be:

> "flat, fast organizations, with even the newest employees engaged in helping the company succeed. Employees given the chance to share in the invention of their companies—given a voice in a pluralistic process—will embrace the institutional change necessary for leading in the new millennium. Using technology to support energetic and engaged staffs—to free up employees to team, to dream, to invent—may be the key to future success."[1]

It's not just the availability of digital networks that is driving change, however. This century is witnessing an explosion of information and other diverse economic and societal trends that is creating a far more complex society. This convergence of factors coupled with the availability of digital networks is driving change at an unprecedented pace.

In chapter 2, you will examine the technology and its impact on workplace environments. The ability to use technology to enhance individual, work-group, and organizational performance will become increasingly important in the twenty-first-century workplace. This ability requires a thorough understanding of organizational development and change leadership as well as information technology skills. The technology will advance much faster than the ability to use it. The ability to understand the implications of new technologies for how we work, to break old behavior patterns, and to change our paradigms unfortunately comes much more slowly.

2.2   THE CHANGING WORKPLACE (PROCESS)

Probably the most profound impact on the workplace over the next few decades will be the impact of the Internet and other networking technologies. Digital networks will transform the workplace in ways that most people hardly can imagine today. As we look back 100 years and compare life in 1900 to our life today at the dawn of this new millennium, the changes are profound. Among the myriad of new technologies, the twentieth century has brought electricity, cars, televisions, airplanes, telephones, microwaves, rocket ships to the moon, guided missiles, computers, and the Internet. Each of these technologies has brought wide-ranging cultural changes, as well. Take the automobile, for example. Whereas paved roads, gas stations, repair shops, and tire manufacturers may not have been too difficult to predict, how many do you suppose foresaw today's superhighways, motels, the RV industry, drive-in restaurants, drive-up banking, car washes, commuter traffic jams, and automobile insurance among the hundreds of spin-off industries and cultural changes? Although few if any may foresee or predict, we can be certain that the changes that will occur over the next 100 years will be as great if not greater in magnitude.

Digital networks will transform not only the workplace but many other aspects of modern life, as well. This transformation is underway already. Networked organizations foster virtual environments where people work from home and remote locations. Work teams are spread out around the world, not just in business but in almost every field of endeavor including science, politics, medicine, art, and music. The Internet has spawned new virtual learning environments and virtual communities brought together around common interests. The impact of technologies—such as webcasting, Internet telephones, streaming audio and video, net meetings, wireless computing, and much more—is just beginning to be felt.

Enterprises must leave behind aging models and career paths that evolved out of the Industrial Revolution. "In the old-fashioned career path, employees came to the same building for the same hours, paid their dues and climbed the ladder," says Bruce Tulgan, founder and CEO of Rainmaker's Thinking, Inc., a workplace consulting firm based in New Haven, Connecticut. "But a smaller and smaller number of employees fit that model. You have to do business now with a fluid talent pool. It means a fundamental rearrangement in the way you organize your business and the way you handle staffing, a new way of looking at your human resources, a new way of motivating employees that goes beyond simple retention strategies."[2]

Digital networks are having their greatest impact in creating new and powerful bonds among customers, suppliers, and business partners. In the digital economy, speed and agility are paramount. The impact goes far beyond business, however, touching every aspect of life in America and, perhaps even more significantly, the world. A *Newsweek* issue devoted to e-life (see Spotlight, The Dawn of E-Life, page 43) concluded, "What is certain is that America has digitized, and there's no going back. . . . The corner has been turned, but only just. We're at the beginning of a new way of working, shopping, playing, and communicating."[3]

Although this text focuses primarily on business, digital networks are having a profound impact on many aspects of life. In this section, we examine briefly some of the workplace changes that various sources are observing or forecasting as digital networks reach critical mass.

2.2.1 Anytime, Anyplace Environments

In networked enterprises, workers will have access to almost everything they need via the desktop and portable PCs. We're moving to a world where fairly simple personal companion devices will proliferate side-by-side with powerful PCs that support knowledge work at home or the office—or anywhere in the world. Workers can carry with them incredible amounts of information or be connected to anyone or anything in the enterprise as they need it from anywhere.

An Internet presence makes enterprises instantly global, opening up new opportunities for products and services, but also making new demands upon the organization. The boundaries of what we think of as an organization are going to blur. How work is transacted will change in ways yet unforeseen.

As Internet capacity expands, we are seeing a convergence of data-, text-, voice-, and video-enabled applications. People have greater access to bandwidth from home and office. In fact, it is becoming so easy to stay connected and plugged in that the distinction between private and public enterprises and between our private and pubic lives is blurring. If you have full access to your desktop from home, hotel, plane, and even a vacation cottage, when are you on the job and when are you off the job? It works the other way, as well. With cellular phones, pagers, instant messaging, and computer monitoring, parents can more easily keep in touch with children from the office or anywhere. Day care centers are even beginning to install computer monitors so parents can check in and see their children at work or play, reassuring themselves that all is well.

2.2.2 A 24/7 Global Digital Economy

The twenty-first-century workplace never sleeps. Global enterprises operate on a 24-hour clock, 7 days a week. Although the New York office may be closed, employees in China or Australia are in the middle of their day. They may need access to information from company operations in New York or San Francisco.

Some call it the digital economy. Some call it the knowledge economy. Whichever you prefer, today's global information infrastructure provides instant access to information that enables executives to react quickly to opportunities that emerge anywhere in the world. Billions of dollars can be moved around the world in seconds to take advantage of changing opportunities.

In 1998, the Commerce Department issued its first report on the emerging digital economy, revealing that about one third of the nation's real economic growth

THE DAWN OF E-LIFE

WAS THERE A SINGLE MOMENT WHEN WE TURNED THE CORNER? When we moved from a culture centered on network television, phones with wires, information on paper and stock prices based on profit into a digital society of buddy lists, streaming video, Matt Drudge and 34-year-old billionaires in tennis shoes? Did the transition come with the Deep Blue chess match, when millions of Web surfers watched a stack of computer chips dominate the world's greatest player in a test of "intelligence"? Could the global outburst of online mourning after the death of Princess Diana have marked our passage? Did it come last Christmas, when hundreds of thousands of shoppers avoided malls and clicked through their gift lists? Or was it the online lingerie fashion show? The online birth? And just when did putting an e-mail address on a business card stop marking you as ahead of your time?

Let the chat rooms debate what marked the turning point. What's certain is that America has digitized, and there's no going back. Worldwide there are almost 200 million people on the Internet. In the United States alone, 80 million. The numbers tell just part of the story: The Net is no longer a novelty, an interesting way to pass the time. A third of wired Americans now do at least some of their shopping on the Net, and some are already consulting doctors on the Net, listening to radio on the Net, making investments on the Net, getting mortgages on the Net, tracking packages on the Net, getting news on the Net, having phone conversations on the Net, checking out political candidates on the Net. Each of these activities is impressive, but the aggregate effect is a different kind of life. Our goal in this special issue of *Newsweek* is to examine what's happened, why, and how the Internet is changing the way we live now.

It's been 30 years since the Internet's predecessor, the Arpanet, was switched on to help academics and government wonks get connected. Almost 25 years since the first software for personal computers (co-written by some kid named Bill Gates). About 5 years since the Net became in effect the world's grandest public utility, driven by a combination of cheap, powerful PCs, a remarkably scalable infrastructure that sped up our connections (though not enough), and easy-to-use browsing software that took advantage of the Net's open rules. And maybe 3 or 4 years since concocting Internet business schemes became the world's most desirable creative outlet, the contemporary successor to writing the Great American Novel.

The triumph of tech, for better or for worse, is far from complete—in schools, businesses, operating rooms, labs, banks or the halls of government. Just about everything we've ever done that has to do with communication and information has been digitized, and now we're going to start tackling stuff that hasn't been done because you can do it only with the Internet. And if you think up something that fits that bill, there's a venture capitalist in Palo Alto who will whip out a huge check for you. Even the most knuckleheaded CEO—the kind of guy who used to think it was beneath him to put a terminal anywhere near his mahogany desktop—now knows that job No. 1 in the firm, no matter what the company does, is to figure out how to become an *Internet* company, because he can be sure that his competitors are.

It's crucial to assess the impact of this shift, because the digital revolution is much more profound than a mere change of tools. The Internet is built on both a philosophy and an infrastructure of openness and free communication; its users hold the potential to change not just how we get things done, but our thinking patterns and behavior. Bound together by digital mesh, there's hope we may thrive together—if some nagging, unanswered questions find felicitous answers. Can a spirit of sharing be maintained in the face of the need to recoup huge investments? Will persistent security holes—both personal and national, with the threat of cyberwar—erode our confidence in this new medium? Is it really possible for governments to forgo their impulses to regulate the Net with their usual heavy-handedness? How will the bounty of the digital age be distributed fairly?

The corner has been turned, but only just. We're at the beginning of a new way of working, shopping, playing and communicating. At *Newsweek* we're calling this phenomenon e-life, and it's just in time. Because the day is approaching when no one will describe the digital, Net-based, computer-connected gestalt with such a transitory term. We'll just call it life.

came from information technologies. This revelation has led economists to begin looking for a new definition of output transcending the industrial era concept of widgets coming off the assembly line. New terminology, such as *knowledge assets* and *intellectual capital,* are creeping into the language of economics.

Renowned economist and best-selling author Lester Thurow believes that "knowledge-based capital, along with the advent of electronic commerce and a true global economy, are changing the very rules of economics and society." In his book *Building Wealth: The New Rules for Individuals, Companies and Nations in a Knowledge-Based Economy* (HarperCollins, 1999), Thurow says that the basis for the new economy is the proliferation of knowledge.[4]

This new digital or knowledge economy is increasingly innovative and entrepreneurial in contrast to the slow-changing, more static economy of the industrial era. Enterprise leaders wishing to succeed in the new digital economy must embrace and adapt quickly to change. Technology increasingly will be a driver of business change, as faster, broader networks become more ubiquitous. Business leaders and CIO's, or technology leaders, must work in closer partnership. End users across the enterprise must become more savvy about how to harness the technology at their desktop to improve their own productivity, as well as to enable and support business innovation and change at all levels.

2.2.3 Teamwork and Collaboration

Society has become too complex for individuals to work meaningfully alone. Companies that hope to win in the twenty-first century must find new ways to foster and reward information sharing and collaboration. This need for collaborative work processes flies in the face of long-engrained hierarchical structures and management practices. Breaking established patterns of thought and action can be near impossible, especially when reward structures are still geared to recognizing individual performance. Implementing collaborative tools, such as *Lotus Notes,* has minimum impact on how people work unless the business processes change, as well. In fact, some sources estimate that no more than 10 percent of *Lotus Notes* projects actually employ its collaborative functions, such as discussion databases.[5] The collaborative aspects are underutilized not because of faulty technology, but because the technology often is deployed without considering how the organizational structure must change to support it.

Collaboration is fundamental because it gets to the notion of participation, which is necessary to understanding. What you learn from a lecture or reading is transformed into personal knowledge when you debate in groups and start to solve problems. We learn from and with each other. The question is how to build a culture in which that kind of learning is deeply honored. In today's knowledge economy, we need to look at how communities can work together to create shared understandings.[6]

In the digital economy, collaboration is no longer an option. Collaboration will be an essential ingredient for success in the years ahead. It is the key to unleashing the energy in people, bringing the benefits of diverse thinking to solving problems, and fostering a culture of innovation.

To succeed in twenty-first-century enterprises, workers must collaborate effectively so that all of the key people on a project are well informed and energized. Collaboration on a widespread basis makes for a stimulating, energized workplace. When a critical mass of capable people work in concert, it creates synergy. New ideas are generated through cross-stimulation, and less-experienced employees are pulled along to a higher level. The company as a whole works smarter.[7] The ultimate goal is for work teams to identify and develop the best ideas from throughout an organization and then act with the same unity of purpose and focus that a single, well-motivated person would bring to bear on a situation. Digital networks, which facilitate information sharing and communication, can help bring about this group cohesiveness. The technology in itself doesn't make a collaborative culture; that starts from the top. Digital information flows, however, reinforce collaboration, making it possible for bright people all over a company to be in touch with each other.

2.2.4 Fast Moving and Flexible

Increased global competition and rapidly changing customer behavior are driving shorter business cycles. Decision makers must be able to act quickly in this brutally competitive environment. Accurate and timely information is vital to defending, maintaining, and advancing an enterprise's position in the market.

In the digital economy, market environments change fast. New business models, like that employed by Amazon.com, can change the rules of the game and transform an industry. *Time* named Amazon.com's CEO, Jeff Bezos, as "person of the year" because "e-commerce is changing the way the world shops." The same *Time* edition also features the story of e-Bay, "the other e-commerce revolutionary." These .com companies deploy two very different approaches, both of which are shaking up old industrial world models. "E-Bay's many-to-many approach to selling—the world is just one big auction—completely opposes Amazon.com's one-to-many, fixed-price model, and it has been profitable from day one." Both companies made the rest of the retail industry scramble. Moreover, rather than being a cold, impersonal world, cyberspace is giving new meaning to the word *community.* "For many people e-Bay does what communities have traditionally done. It not only provides them financial systems, but also draws them together with like-minded folk, offering encouragement, rewarding unique talents and interests, giving them an outlet for their eccentricities and individuality. And in some cases, rescuing them from the margins where they would otherwise languish alone." Fans suggest that e-Bay represents a return to earlier one-to-one sociability or perhaps even improves on it, because the Internet diminishes the traditional divisions of geography and class.[8]

To compete in the twenty-first century, enterprises must be fast moving and flexible. The chairman of Microsoft Corporation, Bill Gates, sees it this way:

> The twenty-first century will be about velocity: the speed of business and the speed of change. To stay up with and anticipate change, businesses need radically better information flow. To get a better flow of information to develop the right processes and strategies, they need a digital nervous system. Most organizations don't have enough data to understand key aspects of their business well enough. A digital nervous system will help you understand your business better and then act more effectively on that understanding. An infrastructure designed around information flow will be the "killer application" for the twenty-first century.
>
> If the 1980s were about quality and the 1990s were about reengineering, then the 2000s will be about velocity. About how quickly the nature of business will change. About how quickly business itself will be transacted. About how information access will alter the lifestyle of consumers

and their expectations of business. Quality improvements and business process improvements will occur far faster.

We have infused our organization with a new level of electronic-based intelligence. I'm not talking about anything metaphysical or about some weird cyborg episode out of *Star Trek*. But it is something new and important. To function in the digital age, we have developed a new digital infrastructure. It's like the human nervous system. The biological nervous system triggers your reflexes so that you can react quickly to danger or need. It gives you the information you need as you ponder issues and make choices. You're alert to the most important things, and your nervous system blocks out the information that isn't important to you. Companies need to have that same kind of nervous system—the ability to run smoothly and efficiently, to respond quickly to emergencies and opportunities, to quickly get valuable information to the people in the company who need it, the ability to quickly make decisions and interact with customers.

The successful companies of the next decade will be the ones that use digital tools to reinvent the way they work. These companies will make decisions quickly, act efficiently and directly touch their customers in positive ways. I hope you'll come away excited by the possibilities of positive change in the next ten years. Going digital will put you on the leading edge of a shock wave of change that will shatter the old way of doing business. A digital nervous system will let you do business at the speed of thought—the key to success in the twenty-first century.[9]

In the digital economy, market environments change faster than the most competitive company can respond on its own.[10] This is one of the factors driving corporate mergers. Enterprises can acquire expertise and knowledge faster than they can develop it in-house. From the knowledge management perspective, the best merger partners are those with complementary strengths. "Increasingly," wrote Tom Davenport and Larry Prusak in *Working Knowledge*, "firms acquire other companies specifically for their knowledge."[11] Twenty-first-century enterprises need to be fast and flexible.

2.2.5 Just-in-Time

The byword in networked organizations is *just-in-time*. It started with just-in-time supply methods and stockless inventory systems. Strategic systems for linking customers and suppliers have changed the way many enterprises—including factories, hospitals, and retailers—handle the supply and inventory requirements of their businesses. Just-in-time supply methods reduce inventory requirements by tightly integrating the ordering and delivery of materials, thus greatly reducing inventory levels and associated costs. Stockless inventory goes a step further, delivering goods to the floor as they are needed, effectively eliminating inventories entirely and outsourcing responsibility for inventory management to the supplier. Wal-Mart's legendary inventory replenishment system, which is triggered directly by point-of-sale purchases, has propelled it to the position of number 1 retailer in the nation.

The concept of just-in-time has many other dimensions, as well. Online help and electronic performance support systems provide just-in-time job aids, which are context specific. Corporate universities deliver training at the desktop to knowledge workers just-in-time as new assignments require.

2.2.6 Process Oriented (Versus Functional)

Digital networks offer enterprises fundamentally new ways to expand their markets, streamline their corporate business processes, and attract and retain customers in new and innovative ways. By becoming more process oriented, enterprises are reducing the influences of bureaucracy and linking their internal operations more directly to meeting customer and market demands.

A *business process* refers to the unique way in which an enterprise organizes and coordinates work activities and resources to produce a product or service. Business processes are generally cross-functional, transcending the boundaries between sales, marketing, manufacturing, research and development, accounting, and human resources. A business process generally represents a concrete work flow that is linked directly to serving customers. Examples include new product development, which turns an idea into a manufacturable prototype, and order fulfillment, which begins with receipt of an order and ends with payment for a delivered product or service. The order fulfillment process generally transcends the functions of sales, accounting (credit checking, billing, and accounts receivable), manufacturing, shipping, and possibly installation of complex equipment, for example.

E-business has escalated the focus on business processes, often fundamentally changing the business model underlying how business has been conducted traditionally. The business process view provides the basis for reengineering and other corporate change efforts. By focusing on a complete business process that is linked directly to achieving corporate objectives and meeting customer and market demand, enterprises have been able to streamline work flows, significantly reducing cycle times and costs. The most successful efforts have been associated with radical changes in the underlying business models—often having a major impact on an entire industry. The success of new business models on the Internet, such as those underlying Amazon.com and e-Bay, have underscored the critical importance of enterprises focusing on their key business processes and executing them well. Business reengineering and organizational change are discussed in more detail in chapter 11.

2.2.7 Innovation

Innovation isn't just the new strategy; it's the only strategy for businesses that want to thrive in the new millennium.[12] Innovation always has been something at which U.S. industries have excelled. In the new, global knowledge economy, the need to continue to invest in innovation has become even more urgent.

Although innovation can start anyplace in the enterprise—manufacturing, marketing, even IT—it cannot succeed without a lot of support from senior management. According to *CIO Magazine,* innovation is core to the culture of most enterprises that made the CIO 1999 List of Top 100 Leaders for the Next Millennium. "Senior executives have opened their doors to new ideas and new ways of doing business. They have found creative ways to motivate and reward employees at all levels of responsibility to rethink their jobs—to concentrate less on the task at hand and more on tomorrow's needs and solutions."[13]

With a shorter and shorter grace period for companies to grab market attention for their products, technological breakthroughs can no longer assure a company dominance for years to come. Innovation must be an integral part of a company's culture, and enterprises need to provide the support and resources for workers to excel at it. For instance, 3M asks employees to spend 15 percent of their work-week daydreaming about new inventions. Nokia routinely polls employees for product suggestions. Such policies must be seen as potential revenue builders—not as overhead. It's a leap of faith that companies must be willing to make.[14]

2.2.8   Knowledge Age Learning Organizations

Competition and decision making are increasingly knowledge based. As firms become more far flung, employees become even more mobile, and business grows ever more complex, keeping tabs on corporate knowledge has become increasingly challenging. The problem today is not information; it's information overload. In essence, the problem of putting your finger on the right information at the right time has been compounded. It's not just information; it's information in context. It's knowing who's working on what and who knows what. It's about how to better leverage the experience and expertise of people and to provide an environment for knowledge sharing. In the networked organization, the need for coordinating information flow and managing knowledge across the enterprise has grown exponentially—and so have the options for addressing this need.

One of the most dominant trends to emerge in the past couple of years is the concept of *knowledge management (KM)*, which is managing knowledge for strategic advantage. When the earlier edition of this text was published, the term *knowledge worker* was just emerging, and terms such as *knowledge management, Knowledge Age, knowledge economics*, and *enterprise portals* didn't even exist. The American Productivity and Quality Center (APQC) in Houston describes KM as a conscious strategy of getting the right information to the right people at the right time so that they can take action and create value. A new trade magazine titled *Knowledge Management* began publishing in October 1998. According to the magazine editors, KM as a discipline has been on a slow but sustained growth curve that is likely to continue ascending for years to come. KM is multidimensional in nature and hard to define. It cannot be purchased in a box. It is not simply a market opportunity, nor just a management approach. It is not the exclusive province of the employer or the employees. It is not wholly owned by IT, human resources, executive management, or the lines of business. Most of all, based on tracking KM trends, issues, products, and applications it is not just another management fad.[15]

Managing knowledge and transferring best practices is simple in concept but difficult in execution. Knowledge management is discussed in detail in chapter 5.

An even more recent concept is the *enterprise portal*, a single, browser-based point of entry to all of an enterprise's knowledge assets. In a nutshell, an enterprise portal is a Web-based front end to internal and external information that is classified according to a company-specific information taxonomy. One important characteristic of enterprise portals is that they bring together structured information from corporate database systems and unstructured information from document management systems, e-mail, and Web pages. Another important characteristic is that they use some form of automated classification technology to sort information into useful content categories.[16]

Ultimately, KM will have profound implications for the roles of individual workers. While it may be difficult to define KM precisely, real benefits are to be gained from engaging people throughout an enterprise to focus their intellectual abilities on innovation and hard-to-solve problems, rather than simply dealing with and maintaining routine tasks. Digital networks open up new options for enabling the flow of information and data within an enterprise. Our Information Age society has become too complex for individuals to work meaningfully alone. Even the medical profession has been affected:

At the moment, only one physician in four even uses a computer at work. But that is sure to change. I see patients in the office and the hospital. I do house calls. I'm on call at the hospital tonight. And the care I give depends on the information I command. Medicine has gotten too complex to practice from a dog-eared textbook. Fortunately, there is now an alternative. InfoRetriever and other portable databases won't make doctors obsolete. But doctors who lack them may soon be just that.[17]

Another major trend in response to the increased demand for continuous learning is *corporate universities.* According to Corporate University Xchange Inc., a New York City-based consulting and educational research group, more than 1,600 companies, including nearly half the Fortune 500 companies, maintain corporate universities. Corporate universities are "less a place to go to for training than a metaphor for continuous learning."[18] To illustrate the magnitude of these efforts, average annual budgets in 1999 were $17 million, up from $13 million in 1998.

Corporate universities have evolved primarily in response to the increased need for continuous learning in the fast-paced, digital economy. Ninety percent of those 1,600 companies offer at least some virtual training. Proponents expect the growth of the virtual university component to continue because it fits well with a knowledge-based digital economy. Enterprises need to train more people on more topics and to do it faster, on a worldwide basis, and at lower cost. Web-based technology allows enterprises to provide that training anywhere, anytime. Workers study at their own pace, skip sections that aren't relevant, repeat sections as needed, and do it right from their desktop or home computers. Corporations are also finding that Web-based curriculums provide an effective tool for creating a unified culture, which is particularly important as companies grow, merge, and globalize. Corporations can use it, for example, to make training available to geographically dispersed teams and to share lessons learned by a team in Japan with others in dozens of locations around the globe.

Bain Virtual University, launched in June 1998 by Bain & Company, a Boston-based consultancy, wanted to create a central, consistent, constantly updated learning source available all the time to all employees at 25 offices worldwide. Cox University, launched in July 1998 by Cox Communications, serves 50,000 employees in 200 locations. Its mission is to help Cox meet its business goal of becoming the leading telecommunications and media company in its market. Conoco University elected to go virtual because "We are a global corporation that happens to have a Houston headquarters. The university had to live in the conference rooms and corridors of Conoco around the world, not just be an initiative from Houston."[19] Conoco offers Web-based learning programs around three major themes: executive development (open to only the top 200 to 300 leaders), shared purpose and direction, and fundamentals for the future.

2.3 THE TWENTY-FIRST CENTURY WORKFORCE (PEOPLE)

How will the third millennium workforce differ from that of the twentieth century? For starters, "perhaps they'll banish the term *human resources,* an Industrial Age invention that seems to imply individuals, like coal, conveyor belts or chairs, are commodities to be maintained."[20] In the meantime, some of the new position titles that are emerging are revealing. Figure 2-1 shows a number of titles gathered randomly from recent computer trade magazine articles.

Forecasters say that the average worker of the future will have six or seven different careers, each requiring new skills, new attitudes, and new values.[21] Continuous learning is now a hallmark of careers in the new economy. Post-secondary institutions no longer produce fully and permanently qualified professionals. Students and graduates planning careers can no longer predict what skills and competencies will be required in the years to come. Success increasingly depends on continuous learning and knowledge management, both of which can be aided by information technology.[22]

No one can foresee all the changes that will happen to workers, organizations, governments, and society as we move into the digital age. What is sure is that life in cyberspace enterprises will be significantly different than in the industrial firm. In the sections that follow, you will explore some of the ways in which digital networks are transforming the workforce.

2.3.1 Shifting People into Thinking Work

Information work is thinking work. Most routine, repetitive work has been automated or, if not, ought to be. That's what computers do best—routine, repetitive tasks. At the same time, people are freed up to do the thinking work—answer questions, handle the exceptions, solve problems, and create better products and services. Yet, many companies still hire and manage staff as they did 30 years ago when routine, repetitive tasks made up the majority of work. Consequently, problems do not surface until irate customers call. Customers are told that's the way the system works, and they spend hours on the telephone being passed from one department to another to resolve problems.

Enterprises need to reexamine the ways in which they use IT to handle routine tasks. Digital networks give enterprises new opportunities to provide the human touch where it matters. Service levels that were acceptable in the past no longer meet the expectations of today's more demanding consumers. The difference is dramatic between getting a note that was clearly written by a person versus a computer-generated form letter, or receiving a phone call about a billing problem or order from a person versus a computer. It's of tremendous value to have a person working with a customer who is unhappy about something important or who has special needs. With the aid of smart systems, a service worker's span of control can be expanded easily to shift responsibility from executing transactions to satisfying clients. In a hotel, for example, digital networks can streamline the check-in and check-out processes dramatically and solicit routine feedback, freeing up staff time. Guests who prefer might simply walk up to a lobby kiosk and check themselves out or do it from the room before leaving. How much value would hotel guests gain if half a dozen additional people were acting as concierges instead of as clerks? Improvements could include answering the phone before the second or third ring, not being left on hold, getting prompt assistance with service needs, or perhaps offering new services.

Having workers focus on whole processes allows them to tackle more interesting, challenging work at the same time that it improves customer service. It also engages them, fosters a greater sense of responsibility, and helps keep the focus on the end in mind. One-dimensional jobs (tasks) can be eliminated, automated, or rolled into a bigger process. One-dimensional, repetitive work is what computers, robots, and other machines are best at and what people are poorly suited to and generally find boring and distasteful. Managing a process instead of simply executing isolated tasks makes someone a knowledge worker. Digital networks make it all possible.

2.3.2 Diversity

Demographic diversity will continue to have a striking impact on business, education, and many other aspects of life. Diversity is not only tolerated, it is a distinct advantage for competing in the global marketplace. Dissent is to be encouraged because it encourages workers to think for themselves. The ability to appreciate diverse thinking and constructively manage conflict are critical skills for twenty-first century workers. *Failure* should never be a dirty word because fear of failure begets fear of risk. Creating such a culture is not an easy task. It is a critical one, however, because timidity and conservatism can cause a company to lag behind.

2.3.3 Taking Ownership, Empowerment; Broader Jobs

A culture of empowerment is key to succeeding in a knowledge economy. It is knowledge workers and business managers who benefit from more and better information, not just senior managers. When workers get access to digital networks and IT tools that deliver better results, they demand more. Moreover, with the support of digital networks, scope of responsibility can be expanded, effectively shifting the horizon of workers from completing isolated tasks to contributing toward corporate goals. Twenty-first century corporations must empower knowledge workers and organize for learning:

> Aim for distributed power. Concentrating power in a few people at the top is contrary to competitive output. Concentrated power creates expectations that decisions are made "somewhere up there." It sub-optimizes available brain power, creating an enormous under-utilization of the intellectual abilities available lower down in the organization. While distrib-

Figure 2-1
Emerging new job titles

Senior adviser on learning and organization development, BP Amoco
Vice president of business development process change, Gateway
Vice president of electronic commerce, Gateway
Vice president of global architecture, Gateway
Vice president of knowledge management, Gateway
Vice president of global applications, Gateway
Knowledge architect, Hallmark
Senior director, knowledge management, Pillsbury
Ernst & Young chief knowledge officer (CKO)
Mentoring director
Staff strategist
Communications facilitator
Manager of strategic innovation
Career coach
Internet strategist

uted power may be time-consuming and frustrating, history has shown it very effective in business. When top managers end the frustration by stepping in, they destroy the conditions for maximizing available talent.[23]

Knowledge empowers. The old corporate cliché about distributing information on a need-to-know basis is antithetical to empowerment. It suggests that somehow someone "up there" knows what everyone else in the organization needs to know. It suggests that knowledge workers are still Industrial Age cogs who should be doing repetitive, single-task jobs. It suggests that workers should not step outside the box. Progressive CEOs agree:

> A company's middle managers and line employees, not just its high-level executives, need to see business data. It's important for me as a CEO to understand how the company is doing across regions or product lines or customer segments, and I take pride in staying on top of those things. However, it's the middle managers in every company who need to understand where their profits and losses lie, what marketing programs are working or not, and what expenses are in line or out of whack. They're the people who need precise, actionable data because they're the ones who need to act. They need an immediate, constant flow and rich views of the right information. These employees shouldn't have to wait for upper management to bring information to them. Companies should spend less time protecting financial data from employees and more time teaching them to analyze and act on it.[24]

Fast, open communication will play a critical role in shaping organizations in the digital economy. Changing the way individuals can communicate, will also change how most organizations work. For instance, e-mail has helped flatten many corporate hierarchies by providing entry-level employees unprecedented direct access to top decision makers. Traditionally, it was viewed as an act of warfare if an employee carbon-copied the boss's boss on paper. In e-mail, however, individuals do it all the time—without repercussions. Empowerment requires creating a culture where people at all levels of responsibility are listened to and encouraged to report the bad news as well as the good. For example, the impetus for Microsoft's response to the Internet, according to Bill Gates, did not come from him or the other senior executives. It came from a group of dedicated employees who recognized the power of the Internet early on and took advantage of Microsoft's policy that smart people anywhere in the company should have the power to drive an initiative. In many ways, according to Gates, technology has shaped the policy. "Do people all over my company feel free to send me e-mail because we believe in a flat organization? Or do we have a flat organization because people have always been able to send e-mail directly to me? For years, everybody at Microsoft has had a PC and e-mail access. It's a famous part of our corporate culture, and it's shaped the way we think and act."[25]

2.3.4 Pay for Performance

The pursuit of a job for life no longer drives employees in today's knowledge economy. Instead, flexible career paths are becoming the norm. Employees look for opportunities to continue to expand their knowledge and experience and to enhance their resumes or portfolios in the process of completing assignments and contributing to projects. Many employees today want a challenge as well as a paycheck.

The changing marketplace is forcing enterprises to come up with inventive, new ways to inspire and reward good performance. In response to changing competitive pressures, enterprises need greater flexibility to assign and reassign workers. As workers rotate on different projects, they may no longer report to one manager long enough for the old standard, annual performance review processes to be valid. Enterprises are focusing more on the requirements of specific projects and needs as they arise. They are developing inventories of employee competencies and skills and assigning and reassigning workers when and where needed. Compensation is based on the level of knowledge, skills, and experience and demonstrated performance as opposed to time in the job.

Face time and seniority count for less than they did formerly when it comes to recognition or promotion. Speed and efficiency are what matter most. The worker who boasts that he or she spent 80 hours in the office this week on a project will not win. Instead of "that's great," the response is likely to be "you needed 80 hours for this?"

Work assignments are increasingly defined in terms of specific results to be delivered within a certain time frame. Parameters and requirements are agreed upon, and the work does not necessarily have to be done in the office from 9 to 5. Work can be completed anytime, any place.

2.3.5 Telecommuting, Flexible Work Hours

New work styles include more relaxed work environments and dress. Flexible work hours, job sharing, and telecommuting are becoming increasingly commonplace. On-site or company subsidized day care, mother's lounges, and childbirth and adoption leaves for men and women are among the benefits designed to make the workplace more flexible to attract and retain high quality workers. Savvy enterprises recognize that to attract and retain quality employees, their workplaces must be transformed into truly diverse, flexible environments that enable workers to balance their personal lives with their professional lives.

2.3.6 Work Groups without Borders

Teams and work groups increasingly have no borders but are geographically dispersed. As more and more business happens almost entirely online—and as the lines among companies and their partners, suppliers, and service providers blur—the new collaborative applications are becoming essential for completing projects or executing business transactions without being hampered by the limitations of time and geography. As indicated by a recent survey of 400 professionals from various industries, shown in Figure 2-2, a new generation of workers is embracing "boundary-less" work arrangements. Whereas the over 50 set is apprehensive about breaking down the corporate office, feeling that boundary-less workers are less respected and may have reporting problems, younger workers feel just the opposite.

Digital networks change what is possible and practical. The costs of information and coordination are dropping. New avenues are available for coordinating the efforts of globally dispersed workforces. Instant messaging and real-time collaboration can be highly effective in coalescing geographically dispersed work groups. Applications like customer–relationship management and online customer service can take advantage of real-time collaborative software to provide customers and partners with an immediate, high-touch level of communications. Team members can use instant messaging to exchange just-in-time messages, the equivalent of shouting over the top of the cubicle wall for help.

2.4 LIFE IN THE WORLD OF E-BUSINESS AND E-COMMERCE (ORGANIZATIONAL STRUCTURES)

Digital networks have opened new ways for conducting business inside (e-business) and outside (e-commerce) the enterprise. Life in the world of e-business and e-commerce is essentially business without boundaries. The Internet provides new channels of communication and interaction that can be used to create closer relationships with customers in marketing, sales, and service. The Internet brings an immediacy and reach to relationships that have no parallel in the Industrial Age economy.

E-commerce offers enterprises fundamentally new ways to expand the markets in which they compete; to streamline their corporate business processes to deliver products and services more efficiently; to attract and retain customers in new and innovative ways; and to deliver better, more personalized customer service. E-commerce is not without risks, however. Market conditions constantly change as new competitors enter markets with new business models. Customer loyalty is fleeting as customers are just a few clicks away from switching to competitors. Moreover, competitive advantage can be short-lived as traditional barriers are rendered irrelevant by technological advances.

Relationships, both business to business and business to consumer, are key as firms learn to create online business communities. This concept of community—enabled by electronic networks—runs contrary to the individualistic competitive models of the past century. According to Don Tapscott, chairman of the Alliance for Converging Technologies, "Driven by the need to reduce supply chain costs and respond more quickly to end-user demands, communities of companies are using networks to trade with one another and create products or services that draw on the talents of many players. Digitally savvy firms in every industry are beginning to use this model to establish the conditions for value creation and dominance."[26]

In the long run, e-business—the use of Internet and other digital technology for internal organizational communication, collaboration, and coordination of business processes—may have an even greater impact than e-commerce. The use of internal networks based on Internet technology—called Intranets—is soaring. Their ease of use and low cost provide a huge advantage over other internal networks. The seamless interface with the Internet provides another major advantage. Internal applications are expanding rapidly and include publishing personnel policies, electronic forms, catalogs, employee handbooks, and many other types of proprietary documentation; reviewing account balances; scheduling; revising design documents; and hundreds of other applications. Even more far reaching, perhaps, are the new opportunities to create collaborative environments, in which knowledge workers can share information, exchange ideas, and work together on projects and assignments regardless of geographic location. Collaborative tools include e-mail, fax, voice mail, bulletin boards, newsgroups, groupware, discussion boards, chat rooms, teleconferencing, and more. These tools are described and discussed in chapter 4.

Both e-business and e-commerce can fundamentally change the way business is conducted. They open up new horizons for what is economically and practically feasible by reducing the cost of information and coordination. More than ever companies are in a position to create wealth by adding knowledge to each product at each step.

Welcome to the post-industrial live-work space. Corporate dress codes have eased, and now the corporate work environment is becoming amorphous. We're seeing the age of the regimented company left behind as we step toward the new millennium, where technologies are not only providing new business opportunities but are also enabling workers to balance their personal lives with their professional ones. Ceridian Employer Services, *a human resources solutions company, surveyed about 400 professionals from a number of industries and found that the younger element of the workforce is embracing what they call a "boundary-less" work arrangement. The breaking down of the corporate office structure includes working in virtual teams, telecommuting, flexible work plans and temporary, project-based contracting.*

Boundary-less Work Arrangements are Here to Stay
Most employees said they or their companies use some type of boundary-less work arrangement with the breakdown of usage as follows:

Temporary professionals	67%
Flexible work plans	66%
Virtual teams	42%
Telecommuting	35%
No Boundary-less workers	9%

Tools offer flexibility

Surprisingly, senior executives and HR managers were the least interested in investing in technology tools, while workers and their managers saw extreme benefit in online training, the Internet and home fax machines. The Internet ranked number one as the tool that best supports working away from the office or in some other "boundary-less" format.

Boundaries are out

Most companies offer some sort of "boundary-less" work plan—whether it's virtual teams, flexible work schedules or employing temporary professionals. But the younger companies, like their younger employee counterparts, are trailblazing the flexible corporate landscape. Companies younger than 10 years old are almost twice as likely to increase their use of virtual teams as older companies.

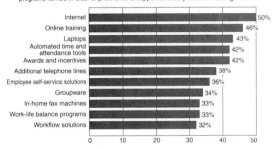

Boundary-less Work Arrangements Require Technology and Support
Overall respondents were interested in using the following technology tools, resources and programs ranked in order of preference to support boundary-less work arrangements

Internet	50%
Online training	46%
Laptops	43%
Automated time and attendance tools	42%
Awards and incentives	42%
Additional telephone lines	38%
Employee self-service solutions	36%
Groupware	34%
In-home fax machines	33%
Work-life balance programs	33%
Workflow solutions	32%

Keeping your talent

Employees are quick to jump ship nowadays for sweeter deals with the competition. Among the incentives are money, training, advancement opportunities and more lately, flexible work environments. Giving a worker more control over his career will likely keep that person around longer.

HR Pressures Force companies to Use Boundary-less Work Arrangements
Highly successful for attracting and retaining qualified workers

	Attracting	Retaining
Virtual teams	50%	66%
Flexible work plans	52%	64%
Telecommuting	52%	60%
Temporary professionals	46%	43%

■ Attracting qualified workers
☐ Retaining qualified workers

Generation gap

Those free-loving participants of the '60s Generation take the conservative road here, while their offspring and their younger cousins, Generation X, embrace a boundary-less arrangement with open arms. Those over 50 are particularly apprehensive about breaking down the corporate office, feeling that boundary-less workers are less respected and will have more reporting problems. The younger—and likely more technologically savvy—workforce feels just the opposite.

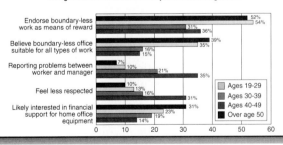

Younger Workers Embrace Boundary-less Work Arrangements

	Ages 19-29	Ages 30-39	Ages 40-49	Over age 50
Endorse boundary-less work as means of reward	52%	54%	31%	36%
Believe boundary-less office suitable for all types of work	39%	35%	16%	15%
Reporting problems between worker and manager	7%	10%	21%	35%
Feel less respected	10%	13%	16%	
Likely interested in financial support for home office equipment	31%	31%	23% / 19%	14%

Figure 2-2
A new generation of workers embraces the "boundary-less" company

Source: Survey conducted by Ceridian Employer Services and published in *Knowledge Management Magazine,* 2 (May 1999) p. 32.

In the sections that follow, we will highlight some of the significant ways in which information technology and digital networks are shaking up assumptions fundamental to industrial era enterprises. Understanding the significance of these changes is key to transforming industrial era enterprises into winners in the new digital economy.

2.4.1 The Customer Is King

With so much competitive information easily accessible on the Internet, consumers are becoming far more savvy and demanding. Consumers can determine quickly which company's product is priced lower or has more features than a competitor's product. Competing in this digital environment requires companies to be faster, more agile, and more creative than was necessary just a few short years ago. With more and more companies replicating features found in competitors' products, companies are finding it increasingly difficult to differentiate themselves in the marketplace. Instead, they are taking a closer look at their customer relationships.

These more complex customer-service strategies and business challenges require powerful computers on both sides of the relationship—vendor and customer. As the capacity of digital networks expands, various electronic means such as voice, video, interactive use of the same computer screen and so on will be incorporated to further augment the new relationships. Thus, after focusing for years on shareholder value, streamlining business processes, and eliminating jobs, enterprises are returning to building their companies on a customer-centric model.

2.4.2 Shift from Transactions to Relationships

Digital networks are changing business in fundamental ways. "Companies that think e-commerce won't affect their businesses are wrong. It is a shift from transactions to relationships in terms of working with the customer. The old rules of customer service don't apply."[27] Unlike the early days of telecommunications, the Internet is not merely about displaying information, transferring data, or conducting transactions. The Internet is about building relationships with customers, business partnerships, and other constituencies. Enterprises are employing a number of new strategies aimed at making this shift from transactions to relationships. Some of the fastest-growing applications today are customer relationship management (CRM), enterprise relationship management (ERM), and sales force automation (SFA).

Customer relationship management links back-office and front-office functions with all of a company's touch points with the customer. It thereby attempts to maximize the relationship with each customer through better service, supported by a technology infrastructure. By linking back and front office functions electronically, firms can make available to everyone within the firm who needs it a wealth of information about customers at a fraction of the previous cost. The objective is to provide a single point of entry that connects customers and their orders to all operations that support order fulfillment—e-mail, e-commerce, call centers, Web conferencing, marketing tools, customer service, sales automation, lead tracking, billing, manufacturing, shipping, and partner and channel tools, all leading to a central database. When well implemented, CRM dramatically increases competitive advantage by streamlining communications and transactions to enhance marketing, sales, finance, delivery, and service efforts.

Enterprise Relationship Management (ERM) extends CRM to include other relationships, such as those with business partners and suppliers. The ability to share information with business partners and suppliers over digital networks opens new avenues for closer collaboration that can lead to reduced cost and improved service.

Sales Force Automation (SFA) employs software that automates routine tasks such as tracking customer contacts and forecasting, thereby freeing up the sales force to concentrate more on selling. Getting sales representatives to buy in and use technology, however, can be a major challenge.

2.4.3 Mass Customization

Whereas the industrial era was characterized by mass production, the digital era is characterized by mass customization. Contrary to popular notions about dehumanized technological environments, digital networks are leading to increased personalization. A new strategy for a growing number of enterprises is one-to-one marketing, which is an approach that targets individual customers with customized products and services. (see Figure 2-3)Companies like Amazon.com strive to get to know their customers on a personal basis. Then they use customer information and history to tailor future transactions. When *Time* named Amazon's Jeff Bezos as "Person of the Year," they noted the company vision of being "the world's most customer-centric company." However, it is not just the new upstarts that are concentrating on customers. Mass customization has become the strategy of long-standing veterans like Ford Motor Company, Dell Computers, and Levi Strauss, as well.

This trend "represents a 180 degree turn from previous years when it was the company, not the customer, that dictated what appeared in the market. You wouldn't have dreamed of asking Levi Strauss & Company years ago to custom-fit a pair of jeans for you—now the company will do it and it won't break your trouser budget. Nor would you have considered asking a car manufacturer to build a car that suited your individual tastes. Today, the car of your dreams is only a few clicks away."[28]

2.4.4 Transforming the Enterprise

Business leaders are finding that they have squeezed all the efficiencies they can from flattened organizations and reduced budgets. In the digital economy, it's the rapid flow and analysis of information that differentiates the winners from the losers. The big advantage lies not just in reengineering or total quality management. It lies primarily in sharing information and making decisions faster than your competitors can. The ability to capture and share knowledge is critical. Digital networks are hastening the transition from hierarchical, bureaucratic organizations to networked organizations where information and decision making move horizontally within flat organizations.

By taking advantage of advances in IT and digital networks, enterprises are streamlining the mundane, day-to-day tasks like invoicing, purchasing, and inventory control. In the process, they are making this information more accessible at every point of contact with clients and vendors. This automation of internal operations—sometimes referred to as e-business—often doesn't have the glamour of e-commerce, but many industry forecasters believe that it is in this back office of business where the biggest productivity dividends will be achieved—in the wholesale automation of corporate transactions and procedures.

Reengineering is taking on new significance as enterprises attempt to redefine themselves to extract greater advantage from networking technologies. Work in the twenty-first century has become an exercise in managing change. In a society where change is a constant, a talent for exploiting change with IT is invaluable. The challenge for enterprises is seldom a lack of ideas; it's the ability to put ideas into action—to make them happen. Technology is merely an enabler. People, not technology, accomplish organizational change. Putting new ways into action requires more than technology savvy. It requires business knowledge, foresight, and an understanding of the end-user environment. The biggest challenge is how to harness the technology to create an optimal workplace environment that enables workers to be more productive, affords them greater fulfillment, improves decision making, and makes organizations more competitive. The challenge is to create workplace environments that attract, retain, and challenge workers on every level to excel.

2.4.5 Eliminating Intermediaries

Digital networks provide enterprises with direct links to clients and business partners, effectively eliminating the traditional intermediaries. Whether it's e-trading of equities, travel, banking, shopping, shipping, or whatever the industry, traditional distribution channels are being challenged by the Internet.

Bill Gates used the term *friction-free capitalism* to describe "how the Internet was helping create Adam Smith's ideal marketplace in which buyers and sellers can easily find one another without taking much time or spending much money. Achieving Smith's 'perfect price' comes not just from eliminating the middleman but also

Figure 2-3
E-commerce innovations that foster one-to-one relationships with consumers

10	E-Trade's Smart Alerts (www.etrade.com) Notifies investors via e-mail, Web, or pager when a stock hits a particular trigger point.
9	*The Wall Street Journal Online's* Personal Journal (www.wsj.com) Allows subscribers to select up to eight key words, categories, or company names of particular interest. All stories that match the key words are then saved into folders for later viewing.
8	Ticketmaster Online/City Search Online Viewer (www.myticketmaster.com) Simulates the view you can expect from your seats for many venues around the country. (See "That's the Ticket," *CIO* Section 2, June 15, 1999.)
7	Amazon.com's "1-Click" Ordering System (www.amazon.com) Accesses shipping and billing preferences for each customer automatically and places the order.
6	S&P Personal Wealth's Asset Allocator (www.personalwealth.com) Provides customized portfolio advice.
5	Peapod.com's Recipe Generator (www.peapod.com) In partnership with Kraft Foods, this program allows consumers to enter the contents of their refrigerator into the site and receive recipes that incorporate all or most of the items.
4	Lands' End's Personal Model (www.landsend.com) Customers enter information about their height, build, and hair coloring to create a virtual model. They can try different clothing on the model to get a sense of how it will look on them.
3	Dell's Online Product Configurator (www.dell.com) Customers who purchase a PC can configure 21 different features, such as hard drives, printers, and speakers. Each feature provides an additional 3 to 10 options that allow for millions of configurations.
2	Cisco Systems' Customizable Online Knowledge Base (www.cisco.com) Gives customers access to the same customer service knowledge base that Cisco's technical support personnel use.
1	Amazon.com's Recommendations System (www.amazon.com) Suggests books, CDs, and videos to its customers based on past purchases. —*D. Duffy*

Source: Reprinted through the courtesy of *CIO.*

from the additional information available online. The Internet makes it easy for a buyer to get background information about a product—how it's rated by consumer organizations or other independent reviews—and to compare prices easily. Buyers also can tell sellers more about their requirements, and sellers will be able to target their wares to the people most interested and to cross-sell related products."[29]

Empowered by the Internet to deal directly with manufacturers and service providers, customers gain little added value from intermediaries who simply transfer goods or information. The value of a pass-through intermediary's work is falling quickly to zero. For example, travel agents who simply book plane fares are at risk. This kind of high-volume, low-value transaction is perfect for a self-service Internet travel reservation site. The key question for the future is what value travel agents will add to the process. Can they, for instance, create a total travel adventure or highly personalized tour packages with benefits that would be difficult for any but the most savvy of travelers to duplicate for themselves?

2.4.6   Building Partnerships and Alliances/Open Systems

In the digital economy, the nature of competition as it evolved in the industrial era is being challenged. In good relationships, wise buyers sometimes go out of their way to help their vendors. Although conventional wisdom holds that buyers squeeze the most they can out of their sellers, the opposite is often true in good relationships—a phenomenon called "discretionary collaboration." This concept may be critical in the information management process and distributed environments of today's global enterprises. "Companies must learn to coevolve with others in their environments—in a process that involves not only conflict, but collaboration, shared visions, alliances, and other complex relationships for which there is very little precedent."[30]

"The key to competitiveness right now is business model innovation, and the new models that work are partnerships," according to Don Tapscott, author of *Blueprint to the Digital Economy: Creating Wealth in the Era of E-Business.* Based on his study

SPOTLIGHT ON SOLUTIONS → Technology, People, Structure, Processes

---

ABOVE THE CROWD

The concept, known broadly as mass customization, is best exemplified by Dell Computer, which builds millions of computers each year, each to the specifications desired by the buyer. For one big customer, Ford, Dell has established different PC configurations designed to suit different employees in many different departments. When Dell receives an order for a PC via the Ford intranet, it knows immediately what type of machine the worker is ordering and what kind of machine he or she should get.

Ford pays a premium for such personalized service. Is the price worth it? Consider the alternative. Ford could purchase its PCs from a local distributor. The distributor would send boxes over to Ford. Those boxes would need to be opened and configured by a systems worker. This process, which is common at most companies, typically requires 4 to 6 hours of a professional's time for each computer and often results in configuration errors. Clearly, Dell's customization is worth the higher price.

The same is true for other custom products. Levi Strauss is able to charge more, not less, when it customizes a pair of jeans, and Mattel can be sure that little girls will pay a higher price for a personalized Barbie doll. So there's no doubt: Companies are beginning to use technology to push margins higher.

Source: J. William Gurley, "Productivity Paradox."

---

of 120 new, partnership-based businesses, Tapscott says that, "We've been talking about partnerships forever, but what we're seeing now is completely different." He believes that in the future, manufacturing companies won't make things, partnerships will. Partnerships will be the foundation for the design, production, marketing, sales, and support of products and services. These new partnerships and alliances call for sharing information not only among members of the firm, but with clients and business partners, as well.[31]

Enterprises of all types—corporations, universities, medical facilities, and so on—are becoming more open systems. In today's emerging systems, the key concepts no longer are authority and control but rather partnership, collaboration, and cooperation—and perhaps even creative chaos. The Internet is surely a precursor of the ultimate open system.[32]

2.4.7   Virtual Communities

Virtual corporations result when decision makers decide to partner with other corporations to achieve competitive success. Instead of hiring additional staff to manufacture a needed product, a corporation examines its strengths and then joins with other businesses for those products. Corporations achieve this by linking their computers with those of other companies. Suppliers can use the computer links to make forecasts on demand for their products, and retailers can use the links to reduce inventory and improve availability.

Perhaps even more significant is the concept of *virtual communities,* which are groups that coalesce around common interests or needs. This concept runs contrary to fears people often have about technology leading to impersonal, detached, isolated environments.

> Community building is going to be one of the biggest growth areas in the next few years on the Web. The Web dramatically increases the number of communities you can bond to. In the past, you might have had time to be a part of your neighborhood community and one or two social organizations you took the trouble to join. In the Web lifestyle, you are limited only by your interests. One of the most powerful socializing aspects of the Web is its ability to connect groups of like-minded people independent of geography or time zones. If you want to get together a group of avid bridge players, or talk issues with people who share your political views or stay in touch with your ethnic group scattered all over the world, the Web makes it easy to do. If you want to keep up with the goings-on in your hometown, the Web can help. . . . A Web site such as Third Age, which offers an electronic community space for seniors, illustrates the power of electronic community building. The site provides advice on family, health, and technology; warnings about scams targeting seniors; and discussion groups on topical issues.[33]

Savvy enterprises, universities, and organizations of all types are shifting the approach to their Web sites from one-way communication to fostering two-way communication. Thus, Web sites are becoming increasingly interactive. The concept of virtual communities moves beyond interactive communications, however, to fostering one-to-one relationships. This introduces the concept of recognizing the individuality of users, which is a fundamental ingredient for building a true relationship. It starts with the notion of a personalized home base. Customers, partners, and employees can tailor the home base, making it a far more interesting and advantageous place to exchange information. As an alternative, the enterprise, making use of intelligent agents, can tailor the site to users based on their previous interactions and patterns of use. By tailoring services and making use of interactive communications features such as e-mail, chat rooms, and collaborative tools, enterprises can enhance the value and effectiveness of their relationships with constituencies. One example of this type of relationship is Web-based Help Desk support (see chapter 7). Enterprises are able to provide access to technical information tailored for a client's make and model of equipment; share experience among users through frequently asked questions; promote interaction among users through, for example, posting questions that other users can respond to; maintain a record of prior questions or problems and their resolution; submit questions to technical assistants; and talk directly with users through real-time chat sessions. In essence, the paradigm—or business model—becomes more of a *communications center* than today's notion of a Web site.

As illustrated in this chapter's Spotlight Creating Virtual Communities, colleges and universities are capitalizing on this approach to create richer learning communities and foster lifelong relationships with alumni and other important constituencies.

2.5   THE KEYS TO SUCCESS IN A TECHNOLOGY-DRIVEN ECONOMY

What are the keys to the new millennium? According to a survey conducted by *CIO Magazine,* the number one key is people. To win in a technology-driven economy, companies must focus on people within and outside the enterprise.[34]

An 18-member panel, which included academicians, analysts, and consultants with expertise in a broad range of industry and technology areas, selected 100 companies that they thought were best positioned to prosper in the new millennium. Predicting future success is always rather shaky ground, but several dominant themes emerged among these 100 companies. These themes confirm many of the trends discussed elsewhere in this chapter and throughout the text and are summarized briefly in the sections that follow:

- Cater to customers
- Invest in people
- Embrace creativity
- Rethink your business
- Seize the Web
- Care about others

2.5.1   Cater to Customers

Know your customer is the mantra for companies moving away from simple cost cutting to actual growth in revenues in the coming millennium. Across all industries, the increasing transformation of products into commodities has created a dilemma for companies attempting to stand out in the marketplace. Consequently,

CREATING VIRTUAL COMMUNITIES

Universities are leveraging the power of the Internet and digital networks by implementing systems for technical, administrative, and instructional support that tailor meaningful communications to students, faculty, staff, and alumni. The most forward thinking are going even further in an effort to create lifelong virtual communities.

Like the far-flung families that are becoming typical of Baby Boomers and Generation X, higher education is struggling to maintain a sense of community and loyalty among its constituents. Geographical restrictions have fallen. Distance learning technologies offer a plethora of choices—students can pick from an array of education providers, changing their future alma mater almost as easily as changing their long-distance provider. Forecasters say that the average worker of the future will have six or seven different careers, each requiring new skills, new attitudes, and new values. Already, traditional undergraduates, those 18 to 22 years old, attending full time and living in college housing, account for less than 25 percent of all students in higher education. Lifelong learners—mature adults who require continuing education—already comprise 44 percent of the student population. Even traditional students are expecting round-the-clock access. In response, more than 80 percent of traditional U.S. colleges and universities will use distance-learning technologies and techniques in one or more "traditional" academic programs by the year 2002, according to the GartnerGroup.

"The feeling of remoteness is the biggest barrier to distance learning," according to Mike Rebbechi, executive director of Information Technology at Charles Sturt University (CSU), New South Wales, which serves a student population of nearly 18,000 distance learners. In response, CSU and other universities are attempting to use technology, which ironically is often viewed as cold and impersonal, to create a sense of community. "We are trying to make any services and faculty we have available to on-campus students, also available to off-campus students. In addition, we want to provide the best modes of delivery and services available to our on-campus students," Rebbechi explains.

Higher education is providing access and community to distance learners through the World Wide Web, e-mail, computer conferencing with selected audio/video streaming, two-way audio/video computer conferencing, multi-media, virtual reality, and even offerings on business networks. The capacity and capabilities for virtual communications will continue to proliferate. Ultra-intelligent networks, digital wireless, and Web channels will become more affordable and available.

"It's important that we do depict it as a learning environment and not as a cold technological world," says Gary Kerr, academic vice president at the Southern Alberta Institute of Technology (SAIT). "We'd better be able to differentiate ourselves in the marketplace by providing highly interactive communications strategies and learning strategies that will engage the learners and keep them moving along."

Toward this end, some universities are striving to create a "home base" for learners as a platform for building a true relationship based on individual needs and interests. Home base, in Internet terms, is where users ultimately spend the majority of their time on the Web. Like the home page that greets users of America Online, it is a secure communications center where users get the most from their time spent on the Net. In higher education, home base is the page where students, faculty, and administrators will return over and over again. The university's home base can be an exclusive provider of electronic communication by delivering services such as e-mail, collaborative tools, voice mail, customized personal and campus content, and e-commerce, all through a secured access path.

"The value of the home base is that learners can tailor it, making it far more advantageous and far more interesting to them to go to receive information. It will increase their utilization of the page, and that increases my ability to communicate with them," says Eric D. Weber, dean of student services, Salt Lake Community College. "The personalized home base gives us an opportunity to develop a much better relationship with our learners and reinforces the personal, interacive kind of learning environment that we want to create," adds Gary Kerr of SAIT. "A key feature is the ability of learners to interact with us, in the chat rooms, for example. It gives them the ability to question our people so we can respond. The more interactive the tools appear to the learner, the better the quality of the relationship we can establish with the customer."

The benefits of the communications center—and the opportunities to better serve students—are increased exponentially by integrating the center to a university's existing administrative software and hardware. The result is dynamic and personal event-driven applications that maximize the content in a university's existing database by delivering data automatically to the user based on some set criteria. By linking the communications center to a university's database and enabling it with event-driven technology, higher education can deliver tailored, meaningful communications to students, faculty, staff, and alumni. By enabling 24-hour access to curricula, as well as administrative services, institutions can meet the service expectations of today's consumers. "The capability to communicate to a wide audience, yet with different messages, is the greatest benefit of the technology," says Curt Guenther, interim director of media relations at the University of Memphis. "We can deliver individualized messages to alumni, parents, students, and prospective students, messages they will be most receptive to, messages they want to hear. It makes our job easier."

Gary Olsen, assistant vice president, alumni affairs at Villanova University, sees the technology supporting long-term relationships with alumni and donors. "It will allow us to disseminate information in a very personalized and individualized way to our students, our faculty, our staff, and our alumni. It has the potential to bring our campus community and our university community closer. . . . It will allow us to bring our 80,000 alumni to our campus without their having to leave their homes. It's a very, very exciting propsect for the future."

In the Information Age, consumers are at the center, requiring greater choices, heterogeneity, and personalization from businesses. Whether you're selling books, or degrees, your network must support increased application functionality, user friendliness, and flexibility. While many vendors are hoping to catch the prospect's interest for a second, the more savvy companies are trying to hold on for a lifetime, building a lifelong relationship with the prospect. Higher education is possibly the most likely market to build such a relationship with its constituents. People understand that, unlike the choice of computers, car insurance, or stereos, the choice of a college or university will impact their lives.

Source: Adapted from Rodney L. Everhart, Creating Virtual Communities, *Syllabus, http://www.syllabus.com,* April 1999, (12:8) 14–16.

they are turning to strategies to differentiate themselves through services. Many companies are embracing the concept of *customer relationship management (CRM),* but few so far have taken the steps necessary to truly implement it—to link the back and front offices directly to the customer.[35]

Beyond the ability to tailor marketing initiatives, forward-looking companies are using customer relationship management to increase market share by customizing products and services and building consumer loyalty. Customization is at the heart of the marketing strategies of companies like Capital One Financial Corporation, based in Falls Church, Virginia. Instead of standardizing credit programs to maximize efficiency, Capital One provides multiple variations of programs built upon the interests of individual consumers. Capital One began life in 1988 as the Signet Bank with 1 million customers and $1 billion in managed loans. Signet spun off the division in 1994, and it currently has 18 million customers and $17.4 billion in managed loans. They offer more than 3,000 different credit card products, whereas most of their competitors have only a few standard offerings. By using massive databases, Capital One sales representatives are able to access information instantly on individual customers in order to suggest further services.

Recent initiatives by Kraft Foods Inc. provide another example of this customization trend. Kraft mounted a multifaceted effort to raise sales for its retail partners, and thereby itself, through the use of the Web with data warehousing and data mining technologies. An internally developed retailer software program helps grocery stores analyze customer preferences and stock shelves accordingly, resulting in 5 percent sales growth and reducing the time it takes retailers to manage the process from days to hours. Meanwhile, the Krafts Interactive Kitchens Web site (www.kraftfoods.com) offers consumers extensive information about nutrition and helps them build meal plans. Kraft is working now on linking up information obtained from the Web site, its toll-free number, and e-mail messages to further aid grocery stores in managing stock and raising sales through more customized service.

2.5.2 Invest in People

Getting the best people and inspiring them to pull ahead of the competition will be the primary challenge in the coming years. Increasingly, companies are turning to unconventional approaches to attract, retain, and empower the best in their industries. Companies are employing fewer full-time and more contract employees.

The trend is clearly for companies to equip all employees with access to everything they need at their desktop or with mobile units. Job sharing, flexible work hours, and telecommuting are becoming more common. Companies offer extensive training programs through corporate universities. In addition to the more traditional classroom type of workshops and seminars, however, corporate universities offer extensive Web-based training options available on demand from anywhere. Digital networks, collaborative software, mobile communications, and videoconferencing technologies harness the power of teams.

Long-standing management practices are beginning to change, as well. Indicators point to a reversal in the 1980s and 1990s trend of reducing middle-management ranks as the role of management becomes more important. Companies are looking for a new breed of managers, however, who will be leaders and coaches rather than the supervisors of the past. Managers must lead by engaging their staff in working as a team. Longevity with the company will no longer be enough for middle managers to qualify for positions. The most-sought-after competencies will be the ability to work with employees to set concrete goals and deadlines, create clear performance specifications, give fast feedback, and avoid micromanaging.

2.5.3 Embrace Creativity

Many of the reengineering efforts of the 1990s simply meant cutting staff and squeezing the life out of budgets. The survey showed that companies now are beginning to understand that the only real path to maintaining growth and creating new value for customers is innovation. Companies are acting to make innovation an integral part of the culture and to provide the room and encouragement for staffers to excel at it. For instance, Tom Peters, in his book *In Search of Excellence*, points out that excellent companies are better listeners. They get a benefit from market closeness because most of the real innovation comes from the market. When Procter & Gamble (P&G) began putting the toll-free 800 telephone number on all its packaging—it got 200,000 calls the first year with customer ideas or complaints. P&G responded to every one of those calls, and the calls were summarized monthly for the board meetings. Insiders report that the 800 number is a major source of product improvement ideas. According to Peters, there is surprising and powerful theoretical support for what P&G and others are doing. Eric von Hippel and James Utterback of the Massachusetts Institute of Technology are long-time students of the innovation process. Studying the source of innovation in the scientific instruments business, they found that out of the eleven "first of type" major inventions they looked at, all came from users;

of 66 "major improvements," 85 percent came from users; and of 83 "minor improvements," 66 percent came from users.[36]

2.5.4 Rethink Your Business

Rethinking the company, whether in response to increased competition, globalization, or any of the other factors driving businesses today, was another post-2000 success trait among the CIO-100. Reengineering took many forms, often changing a company's underlying business or substantially altering its corporate structure or culture. For example, Enron Corporation, an energy company based in Houston, made reinvention a central theme of its strategy of rapid new business development.

Sometimes, business reengineering was a desperate response to failure. One CIO-100 company, Yellow Corporation, a freight transportation company based in Overland Park, Kansas, was caught off guard when deregulation hit in 1980. A strong internal focus left it ill-prepared to compete in an increasingly crowded industry. Near failure drove Yellow to look outside and determine what its customers were demanding. It learned that customers wanted just-in-time deliveries and specialized services such as electronic data interchange (EDI). In response, Yellow hired a consulting firm to develop a new client/server-based information system and two call centers to help the flow of freight information. The company also overhauled its old Web site, which was used primarily to post company information. Customers now can use the site to track their shipments and link to the call center. Usage of the Web site went from 10,000 hits per month in 1998 to 4 billion a month in 1999. The company also installed mobile data terminals in all trucks so that dispatchers can keep better track of where shipments are heading. According to one company executive, "Whereas Yellow was once a company whose philosophy was if we are efficient, then the customer will come, it is now a rapidly growing organization using technology to get closer to its customers."[37]

2.5.5 Seize the Web

"The barriers to entry for the Internet are very low; . . . but the barriers to really succeeding are very, very high."[38] Survey findings underscore just how different business on the Web truly is. One of the lessons that companies learn early on is that online customers have different expectations about service than traditional customers do. Web customers want speed, reliability, and consistency. For example, E-Trade Group Inc. finds that "most customers are pretty technically savvy, so when they speak to a customer service rep, they want someone who can speak their language."[39] The electronic environment seems to subtly raise people's expectations and diminish patience and social politeness. Thus, Web business demands much better service than in the physical world.

Some industry leaders believe that because the cultures and expectations are so different, established companies that want to become a competitive force on the Web are at a disadvantage—that it is next to impossible for those companies to be focused on both the Internet space and the physical space. Cyber and brick-and-mortar companies operate so differently that even offering the same product requires a radically different way of thinking about issues like marketing and customer service.

2.5.6 Care about Others

Growth in environmentally conscious companies was another noticeable trend in the CIO-100 survey. For some new economy companies, caring for employees does not go far enough. They are going a giant step further to incorporate socially responsible behavior in the core corporate culture, as well. Some of the companies that made the CIO-100 list, like Patagonia Inc., based in Ventura, California, believe that treating employees well and weaving environmentalism into its business model are critical to corporate profits. Advocates argue that in the twenty-first century, companies with a social agenda as their underpinning will thrive better than companies that focus solely on the bottom line.

2.6   THE DIGITAL DIVIDE

According to government statistics and other sources, equitable access to computers and the Internet is a growing concern in the United States and worldwide. The so-called *digital divide* threatens to exacerbate an already widening income gap between the rich and the poor. Access to computers is expanding rapidly. In 1998, more than 40 percent of American households owned computers, and 25 percent of all households had Internet access. Community technology centers are springing up, and inner-city schools are being wired quickly thanks to federal dollars provided through the government's reduced E-Rate program. In the meantime, the divide is getting worse. According to a new Commerce Department report, "Falling Through the Net" (ntia.doc.gov), the gap in Internet access between those at the highest and lowest income levels grew by 29 percent in one year alone.

Although some expect the access gap to narrow as prices of computers continue to fall and incomes rise, an even bigger concern is the gap in being able to use the technology in meaningful ways. "Access won't by itself level the playing field: If you wire them, they won't necessarily prosper. Computers might become as common as TVs, but they require initiative and creativity to use fully. Knowing how to play computer games is not the same as knowing how to design them."[40]

2.7   NEXT GENERATION INTERNET (NGI)
AND INTERNET2

As individuals and organizations race to take advantage of the opportunities and challenges of the Internet and World Wide Web, multiple efforts are underway to develop the Next Generation Internet. Two major research efforts are promoted and heavily funded by the U.S. government. The first, the *Next Generation Internet (NGI)*, is a U.S. government-led initiative focussed primarily on commercial and governmental applications. The second, the *Internet2 Project*, is a university-led collaborative effort with the objective of accelerating the next stage of Internet development in academia. We'll take a brief look at each and how they are working together on the Abilene network.

2.7.1   Next Generation Internet (NGI)

The Next Generation Internet (NGI) was initiated on October 10, 1996, in Knoxville, Tennessee, when then President Clinton and Vice President Gore announced a three-year commitment of $300 million to improve and expand the Internet. Built on the base of already federally funded research and development, the NGI initia-

Dell Computer Corporation recently responded to a disgruntled customer by building a better box—a shipping box, that is. The customer was one of many who had been invited to the company's usability lab to test the length of time needed to get a new PC up and running. While unpacking a Dell Dimension tower, the customer struggled and struggled with the shipping box. He finally became so frustrated that he picked it up and turned it upside down. The tower fell to the floor—and died. Although the purpose of the test was to learn how long it took a customer to install a computer, seeing someone destroy a tower was so startling that executives quickly decided to redesign the box and its packing materials.

Source: Adapted from Louise Fickel, "Know Your Customer," *CIO,* 12:21, August 15, 1999, p. 63. Reprinted through the courtesy of *CIO.*

tive calls for substantial matching funds from private sector partners. The initiative is built on partnerships between researchers developing advanced networking technologies and researchers using those technologies to develop advanced applications. Partnerships also involve federally funded network test beds and commercial network service and equipment providers that participate in these test beds to test concepts for the future commercial Internet. In addition, NGI will focus and stimulate other federal programs, from research and development to shaping future information technology procurement visions.

The NGI Vision is as follows:

In the twenty-first century, the Internet will provide a powerful and versatile environment for business, education, culture, and entertainment. Sight, sound, and even touch will be integrated through powerful computers, displays, and networks. People will use this environment to work, bank, study, shop, entertain, and visit each other. Whether at the office, at home, or on travel, the environment will be the same. Security, reliability, and privacy will be built in. The customer will be able to choose among different levels of service with varying prices. Benefits of this environment will include a more agile economy, a greater choice of places to live or work, easy access to lifelong learning, and better opportunity to participate in the community, the nation, and the world.[41]

To reach this vision, three goals have been established, each with a strategic approach and each with metrics of success. The three goals are:

1. Experimental research for advanced network technologies
2. Next generation network fabric
3. Revolutionary applications

As one of its goals, the NGI initiative enables advanced network-based science, health, education, and environmental network applications. These applications are selected from the participating agencies and other government missions and are carried out in partnerships between the initiative and other programs. The role of applications in the initiative is to demonstrate the value of advanced networking and to test advanced networking services and technology.

2.7.2 Internet2

Internet2 (I2) is a project of the University Corporation for Advanced Internet Development (UCAID), involving more than 160 U.S. universities, working together with partners in industry and government. The Internet2 project is not a single separate network, but rather joins member network application and engineering development efforts together with many advanced campus and regional and national networks. The goal is to develop advanced Internet technology and applications vital to the research and mission of higher education (see Figure 2-4). Internet2 is working to enable applications, such as telemedicine, digital libraries, and virtual laboratories, that are not possible with the technology underlying today's Internet.

The Internet2 project is bringing focus, energy, and resources to the development of a new family of advanced applications to meet emerging academic requirements in research, teaching, and learning. Internet2 universities, working with government and others, are addressing the major challenges facing the next generation of university networks by:

- First, and most importantly, creating and sustaining a leading edge network capability for the national research community.
- Second, directing network development efforts to enable a new generation of applications to exploit fully the capabilities of broadband networks.
- Third, working to transfer rapidly new network services and applications to all levels of educational use and to the broader Internet community, both nationally and internationally.

Just as today's Internet arose from the academic and federal research networks of the 1980s, Internet2 is helping develop and test new technologies, such as Internet Protocol Version6 (IPv6), multicasting, and quality of service (QoS), which will enable a new generation of Internet applications. This research ultimately will benefit all sectors of society. Just as e-mail and the World Wide Web are legacies of earlier investments in academic and federal research networks, the legacy of Internet2 will be technologies adopted by and deployed in commercial networks.

Internet2 is not a physical network that will replace the Internet. Rather, Internet2's goal is to bring together institutions and resources to develop new technologies and capabilities that can then be deployed in the global Internet. Universities will maintain and continue to experience substantial growth in the use of existing Internet connections, which they still will obtain from commercial providers. In fact, the commercial sector is a full partner in the Internet2 project and will benefit from applications and technology developed by Internet2 members. The Internet2 project has more than a dozen leading companies as partners.

Participation in Internet2 is open to any university that commits to providing on-campus facilities that will allow advanced applications development. The investment this requires may be more than many institutions can manage right now. However, Internet2 intends to transfer rapidly the results of its work to the broader networking community. Fifteen years ago, connecting to the Internet could be as expensive as participating in Internet2 is today. As the technology dropped in price, the entire academic community benefited from the efforts of the initial research participants. It is anticipated that deployment of Internet2 technology will follow a similar pattern.

A key goal of the Internet2 project is to accelerate the diffusion of advanced Internet technology, in particular into the commercial sector. In this way, Internet2 will help to sustain U.S. leadership in networking technology. Internet2 will benefit nonuniversity members of the educational community as well, especially grades K through 12 and public libraries. Internet2 and its members aim to share their expertise with as wide a range of computer users as possible.

Mission
Facilitate and coordinate the development, deployment, operation, and technology transfer of advanced, network-based applications and network services to further U.S. leadership in research and higher education and accelerate the availability of new services and applications on the Internet.

Goals
- Enable a new generation of applications.
- Re-create a leading edge research and education network capability.
- Transfer new capabilities to the global production Internet.

Additional Objectives:
- Demonstrate new applications that can dramatically enhance researchers' ability to collaborate and conduct experiments.
- Demonstrate enhanced delivery of education and other services (e.g., health care, environmental monitoring) by taking advantage of virtual proximity created by an advanced communications infrastructure.
- Support development and adoption of advanced applications by providing middleware and development tools.
- Facilitate development, deployment, and operation of an affordable communications infrastructure, capable of supporting differentiated Quality of Service (QoS) based on applications requirements of the research and education community.
- Promote experimentation with the next generation of communications technologies.
- Coordinate adoption of agreed working standards and common practices among participating institutions to ensure end-to-end quality of service and interoperability.
- Catalyze partnerships with governmental and private sector organizations.
- Encourage transfer of technology from Internet2 to the rest of the Internet.
- Study impact of new infrastructure, services, and applications on higher education and the Internet community in general.

Figure 2-4
Internet2 mission and goals

Source: www.internet2.edu. Reprinted with permission of Internet2.

Over the past decade, federal government R&D agencies, the university community, and private companies have worked together to develop many of today's Internet technologies. That partnership created a multibillion-dollar industry. By renewing this partnership, Internet2 will develop and diffuse new technology needed by all network users, helping to ensure continued U.S. leadership in computers and communications.

2.7.3 What Is the Relationship between Internet2 and NGI?

The university-led Internet2 effort and the federally led NGI initiative are complementary and are already working together in many areas. For example, the Internet2 program is in partnership with the National Science Foundation (NSF) merit-based High Performance Connections program. More than 90 Internet2 universities have received competitively awarded grants to support connections to advanced backbone networks such as UCAID's Abilene and the high-performance Backbone Network Service (vBNS) developed by the NSF and MCI/Worldcom.

The Abilene backbone network is named for a frontier railroad established in Abilene, Kansas, during the 1860s. Just as the railroad changed the way people worked and lived, the Abilene Project is expected to transform the work of researchers and educators into the next millennium. The Abilene network spans more than 10,000 miles and operates at 2.4 gigabits per second, which is 45,000 times faster than a 56K modem. More than 70 Internet2 universities and research facilities were connected to Abilene by the end of 1999. As with Internet2, Abilene supports the NGI and will link with existing federal research networks, such as the high-performance Backbone Network Service. The vBNS ultimately is expected to be replaced by a commercial network, but Abilene is expected to remain a test bed network to provide a place for continuing to try out new ideas—a place where ideas can fail as well as succeed.

Internet2 also is participating in the NGI Joint Engineering Task Force (JET) to ensure the cohesiveness and interoperability of the technologies Internet2 is developing. Additional cooperative relationships are being planned as part of NGI implementation. As Internet2 develops among university members, NGI programs go forward at federal agencies, and commercial vendors and other organizations continue to create new backbone networks, it will be crucial to ensure the interoperability of these networks and the widest possible availability of advanced services and applications.

2.7.4   What Do Internet2 and NGI Mean for Businesses?

The ramifications for commercial use are expected to be far reaching. Early commercial applications are expected to start entering the marketplace by the end of 2000. "The result for the world's businesses is that everything changes—from strategic business models to business processes and staffing skills. Companies will have to rethink how they work, how they build and sell products, and how they manage their network assets. In an age of Internet time, it becomes even more critical to understand high-speed network technologies and the capabilities they will enable."[42]

Some of the most far-reaching effects will be in the way people work and collaborate in organizations. The types of applications and functionality that can be delivered to the desktop and to wireless portable devices will expand dramatically. The combination of high bandwidth, full-screen video; 3-D multimedia display; and CD-quality audio opens up extraordinary possibilities for business use. Imagine, for example, a videoconference in which the images of participants are captured by 180-degree surround camera and then projected thousands of miles away onto a wall—life size and with directional voice.[43] Or, picture a virtual team in Tokyo, Milan, New York, and London collaborating in real time, spontaneously discussing, viewing, exchanging, and editing documents and complex technical drawings. The implications are far reaching.

2.8   INFRASTRUCTURE AND PLATFORMS FOR EUIS

The desktop of the future will put everything knowledge workers need right at their fingertips. Moreover, it will be portable to anywhere in the world. In all likelihood, it also will be wireless or at least capable of wireless operation in some locations if not everywhere in the world.

In addition to a suite of productivity tools on the local hard drive, the desktop will be Web-based and provide end users with a personalized, single view into the network. It will include collaborative services, links to corporate information, the Web, and updates from customers and suppliers. It will be a gateway to the corporate university. Most importantly, it will provide a customized gateway to all the knowledge and business intelligence essential to the job or projects relevant to the knowledge workers' current assignments. The knowledge and tools will be accessed easily and shared among colleagues; at the same time, they will be integrated tightly with other Web and desktop applications. In essence, knowledge workers will have just-in-time access to everything they need to do their jobs right at their fingertips. In addition, they will be connected easily with almost everyone with whom they need to collaborate or share information.

Knowledge workers will be able to collaborate with colleagues and customers near and far over an Internet with greatly expanded capacity as described. Doing so will probably be as natural as dialing the telephone is today.

Developing, implementing, and supporting this environment is the challenge for end-user computing. Successfully implementing the desktop of the future all hinges on being able to answer critical questions about how end users work and what knowledge is needed to support innovation and exceptional performance. What information is required? Where do they get it? How do they use it? How do they keep their knowledge current? This challenge is the hard part and is a primary concern of EUIS.

2.9 SUMMARY

Chapter 2 examines the rapidly expanding impact of information technologies and digital networks on workplace environments—people, processes, and organizational structures. It also looks at implications of the economic environment, the digital divide, and the Next Generation Internet.

The ability to use technology to enhance individual, work group, and organizational performance will become increasingly important in the twenty-first-century workplace. Technology is advancing much faster than the ability to use it effectively. The technology provides powerful new capabilities, but understanding how to implement them is far more difficult than most people realize. Workplace changes examined include anytime, anyplace environments, a 24/7 global economy, increased need for collaboration, shorter business cycles, just-in-time operations, the shift from a functional to a process orientation, a focus on innovation, and new strategies for managing knowledge and learning.

Expectations of and requirements for the twenty-first-century workforce are changing. Life in cyberspace enterprises will be significantly different than in industrial firms. Some of the more prevalent effects on the workforce include shifting people into thinking work, increased value placed on diversity, renewed focus on empowerment, pay for performance, flexible work environments, and a blurring of boundary lines. Many as yet unanticipated changes are likely as well.

Digital networks have opened new ways of conducting business both inside (e-business) and outside (e-commerce) the enterprise. E-commerce offers enterprises fundamentally new ways to expand the markets in which they compete, customize products and services, and streamline marketing, sales, and delivery. In the long run, e-business—the use of Internet and other digital technology for internal organizational communication, collaboration, and coordination of business processes—is expected to have an even greater impact than e-commerce. Both e-commerce and e-business open up new horizons for what is economically and practically feasible by reducing the cost of information and coordination. Some of the significant ways in which digital networks are shaking up industrial era assumptions include putting customers in the driver's seat, shifting the client focus from transactions to relationships, mass customization, eliminating middlemen, forging new partnerships and alliances, and creating virtual enterprises.

As individuals and organizations scramble to take advantage of today's digital networks, major research efforts are underway to develop the next generation Internet. The first, the Next Generation Internet (NGI), is a U.S. government-led initiative focussed primarily on commercial and government applications. The second, the Internet2 Project, is a university-led collaborative effort with the objective of accelerating the next stage of Internet development in academia. These initiative are complementary and are already working together in many areas, including development of the Abilene backbone network, capable of operating 45,000 times faster than a 56K modem.

KEY TERMS

- Abilene network
- Corporate University
- Digital divide
- Digital economy

- Digital workplace
- Enterprise portal
- Internet2
- Knowledge economy

- Knowledge management
- Next Generation Internet (NGI)
- Virtual communities
- Virtual corporations

DISCUSSION QUESTIONS

1. What impact are digital networks having on businesses and other organizations worldwide?
2. Why is the twenty-first century being called the Digital Era? What are the implications?
3. List at least six ways in which the Digital Age workforce differs from the Industrial Age workforce.
4. Why do advances in technology outstrip our ability to use them?
5. How are e-commerce and e-business changing the dynamics of the marketplace? What are the implications for consumers? For business enterprises? For governmental and other nonprofit organizations?
6. What is the Next Generation Internet (NGI)? What is the relationship between NGI and Internet2?
7. Briefly describe several of the expanded capabilities and benefits of the Next Generation Internet.
8. What is the Abilene network? How did it get its name?
9. What do Internet2 and NGI mean for business?
10. Describe the desktop environment that typical Digital Age workers can expect to find in the workplace.

APPLICATION EXERCISE

1. Working with a group of your classmates, pick a business with which you are familiar or have an interest. Imagine that you and your classmates have just been appointed by the CEO to head up a task force to reinvent the company as an e-commerce business or to create an e-commerce division of the company. How would you restructure the business? Describe how you would operate from the customer perspective. How would you build relationships with your customers? Describe the experience that a typical customer would go through in doing business with your firm. What will the customer do? What will you do? How will the customer feel about the experience? How will it be different than doing business with the brick-and-mortar business? What will be the benefits for the customer? For your firm?

SUGGESTED READINGS

Bill Gates with Collins Hemingway (1999). *Business @ the Speed of Thought: Using a Digital Nervous System.* New York: Warner Books.

Don Tapscott (1998). *Blueprint to the Digital Economy: Wealth Creation in the Era of E-Business.* New York: McGraw-Hill.

USEFUL WEBSITES

www.speedofthought.com/getting/explore.html

The official Web site for Bill Gates's book, *Business @ the Speed of Thought.* It includes a video interview with Bill Gates and many excellent examples and cases that illustrate how digital technology can be applied to empower employees, streamline business operations, and thrive in a digital era.

www.internet2.edu/html/about.html

Internet2 Web site for more information about the Internet2 project.

www.kraftfoods.com

Kraft Interactive Kitchens Web site offers consumers extensive information about nutrition and helps them build meal plans.

www.CIO.com/printlinks

CIO Magazine covers leading issues for IS executives. You can view the latest surveys, articles, and much more at the Web site.

www.ntia.doc.gov

Source for U.S. Commerce Department report, "Falling Through the Net."

www.officeteam.com

OfficeTeam Career Center provides a variety of interesting information about workplace and employment trends. OfficeTeam is an international firm specializing in administrative staffing. A list of emerging top job titles and descriptions was available at *www.officeteam. com/OT/TopJobTitles* at the time this text went to press.

ENDNOTES

1. Mindy Blodgett, "Fast Forward: What's the Key to Success in a Technology-Driven Economy? Twelfth Annual CIO-100 Leaders for the Next Millennium," *CIO Magazine* 12 (August 15, 1999): 58.
2. Ibid., 48.
3. "The Dawn of E-Life," *Newsweek* Special Report (September 20, 1999): between page numbers 41 and 42.
4. Warren Karlenzig, "Interview with Lester Thurow, Balancing Chaos and Order," *Knowledge Management Magazine* 2 (September 1999): 30.
5. Carol Hildebrand, "A Little of That Human Touch," *CIO Magazine* 9, Special Issue on How to Build a Collaborative Enterprise (March 1, 1996): 64.
6. Ibid., p. 65.
7. Andrew Ferguson, "Auction Nation," *Time* (December 27, 1999): 82.
8. Steve Barth, "Knowledge-Age Mergers: Finding the Perfect Fit," *Knowledge Management Magazine* 2 (May 1999): 52.
9. Bill Gates (1929), *Business at the Speed of Thought: Using a Digital Nervous System. New York: Warner.*
10. Stuart Silverston, "A Pictorial Interview with John Seely Brown, Exchange Practice Insights," *Knowledge Management Magazine* 2 (May 1999): 39.
11. Davenport, Thomas H. and Laurence Prusak. (1997). *Working Knowledge: How Organizations Manage*

What They Know. Boston: Harvard Business School Press.

12. Tom Field, "Unleash Innovation: To Stay Competitive in the Years to Come, Companies Must Keep the New Ideas Flowing," *CIO Magazine* 12 (August 15, 1999): 111.

13. Ibid., 114.

14. Mindy Blodgett, "Fast Forward: What's the Key to Success in a Technology-Driven Economy? Twelfth Annual CIO-100 Leaders for the Next Millennium," *CIO Magazine* 12 (August 15, 1999): 50.

15. Dan Ruby, "Fin-de-Siecle Knowledge Management," *Knowledge Management Magazine* 2 (December 1999): 8.

16. Peter Ruber, "Framing a Portal Strategy," *Knowledge Management Magazine* 2 (May 1999): 41.

17. Geoffry Cowley and Anne Underwood, "Finding the Right Rx: Portable Databases Can Make Doctors More Efficient, but This One Helps Them Practice Better Medicine," *Newsweek* (September 20, 1999): 67.

18. Anne Stuart, Continuing Education. *CIO Web Business*, Section 2, (12:22) September 1, 1999: 32.

19. Ibid., 42.

20. Gary Abramson, "Invest in People," *CIO Magazine* 12 (August 15, 1999): 85.

21. Rodney L. Everhart, "Creating Virtual Communities," *Syllabus* 12 (April 1999):12.

22. Diana G. Oblinger, "Is Your Mission Ready for the Information Age?" *Trusteeship* 7: 22.

23. Stuart Silverstone, "Interview with Arie de Geus: Organize for Learning," *Knowledge Management Magazine* 2 (September 1999): 37.

24. Bill Gates, *Business @ the Speed of Thought*, Chapter 23.

25. Bill Gates, *Business @ the Speed of Thought*, Chapter 10.

26. "Anatomy of IT Partnerships," Conference Supplement in *CIO Magazine* 12 (August 15, 1999): no page number.

27. Paul Saffo, a futurist and research director with the Institute for the Future in Menlo Park, California. Quoted in Karthrine Noyes, "Trendlines: News, Insight, Humor, Reviews," *CIO Magazine* 12 (August 15, 1999): 26.

28. Paul Cole quoted in Louise Fickel, "Know Your Customer," *CIO Magazine* 12 (August 15, 1999): 64.

29. Bill Gates, *Business @ the Speed of Thought*, Chapter 5.

30. Syracuse University School of Information Studies. Written and produced by Raynor & Roen. 1999, p. 20.

31. David Pearson, "IT Takes Two: One Is the Deadliest Number Business Ever Knew." Conference Supplement to *CIO Magazine*, (August 15, 1999): no page number.

32. Donald N. Langenberg, "All Systems Go." *Trusteeship* (December 1999): 17.

33. Bill Gates, *Business @ the Speed of Thought*, Chapter 7.

34. Mindy Blodgett, "Fast Forward: What's the Key to Success in a Technology-Driven Economy? Twelfth Annual CIO-100 Leaders for the Next Millennium," *CIO Magazine*, (August 15, 1999): 46–58.

35. Ibid., 54–55.

36. Thomas J. Peters and Robert H. Waterman, Jr. (1982) *In Search of Excellence*. New York: Harper & Row, p. 193–4.

37. Ibid.

38. Daintry Duffy, "Seize the Web," *CIO Magazine*, 12 (August 15, 1999): 140.

39. Ibid., 146.

40. Jonathan Alter, "Bridging the Digital Divide," *Newsweek* (September 20, 1999): 55.

41. NGI Concept Paper released 23 July, 1997, *http://www.ccic.gov/ngi/concept-Jul97/ngi_vision.html*.

42. Rochelle Garner, "Internet2 . . . and Counting," *CIO Web Business*, Section 2, 12 (September 1, 1999): 45.

43. Ibid., p. 47.

Case Study   Putting Organic *in the* Org Chart

Network Analysis Replaces Hierarchy with Real-World Webs

Organizational Charts Obsolete: Treelike hierarchies and linear value or material chains are obsolete in today's connected economy. Instead, many observers advocate mapping the organizational terrain to determine the hubs and webs through which flow the interactions among people, products, and information.

Organizational X Rays: To help companies evolve into adaptive organizations, Valdis Krebs, an organizational behavior consultant based in Cleveland (www.orgnet.com), uses social network analysis to identify the emergent knowledge networks inside and among organizations. "The most fundamental flaw of the org chart is that it reveals only who works where and who reports to whom. Yet many people still take it as a picture of reality in the business world," says Krebs, who predicts that organizational hierarchy will fade into a background support role. The org chart does not show many things that are critical in today's connected knowledge economy: who knows what; who knows who knows what; key business relationships that connect the organization to the marketplace; the location of core competencies; emergent leaders, experts, and influencers; and the diffusion of innovations, new ideas, and best practices.

For example, in the market planning department of a Los Angeles financial services firm, both morale and productivity were failing. Krebs found that work in this department

flowed according to the treelike structure of a traditional org-chart hierarchy—except that, in practice, this hierarchy placed the director at the center of a hub because he was the intermediary for every step of the process. As these diagrams show, the organization was able to evolve from an ineffective, inflexible organization into one that could adapt dynamically and organize itself according to the environment and the needs of customers and other key stakeholders.

Highlighting Bottlenecks: The hierarchy and its formal work groups are clearly shown in the department's first network diagram (Figure 1), which looks like a bird's-eye view of an org chart. An analysis of the workflow (Figure 2) confirms that this is a counterproductive structure that makes the role of the director, Thomas, too rigid for the flow of work and information, although it also identifies Martha as an emergent leader in the group.

Dynamic Networks: New rules formalize Martha's status as owner of the daily work flow and allow knowledge workers to interact directly (Figure 3). Employees enjoy new freedom and responsibilities, while management can take comfort in improved performance. The next step would be to further enable this transformation through recognition and support of communities of practice, which better reflect the way a network's nodes—or, in this case, workers—naturally cluster.

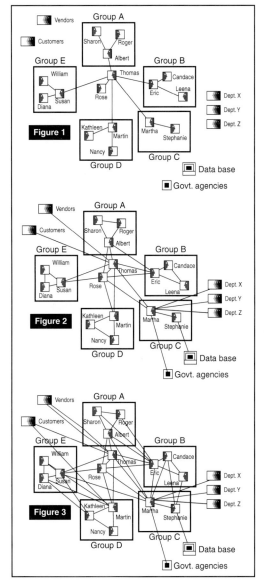

Source: Reprinted from April 2000 issue of *Knowledge Management Magazine.*

CASE STUDY QUESTIONS

1. What is the significance of the change from a hierarchical to a networked organization structure?

2. Do you agree with the case's conclusion that this is the way of the future for most organizations? Why or why not?

3. How have information systems, and especially digital networks, influenced this direction in organization?

4. In which type of organization would you personally prefer to work—the traditional hierarchical organization or an empowered, networked organization? Why? What difference do you feel it would make in the way you work on a day-to-day basis? In career opportunities and growth?

End-User Information Systems: Business Solutions

In part II, the emphasis is on understanding requirements of individuals and work groups, and selecting or designing appropriate software solutions to meet identified business needs. The discussion of productivity tools focuses on improving individual, work group, and organizational performance. It offers a sampling of current hardware and software tools but is not intended to be all inclusive, or to suggest limitations of tools to particular personnel or tasks. As the e-business revolution continues to sweep the workplace, the use of information technologies by knowledge workers is no longer optional. The objective here is to expand horizons for identifying innovative business solutions.

Chapter 3, "Productivity Tools for Individuals," focuses on individual work requirements at all levels of the enterprise. It looks especially at the needs of individuals in four major categories—managerial, professional/technical, sales/marketing, and administrative support—in the light of changing workplace demands and new practices such as customer relationship management and e-business. A variety of software solutions are discussed in relation to their ability to improve individual performance, including desktop productivity tools, activity management, end-user computing, communications, decision support, and sales and marketing automation. The chapter also offers specific guidelines for evaluating software features and matching them to user needs.

Chapter 4, "Work Group Computing," provides an overview of the promises and challenges related to effective groupware choices and implementation. Groupware is described as a useful infrastructure to support teams, departments, and organizations. The chapter explores a wide range of increasingly sophisticated communications and decision support technologies and how these tools are enabling virtual work and challenging virtual workers and their managers.

Chapter 5, "Knowledge Management," explores the emergence of an important new discipline intended to manage and leverage knowledge and experience systematically and actively within an organization. The past decade has witnessed the rapid evolution of concepts such as the knowledge worker, knowledge economy, intellectual capital, and knowledge as a tangible asset. Knowledge management programs have been launched at countless companies. Management of organizational knowledge may be especially relevant in flattened or networked organizations where layers of management have been eliminated and empowered workforces need a high level of knowledge to operate effectively in a twenty-first-century global marketplace.

Chapter

Productivity Tools for Individuals

Learning Objectives

Upon completing this chapter, you should be able to:

➤ Identify characteristics of managerial work and relate them to requirements for EUIS.

➤ List characteristics of useful information for decision making.

➤ Give examples of useful productivity tools for managers and explain how they improve performance.

➤ Describe the characteristics of professional and technical work and relate them to requirements for productivity tools.

➤ Discuss end-user computing, offering reasons for its growth.

➤ Evaluate the impact of word processing as an authoring tool.

➤ Discuss the impact of information technologies on medical and legal practices.

➤ Describe characteristics of sales and marketing work and relate them to requirements for effective sales solutions.

➤ List examples of productivity tools for sales applications and describe how they affect performance.

➤ Identify major administrative applications for EUIS technologies.

➤ Understand the basic concepts of administrative support.

➤ Differentiate between the word processing needs of clerical and administrative personnel in a production environment and those of casual users such as managers and knowledge workers.

- ➤ Explain how technology is changing the roles of secretaries, administrative assistants, and clerical workers.
- ➤ Discuss how the prevalence of digital networks is changing administrative services.
- ➤ Discuss the problems in managing information in digital, image, and paper formats.
- ➤ Describe image processing systems, and explain how they can be used to improve work flow and business processes.

3.1   INTRODUCTION

We call them PC productivity tools, but have they really led to increased individual productivity? Some say yes; some say no. In fact, results have been mixed. If you were to stroll through a typical corporate office, you would see some desktop devices being used constantly and others collecting dust. What accounts for these differences? That is the subject of this chapter.

The end-user information systems field deals with meeting the needs of individuals and work groups. Thus, understanding how users work and, most importantly, how that work can be changed or transformed through the use of information technology to improve performance, is critical. It is seldom sufficient just to provide new tools. Effective use of Web technology and desktop productivity tools requires transforming the way work is done, not merely automating what is done currently or adding on some new technology solutions. As most organizations have discovered, transforming the way work is done is tough and takes considerable planning and effort to implement successfully. Even in an empowered environment, workers need management support and often the assistance of outside consultants. Generally, the interrelationships are very complex between how individuals perform their jobs and the dynamics of the work group of which they are a part, other work groups with which they interface, and the broader organization. Thus, it is hard to change individual performance without affecting everything else, and a great deal of planning and collaboration are needed to make meaningful changes.

To improve individual performance realistically starts with an understanding of what performance or end results are required in a particular situation and the critical success factors for achieving them. All too often, the approach has been "build it and they will come." This approach has proven successful in only a small percentage of cases. More often than not, it has resulted in underutilization or disuse.

This chapter focuses on individuals at all levels of the enterprise. It looks especially at the needs of individuals in four major areas: managerial, professional/technical knowledge, sales and marketing, and administrative support.

3.2   UNDERSTANDING NEEDS OF INDIVIDUALS

It is difficult to generalize about the needs of individuals. Even in the same company, considerable variation can exist among similar jobs across various functions or business processes within an organization. Job responsibilities for administrative assistants, for example, can vary considerably among the accounting department, the sales department, the legal division, and the manufacturing division. This variation among jobs for managers, knowledge workers, technical professionals, administrators, and sales and marketing positions becomes even more widespread across different industries. Requirements for underwriters, for example, vary considerably among banking, brokerage, and insurance. Even within just insurance, needs vary considerably among underwriters depending on whether they specialize in life, health, or property and casualty insurance.

Although the same basic principles apply, analysts must assess the needs of each situation on its own merits. Broad generalizations are not useful when the objective is improving performance on an individual or work group level. The unique requirements of each situation must be assessed with specific improvement goals in mind.

In the sections that follow, we discuss characteristics of various jobs and how these characteristics shape information technology needs. The discussion is intended to provide a foundation for performing needs analysis and designing appropriate EUIS solutions.

3.2.1 Analyzing Managerial Work

PC productivity tools have been making their way slowly and steadily onto executive desktops. Although the concept of computer support for management decision making, usually called decision support systems, has been around for more than 20 years, use was fairly limited until the advent of the Internet and e-business. Decision support systems (DSS), although not well defined, generally refer to automated tools intended to help managers monitor their companies' (departments'/ divisions') performance, analyze business problems, and formulate decision alternatives. Analysts generally attribute the low acceptance of DSS in the past to limitations of the technology and a failure to meet management needs. Newer PC productivity and communications tools, with graphical user interfaces, have gained much broader acceptance. By far the most widely used tool by managers today is e-mail, and the explosion of e-business makes PCs and digital networks essential tools for every modern manager.

A survey by the San Jose, California, *Mercury News* indicated that senior-level executives average a 57.5-hour workweek. Such demanding schedules underscore the need for new and better ways to manage organizations in today's fast-paced, global economy. In an age when information often equals power, managers who have access to timely, accurate information are more likely to have the upper hand.

Most top officers in *Fortune* 500 companies now use PCs in the office and at home. In contrast, in 1996, only 34 percent of these managers used PCs in the office and in 1982, only 8 percent. In *Leadership and the Computer*, Mary Boone suggests that computers extend human intellect, and are therefore thinking tools that are relevant to executives.[1] Some technology proponents predict that increased use of computers by executives will have a major impact on reshaping traditional organizational structures (see chapter 11).

The concept of improving a manager's performance through support tools is not new. A primary function of the business office always has been to provide support to managers to leverage their time and maximize productivity. This support has two primary components:

1. Delegation of work to support staff.
2. Time and activity management.

Support staff to whom managers delegate work generally include some combination of secretaries, administrative assistants, and technical specialists. In delegating tasks, managers give up a certain amount of control over precisely how the work is accomplished. They also must rely on information that is filtered through others rather than personally garnered from primary sources. The time that managers save by delegating is offset partially by the time they must devote to supervising and coordinating the work of others. Generally, as the scope of a manager's accountability expands, so does the size of the staff that supports the work.

In addition to delegation, managers typically use various tools and techniques to prioritize and manage the demands on their time. Traditional time and activity management tools include telephones, dictation machines, calculators, calendars, tickler files, Rolodexes, and to-do lists.

Managers must decide which tasks to delegate and which to perform themselves. The goal is always to maximize the manager's efficiency and effectiveness, which adds up to productivity. *Efficiency* is a measure of the time and effort required to complete tasks, whereas *effectiveness* is the ability to discern the right tasks to spend time on in the first place. Because effectiveness is more difficult to quantify than efficiency, however, benefits are more difficult to measure. Benefits in effectiveness also take longer to realize because they require changes in behavior. For example, if a manager uses an electronic spreadsheet to produce a monthly report in two hours instead of six, the increased efficiency is obvious. If, however, the manager continues to take six hours to produce the report but includes additional analyses and graphs, is the manager still more efficient? Is the report more effective? The evaluation now becomes more subjective.

An important way in which information technologies increase effectiveness is by changing the delegation equation: Which tasks are most productive for managers to do themselves and which should be delegated? Computers can save time and help managers gain back some of the control over their organizations that was given up as the price of delegation. With better computer support tools, executives are able to extend their span of control (the number of people or departments one manager can oversee effectively). Computers can provide improved access to information, better monitoring and control of operations, and improved communications. Managers who adapt their working styles to capitalize on the new technologies stand to improve both their efficiency and effectiveness.

3.2.1.1 Understanding How Managers Work

Most management studies have focused on decision and information requirements of managers rather than on the process by which information is obtained and decisions are translated into actions to achieve results. Management science has little to say about how the physical limitations of communications restrict the complexity of management tasks that an organization can accomplish.

To determine the complexity of management activities, Booz·Allen & Hamilton provided a number of insights into what knowledge workers (managers, supervisors, professionals, and technical workers) do.[2] They studied 300 professionals in 15 major U.S. corporations and developed a series of in-depth case studies by interviewing knowledge workers and recording managers' use of time. To record their use of time, participants in the study carried a walletlike folder containing a device that beeped at 20-minute intervals. Each time the device beeped, managers recorded what they were doing at the time and rated its importance on a scale from 1 to 10. The participants also recorded other factors relating to work output, activities, and habits. The purpose of the study was to determine how end-user systems could be justified in terms of supporting managerial/professional performance. Investigators used productivity and quality as the two principal criteria by which to analyze that performance. The results of the study provided interesting insights into work habits of knowledge workers. Booz·Allen & Hamilton concluded that most organizations could save 20 percent or more in operating costs by taking advantage of EUIS systems. They concluded that EUIS systems could reduce office support costs and improve managerial and professional productivity at the same time. Specific findings regarding how managers work included the following.

1. High-level managers make little use of available computer tools. They spend less than 2 percent to 3 percent of their time looking at computer printouts or dealing with information retrieval machines such as terminals or intelligent workstations.
2. Managers spend too much time on nonproductive activities, such as looking for information and on telephone calls that are incomplete, and not enough time on analytical and planning activities, updating professional skills, or taking part in decision-making processes.
3. Roughly 90 percent of all hard copy activity involves words:
    • Graphics are involved in only 5 percent of all hard copy activities.
    • A combination of words and numbers occurs in almost 50 percent of hard copy activities.
    • Numbers account for only 7 percent of all hard copy activities.
    • Nonmanagers use computer printouts twice as often as managers do.
4. In rating uses of managers' time, telephone use was rated low except for outgoing external calls because of a combination of the disruptive nature of incoming calls and the less productive time spent seeking people on outgoing calls.

Because managers accomplish tasks through other people, good communication of information is extremely important for effective management. Managers need the right information at the right time. Simply providing more information is not necessarily the answer. A major problem for most managers is filtering through vast amounts of information to find what they need. Unfortunately, technology often simply provides more information more quickly. Systems are most beneficial when they help sort and condense information so that managers receive only the information they need to perform their jobs effectively—at the right time and place and in the right format.

Henry Mintzberg conducted some of the most useful research regarding the work of managers in terms of what they do and how they do it. In *The Nature of Managerial Work,* he indicated that the classic description of management as planning, organizing, coordinating, and controlling does not accurately reflect how managers spend their time or what they do. Familiarity with Mintzberg's work and that of other researchers who have studied management behavior is important to EUIS analysts and consultants charged with providing tools to assist managers. Some highlights of Mintzberg's findings that are especially relevant to information technology are summarized here.

1. Managers work at an unrelenting pace. Their activities are characterized by brevity, variety, and discontinuity. They are action oriented and dislike reflective activities.
2. Managers play a key role in securing "soft" external information (much of it available to them because of their status) and in passing it along to subordinates.
3. Managers' prime media for dealing with information are verbal: telephone calls, meetings, and observational tours. Managers spend 65 percent to 75 percent of their time communicating orally. Mail provides only 13 percent of information of specific or immediate use. A small percentage of the manager's information comes from formal reports, documents, or computer printouts. Mintzberg suggests this fact as the main reason why MIS systems rarely are used by managers.
4. Because of its reliance on verbal information, according to Mintzberg, the chief strategic data bank of the organization is not in the memory of its computers but in the minds of its managers.
5. Manager reliance on verbal media also helps explain why it is frequently difficult for them to delegate many tasks. In order to delegate, managers have to "dump memory," meaning they must tell everything they know about the subject.[3]

Mintzberg described the manager's job in terms of various roles or organized sets of behaviors identified with position. Formal authority gives rise to three interpersonal roles, which in turn give rise to three informational roles. The first two roles then enable the manager to play the four decisional roles. Mintzberg's description of these ten roles is shown in Figure 3-1. These roles are closely integrated and inseparable.

3.2.1.2 Managers' Information Dilemma
Managers face a dilemma of growing proportion in today's information society. Although they are receiving more information than ever before, that information is not necessarily useful. Information may be irrelevant, unreliable, late, incomprehensible, or contradictory. In many ways, it has become more difficult to isolate key information. Although little conclusive research is available on what constitutes the most useful information for managerial decision making, experience indicates that the following characteristics are important.

- *Significance.* Managers need information relevant to the critical aspects of business operations. It must help them evaluate organizational performance in key areas and monitor progress toward organizational goals. For example, a marketing vice president needs information to answer questions such as "Why have sales for Product X declined by 20 percent?" or "How much does Product X contribute to the profitability of the company?" Typical computer reports merely summarize historical results. They do not report why performance is at a certain level or what needs to be done to improve it.

- *Reliability.* Managers need reliable information to assess organizational performance and make decisions. Data do not necessarily have to be precise by accounting standards. They must be valid, however, and come from a source that has integrity.

- *Consistency.* Information from various sources both inside and outside the organization should be consistent. The marketing vice president should get sales

Figure 3-1
Managerial roles
stemming from formal
authority and status

Source: Reprinted from *The
Native of Managerial Work* by
Henry Mintzberg, 1973.
Harper Collins.

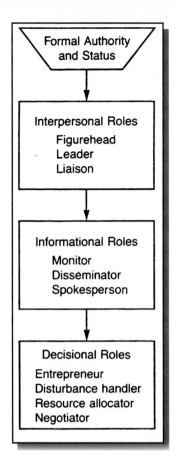

figures from the sales force that are consistent with production figures from the
manufacturing division and delivery figures from the shipping department.

- *Timeliness.* Information is most useful when it enables managers to anticipate
  problems and business requirements. Receiving information after damage is
  done or after the competition has gained the lead is ineffective.

- *Comprehensibility.* To be useful, information must be understood easily. Managers cannot devote hours to culling essential facts from a morass of details.

- *Action-oriented impact.* Information must help managers take action. They need
  to identify actions that have been completed and tasks that remain undone.
  Information should suggest alternative solutions. Managers need to assess
  what steps can or should be taken next and the probability of success for various options.

More often than not, executives receive information that is an unfocused by-
product of the operational and transactional computer systems of the business. These
systems contain data that support record-keeping requirements and operational decision making. They are designed to help supervisors monitor the business on a day-
by-day basis, not to help executives manage the organization. Although information
summarized from these systems is usually accurate and reliable, it often is not significant, vital, and action oriented to management. Although it is apparent that managers
need understandable, action-oriented information, it is unclear how to identify this
information and implement support systems that provide it in an easy-to-use form.

PC productivity tools, such as word processing, spreadsheets, graphics, and databases, often go unused by executives because they assign other people to do most of what needs to be done. Considerable effort and research are being expended now on developing computer tools tailored to the needs of managers. This task is difficult because the size and nature of the organization affect the needs of every manager. In large organizations, the needs of high-level executives differ considerably from those at lower levels (especially first-line supervisors). The failure rate among systems designed for managers has been high. Some estimates are that high-level executives spend an average of 10 percent of their day on information processing tasks. Lower-level managers might spend considerably more time. It is important to keep these differences in mind.

3.2.1.3 The Changing Management Climate

In response to economic conditions, global competition, greater workplace diversity, and technology, management structures are changing. Enterprises are restructuring the way work gets done. Hierarchical systems designed to control workers and break down production into its smallest component tasks are becoming obsolete. They are steadily giving way to looser, more decentralized arrangements that give workers more autonomy and responsibility. The objective is to empower workers to encourage individual contribution, judgment, and creativity. Although efficiency can be quantified, quality (effectiveness) is hard to measure. Moreover, because quality, a crucial component of competitiveness, is an attribute that resides in every part of the process, it must be put in by every producer, not just sprinkled on later.

Such fundamental restructuring demands new management skills and approaches. Decision making is based on shared power and informed judgment instead of gut feel or personal judgment. Corporations are calling on managers to provide greater leadership. Consensus building, coaching, and facilitation skills are at a premium. New empowerment models call for broader access to information. Group processes are needed to focus decision making on the problems and drive issues to resolution. Enterprises are looking to information technologies to help meet the challenges. Even more compelling is the need for business leaders who understand the power of technology to drive business innovation.

3.2.2 Analyzing Professional and Technical Work

In recent years, EUIS specialists have focused on providing IT support for professional and technical workers—the so-called knowledge workers who constitute a growing proportion of the workforce. Desktop PCs are standard equipment for knowledge workers in today's digital workplace. However, the desktop is no longer necessarily located in a conventional office. It might be at home, in the field, or halfway around the world. Yet despite their ubiquity, PC productivity tools are not used to anywhere near their potential according to most surveys and corporate executives. Moreover, the typical knowledge worker is putting in more hours today than in the past and has a more demanding work schedule. Who are these knowledge workers? What do they do? How do they work? What's important to their success? How can PC productivity tools help?

Knowledge workers are well-trained, specialized personnel who exercise considerable autonomy in carrying out their responsibilities. Their work usually "requires a high degree of specialized training and education and mental, rather than physical, effort."[4] They frequently serve in staff or advisory roles to managerial personnel. They occupy most of the jobs in staff functions in personnel departments, financial services, accounting, legal departments, information technology, and computer services. They also increasingly fill the ranks of engineers, manufacturing, research, and many more areas. Most knowledge work positions are salaried, and thus exempt from hourly wage laws and overtime pay regulations. Thus, if overtime is required to meet job responsibilities (and it often is), knowledge workers seldom can expect additional compensation.

Knowledge workers include accountants, architects, auditors, lawyers, computer analysts and programmers, researchers, editors, market analysts, actuaries, underwriters, economists, public relations specialists, financial analysts, engineers, scientists, and others. They work primarily with information. They also include the ranks of many small business professionals and entrepreneurs. Researching, sorting, analyzing, calculating, summarizing, and presenting information are their stock and trade. Collectively, these personnel represent the intelligence of the organization, possessing considerable technical expertise about the enterprise's products and services and the legal and competitive environment in which it operates. Many knowledge workers have direct responsibility for servicing customers, or they contribute directly to the value chain for products and services. With the growing emphasis on quality service, these workers are often the focus of efforts to redesign business processes to improve delivery of products and services.

In the broadest sense, knowledge workers also include managers and executives—although generally the term applies to nonmanagerial personnel. In many ways, middle managers have information processing requirements more similar to those of knowledge workers than to senior and executive managers, because the responsibilities of first-level supervisors and operating management often require close involvement in daily business. The reader is reminded once again that business needs, rather than hard and fast rules, determine appropriate applications of end-user information systems.

Unlike executives and managers, knowledge workers generally have little secretarial and clerical support in carrying out job responsibilities. The level depends somewhat upon the organization, but the trend has been to provide one-on-one secretarial or administrative support only at senior levels. Middle managers and professional/technical personnel share administrative resources. In some organizations, knowledge workers are supported by word processing centers. Other organizations employ departmental secretaries who handle support service for the entire department. Most commonly, however, knowledge workers perform a number of tasks for themselves that fall into the category of clerical or administrative.

3.2.2.1 Understanding the Needs of Professional and Technical Knowledge Workers

Factual information about how professional and technical knowledge workers work is even sketchier than that about managers. Little research has been done in this area. The work of professional and technical knowledge workers shares several commonalities with the work of managers. Their work, however, is more information intensive than that of their managers. They generally serve as specialists in one or more aspects of a business. Examples include business analysts, marketing researchers, government policy researchers, public relations specialists, legal advisers, and many others. Although information about knowledge workers is limited, the following generalizations can be made.

- The knowledge worker spends considerable time probing complex problems.
- The knowledge worker depends on accurate, timely information and decisions by managers.
- With the increased complexity of today's business environment, the typical specialized knowledge worker must deal with mountains of information and a sea of detailed procedures. A typical job requires intensive preparatory training and a learning curve of 6 months to 24 months before the employee is proficient on the job.
- Managers are coming to rely more and more on knowledge workers, such as staff specialists and business analysts, for detailed computer analyses of information.
- Knowledge workers spend most of their time in informational roles. They are the experts who are supposed to have the facts. Other people and parts of the organization look to them for advice. They frequently are involved directly in designing an enterprise's products and services.
- Knowledge workers spend considerable time analyzing, manipulating, and summarizing information. They need to look at information and organize it in different ways. They frequently require different views of the same information.
- Knowledge workers often work in teams or groups, and increasingly these groups are dispersed geographically. For example, automobile design often is done now by international teams working across borders. Consulting teams are also increasingly international operations.
- Knowledge work often involves a high level of collaboration among various specialists.

Access to information is critical for professional and technical knowledge workers. Business needs for these specialists include the following.

1. *Tracking systems.* Knowledge workers often have to track the status of events or actions related to their organization. For example, public relations specialists may track local, state, and national legislation that relates to the business.
2. *Forecasting.* Knowledge workers may play a role in trying to estimate future trends or happenings that pertain to their firm or industry. Business forecasts might include short- and long-term forecasts of sales, price forecasts for important raw materials and equipment, market demand for new products, and a host of other matters of specific interest.
3. *Modeling.* Knowledge workers use models to explain phenomena, clarify certain aspects of problems, or help analyze constraints and potentials. Models represent an abstraction of reality: what things *were* like, what they *are* like, what they *could* be like, or what they *should* be like. The objective is to highlight certain important relationships and key interactions.
4. *Statistical analysis.* Knowledge workers often need to analyze information using various statistical techniques.
5. *Graph production.* Knowledge workers frequently use graphs and charts to analyze trends, illustrate statistical information, or clarify data.
6. *Report generation.* Information must be summarized in written format so that it can be disseminated. Often, various forms of media are needed.

7. *Access to corporate information resources.* Availability of accurate, timely corporate information, such as sales figures, manufacturing costs, budgets, and other data, is essential for knowledge workers to do their jobs.

8. *Access to outside reference sources.* Knowledge workers require business information such as economic data, stock quotations, interest rates, demographic information, technical information, or any of hundreds of topics.

9. *"What if" analysis.* Knowledge workers often need to look at information in different ways, changing one factor while holding other factors constant. For example, a business analyst may study the effect of various interest rates on a business investment decision.

10. *Communication.* Knowledge workers frequently must share information and communicate information effectively to others. They often are called upon to present complex information to managers or others for decision making either individually or in group settings.

In summary, knowledge workers make up a growing percentage of the workforce. Their work is information intensive. They spend considerable time researching, analyzing, manipulating, and summarizing information related to products, services, or other business requirements. As indicated by the preceding list, knowledge workers have a wide variety of needs that EUIS tools can help address. In fact, the value that knowledge workers add has increased as computers have improved their ability to deliver detailed, accurate, timely information. The EUIS specialist must have an accurate understanding of the knowledge worker's business needs as a basis for selecting the most appropriate tools.

3.2.3 Analyzing Sales and Marketing Work

E-commerce is turning the sales world upside down. The rules have changed. The customer is in control. The marketplace is now demand driven rather than product driven. Sales personnel, who often resisted technology in the past because they believed that sales is a people business, now find themselves being pulled rapidly into the world of e-commerce. The Internet gives customers a direct line, access to product information, and the ability to comparison shop or purchase online. It is changing the dynamics and opening up many new opportunities to connect more closely with customers and enhance service.

Sales and marketing positions vary considerably, depending upon the nature of the product or service and industry. Typical positions include manufacturer's and wholesaler's representatives, service sales representatives, insurance agents, retail sales personnel, travel agents, real estate agents and brokers, security and financial service sales representatives, and sales engineers.

Companies have compelling financial reasons for trying to improve sales force productivity. The average industrial products salesperson makes $36,000 to $50,000 a year and calls on three to eight customers daily. Excluding compensation, the average sales call costs $102. Most sales representatives spend only 35 percent of their time actually selling, 35 percent traveling, and 30 percent on paperwork. Sales managers find that selling time can be increased by as much as 50 percent with better time management. More selling time generally translates into higher sales and profits. Companies can use EUIS technologies to improve sales management and support. A wide range of technologies can help reduce paperwork, make better information available faster, focus on the best leads, and provide customer service.

Sales representatives must know their business and the business of their clients so that they can understand how company products and services can meet customer needs. With the diverse array of products and services offered by industries today, this is not easy. Just think of the options available to today's consumer, for example, in stereo equipment. Making an intelligent choice requires considerable time and research by the consumer, and a well-informed salesperson can be helpful. Now think about the manufacturer's representatives selling to retail outlets, competing for display space in the store. Think about the product knowledge, vendor support, and training needed. Moreover, customers often look to salespeople for product availability, shipping, invoicing, and account information. Technology can provide sales representatives with a wealth of such information at their fingertips. Sales reps also may help install new equipment, train employees, and resolve any problems with or complaints about the merchandise.

Until recently, computer-based sales support was rare. One software service and consulting firm estimated that in 1986, less than 2 percent of corporate resources among Fortune 1000 companies was applied to sales and marketing functions. Another estimate showed that in 1987, about 20 percent of all companies were using some form of sales and marketing software. Today, PCs, laptops, networking, and software tools are providing new solutions to a variety of problems.

Changes in sales and marketing are being driven by more than today's powerful software tools, however. The heyday of mass marketing is fading. Busy consumers expect more from the companies with which they do business. Consumers are increasingly sophisticated and demanding. Thanks to the Internet, they have many more shopping options. They can let their fingers roam the PC keyboard as they comparison shop on the Net. The customer has much more control with companies today.

Consequently, companies have shifted their focus from pushing products to building relationships with customers. Enabled by sophisticated technology tools, companies are employing a strategy known in the industry as customer relationship management (CRM). The name of the game is not only getting customers, but keeping them. Powerful databases make it possible to collect information as the customer interacts with the company—whether in person, online, by phone, or by mail. CRM software uses complex logic and algorithms to analyze these data to identify buying patterns and preferences and, most importantly, to anticipate future needs or customize promotions and communications to customers' interests and needs. It's a win-win situation. The marketer saves by being able to target promotional dollars better and avoid wasting money sending expensive catalogs to consumers who don't want them. Customers benefit by getting what they want when they want it.

3.2.3.1 *Characteristics of Sales and Marketing Work*

A sales professional usually is responsible for achieving sales results for a defined territory. The size of an appropriate territory varies widely with the nature of the products being sold. Within the norms of a particular industry, the size of a salesperson's territory is based on the convergence of two factors.

1. Sales representatives want their territory to be as large as possible because the larger the potential customer base is, the higher the salesperson's potential earnings are.
2. Time constraints limit the size of a territory that a sales representative can cover. It is in the best interest of a company to ensure that territories are small enough to service thoroughly.

For the sales representatives then, managing a territory is a balancing act between ambition and available time. The salesperson must spend as much time as possible selling and as little time as possible on administrative tasks. Ideally, sales representatives spend minimum time at their desks and maximum time in clients' offices. In reality, a sales representative's "office" is often a car or hotel room. Most sales representatives spend only 35 percent of their time selling and another 35 percent traveling. Monthly sales reports require an average of four to six hours of preparation. If time can be saved and converted into additional selling opportunities, it can directly affect earnings.

Sales is a high-turnover occupation, and salespeople tend to be mobile and widely dispersed. Thus, EUIS specialists are likely to be dealing with novice end users who are spread across the country and are replaced frequently. Sales reps are highly goal oriented and usually must meet sales goals or quotas set by management. They often have little tolerance for computers. Anything that requires time is seen as directly decreasing their selling time. Hence, ease of use and fast response time are paramount. If they cannot get their answers immediately, they will be quick to give up on the system.

Efficient and effective information processing is important for good time management. Typical sales representatives use card files of contacts, appointment books, and folders of good prospects. Business requirements for sales representatives include the following.

- *Lead generation.* Obtaining new accounts or clients is an important part of the job. Sales reps follow leads from other clients, track advertisements in trade journals, participate in trade shows and conferences, and visit potential clients unannounced. They may spend considerable time meeting with and entertaining prospective clients during evenings and weekends.

- *Prospect management.* Salespeople need a procedure for identifying and maintaining lists of potential clients. Effective time management depends on the ability to discern those prospective customers who are most likely to purchase a particular product. This process, referred to as qualifying prospects, is a valuable method for targeting sales calls.

- *Client information and purchasing history.* The ability to understand clients and a client's product needs enables a salesperson to serve that client more effectively.

- *Sales presentation materials.* The most effective way to convince potential customers that a product meets their needs is to tailor the sales presentation to their requirements. Individually tailored sales materials can be powerful selling tools.

- *Product information and prices.* Information must be accurate, current, and readily accessible. Sales reps often analyze sales statistics. They study literature about new and existing products and monitor the sales, prices, and products of their competitors.

- *Communications.* Both telephone and written correspondence are essential for establishing contacts and appointments and following up on sales calls. Increasingly, these are being replaced or enhanced with faxes, e-mail, and online CRM systems.

- *Paperwork.* Purchase orders and various other paperwork must be submitted, depending on the nature of the product. When salespeople use manual methods to send follow-up correspondence after completing a call, they must sit down and write a letter in longhand (or dictate it), give it to a secretary upon returning to the office, wait for it to be typed, and then proofread and sign it. The process could take three or four days.

CUSTOMER RELATIONSHIP MANAGEMENT (CRM) HELPS MURPHY BREWERY SERVE UP A CUSTOMER-FOCUSED OPERATION

In Ireland, the success of a brewery depends upon its ability to build brand reputation for the beers and lagers it manufactures, markets, and distributes. Murphy Brewery, owned by Dutch brewers Heineken N.V., has approximately 9,000 customers, including pubs, hotels, off-licenses, and supermarkets. When a self-commissioned survey highlighted the need to enhance the level of customer service the company was providing, Murphy Brewery took a comprehensive look at customer relationship management.

The main issue was that customers were presented with various points of contact within the company without any one individual taking responsibility for a specific order, query, or request. The first step toward a solution was to build a dedicated Customer Care Center totally responsible for handling all customer queries from the point of capture through final resolution. The main objective of the Customer Care Center is to make it easy for customers to do business. To do this the company is using a combination of technology, improved business processes, customer relationship building strategies, and an experienced service staff.

The Customer Care Center was only the first step in a wider initiative to equip not only service staff but also the company's sales and marketing teams with access to detailed customer account information. Murphy Brewery wanted every customer-facing agent within the organization to be able to call up information at the click of a button, and use it to gain a detailed understanding of a customer's buying patterns and service needs. This meant that they needed more than just a call-handling application; they needed an end-to-end Customer Relationship Management (CRM) solution. The software selected was Siebel Call Center and Siebel Sales Enterprise.

Siebel Professional Services and Pricewaterhouse Coopers managed the implementation of Siebel Call Center, and the Customer Care Center project went live in just 7 months. In addition to providing technical support, Siebel End User Education developed a customized program to train Murphy's staff on using the new Call Center system. The trainers took the business processes that Murphy had defined and worked them into the training program to create a highly relevant and effective training package. Following an intensive three-day training event, the trainers remained on hand to support the users.

Murphy Brewery Customer Care Center now handles an average of 700 inbound and up to 1,000 outbound calls a day. When a call comes into the Center, agents use the Call Center system to identify the customer from the underlying database. The agent then sees a single screen that holds all the relevant information about that particular customer account. The agent also can see the customer's order history. Answering queries or placing new orders is quick and easy.

Following the success of the Customer Care Center, Murphy Brewery is continuing to roll out Siebel Sales Enterprise to its field sales representatives, marketing, and technical staff. Implementing the front office applications is an even bigger project than the Call Center, but will give Murphy the power to explore how they can build better relationships with their customers, not just by responding to their needs but also by anticipating them. Working hand in hand with customers, they now plan to build better business opportunities across all customer touchpoints and channels.

To Think About: How does CRM differ from traditional sales approaches? How important are information systems and digital networks for CRM? To what extent must Murphy Brewery reengineer their business to take advantage of CRM? How significant a role did the customized end-user training play?

Source: Microsoft Industry Solutions, Siebel Systems and Murphy Brewery Case, *http://www.microsoft.com/industry/crm/casestudies/siebel-murphy.asp.,* accessed 8/2000.

- *Client services.* A good salesperson keeps careful track of the status of customer orders and follows up to ensure that the customer is completely satisfied. Salespeople must avoid walking into a client's office with a big smile when the client is already furious about overdue orders.

In summary, sales representatives can benefit from EUIS tools that enable them to reduce time spent on administrative tasks and to increase the time available for selling. EUIS can help sales reps identify and manage prospects, make effective sales presentations, and follow up on orders and deliveries. New, dynamic, customer-driven business models are emerging that link front office and back office operations and provide real-time access to all the information needed to interact more effectively with customers.

3.2.4 Analyzing Administrative Support

All enterprises need timely, effective *administrative support* to operate efficiently. Clerical and administrative personnel provide a diverse network of support services that keep information flowing into, within, and out of the enterprise. Increased use of desktop productivity tools, digital networks, and business restructuring continue to have significant impact on clerical and administrative positions. Although specific functions vary considerably, these personnel perform four primary functions.

1. Processing information to support decision making.
2. Processing information to support operations.
3. Providing services (or support) to clients or customers.
4. Operating the physical facilities of the office.

Clerical and administrative support covers a broad spectrum of jobs. At one extreme, executive assistants, who are the elite of the secretaries, command salaries beyond $50,000 a year. Closely aligned with the executives for whom they work, these secretaries exercise subtle power and often supervise staffs of their own. At the opposite extreme, a variety of entry-level positions require little skill and pay minimum wage. Figure 3-2 shows the job titles under the category of administrative support listed in the U.S. Department of Labor's *Occupational Outlook Handbook*. It is estimated that two-thirds of the more than 5 million jobs within the administrative and clerical category are held by women.

Information technology and corporate restructuring continually change the support services provided by clerical and administrative personnel. Notions about who performs what work in the office are being redefined. EUIS technologies provide much of the support previously performed manually. With desktop productivity tools, managers and knowledge workers now handle many tasks previously delegated to support staff. Using e-mail, for example, managers and knowledge workers compose and distribute their own memos. Formerly, they would have dictated the memo using a dictating machine or stenographer, a transcriptionist would have typed the memo, and mail personnel would have distributed it. That process is viewed now as much too slow and inefficient. E-mail can be transmitted anywhere in the world in seconds, whereas standard mail can take a week or longer. Even most high-level executives today have desktop PCs and handle much of their own e-mail.

- Adjusters, investigators, and collectors
- Bank tellers
- Communications equipment operators
- Computer operators
- Court reporters, medical transcriptionists, and stenographers
- Information clerks
  - Hotel, motel, and resort desk clerks
  - Interviewing and new accounts clerks
  - Receptionists
  - Reservation and transportation ticket agents and travel clerks
- Loan clerks and credit authorizers, checkers, and clerks
- Mail clerks and messengers
- Material recording, scheduling, dispatching, and distributing occupations
  - Dispatchers
  - Shipping, receiving, and traffic clerks
  - Stock clerks
- Office and administrative support supervisors and managers
- Office clerks, general
- Postal clerks and mail carriers
- Records processing occupations
  - Billing clerks and billing machine operators
  - Bookkeeping, accounting, and auditing clerks
  - Brokerage clerks and statements clerks
  - File clerks
  - Human resources clerks, except payroll and timekeeping
  - Library assistants and bookmobile drivers
  - Order clerks
  - Payroll and timekeeping clerks
- Secretaries
- Teacher assistants
- Word processors, typists, and data entry keyers

Figure 3-2
Administrative support occupations, including clerical

Source: U.S. Department of Labor, Bureau of Labor Statistics. *Occupational Outlook Handbook,* *http://stats.bls.gov/oco/oco1005.htm,* last updated April 19, 2000.

Nonetheless, a significant portion of information processing and support probably will continue to be performed by administrative personnel. The nature of this work is changing, however. Computer competency is now a requirement for most administrative positions, and administrative personnel have been handling increasingly complex tasks. For example, with desktop publishing tools, many publications previously outsourced to print shops are now done in house. Most administrative personnel now are viewed as members of the team or workgroup with their own responsibilities rather than just following the directions of a boss.

A recent survey of administrative support personnel indicated that, as a result of corporate restructuring in the 1990s, secretaries and administrative assistants have picked up many of the duties of middle-management positions, such as purchasing office materials, personnel hiring, training and supervision of other administrative personnel, project management, and implementing or supervising quality management programs. In so doing, they have gained increased recognition and significantly larger workloads, but not always additional training and compensation. Nearly 78 percent of those surveyed reported working the equivalent of two or more prior positions.[5]

Whether evaluating individual productivity tools or implementing office networks, EUIS analysts must take into consideration the entire spectrum of administrative support functions. Digital networks and business on the Internet are driving enterprises to streamline office operations and link front office and back office operations into a seamless network focused on building customer relationships. EUIS analysts must be able to see and understand the big picture and how all the pieces fit together. Even small projects should not be addressed in isolation without regard to the broader picture.

3.2.4.1 Characteristics of Administrative Work

As with the knowledge workers discussed in the three preceding sections, much more is known about what clerical and administrative personnel do than about how they do it. Here, too, the how is as important as the what for designing effective office systems. Far too many systems are underused because they miss the target of being truly useful to the personnel for whom they were designed.

The following generalizations can be made about clerical and administrative personnel.

1. *No standard job description.* The makeup of clerical and administrative jobs varies from one office to another, depending on the type of enterprise, its size, and the assignments involved. Many clerical jobs are routine and repetitive in nature. Others are extremely diverse and include a wide variety of duties and responsibilities. One employee in a small office may perform a variety of duties that are divided among several specialized jobs in a large office. In information industries, such as banking, insurance, and brokerages, administrative positions comprise the majority of the non-exempt (hourly paid) employees. Only a small percentage of these could be considered secretarial positions. A few examples of the many diverse clerical titles include new business service representative, client service analyst, benefit analyst, order processing clerk, claims specialist, mortgage clerk, and billing clerk.

2. *Direct interface with clients and business associates.* Clerical employees often are an organization's primary interface with its customers as they receive payments, take orders, answer telephone inquiries, and handle complaints. They may need to locate information, resolve problems, handle exceptions, and smooth the ruffled feathers of irate customers. Often, they have a more accurate knowledge of the day-to-day operations of a business than their managers do. They understand the requirements of their jobs, take pride in performing them well, and appreciate technologies that improve their performance. During EUIS projects, clerical and administrative personnel can be a valuable resource for aiding management in streamlining procedures, improving customer service, and controlling costs.

3. *Various levels of authority.* Jobs range from entry-level to supervisory and management positions. An office manager may be an individual running a one-person office or someone who supervises dozens of employees and has responsibility for an entire service operation. High-level administrative assistants or executive secretaries wield considerable responsibility and authority. An executive secretary may have great latitude in screening mail and visitors, handling administrative details, and keeping an office running when the executive is away. They often hire, train, and supervise junior-level personnel and act on behalf of the executive.

4. *Loosely structured tasks.* Although clerical and administrative services often are considered routine and repetitive, many of these tasks are not well structured. In fact, contrary to popular perceptions, the use of computers has made many clerical positions less, rather than more, routine. Online transaction processing systems usually automate the routine, repetitive tasks but leave less structured tasks such as correcting errors, handling exceptions, and resolving problems to be handled by administrative personnel. Some secretarial, administrative, and clerical jobs have been redefined, others eliminated, and new ones added. Many office jobs require teamwork. The ability to see another employee's problem and to help whenever possible is important. Staying with a task until it is finished, adaptability, and tact are often requirements.

5. *Production environments.* Office work can require working under pressure. Clerical workers frequently work under constant deadlines. Reports must be ready for an upcoming meeting, contracts have to be in the mail by the first day of the month, or all orders must be processed within 24 hours of receipt. Production quotas might be monitored closely.

6. *Paper intensive.* Most administrative and clerical jobs are paper intensive. Walking through a typical office environment, one is likely to see stacks of files and papers everywhere. In many instances, computers, high-production printers, and copiers have exacerbated the problem. With advances in EUIS technologies such as e-mail, Intranets, imaging, groupware, and workflow managers, the situation is improving slowly, but most offices have a long way to go to approach the vision of a paperless office.

To meet the diverse needs of clerical and administrative personnel, EUIS specialists must analyze each situation carefully. Some of the general information processing requirements of clerical and administrative employees are described in the following sections, but these requirements often vary from organization to organization.

3.2.4.2 Administrative Assistants

The traditional *administrative assistant* supports one manager, working in a close, team relationship. The number of traditional administrative assistants has declined with the growing use of PC productivity tools by knowledge workers and managers. In many organizations, only officers and senior-level people have their own administrative assistants. Administrative assistants to top executives handle diverse responsibilities and channel much of the information and communication to and from the executives with whom they work. An administrative assistant typically handles correspondence, manages the executive's calendar, screens visitors and telephone calls, plans travel itineraries, and tracks a myriad of details. High-level administrative assistants frequently manage special projects, as well. An effective team relationship with an administrative assistant, who anticipates requirements and works with minimum direction, can be one of an executive's most valuable means for leveraging time. Otherwise, much of the potential time the executive can gain by delegating responsibilities is lost. Administrative assistants are often primary users of Executive Information Systems, sometimes becoming the trainers for their principals. Typical duties of a administrative assistant are listed in Figure 3-3.

The trend in many offices is for knowledge workers and managers to share administrative assistants. Thus, administrative assistants increasingly support systems or units. This approach often means administrative assistants assume added

An increasingly vital and skilled role in today's (and tomorrow's) office . . .

a. The administrative professional's job today requires skills in management functions and technology, including:

- Project management
- Integrated computer software applications
- Organization and scheduling
- Internet, intranet communications and research
- Document preparation, storage, and retrieval, with emphasis on electronic record-keeping
- Customer service and public relations

b. **A typical day for today's administrative assistant can include:**

- Developing a production report using spreadsheet software
- Preparing charts, slides, and handouts for a management presentation
- Corresponding via phone, fax, or e-mail with clients all over the world
- Researching a topic on the Internet
- Coordinating a videoconference
- Scheduling an airline flight and purchasing tickets over the Internet
- Supervising and training a coworker
- Effectively representing management at a meeting

Administrative professionals often handle duties such as preparing reports and presentations, contributing to project teams, and planning meetings and events. According to a 1997 International Association of Administrative Professionals (IAAP) benchmark study, one-third of IAAP members supervise others: 45 percent train others, especially on computer skills; and 78 percent recommend or make purchasing decisions for the office.

Figure 3-3
The twenty-first-century administrative professional

Source: International Association of Administrative Professionals (iaap). *http://www.iaap-hq.org/ResearchTrends/21centuryadmin.htm.*

responsibilities and are seen as valuable members of a team. These departmental administrative assistants, on the other hand, usually must be jacks of all trades, doing everything for everyone. They must juggle the work of many principals diplomatically. They might have to handle multiple calendars and telephone lines, and track and follow up on details. Their responsibilities might include any assignments the principals ask them to handle, plus general department administration and filing.

Information processing tasks performed by administrative assistants include the following:

1. *Word processing.* Administrative assistants produce documents ranging from simple notes and one-page memoranda to complex statistical reports and manuals several hundred pages in length.
2. *Dictation and transcription.* Since ancient times, when early stenographers recorded the words of Greek orators, one of the information processing tasks of secretaries (the keeper of secrets) has been to record the spoken word. With the growing use of word processing as an authoring tool, the amounts of dictation and transcription have declined significantly. Shorthand dictation is virtually extinct and remaining dictation is handled by recording devices. The use of direct voice dictation to word processing is growing although accuracy is still a problem.

3. *Copying and duplicating information.* Multiple copies of documents frequently are required to communicate information to all who need to be informed. To some extent, the need for copying is being replaced by electronic document distribution and Web publishing. However, in many instances, electronic distribution is shifting the point at which documents are printed rather than eliminating print.

4. *Arranging meetings.* Setting up meetings frequently involves numerous telephone calls to check availability of participants and to agree on a time and place.

5. *Handling telephone calls.* Handling telephone calls might be the major portion of a clerical person's job or only one of numerous responsibilities. Telephone calls can be a source of constant interruption. Administrative assistants must screen calls, determining which inquiries to handle themselves and which to direct to others. If the intended recipient is not available, they must direct the caller to phone mail or take accurate messages and deliver them to the appropriate party. Because telephone calls might be the major (or only) contact clients or customers have with an organization, good telephone etiquette is important to building goodwill and a good public image. The telephone is a major tool for securing or transmitting information. Formerly, administrative assistants spent much time placing telephone calls for others; today it is common for individuals to place their own calls. With new phone mail systems, many incoming calls now are handled directly, as well.

6. *Handling visitors.* Administrative assistants frequently greet and assist visitors, sometimes screening those who wish to meet with principals.

7. *Calendaring.* Administrative assistants are usually responsible for scheduling time and making appointments for managers and professionals.

8. *Tracking and follow-up.* Administrative assistants must track and follow up on activities such as responses to inquiries, replies to correspondence, renewal dates, delivery dates, invoices, and the like.

9. *Filing and retrieving information.* In large organizations, records management is a full-time responsibility with specialized personnel. In small organizations and for departments and individual offices, filing and retrieving information may be one of many responsibilities of an administrative assistant. Centralized record departments follow generally accepted practices for categorizing and indexing records. Formal procedures are employed to safeguard records and periodically dispose of outdated materials. Departmental and individual files are more often than not organized intuitively rather than according to formal rules.

10. *Travel arrangements.* Administrative assistants make travel arrangements, organize itineraries, and submit travel expense reports. These activities require administrative assistants to be thoroughly familiar with their principal's preferences or to work closely with the principal. Large corporations may have their own travel departments.

11. *Budgeting.* Administrative assistants generally track expenditures against projected expense allocations. They may be involved in developing department budgets, although the principal or department manager is accountable for the budget. Administrative assistants frequently maintain petty cash accounts.

3.2.4.3 *Paraprofessionals*

The number of paraprofessional positions has increased in recent years. *Paraprofessionals* are high-level administrators such as paralegals (or legal assistants), medical assistants, and customer service representatives. Paralegals perform varied duties: searching and checking public records; preparing probate inventories; assisting with tax returns; contacting clients for information; conducting interviews; drafting wills, deeds, and trusts; and making arrangements for depositions and hearings to name a few. Medical assistants handle a variety of patient-care responsibilities in addition to clerical functions. Customer service representatives manage customer accounts, such as insurance policyholders or bank clients. After a group insurance contract is sold, for example, a group representative may be responsible for implementing the program at the customer's enterprise. Paraprofessional jobs require a good understanding of the business and its products, as well as information processing skills.

Paraprofessionals are often customers' primary contact with an organization. Automation can provide better access and control of essential information, document management, and other time-saving features that offer new opportunities to improve customer service.

3.2.4.4 Mail Services Personnel

As the volume of mail has increased, so have the demands on mailroom operations. Electronic communications and distribution increase the competitive pressure to move more information faster, both within and between organizations. Efficient, economical, dependable service has become a major challenge for mailroom personnel. Historically, mailrooms have been staffed with entry-level personnel who were expected to work temporarily in the mailroom before moving up to better positions. Mailroom equipment and furnishings were minimal and operations were likely to be housed in the basement or some back-office hideaway. Because mail services in large organizations handle millions of pieces of mail each month at substantial cost, the old attitude and approach are changing. Today's technology offers many opportunities to increase the efficiency and effectiveness of mail services and to provide better integration with other information processing components.

The job titles of mail services personnel vary considerably among organizations. The major tasks handled by mail personnel include the following.

- Processing incoming mail
  - Receiving and opening mail
  - Sorting and time stamping
  - Distributing mail
- Processing outgoing mail
  - Collecting and sorting by destination
  - Inserting, sealing, and stamping
  - Posting mail
- Supervising bulk mailings
- Messenger services
- Express mail services

3.2.4.5 Records Management Personnel

Records management personnel maintain information and make it available as needed. They are responsible for storing, retrieving, protecting, archiving, and purging records. (A *record* is any form of recorded information.) *Records management* traditionally has been defined as the science of managing records and information from their creation to final disposition. Records and information increasingly are stored in digital format, but still are found in many other forms as well: paper documents, computer printouts, microforms, videotapes, optical disks, voice recordings, photographs, and many others. Many records management requirements, such as what documents must be kept and the retention period, are established by regulatory bodies.

To manage information resources efficiently, organizations must have a comprehensive program that establishes policies and procedures for storing, accessing, protecting, and purging information, regardless of format. A comprehensive program can eliminate expensive duplication of effort and optimize operations. The trend today is to think in terms of managing knowledge rather than managing records.

Large organizations generally have a separate records department, which may include an active-records supervisor, a center (inactive-records) supervisor, forms supervisor, micrographics supervisor, and clerical personnel within each function. Small organizations often do not have separate departments. The records management function might be controlled by an office manager, secretary, clerk, or accountant.

Statistics can help put the size of the task in perspective. In the United States, more than 1 million documents are created every minute. Office workers file 180 million papers and produce 600 million pages of printout every day. In addition to hard copies, organizations must deal with millions of tapes, disks, microfiche, and cassettes.

Paper filing systems consume a large part of a budget. It costs between $12,000 and $13,500 annually to maintain 10 five-drawer vertical file cabinets (based on a cost of $20 per square foot for office space and an average clerical salary of $195 per week, plus supply costs). Seventy percent of filing costs go to salaries, 20 percent to space, 5 percent to supplies, and 5 percent to equipment. The cost of space, rent, and new construction is rising rapidly. Annual energy and maintenance costs are estimated at more than $5 per square foot. Off-site storage costs are up by 50 percent.

3.2.4.6 Clerical Accounting and General Clerical Personnel

Accounting clerks, working primarily with figures, perform in such areas as payroll, general ledger, accounts payable and receivable, and cost accounting. In small offices, accounting clerks may do all the bookkeeping, with an outside accountant verifying their work periodically or annually. Automated accounting and spreadsheet programs offer many opportunities for improving productivity.

General clerical workers have the most diverse job descriptions of any support category. This group encompasses data-entry personnel, insurance claims processors, shipping clerks, order-entry clerks, receptionists, clerk-typists, and many other specialized positions (which vary depending on the nature of the business).

Administrative personnel often are responsible for maintaining department budgets and tracking expenses. Spreadsheet programs can reduce the time and effort required for these duties and provide better control for tracking expenses against budgets. With the aid of spreadsheets, many other administrative and clerical tasks now are completed more effectively and with much less time and effort. Among these tasks are the following.

- Office bookkeeping
- Petty cash funds
- Expense reports
- Invoicing

- Billing
- Time card calculations
- Bank reconciliations
- Local taxes and reporting forms
- Depreciation schedules
- Physical inventory records

Virtually any repetitive administrative task that requires itemizing information in columns and rows is an appropriate application for a spreadsheet. Most administrative assistants, secretaries, and clerical personnel welcome the challenge of setting up spreadsheets once they have had basic training in their use. Applications such as index cards, Rolodex files, notebooks, forms, and other recordkeeping aids can be handled using database programs.

3.2.4.7 Reprographics Personnel/Graphic Services

Reprographics encompasses the various means for reproducing or duplicating information, including copying, printing, and facsimile reproduction and digital, graphic, and voice replication. Although microfilming also is used, it is generally part of records management. Reprographics personnel include phototypesetting operators, copier operators, receiving and distribution clerks, collators, binders, and quality-control personnel. This category also includes professional/technical employees such as graphics artists, job estimators, and printing press operators.

Reprographics is a rapidly expanding field because new developments are providing lower costs, increased output, higher quality, and greater flexibility. As in other areas, the lines between reprographics and other information functions overlap. As pointed out previously, distinctions between word processing and photocomposition have blurred. The formatting, font, and graphics features incorporated into high-end word processing software meet many office needs. New electronic copiers offer many capabilities formerly available only with expensive offset printing. Computer graphics and desktop publishing software are redefining the boundaries between in-house printing and end-user computing.

3.2.4.8 Forms Design Personnel

Forms design personnel oversee the creation and disposition of forms within an organization. They are responsible for approving and maintaining an inventory of all forms created or purchased. Forms control may reside in a separate department or with the graphics or the records management department. Forms simplify and standardize the handling of recurring but variable data. Traditionally, a form is defined as a piece of paper with standard printed information and systematically arranged spaces for entering variable information. Common examples are application and order forms, invoices, credit memorandums, and bills of lading. According to estimates, 50 percent to 75 percent of all documents stored in records systems are forms.

The proper designing of office forms requires specialized skill. The designer often enlists the assistance of persons performing the office work, systems analysts, and work simplification specialists. Effective forms are *simple* forms. Well-designed forms must capture all required information, make it easy to enter and use information, minimize chances for errors, and reduce the costs of printing and using the form. EUIS technologies assist with designing, storing, distributing, updating, and controlling forms. However, technology is redefining the boundaries between forms design and end-user computing. Many forms today are distributed, filled in, and submitted online. Tasks previously handled by forms are increasingly automated as part of online processing systems. This trend is expected to accelerate as the use of Internet self-service and information capture applications continue to increase.

3.2.4.9 Facilities Management Staff

Facilities management plays an integral role in the design of office space and workstations. *Facilities management,* as defined by the Library of Congress, is the process of coordinating the physical workplace within the principles of administration, architecture, and the behavioral sciences. According to the International Facility Management Association, "Facility management coordinates the physical workplace with the people and work of the organization. It combines the best management practices with the most current professional and technical knowledge to provide humane and effective work environments."[6] Facilities personnel include building service managers, security personnel, and space planners and designers. Technologies such as computer-aided design and databases save time and enhance services.

3.2.5   Computers in the Professional Office

Professional offices such as legal and medical offices share many characteristics of business offices but have unique requirements. They are good examples of how EUIS are serving the information processing needs of professionals.

3.2.5.1 Legal Offices

Law firms and legal departments within large corporations find information technologies to be extremely beneficial. Originally, only large legal firms could afford computers. Now, they are virtually indispensable for legal work. Legal offices are growing more innovative in using computers for a wide range of applications such as drafting laws by state and federal legislators, adjudicating cases, researching legal precedents, and managing docket calendars—not to mention the obvious need for preparing correspondence and legal documents.

Computers also are changing the way work is done in law offices. According to Isaac Asimov, a leading science fiction writer, "Cold-blooded computers will make the United States legal systems more just and the American public less litigious over the next 70 years." Writing in the *Journal of the American Bar Association,* Asimov said:

> Computers will grow more elaborate and versatile and cope better with the complexities of law, judgments, and precedents and, as a result, there will be fewer appeals, fewer delays, faster and shorter trials, more out-of-court settlements, and, most of all, fewer cases brought to court in the first place. With computers in action, there will be increasingly little chance of an egregious mistake in legal strategy or tactics and a diminishing hope of unpredictability on the part of the judge. [Calling today's courts "uncivilized"]. . . . competing lawyers need not consider results inevitable; they can simply wait for the opposition to make a mistake, or they can wait for a judge to make a blunder or a jury to be hoodwinked. Virtually every case, therefore, is worth trying, for it offers some hope of winning."[7]

According to a growing number of articles in *ABA Law Practice Today,* more and more law firms are "taking it to the next level: redefining technology and revolutionizing services."[8] The most important strategic initiatives for law firms today are "to redefine technology, to create work systems that are more meaningful to lawyers and their clients, and to shift the focus from productivity improvement to generating revenue."[9]

"These efforts are far more complex than administering a server, adding a mail account, or hiring a Help Desk or a training director. These questions are answered only by diving into the processes by which lawyers work. Because they involve allocation of resources and involve nonbillable time, the answers are also political. True technology integration means moving far beyond bits and bytes toward people and processes, and this requires a new breed of lawyer—one who can see the intersection of legal services, marketing, and technology."[10]

The legal technology framework diagrammed in Figure 3-4 suggests a new approach to the challenges faced by today's law firms in integrating technology and transforming business processes. Up to this point, technology investments by law firms have focused primarily on internal processing and productivity improvement (i.e., cost savings). Progressive law firms, on the other hand, are beginning to capitalize on digital networks to shift that focus to the way attorneys deliver their products and services and interact with clients and other constituencies. The emphasis is on business strategy rather than technology and is aligned with business objectives such as cross-marketing, virtual teaming, and client-partnering.[11]

Technology is entering the courtroom, as well. A multimedia system can show text, video, and audio images on a single computer screen at one time. The system can search and retrieve any word or succession of words from a text or videotape of a court proceeding or pretrial deposition. It works simply. While a trial or de-

Figure 3-4
The legal technology framework

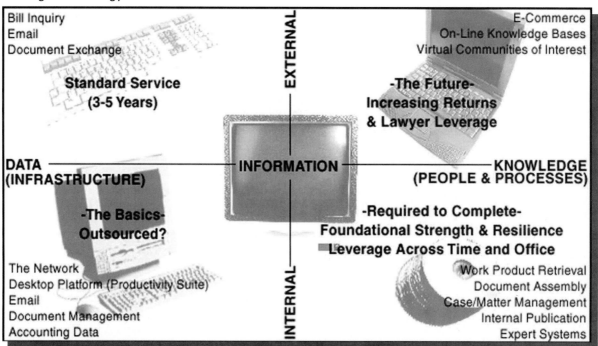

Source: Courtesy John Hokkanen. This figure was derived from a series of grids developed by Professor Richard Susskind. These are fully documented in Susskind's book, *Transforming the Law* (Oxford University Press, 2000) and from his Website, *www.oup.co.uk/law/practitioner/ richardsusskind.*

position is being taped, a court reporter transcribes the proceedings on a steno-graphic device that is connected to a microcomputer equipped with special hypertext software. The videotape is then put into a VCR, and the judge, lawyer, or jury can watch the video of the testimony while reading the written version on the screen. Discovery Video is one of several software vendors that has developed such a system. Its potential for the legal field is unlimited, giving lawyers the ability to manage extremely large cases and find relevant information.

Graphics software also has made its way into the courtroom. Prosecutors are using graphic animation software to reenact the scene of crimes for the jury. For example, graphics animation may show how an automobile accident occurred or how blows or shots were delivered to a body. Though controversial, these new forms of evidence are gaining acceptance in the courtroom.

3.2.5.2 Medical Offices

EUIS can be indispensable in medical practice and research, training, hospital administration, and pharmaceutical distribution. By computerizing their patients' records and billing systems (see Figure 3-5), doctors find they can maintain more detailed, accurate records and save valuable time. Less time spent on administrative chores means more time to spend with patients. Moreover, better records provide many benefits beyond good patient care.

For example, a gynecologist in New Jersey used a personal computer to design and send a questionnaire to patients whose payments were delinquent. Although many patients did not pay because they could not, he discovered that others withheld payment because they were dissatisfied. The questionnaire gave patients an opportunity to express hostility and helped the doctor better understand problems.

SPOTLIGHT ON SOLUTIONS → Technology, People, Structure, Processes

---

AUTOMATION IN LEGAL OFFICES

The legal department at Ryder Systems, a $2.8 billion transportation and business service company, is illustrative of automation in legal offices. Its legal department handles acquisitions, Securities and Exchange Commission work, contracts for the company's seven divisions, and leasing agreements, as well as general corporate legal functions. The office's integrated services provide word processing, calendaring, electronic mail and messaging, and directory service, in addition to communications to public databases and corporate mainframes.

Attorneys communicate with each other through electronic messages and mail, exchanging memos and reports electronically. Attorneys can retrieve items quickly or combine new and previously created (cut-and-paste) text. Several attorneys now keep reminder lists. They keep track of billable time and print out the notes at the end of the day for the billing clerk.

Paralegals find the calendaring function essential for their time-critical work of filing deadlines and tracking cases. Paralegals can research precedents for cases through legal files in public databases right at their desks.

The legal department realized productivity gains in two major areas through its office automation system. First, the distributed word processing has provided much faster turnaround for documents. Documents that used to take a day to produce can now be drafted, revised, and printed in an hour, without anyone standing in line for a terminal or waiting for staff support. Second, the integrated office system has provided the legal office with much more efficient communications. Lawyers and staff can exchange information much faster, even at night or on weekends. The legal administrative assistant has estimated that the system saves her three or four hours a day by reducing the time formerly spent typing, copying, and circulating materials.

To Think About: What level of technology integration does this scenario represent? Is the primary focus productivity improvement or generating revenue? What will it take for this firm to "take it to the next level" as described by the quotes in the text from *ABA Law Practice Today?*

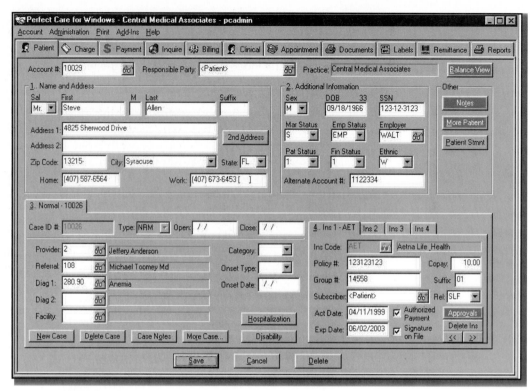

Figure 3-5
Perfect Care for Windows: Patient entry screen

*Source: http://www.ncgmedical.com/products/pcare/pcare_windows/screen_shots/
patient-entry.htm* (accessed 7/21/00).

Moreover, pressing disgruntled patients for payment can lead to unwarranted malpractice charges. Thus, the gynecologist found that computerized billing helped avoid malpractice suits. For patients who could not pay, the system made it easy to develop a payment plan to spread the costs over time.

Software also can help doctors with decision making. For example, a doctor can analyze records to determine whether a procedure is performed often enough to cover the cost of equipment or if it is more cost effective to use an independent laboratory. A doctor also can analyze patients' records to assess trends in treatment or increases in symptoms or diseases.

High-definition television (HDTV) can make expert or second opinions on medical issues quicker and easier to obtain. The high-quality color and resolution of HDTV can offer a doctor at a remote site the feeling of "being there" with a colleague or patient or seeing X rays with no distortions. In addition, high quality videos of, say, a heart operation, are used increasingly for medical education and often provide a better view of medical procedures than if the student were standing by the side of the doctor.

One innovative doctor in Connecticut has a personal computer with a modem in his home. When he receives an emergency call at home, he dials up the computer in his office to check the patient's medical record. The medical office is another example of how computers can be used innovatively. EUIS can reduce time spent on administrative tasks and give medical professionals more time to devote to medicine.

3.3 MATCHING USER NEEDS TO SOFTWARE SOLUTIONS

Many quality off-the-shelf software packages are available today to meet a wide variety of individual needs. Selecting an appropriate solution is a matter of clearly identifying the user needs, establishing specific performance objectives, defining the needed functionality, and then evaluating appropriate software packages against the required functionality.

Although the evaluation process seems straightforward, in practice, it is often a great deal more complex than people think. To make an informed decision, it is important to use a systematic process for matching product features against needed functionality and comparing alternative packages.

3.3.1 Defining User Needs

It takes time and skilled interviewing for an analyst to develop a clear, detailed definition of the specific functionality that a user may require. Because an analyst usually is not familiar with all the details of the user's job, it is easy to miss the significance of some of the needs the user may express. What may seem like minor details sometimes can turn out to be major issues or shortcomings of a software package. For instance, if state laws regulating insurance require reporting on a certain piece of information and a selected software package does not provide a field to capture and store that information, it could be a show stopper even though the rest of the package functionality is an excellent fit. However, if the package is customized, it could add significant additional cost to the project.

Sometimes workflow requirements must be taken into consideration in addition to functionality. The sequence in which tasks are performed may be important, and if software doesn't provide sufficient flexibility, it could be a problem. As a basis for evaluating software packages, the analyst needs to develop a detailed list of required functionality, and verify with users to be sure that nothing important has been overlooked. The analyst may have missed the significance of something, or the user may have neglected to mention an important need.

3.3.2 Clarifying Business Objectives

In addition to documenting specific functionality needs, it is also critical to clarify specific business objectives. Exactly what outcomes are expected from the use of the technology and how are the achievement of those outcomes going to be measured? Is the objective primarily productivity improvement (i.e., cost savings) or delivery of new products and services (revenue generation)? To what extent are individuals going to be required to change behaviors and modify business processes? Are users supportive or resistant? How much training will be required? Will it primarily be on software features or on business processes? Issues and questions such as these must be addressed and provide the framework for selecting an appropriate software solution.

After needs and objectives have been documented thoroughly, the EUIS analyst is ready to begin evaluating alternative software solutions.

3.3.3 Evaluating Alternative Software Packages

To evaluate alternative software packages adequately, the analyst usually has to learn each package and use sample applications to compare the features and performance of each package. Going through the vendor demonstration or randomly sampling product features usually is not adequate to make an informed decision. Without a thorough, systematic evaluation, shortcomings are not discovered until the user has been trained and begins using the package, only to discover that some important functionality is not available. A effective approach for systematically evaluating software is to create an evaluation form to guide the process of collecting information and comparing results.

As software packages are evaluated, features should be checked off systematically against required functionality. Often it is not just the presence or absence of a feature that is important, but how the feature works that is critical. Product marketing literature seldom tells the whole story. All too often, advertised features may fall seriously short of the full functionality that is required by the user. Therefore, the analyst should evaluate the adequacy of each feature against the predefined needs, not just check them off. A sample software evaluation form is shown in Figure 3-6. Note how each vendor or product is listed across the top and is rated on a scale of 0 to 5 on each product feature. A zero indicates absence of a feature, a 1 or 2 indicates limited functionality, and a 4 or 5 indicates not only that the functionality is adequate but the extent to which it matches how the work needs to be performed.

In most cases, making a selection is a matter of tradeoffs. The user will prefer some features in one package and others in a different package. When many features are involved in the evaluation, the best overall fit is not always obvious. After completing the evaluation matrix, the ratings on all features are tallied for each vendor. The highest score usually indicates the package with the best overall fit.

Besides the product features, it is also important to consider factors such as reliability of the vendor, service availability and cost, product upgrades, security issues, and fit with the enterprise's desktop platforms and systems architectures. Appropriate management tools or applications must be selected in conjunction with hardware considerations. When computer systems are already in place, software options will be narrowed to those designed to run on installed systems. If hardware is not a constraint, the tools that best meet business requirements are identified first, and then the appropriate hardware may be selected.

3.4 EVALUATING PRODUCTIVITY TOOLS FOR INDIVIDUALS

The range of productivity tools for individuals today is extensive. The sections that follow provide a sampling of available tools. It is meant only to be representative—not definitive or comprehensive. The focus is on factors to consider in choosing among alternative packages rather than on details about product features.

3.4.1 Desktop Productivity Suites

Productivity suites have become the standard platform for desktop computing. The industry leader by far is Microsoft Office Suite. Other current contenders are Corel WordPerfect Office, Lotus Development eSuite Workplace, Apple Computer AppleWorks, and StarOffice by Sun MicroSystems. Productivity suites bundle word

FEATURES/CONSIDERATIONS	RATINGS (0 LOW TO 5 HIGH)			
	ALTERNATE 1	ALTERNATE 2	ALTERNATE 3	COMMENTS
System Requirements				
Necessary hardware and networking resources				
Compatibility with enterprise architecture				
Graphical presentation				
Data handling				
System flexibility				
Interface with other existing systems				
Ease of Internet interface				
Security				
Scalability				
Installation requirements? Does the vendor install the software? If not, is any special training involved?				
Is there a trial period with little or no obligation?				
Software Features/Functionality				
Feature 1				
Feature 2				
Feature 3				
Feature 4				
ETC				
Training				
Required training (learning curve) for **developers?**				
Required training (learning curve) for **users?**				
Is training provided by the vendor? On-site? Vendor site?				
Is there tutorial and online help?				
Vendor Considerations				
Cost and financial terms				
Upgrade policy and cost				

(continued)

Figure 3-6
Sample software evaluation matrix

| FEATURES/CONSIDERATIONS | RATINGS (0 LOW TO 5 HIGH) | | | |
	ALTERNATE 1	ALTERNATE 2	ALTERNATE 3	COMMENTS
Vendor's reputation and reliability				
Vendor's success stories (Will vendor supply reference list of current users?)				
Ongoing technical support and vendor availability for help				
Availability and quality of documentation				
Will vendor customize the software to meet individual needs?				
Will vendor allow the user to customize the software? (Permit access to source code for customization?)				
Product quality and performance guarantees				

Figure 3-6
(continued)

processing, spreadsheets, databases, presentation software, communications, and a Web browser into a highly integrated package. The newest suites support both desktop publishing and Web publishing.

Word processing is turning out to be a major business application for knowledge workers and managers. Originally considered a replacement for the typewriter, word processing has become an authoring tool—a replacement for pen and pad. Word processing no longer is viewed as something that "real managers" don't do. Most knowledge workers today draft their own letters, memos, and documents. Administrative assistants also may key in drafts, which managers then edit (or vice versa). Consequently, administrative assistants do less typing than they formerly did, especially in offices where word processing is coupled with electronic mail. In fact, the old excuse "It's on the administrative assistant's desk to be typed; you'll have it tomorrow" is losing its credence in management circles. Today, the response is likely to be "if you had used word processing (or e-mail), I'd have the draft in my hands now."

The benefits of word processing as a replacement for dictation are less clearcut. Ultimately, its use is a personal choice. Knowledge workers who learned to think and compose with a microphone in hand might continue to find dictation more effective. For capturing words, audio-tape dictation systems are more efficient, except perhaps for the fastest keyboarders. Most dictation systems do not lend themselves to revising, however. Using word processing, on the other hand, authors can edit and refine their texts easily. Most people work in a draft-and-edit style; few people can create a final draft the first time. Many knowledge workers are discovering that they write more effectively with word processing. The ease of editing and reorganizing text encourages revision. It even changes people's approach to the writing process. With word processing, authors tend to get their key ideas down quickly and then go back to fill in the details and refine the prose.

However, as voice-recognition systems become more sophisticated and easier to use, voice rather than keyboarded input may become more prevalent. As discussed in chapter 10, Human Factors, speech recognition systems such as Dragon System's NaturallySpeaking Preferred, support dictation up to 160 words per minute, with words transcribed immediately into software application packages, e-mail, and chat rooms.

For knowledge worker solutions, editing and revision may be the most important word-processing features. High-powered word-processing packages include the ability to track editing changes and document versions. When evaluating the needs of knowledge workers, it is important to understand the document creation process. Many complex documents have multiple authors and go through multiple editing cycles. Word-processing features that support collaborative writing and track editing changes can be extremely valuable in streamlining what often can be an arduous process.

Another key factor to consider is the ability to interchange documents easily. Users want to be able to interchange electronic documents as easily as paper documents, which is one of the primary reasons that Microsoft Office has become a de-facto standard worldwide. This point often is missed by technologists who are caught up with quantity of features. Few users actually use more than 20 percent of package functionality. They usually do not care nearly as much about the latest and greatest features as they do about ease of use and the ability to interchange documents. The time needed to perform a task used only occasionally is dwarfed by the time saved in being able to interchange documents. Thus, it is critical when selecting a desktop productivity platform to understand the need for interchanging documents and information among different software programs.

3.4.2 Activity Management

Activity management tools are designed to manage time and events. The most common applications are *calendar management* and *personal digital assistants (PDA)*, with tools such as appointment books, to-do lists, electronic notepads, address books, and calculators. Improved networking and the growing use of portable PCs and the newest palm-sized devices are giving these tools the flexibility and transportability needed to gain widespread use. A key factor when selecting activity management tools is whether they are intended for individual use or for facilitating scheduling of meetings and coordinating events across groups or enterprises.

3.4.2.1 Calendar Management

Calendar management software can streamline the process of scheduling meetings and notifying attendees. This software virtually eliminates the multiple phone calls required to schedule meetings with several attendees; a meeting for ten individuals can be scheduled as quickly as a meeting for two.

To schedule a meeting, the manager or administrative assistant simply instructs the computer to select the times when all attendees are available. To do this, the computer needs three items of information: (1) a list of attendees, (2) the duration of the meeting, and (3) the acceptable range of meeting dates (e.g., between March 2 and March 4). Once the manager or administrative assistant specifies these parameters, the computer reports a list of available time slots that meet the criteria. For example, a request for a one-hour meeting among six managers within the next three days might produce a list of four meeting times when these managers would be available at the same time. With some software, meetings can be assigned priorities, so that lower-priority meetings can be bumped for those with higher priority.

After the meeting time is selected, attendees may be notified in one of two ways. The system either can send meeting notices electronically to all intended participants, who schedule their own calendar, or the meeting may be scheduled directly on each attendee's calendar. The best way is more a matter of individual preference than efficiency.

One of the biggest advantages of calendar management systems, such as the one in Figure 3-7, is that anyone who is authorized to view a manager's calendar always sees the same version; thus, the need for managers and administrative assistants to maintain multiple copies is eliminated. Users can avoid problems such as double bookings or missed meetings when appointments are inadvertently omitted from one version of the calendar. Recurring meetings can be entered just once, with successive dates scheduled automatically. For example, a staff meeting at 9:00 A.M. every Friday needs to be entered only once. Then, in one step it is copied as a weekly meeting for the specified duration.

The same calendar may be viewed and printed in multiple ways. An individual may view one day at a time, a week at a time, or an entire month. Access can be controlled to permit only authorized individuals to view calendars. Even when managers grant access to others, they can schedule undesignated times or keep private notes about meetings. The calendar may be searched easily for a specific event,

Figure 3-7
A typical electronic calendar: Microsoft EXCHANGE

Source: Microsoft Corporation.

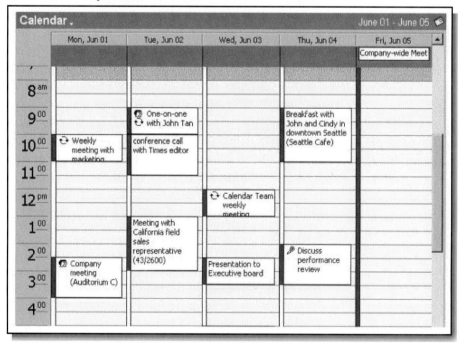

such as an appointment with a particular person or even a list of the days that a manager will be out of the office.

When evaluating calendars, analysts should clearly define and prioritize required functionality. Important considerations from a manager's perspective, for example, include the following.

1. Provide all the scheduling information the job requires. (Otherwise, the manager will need to supplement it manually, resulting in wasteful duplication of effort.)
2. Include access to calendars of all individuals in the company with whom a manager regularly meets.
3. Offer easy access and reference.
4. Provide printed output. If managers are accustomed to carrying a calendar in their pockets, they should be able to obtain a printout in a format convenient for carrying.
5. Be easy to learn and use.
6. Work the way the users work.

From the administrative assistant's perspective, priorities might be different. For example, when administrative assistants manage calendars for several managers, they must be able to "flip" directly from one calendar to another. Otherwise, working with multiple calendars is too cumbersome to be practical.

Another factor to consider is the extent to which managers can control access by designating who is authorized to view the calendar and who is authorized to change the calendar. Administrative assistants, for example, might be authorized to schedule only the calendars of managers in the work group they support. Meeting attendees who are outside the immediate work group would be notified of meetings but would schedule their own calendars.

Calendars also can be used to schedule conference rooms or other facilities. The facility is assigned a calendar on the system, which means that it can be scheduled, displayed, and queried. When scheduling a meeting, the requester includes the name of the meeting room, along with the list of attendees.

Electronic calendars can be effective on centralized systems or a local area network. If considering the use of calendar software in a inter-networked environment, it is critical to verify the level of integration across networks. A calendar system that does not provide full support for scheduling meetings will not be used.

3.4.2.2 *Personal Digital Assistants (PDAs)*

Personal digital assistants (PDAs), such as the Palm Pilot, Visor, and Cassiopeia, are designed for personal time management (see Figure 3-8). These highly portable devices, which are small enough to slip into a pocket or purse, include calendars, address books, to-do lists, electronic notebooks, and tools such as calculators and clocks. Off-the-shelf, add-on software is readily available, and they can be programmed for customized applications. The devices come with a PC desktop interface or can interface with other popular desktop programs, such as Microsoft Exchange. E-mail can be downloaded and read or saved on the PDA. Higher-level models can connect to the Internet, so, for example, the knowledge worker easily can access favorite sites, monitor stock prices, or execute trades from the PDA.

To-do lists, or reminder lists, are tools for prioritizing and tracking tasks. To-do lists serve as a working scratch pad of tasks and priorities or as a permanent record of daily activities. Because to-do lists generally are linked with an electronic calendar, a manager easily can list in priority order tasks to be completed on or by a certain date. If priorities change, the manager can reorder the list at any time. When items are completed, the user simply checks them off. Unfinished items automatically are carried over to the next day. A manager can keep detailed notes about any of the items on a separate page.

Electronic notebooks (not to be confused with notebook computers) are designed for storing random items in the format of a notepad. The user can jot down ideas, addresses, status notes, telephone messages, or other types of notes. Electronic notebooks offer flexible indexing that allows the manager to store information by categories, classes, and subjects. Information can be transferred directly from calendars, mailboxes, to-do lists, or other features to the notebook.

As substitutes for their paper cousins, electronic notebooks offer several advantages. Information is located easily simply by keying in the subject and allowing the computer to locate the information. With some electronic notebooks, a manager can search for information by any word within a note. Notebook pages can be printed if desired.

3.4.3 Communications/Networking

Automated communication tools include voice messaging systems, smart phones and wireless communicators, and desktop business meetings. Their usefulness depends on business requirements and the willingness of individuals to change the way they traditionally have communicated. For example, medium-size companies, residing in a single building, may use a voice message system much less than a large company with geographically dispersed divisions and managers who travel frequently.

Figure 3-8
Personal digital assistant
Source: Palm Inc., Santa Clara, CA

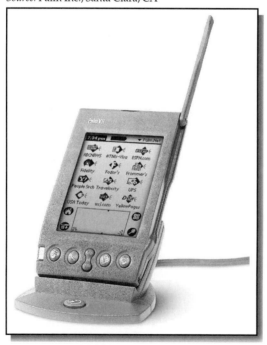

Part II   End-User Information Systems: Business Solutions

A FURNITURE MANUFACTURER USES VOICE MAIL TO IMPROVE DECISION MAKING

The case of a Midwestern furniture manufacturer illustrates how a voice mail system can be used to improve business. Corporate management at manufacturing headquarters depended heavily on telephone communication. Decisions often had to be made quickly and required gathering information and opinions from peers and subordinates. Final sign offs for pricing decisions, contract negotiations, personnel decisions, and company reorganizations required fast input and fast distribution. Executives traveled frequently, which made coordination of meetings and telephone communication difficult. Executives wanted to communicate the context of decisions as well as the content. Such attitudes as "We have to pursue this, but there are likely to be problems" were difficult to communicate by letter or memo. Moreover, information was often confidential. Pink-slip telephone messages or written letters were considered less than confidential.

After a careful analysis of its requirements, the company selected a digital voice mail system. The company developed a comprehensive implementation strategy that included careful selection of the initial users and applications, a training program, and continuing education. All upper-level management, the entire sales force, and other key departments in the sales communication network, such as the shipping and order entry departments, were given access to the voice mail system.

After several months, the manufacturer reported that the system was adopted quickly and heavily used. A series of interviews assessed the impact of the system on corporate managers, and the research report cited the following benefits.[12]

1. *Increased corporate control.* Executives felt that the message system made it easier and faster to communicate corporate decisions, thus increasing their organizational control. For example, one executive distributed a message simultaneously to all managers about a reorganization of their division before rumors had time to spread. By receiving information through the phone mail system in advance of the official announcement, managers were prepared to handle organizational changes more calmly and efficiently. Before another executive forwarded a message to the entire sales force concerning a large contract that had im-

plications for the industry as a whole, it was sent to the regional sales managers, who added their own introductions to indicate the local context.

2. *Increased ability to communicate context.* Executives used phone messages, instead of memos, when it was important to communicate message context as well as content. The tone of voice can indicate the level of support for a given decision, which in turn might have consequences for the strategies subordinates use to implement a decision.

3. *Increased speed of decision making.* Executives were able to participate in negotiations and to give final sign offs while they were traveling. They reported instances in which complex contract negotiations, involving millions of dollars, were carried out among three or four decision makers in different cities. Because detailed messages could be communicated to the right people within a day's time, they did not have to wait for formal meetings to complete these transactions.

4. *Improved quality of information for decision making.* Executives reported being able to secure information from more people in less time, providing better-quality information for decision making. Executives reported receiving from 10 to 20 messages per day. The system proved effective even for detailed messages, several minutes in length, if they were well organized. Consequently, executives felt that the message system provided a vehicle not previously available for making business decisions.

5. *Decreased interruptions.* Subordinates learned to use the message system to request information instead of interrupting the executives during their limited time in the office. The executives could respond to such messages while they were on the road and after hours when they were less pressured.

6. *Decreased dependence on administrative support.* Communication via a message system is a direct process that requires no intervention from support personnel. Thus, complex negotiations could be carried out among decision makers without the support of secretaries. When meetings were desired, using the message system reduced the amount of time required to set them up. One support person reported that the average three days to set up meetings for 4 to 12 executives was reduced to one day.

7. *Increased control over when information is accessed.* Executives could access the system at any time of the day or night from a telephone anywhere in the nation. They were able to carry out complex communications after hours or between meetings, which had the effect of increasing their overall efficiency.

To Think About: What changes were required in the way executives worked in order to capitalize on the benefits of voice mail? How did voice mail impact performance?

3.4.3.1 Voice Mail Systems

Voice mail or *phone mail systems,* which create and send digitized voice messages over standard telephone systems, have become so commonplace over the past 10 years that they hardly bear mention. Yet they often are not well used. Users can access messages from any tone-generating telephone at any time of day or night. Especially useful features enable users to distribute a message to multiple recipients in many locations and to create and store distribution lists. A recipient may forward a message to someone else and preface it with an explanatory introduction. Voice mail systems eliminate time-zone problems in communication across the country or internationally. Managers often use passwords to restrict access to their messages. An often overlooked feature is the capability to delete and re-record messages. For particularly sensitive messages, users can listen to the message and re-record until the message conveys precisely the right meaning and tone, an alternative with much lower risk of misinterpretation than e-mail or a written document. As with any technology, it is important to identify user needs and provide for adequate training to achieve business objectives.

3.4.3.2 Electronic Mail

Electronic mail systems, usually referred to as e-mail, have become ubiquitous in just a few short years. Around since the 1980s, their use virtually took off with the introduction of Internet-based e-mail. Users easily send and receive messages, memos, and reports in a variety of formats. These formats include text files, programs, data files, and images. Electronic mail provides fast, direct communication anywhere in the world. No intermediaries—administrative assistants, mail clerks, postal employees—are required. E-mail rapidly has become the number one application among managers. Most business cards and letterhead today include an electronic mail identifier along with the telephone number and address.

No longer a mere device for simple messages, e-mail is viewed by progressive enterprises as a strategic business tool to improve communications between employees and with trading partners. E-mail provides the kind of communication needed to facilitate restructuring to flatter, more fluid, and decentralized organizations.

With new Web-based e-mail, users no longer need a PC linked to a proprietary e-mail system on the corporate LAN. Users can check their e-mail from any computer device—incuding PDAs or cell phones—linked to the Internet. This convenience of anytime, anywhere access, however, currently comes at the expense of functionality to which most users have become accustomed with LAN-based e-mail systems. Moreover, the functionality among current Web-based mail systems—such as Lotus iNotes, Novell Groupwise WebAccess, Ipswitch Imail, Microsoft Exchange 2000 Server Outlook for Web Access, Critical Path InScribe, and Novell Internet Messaging System—varies considerably. Careful analysis of user preferences and patterns of use will be critical to making a wise decision about future directions for a particular enterprise.

3.4.3.3 Smart Phones and Wireless Communicators

These devices will combine the best features of cellular phones with those of computers. Smart phones will store thousands of telephone numbers, retrieve voice mail and e-mail, and access the Internet. They also will be compatible with the desktop PC. To dial a phone number, the user issues a voice command or touches the screen. He or she also will be able to send voice mail messages as e-mail attachments or hear audio versions of e-mail messages via voice mail.

3.4.3.4 Desktop Business Meetings

Currently in limited use, meeting software allows individuals sitting at their own PCs to meet in real-time conferences in virtual meeting rooms on the Internet. In the future, dozens of people in dozens of locations will meet at the same time in cyberspace to collaborate, brainstorm, share information, and make decisions. These software programs will include video and data conferencing and help members of work groups and task forces streamline decision making. Users will be able to review each team member's input without time-consuming group discussion and enter their own comments and feedback. Voice and fax software will be ideal for entrepreneurs and small businesses, as these packages track incoming and outgoing calls, send auto pages, take messages, and feature fax-on-demand capability.

3.4.4 Decision Support

Decision support software is designed to aid in creative tasks and decision making. Tools in this category have proven to be among the most difficult to implement successfully. Business needs and objectives are often more specific in nature than for other desktop productivity tools and more closely aligned to the business context. Thus, it is especially important that EUIS analysts understand the specific needs of the intended users and the business objectives to be achieved. Careful analysis is required to ensure that the right tools are selected for the job at hand. Considerations related to several examples of decision support software are discussed in this section, including decision modeling, data warehousing, online analytical processing and datamining, project management, geographic information systems, statistical and mathematical analysis, and executive support systems.

3.4.4.1 Decision Modeling

Model-driven decision-support systems are generally stand-alone, independent systems that use some type of model to perform "what if" and other analyses of business problems. Knowledge workers and managers use *decision-modeling software* to collect and organize their thoughts on a particular problem, narrow the number of alternatives, and present logical plans of action. Decision-modeling software allows them—either personally or through a subordinate—to create and manipulate complex business models on an interactive basis, without the help of programming specialists.

Using decision-modeling software, a manager keys commands into the system that resemble spoken business terminology and may be phrased with great latitude. Some of the new planning software allows models to be created in a nonprocedural way; that is, managers may describe the characteristics of a model in whatever order they think of them, rather than specifying the procedure to be followed in solving the model. Simple models may be set up in a few hours, and even complex ones in a few days. Alternatives may be chosen and new solutions obtained in a few minutes, and the results may be presented in any format to suit the manager's understanding. Decision-modeling programs offer guidance on many problems, from improving a subordinate's performance to locating a new branch or plant.

A model can help the decision-making process, analyze raw data, enhance understanding of business relationships and alternatives, or compare the alternatives to select the best one (together with contingency plans). Models or inter-related networks of models may be set up and maintained for continuing corporate planning, forecasting, and control. Alternatively, models may be created on an ad-hoc basis for decisions on specific projects. Models may be manipulated as part of private or group deliberations. In any case, a model becomes a virtual extension of an executive's mind in exploring the probable consequences of alternative decisions.

Not all decision-modeling software is alike; various programs take different approaches to the modeling process. Some programs provide guidance for business- or personnel-related problems, offering recommendations and options. Others use a statistical approach whereby managers compare alternatives against criteria they have defined. Results can be compared on graphs and charts. A third variety prods the manager with questions in an effort to isolate the factors that have contributed to the problem before it offers suggestions or solutions.

Consider the following examples of the use of decision support software.

- An account supervisor at a San Francisco advertising agency found that using a decision-modeling software package helped him convince clients of the need to change their advertising strategy. It enabled him to focus discussions with clients on objective criteria—something he was not able to do before.
- The president of a consulting company reported using a micro-computer package called Expert Choice by Decision Support Software to help clients, primarily health care facilities, reach decisions about purchasing computer systems. The software helps consultants cut through information overload, sort out sub-issues, and reduce the inclination to make decisions on subjective or gut-level feelings. The consultants found that the program helped eliminate the rhetoric that frequently accompanies group decision making and helped participants focus on the issues. It was easier to go through the process of rank ordering alternatives. According to the president, use of the decision-modeling package allowed them to make decisions in about half the time it took before.

The strength of decision-modeling software is primarily its organizational capabilities. It does not make final decisions; it provides information so that the manager can better determine what the solution might be. Whether or not managers could use a decision support program depends on the kinds of decisions they make on a regular basis. If managers make snap judgments most of the time, they are probably not good candidates for such a package. If managers evaluate situations and weigh alternatives, however (such as where to test-market a new product), they may find such a program helpful.

3.4.4.2 Data Warehousing, Online Analytical Processing (OLAP), and Datamining

Data warehousing assembles and organizes data from enterprise operations, such as transaction processing systems (order systems, reservation systems, cash register checkout systems, etc.), and stores this data in a format—called a data warehouse—that knowledge workers and managers can analyze. Enterprises are beginning to build data warehouses to collect data from their Web sites, as well. The data are made accessible through various tools, such as online analytical processing (OLAP) and datamining, for individuals in need of detailed information.

In the past, traditional database queries answered questions such as how many units of product X were shipped in January. OLAP is multidimensional and supports much more complex queries for analysis of problems such as comparing the sales of product X relative to plan by region, by quarter, for the past three years. There are many different types of OLAP tools for analysis of different database systems. These include desktop OLAP (DOLAP), multidimensional (MOLAP), and relational (ROLAP).

Datamining offers end users an even more powerful tool for data analysis. With OLAP, like other query-oriented data analysis tools, knowledge workers still are required to have a good understanding of the information for which they are looking. Datamining, on the other hand, is more discovery oriented. It can find hidden patterns and relationships in large databases and infer rules from them to predict future behavior. Thus, it provides a powerful tool for gaining insight into corporate data and is especially popular for analyzing customer buying patterns and behaviors. It can answer questions such as which customers are most likely to reply to my next promotional campaign and why?

The types of information that can be inferred from datamining include associations, sequences, classifications, clusters, and forecasts. Datamining technology makes use of statistical analysis tools, neural networks, fuzzy logic, genetic algorithms, and rule-based reasoning and other artificial intelligence techniques.

In its simplest form, data warehousing is basically a sophisticated database. What sets it apart is that the information it contains is intended for analytical tasks rather than for operational purposes—everything from identifying new market segments to corporate brainstorming. Data warehousing has put new zip into decision support systems, which have been around since the 1970s. In fact, some would say that it is ushering in a whole new paradigm for corporate decision making—taking it far beyond the past focus on recording and reporting what happened to making it much more proactive and forward looking. Some companies are using data warehousing and datamining "to build relationships with their most important customers by aggregating information about individual and group buying patterns. Some use it to rationalize inventory and supply, to the extent of driving production cycles at their key suppliers. Still others have discovered that the timely access to complex data can be a new business in itself."[13]

Designing and implementing a data warehouse is a complex and expensive undertaking. Moreover, it has organizational and cultural implications. When enterprises start giving end users data warehouse tools, it can raise many political issues, as well.

3.4.4.3 Project Management

To plan and control a large project, managers typically subdivide it into logical tasks and calculate the time and resources required to complete them. *Project management software* enables the manager to outline all required tasks, estimate starting

COMBE, INC.
HARD CODED REPORTS GIVE WAY
TO ONLINE/WEB ANALYSIS

You can learn a good deal about a customer's buying habits and forecast your own sales better if you have timely access to relevant sales data. For Combe of White Plains, New York, the maker of some of the most widely used family care and pet products in the world, getting sales data to the field sales force was a challenge. A standard hard copy sales report sent to the field was outdated by the time it might be used. "We found ourselves walking into a buyer's office with the retailer having more information about its buying patterns than we did," said Bob Woods, senior vice president of sales operations at Combe.

At a time when buyers are managing inventories more carefully, not having this critical information readily available was a handicap. The company needed to track routine statistics on customers, products, orders, and sales, as well as changes in those numbers year-to-year.

The company decided to investigate OLAP technology, and after evaluating several vendors, chose Accrue Software's Pilot Analysis Server (PAS) for its ability to perform time series analysis. Pilot Analysis Server provides the ability to pose "what-if" questions on large data sets and obtain detailed information by region, time, product, and other categories.

"It also helps our retailers manage inventory better; and since they try to carry less inventory it is very important that both of us have an accurate picture of what is in stock," Woods said. "This also helps us plan factory production." In addition, Combe uses time series analysis to track the acceptance of new products. "We can tell fairly quickly who orders a new product and, more importantly, who reorders it," he said.

SALES REPS FIND PILOT EASY TO USE

Providing the analysis is important, but getting a group of noncomputer professionals to use it is another matter. The system had to be easy to use so that sales people could feel comfortable performing their daily downloads as well as working with their customers in front of a laptop.

Because most of Combe's sales representatives work remotely, it was also important that they have a way of quickly downloading data that could then be disconnected from the central server. When Combe first adopted Pilot technology, it outfitted sales reps with single-user copies of Pilot's OLAP server. Remote offices received a daily download from headquarters with a slice of that day's sales data pertaining to each region. Sales people then incrementally built a local database.

REPLACING DOWNLOADS WITH THE WEB

The whole downloading process has been replaced recently with a Web application based on the Pilot Internet Publisher. The introduction of Pilot Internet Publisher (PIP) has eliminated the need for data synchronization and download, and researching information is simply a matter of getting to the Web site.

Combe also works with a broker network that is responsible for covering accounts outside traditional sales territories. According to Woods, "Brokers work closely with field sales and although they do not have access to the system, it's very easy to put a slice of data in Microsoft Excel and e-mail it to them."

In summing up his success with Pilot, Woods points out how far the sales team has come in a short time. "Marketing and sales are now on the same page, they access the same data, and know who is driving business."

To Think About: What are the advantages of OLAP software for Combe's management? For sales representatives?

Source: www.combe.com (Combe Incorporated web site); *www.accrue.com/products/Accrue_Pilot/pilot_suite.html; www.accrue.com/successes/casestudies.html*

and ending dates, assign staff resources, and analyze project costs. Key tasks and critical deadlines can be identified. Project management software automates various planning techniques such as Gantt charts, the Critical Path Method (CPM), or the Project Evaluation and Review Technique (PERT), which may be familiar to readers from business management courses.

With computerized project management tools, a manager can compare alternative strategies for completing a project, whether it is the construction of a bridge or building, designing a new product, programming a computer system, or any other large project. The manager can change the variables and assess the results, a process frequently referred to as what-if analysis. What-if analysis can tell the manager the effect, in both time and money, of accelerating or decelerating various activities. For example, a manager can answer questions such as the following: How much more will it cost to complete the project a week sooner? What is the best way to improve the schedule by one week? Can I save money by paying overtime for critical tasks? Figure 3-9 illustrates comparing alternative strategies with the aid of project management software.

After the project begins, the manager can track its progress with a chart of related activities and reports of costs and resources. He or she can spot tasks that are behind schedule or costs that exceed the budget. The manager then can assess alternatives and take corrective action based on how critical the task is and its impact on other phases of the project.

Good project management contributes to effective management of all organization resources. Once all projects are entered into a computerized database, responsibilities and strategies common to a number of projects can be identified for cost and time savings. Resource-leveling techniques can be employed to minimize costs by scheduling noncritical activities to minimize peak demands on resources.

The major advantages of project management software are their speed and capacity to handle complex projects and relationships. Project management techniques have been part of good management practices for many decades. Automating them has greatly extended their practicality and usefulness. The Spotlight on Solutions: Project Management describes the use of project management software at Eddie Bauer, Inc.

3.4.4.4 *Geographic Information Systems (GIS)/Visualization*

Once the province of specialists, desktop-mapping software—also called *geographic information systems (GIS)*—is gaining in importance as a general purpose decision support and presentation tool. GIS use digitized maps as a framework for storing, manipulating, and displaying information, tying it to points, lines, and areas on the map. GIS provide valuable data for planning and decision making. They include modeling capabilities that allow decision makers to change data and revise business scenarios to evaluate alternative solutions. GIS are useful in situations that require knowledge about the geographic distribution of people and other resources. They are used commonly for municipal facilities management, property mapping for municipal development and tax records, scientific research, sales territories and product distribution, site analysis for location of plants or facilities, designing delivery routes, and a growing number of other applications.

For the insurance industry, for example, mapping holds the potential to change how underwriters analyze risk and rate setters compare competitive positions, as well as how sales and marketing executives organize their efforts. For one company, spatial analysis of demographics and historical loss experience revealed that its large ratings territory was at a disadvantage compared with competitors, which had divided the territory into smaller areas, each with a different rate. Beginning with the 1990 Census, the U.S. Census Bureau began making census data available in GIS form. The Topological Integrated Geographic Encoding and Referencing file (Tiger) is a digital version of the Census street map for the entire country, including U.S. territories. The Tiger database is accompanied by a separate file of demographic data. This is just one of the examples of the benefits of GIS, which is spurring much of the commercial interest.

Mapping packages combine the visual presentation of a map with the power of relational database technology. A considerable range of data-driven mapping packages is now available, starting with inexpensive presentation products and moving upscale to complex geographic information systems.

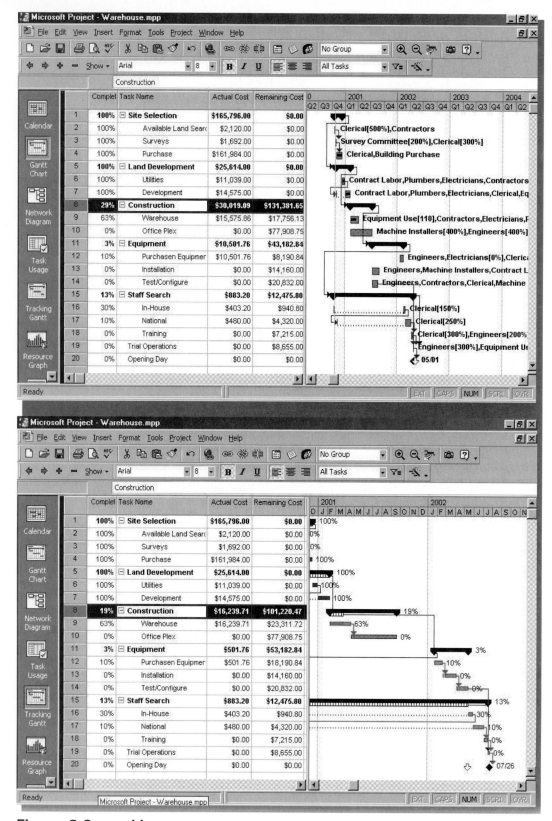

Figure 3-9a and b

Using project management software to compare alternative strategies. Project managers use Gantt charts to analyze project data and to make correct decisions for keeping projects on schedule and within budget.

PROJECT MANAGEMENT
AT EDDIE BAUER, INC.

It's a significant challenge to coordinate a team involving more than 100 people pulled from dozens of departments across a company—especially when that team was responsible for taking on year 2000. At Eddie Bauer, a Redmond, Washington-based retailer that employs 15,000 people, Microsoft Project 98 helped the Y2K team stay on top of its work with such features as consolidation, linking, filters, Web publishing, and what-if scenarios. This ambitious effort covered everything from mainframe and client/server software and hardware to telecommunications, facilities, and security.

As team manager, Paul Karas explains, Y2K planning had to be divided into many parts in order to complete the project on schedule. At the same time, the parts had to be properly connected for management to have a clear view of resource allocation and costs. Resource allocation was especially difficult at Eddie Bauer because team members were continually being moved from one part of the project to another. Thus, the resource-allocation tools in Microsoft Project 98 were especially useful. "Resource allocation involves a lot of guessing, projecting, and finding out that things don't happen the way you might think. It can be hard to express all that in most project-planning tools," Karas says. "The multiple-views capability of Microsoft Project 98 allowed us to see exactly where resources were over- or under-allocated. We then could convey that information clearly to management."

Consolidation and linking are two other Microsoft Project 98 features that helped Eddie Bauer stay on top of their otherwise-unwieldy job. "Consolidation is useful because it helps us manage resource allocation across the entire project," Karas says. "Linking enabled us to join smaller subplans into a single master plan while, at the same time, keeping resource allocation among the subplans separate." At Eddie Bauer, the overall Y2K plan consisted of 77 subplans, focusing down to the smallest detail of every desktop application. Using linking, these subplans were consolidated into increasingly higher-level plans and then were joined with the master plan. Organizing the work in this way enabled team members to report on different levels and parts of the work to various levels of management.

The filters in Microsoft Project 98 provide yet another way of hiding some kinds of information while revealing others to make reports easy to understand. In addition to enabling users to select the information they want to view, filters can help reformat that information. The Y2K team created a custom html filter to ensure a consistent format for weekly status reports that were published on the company intranet. Once the report was posted, executives, members of the Y2K team, and other employees used built-in Microsoft Project 98 filters to select the information view that was most useful to them.

Filters were also handy for tracking costs. Because the Eddie Bauer Y2K team members came from so many different divisions, it was crucial to track costs accurately for each and every one of them. With Microsoft Project 98 filters, this could be done easily on a practically up-to-the-minute basis. For projecting future costs, Microsoft Project 98 what-if scenarios were especially worthwhile. With these scenarios, management could see exactly how adding or decreasing resources could make a difference. That's because Microsoft Project 98 makes it easy to juggle scheduling and costs in an easy-to-explain fashion.

Microsoft Project 98 integrates with other Microsoft Office products. Thus, when management wanted additional details, such as the percentage of program units that had been tested for compliance or the number of applications that had contingency plans in place, data from Microsoft Project 98 could be moved smoothly into Microsoft Excel for additional analysis. From the outset, integration capabilities were important to the Eddie Bauer Y2K plan. "When we were selecting a management tool for Y2K, a major factor in Microsoft Project 98's favor was the integration capability of the program with all the other products in the Microsoft Office suite," says Nancy Salcedo, who led the company's Y2K year-end readiness project. This project, just one part of the overall Y2K effort, addressed cross-company communication and planning, shutdown and startup requirements, and other events slated to occur directly before and after January 1, 2000.

The result? The Eddie Bauer Y2K team completed inventory and remediation, finished unit and application testing, and began system testing on schedule by the end of 1998 to meet the goal of having all systems fully tested by the third quarter of 1999. The company experienced no business disruptions when January 1, 2000, arrived. Such success shows the value of a strong team effort, and the added value Microsoft Project 98 brings to that team. Rod Shogren, Eddie Bauer Information Services applications manager, concurs. "Y2K planning is like any other large corporate project—lots of people involved, lots of very serious work that must be done—and a deadline that stares you in the eye and doesn't blink," he says. "With

Microsoft Project 98, we've found a way to stare back."

To Think About: What advantages does project management software provide over paper-based tools? Does using project management software have any drawbacks? What were the main advantages that Eddie Bauer derived from using Microsoft Project 98 for managing their Y2K effort?

Source: Microsoft Office Case Studies, *http://www.microsoft.com/office/project/EdBauer.htm,* accessed 9/10/00.

Low-end, presentation-mapping packages are used primarily for preparing presentation materials, rather than for analysis and planning. A user who needs to develop only a few maps, defining, for example, sales districts across the country, may be satisfied with such packages. In fact, basic presentation mapping doesn't require a dedicated package. Many clip art packages include a variety of maps that can be imported into most drawing programs. Efficient data-driven mapping, however, requires a true presentation-mapping program, such as Software Publishing Corporation's Harvard GeoGraphics or Strategic Mapping Inc.'s Atlas MapMaker for Windows. Both programs provide a variety of mapping and annotation tools that users can combine with spreadsheet or database data to produce presentation maps.

High-end geographic information system software, such as Caliper Corporation's GIS+ and Environmental Systems Research Institute Inc.'s (ESRI) ArcView GIS and ARC/INFO, are used for data-intensive tasks such as geologic exploration, contour mapping, street mapping, and city planning. GIS are being used typically by municipalities and engineers for construction, zoning, and managing utilities and services. Figure 3-10 depicts output from a GIS that matched census data with neighborhood maps to help school administrators understand enrollment patterns. These systems move up in order of magnitude in product complexity and are capable of three-dimensional mapping driven off large databases.

3.4.4.5 Statistical and Mathematical Analysis

Statistical packages can compute statistics such as means, medians, modes, analysis of variance, and regression analysis, as well as linear programming, factor and component analysis, discriminant analysis, and other multivariate procedures. Data can be input at the keyboard or stored in other computer programs. Statistical analysis programs also produce graphics and reports. Two statistical application packages widely used in business are the Statistical Analysis System (SAS) from the SAS Institute, and the Statistical Package for the Social Sciences (SPSS) from SPSS, Inc. Both packages were developed for the mainframe and now are available in PC versions with graphical user interfaces. Other PC-based statistical packages include MiniTab, Systat, PC-Statistics, and Statview.

Statistical packages such as the SAS System also incorporate decision support, forecasting, and an applications development environment. SAS provides multidimensional electronic spreadsheets as well as tools for time series analysis, econometrics, and financial modeling. For even more specialized tasks, SAS provides integrated tools for statistical quality improvement, experimental design, and laboratory data analysis. There's even an interactive matrix programming language

Desktop mapping linked to pupil information systems provides a useful new tool for school district administrators in their search for more effective use of resources.

As school-age populations increase or decline, as families with children move from one part of a community to another, or when new residential areas are built, some schools become overcrowded and others may be underutilized. While these enrollment changes may lead to the construction or closing of schools, they often result in the need to redraw attendance area boundaries to match pupil enrollments to school capacities. Other factors enter into this *redistricting*, such as maintaining a racial and ethnic mix, reducing transportation time, and assuring parents, students, and teachers that the redrawn attendance areas will remain stable for four or five years.

A recurring problem for school administrators is how to make accurate projections of pupil populations by attendance areas. Most public school districts in the United States have computerized financial and pupil accounting systems and use microcomputer spreadsheet programs for budget analysis, demographic projections, and long-range planning. School districts are required to keep detailed records on enrolled pupils. They maintain extensive computer databases containing pupil, parent, or guardian names and addresses, school and grade attended, and similar information.

Typically, school district administrators and planners use cohort survival and grade progression techniques to extrapolate from historical enrollment patterns and project future enrollments for the school district as a whole. These projections in the aggregate are relatively accurate. Grade progression is quite uniform: Each grade cohort moves up one grade annually—this year's kindergartners are next year's first graders. Of course, in- and out-migration patterns must be taken into account.

Traditionally, time-consuming dot or pin maps are constructed to show pupils' residences by neighborhoods. Then when an attendance boundary is shifted, the number of affected students can be determined by inspection.

GIS permits electronic pin maps to be created easily by using street maps derived from Census Bureau Tiger files that contain address ranges. Pupils' addresses are then matched to precise latitude and longitude locations on the street maps. (See the lower left inset in the accompanying map.) Once addresses are matched, the number of students at each grade level located within particular bounds can be determined in seconds.

The mapped attendance area boundaries can be moved with a few keystrokes and a touch of the cursor to add or subtract several more city blocks. Not only can the number of students affected by the boundary shift be determined, but their parents' names and addresses can be listed to receive information about school (re)assignments.

To project enrollments more accurately on a school-by-school basis, health department records of live births are used. By matching addresses on newborns, the future kindergarten cohort for each school can be readily identified. This plan assumes that children born in one year will, on the average, enter kindergarten five years later. After adjusting for a historical pattern of gains and losses in the number of newly admitted pupils in proportion to the number of births five years earlier, the school district has solid information based on the number of youngsters already residing in the community. Each dot on the subneighborhood map represents a child who will enter school over the next five years. The linked database will show both *where* and *when* that classroom space is needed.

Finally, easily understood, presentation-quality maps can be produced showing boundary adjustments, enrollment patterns, classroom utilization, and the need for change. Maps of alternative ways to redistrict can inform the policymaking debate to give decision makers, parents, teachers, and students an opportunity to contribute effectively to school district planning.

(continued)

Figure 3-10
GIS application in school district planning
Source: Dr. Robert Burnham, New York University, New York, NY.

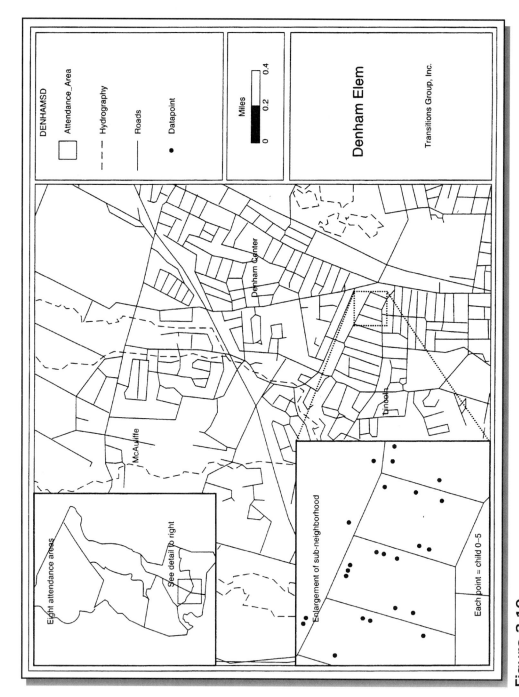

Figure 3-10
(continued)

126

for advanced mathematical, engineering, and statistical needs. SAS includes powerful graphics capabilities, as well.

By automating laborious manual calculations, computers have turned statistical analysis into a practical tool for market research, survey compilation, and other business research. For example, a marketing research department within a nationwide travel agency uses the SPSS program to compile customer demographics and service patterns. Data analysis helps them plan programs to attract and serve business travelers. In another case, a division of the U.S. Army uses SPSS to analyze data and build models from surveys, studies, and personnel data on hundreds of thousands of recruits. Analysis of their data enables the Army to improve its recruitment campaigns.

3.4.4.6 Executive Support Systems (ESS)

Executive support systems are designed to provide support for unstructured problem solving, focusing on the information needs of senior-level managers and executives. Their use is not limited to top executives, however, and may be more prevalent among subordinates than top executives.

ESS usually incorporate advanced-level graphics and communications and combine internal and external information. The challenge is providing comprehensive information while avoiding information overload. To this end, ESS often use a technique referred to as drill down, providing the user with highly summarized information with the ability to drill down through successive levels of detail as desired.

New graphical-based products, such as Lightship by Pilot Executive Software, Inc., have made it easier and less expensive to design executive information systems that are tailored to executive needs. Many of the more successful projects have started on a small scale, targeting specific problems and delivering information that is badly needed. Seasoned veterans advise analysts to avoid the temptation to try to build a global anything until they have had successes delivering something concrete. Timeliness and accuracy of information are important, but presentation is equally important so that executives can grasp the information easily and quickly.

Today's ESS are likely to encompass a range of tailored desktop analytical tools and online data displays. However, despite being around for some 20 years, ESS still are considered to be in their infancy. The following features are likely to be incorporated in the future.

1. *Speech recognition.* Speech recognition systems range from those capable of understanding voice commands to speaker independent systems that take dictation at 160 words per minute.
2. *Expert systems.* Executive workstations of the future will include expert support systems that learn from experience and aid in decision making.
3. *Increased use of video.* Future workstations will include capabilities for video-conferencing and videotape windows for visual aids in learning.
4. *Executive support software.* The concept of an ESS usually implies customized software. The efforts of some organizations to develop executive support software are discussed in the next section.

Executive support software customizes databases to fit executives' specific needs. The objective is to provide managers with status access—the ability to get information about the status of the corporation at a glance, in graphic form, without developing any particular computing skill. These systems are designed to collect large amounts of data from disparate sources, including mainframe databases and outside services, and put it into a format accessible on executive workstations. The systems generally are menu driven, and using them requires only a minimal number of keystrokes or a mouse. For example, an executive support system may be programmed to process time-series data so that the executive can review operating results at the press of a key or click of the mouse. Some analysts predict that these systems will supersede such software as modeling systems, spreadsheets, and integrated packages.

One major corporation that is trying to make the use of database information easier for its executives is the Clorox Company of Oakland, California. At Clorox, key marketing executives use a support system that allows them to combine data from a variety of research firms with information from Clorox's internal computer systems. For instance, an executive could obtain information from outside sources, such as the marketing research unit of A.C. Nielsen Company and Time Inc.'s Selling Areas-Marketing Inc. (SAMI), and combine it with internal marketing data.

The system used by Clorox consists of four elements: an executive workstation, a database server, a file server, and a communication server that extracts data from the company's mainframe computer systems. It also includes proprietary interactive software for information retrieval. Once retrieved, information can be viewed and incorporated into reports or used with the available spreadsheet, graphics, or other analysis tools. To make the system easy to learn and use, it is built almost entirely on icons (pictures). Instructions are entered with the click of a mouse. Output can be displayed graphically, and several items can be displayed simultaneously in windows on the screen. Once a manager performs a procedure manually, the system "remembers" each step and repeats it, upon request, to obtain updated information. Even managers who have never used a computer can access the corporate data they need within minutes.

3.4.5 Desktop Publishing/Multimedia

Desktop publishing is one of the fastest-growing job areas today. Desktop publishing allows companies to produce high-quality documents by combining word processing software with design elements, graphics, and special layout features. Multimedia is becoming more prevalent. Business presentations today not only make use of powerful PC presentation tools such as PowerPoint, but increasingly incorporate multimedia, as well.

With desktop publishing, knowledge workers can combine text, graphics, and quality artwork from commercially produced disks, the Web, scanned images, or digital cameras to create newsletters, advertising, fliers, training materials, forms, and other types of printing. U.S. companies are the biggest producers of forms, brochures, circulars, catalogs, and other printed materials. In fact, corporations are the largest segment of the U.S. publishing industry. Most of these formats are produced with offset printing by commercial printers or in-house print shops. Desktop publishing now offers a fast, low-cost alternative for printing some of these materials right in the office.

3.4.6 Web Publishing

More and more information used by enterprises is being published online using Internet-based technologies. The data may be available to external audiences via the Internet; to internal audiences via Intranets; or to customers, vendors, suppliers, and other constituencies via an Extranet. Not only does Web publishing provide immediate, universal access to the latest version of information, but it changes the dynamics, as well. Unlike paper, the Web is a dynamic medium, not static. Thus, it is much more than a giant bulletin board. Effective Web publishing creates a collaborative environment for sharing and exchanging information.

Effective Web publishing is a combination of content development, writing skill, graphical presentation, and increasingly multimedia. It requires a whole new approach to analyzing, organizing, and presenting information to achieve specific business objectives for the intended audience.

A growing number of tools are available for Web publishing. The language of the Web is html, but many software packages allow users to create Web pages without learning html. Some of the more popular tools include Microsoft Front Page2000, Adobe PageMill, Jasc Software Paint Shop Pro, Dreamweaver, and others. Many companies have one or more Web Masters to develop, support, and maintain their company Web site.

3.4.7   End-User Computing (Programming)

Programming (application development) by knowledge workers is frequently referred to as *end-user computing (EUC),* a term carried over from technical data processing terminology. End-user computing is defined as computer applications developed or maintained by an end-user area whose management accepts responsibility for the integrity of the results. End-user computing is used primarily to support local business functions and to build decision support environments. When end users need to access corporate information from central processing systems, they work with the Information Systems organization to define their requirements so that IS can prepare and deliver the needed data.

The idea that users could do some of their own computing was revolutionary in the early 1970s. Management information systems or data processing (MIS/DP) departments often resisted such efforts. Businesspeople had needs that could be met by the new technologies, however, and they used them with or without corporate approval. The match between need and new technology ushered in end-user computing, similar to the way in which mushrooming paperwork and word processors fueled the growth of secretarial automation in the 1960s. The technologies that gave rise to EUC were nonprocedural, fourth-generation computer languages for mainframes and easy-to-use business software for microcomputers, especially databases such as D-Base and Paradox. Today's powerful PC databases, such as Access and SQL query language, have expanded the capabilities greatly, as well as making them easier to use.

As with most grassroots efforts, implementation took various forms in different enterprises. Issues of ownership and responsibility created internal conflict and organizational changes. Information centers were introduced in many large enterprises to promote and support end-user computing. Most enterprises today consolidate support for end-user computing within the EUIS department, which provides a logical point for supporting computing at the desktop.

The philosophy of end-user computing is that for some types of applications, it is more efficient to teach businesspeople to do their own computing than to teach data processing professionals about business requirements. This philosophy is reflected in the ancient proverb: "Give a man a fish and you feed him for a day; teach a man to fish and he can feed himself for a lifetime." Applying this principle to end-user computing, an appropriate paraphrase might be: "Develop a computer application for an individual and you solve one problem; teach individuals to compute and they can solve their own business problems for a lifetime."

Therefore, the ideal applications for end-user computing are those that require a high level of business knowledge and understanding and a relatively low level of computing complexity as illustrated in Figure 3-11. Arrows indicate the increasing complexity of both business knowledge (vertical arrow) and computer complexity (horizontal arrow). The more that business knowledge is required and computer complexity is low, the more appropriate the application is for end-user computing. The more complex the processing (computer complexity), the more appropriate that information systems technical personnel support be involved in systems development.

Moreover, the volume of potential applications in the office makes it impractical for one department of computer specialists to develop all of them. Productivity improvement in the office generally results from the cumulative impact of hours saved on hundreds of small applications rather than a few major applications. Experience demonstrates that the most innovative ideas originate from business specialists who can apply technology to their own needs.

3.4.7.1 Fourth-Generation Languages

The introduction of *fourth-generation languages* (4GLs) marked a quantum leap in productivity and opened the door to computer programming by nondata-processing professionals. Earlier programming languages were procedural in nature, meaning that the programmer had to concentrate on *how*, step by step, the computer should accomplish a task. In the late 1960s, nonprocedural 4GL programming techniques were introduced. A nonprocedural language enables the programmer to concentrate on *what* should be done instead of the details of *how*.

For example, 4GLs provide verbs like *sum* or *count* to indicate addition, rather than requiring several steps to detail how the process is to be carried out. By reducing the level of detail in a program, 4GLs significantly reduce the time required to create an application program. Their use also requires considerably less knowledge about how a computer processes data.

Although a 4GL is more productive for the programmer, it is less machine efficient. For small applications, the difference in speed may be insignificant, but for major transaction processing systems it may be substantial. For this and other reasons, such as data integrity, security, and maintenance, traditional programming languages such as COBOL and C continue to be used widely by corporate IS

Figure 3-11
Matrix of computing applications

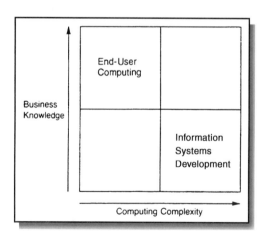

departments. The use of 4GLs is growing, however, for developing new data processing systems and for end-user computing.

Not everyone agrees on precisely what constitutes a fourth-generation language. Generally, however, 4GLs have the following characteristics.

- They are nonprocedural.
- They are appropriate for nonprogramming professionals. (Some languages, however, are too sophisticated and technical for end users.)
- They are easy to learn and user or programmer friendly. (A two-day rule often is applied; a user must accomplish useful work after two days of training.)
- They contain built-in functions, including an integrated database management system (DBMS) and some or all of the following: query language; report generator; screen definition facility; graphics generator; decision support, financial modeling, or spreadsheet; statistical analysis.
- They are capable of generalized application development.

Examples of 4GLs appropriate for end users are Focus, Nomad2, SAS, CA-Universe, and APL. The most popular language today is probably SQL— structured query language. Additional 4GLs that are primarily for data processing professionals include ADS/On-Line, Ideal, Mantis, and Natural.

3.4.8 Customer Relationship Management

Customer relationship management (CRM) is forcing companies to better integrate their services across former functional lines, bringing back office and front office operations much closer together. An important objective of CRM is to provide a complete view of the customer relationship at every touch-point with the customer. Some in the industry are calling it a 360-degree view of the customer. So even if the credit department is located in Denver, the customer purchased from an outlet in California, and the product will be shipped from North Carolina and serviced from Detroit, everyone has the entire history not only of this transaction but the customer's complete history with the firm.

This vision is a long way off for many businesses that still manage different aspects of customer relationships with multiple information systems. Such fragmentation weakens customer service and total sales potential. Thus, the concept of CRM looks beyond automating sales and marketing functions to providing integrated solutions across all customer information systems to tie together the front and back offices for a complete view of the customer.

The applications generally included in the category of CRM are continually evolving, reflecting emerging new technologies and changing business requirements in response to competitive pressures and expectations of consumers. The rapid acceptance and integration of the Internet has caused the most significant change in CRM applications as they increasingly use Internet-based architectures.

CRM has several major components, all of which involve much of the same technology and deal with many of the same management and implementation issues. However, each has unique perspectives, business processes, and needs.

- *Sales Automation.* Sales automation provides sales representatives with access to critical customer information and tools that enhance their ability to sell as well as manage their time effectively. Examples include contact management, calendaring functions, forecasting tools, and configuration models.

- *Marketing Automation.* Marketing automation solutions are maturing rapidly as the Internet is making personalized, one-to-one marketing a reality. Marketing automation solutions provide marketing departments with campaign management, lead generation, and datamining tools. Closed-loop lead management is one of the most important functions of marketing automation and relies on integration with the CRM data repository and related applications.

- *Customer Service and Support.* Customer service automation focuses on serving the needs of customers after the sale and entails operations such as call centers, technical support, and customer service operations. Enterprises seek solutions that enable them to address customer questions, problems, or issues effectively and efficiently. Although customer satisfaction is usually the primary goal, many enterprises also are seeking to use their customer service operations to increase revenues through cross selling.

- *Channel Management/Partner Relationship Management (PRM).* Channel management, also called partner relationship management, extends CRM capabilities to the needs of extended selling channels such as distributors and value-added resellers. PRM applications enable companies to distribute leads and manage promotions outside the enterprise sales team.

CRM is a major goal of most e-commerce efforts. Simply opting to implement an e-commerce solution does not guarantee improved customer relations, however. To achieve that goal, a company must thoroughly plan the execution of its e-commerce strategy to transform business processes with the goal of enhancing customer relationships. Results must be tracked through a set of predefined measures to see if that goal is being achieved. According to a May 2000 *InformationWeek* research study, three-fourths of executives who are reinventing their corporate culture

SPOTLIGHT ON SOLUTIONS → Technology, People, Structure, Processes

HELLODIRECT MEETS NEW MEASURES

When San Jose, California, based HelloDirect CIO Michael Young came to work at the company, he was impressed with the company's 1.5 million customer name and address database, the fact that it annually mails out 30 million catalogues and that it typically engages its 165,000 customers in at least two conversations a year. "But we still didn't do a very good job of knowing which portions of the house file bought what and how we could up-sell and cross-sell," says Young. "The first thing that I wanted to do was create a customer relationship and use software to help our agents do that."

CRM efforts at HelloDirect have been especially important from a strategic standpoint because in the years since 1995, the company has undergone a radical shift from entirely catalogue-based inbound sales to an environment where less than 30 percent of sales are inbound sales, the Internet accounts for 20 percent and outbound has grown from 0 to 55 percent.

Because sales to existing house accounts were four times as effective as the others, a major drive was made to cross-reference the customer sales database with the products they historically buy. As with any CRM project, it can be a stretch to say that a single application, or even any given set of applications, produced a single, specific return. There is typically much more going on that makes it harder to quantify. "It's hard to put it on the system because it's not just the system," admits Young. "But the system has enabled us to change our philosophies and to change our policies, practices, procedures and our sales and support process." In the larger view, it is this wide impact that is exactly what companies are expecting from CRM. Those widespread changes suggest that the company is doing what it can to remain competitive in a changing world.

Source: Pixion Website. (*pixion.com*) Case study: synergistic

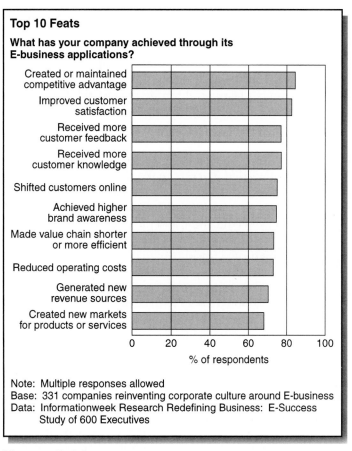

Top 10 Feats

What has your company achieved through its E-business applications?

Figure 3-12
Payoffs from e-commerce. Most managers report that e-commerce strategies have given their companies a competitive market advantage and more satisfied customers.

Source: Chris Murphy, Senior Editor, "Behind the News: Behind the Numbers: Customers Dominate E-Business Strategy," *Information Week* (May 29, 2000): 208. CMP Media, Inc.

around e-business cite greater customer feedback and more customer knowledge from their e-business applications. More than 80 percent list improving customer satisfaction as a key to building loyalty (see Figure 3-12). CRM and e-commerce are expected to converge into a customer-centric solution, which allows organizations to interact with, sell to, and service customers through all channels.

3.5 SUMMARY

Selecting and implementing productivity tools for individuals begins with understanding how users work and, most importantly, how that work can be changed or transformed through the use of information technology. It is seldom sufficient just to provide new tools. Effective use of desktop productivity tools and other information technologies requires transforming the way work is done, not merely automating what is done currently or installing new technology. This chapter focuses on individuals at all levels of the enterprise in light of changing workplace demands and new practices such as customer relationship management and e-business. It looks especially at the needs of individuals in four major areas: managerial, professional/technical knowledge workers, sales and marketing, and administrative support.

Today's fast-paced competitive world demands new and better ways for managing organizations. Executives faced with too much information must filter out the pertinent and timely facts needed for decision making. To be useful for managerial decision making, information must be significant, reliable, consistent, timely, comprehensible, and action oriented.

Knowledge workers make up a growing percentage of the workforce. These well-trained and specialized personnel exercise considerable autonomy in carrying out their responsibilities. Their work usually requires a high degree of specialized training and education, and mental rather than physical effort.

Sales and marketing, which have been fairly resistant to technology in the past, are being turned upside down by e-commerce. The Internet has given customers a direct line, access to product information, and ability to comparison shop or purchase online. It is changing the dynamics and opening up many new opportunities to connect more closely with customers and enhance service. Sales and marketing positions vary considerably depending on the nature of the product or service and the industry. CRM is forcing companies to integrate their services across former functional lines, merging front office and back office operations. In the process, it is transforming the ways in which sales, marketing, and service personnel interact with clients.

Administrative support and clerical workers provide a diverse network of support services that keep information flowing into, within, and out of the enterprise. Increased use of productivity tools, digital networks, and business restructuring continue to have significant impact on clerical and administrative positions.

Software evaluation is a systematic process for matching product features against required functionality and comparing alternative software packages. The process begins by defining user needs and clarifying business objectives. Information gathered during this process usually is turned into an evaluation form, which serves as a framework for systematically evaluating software features and comparing alternative packages. Final selection of the solution is usually a matter of tradeoffs, with users preferring some features in one package and different features in other packages. The final decision should represent the best overall fit.

The range of productivity tools for individuals today is extensive. This chapter provided a sampling of available tools, including desktop productivity tools, activity management, communications/networking, decision support, end-user computing, desktop publishing, Web publishing, and customer relationship management. The focus was on factors to consider in choosing among alternative packages rather than on details about product features.

KEY TERMS

- Administrative assistant
- Administrative support
- Calendar management
- Customer relationship management
- Data warehousing

- Decision modeling
- Decision support systems (DSS)
- Desktop publishing
- Direct response marketing
- End-user computing

- Executive support systems (ESS)
- Facilities management
- Fourth-generation languages (4GL)
- Geographic information systems (GIS)

- Knowledge workers
- Paraprofessionals
- Personal digital assistants (PDA)
- Project management
- Prospect management
- Record

- Records management
- Sales automation
- Sales illustrations
- Sales force automation (SFA)
- Telemarketing

- To-do lists
- Tracking and follow-up systems
- Voice response systems
- Web publishing
- Web master

DISCUSSION QUESTIONS

1. Of the tools described in this chapter, which appear to have the most potential for today's manager? Defend your answer.
2. What are the six characteristics of useful information?
3. What is calendar management software? What aspects do users like most about it? Least?
4. What advantages do personal digital assistants (PDAs) have over paper and pencil? Disadvantages?
5. Video technology will be part of the managerial workstation within this decade. Do you agree or disagree? Support your response.
6. Decisions made via teleconferencing are frequently better than those made in a traditional meeting. True or false? Discuss.
7. What is decision-modeling software? What are the three approaches various programs take in the decision-modeling process?
8. What advantages does project management software offer over paper-based techniques?
9. What are executive support systems? How can they help improve the job performance of managers?
10. What is customer relationship management (CRM)? What role do e-commerce and sales force automation tools play in CRM?

APPLICATION EXERCISES

1. Design the ideal student workstation or knowledge management portal (see chapter 5). Of the applications discussed in this chapter, which would you include? Would you add any others?
2. Read two articles related to activity management software in *PC Week* or a similar microcomputer publication. Identify potential uses of the software.
3. Interview a high-level manager in a local organization. Describe his or her workstation. Which features does the manager rely on most? Which could the manager do without?
4. Pick a business with which you are familiar. Develop a conceptual design for an executive information system that could aid in managing the business. What information and tools would you make available? Explain how you think the EIS would help the executive manage the business more effectively.
5. *Software needs analysis project:* Working individually or in your assigned group, locate and download a software evaluation form off the Web or design your own form. Select one of the four job areas discussed in the chapter (managerial, professional/technical, sales and marketing, or administrative support) and research additional job information on the Web or at the library. Potential sources of information include the *Occupational Outlook Handbook*, industry trade publications, professional organizations, and career literature. Interview someone you know to

identify and document details about a current business need. Define objectives, and develop a detailed list of required functionality for software evaluation.

6. *Software evaluation project:* Based on the needs analysis completed in the previous project, select two or three software packages and evaluate them. Use the evaluation matrix created in the prior project to document and compare features. Evaluate the results and recommend the best solution. Explain your choice. Your instructor may ask you to present your findings and recommendation to the class.

SPOTLIGHT ON SOLUTIONS → Technology, People, Structure, Processes

ONLINE MORTGAGE LENDER DITECH IS CUTTING COSTS AND BOOSTING PROFITS WITH MARKETING AUTOMATION SOFTWARE

It was with a bit of frontier spirit that DiTech Funding entered the mortgage loan market. In the five years since it was founded, the Costa Mesa, California-based company, now called DiTech.com, has shaken up stodgy lending practices by pioneering a unique combination of innovative loan offerings, technology-enabled services, and aggressive advertising. The unconventional approach is paying off. With a 1999 loan volume of more than $5 billion, the company is one of the largest direct discount lenders, and has developed strong brand-name recognition in a highly competitive marketplace, as well as a reputation for great customer service.

Now DiTech is at it again. At a time when other lenders are warily circling the idea of e-commerce, DiTech is forging ahead into Internet territory armed with its new name, a sophisticated Web site, and a belief that ultimately customers will be best served online.

BLAZING A TRAIL ON THE WEB

For a company that prides itself on customer service, migrating to an Internet model means more than changing the corporate mantra from "Call 1-800" to "Type www. DiTech.com." New channels present challenges as well as opportunities, and in a typically trail-blazing fashion DiTech.com is leveraging an emerging class of software—enterprise marketing automation—to help manage the transformation. EMA software automates the planning, execution, management, and measurement of online marketing campaigns. At its core, though, EMA is more about establishing personalized, long-term relationships with customers over the Internet, and that is what attracted DiTech to San Mateo, California-based Rubric, an EMA solution provider. (In December 1999, Rubric was acquired by Broadbase.)

"For us, it's not so much about marketing as it is about customer care. We're still relying primarily on billboards and television for marketing, but we will be using Rubric to get back to the customers who visit our Web site, to keep those customers informed about developments that might interest them, to maintain the customer relationship, and, most important, to improve the quality of it," says Matt Ghourdjian, CIO of DiTech.

The software was installed in early November 1999. By the end of December, DiTech had yet to bring Rubric online for regular use, but one trial campaign had yielded promising results. Planned and executed over the course of just a few days, the e-mail effort generated a higher rate of return than any traditional marketing campaign and cost practically nothing (not including the approximately $200,000 spent on the Rubric package).

Using the Rubric software, DiTech sent out a general e-mail message to 30,000 addresses culled from the operational database and received 1,400 responses. Out of those responses, DiTech generated 146 loan applications. By mid-December, 53 respondents had closed loans and approximately 30 were still in progress. Those 53 closed loans generated $220,000 in gross revenue with total revenue expected to increase due to the pending loans, according to Lee Furnival, e-business manager for DiTech.

Generating $220,000 in gross revenue in a speedy campaign at negligible cost is significant, but for DiTech it simply represents the tip of the benefit iceberg e-marketing is expected to bring to the company. Though the campaign itself was only a test and was not as targeted as future campaigns are expected to be, Furnival expects the final number of completed loans to top out between 57 and 60 percent of total applicants. If that happens, it would represent a capture rate 2 percent to 10 percent higher than traditional campaigns, with more-targeted campaigns potentially netting even higher capture rates.

In addition to personalized, ongoing communications with customers, DiTech is investing in marketing automation to streamline the loan process as well as enhance the company's ability to react to market forces. Although DiTech is already known for rapid transactions—completing the entire loan process in anywhere from 5 to 20 days as opposed to the 30 days or more by a traditional lender—the Internet promises to increase efficiencies even more.

Source: Adapted from *Sales and Marketing Automation, March 2000,* pp. 65–66.

SUGGESTED READINGS

Boone, Mary, *Leadership and the Computer.* Rocklin, CA: Prima Publishing, 1991.

Kanter, Rosabeth Moss, "Transcending Business Boundaries: 12,000 World Managers View Change," *Harvard Business Review,* Reprint No. 19308 (May-June 1991): 151–161.

Panko, Raymond R. "Managerial Communications Patterns," *Journal of Organizational Computing* 2 (1992): 95–122.

USEFUL WEBSITES

www.iaap-hq.org. Web site for the International Association of Administrative Professionals.

www.officeteam.com. The Office Team Web site provides much interesting information and research related to the changing workplace. OfficeTeam is a firm that specializes in administrative staffing.

www.aba.com. American Bar Association Law Practice Management

www.smamag.com. Web site for *Sales and Marketing Automation Magazine.*

ENDNOTES

1. Boone, Mary (1991). *Leadership and the Computer.* Rocklin, CA: Prima Publishing.
2. Booz · Allen & Hamilton. *Study of Managerial/Professional Productivity.* New York: Booz · Allen & Hamilton, Inc., June 1980.
3. Mintzberg, Henry (1973). *The Nature of Managerial Work.* New York: Harper and Row, p. 59.
4. Mandt, E., "Managing the Knowledge Worker of the Future," *Personnel Journal* (March 1978): 138.
5. The Impact of Restructuring on the Secretarial Profession: A Survey of Office Professionals. Holland, MI: Administrative Development Institute, 1994.
6. Sandquist, Nancy, "Facility Management: A Strategic Function," *The Office* (March 1987): 41.
7. Asimov, Isaac, "The Next 70 Years for Law and Lawyers," *ABA Journal* (American Bar Association, January 1985): 56–59.
8. Hokkanen, John, "Taking It to the Next Level: Redefining Technology and Revolutionizing Services," *ABA Law Practice Today* (May/June 2000).

http://4.21.247.201/magazine_article.asp?artnum=11934. (accessed 7/21/00) p. 1 of 4.
9. Martin, Kingsley, "Charting Legal Technology Strategy: Advancing On All Fronts," *ABA Law Practice Today* (May/June 2000). *http://4.21.247.201/magazine_article.asp?artnum=11935.* (accessed 7/21/00) p. 1 of 3.
10. Hokkanen, op. cit., p. 1 of 4.
11. Ibid., 3.
12. Ehrlich, Susan F., Elizabeth A. Akiba, and Vernell K. Munson (November 1983). *Research Report: The Organizational Impact of Voice Store and Forward Technology.* Lowell, MA: Wang Laboratories.
13. Fisher, Lawrence, "Along the Infobahn: Data Warehouses," *Strategy and Business,* from Booz Allen & Hamilton. *http://www.strategy-business.com/technology/96308/page1.html.* Third Quarter, 1996. (accessed 7/21/00), p. 1 of 2.

Case Study   Working Smart: Maximizing the Payoff from IT

WearGuard, a division of Aramark, is based in Norwell, Massachusetts. The company began in the 1950s as a one-person business, providing custom uniforms to a local clientele. In the four decades since then, it has grown into a national leader in direct marketing of work-related clothing, including heavy-duty pants and jackets. These days it even sells internationally. While some things, like a focus on service and quality and a 100 percent satisfaction guarantee, have remained the same, other aspects of the business have had to change to support and sustain growth. In particular, the crucial Business Sales Group (BSG), which focuses on the potentially lucrative market between individual mail-order consumers and giant *Fortune* 1000-size accounts, had been targeted for attention late in 1996.

According to Judy Franciosi, business sales manager, the company sends out a total of 40 million catalogs a year to individuals as well as small and mid-size businesses. BSG, Franciosi explains, was developed to target the 60,000 mid-size businesses that receive the catalogs, "where we have enormous potential to increase sales." However, to fully capitalize on the opportunity WearGuard saw, they needed to reinvent BSG as a modern sales organization, leveraging sales force automation tools and linking, wherever possible, with existing IT investments.

Until introducing sales-force automation (SFA), the WearGuard Business Sales Group (BSG) put its faith in a manual system of shoe boxes filled with Post-it Notes and index cards to track leads and customer information, says Barry Meltzer, project manager for application development at WearGuard. Although the BSG had access to the company's Unix-based order-entry and customer-service system via Windows-based clients, they did not have automated tools that helped them in the sales process. Instead, they had to rely on their own homemade manual methods. As a result, when salespeople left the company, critical client histories often went with them. New sales representatives had to start from scratch—a waste of time considering that each sales representative tracks between 700 and 1,200 accounts from small to mid-size businesses. It was also a source of frustration for clients who had to start all over again with a new sales representative.

In late 1996, WearGuard executives decided to expand BSG to concentrate more on the corporate clothing market and realized that a larger sales force would require an investment in sales-force automation technology. BSG chose GoldMine contact management software from GoldMine Software Corporation of Pacific Palisades, California, be-cause it had the features BSG needed and could be linked with minimal trouble to WearGuard's legacy Oracle database. The MIS group built a link from the company's master Oracle database to feed the GoldMine SFA application with customer data and also built a link between GoldMine and the order-entry system. An icon on each desktop connects users to customer information in the GoldMine database via the Novell network server. Information updates from Oracle to GoldMine run automatically every evening. A hot button on WearGuard's order-entry system can bring up customer contact and call-back information stored on GoldMine.

WearGuard tested the software on the task force and a group of six sales representatives. The companywide roll-out kicked off in June 1997 and took about 4 months. The biggest challenge, according to Meltzer, was getting everyone to use the technology because sales staff had a wide range of computer skills, and many sales reps had previously avoided using computers. Changing the minds of salespeople is a tough but critical task; SFA cannot prevail without user commitment. Sales reps must be convinced of direct benefits for them before they are willing to abandon the tried-and-true for new ways of selling. Using the new system, BSG's 87 sales reps now can track all calls to customers who receive the company's catalog. It prompts them to follow up on old sales leads and maintains call histories of prospects. The system provides customized screens for adding notes, as well as a scheduling calendar so that sales reps no longer forget to make calls or randomly call contacts from their account lists.

WearGuard's system administrators also hail GoldMine's attributes. For instance, the Goldmine file system structure eases management of multiple independent systems and makes the creation of test systems quick and painless. Adding licensees and performing version upgrades is easy using GoldMine version upgrade executables. In addition, client-side installations are a breeze because they require only a shortcut on the user's desktop.

Since implementing the system, customer service has improved. It is hard to tell how much growth is due directly to the new system, but accounts increased from 65,000 to 80,000 in the year following implementation. WearGuard now is focusing on using the system to facilitate much more targeted selling. Reps will be able to pull specific information from the system to help them sell on the fly. For example, if a blizzard hits a particular state, WearGuard can download all customer names from that area and immediately send sales information on subzero temperature work clothes. According to Judy Franciosi, Business Sales Manager, "the implementation has not only improved our sales productivity, it has also ensured our relationship with customers."

Source: Kim Girard, "Working Smart," *CIO Magazine* (January 15, 1999), *http://www2.cio.com/archive/printer.cfm? URL-011599_smart_print.cfm,* accessed 7/22/00.

CASE STUDY QUESTIONS

1. Why is user commitment critical to the successful use of sales force automation tools?
2. Why do you think salespeople have been especially resistant to computer tools in the past? What are some things a company might do to help gain sales force commitment for SFA?
3. How did the work of the sales representatives change when WearGuard implemented SFA?
4. What benefits did WearGuard gain from sales force automation?

Chapter 4

Work Group Computing

Learning Objectives

Upon completing this chapter, you should be able to:

➤ Summarize the growing impetus for groupware development.

➤ Match specific categories of groupware tools with group communications and decision-making tasks.

- Point out how e-mail technologies have become foundations for the development of other groupware tools.
- Explain how the effective implementation of groupware requires both technology training and organizational culture changes.
- Identify the hardware and software required for desktop videoconfencing systems.
- Appraise the potential for the growth of group support systems.
- Differentiate the functionality of distance learning technologies from more generic conferencing tools.
- Give examples of how software agents could assist in group communications and decision making.
- Describe the functionality of virtual office software.

4.1 INTRODUCTION

Words such as *downsizing* (or its more positive corollary, *rightsizing*), *outsourcing, reengineering, empowerment,* and *quality assurance* are on the lips of everyone in large organizations today. Such words have crept into common use as organizations attempt to become meaner and leaner—as they attempt to do more with less. Technologies were not the cause for the crises that spawned such measures; however, technology definitely can play a new role to facilitate the flat organizational structure that is increasingly the norm in business. Technology *is* the catalyst for the virtual workplace. Today's anywhere, anytime, anyplace work environment is made possible by a wide range of increasingly sophisticated communications and decision support technologies referred to as groupware.

This chapter gives an overview of the promises and challenges related to effective groupware choices and implementation. Groupware has been described as a useful infrastructure to support teams, departments, and organizations.[1] First, groupware tools are overviewed, and then a discussion of how these tools are enabling virtual work and challenging virtual workers and their managers is discussed.

4.2 GROUP COLLABORATION AND ITS IMPACT

In his classic *Harvard Business Review* article "The Coming of the New Organization," Peter F. Drucker predicted that by the year 2008, large businesses would have fewer than half the levels of management of their counterparts in 1988, and no more than a third the managers.[2] Drucker explained that such a structure would be possible because organizations would become information based. This flat organization would be "composed largely of specialists who direct and discipline their own performance through organized feedback from colleagues, customers, and headquarters."[3] Drucker was, indeed, ahead of his time, and his predictions have come to pass sooner than he thought.

Today's organization, based on information sharing, needs software tools to help groups, which may or may not be in the same location, solve problems and make decisions. These groups or teams (*teams* are defined here as "groups with a purpose") are often ad hoc rather than standing (e.g., individuals will work together to achieve a specific goal and once that goal is met, the ad hoc team dissolves). Thus, the role of the individual changes from that of solely a subject-matter expert to that of a team member. Companies already are restructuring their management compensation systems to reflect rewards for what a person knows and for team, not individual, performance.[4]

Team performance mandates shared information. If I have a dollar and give it to you, then you have the dollar and I don't. However, if I have information and give it to you, then we both have the information. This sharing of information will become more and more vital, assigning the computer the role of coordination and communication over and above the traditional roles it plays in transaction processing or decision support.

4.3   GROUP TECHNOLOGIES

This section is an overview of groupware products to support this flattened, team-based organization. As more employees become involved in teams, the need for tools that support group processes is increasing. Such technologies are referred to generically as groupware, with emphasis on *group* because the human side is always more important than the *ware*.[5] Groupware tools go by a variety of names, including group support systems (GSS), group decision support systems (GDSS), computer support for collaborative work (CSCW), electronic meeting systems (EMS), collaborative technologies, or simply teamware. "Groupware has been hailed as the hallmark of an empowering organization, as it goes beyond the scope of traditional e-mail systems to allow people to collaborate electronically, fostering creativity and teamwork in the process."[6]

Groupware technologies are expanding in functionality, and the number of vendors that are producing these technologies is expanding by leaps and bounds. Most development efforts are being driven by the Internet. The Internet is a technical environment that is enabling many new applications because it allows the user to gain access to applications with any computer that has a Web browser and a user with a password. Few compatibility issues exist. The Web also has resulted in groupware systems that are easy to use, more visual, and inexpensive. Market researchers have predicted that software developers will have revenues of $2.6 billion by 2003[7] in groupware products alone.

Although it is difficult to put these versatile tools into categories, groupware products can be organized by their complexity and the length of time they have been on the market. Level 1 groupware products support communications. Level 2 systems include software tools with statistical features designed to help groups solve complex, unstructured problems. Level 3 systems, in various stages of development, are behind-the-scenes software agents that can operate to keep projects on track as a virtual team member or serve to facilitate information-gathering needs of group members. Figure 4-1, The Time/Place Dimensions of Groupware, depicts e-mail as the enabler, or hub, of group technologies that support same time (synchronous) and different time (asynchronous) communications from different places, and the Internet as the increasingly empowering environment for the delivery of all such services.

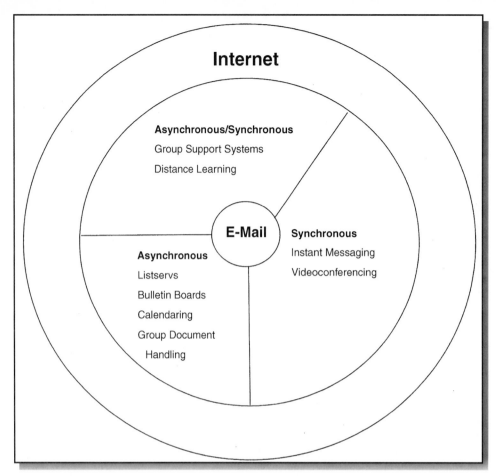

Internet

Asynchronous/Synchronous

Group Support Systems

Distance Learning

E-Mail

Asynchronous

Listservs

Bulletin Boards

Calendaring

Group Document

Handling

Synchronous

Instant Messaging

Videoconferencing

Figure 4-1
The time/place dimension of groupware

4.3.1 Level 1 Groupware Products: Supporting Asynchronous Communications

The simplest and most prevalent of groupware products are those that support group communications. Asynchronous products in Level 1 groupware include e-mail, listservs, calendaring, group document handling, and virtual office software.

4.3.1.1 E-mail

Full-service electronic mail (e-mail) systems send messages or documents from location to location without the need for physical transfer of paper. Almost overnight, e-mail has become the preferred communication medium of millions of users. In addition to short text messages, full-service systems allow users to send and receive full-page memos, letters, and reports and access other documents such as mailing lists, directories, and bulletin boards. Although e-mail systems are considered one-to-one communication, messages can be sent to multiple recipients simultaneously and documents can be annotated and forwarded. Moreover, the Internet is transforming e-mail systems from an era of closed, proprietary systems that work only at one location to systems that provide anytime, anywhere access to messages.

Eudora	Qualcomm Inc.	qualcomm.com
Imail	Ipswitch, Inc.	ipswitch.com
CommuniGate	Stalker Software	stalker.com
N-Plex Globa	Isocor, Inc.	isocor.com
Outlook	Microsoft Corp.	microsoft.com

Figure 4-2
A sampling of e-mail products

By themselves, electronic mail systems move mail messages or documents among users. To be the foundation for groupware products, however, additional features are needed such as application development tools and hooks to end-user applications. A growing number of vendors are attempting to deliver these enhancements and position their products as the foundation for groupware products. These features include e-mail across the Web, fax or paging gateways, mail lists, aliases, e-mail forwarding, and auto reply features such as vacation notices. Sophisticated systems also are capable of spam filtering, archival/storage of old messages, and serving as hooks for antivirus software—checking messages and attachments for viruses. Simple Network Management Protocol (SNMP) can stop advertisers from overpowering the system. User accounting features can generate per-user reports based on message number and size of messages transmitted or received, or on the amount of disk space used. Figure 4-2 is a listing of popular e-mail products and their vendors.

IT managers are concerned about a wide range of issues relative to the effectiveness and efficiency of their e-mail systems. In addition to ensuring that the system is operable at all times, issues related to data security and privacy are uppermost in IT managers' concerns. Moreover, policies that attempt to lessen its misuse are increasingly the norm in organizations. Policy statements, for example, may require users to limit their use of the e-mail system for personal use. Most organizations are clear that e-mail messages are subject to random monitoring. Use of e-mail systems has resulted in new vocabulary that describes technology features and issues (see Figure 4-3).

Other issues are poorly written messages. In fact, one organization found that almost 60 percent of its e-mail messages failed, as they did not include the right information for the user to act. In this same report, e-mail users cited issues related to misinformation, grammar, spelling, poorly constructed sentences,[8] and the

Figure 4-3
E-mail vocabulary

Spam:	Unwanted, unsolicited e-mail
Alias:	Shorthand for an individual's e-mail address; may also be an e-mail mailing list
E-mail filter:	Software that scans a user's incoming e-mail and prioritizes messages based on user's preferences
Electronic arrow:	Misdirected e-mail
Flaming:	Term used to describe quick and angry e-mail

proper etiquette for using e-mail (see Figure 4-4). However, the biggest issue from the user's point of view may be how to respond to, file, store, and retrieve the thousands of e-mail messages received.

4.3.1.2 Listservs and Bulletin Boards

Although e-mail is typically one-to-one communication, *listservs* and *bulletin boards* are one-to-many communications. Because the capabilities of listservs and bulletin boards increasingly are being integrated into e-mail systems, their distinctions are blurring. However, listservs and bulletin boards traditionally have supported self-selected groups and have provided a means of message distribution. Most professional associations have these services, which allow members to stay up to date on issues and announcements. Automated listservs, such as Lyris, provide easy-to-use, sophisticated communications capabilities such as conversation threading, file archiving, and search capabilities.

4.3.1.3 Calendaring

Initially, *calendaring* systems were considered tools for secretaries and administrative assistants to schedule meetings for others. It wasn't until users took control of the systems themselves that they began to gain in popularity.

Calendar management software can improve control of appointment scheduling and time management. Calendar entries, scheduled by date and time, may include locations, descriptions, and agenda items. Electronic appointment calendar systems can be synchronized with handheld personal organizers. Software can help the user schedule appointments, manage contacts (e.g., digitize information from business cards), make to-do lists, keep notes, and share calendars. Many products are Internet based.

4.3.1.4 Group Document Handling

Document management refers to a systems approach to handling complex documents. It entails managing all steps in preparing and producing documents from their creation to subsequent editing, formatting, composition and makeup, printing and reproduction, distribution, presentation, and storage. The approach encompasses four elements:

1. Integrating the various activities that go into composing documents.
2. Reducing the number of steps required to produce complex documents.
3. Distributing the documents electronically.
4. Presenting documents in the most appropriate medium.

Group document handling systems enable users to communicate, create and share databases, and create and share documents. Lotus Notes was the pioneer product in this category and remains a popular choice. Notes, a customizable en-

Figure 4-4
E-mail etiquette

AVOID TYPING IN ALL CAPS (virtual shouting)
avoid typing in all lowercase (virtual whispering)
Address your recipient by name
Limit the number of issues/ideas per message
Use a descriptive subject line
Proofread messages before sending

QuickPlace	LotusDevelopment Corp.	lotus.com
Livelink	Open Text Corp.	opentext.com
Teamspace	Involv Corp.	involv.com
ActiveProject	Framework Technologies Corp.	frametech.com

Figure 4-5
Project management groupware products

vironment, acts as central access to both structured and unstructured data, and stores and manages documents. Lotus Notes R5 also includes integrated e-mail, calendaring, group scheduling, Web access, and information management. Lotus Notes Reporter is a read-only report writing and analysis tool offering drill-down to databases, allowing the user, for example, to see the detailed data underlying chart summaries. Another example is X-Collaboration.com, which lets users in emerging enterprises work together on projects and documents on the Web, facilitating data gathering and document assembly, organization, publishing, and archiving—in other words, enabling digital group document handling.

A more specialized application of group document management systems is project management. Project management software initially was limited to software that supported project planning and costing. However, the Web has spawned a number of products that go beyond, allowing groups to set up document libraries for nonspecialized, short-term projects and to support other aspects of their work, including document sharing and calendaring. Using a browser interface, teams can share documents, post graphics and photos, interact with others, and alert participants to changes. Web-based groupware can be an inexpensive alternative to Intranet groupware products. Figure 4-5 is a listing of project management groupware products.

4.3.1.5 Virtual Office Software

The virtual office is any location where a worker uses groupware technology to stay in touch with the office or clients. An independent agent for an insurance agency, for example, described his technology needs as a laptop; a four-in-one printer that prints, faxes, scans, and copies; and two phone lines.[9] Other support technologies could include a Personal Digital Assistant (PDA) for tracking clients and keeping a calendar. Cellular telephones also are considered must-have devices.

One way that small companies can support the groupware needs of their workforce is to subscribe to an Intranet or Internet service such as those listed in Figure 4-6. These (usually) Level 1 groupware services may be free when bundled

Figure 4-6
Virtual office products

HotOffice™	Virtual Office Service	hotoffice.com
Instant TeamRoom	Lotus Development Corp.	lotus.com
NetMeeting	Microsoft Corp.	microsoft.com
Virtual Office	Netopia, Inc.	netopia.com
Innovative Network Integration	Ininet, Inc.	ininet.com

with other software products or can be leased for a monthly fee. These products can be used to share and retrieve documents, send and receive e-mail, maintain threaded discussions, update calendars, host bulletin board discussions, hold on-line conferences, make travel arrangements, and the like. These inexpensive services are useful for organizations that want to avoid the costs associated with developing their own software and hardware and supporting IT personnel.

4.3.2 Level 1 Groupware Products: Supporting Synchronous Communications

Synchronous or real-time conferencing refers to those communications or decision-making meetings that connect group members at the same time. Real-time conferencing tools discussed here are instant messaging and chat sessions, and desktop video teleconferencing tools.

4.3.2.1 *Instant Messaging and Chat Sessions*

Instant messaging allows users to see who else is online. A user can send a message that instantly pops up on the addressee's screen, and two or more users can have an interactive discussion. Chat sessions allow (usually) larger groups to communicate either publicly or privately by typing to each other. However, some products in this category are blurring distinctions between instant messaging and chat sessions to include audio and video. For example, the instant meeting technology in Lotus's Sametime product builds on the product's existing real-time chat technology. Sametime lets users know when others in their group are online and instantly convenes an interactive data conference, complete with documents, spreadsheets, interactive presentations, and other applications. Vendors, such as those listed in Figure 4-7(a), also are creating audio and video add-on products to their instant messaging and chat tools. Figure 4-7(b) shows screen shots from Lotus's Sametime online meeting room. A discussion of desktop video conferencing systems appears later in this chapter.

Information technology managers tend to discount the value of instant messaging and chat systems, but end users are increasingly enamoured with them. IT managers, struggling with issues related to the working and security of their e-mail systems, often consider such tools as unnecessary as they say their existing e-mail and groupware systems work fine.[10] However, user demand may force IT managers to support these products; in fact, it is anticipated that as instant messaging becomes more standardized, it will be part of every e-mail system.

Most instant messaging today is by typed conversations; in the very near future, instant messages may be real-time video, voice, or text. Moreover, users will be able to send "smart" messages that find the recipients wherever they may be and through whatever medium they may be using at the time—a desktop PC, a wireless phone, or a TV.[11] This vision will be enabled by the interoperability of Internet-based systems.

4.3.2.2 *Desktop Videoconferencing*

Videoconferencing originally was marketed as a means for lowering executive travel costs. Today, however, the conference's biggest selling point is the timeliness and convenience it offers: quick communication with little disruption in normal work patterns. Videoconferencing allows for facial expressions and body language, which is lost in text-based, audio-only, or chat conferencing.

Instant Messenger	America Online	aol.com
Sametime	Lotus Development Corp.	lotus.com
NetMeeting	Microsoft Corp.	microsoft.com
CoolTalk	Netscape Communications Corp.	netscape.com
Netscape Conference	Netscape Communications Corp.	netscape.com

Figure 4-7a
Instant messaging and chat tools

Room-sized videoconferencing systems were initially expensive and difficult to use. However, as costs come down and the need for one-to-many or many-to-many communications increases, users are finding room-sized conferencing systems, such as those offered by PictureTel, versatile and cost effective.

The discussion here centers on desktop videoconferencing systems, which are incredibly inexpensive and simple. These systems support one-to-one and one-to-many communications. For one-to-one communications, the only technology required is a small camera that sits on top of the user's microcomputer, a microphone,

Figure 4-7b
Lotus Sametime instant messaging and meeting room

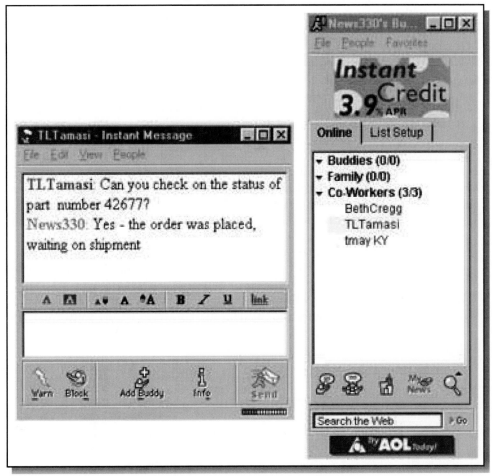

Source: Reproduced with permission from Lotus Development Corporation.

and software to compress the audio and video files. The software allows the user to send and receive information that is stored on the computer. Because users are in their offices rather than a conference room, conferences can be set up quickly and conferees have instant access to everything on their computers.

The features of desktop videoconferencing systems are similar. Video quality depends on the bandwidth of the network at both ends of the connection. The quality of images when POTS (plain old telephone services) lines are used can be shaky, and because the audio and video often are not synchronized, an annoying, 1-second delay is the result. However, addressing bandwidth issues are Digital Subscriber Lines (DSL) that can push data more quickly over POTS lines and direct-broadcast satellite. Also addressing these issues are Internet2, a development effort funded by the U.S. Government, a separate network offering data transfer rates 100 to 1,000 times faster than the Internet (see chapter 2). It is anticipated that once desktop systems are Internet-based, multimedia communications will be more standard. Figure 4-8 lists several popular desktop videoconferencing products.

4.3.3 Level 2 Groupware Products: Supporting Group Processes

Level 2 groupware products are software and hardware tools that add value to the group communication process by adding functionality to the group's deliberations, whether the task at hand is a meeting or learning. Groupware products under two functional areas, electronic meeting management and distance learning, are discussed in this section.

4.3.3.1 Group Support Systems

Group support systems (GSS), often referred to as electronic meeting systems, are software tools that support group processes such as brainstorming, voting, consensus building, and group writing, adding functionality way beyond the communications supported by chat rooms or videoconferencing. Dissatisfaction with the inefficiencies and ineffectiveness of meetings is nothing new; see Figure 4-9. GSS, by adding structure and data analysis tools, have the potential to improve meeting quality and effectiveness. Figure 4-10 is a list of popular GSS systems, and Figure 4-11 is a listing of the tools of one groupware product, from groupsystems.com. Meetings can be same time/same place, same time/different place, or different time/different place.

When used in a same time/same place dimension, users sit at individual workstations that are linked to a file server via a local area network, and users supplement their verbal interaction by using the software tools. At his or her workstation, the user views work privately before sending ideas anonymously to the file server for display on a public screen and/or data manipulation by the software.[12] The

Figure 4-8
Desktop videoconferencing products

CU-SeeMe	White Pine Software, Inc.	wpine.com
NetMeeting	Microsoft Corp.	microsoft.com
MeetingPoint	White Pine Software, Inc.	wpine.com
PictureTel	PictureTel Corp.	picturetel.com
PictureTalk	Pixion, Inc.	pixion.com

Nothing is ever accomplished by a committee unless it consists of three members, one of whom happens to be sick and another absent.

Hendrick W. Van Loon, *Reader's Digest*, 1934

A committee is a cul-de-sac down which ideas are lured and then quietly strangled.

Sir Barnett Crocks, 1973

I love meetings. NOT!

Professor Mary Driscoll, 1992, after seeing the movie *Wayne's World*

Figure 4-9
Perceptions of meetings

GroupSystems	groupsystems.com	ventana.com
Council Services	CoVision	covision.com
Facilitate	Facilitate.com, Inc.	facilitate.com
Meeting Works	Meetingworks.com, Inc.	entsol.com

Figure 4-10
Group support systems products and vendors

Figure 4-11
GroupSystems® overview

GroupSystems is a suite of team-based decision software tools with the power and variety to help groups reach decisions. The suite consists of the following tools:

Standard Tools
The Standard Tools support business needs such as strategic planning, activity-based costing, business-process reengineering, innovative problem solving, product definition, knowledge management, and many more. To support these needs, the Standard Tools use group processes such as brainstorming, list building, information gathering, voting, organizing, prioritizing, and consensus building.

Survey
Survey expands the horizons of online surveys. Use Survey for face-to-face or distributed groups across local area networks, e-mail, the Internet, or your company's Intranet—and then collect and analyze results with push-button ease.

Alternative Analysis
Alternative Analysis allows your group to explore the strengths and weaknesses of strategic plans, select candidates, determine the impact of a plan on stakeholders, generate and prioritize product requirements—and much, much more.

Source: Reprinted with permission from groupsystems.com.

same set of tools can support groups that are not meeting at the same time or in the same location. In such cases, advance work on the part of a team leader and the technology facilitator is important.

GSS cannot make a poor team function better, but it can help a good team work more efficiently and often more effectively. Evidence shows that GSS tools have the potential to reduce conflict and improve satisfaction with outcomes. For example, GSS tools may support communication and participation among members, reduce domination by overpowering individuals, allow for individual differences, and lessen the amount of time wasted.[13] Studies also have shown that GSS-supported groups spend more time making decisions and make better decisions. However, other studies have shown just the opposite effect, perhaps because of decreased body language cues and a hesitancy to change the way decisions traditionally are made. Anonymous communication may reduce the risk associated with contributing unpopular ideas, but it will not deal with why such risk is not encouraged face to face, and it does not give credit for good ideas.[14]

4.3.3.2 *Distance Learning*

When learning is the goal of a conference and groupware technologies are being used, conferencing events are labeled distance learning. In some distance learning programs, technology supports asynchronous (different time/different place) communications; other times, distance learning programs are synchronous (same time/different place). Some programs are combinations of both.

Distance learning products from groupware vendors add the functionality of classroom management and/or presentation strategies designed to support either self-paced materials or live interaction with an instructor and other students. Products, which are typically instructor controlled, can support registration, discussions, multipoint audio and video, whiteboards, class assignments, interactive quizzes, and course development. Internet streaming—both audio and video—allows learners to replay educational lectures on demand. A total distance learning solution can integrate other products that support data and/or video transmissions. Software components can include an instructor client, a student client, and a server. Figure 4-12 is a listing of vendors and their products for distance learning. Figure 4-13 is a virtual college screen shot. Chapter 6 offers more discussion on this topic.

4.3.4 Level 3 Groupware Products: Supporting Software Agents

Software agents, self-contained pieces of computer code, carry out specific, electronic tasks for their human masters.[15] These agents are sometimes referred to as knowbots (or shopbots if they are used in electronic commerce applications). These agents learn your preferences. For example, software agents can sort electronic mail by analyzing a user's reading habits.[16] Electronic mail can thus be sorted by whom the user typically responds to quickly, such as her CEO, her boss, or her favorite aunt. Bruce Springsteen is in town? Your knowbot can get you aisle seats.[17] Shopbots can automate comparison shopping for tasks such as choosing mortgages or cars. For discussion here, software agents that cooperate with each other or with groups of users are considered groupware. Although they remain in the developmental stage at this time, consider, for example, an agent that could serve as project manager, reminding team members of deadlines and tasks. The team's agent also could perform routine tasks for users such as finding critical information or accessing other team members' calendars to set up a video teleconference.

PAY-FOR-TEAM PERFORMANCE: BAILEY AND BAILEY

Bailey and Bailey, Inc. [pseudo name], a specialized financial-guarantee insurance company based in New York City, has a practice of giving biannual bonuses to its employees. The medium-sized organization's structure is flat, with group work being the norm. The corporation has a history of using computers in all phases of their everyday work. Work is organized around "deals," whereby a project director assigns the right mix of individuals to work together. Rarely does the exact same team work on a given deal, and deals could take as little as two hours or as long as six months to complete.

The organization's Policy Committee makes bonus allocations based on profit figures and performance reviews describing the contributions of employees. This year, the committee wanted additional data on how effective employees were as team members as measured by their peers. The organization had previously used GroupSystems, a Level 2 groupware product, in a face-to-face strategic planning activity, and the CEO mandated that it should be used for this purpose. The Human Resource Director suggested several important guidelines: Employees would need to be assured of confidentiality, and the evaluation would have to take place in a different time/different place environment, allowing employees to complete their reviews in the privacy of their own offices. The HR director was responsible, too, for developing the measures and ensuring training.

Employees had access to the software via a local area network connected to their office computers and to a central file server. Within GroupSystems, the reluctantly complying information systems director had established an electronic folder for each specific deal, and individual reviewers had access to only those folders for which they were a deal participant. Signing on required users to click on the Agenda icon and then identify the deal in which they participated. At that point, eligible reviewers automatically were ushered into the vote tool, where they were asked to "click" the name of the individual they were rating, then asked to rate the individual's team contribution on a scale of 1–7, where $1 = $ low and $7 = $ high. Planners also wanted qualitative data in the form of critical incidents to back up the evaluation score. For example, an item measuring support read:

He/she has good communications skills; motivates the team; serves as a role model; takes time to mentor/coach; provides timely feedback; is approachable; demonstrates sensitivity; does not favor one team member over another.
Rating: ____
Critical Incident:

As to the use of GroupSystems to enable the evaluation, users were pleased, although not completely satisfied that their evaluations were confidential. The Information Systems Director initially had difficulty in providing reports (perhaps because of low personal enthusiasm about the project in the first place). However, data were used by Bailey and Bailey, and in their next attempt to use the groupware for this project, planners will have learned from what went right—and what went wrong.

Source: Adapted from *Informing Sciences International Journal of an Emerging Transdiscipline,* Vol. 2, No. 1, pp. 11–18.

4.4   AN OVERALL VISION FOR GROUPWARE

David Coleman, founder and Managing Director of Collaborative Strategies and author of *Groupware: Collaborative Strategies for Corporate LANs and Intranets* (Prentice Hall, 1997), has done extensive research in the area of groupware tools and implementation issues. He reports that groupware tools typically are implemented by organizations piecemeal: "e-mail in this department, calendaring and scheduling in another department, Notes over in finance. To make matters worse, the technical/MIS people don't believe in groupware at all."[18] His vision of a fully integrated groupware system would include a work-flow tool that would track and route tasks and assignments with time and date stamps. His overall architecture for this vision is shown in Figure 4-14.

Learning Space	Lotus Development Corp.	lotus.com
ClassPoint	White Pine	wpine.com
Course Info	Blackboard	blackboard.com
Web CT	Web CT	webct.com
e-education	JonesKnowledge.com, Inc.	jonesknowledge.com
Collegis	Collegis	collegis.com
Web Course in a Box	Mad Duck	madduck.com
TopClass	WBT Systems	wbtsystems.com
eCollege	eCollege.com	ecollege.com
Convene	Convene.com	convene.com

Figure 4-12
Distance learning technologies

Figure 4-14 illustrates the solid link between groupware tools and the previous chapter, Knowledge Management. Note how tools including calendaring, electronic meeting systems (group support systems), project management systems, and work-flow systems come together in this chart to provide a means for sharing data, storing data, and coordinating tasks to achieve organizational goals.

Figure 4-13
Screen shot from ClassPoint

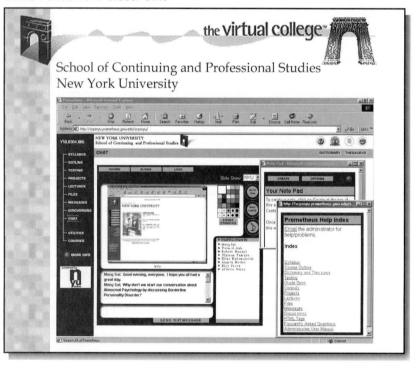

Source: Reprinted with permission of Whitepine Software.

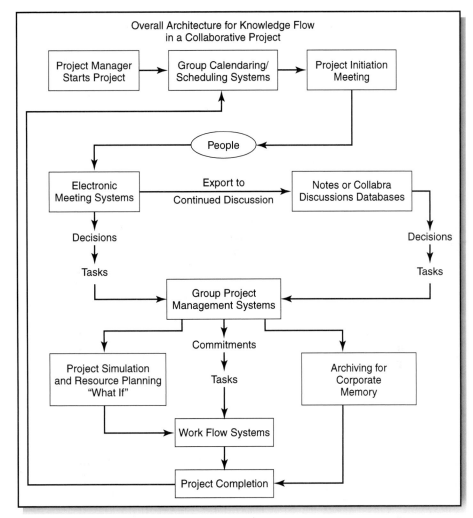

Figure 4-14
Overall architecture for knowledge flow in a collaborative project

Source: GroupWare by Coleman © 1998. Reprinted by permission of Prentice-Hall, Inc., Upper Saddle River, NJ.

4.5 SUMMARY

Groupware technology selection and successful implementation has been described as a task that requires technical know-how and knowledge of the organization's culture and how individuals prefer to work. Discussed in this chapter were descriptions and issues related to three levels of groupware products. In all categories, the ubiquitous Web, because it eliminates compatibility issues, is the empowering technology that is pushing for improved and new products and services that support the way groups work.

Level 1 groupware products are those software (and sometimes hardware) tools that support communications. E-mail is usually one-to-one communication. Instant messaging facilities allow users to communicate (usually by typing) to each other in real time. Listservs and bulletin boards support one-to-many communications. Calendaring systems allow groups a variety of options related to scheduling meetings, managing contacts, and keeping notes. Group document handling products allow users to share in the creation and sharing of databases and documents. Desktop videoconferencing systems are inexpensive, easy-to-use tools that add a visual dimension to communications. E-mail is considered an enabling technology for most group communications tools, including those described here as Level 2 groupware products.

Virtual Office Software is a separate category in this chapter because tools in this category tend to be those that support small organizations that typically do not have the interest, time, or money to support their own Intranet-based systems. Internet-based and free when bundled with other software products or inexpensively leased, virtual office products provide a large range of (usually) Level 1 groupware tools.

Level 2 groupware products go a step further than supporting communications needs. This level includes products that actually support group processes such as brainstorming, voting, and evaluating by adding functionality to tabulate, summarize, and provide quick statistical analysis of actions, such as a vote tool that can calculate means, modes, medians, and standard deviations. Level 2 products that support learning are labeled distance learning tools. Distance learning tools add classroom management and communications capabilities to the groupware mix, bundling a wide range of activities such as class registration, instant quizzes, document sharing, and even videoconferencing. Although the use of Level 1 tools is increasingly the way business (or education!) is done today, getting buy in and support for Level 2 tools is frequently a challenge because these tools can change the way work is done, not just automate information sharing.

Level 3 tools, software agents, are more than pie-in-the-sky applications. Software developers and organizational decision makers are increasingly intrigued by the potential of such automated team members (agents), and we can expect these agents to expand in currently envisioned functions such as project management or information gophers.

KEY TERMS

- Bulletin boards
- Calendaring
- Chat sessions
- Desktop videoconferencing
- Distance learning

- Document management
- E-mail
- Electronic meeting systems
- Group support systems
- Groupware

- Instant messaging
- Listservs
- Project management
- Software agents

DISCUSSION QUESTIONS

1. List features of e-mail systems. How many of these features are on the system you currently use? Which are most beneficial to you?
2. Summarize the evolution of groupware products. Draw a diagram with e-mail products at the bottom and knowbots at the top. Where would you put the other tools in this hierarchy?
3. Match the following group tasks with appropriate groupware tools:
   - Notifying a group of a meeting
   - Writing a proposal for governmental funding
   - Processing an insurance claim
   - Training program delivery
   - Deciding who to hire for a specific position in the organization
4. Assume that you are responsible for implementing a Level 2 group support tool. Prepare an "elevator speech" (no longer than 1 minute) explaining how it could be useful to someone who needs to be convinced of its value.

5. It's been said that a picture is worth a thousand words. What other value does desktop videoconferencing add to communications?

6. Identify business needs that point to the future success of groupware systems and list barriers to effective implementation.

APPLICATION EXERCISES

1. Check out the Web site of a Virtual Office Products vendor. Identify how the vendor's most recent product offering could help a small business with its groupware needs.

2. Survey three or four executives from varying industries to see how they use groupware in their environments.

3. Read reviews of new groupware products in journals such as *PCWeek* or *PCWorld*. Summarize those reviews in a report to your class.

SUGGESTED READINGS

Coleman, David. *Groupware: Collaborative Strategies for Corporate LANs and Intranets.* (Upper Saddle River, NJ: Prentice Hall, 1997, p. 35).

Mankin, Don, Susan G. Cohen, and Tora K. Bikson. *Teams and Technology: Fulfilling the Promise of the New Organization.* (Boston: Harvard Business School Press, 1996).

McGrath, Joseph E., and Andrea Hollingshead. *Groups Interacting with Technology.* (Thousand Oaks, CA: Sage Publications, 1994).

O'Hara-Devereaux, M., and R. Johansen. *GlobalWork: Bridging Distance, Culture & Time.* (San Francisco: Jossey-Bass, 1994).

ENDNOTES

1. Amy D. Whol, "The Evolution of Groupware," *Beyond Computing* 8 (September, 1999).

2. Peter F. Drucker, "The Coming of the New Organization," *Harvard Business Review* (January/February 1988).

3. Ibid.

4. Andrea Gabor, "After the Pay Revolution, Job Titles Won't Matter," *The New York Times,* March 17, 1992, p. F5.

5. M. O'Hara-Devereaux, and R. Johansen, *GlobalWork: Bridging Distance, Culture & Time* (San Francisco: Jossey-Bass, 1994).

6. Y. Merali, "Informed decisions," *People Management* 5 (June 17, 1999).

7. S. M. Dugan, "Groupware Still Going Strong," *InfoWorld* 21 (July 5, 1999).

8. "You've Got (Way Too Much) Mail," *Workforce* (February, 1999).

9. Amanda Levin, "Virtual Agencies Are Becoming a Reality," *National Underwriter* (August 9, 1999).

10. D. Deckmyn, "Valuable Tool or Distraction?" *ComputerWorld* 33 (July 12, 1999).

11. Mike Snider, "Instant Messaging on Fast Track; Today's Chats Could Spark a Multimedia Information Revolution," *USA Today* (August 11, 1999).

12. Susan R. Feather, "The Impact of Group Support Systems on the Development of Groups Engaged in Collaborative Learning" (Doctoral Dissertation, New York University, 1998).

13. Margaretta J. Caouette and Bridget N. O'Connor, "The Impact of Group Support Systems on Corporate Teams' Stages of Development," *Journal of Organizational Computing and Electronic Commerce* 8 (1998).

14. Poppy Lauretta McLeod, "A Literary Examination of Electronic Meeting Systems Use in Everyday Organizational Life," *The Journal of Applied Behavioral Science* (June, 1999).

15. Christopher Barnatt, "Our New Working Class: The Business Implications of Software Agents," *Journal of General Management* (Winter 1997).

16. Ivars Peterson, "Agents of Cooperation," *Science News* (January 2, 1999).

17. "Getting to Know Your Knowbot," *Kiplinger's Personal Finance Magazine* (January, 1997).

18. David Coleman, *Groupware: Collaborative Strategies for Corporate LANs and Intranets* (Upper Saddle River, NJ: Prentice Hall, 1997, p. 35).

Chapter 5

Knowledge Management

Learning Objectives

Upon completing this chapter, you should be able to:

➤ Define knowledge and knowledge management within a business context.

➤ Explain the importance of knowledge management in contemporary enterprises.

➤ Identify technologies that are most useful for capturing, organizing, distributing, and sharing knowledge within an enterprise.

➤ Discuss the impact of Intranets and groupware on knowledge management.

➤ Explain how to formulate a knowledge management strategy.

➤ Identify major requirements and issues for designing an enterprise knowledge architecture.

➤ List and describe the steps for implementing knowledge management projects.

➤ Identify common pitfalls for enterprises seeking to implement knowledge management and explain how to avoid them.

5.1 INTRODUCTION

Knowledge management (KM) is an emerging but important area of study and practice. The past decade has witnessed the rapid evolution of concepts such as the knowledge worker, knowledge economy, intellectual capital, and knowledge as a tangible asset. More and more, business leaders and consultants talk about knowledge as the chief asset of organizations and the key to a sustainable competitive advantage. Knowledge management programs have been launched at countless companies. The growing interest in this movement has even spawned new executive titles such as Chief Knowledge Officer (CKO), Director of Knowledge Networking, Corporate Knowledge Strategist, Vice President for Strategic Technology and Knowledge Management, Knowledge Management Initiative Leader, and Chairman for Knowledge Sharing. Additional details about emerging KM jobs are provided in Figures 5-1 and 5-2.

The worldwide market for KM software is forecast to grow from $515 million in 2000 to $3.5 billion by 2004, according to a report by the market research firm Ovum. Most major software vendors recently have made major commitments to

Chief Knowledge Officer (CKO)
Director, Knowledge Networking
Consultant, Corporate Quality
Head of Knowledge and Differentiation Program (IBM United Kingdom Limited)
Knowledge Management Initiative Leader (Hewlett-Packard Consulting)
Chairman for Knowledge Sharing (Buckman Laboratories)
Director, Collaboration and Knowledge Sharing (Texas Instruments)
Corporate Knowledge Strategist (National Security Agency)
Senior Technical Associate—Knowledge Management (Shell Chemicals)
Program Director, Knowledge Management (World Bank)
Vice President, Strategic Technology and Knowledge Management
Information Technology Analyst

Figure 5-1
Emerging job titles

this market, including IBM/Lotus Development and Microsoft. U.S. businesses paid $1.5 billion to consultants for KM advice in 1999 and are forecast to pay $5 billion a year for it by 2001, according to the Gartner Group marketing research firm. In a 2000 survey by Ernst & Young's Center for Business Innovation and Business Intelligence, 94 percent of respondents said they believe that they could leverage the knowledge of their organizations more effectively through deliberate management. In the same survey, more than 40 percent said they already had started or completed KM projects; another 25 percent said they planned to do so within the next year.

How are enterprises using knowledge management? What are the most common applications? Figure 5-3 shows objectives of knowledge management cited by major corporations in a recent benchmarking study conducted by the American Productivity and Quality Center.[1] The most common objective in this survey was transferring best practices, followed by increasing employee capabilities, providing customer/market information, supporting business process improvement, and leveraging intellectual capital.

Some of the major corporations that have adopted knowledge management include British Petroleum, Monsanto, Hewlett Packard, PricewaterhouseCoopers, Andersen Consulting, Chevron, and Texas Instruments. Chevron calculates that it has saved more than $650 million since 1991 by sharing best practices among managers in charge of energy use at its oil refineries. General Motors has created an electronic performance support system (EPSS) that captures knowledge that is created when employees are working. Mechanics use notebook-sized computers that deliver learning materials and job aids when and where they are needed. When mechanics complete their repair work, they describe the problem and its resolution using voice recognition to relay information into the computer. This information is reviewed by technicians back at headquarters, and new competencies and experience get turned into new knowledge for the EPSS system. The system is changing not only the way the mechanics learn but also how they work. Mechanics can work on a wider variety of vehicles because the knowledge they need is built into the EPSS.

Based on more than a decade of knowledge work, Debra Amidon, founder of Entovation International, and Clint Ackerman, CEO of the Network Connection and Knowledge Jobs, have devised a classification system that divides knowledge professionals into eight categories based on skill sets and backgrounds. They use the classification system to help candidates determine what positions are appropriate for their skills and to help companies determine what kinds of professionals they need.

Knowledge and innovation professionals:

Individuals have strong backgrounds in shaping and formulating knowledge-based programs. Many have developed best practices for global Fortune 1000 companies. Most are highly skilled in a variety of disciplines, including business process improvement, innovation, performance measurement and modeling, case history, facilitation, strategic integration, and developing best practices. Chief knowledge officers are part of this group, as are consultants.

Knowledge management professionals:

KM professionals have expertise in implementation. They ensure that a company gains from management of knowledge. They are involved in all phases of innovation (knowledge creation, knowledge acquisition, knowledge sharing, knowledge conversion, and knowledge commercialization). Their career background could be in any of a number of functions, including finance, human resources, quality, IT, R&D, manufacturing, sales, or customer service.

Knowledge catalogers, researchers, and media specialists:

These are Web site, Internet and intranet developers, librarians, catalogue specialists, content developers, communicators, software designers and developers, middle managers, and others who create the knowledge networks and links.

Knowledge and competitive intelligence professionals:

The emphasis for these professionals is on competitive intelligence. They are heavy on research and have the ability to create and develop solid analyses. They have online research savvy mixed with the ability to cogently and concisely present ideas. Their writing and presentation skills are strong.

Knowledge and strategic integration professionals:

Composed of top strategists, thinkers, planners, marketers, and individuals with senior management experience, these workers make planning and strategy the engine for business improvement and growth.

Knowledge academicians, theorists, and visionaries:

This group focuses primarily on discussion within an academic setting and developing and testing models and applications. Visionaries are thought leaders who are frequently well in front of the practice. These individuals make outstanding speakers and can stimulate your organization's thinking.

Knowledge facilitators, trainers, and corporate educators:

These individuals focus on learning and education in a corporate setting. Many have created outstanding models and programs for linking external and internal audiences, designing and developing curriculums, implementing distance learning, and creating custom-tailored courses for executives and senior managers.

Knowledge and expert systems professionals:

One facet of knowledge and knowledge management is expert systems and how to institutionalize corporate knowledge. Individuals in this area include systems specialists, technologists, chief information officers, technology transfer specialists, expert systems engineers, project managers, and others who primarily focus on information technology.—E.J.

Figure 5-2

A taxonomy of K-careers

Source: Ellie Jones, "Fast-Track Knowledge Careers: Managers Who Combine Technical, Business and Social Skills Will Be the Winners in the KM Career Game." *Knowledge Management Magazine* 2 (September 1999): 40.

Part II   End-User Information Systems: Business Solutions

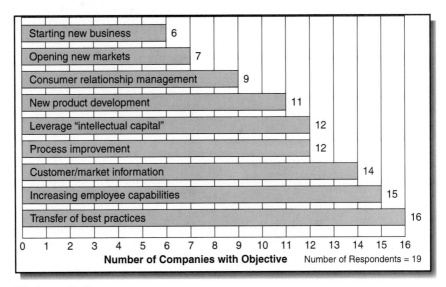

Figure 5-3

Objectives of knowledge management

Source: Reprinted with the permission of The Free Press, a Division of Simon & Schuster, Inc., from *IF WE ONLY KNEW WHAT WE KNOW:* The Transfer of Internal Knowledge and Best Practice by Carla O'Dell and C. Jackson Grayson, Jr. with Nilly Essaides. Copyright © 1998 by Carla O'Dell and C. Jackson Grayson, Jr.

5.2   WHAT IS KNOWLEDGE MANAGEMENT?

Knowledge management as an emerging concept is not yet well defined. As a construct, it has come to mean many things to many people. It includes work flow, document control and distribution, e-mail, performance support, best practices, and collaborative computing. It also can include Intranets, Extranets, e-business, customer relationship management, business intelligence, data mining, and knowledge portals. All of these are discussed in various ways by different sources in relation to knowledge management.

The idea of the importance of knowledge is not new. Yet as a concept and an organizational process, knowledge management takes on an entirely different meaning. The rapid growth in popularity of this concept has made it difficult to sort out the hype from the reality. As often happens when a new concept becomes popular, there has been a rush to rename existing technologies or products to make them more marketable. As a result, systems that have been around for a long time, such as artificial intelligence (AI), expert systems, databases, and document management systems, now are touted as knowledge management systems. What, then, are we talking about when we say knowledge management? Many sources offer definitions of KM with varying degrees of consistency.

The American Productivity and Quality Center defines the term *knowledge management* as "the broad process of locating, organizing, transferring, and using the information and expertise within an organization."[2] According to O'Dell and Grayson in their book *If Only We Knew What We Know,* "Knowledge management is a conscious strategy of getting the right knowledge to the right people at the right time and helping people share and put information into action in ways that strive to improve organizational performance."[3]

The Gartner Group, a prominent marketing research firm, defines knowledge management as:

> . . . a discipline that promotes an integrated and collaborative approach to the process of information asset creation, capture, organization, access and use. Information assets include databases, documents, and most importantly, the uncaptured, tacit expertise and experience resident in individual workers.[4]

In his book *Business @ the Speed of Thought,* Bill Gates describes KM this way:

> Knowledge management as I use it is not a software product or a software category. Knowledge management doesn't even start with technology. It starts with business objectives and processes and a recognition of the need to share information. Knowledge management is nothing more than managing information flow, getting the right information to the people who need it so that they can act on it quickly. It goes back to Michael Dertouzos' idea that information is a verb, not a static noun. And knowledge management is a means, not an end.[5]

The editors of *Harvard Management Update* define knowledge management simply as a formal, directed process of figuring out what information a company has that could benefit others in the company, then devising ways of making it readily available.[6]

Knowledge management, according to Daniel Tkach, IBM worldwide marketing manager for Knowledge Management Solutions says:

> Knowledge management is a discipline used to systematically leverage expertise and information to improve organizational efficiency, responsiveness, competency and innovation. Systematically means that the discipline does not rely on just water cooler conversations, but on planned processes, technology and behaviors. Knowledge management leverages all the key resources that a company has already and that can be put to use in a more effective way.[7]

According to Thomas Davenport (professor at the University of Texas and noted KM guru),

> Knowledge management caters to the critical issues of organizational adaptation, survival and competence in the face of increasingly discontinuous environmental change. Essentially, it embodies organizational processes that seed synergistic combinations of data and information processing capacity of information technologies, and the creative and innovative capacity of human beings.[8]

In summary, knowledge management is the concept of managing organizational knowledge, but in the sense of facilitating learning and collaboration—not in the old sense of controlling information. The old concept of sharing information on a *need-to-know basis* was a control concept as if information were a finite resource. In contrast, knowledge management recognizes knowledge as an infinite resource or asset. As pointed out by Jan Duffy in *Harvesting Experience: Reaping the Benefits of Knowledge,* knowledge is different and much more difficult to manage than other assets. Rather than become less as it is used, new knowledge is developed as existing knowledge is shared. Knowledge is a dynamic, evolving product that depends on an organization and its network of relationships for its existence. Processes that encourage creativity and innovation—processes that are seeded by new knowledge as it is being created—enhance the value and growth of knowledge. Knowledge value comes from processes that allow continuous progress and that minimize regressive relearning and reinvention of the wheel. The value of knowledge increases dramatically when it is used and diminishes when it is allowed to atrophy.

Perhaps the best way to think of knowledge management is as knowledge plus process.

Knowledge management = knowledge + process

Let's briefly examine both components of this equation. What precisely is *knowledge,* and how is it different than data and information? Organizational knowledge consists of *explicit knowledge* (knowledge that is documented and public) and *tacit knowledge* (undocumented and personal). Explicit knowledge generally comes in the form of documents, manuals, financial statements, databases, books, and other print or electronic formats. Tacit knowledge, in contrast, is found in the heads of employees. It is context sensitive, dynamic, experienced-based, and often subjective or intuitive. It consists of such things as judgment, know-how, and perception and is difficult to document and explain. Both types of knowledge are important.

Knowledge is broader than intellectual capital, which generally refers to the commercial value of trademarks, brand names, patents, licenses, and other intellectual property. It also is bigger than information or data although it is related to both. Organizations are flooded with data and information, but until people use it, it is not knowledge. Although it has meaning, information without context adds little value to the decision-making process. Knowledge is information that has been validated and that has context, which provides the understanding associated with knowledge. Knowledge comprises a fluid mix of contextual information, data, experience, values, and insight that provides a framework for evaluating and incorporating new experiences and information. A simple working definition is: "Knowledge is information in action."[9]

Although knowledge creation is a natural phenomenon, the *process* part of the knowledge management equation implies that an organization can improve performance by employing purposefully designed strategies for creating, identifying, collecting, organizing, and sharing or transferring knowledge. Note that it does not imply management in the sense of control, but rather in the sense of facilitating and nurturing the creation and sharing of knowledge. It suggests the concept of the learning organization, as articulated by Peter Senge in *The Fifth Discipline*. In formulating strategies, some enterprises have adopted a mantra of becoming a learning organization while other enterprises use the rhetoric of leveraging knowledge as an intellectual asset. Although the rhetoric may vary, the intent is the same: making shared learning or knowledge management a high priority.

5.2.1 Evolving Concepts and Directions

The knowledge management industry has roots in several disciplines. KM appears to represent a synthesis of these various distinct markets or disciplines—not a progression from any one of them. Perhaps it is this convergence of several threads that accounts, more than any other factor, for what seems like a sudden explosion of interest in KM. Moreover, this convergence is consistent with emerging models of organizations. Most modern business models involve people in teams coming together on a project basis, then moving on to new relationships. All these models are process oriented, not bound by functions, industries, or structures. Knowledge underpins their continuous existence.

Key disciplines or threads from which KM has roots are summarized in the sections that follow. These varying roots account at least in part for some of the current variation in terminology, perspectives, and recommended approaches to KM.

1. **Best practice transfer.** One of the most dominant themes is the systematic transfer of best practices. According to a study conducted by the American Productivity and Quality Center, best practice management was the one strategy pursued by 100 percent of the firms implementing knowledge management approaches.[10] This is the approach emphasized by O'Dell and Grayson based on research and work with numerous *Fortune* 500 firms.

2. **Information and records management.** KM also has roots in document management, both paper and image. The Association of Information Image Management (AIIM) and ARMA International, the former Association of Records Managers and Administrators, have a huge presence in the knowledge management market. This approach reflects a strategic view of managing and safe-guarding information resources from a corporate perspective. It is the approach reflected by Jan Duffy, in *Harvesting Experience: Reaping the Benefits of Knowledge.*

3. **Organizational learning and innovation.** The concept of the learning organization generally is associated with Peter Senge, author of *The Fifth Discipline.* It embodies the notion that organizations as well as individuals can learn from experience, and it emphasizes the need for information sharing and collaboration. Senge defines the learning organization as "a group of people continually enhancing their capacity to create what they want to create."[11] This is essentially a human resources approach and reflects the changing view of organizations from a mechanistic industrial era to the information age, from a structural view to a process view, and from adaptive learning to generative learning. Whereas adaptive learning has to do with coping, "generative learning emphasizes continuous experimentation and feedback in an ongoing examination of the way organizations go about defining and solving problems."[12] Generative learning, in Senge's view, requires systems thinking, shared vision, personal mastery, team learning, and creative tension. The concept of the learning organization is increasingly relevant given the growing complexity and uncertainty of the twenty-first-century organizational environment.

4. **Electronic performance support systems (EPSS) and computer-based training (CBT).** One of the early precursors of KM is electronic performance support, the concept of just-in-time delivery of online reference, training, and help. During the 1980s hundreds of firms focused on creating online performance support and computer-based training using tools such on Goal Systems Preference and Phoenix CBT authoring system. This approach is described in books such as *Designing Electronic Performance Support Systems* by Gloria J. Gery and *Designing and Writing Online Documentation* by William K. Horton.

5. **Database management and data warehousing.** Another school of thought that has received a great deal of attention is based on IS methodologies related to data warehousing and data mining. This approach is represented in works such as the book by Thomas H. Davenport and Laurence Prusak, *Working Knowledge: How Organizations Manage What They Know* (Harvard Business School Press, 1997).

6. **Internet and e-business** (and more recently customer relationship management, business intelligence, and portal technologies). This appears to be the dominant focus *of Knowledge Management Magazine, Business Intelligence for Strategic Decision Makers,* aimed at executives interested in organizational and technological knowledge-management strategies.

7. The knowledge economy and knowledge as a corporate asset. Another perspective is based on economic concepts related to productivity and measuring economic value in the new economy. Economists and business leaders today are concerned with whether traditional accounting and statistical models are capable of calculating the true productivity gains created by knowledge in the new economy. Recent works in this area include those by Paul A. Strassmann, columnist on knowledge metrics for *Knowledge Management Magazine* and Thomas A. Stewart, author of *Intellectual Capital: The New Wealth of Organizations.*

5.2.2 Major Trends in Knowledge Management

When *Knowledge Management Magazine* started publishing in October 1998, the notion of KM for strategic advantage was treated with more than a little skepticism by much of the business community, including many opinion makers in the corporate computing market. By the end of the century—just 15 short months later—the landscape had changed considerably, with explicit support coming from the likes of Xerox, IBM, the Big Five accounting firms, Bill Gates and even Federal Reserve Board Chairman Alan Greenspan. More significantly, the connection of knowledge to almost every other aspect of business grew more evident, such that the concepts of the knowledge worker, the Knowledge Age, and the knowledge economy—if not necessarily of knowledge management—now are recognized widely among the general public.[13]

A list of top 10 trends in KM, compiled by *Knowledge Management Magazine* in December 1999, included the following:[14]

1. The rise of the corporate portal as the defining KM application. The advent of corporate portals according to the editors of *KM Magazine,* crystallized a union of technology, function, and need. The *portal,* in effect, makes collaboration, business intelligence, and unstructured text-search capabilities available through a single interface. The portal is a natural evolution of e-commerce and Internet and Intranet technologies.
2. The recognition of knowledge economics as the context for next-century business. Economists in the U.S. Labor Department have acknowledged the new economy with a substantially revised economic classification system— the first such revision since the 1930s. The old Standard Industrial Classification (SIC) code system will be replaced with a new North American Industrial Classification System (NAICS), which will be expanded 35 percent to accommodate information technologies and information-based industries. In a September 1999 speech, Federal Reserve Board Chairman Alan Greenspan endorsed the notion that a combination of intellectual capital, technology, and evolving know-how are responsible for increased economic productivity in the United States. According to Greenspan, such icons of America's earlier might as steel mills, petrochemical complexes, auto assembly plants, and skyscrapers are being replaced with "economic value best symbolized by exceedingly complex, miniaturized integrated circuits and the ideas—the software—that utilize them. Most of what we currently perceive as value and wealth is intellectual and impalpable."
3. Corporate initiatives target strategic KM. Bipen Junnarkar, vice president of KM/chief knowledge officer at Gateway, pointed out that companies now are looking clearly at KM as a way to differentiate their companies from the competition and create tangible value. "The focus in KM has evolved from

integrating information to leveraging human interactions to just beginning to apply knowledge-based products and services for the extraction of value." Another sign of KM's ascending strategic role in the enterprise is that the Big Five firms such as PriceWaterhouseCoopers, Ernst & Young, and Andersen Consulting started up substantial KM consulting practices in 1999.

4. Organizational behavior focuses attention on human-resources aspects of KM. Recognition is growing that the cultural factors influencing KM are paramount to its success. Accordingly, the movement is broadening its impact from within the IT department to organization-wide management initiatives focused on organizational learning, collaborative work processes, and change management. "There's a much greater degree of interaction between knowledge management and those concerned with human resources, training, and management development issues. If there's a dominant group talking about KM issues now, it's shifted to HR people."[15]

5. Microsoft also embraces KM. In *Business @ the Speed of Thought*, Bill Gates prescribes knowledge-focused strategies for e-business. Microsoft has announced a platform-wide KM initiative, introducing a new portal-like product, Digital Dashboard, which was announced as the front end for other KM components such as file-sharing on the Web, mobile connectivity solutions and enhanced computer interfaces.

6. Intellectual capital as a corporate asset. Intellectual capital, which has long been regarded as an intangible quality of individuals and organizations, is gaining ground as a tangible line item on the corporate balance sheet. The most prevalent model has been the *balanced scorecard approach,* which makes the assumption that "innovation" and "learning and growth" relate directly to future organizational performance. Various accounting bodies and economists are making progress in developing methodologies to measure the value of intellectual capital.

7. Theory gives way to emergence of practical KM. Enough people have been implementing knowledge management projects to compile a significant body of knowledge about what works and what doesn't. More and more KM projects are being initiated by line-of-business managers without necessarily labeling them as knowledge management projects.

8. Customer successes show tangible results. A growing number of KM success stories show significant benefits in streamlining work flow, improving customer relations, reducing cycle times, or increasing capacity to process business.

9. Alignment of IT priorities and business strategy. Implementing KM demands a close alignment between the IT side and the business side of the house. KM is not a discipline unto itself. Rather it is a series of tools, techniques, processes, and concepts that are an aspect of the larger domain of executing business processes.[16]

10. IBM and Lotus led the convergence of business intelligence and knowledge management by coordinating their approaches to KM. Thus, IBM become an advocate for the convergence of structured and unstructured information even before corporate portals began to make that convergence a reality. In addition, IBM's Global Services consulting group focuses on the KM service element, and its Institute for Knowledge Management has emerged as a center of thought leadership for the KM community.

An enormous amount of valuable knowledge, both explicit and tacit, is available within most enterprises. Information technologies can provide access to vast reservoirs of knowledge. For example, workers can surf the Internet to seek out new ideas and developments. Industry associations provide online knowledge-sharing forums. Enterprises are working more closely with suppliers and customers, sharing information and experience to streamline operations. Moreover, partners, alliances, mergers, joint ventures, and even customers are potential sources of valuable knowledge. Seven primary sources of knowledge that enterprises commonly tap into when implementing knowledge management systems are described briefly here.

- Best Practices. One of the fastest, most powerful ways that companies can manage knowledge is through the systematic transfer of best practices. *Best practices* can be defined as "those practices that have produced outstanding results in one situation and that could be adapted for another situation."[17] "Managing knowledge and transferring best practices is simple in concept but difficult in execution."[18]

- Corporate Memory. Corporate memory refers to the enterprise's corporate records, official documents, reference manuals, procedure manuals, policies, and other pertinent business knowledge. For most contemporary enterprises, it includes a vast archive of digital records, as well. It also encompasses the accumulated knowledge, experience, expertise, strategies, stories, assumptions, methodologies, and history of an enterprise as these exist in its employees.

- Data Warehouses and Other Corporate Databases. Most large organizations today have vast amounts of data stored in computer files and databases. Data warehouses and data mining are ways of trying to get at this information to make it more useful for multiple purposes.

- Communities of Practice. *Communities of Practice* are naturally occurring groups of people who come together out of a common interest either on an informal or a formal basis. Participants are motivated by a desire to use and develop their skills and competencies and to work together on issues of common interest.

- Current Operations. Enterprises constantly are generating new knowledge from operations. In today's fast-paced environment, it is extremely important to capture and share this new experience. Enterprises frequently fail to learn from success stories and failures alike, which often go relatively unshared and unanalyzed. Equally devastating, enterprises often learn the wrong lessons or draw the wrong conclusions from current successes or failures. This occurs either because the experience is not adequately evaluated or because it is interpreted in light of past experience (i.e., old paradigms), which may no longer be applicable in today's changing business environment.

- Innovation and Generation of New Knowledge. It is clear that the best knowledge management systems foster and capture new learning and innovation, not just share existing knowledge.

- Outside Information. In addition, enterprises are looking outside their own walls for sources of important knowledge. As enterprises form closer alliances with suppliers, outsourcing vendors, and others, these partners also are being looked to as sources of critical knowledge. Outside contacts can be important sources of knowledge about industries, economics, marketplace trends, customers, and so on.

5.3.1 Knowledge Management and Individual, Group, and Organizational Performance

Much of the current focus on knowledge management deals with managing knowledge on an enterprise level. However, KM also applies on the group and individual levels, and these projects can yield significant benefits. Despite what the conventional KM wisdom suggests about serious efforts to manage organizational knowledge requiring broad scope, top management commitment, and major resource allocations, smaller-scale projects can and do pay off. KM programs also can start small and grow from the ground up.[19] On the other hand, it cannot be assumed that an increase in individual learning automatically leads to an increase in organizational learning. For knowledge to be transferred effectively across the enterprise, attention should be given to how work groups might learn from one another and how this will facilitate continuous improvement.

Thus, it is important when initiating KM projects to be clear about which level(s) is being targeted and what the objectives are. Attention must be paid to the connections between knowledge and learning at the individual, group, and enterprise levels. Explicit strategies are needed to capitalize on knowledge resources in a systematic way to increase innovation, productivity, and performance.

5.3.2 Enterprise Knowledge Management Environments

Thomas Davenport and Laurence Prusak studied various KM projects and identified three broad types of KM objectives on an enterprise level.[20]

1. Attempts to create knowledge repositories. The typical goal of knowledge repositories is to take knowledge embodied in documents—memos, reports, presentations, articles, and so forth—and organize it so that it can be stored and retrieved easily. A somewhat less structured forum of accumulating knowledge is the discussion database, in which participants record their own experience on an issue and react to others' comments. Three basic types of repositories are:
   External knowledge (e.g., competitive intelligence);
   Structured internal knowledge (e.g., research reports); and
   Informal internal knowledge (e.g., discussion database full of know-how).
   Davenport and Prusak studied an automobile company that compiled an external repository of competitive-intelligence knowledge, encompassing analyst reports, trade journal articles, and external market research on industry competitors. Using a software tool called GrapeVINE, the knowledge managers for this project could route information or knowledge on different topics to managers with a specified interest in that topic. Items of particular importance could be prioritized and sent to everyone, thus making the information or knowledge in the system more accessible and useful.
2. Attempts to create knowledge access. Another type of project is providing access to knowledge or facilitating its transfer among individuals. Whereas knowledge repositories capture knowledge itself, knowledge access projects

focus on the possessors and prospective users of knowledge. The primary objective is to find the individual with the knowledge one needs, and then successfully transfer that knowledge from one person to another—a sometimes daunting process. Furthermore, knowledge access projects vary in their technological orientation.

3. Attempts to improve knowledge environment and cultures. A third type of project is to establish an environment conducive to knowledge management. This type of project intends to measure or improve the value of knowledge capital. Objectives include building awareness and cultural receptivity, changing behavior as it relates to knowledge, and improving the knowledge management process. For example, at one direct marketing firm, the goal of KM efforts was to increase awareness and reuse the knowledge embedded in client relationships. The chief knowledge officer, who had no staff, worked through the education and exhortation of others.

Industry studies show growing adoption and growth of KM in business.[21] Although KM gained its first solid foothold in professional services and a few other industries, many other organizations today are actively developing KM programs, including communications, manufacturing, financial services, and government. KM also is becoming less technology focused and more driven by specific business goals. The applications that enterprises are focusing on to achieve their goals, according to the survey, involve knowledge sharing, best practices, and customer-relationship management (see Figure 5-4).

5.3.3 Small-Scale Knowledge Management Projects

As pointed out earlier, many KM proponents believe that KM does not have to be implemented on an enterprise scale to be effective. Although no one denies the value and desirability of having an enterprise knowledge management strategy and top-level leadership in fostering a culture of learning and collaboration, ample evidence exists of good results achieved with smaller-scale KM projects. Thus,

Figure 5-4

Current business applications of KM initiatives

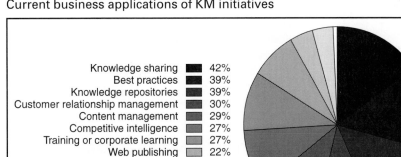

Knowledge sharing	42%
Best practices	39%
Knowledge repositories	39%
Customer relationship management	30%
Content management	29%
Competitive intelligence	27%
Training or corporate learning	27%
Web publishing	22%
Intellectual property management	11%
Supply chain management	10%
Other	2%

Source: Greg Dyer, IDC State of the Market Survey: KM Crosses the Chasm, published in *Knowledge Management Magazine* 3 (March 2000): 52.

sometimes the most effective approach to implementing a KM initiative is to look for low-cost small wins in a single department or community of practice.[22]

When planned and implemented effectively, a small, local KM project can produce immediate benefits and be integrated effectively with the corporate KM program later. Even if it ultimately has to be redesigned to integrate with corporate directions, chances are that everyone involved with the project learned a great deal about what works and what doesn't, which will help ensure the success of future projects. Moreover, early successes can help build needed support for larger-scale projects. "In fact, a collection of carefully conceived, small-scale knowledge projects are more likely to have a positive cumulative impact than any single attempt at enterprise-level change, which often requires enormous amounts of time, resource, and cultural adjustment."[23]

With smaller-scale projects, it is especially important to define the project scope carefully and to develop a realistic estimate of the time and resources required to complete it. In most cases, the scope should be limited to achieving a few clearly defined goals and staying focused on achieving them. One of the best ways to do this is to avoid starting by attempting to define what knowledge or information is needed. It is better to concentrate on why the information is needed and how it is going to be used. Is the goal to expand the scope of a specific group of workers? Is the goal to empower workers who previously did not have adequate information to make important decisions? Is the goal to improve customer service by providing access to customer records so that service representatives can answer inquiries on the first call? Once the goal is clear, it is much easier to define the scope of required information and knowledge and the most appropriate way to organize, capture, and present it.

The other critical point in controlling the scale of a project is the selection and integration of technology. It's important to remember that technology is the enabler, not the goal. Options might be limited by budget, but that does not necessarily have to handicap the project. A limited budget doesn't mean working with outdated or inadequate technology. The technology selected needs to be appropriate for the defined purpose. The latest all-powerful software program might be great, but a number of lower-cost alternatives might achieve the desired results at a much lower cost.

Required approvals will depend upon the project scope and people who will be affected. While top management support could be helpful, it might not be necessary. The most important support is the support of the people who will be affected—the ones who need and will use the KM system.

Ultimately, success at a small-scale KM system might be the best avenue to approval for more extensive projects in the future.

5.4 Second-Generation Knowledge Management

Most proponents of KM stress that it is more about process than about technology. Despite the process rhetoric, much of the recent activity and hype have focused on aligning KM with various technologies and applications. Many software vendors have been repositioning their products for the knowledge management market.

Part II   End-User Information Systems: Business Solutions

CLARICA LIFE INSURANCE: ALIGNING THEORY AND PRACTICE

Clarica is the new name of Mutual Life of Canada, adopted following its demutualization and transition to a public company. Clarica's new brand emphasizes "clarity through dialogue" in the way its 3,000 agents and representatives guide customers through the decision-making process of choosing insurance and investment solutions. The firm, founded in 1870, serves 3 million Canadians and 250,000 Americans from 100 offices across Canada and in two major U.S. cities. It employs 7,000 workers overall.

Clarica has built knowledge management into its organizational structure. It created a strategic capabilities unit (SCU) to support individuals (Clarica calls employees "members") and teams. Individual capability is about developing all of the individuals in the organization, putting learning resources at their disposal, and providing an environment and structure that encourages application of their talents. The individual capability practice leader supports Clarica's membership service group (which has replaced human resources), where both members and their managers access services through the company intranet on a self-initiated basis. For instance, through the Knowledge Depot, members can access just-in-time learning as part of their everyday work.

Organizational capability requires alignment across the enterprise of five components: strategy, structure, processes, culture, and leadership. An organizational capability consultant sits on each of the 12 key business teams in the organization to ensure that these five components are aligned to encourage optimal team performance.

In between is the knowledge team, which provides the enabling technology infrastructure and knowledge architecture as a platform to accelerate learning among individuals and teams, and between the organization and its customers. Six knowledge architects are responsible for learning, career development and achievement management, reward and recognition, workforce planning, competencies and capability modeling, and staffing and recruitment. The knowledge team is responsible for the architecture and the approach to knowledge.

The practice leader for organizational capability focuses at a fundamental level on the shaping of the culture and the development of values-centered leadership.

To Think About: Is Clarica taking an organizational learning (OL) approach or an intellectual assets approach? What benefits did Clarica achieve through KM? How did their KM efforts affect the company's culture and how people work?

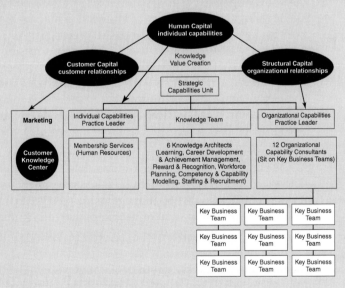

Source: Adapted from Steve Barth, "Clarica Life Insurance: Aligning Theory and Practice," *Knowledge Management Magazine* (May 2000): 24.

Some KM proponents have expressed concern that an overemphasis on technology could be placing the credibility of KM, as a relatively new concept, at risk.

The term *second-generation knowledge management* (SGKM) has emerged among supporters of a less technology-centric view of KM. Second-generation thinking is more inclusive of human resources and process initiatives. Although KM and organizational learning take different approaches at the strategic level, they are increasingly similar in terms of tactics and tools. Supporters of second-generation KM contend that "While much of KM has been made possible by technology, many IT-centric approaches have had limited success. For long-term success, the underlying cultural factors and support systems are key factors."[24] A fundamental flaw in viewing KM as a technology issue is that technology is not holding organizations back. Rather, it is a lack of strategy and a failure to build KM into the organization's day-to-day operations and its culture, and consequently, a failure to gain end user buy-in.[25]

Mark McElroy, a principal with IBM's Knowledge Management Consulting Group, argues for embracing SGKM. "The arrival of second-generation knowledge management," he argues, "includes the introduction of some new terms, new concepts, and new insights that give it some real depth and distinction when compared to first-generation models."[26] These second-generation ideas fall into the following seven categories.

- Supply-side versus demand-side KM
  Whereas first-generation KM emphasizes sharing existing knowledge (i.e., supply-side view), SGKM emphasizes the generation of new knowledge (i.e., a demand-side approach). Thus, SGKM focuses on enhancing the conditions in which innovation and creativity naturally occur. The emphasis is on high-performance learning. "The emergence of SGKM thus signals the convergence of the knowledge management and organizational learning (OL) communities."[27]

- The knowledge life cycle
  SGKM takes a life cycle view of knowledge management, as illustrated in Figure 5-5a. Because first-generation KM approaches tend to assume that knowledge already exists, projects usually begin by stressing codification and transfer issues, after which they invariably turn to technology. In contrast, the SGKM life cycle view starts with creating and validating new knowledge. Knowledge that survives the validation process is then operationalized systematically through codification and knowledge transfer processes. Ultimately, new knowledge displaces old, completing the life cycle.

- Knowledge processes
  SGKM puts the focus on three fundamental knowledge processes: production, validation, and integration. Thus, SGKM proponents advocate new terminology: knowledge PROCESS management. "Feed the processes that spawn the production and integration of new knowledge in human affairs, and innovation and better organizational performance will follow."[28]

- Knowledge as rules
  The theory of SGKM sees both declarative knowledge (know-what) and procedural knowledge (know-how) as rules held collectively by people in organizations, which are practiced en masse from one day to the next. Thus, all knowledge can be expressed in the form of rule sets, such as the example shown in Figure 5-5b.

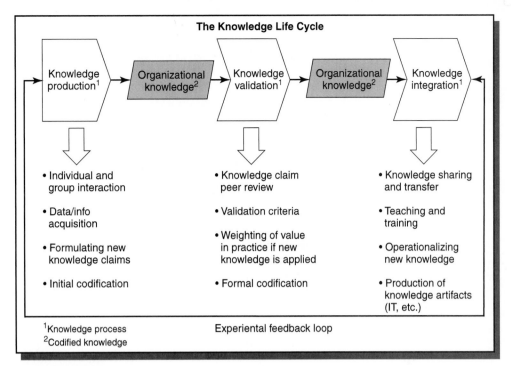

Figure 5-5a

Second-generation knowledge management

Source: Mark McElroy, "White Paper: The Second Generation of KM." *Knowledge Management Magazine* 2 (October 1999): 86.

Figure 5-5b

Second-generation knowledge management

Source: Mark McElroy, "White Paper: The Second Generation of KM." *Knowledge Management Magazine* 2 (October 1999): 86.

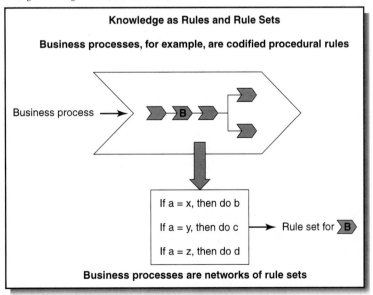

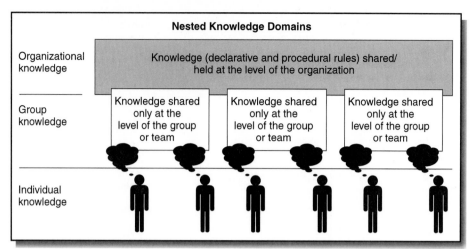

Figure 5-5c
Nested knowledge domains

Source: Mark McElroy, "White Paper: The Second Generation of KM." *Knowledge Management Magazine* 2 (October 1999): 86.

- Knowledge structures
  SGKM views business processes and business strategies as examples of knowledge structures, each of which holds embedded organizational knowledge or codified rule sets. Not all knowledge structures take conventional forms, however; informal storytelling also can play a valuable role.

- Nested knowledge domains
  SGKM clearly distinguishes between individual and organizational learning, something first-generation KM failed to do. SGKM is focused squarely on organizational learning. Its techniques stress the importance of focusing on knowledge processes in knowledge life cycles. SGKM sees knowledge held by individuals as nested within the broader domain of organizational knowledge, as illustrated in Figure 5-5c. The dynamics between these levels give rise to new knowledge through "creative tension."

- Organizational learning (OL)
  One of the most striking distinctions made by SGKM is the explicit connection between knowledge management and organizational learning, in the tradition of Peter Senge. OL is widely regarded as the only sustainable advantage in business: the ability to learn faster than your competitors can. The primary objective of SGKM is seen as increasing an organization's ability to learn effectively.

SGKM provides a new theoretical framework—a theory of knowledge—that up to this point has been absent from KM practice. At this point, the concept is still too new to determine how much influence it will have on the future direction of KM.

5.5 TECHNOLOGY INFRASTRUCTURE FOR KNOWLEDGE MANAGEMENT

Most enterprises already have an information technology infrastructure in place. The typical knowledge worker has a personal desktop with an array of productivity tools linked to the enterprise network and the Internet. This remarkable increase in the availability of information and the equally remarkable increase in the need to apply knowledge to everyday tasks have directly influenced the evolution of knowledge management.[29] A powerful synergistic relationship exists between KM and technology. Technology has made it realistic to share knowledge not only within the enterprise, but across the continent and around the world.

5.5.1 IT as an Enabler for Knowledge Management

Information technology is critical; however, it is not sufficient to enable knowledge management. IT provides the infrastructure for sharing knowledge but does not make it happen. One of the most common mistakes made by enterprises in implementing knowledge management is assuming that putting the technology in place is the major part of the effort. Enterprises must create an environment that supports and rewards information sharing and have a clear strategy and a structured process for achieving it. KPMG Consulting concluded in their *Knowledge Management Research Report* 2000 that "It is not the technology that is holding organizations back but a lack of strategy and a failure to build KM into the organization's day-to-day operations and its culture in order to encourage end-user buy-in."[30] According to Thomas Davenport, "If you're spending more than one-third of your energy on the technology side, you're probably not going to be successful."[31]

Using technology to share data and information is not a startling new concept. Enterprises have been using tools such as mainframe-based e-mail systems, list serves, bulletin boards, conferences, and so forth to share information for more than 15 years. Mainframe-based online reference systems also have been available and used by many companies to create effective performance support systems. What has changed? The answer is the pervasive use of Internet and Intranet technologies and groupware along with the giant leaps in ease of use that they represent. Moreover, widespread exposure to dot.com enterprises has raised awareness of the power of digital networks. In fact, knowledge management is a huge part of e-business.

A growing number of excellent tools can be crafted into solutions tailored to meet an enterprise's needs. Two critical considerations in selecting technologies for knowledge management are ease of use and the ability to integrate it into the process of doing the work. Most authorities stress, however, that selecting the right technologies is only half of the solution, and not the bigger half. The biggest challenge is in deciding how the actual KM solutions will be used and maintained.

KM solutions must support the way in which individuals and groups are organized and how they work. People interpret, understand, use, and share information in situation-specific and task-specific contexts, and they relate knowledge objects to other knowledge objects in different ways. For example, knowledge about customers is interpreted and used differently by a credit manager than by a sales representative. As a general rule of thumb, the simpler the solution is, the better.

5.5.2 Information Technologies That Support Knowledge Transfer

What technologies support and enable knowledge management? Different sources emphasize different technologies, depending somewhat on how broadly they define KM. Viewpoints are evolving and changing rapidly. One point on which everyone seems to agree is that no one out-of-the-box solution exists for KM because it is not something that a single product can provide. Firms apply a wide variety of technologies to the objectives of KM, some of which have been available for years. However, it is the availability of Internet-based systems and collaborative tools, such as Lotus Notes, that many authorities believe were most instrumental in catalyzing the KM movement. The convergence of these networking tools along with a common set of tools for word processing, presentations, spreadsheets, databases, search engines, and more have created an infrastructure for digital information flow that has reached critical mass. A standardized company-wide architecture is important to ensure the sustainability and scalability of KM efforts. Knowledge and best practice sharing are difficult when companies allow the proliferation of separate systems. If a firm does not have the architecture of an organization-wide solution in mind when designing local KM/IT solutions, then the organization will, over time, face problems in integration and scalability; subsequently, it stands to lose much of the leverage knowledge management can create.[32]

The sections that follow provide a brief discussion of key technologies currently used to support KM solutions. The process of selecting and implementing technologies for KM is fundamentally the same as it is for all end-user technologies (see chapters 15 and 16). The three basic steps in selecting a KM technology infrastructure are:[33]

- Determine what you want to be able to do. (What functionality do you need?)
- Design an architecture that will allow you to do this.
- Select the technologies that will accomplish your objectives best.

5.5.2.1   Intranet-Based Solutions

Intranets are private, company-wide networks for posting and disseminating company information. Some authorities credit the emergence of Intranets as the single biggest boost to the concept of KM. In fact, Intranets are credited with enabling groupware and KM systems. Intranets have been successful because they have a single computer interface, which makes them easy to learn and use. The technology makes it possible to merge data streams from different sources in ways that make sense to users or that serve specific needs. Additionally, it allows information displayed to be customized based on specific objectives, such as by work groups; by hardware; or through filters, alerts, and searching.

The single biggest caution is that simply making an Intranet available is not KM. KM is not simply a case of "build it and they will come." An Intranet is nothing more than the platform to enable the building of KM solutions. It is a starting place, not the finish line.

5.5.2.2   Groupware, Especially Lotus Notes

Groupware supports groups and people working together and is built around three key principles: communication, collaboration, and coordination. It allows groups to work together on documents, schedule meetings, route electronic forms, access shared folders, develop shared databases, and send e-mail. Companies use groupware for a variety of reasons ranging from sharing knowledge within work groups to supporting collaborative efforts among geographically dispersed teams. (See chapter 4.) For example, some insurance companies use Lotus Notes to set up on-location claims-paying operations when massive disasters, such as hurricanes, call for prompt handling of large numbers of claims. The World Bank relies on Lotus Notes to help its traveling staff members say in touch when on missions. Ernst & Young, one of the Big Five accounting firms, used Lotus Notes to create a global collaboration environment to help teams in different locations work together on projects.

The Web has spurred development in groupware and collaborative tools. Now virtually every groupware maker has come out with a Web-based version. This means that a combination Web/groupware server lets Web users search company application databases, view contents, and create, edit and delete documents, as well as have interactive forms, threaded discussions, and personal Web pages. Using a browser and a password, employees all over the world can access, share, and track documents.[34]

5.5.2.3 Knowledge Portals

Virtually overnight, portal technology has taken over the function of operating systems, allowing content and data from disparate systems to move in and out of repositories more easily and in the forms users need. Portals enable enterprises to extend knowledge management and business intelligence initiatives within and beyond the walls of their organization in ways that could not have been envisioned just a few years ago.[35] Figure 5-6 illustrates conceptually how portal applications can serve as a hub for organizing various types of KM activities with examples of related products.

Portal software comes in a variety of types designed for different purposes, but the technology is evolving so rapidly that this is expected to continue to change for the foreseeable future and eventually result in consolidations. Some clear, use-defined segments include business to business (B2B), business to employee (B2E), business to consumer (B2C), and vertical portals (vortals) that target specific

Figure 5-6

Portal applications can serve as the hub for organizing various types of KM activities and related products

Source: Peter Ruber, "Portals on a Mission: Second-Generation Portals Combine Knowledge Management and E-Business Applications to Meet Market Requirements," *Knowledge Management Magazine* 3 (April 2000): 44.

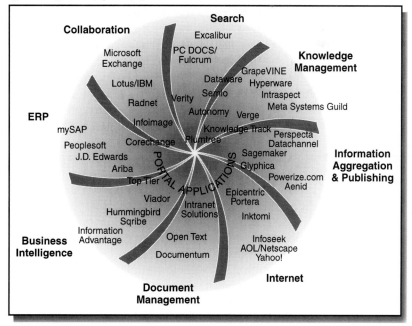

industries. These segments include subcategories or technological classifications such as structured and unstructured data portals, mobile portals, hosted portals, collaborative portals, and application integration portals.[36]

Currently, the business-to-business and collaborative portals are of most interest for KM. Business-to-employee portals provide a point of aggregation for corporate knowledge bases, which departmental employees can search with a desktop browser. Web-based portals for collaboration and project management are coming to market. These portals can be set up by groups of users, and these work groups can align and realign as needed. Early adopters include professional service firms, which use collaborative portals to manage internal knowledge bases and collaboration with clients.

5.5.2.4 Knowledge Transfer and Exchange

A number of KM tools fall into the category termed *knowledge transfer and exchange*.[37] Discussed here are structured document repositories, pointer systems, document exchange, document management, workflow/process management, and videoconferencing.

Structured document repositories organize content into short descriptions that can be stored in conventional relational databases. Some companies have created repositories of best practices with short descriptions and perhaps pointers to contacts in the firm who have knowledge about those best practices. Other examples include databases that provide customer data or competitor intelligence. Knowledge repositories also include computerized databases of published materials, such as Lexis/Nexis and Dialog, which have been around for decades. *Discussion databases* might include listserves, bulletin boards, news groups, threaded electronic discussions, or groupware-based discussion groups.

Pointer systems are directories of internal expertise, human resource listings, personnel profiles, or other corporate skills repositories. The objective is to make it easy to identify and contact workers who have specific skills or knowledge.

Document exchange now is handled primarily through e-mail. In fact, it has become so fast and easy to exchange documents that some workers complain of information overload. The downside of e-mail is that it is largely unfiltered and uncategorized.

Document management is a way of storing, locating, and controlling documents throughout their life cycle on local or wide-area networks. Gartner Group estimates that most knowledge workers spend as much as 20 percent to 40 percent of their time managing documents. Document management occurs on the individual, work group, and enterprise levels. At the enterprise level, document management is generally a highly structured process. At the work group level, it is usually far less structured, and at the individual level there are seldom structured efforts to provide any level of consistency or coordination.

Workflow/process management systems route work from one activity, role, or process to another, based on business rules. They tie activities together in a logical sequence and track the status of work as it moves through the system. Users easily can determine the status of work at any point in the flow. A workflow system, for example, might support processes triggered by outside events, such as customer or supplier transactions, and facilitate moving those transactions step by step through the system to completion.

Videoconferencing is growing but not yet commonplace on the desktop. As newer Internet-based technologies evolve and camera prices continue to drop, it is anticipated that videoconferencing at the desktop will continue to grow.

5.5.2.5 Search and Retrieval

Search engines are tools for locating specific information or sites on the Internet or an Intranet. Search-and-retrieval vendors have made KM the cornerstone of their recent product plans and marketing campaigns. Dataware Technologies, Excalibur, Fulcrum, and Verity offer engines that in one query will search hundreds of document formats across multiple repositories. Users can create agents that perform specific searches regularly and deliver the results via personalized Web pages or push technology.

5.5.2.6 Databases

Database vendors are positioning a new class of database management system, so-called universal databases, to play a central role in KM architectures. IBM, Informix Software, Oracle, and Sybase all have introduced variants on the universal database. The systems manage data in many different forms—documents, spreadsheets, photographs, video clips, or sound bites—and that makes them ideal KM platforms, the database vendors say. Oracle has developed a text-search engine, called Oracle Context Cartridge, that works with the Oracle8 database and allows e-mail, spreadsheets, and documents to be searched and summarized in the database with the same security, backup, and recovery capabilities of relational data.

5.5.2.7 Performance Support Systems

Performance support systems (PSS) are used to support individual job performance and learning—a kind of just-in-time learning and help. Gloria Gery, an expert in performance support, says that the goal of an electronic performance support system is to provide whatever is necessary to generate performance and learning at the moment of need. This kind of support always has required human beings in the past. We now have the means to model, represent, structure, and implement that support electronically—and to make it universally and consistently available on demand any time, any place, and regardless of situation, without unnecessary intermediaries being involved in the process.[38]

PSS can be implemented in many and diverse ways depending on requirements, available technology, developer skill, and resources, and they can be more or less powerful. The common denominator that differentiates a PSS from other types of systems, according to Gery, is the degree to which it integrates information, tools, and methodology for the user. These systems are generally most useful for complex jobs that require a high level of training and expertise, especially when continual learning is required to keep up with changing regulations, rules, or technologies, for example.

Sales and call center support systems are good examples of this type of solution. These systems usually support direct customer interaction and rely heavily on effective training and expertise. A call center might provide customized guidance for resolving different types of problems at varying levels of detail, which the user could select as needed. It might incorporate scripts for customer interaction (tacit knowledge made explicit) and expert systems to aid in problem identification and resolution.

At MassMutual Financial Group, managers realized that the growing complexity of financial products made it hard to keep the hundreds of life insurance customer support representatives around the country trained and up to date. When they developed a new application processing system, they incorporated an extensive electronic performance support system that provides just-in-time help and online reference. The PSS provides help and information at varying levels of detail depending on the needs of the user at the moment. The user can start at the most concise level and drill down for additional detail, if needed. The help is context specific. For example, if the user were required to select options for an insurance policy, only those options applicable to the specific type of policy in the applicant's state of residence would be displayed (perhaps a list of six options out of hundreds of possibilities). If the user were unfamiliar with any of these choices, he or she could drill down for additional detail as needed.

5.5.2.8 Data Analysis Systems

Data analysis systems (also called analytical processing) discussed here include data mining and simulation software. A number of other analytical processing tools also may be used as part of KM systems, such as on-line analytical processing and knowledge discovery.

Data mining tools are used to analyze data from data warehouses and convert it into usable knowledge for decision making. A data warehouse consolidates data from many sources and in many forms. The data are converted into a consistent, uniform format (i.e., cleansed) and organized so that users can extract data for their business purposes. Note that most KM authorities do not consider the data in data warehouses as knowledge. Data mining tools are used to identify trends, to uncover implicit relationships that would be extremely difficult for people to spot in a sea of data, and to extract hard-to-get data. Data mining has become popular with retail chains, airlines, financial institutions, and other businesses for analyzing customer activity and tailoring services. For example, airlines mine customer data to determine optimum fares on particular routes. Retail chains mine data from the point-of-sale registers (checkout counters) to analyze patterns in the way customers shop and use it to optimize store displays or target sales promotions, for instance.

Simulation software allows users to test decisions before putting them into practice. Simulation software can be purchased off the shelf or custom designed. Custom-designed systems can be expensive to produce, but off-the-shelf systems, such as project management, provide a cost-effective training tool that goes beyond classroom lessons to give workers simulated application experience.

5.5.2.9 Artificial Intelligence (AI)

Although AI has been around for a long time, KM has spurred a rebirth of interest in AI. The goals of AI sound remarkably like those of KM. Researchers at MIT's AI lab foresee AI linking human and computer expertise; anticipating and distilling needed information; and providing decision makers with the right information at the right time, in the right quantity, and in the right form.[39] AI technologies—such as genetic algorithms, neural networks, bayesian reasoning, rule induction algorithms, fuzzy logic, fuzzy concept mapping, case-based reasoning, and expert systems—are all finding their way into products for the KM environment. Two—case-based reasoning and expert systems—that appear to have the most widespread applicability initially are discussed here.

Case-based reasoning (CBR) tools are problem resolution systems that allow companies to retain, retrieve, and reuse solutions, called cases. These cases generally are expressed as a series of problem characteristics or probable scenarios coupled with proven solutions. CBR takes users through iterations of questions and answers to locate relevant experiential knowledge to help classify the problem and solve it. Users may add cases as new problems or solutions are identified. Typical applications include Help-Desk operations, customer service centers, medical diagnosis, equipment maintenance, and other areas that involve recurring questions or problems.

Expert systems can be used to develop job aids for decision making. An expert system has a knowledge base, which contains the logic of how the human expert makes a specific decision, plus an inference engine that uses the facts and rules in the knowledge base to arrive at a conclusion for a specific problem. Users interact with the expert system much as they might a human expert. When provided a problem, the system might provide a single answer or pose several alternatives. The response generally includes an explanation of how the system arrived at the recommended solution. Use of expert systems generally is limited to well-structured problems, such as granting credit, that can be limited to no more than a few thousand rules.

5.5.2.10 Intelligent Agents

Intelligent agents are software programs that work in the background to carry out specific, repetitive tasks for an individual user, business process, or software application. The agent uses a built-in or learned knowledge base to accomplish tasks or make decisions on behalf of the user. The use of intelligent agents is growing. Some of the most familiar intelligent agents are the Wizards found in Microsoft Office Suite and agents used to cruise networks, including the Internet, in search of information. They are becoming especially popular in e-commerce applications to help users find products or services and compare prices or features. Users of Yahoo! and Excite, for example, can avail themselves of a "shopping agent" to help them shop for certain products, such as music, toys, or books. The shopper simply enters information about the desired product into a form and sends the shopping agent off to search. The agent reports back with a list of Web sites that sell the product along with prices and a purchase link.

5.5.2.11 Visualization

Visualization refers to presentation of data by technologies such as digital images, geographical information systems, multidimensional tables and graphs, virtual reality, three-dimensional presentations, and animation. Visualization software packages offer users capabilities for self-guided exploration and visual analysis of large amounts of data.

Virtual reality systems, for example, have simulation capabilities that go way beyond conventional computer-aid design (CAD) systems. They use interactive graphics software to create computer-generated simulations that are so close to reality that users feel like they are participating in a real-world situation. Visualization is just starting to provide benefits in business, educational, and scientific work. At Boston's Brigham and Women's Hospital, for instance, surgeons are using virtual reality systems in which a three-dimensional representation of the brain using CT and MRI scans is superimposed on live video. Using this system, surgeons can pinpoint the location of a tumor in the brain with 0.5 millimeter accuracy. Virtual reality applications are being developed for the Web using a standard Virtual Reality Modeling Language (VRML). VRML is a set of specifications for interactive, three-dimensional modeling on the World Wide Web that can organize multiple media types, including animation, images, and audio, to put users in a simulated, real-world environment. VRML is platform independent, operates over a desktop computer, and requires little bandwidth. Users can download a three-dimensional virtual world designed using VRML from a server over the Internet using a Web browser.

5.5.2.12 *Knowledge Management Software*

Although no single out-of-the-box solution exists, a number of vendors market niche KM products. Firms vying for leadership in KM software include startups like FireDrop Inc., Semio Corp. (Taxonomy), and Tacit Knowledge Systems Inc. (Knowledge Mail). Other contenders include established business-intelligence tool vendors such as Cognos Inc. and document-management software suppliers such as Documentum Inc., that are tailoring their products for KM projects.

IBM/Lotus's KM server, code named *Raven,* has a core discovery engine made up of two components: an expertise locator and a content catalog. The expertise locator, a searchable repository of profiles of fellow employees and information about their skills and areas of expertise, serves as a "Who's Who" within an organization. The locator creates the profiles based on the content of documents that people write and post to a network. The content catalog provides users with a means of tracking down documents (including Word files, spreadsheets, and e-mail) within a corporate network, data within database systems, and external HTML-based content. Atop this engine is a KM portal that provides individuals with a means of aggregating and managing the content to which they have access, and personalizing their view of the content and applications that run on Raven. The KM system also includes collaboration capabilities. This package puts together multiple KM functions in a single integrated package.

Microsoft crafted Exchange 2000 with KM in mind. It offers workflow features, as well as improved content-indexing and retrieval capabilities. Microsoft also has structured data within its SQL Server database and documents created with Microsoft Office, all accessible through its Digital Dashboard portal.

A somewhat more structured technology for bringing external knowledge into an organization, GrapeVINE (GrapeVINE Technologies) is used by firms such as Hewlett Packard, Arthur Andersen Consulting, and Ford Motor Company. It can be combined with Lotus Notes for purposes of distribution and alignment with other knowledge management applications. GrapeVINE searches through external databases not on the basis of simple keywords, but rather on a "knowledge chart"—a hierarchical map of an organization's knowledge terms and relationships. The chart is not easy to construct and maintain, but it can allow a more strategic perspective of what knowledge really matters to the organization. GrapeVINE also allows designated knowledge editors to comment on and prioritize—in other words, add value to—external data captured by GrapeVINE.

5.6 MEASURING THE VALUE OF KNOWLEDGE AND KNOWLEDGE MANAGEMENT

The concept of knowledge as an asset that has economic value to an enterprise has evolved. Although most people would agree intuitively that knowledge has value to a firm, quantifying it as an asset on the balance sheet is another matter.

Measuring the economic value of knowledge management initiatives is a critical challenge for enterprises. The more closely a project is tied to specific business objectives, the easier it is to quantify the benefit. For example, if a KM system is developed to support a Help Desk or customer service operation, the benefits could be quantified against benchmarks established prior to implementing the KM system. Typical benchmarks in this situation might include number of problems resolved on the first call, average time to resolve a problem, customer satisfaction measures, and number of staff required to handle call volumes.

KM initiatives with broader objectives related to information sharing, innovation, continuous learning, and raising the enterprise's overall knowledge IQ are harder to quantify. Difficulties relate to a number of factors. The most ambitious KM efforts aim to transform how people work so that the organization as a whole will become more innovative and flexible. Transformations happen slowly and generally do not yield quick benefits. Proponents of KM projects are often in a position where they know the investments will provide important benefits but cannot define precisely what the benefits will be or when they will come. Nonetheless, comprehensive KM efforts are rightly directed at long-term, systemic change, rather than more immediate and easily measurable efficiencies.

Another difficulty in assessing economic value is that many knowledge benefits are intangible. Better decision making, higher-quality work, more sharing, better morale, a more collaborative culture, and more responsiveness to customers are descriptions of qualitative improvements that are hard to quantify. Some measures used to assess knowledge project success, such as the number of documents in a repository, the number of times a particular piece of intellectual content is downloaded from a system, or the amount of traffic on a system, tell nothing about the value of the content stored or shared, or whether it actually helped anyone in the firm do better work.

5.7 BARRIERS TO INTERNAL TRANSFER OF KNOWLEDGE

Although the idea of identifying, sharing, and transferring knowledge and best practices seems logical and simple, implementing it is much more complex and time-consuming than most people imagine. Efforts tend to be thwarted by a variety of logistical, structural, and cultural hurdles and deterrents present in organizations, which act as *barriers* to knowledge transfer. Research has revealed that a practice can go unrecognized and unshared for years in a company. Even when recognized, it still took more than two years on average before other sites began to try actively to adopt the practice, if at all. Research identified four primary barriers to the effective transfer of knowledge and best practice within enterprises.[40]

Reason 1: Ignorance. Those who have the knowledge are not aware that others may find it useful. At the same time, those who could benefit from the knowledge have no idea that someone in the company already has it.

Reason 2: No absorptive capacity. Even when workers knew of the knowledge or best practice, they lacked the money, time, and management resources to pursue and study it in enough detail to make it useful.

Reason 3: The lack of preexisting relationships. People absorb knowledge and practice from other people they know, respect, and—often—like. If two managers have no personal bond or link that preestablishes trust, they are unlikely to incorporate each other's experiences into their own work.

CULTURAL EVOLUTION: CENTRALIZED KNOWLEDGE MANAGEMENT STRATEGY PERPETUATES KNOWLEDGE-SHARING ENVIRONMENT AT ASTRA PHARMACEUTICALS

Research and development (R&D) is the pharmaceutical industry's knowledge-intensive strong suit or its Achilles' heel, depending upon how companies fare in the race to get products to market. Astra Pharmaceuticals has developed a cross-enterprise Knowledge Management Program Office (KMPO) to oversee knowledge-sharing processes and technologies so that new knowledge is leveraged instead of being replicated.

Creation of this office, said Beverly Buckta, knowledge management leader of the KMPO, came out of a need to start addressing information overload and to try to coordinate better. "We wanted to have more dynamic content and enable more effective decision making," Buckta said.

Astra Pharmaceuticals, the U.S. marketing and product development arm of Sweden's Astra AB, was created in June 1998 from the merger of Astra Merck and Astra USA. The twelfth-largest pharmaceutical company in the United States, Astra Pharmaceuticals reported net sales of $3.6 billion in 1998. Organized around cross-functional teams, it makes extensive use of information technology and encourages a corporate culture of sharing knowledge.

Astra put the KMPO under the umbrella of Knowledge Services & Information Resources, which provides enterprise-wide information technology (IT) and infrastructure services. Although it is not unusual to see KM projects tied to IT, Astra Pharmaceuticals made the much less common decision to include people from the world of library and information science in key KMPO positions. The two individuals most responsible for the implementation of KM at Astra, Buckta and Jennifer Klein (director of knowledge services and information resources), have backgrounds in this discipline. According to Klein, "Rather than having an unmanageable flow of information, we are trying to build the paradigm where the information that you need and keep track of will be kept current. Our backgrounds in library science enable us to effectively address the challenge of creating and managing a knowledge management infrastructure." The combination of IT and information science provides the KMPO with strong competencies in the principles of information management, content organization, indexing, search and retrieval, content development, and database design. The melding of IT and information science is a very powerful one.

The KMPO is responsible for providing a framework for implementing an enterprise-wide KM infrastructure, designing and implementing the company's intranet growth strategy, and managing the process for adding content to the intranet. An enterprise-wide perspective allows the KMPO to identify redundancies, common needs across teams, and orphaned or out-of-date content. It also means that the KMPO can be more neutral in working across team and department cultures.

When someone wants to publish information—build a Web site on the intranet or create a Lotus Notes database—they fill out a KM submission form. Because teams submit their ideas and plans through a centralized process, the KMPO can easily spot content that already exists elsewhere within the company. When the KMPO receives multiple requests for the same content, it meets with the stakeholders and recommends that one of the teams take responsibility for, or ownership of, that information and manage the Web site. The biggest short-term advantage from KM is in situations where employees do not have to reinvent the wheel. For instance, if a researcher can find somebody that solved a similar challenge with a substructure or someone that has already documented the toxicity profile of a particular family of compounds, they need not duplicate the work.

An early example of KMPO flagging a common request centered on information about team members. By working with the teams to decide who should "own" and manage the content, they were able to avoid the multiplication of sites that would duplicate information already existing at Astra. Initially, everybody who planned to create a departmental home page wanted to include information about team members—for example, pictures, roles, contact information—on their sites. "Rather than have each team build and manage the content specific to their team, we worked with our corporate communications department to create a centrally managed electronic picture book that teams could leverage as they designed their respective home pages," Klein said. "Corporate Communications was identified as the content sponsor based on the historic role they played in creating the company's hard copy picture book." Owners, or sponsors, of content have a responsibility to keep the content current and accurate, while evolving site content as the need grows. The KMPO feels that its efforts identifying and supporting content sponsors creates numerous operating efficiencies, including reduced effort, saved time and money, and miximized organizational expertise.

Typically, as teams begin to build sites on the intranet, they envision only other members from their team as their audience. While some information requires restricted access for legal and regulatory reasons, Buckta said the KMPO encourages teams to make access to the content unrestricted across the whole company. Because of the KMPO's central role, it has been able to point out to reluctant teams that requests for similar information often comes from other teams. These same people get excited, Buckta said, when they see that they have something to deliver that is needed by areas of which they were not aware.

There is no value in building a Web page on an Intranet unless that page is a gateway to the right kind of information. Approaching the Intranet at a corporate level has given the KMPO a holistic approach to KM, enabling it to leverage information, knowledge, and expertise across the enterprise while reducing redundancies and saving time and effort. Perhaps more importantly, the KMPO helps foster a growing knowledge culture at Astra Pharmaceuticals.

To Think About: How did Astra Pharmaceuticals' decision to centralize responsibility for knowledge management influence the results they have achieved? What was the significance of combining the expertise and perspectives of both IT and information science? What benefits has Astra Pharmaceuticals derived from its knowledge management program? What are some of the key factors that have contributed to the success of Astra's cross-functional approach to knowledge management? What is the importance of knowledge management for pharmaceutical companies such as Astra Pharmaceuticals?

Source: Adapted from Michael Robin, "Best Practice: Cultural Evolution: Centralized KM Strategy Perpetuates Knowledge-Sharing Environment at Astra Pharmaceuticals," *Knowledge Management Magazine* 2 (May 1999): 16–17.

Reason 4: Lack of motivation. Workers may not perceive a clear business reason for pursuing the transfer of knowledge and best practices.

Although personal elements are involved, these hurdles are generally the result of organizational structures, management practices, and measurement systems that discourage—rather than encourage—information sharing within an organization. Therefore, it is not sufficient to put in place strategies and platforms for knowledge management. Enterprises must consciously dismantle these systemic barriers, as well.

5.8   PLANNING FOR KNOWLEDGE MANAGEMENT

Introducing and implementing knowledge management strategy on an enterprise level is a major undertaking. It takes strong leadership, commitment, and courage on the part of sponsors and advocates. For most enterprises, it requires not only vision and preparation but major changes in culture and business processes, as well. Whether an enterprise begins with a comprehensive strategy or smaller-scale project, thoughtful planning is important. Fundamentally, the planning process is similar to planning for all EUIS projects (see part V). This section highlights some important considerations for KM projects. A more comprehensive discussion of project planning is covered in chapter 13.

5.8.1 Responsibilities

Identifying the need for a KM officer (KMO) and choosing the right person might be one of the greatest challenges. The role of KMO requires a visionary who has the ability to assess what the company has achieved and position it for future growth. At the same time, the KMO has to have the technical understanding to exploit corporate data and rapidly evolving information technologies, but most importantly, to understand the difference between data and knowledge. A KMO profile includes the following traits.[41]

- Ambition to succeed
- Expressiveness
- Responsiveness: the ability to take immediate, appropriate action
- Leadership
- Articulateness
- Appreciation of others' efforts
- Social skills
- Dependability
- A strong work ethic
- A vision of future growth

One might add to this list an understanding of organizational learning; change management; and the dynamics of innovation, productivity, and performance. Finding an individual with such broad experience and perspective is truly a challenge. Equally critical to visionary leadership is wide involvement in formulating strategies and plans. Project teams should be representative and appropriate given the scope of the project.

5.8.2 Project Strategy, Scope, and Budget

Setting the direction for the KM project and defining the project scope and budget are critical first steps. The strategy should articulate a knowledge management vision, articulate the knowledge management value proposition, and assess readiness for change. In defining the strategy for the project, it is important to identify the goals clearly in measurable terms. At this point, the focus should not be on defining what knowledge is wanted but on why it is wanted. Is it to improve responsiveness to customer inquiries? To increase customer satisfaction? To what level? To increase innovation in product development? Is the intent to empower individuals who previously were unable to make important decisions? Clear, measurable goals will provide a framework for determining key design issues, such as what knowledge is needed, by whom, for what purpose, and in what format.

Clear goals are important not only to determining the project strategy, but also to defining the project scope and budget. Sometimes the best strategy is to plan big and start small. If well planned, this approach provides an opportunity to demonstrate the success and value of KM within a framework that provides for future scalability and flexibility. Regardless, the project scope must be defined clearly at the outset.

Another crucial step is developing a budget. The extent of resources will be determined by the scope of the project. KM projects can be costly but are not necessarily so. Clear goals with measurable outcomes that directly relate to achievement of business strategies can increase greatly the likelihood of budget approval. If the project strategy and scope are defined clearly, it also might be possible to consider alternative designs and technologies that could be less costly but still achieve project goals. If resources are limited or the budget fails to gain approval, the project objectives and scope might have to be reevaluated and scaled back.

These steps are critical in order to gain needed commitment to the plan and to formulate a communication strategy for making KM principles and objectives well understood by the organization.

5.9 A MODEL FOR TRANSFERRING KNOWLEDGE AND BEST PRACTICES

According to O'Dell and Grayson, the overwhelming majority of KM success stories involve the transfer of best practices. Some of the results reported in *If Only We Knew What We Know* include the following success stories.

- Buckman Laboratories credits their transfer of knowledge and best practice system with helping to boost new product-related revenues by 10 percent and sales of new products by about 50 percent. Responding to customer inquiries about products now takes hours instead of weeks.

- Texas Instruments generated $1.5 billion in annual increased fabrication capacity by comparing and transferring best practices among its existing 13 fabrication plants. Plant managers and teams from Texas Instruments's Semiconductor Group, led by that group's president (now TI president and CEO) Tom Engibous, created the equivalent capacity of an additional semiconductor wafer fabrication plant, thereby avoiding a $500 million investment and providing needed capacity to customers. They called it a "free fab" and have repeated this triumph two more times, for a total of more than $1.5 billion in cost avoidance, in addition to going from last (1992) to first (1994) in on-time delivery satisfaction in customer rankings.

- At Dow Chemical, early efforts to manage intellectual capital brought an immediate kickback in the form of $40 million in savings. Analysis of existing patents to determine which technology streams were the strongest and which were weakest allowed more effective negotiations with joint venture partners.

- At Kaiser Permanente, benchmarking of their internal best practices helped drastically cut the time it took to open a new Woman's Health Clinic. In addition, it opened smoothly with no costly start-up problems.

- Skandia has leveraged internal know-how to dramatically reduce start-up time for new ventures to 7 months, compared to an industry average of 7 years.

- At Andersen Consulting, a Global Best Practice Knowledge base has improved the quality of services, helped lower research costs, and shortened delivery time in business consulting.

- Chevron's network of 100 people who share ideas on energy-use management has generated an initial $150 million savings in Chevron's annual power and fuel expense by sharing and implementing ideas to reduce company-wide energy costs. Chevron credited this best-practice transfer team with generating more than $650 million in savings.

Based on several years of research and experience with more than 70 companies, O'Dell and Grayson have developed a model for knowledge and best practice transfer. This model has three major components:

1. The value proposition
2. The enablers
3. The four-phase change process

These three components are described briefly in the sections that follow and are illustrated in Figure 5-7.

1. *The value proposition.* The first step toward profitable management of knowledge assets is having a clearly defined purpose—the right value proposition. The enterprise starts by identifying the problem or process that will be targeted for improvement. Every enterprise has different reasons for wanting to transfer knowledge and best practices. Value propositions tend to fall into three basic categories:
   - Customer intimacy. This strategy focuses on capturing and using knowledge across the company about how to market, sell, and service customers more efficiently and effectively.
   - Product-to-market excellence. This strategy focuses on using best practices in product development to accelerate time to market.
   - Operational excellence. This strategy focuses on boosting operational excellence by transferring best practices from one plant or location to receptive sites throughout the global organization.
2. *The Four Enablers.* The second component is creating the right environment for transfer of knowledge and best practices. Four key enablers that must be understood and leveraged are culture, technology, infrastructure, and measurement.
   - Culture. A culture supportive of knowledge management has strong professional ethics and pride supported by well-honed skills in teaming, including cross-functional teams. It also helps to have a common approach for thinking about work, improvement, and process. If an enterprise is not so fortunate as to start with a supportive culture, it must be willing to expend efforts to create such a culture or risk failure.
   - Technology. Technology—especially the Internet, Intranet, and groupware—provide the platform for KM. However, technology is necessary but not sufficient. The key is understanding the limitations as well as the power of technology.
   - Infrastructure. To work effectively, KM must be institutionalized into the enterprise through the creation of new support systems, new job responsibilities, new teams, and new formalized networking. Transfer of knowledge and best practices doesn't happen automatically; it requires a process and an infrastructure of people committed to facilitating the process.
   - Measurement. While this is the least-developed aspect of KM, it is important to measure the projects and business processes that are being improved through knowledge management and let the users evaluate the contribution. "Without measurable success, enthusiasm from employees and management will dissipate. And without measurable success, you won't be able to tell what works and what doesn't."[42]

3. *The Four-Phase Process.* The O'Dell and Grayson model provides a simple four-phase methodology for implementing knowledge management programs: plan, design, implement, and scale-up. Although this basic method has proven to be effective for a broad range of knowledge management projects, every enterprise is different and the actual steps and issues are never identical. Moreover, it takes more than good project management; excellent diagnostic and change management skills are also critical to meaningful design and execution. Details on the four-phase process follow.

1. Plan. The first phase involves assessing the current opportunities, defining specific objectives (the value proposition), identifying a champion for the project, preparing the organization, and defining the business case.

2. Design. The comprehensive design phase involves determining the scale of the initiative, defining the KM process, and outlining the roles and functions of people and technologies, as well as any necessary overlay to the organizational structure and performance measures. The outcome includes a comprehensive action plan with required resources.

3. Implementation. The third phase is to put the plan and design into action. It normally involves a pilot program that will test new ideas and yield lessons in what works and what does not. It involves training participants, providing support, observing, learning, and assessing results.

4. Scale-up. The final phase involves scaling up the pilot to an enterprise-wide process to capture the full benefits of effective transfer. It is important at this point to capture success stories and use them for learning and promoting the contributions of knowledge management. At this point, the enterprise also must be prepared to create new organizational structures to oversee the ongoing process.

Figure 5-7

A model for knowledge and best practice transfer

Source: Reprinted with the permission of The Free Press, a Division of Simon & Schuster, Inc., from IF WE ONLY KNEW WHAT WE KNOW: The Transfer of Internal Knowledge and Best Practice By Carla O'Dell and C. Jackson Grayson, Jr. with Nilly Essaides. Copyright © 1998 by Carla O'Dell and C. Jackson Grayson, Jr.

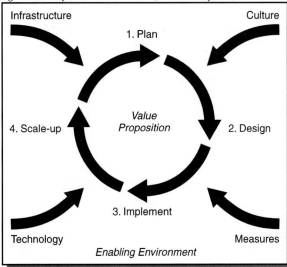

5.10   DEFINING AN ENTERPRISE KNOWLEDGE MANAGEMENT ARCHITECTURE

Many organizations take an enterprise-level approach to knowledge management. The objective is to leverage better the vast information resources and knowledge—both explicit and tacit—that exist within the enterprise. For organizations with well-defined core competencies and business processes, KM can be a logical next step to improve organizational performance. It is also an essential component of establishing the value of knowledge as an asset. Enterprise knowledge management environments can be expensive endeavors to establish and maintain. Thus, an effective business case must be made to identify the objectives and anticipated benefits and to justify the cost. As pointed out earlier, the benefits and payback for enterprises from KM can be substantial.

5.10.1   Knowledge Infrastructure

Building an enterprise-level KM architecture generally begins with a process of identifying existing knowledge resources within the enterprise. The end result is a knowledge infrastructure or knowledge map (K-map). This can be a daunting task, and is, in fact, a place where many enterprises get bogged down early in the KM process. In a large enterprise, it can take several months. Because the enterprise is generally just at the beginning of their KM endeavors, the experience level with knowledge management is probably limited at this point. Therefore, participants in the process may be relatively unsure how KM is going to work and what the benefits will be for them personally. For this reason, enterprises may want to get their feet wet with a few smaller projects or one department or division rather than the entire enterprise—even if they have to go back and rework some areas later.

The project team charged with developing the K-map will include key individuals from various parts of the enterprise. These individuals should be familiar with overall operations and the information resources used within their departments or divisions. It is also helpful to include team members with expertise in information classification, such as records management managers or librarians.

Developing the knowledge infrastructure or map involves many steps. The K-map usually will be representative of the business model. Thus, depending on how well the enterprise's business processes are defined, it may be necessary to go back and review or define business processes as part of developing the K-Map. A knowledge map essentially identifies, organizes, and presents a comprehensive picture of all important knowledge sources and locations throughout the enterprise. Developing this K-map is a typical process of gathering information, analyzing findings, and documenting results. One example of the steps in a typical K-mapping process is shown in Figure 5-8.

5.10.2   Functionality Requirements

Although many potential configurations of knowledge management technology exist, a common set of functions appears to be emerging in the literature. Different sources classify them in different ways. We have elected to use here, as representative, a classification scheme suggested by Jan Duffy in her book *Harvesting Experience: Reaping the Benefits of Knowledge.* The classification scheme outlined here is meant to provide a broad overview of typical functionality for KM environments.

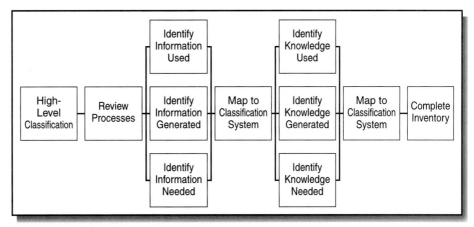

Figure 5-8

Developing the knowledge map

Source: Excerpted from *Harvesting Experience: Reaping the Benefits of Knowledge.* Copyright 1999 by ARMA International. Used with permission.

The objective of a planning team would be to pinpoint the specific functionality needed for their organization to achieve the agreed-upon business objectives.

- Getting where you need to be. Options to consider include pointers to paper or document images, hyperlinks, e-mail hot links, navigation links, internal business application links, and external links.

- Finding what you need. Functionality to consider includes search functions, fuzzy searching, query functions, intelligent push based on a profile or event, and knowledge mining.

- Storing what you've found. Storage options to consider are multidimensional cataloging/indexing, unclassified information, expiration/supersede dates, knowledge rules, and resource directories of subject experts and others.

- Tracking where you've been. Approaches for tracking include personal navigation trail (access path), evolving trail of knowledge (history), and usage audit trails.

- Providing support for using knowledge. Support options include online collaboration and learning, multimedia support, and performance measures support.

5.10.3   Technology Architecture

The technology architecture provides the framework for the various components of the KM system and their relationships to each other. The technology architecture should reflect the knowledge strategy. An example of a knowledge architecture is shown in Figure 5-9. Major components are: user interface, knowledge metamodel, knowledge repository, and knowledge access tools, which are described briefly in the section that follows.

- The user interface.

    A simple, easy-to-understand user interface is critical for acceptance and use of any system. The user should be able to understand easily and relate to the metaphor for representing the classes of information (see chapter 10). An effective metaphor hides the underlying complexities of the system and

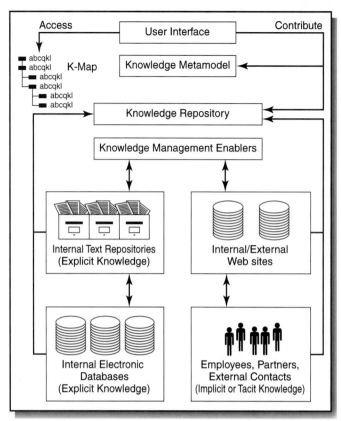

Figure 5-9

Knowledge management technology architecture

Source: Excerpted from Harvesting Experience: Reaping the Benefits of
Knowledge. Copyright 1999 by ARMA International. Used with permission.

presents a logical view of the knowledge objects in the knowledge base. The
interface ideally should behave much like an Internet browser. The more consistent the KM interface is with the desktop technology platform with which
users are already familiar, the easier the learning curve will be.

User input is critical to designing an effective interface. The usability of
the design should be tested thoroughly by representative users during the
design process when adjustments can be incorporated easily into the final
design. Usability testing should not be an add-on at the end of the process.

- Knowledge metamodel.

"The knowledge metamodel is the heart of the knowledge management
environment because it houses the context that makes the knowledge valuable and meaningful." It provides the context or knowledge about knowledge, known to KM professionals as metaknowledge. "Everything in the
knowledge infrastructure works according to the metamodel and the metaknowledge that it contains."[43]

A metamodel usually contains information about the types of knowledge
objects, such as documents, e-mail, data file, person with special expertise, or
other types. It describes the knowledge object, such as creation date, author,
recipient, subject, software used, location, list of persons authorized to access
it, related documents, and more. The metamodel also contains business rules

associated with the use of a particular knowledge object. Since the whole notion of using technology to share knowledge is relatively new, few standards govern KM infrastructure design and development.

If metamodels have been developed independently for other projects, the interfaces may be incompatible. However extensible markup language (XML) is emerging as the metaknowledge language of choice. It defines the syntax and rules that govern the preparation of metaknowledge so that it can be interpreted, processed, and communicated by multiple applications. XML is a subset of standard general markup language (SGML), which is the metalanguage that defines hypertext markup language (HTML).

- Knowledge map.

    The knowledge map or K-map is a visual representation of enterprise knowledge. It identifies the links between existing islands of information and represents all categories of knowledge and the relationships among them.

- Knowledge repository.

    "In implementations where the knowledge repository is a separate physical layer, the repository gathers all of an enterprise's separate knowledge objects from disparate information systems and transforms them into a structured resource. This central repository provides for contributing and retrieving knowledge through a universal access tool, such as a Web browser, while maintaining the functionality and format of the original applications. The knowledge metamodel and its K-map govern the structure and operations of the knowledge repository."[44]

    In many implementations, various kinds of source repositories form the foundation layer of knowledge management architecture. These various repositories of knowledge will be integrated in such a way that the users still will have a single point of access to the organization's knowledge assets—their own user interface. The knowledge architecture can include fileservers, database servers, groupware servers, document management systems, and Web sites. It also can include mission-critical systems, such as financial reporting, human resource management, and sales automation, which represent enormous stores of legacy knowledge about products, customers, and suppliers.

- Knowledge access tools (Knowledge Management Enablers in Figure 5-9).

    The knowledge access layer and the metamodel are totally interdependent, but they need to be kept separate. This is because system management and access tools may change, and if the two layers were to be combined, maintenance could become complicated. The knowledge access layer of the architecture is a complex combination of system administration tools and knowledge management enablers. This layer can include:

    - system administration information
    - location information
    - database type
    - access protocol for database
    - knowledge access tools and engines
    - distribution tools and engines

In organizations with a virtual knowledge repository, automated information request brokers can be used to access, with a single query, multiple repositories housed on an Intranet. Sophisticated search engines can make connections between related knowledge objects, uncovering new insights or previously unknown relationships.

Knowledge Management (KM) is a relatively new concept that is evolving rapidly. It appears to represent a synthesis of a number of disciplines, rather than a progression from any one of them. This factor, at least in part, may account for the rapid explosion of interest in KM. Moreover, this convergence is consistent with emerging models of organizations, which are process oriented and collaborative.

Knowledge Management is not yet well defined. Various definitions are contrasted to provide a sense of similarities and differences in perspective on this rapidly evolving field. In summary, KM is the concept of managing organizational knowledge, but in the sense of facilitating learning and collaboration, not in the old sense of controlling information. Perhaps the best way to think of KM is as knowledge plus process. Although knowledge creation is a natural phenomenon, the process part of the Knowledge Management equation implies that an organization can improve performance by employing purposefully designed strategies for creating, identifying, collecting, organizing, and sharing or transferring knowledge.

Knowledge Management has tremendous potential for improving organizational learning and performance, but it also faces many challenges. Many proponents feel that the current high-level focus on KM is too technology centric, which may ultimately lead to disillusionment. Recent surveys show that many enterprises are failing to grasp the fundamental changes in their day-to-day operations and culture that successful KM implementation requires. Tension is growing between a more technology-oriented approach to KM and an organizational learning focus to KM, leading some KM proponents to propose a strategy for second-generation knowledge management.

At the same time, no one denies the crtitical importance of new digital technologies and networks as an enabler for KM. Many industry watchers credit the rapid growth in Intranets and groupware as major contributors to the emergence of the KM concept. Key technologies used for building KM architectures include Intranets, groupware, knowledge portals, document repositories, data warehouses/ data mining, data analysis, artificial intelligence, electronic performance support, intelligent agents, and knowledge management niche products.

KM is gaining credibility and momentum. Some of the key trends include the rise of the corporate portal as a defining KM application, recognition of knowledge economics as the context for twenty-first-century business, growth in firms undertaking strategic KM projects, KM embraced by major vendors such as Microsoft and IBM, and a growing focus on the behavioral aspects of KM.

Measuring the economic value of Knowledge Management initiatives is a critical challenge for enterprises. Although the idea of identifying and transferring knowledge and best practices is intuitively appealing, implementing it is much more complex and time-consuming than most people imagine. To be successful, enterprises must be prepared to address organizational barriers to the transfer of knowledge. Moreover, creating a KM environment entails significant cultural change that enterprises must be prepared to address in order to succeed.

The most common objectives for enterprise-level KM projects include creating knowledge repositories, creating knowledge access, and improving knowledge environments and cultures. The most common application is implementation of knowledge transfer and best practice programs. Other major applications include Performance Support Systems and training, knowledge repositories, customer relationship management, content management, competitive intelligence, Web publishing, intellectual property management, and supply chain management (see Figure 5-4). The chapter presented a model for transferring knowledge and best practices based on research and practice and a method for defining an enterprise KM architecture.

KEY TERMS

- Balanced score card approach
- Barriers to knowledge transfer
- Best practice
- Case-based reasoning
- Communities of practice
- Data mining
- Expert systems
- Explicit knowledge
- Intellectual capital
- Intelligent agents
- Intranet
- Knowledge management
- Knowledge transfer and exchange
- Performance Support Systems (PSS)
- Portal
- Second generation knowledge management (SBKM)
- Simulation software
- Tacit knowledge
- Visualization

DISCUSSION QUESTIONS

1. How would you define Knowledge Management (KM)? Explain the current variation in definitions for KM.
2. Explain the importance of KM in contemporary organizations.
3. Identify some of the key technologies that support KM. Which are most important in your view? Why?
4. Identify major issues and requirements for designing an enterprise KM architecture.
5. What are some of the common pitfalls for enterprises seeking to implement KM? How can organizations avoid these pitfalls?
6. Discuss the impact of Intranets and groupware on KM.

APPLICATION EXERCISES

1. Conduct a Knowledge Management Assessment. Go to the text Web site and download *The Knowledge Management Assessment Tool (KMAT),* jointly developed by the American Productivity and Quality Center and Arthur Andersen to help organizations self-assess where their strengths and opportunities lie in managing knowledge. Working alone or in an assigned group, select an organization of which you are a member, are employed, or are familiar, and conduct the survey. The survey should take no more than about 10 to 15 minutes to complete. Compile the survey results and report back to your classmates. If you were a KM consultant, what recommendations would you make to this organization for getting started with a KM program? What benefits would you see for a KM program? Develop a KM value proposition statement for this organization.
2. Corporate portals have been touted as the "defining KM application." What is a corporate portal and how do portals support KM? Working individually or in an assigned group, research current developments in portal technology. Use the Web or current trade publications. Look for examples of the use of portals for Knowledge Management applications. Report back to your classmates and share your best KM example. Discuss and compare your findings with those of your classmates.
3. Evaluate and compare the Knowledge Management and e-learning features provided by Microsoft and IBM/Lotus Development. Compare different features and discuss their implications for implementing a KM strategy. What do you see as the major strengths and weaknesses of each of these products?

Suggested Readings

Allee, Verna. (1997). *The Knowledge Evolution: Expanding Organizational Intelligence.* Woburn, MA: Butterworth-Heinemann.

Davenport, Thomas and Laurence Prusak. (1998). *Working Knowledge: How Organizations Manage What They Know.* Boston: Harvard Business School Press.

Duffy, Jan. (1999). *Harvesting Experience: Reaping the Benefits of Knowledge.* Prairie Village, KS: ARMA International.

O'Dell, Carla S. and C. Jackson Grayson, Jr. with Nilly Essaides. (1998). *If Only We Knew What We Know: The Transfer of Internal Knowledge and Best Practice.* New York: The Free Press.

Useful Websites

www.kmmag.com. Knowledge Management Magazine. A magazine of executives interested in organizational and technological knowledge management strategies. It addresses issues of strategy, technology, process, and corporate culture.

www.businessinnovation.ey.cm/mko/index.html. Managing the Knowledge Organization (MKO).Web site for the MKO Consortium, which is a group of business leaders, academics, and researchers brought together by the Center for Business Innovation at Ernst & Young. Their purpose is to "develop a greater understanding of how businesses can better use knowledge to create value."

www.knowledgeinc.com. Knowledge, Inc. Online version of the *Knowledge, Inc.* monthly newsletter produced by the Stamford, Connecticut, consulting firm Quantum Era Enterprises and designed for corporate executives. The Web site is divided into three main areas: Empires of the Mind, The Smart Enterprise, and Leading Lights and includes excerpts from the print publication, interviews with executives and top thinkers on knowledge management and intellectual capital, conferences, links to other sites, and other relevant information.

www.kmworld.com. Web site of *KMWorld,* a monthly newspaper produced by Knowledge Asset Media, Inc., which is focused on creating and managing the knowledge-based enterprise.

Endnotes

1. Carla O'Dell and C. Jackson Grayson, Jr., with Nilly Essaides, *If Only We Knew What We Know: The Transfer of Internal Knowledge and Best Practice* (New York: The Free Press, 1998), 12.
2. American Productivity & Quality Center, *Knowledge Management,* 1998, online, *http://www.apqc.org/km/,* accessed 12/22/00.
3. O'Dell and Grayson, op. cit., 6.
4. J. Bair, "Knowledge Management Is About Cooperation and Context," CD-ROM, *Gartner Group Advisory Services* (Cambridge, MA: Gartner Group Inc., May 14, 1998)
5. Bill Gates with Collins Hemingway, *Business @ the Speed of Thought: Using a Digital Nervous System* (New York: Warner Books, 1999), chap. 14.
6. "Do We Know How to Do That? Understanding Knowledge Management," *Harvard Management Update* 4 (February 1999), 1.
7. Sarah L. Roberts-Witt, "Making Sense of Portal Pandemonium," *Knowledge Management Magazine* (July 1999), 45.
8. Thomas Davenport and Laurence Prusak, *Working Knowledge: How Organizations Manage What They Know,* (Boston: Harvard Business School Press, 1998).
9. O'Dell and Grayson, op. cit., 4.
10. Ibid.
11. Peter Senge, *The Fifth Discipline* (New York: Doubleday, 1990).
12. Ibid.
13. Editors, "The Knowledge Management Movement Gained Traction in Technology, Economics and Organizational Practice. KMM Spots the 10 Strongest Trends," *Knowledge Management Magazine* 2 (December 1999), 35.
14. Ibid., 36-44.
15. Davenport and Laurence, op. cit.
16. John Peetz, CKO of Ernst & Young, quoted in "The Knowledge Management Movement Gained Traction in Technology, Economics and Organizational Practice. KMM Spots the 10 Strongest Trends," *Knowledge Management Magazine* 2 (December 1999).
17. O'Dell and Grayson, op. cit., 13.
18. Ibid., 12.
19. The Molloy Group, White Paper: "KM from the Ground Up," *Knowledge Management Magazine* 2 (June, 1999), 94-96.
20. Davenport and Laurence, op. cit.
21. One example is a 1999 KM survey conducted by International Data Corporation (IDC), Framingham, MA, that looked at the "implementation directions of companies that have expressed interest in KM or are already engaged in KM projects." The 355 respondents answered questions about KM related to five areas: their perceptions; their past, present, and current spending; implementation experiences; project leadership; and future project plans.

22. Michael Charney, quoted in The Molloy Group, White Paper: "KM from the Ground Up," *Knowledge Management Magazine* 2 (June, 1999), 94.

23. The Molloy Group, op. cit., 96.

24. Barth, Steve. "Number Theory: Learning to Learn: Survey Reports Progress in KM and Organizational Learning—and Room for Improvement," *Knowledge Management Magazine* 3 (May 2000): 28.

25. Barth, Steve. "Number Theory: Miles to Go: Many Firms Still Misunderstand the Fundamental Opportunities and Challenges of Knowledge Management," *Knowledge Management Magazine* 3 (June 2000): 31.

26. Ibid.

27. Ibid.

28. Ibid.

29. Duffy, op. cit., 124.

30. Quoted in Steve Barth, "Miles to Go: Many Firms Still Misunderstand the Fundamental Opportunities and Challenges of Knowledge Management," *Knowledge Management Magazine* 3, (June 2000), 31.

31. Quoted in O'Dell and Grayson, op. cit., 87.

32. O'Dell and Grayson, op. cit., 89.

33. Ibid.

34. Sarah L. Roberts-Witt, "Making a Powerful Match: When Knowledge Management and E-Business Come Together, Companies Find Themselves Working Smarter Online," *Knowledge Management Magazine* 3, (June 2000), 33.

35. Peter Ruber, "Portals on a Mission: Second-Generation Portals Combine Knowledge Management and E-Business Applications to Meet Market Requirements," *Knowledge Management Magazine* 3, (April 2000), 35.

36. Ibid., 36.

37. O'Dell and Grayson, op. cit., 95.

38. Gloria J. Gery, *Electronic Performance Support Systems: How and Why to Remake the Workplace through the Strategic Application of Technology* (Boston: Weingarten Publications, 1991), 34.

39. Lee Mantelman, "AI Redux: This Time, People Count," *Knowledge Management Magazine* 2, (June 1999), 84.

40. O'Dell and Grayson, op. cit., 17.

41. Shari Shore and Tina Wang, White Paper: "Knowledge Management Officer Basics," *Knowledge Management Magazine* 3, (March 2000), 94-96.

42. O'Dell and Grayson, op. cit., 37.

43. Duffy, op. cit., 125.

44. Ibid., 129.

Case Study   Cisco Systems

A Matter of Connections: More than an infrastructure supplier, Cisco makes a market dominance a product of knowledge.

Search on "knowledge management" on Cisco Systems' customer portal, the Cisco Connection Online (CCO) Web site, and you won't find much: a fact sheet, some marketing materials for small businesses and a smattering of other documents. But Cisco is an object lesson on how well a company can use knowledge management to reshape its culture and processes without resorting to KM rhetoric.

Knowledge management practices have taken hold in most successful companies, even if they are not called KM. The benefits of working collaboratively, identifying expertise wherever it may reside and sharing key information on a timely basis are well-known; now the necessity of extending knowledge-sharing beyond the enterprise to customers, partners and suppliers also is becoming clear. Cisco has long pursued these strategies, and they have played a significant role in making the company one of the most valuable in the world today.

In practice, Cisco has leveraged its position as a leader in the infrastructure of data networks. It has used the routers, hubs, switches and other products it sells to build open information architectures that link its employees, suppliers and customers to the information and knowledge they need to do their jobs. The resulting channels have allowed Cisco to streamline processes, automate practices and share its knowledge with suppliers to build trusted, mutually profitable partnerships.

Culturally, Cisco promotes knowledge-sharing rather than knowledge-hoarding. It has shrewdly added to its knowledge base by acquiring innovative companies and integrating them into the corporate whole. In an industry notorious for its turnover rates, Cisco is known for hiring and retaining smart employees. All these moves are paying off as the company applies the knowledge gained to its bottom line.

"There are companies doing knowledge management that don't really call it that," says Mark O'Connor, associate director of enterprise knowledge management for the Yankee Group in Boston. "From our perspective, knowledge management is leveraging the organization's intangible assets. In that context, Cisco does a very good job."

Riding the Wave

Cisco owes a great deal of its success to serendipity: It has been in the right place at the right time. The San Jose, Calif., company was founded in 1984 by computer scientists from Stanford University seeking an easier way to connect different types of computer systems. Its core business has been the unglamorous "plumbing" that makes it possible to connect computers and their users. As mainframes and dumb terminals gave way to the client/server architecture, the TCP/IP LANs that Cisco's hardware enables became one of the linchpins of business. Then the biggest of all TCP/IP networks—the Internet—took off, and the rest is history.

Cisco has sustained double-digit revenue growth for more than 38 consecutive quarters. Belief in the value of the company's products and services has become so strong that this year, Cisco's market capitalization surpassed that of General Electric and then of Microsoft; it peaked at $555 billion. Even so, until recently, relatively few people had ever heard of Cisco. "We're like the overnight rock star that took 10 years to get there," says John Sifonis, managing director of Cisco's Internet business solutions group (IBSG).

"Cisco is a fierce competitor that succeeds in nearly every market sector it enters," says O'Connor. "Depending on how you segment it, Cisco positions close to 25 products in seven technology categories, ranging from network interface cards and remote-access devices to routers and ATM/WAN switches. Cisco's objective is to be number one or two in each category, and for the most part it is."

As the network infrastructure business has boomed, the company has prospered while competitors such as 3Com, Cabletron and Nortel Networks struggle. Cisco claims to have captured 85 percent of the market for Internet switching equipment. Yet for so dominant a company, there has been surprisingly little criticism of Cisco in the business press. "They make mistakes like anybody else, but their mistakes are hidden in the dramatic growth they have had," O'Connor says.

"Cisco is one of those firms that are pretty much firing on all cylinders strategically," says Chris Nicoll, who monitors Cisco for Current Analysis, a provider of industry analysis and software in Sterling, Va. "There are some specific blind spots when it comes to carrier voice and optical networking, but strategically it knows how to make itself valuable to its customers—not just with products, but with service and support."

The Internet isn't just Cisco's business: it's also how Cisco does business. Building on the dial-in bulletin board it first posted in 1992, over the past three years the company has opened portals for its customers (CCO), suppliers (Manufacturing Connection Online) and employees (Cisco Employee Connection). This expansion of access to intellectual capital has increased operational efficiencies and reduced costs. Cisco's Web strategy puts a virtual consultant online, offering the customer expertise in configuring systems, closing orders and delivering goods. "The goal is to create a relationship where customers can get access to every aspect of their relationship with our company

over the intranet or Internet," says Pete Solvik, senior vice president and CIO of Cisco.

More than just transaction data flows through Cisco's networks and into its portals. Transmitting an order electronically from the customer straight through to the supplier is one thing; sharing sales forecasts with suppliers and bug reports with customers required a leap of faith. "Early on, in 1991, we took the risk of trusting our employees, our customers and our partners and suppliers with information that normally would be held close to the chest," says Karen Brunett, IBSG marketing director. Cisco gambled that key constituents both inside and outside the organization would learn from each other in mutually profitable ways.

Plans to create its first online technical support database caused a major debate within Cisco, Sifonis admits. Some executives feared that exposing everything—warts and all—would give competitors information they could use to sell against the company. Instead, customers have helped the company find errors in its network operating system. "The reaction was just the opposite [of what was feared]," Sifonis says. "Once our customers knew what our problems were, they also wanted to know what our competitors' problems were."

One-Stop Shopping

The Cisco Connection Online portal is home to a number of customer-facing applications. Customers use CCO to diagnose network problems, find answers to technical questions and order products. They can configure, price, route and submit electronic orders to Cisco on an automated order-flow system. More than half of those orders go directly to Cisco's third-party suppliers, who in turn ship directly to customers. The site is directly linked to Federal Express and UPS package trackers so customers can determine in real time the status of shipments.

This system has shortened Cisco's order cycle by 70 percent—from six to eight weeks to one to three weeks. "We don't touch the product at all," says Brunett. "We saved about $440 million in fiscal 1999 by streamlining that process from order entry to shipment.

Using CCO isn't mandatory. Cisco recognizes that not every customer will prefer this virtual storefront. But CCO is there to greet every current or potential customer that arrives via the Web, since handling routine customer issues through electronic systems frees human sales and service reps to address more difficult or higher-value transactions.

"They have been innovators in using the Web for fulfillment without doing away with the high-touch, personal face," says Nicoll of Current Analysis. "For customers who are self-sufficient and know what they want, the Web offers a quick and secure means of ordering products. Customers who need more hand-holding or prefer to have a more local interface have a familiar body right in front of them."

CCO has contributed to a 25 percent increase in customer satisfaction since 1995, according to Sifonis, who claims that orders arrive at the customer on time and error-free 98 percent of the time. Cisco surveys report that customers prefer to use the Web for technical questions 60 percent of the time and for product information 80 percent of the time. The company sells about $50 million in products on the Web each day, Sifonis estimates.

B2B Benefits

The company also created Cisco Manufacturing Connection Online (MCO), a business-to-business (B2B) supply chain portal for its contract manufacturers, suppliers, assemblers, distributors and logistics partners. MCO provides a central access point for manufacturing applications, reports, tools, forecast data, inventory information and purchase orders.

"They don't have to rely upon faxes, e-mail or phone calls. Everything is done electronically, and there are not many opportunities for errors," says Nicoll. "Cisco operates pretty much on a build-as-you-buy basis. With access to Cisco sales information, suppliers can do their own forecasting, keep a tight handle on their own inventory control and maintain their costs accordingly."

Reducing cycle time cut the company's inventory and that of its manufacturing partners by 45 percent, according to Sifonis. He adds that partner satisfaction has increased as vendors develop a more intimate relationship with Cisco.

The challenge of B2B is that in unmediated exchanges buyers and sellers still have to trade useful knowledge, according to Mark Tucker, senior consultant with the Delphi Group in Boston. "The real intelligence and information value has always been the context that you wrap around the information," he says. "Successful people in B2B will have to automate the management and delivery of context, which is at the heart of knowledge management."

One of the most difficult aspects of building Cisco's supplier Web was transforming a culture where employees and vendors were rewarded for hoarding knowledge into one in which shared knowledge is used to create value for all constituencies. "Building a trust model that the organizations have bought into and are comfortable with is key," says Peter Alexander, vice president of enterprise marketing at Cisco. "It's about extending trust and moving historically confidential information out to suppliers."

"We don't believe in the *Field of Dreams* concept," says Sue Bostrom, senior vice president of Cisco's IBSG. "We actively engage customers [and suppliers] through focus groups and advisory boards to determine what they want, and we develop applications that will meet those needs. If you go to the site, it looks like an interaction and transaction engine, not a marketing tool."

From the Inside Out

On the inside, Cisco's intranet portal, Cisco Employee Connection, applies the self-help model to internal processes. Just as the other two portals are valued by how well they improve customer satisfaction, CEC is designed to boost employee satisfaction, retain human capital and help the company add to its workforce without incurring the additional administrative support costs that usually accompany rapid growth.

Online interaction begins even before employees are hired. More than 80 percent of the 25,000 job applications and resumes Cisco receives monthly come in through the Web. Once hired, employees do almost everything online: hold meetings, learn new skills, order supplies, file expense reports, enroll for benefits, exercise stock options or search for intelligence on competitors.

In the Knowledge Age, companies must strive to keep up. "E-learning is the e-commerce of three years from now," says Bostrom. "The speed at which we need to learn new skills is accelerating." Cisco now does some four-fifths of its sales and technical training online and has saved 40 to 60 percent in costs compared to the expense of traditional classroom training and related travel. According to Tom Kelly, vice president of worldwide training, in one year Cisco converted from doing 90 percent of learning in classroom lectures to 80 percent online.

The company believes that learning must be supported by metrics that put accountability on the part of the learner and the learning content, he says. Employees are not penalized for choosing not to learn but are rewarded if they do. "It's carrot, not stick," says Kelly. Employee scores on learning-related tests become part of their performance evaluations. For salespeople, measurements of their performance on learning-related tests and similar metrics will be built into the sales commission matrix and salary compensation.

One of the best examples of process automation in CCO is expense reporting. Employees receive electronic statements for their American Express corporate cards and can quickly transfer reimbursable charges to their electronic expense forms. Expenses are submitted automatically, and employees are reimbursed in as little as 48 hours.

Cisco's business rules are built into the application, which knows what hotels are approved and at what prices; it will even prompt employees to explain why they stayed in a more expensive hotel. According to Sifonis, only two auditors are now required to handle more than 26,000 users per month.

This convenience for employees also boosts the company's bottom line. Sifonis asserts that by streamlining and automating work processes and employee services, such self-service applications save Cisco about $58 million per year. Yankee Group's O'Connor points out that the productivity value of such initiatives is reflected in Cisco's 1999 income per employee of $690,000; its closest competitor, 3Com, earned approximately $435,000 per worker.

Leveraging Lessons Learned

Cisco's main business is still selling products, but internally it has evolved into a company where knowledge itself is the chief asset. Its understanding of how to reinvent a company is being exported to other companies; Cisco's thought leaders act as high-level advisors to help Ford Motor Co., General Electric, Procter & Gamble and others develop and deploy their e-business strategies.

In nearly every facet of its business, Cisco not only encourages but expects employees to use both private and public networks effective; Slovik credits Cisco's strategic reliance on sharing knowledge in this way for the company's market dominance. Toward this end, Cisco has developed quantifiable ways of measuring the success of information systems. "We measure leading Internet capabilities as a corporate metric," says Alexander. "We can track right down to the organization level. Whether it is finance, HR or lines of business within engineering, marketing or sales, they are required to report on the ways they are using information technology."

Each functional organization first works with Andersen Consulting to determine where it stands in relation to the rest of the industry and then reports directly to CEO John Chambers. "You don't want to be a laggard with regard to Internet applications here at Cisco," says Bostrom.

Because Cisco sells products on the Web, supports customers on the Web and consults on the Web, O'Connor says, "They are their own best customer." With the trend toward e-learning in many industries, by setting an example with its internal training programs Cisco can benefit directly when other companies follow its lead. "By showing people how to do it, they are gaining leverage for the whole argument of network infrastructure technology," he says.

Cisco's evangelism creates a self-perpetuating information feedback loop. "There's a business case that says the more we can help our customers in their business, the more strategic value we add to them, the more they will understand the value of deploying larger infrastructures with Cisco," says Alexander.

Two and a half years ago, the company created its Internet business solutions group to help customers apply to their own e-business efforts the lessons Cisco had learned. "People had heard about our e-commerce and service and support applications, and they wanted to know how we did it," Brunet recalls.

Cisco's consultants apply the company's Global Networked Business model, drawn from Cisco's own experience, which describes an enterprise that strategically uses information and communications to build a network of strong, interactive relationships with all its primary constituencies.

Driven by customer needs and business goals, Cisco has not hesitated to make financial and cultural investments to maximize return on intellectual capital. On one hand, management connects the efforts of employees to actual results by rewarding managers based on the satisfaction of their customers rather than pure sales numbers. And it encourages employees to take risks. "There is an expectation that if you are not making mistakes, you're not trying hard enough," O'Connor says.

"It's not knowledge management for knowledge management's sake," says Bostrom. "You start with the business problem you are trying to solve and ask yourself how this application helps you solve it."

While other companies talk about knowledge management, Cisco has turned theory into practice without adopting KM jargon. Its success speaks volumes about the importance of knowledge initiatives to a company's bottom line. Perhaps unexpectedly, Cisco is now finding that its experience in transforming itself to meet the challenges of the Knowledge Age has become itself a strategic asset. As that knowledge gets exported to customers, suppliers and partners, it is helping to shape our economy in ways previously unforeseen.

Source: Reprinted with permission from: Lee Sherman, "A Matter of Connections," *Knowledge Management Magazine* 3 (July 2000): 42–47.

CASE STUDY QUESTIONS

1. "Early on we took the risk of trusting our employees, our customers, and our partners and suppliers with information that normally would be held close to the chest," says Karen Brunett in the Cisco case. Why do corporate cultures tend to guard information rather than share it? What are the implications of this tendency for KM projects? How did taking this risk pay off for Cisco?

2. How does Cisco use the time saved by making information available via the Web to improve customer service? What has been the payoff for Cisco?
3. How does Cisco's intranet portal, *Cisco Employee Connection,* apply the self-help model to internal processes?
4. How did building Cisco's business rules into its expense reporting system save time and money and improve the process?
5. How is Cisco leveraging its experience with using KM and digital networks to reinvent the company to help other companies and generate additional income?
6. How big a factor is Cisco's strategic reliance on leveraging knowledge to its growth and profitability? How is Cisco measuring this?

End-User Information Systems: Implementation and Support

Parts I and II were all about the EUIS environment and business solutions for knowledge workers. In Part III we take a look at implementation and support for EUIS tools. To be truly effective, new tools must be learned and assimilated into the user's work life. Managers, EUIS professionals, and end users must understand how best to learn to use technologies. Managers must also create policies that address a myriad of implementation issues, including the physical security of the technology and data integrity and security.

Chapter 6, "Training End Users," has as a premise that learning the effective and efficient use of technology cannot be left to chance. Training and supporting a diverse, information-based workforce in the effective use of information technologies is a pressing need in today's enterprises. Workers must continually learn in an environment of change and ambiguity. In Chapter 6, we describe a comprehensive approach to thinking about training, the *training cycle*. Here, you'll find approaches to needs assessment, ways to design learning strategies, perspectives on implementing training programs, and ways to determine the usefulness of training efforts (evaluation). You'll find a discussion of a wide range of learning strategies, based on principles of adult learning, ranging from traditional classroom-based learning to Web-based Training (WBT).

In Chapter 7, "Support and Help Desk Management," we overview learning-related services that are typically the purview of Information Systems Departments (as opposed to training efforts organized by Human Resource Departments). Performance Support and Help Desks are prevalent strategies that provide ongoing support and just-in-time learning for users. Performance support includes online help, expert systems, databases, and hypermedia. Performance support is developed in tandem with system development and is built into many software applications. Help Desks, on the other hand, while they can include access to large databases of questions/answers, typically are supported by live agents who help users work their way through problems. Help Desks are a complex, important aspect of ensuring that users can effectively use technology to do their work.

In Chapter 8, "Management Issues," we focus on risks, opportunities, and concerns that managers face in today's digital workplaces. We examine pressing management issues including establishing policies for EUIS, safeguarding physical hardware and software, controlling access to information, protecting the integrity and confidentiality of data, and a wide range of legal issues.

Chapter 6

Training End Users

Learning Objectives

Upon completing this chapter, you should be able to:

➤ Understand the importance of training in implementing end-user information systems.

➤ Identify the role of organizational, task, and individual analysis.

➤ Select appropriate methods for analyzing training needs.

➤ Apply adult learning principles in developing training strategies.

➤ Choose appropriate methodologies and media for training programs.

➤ Recognize the benefits of well-planned training programs.

➤ Develop performance and evaluation criteria for training programs.

6.1 INTRODUCTION

Organizations and their workers are increasingly dependent upon technology. Key to the effective implementation of individual and collaborative work tools is that users know how to use them effectively and efficiently. When asked what percentage of the workforce requires computer training each year, Elliott Masie, a technology training guru, always replies, "One hundred percent! Every time a piece of technology changes, an upgrade to an application is shipped, a new employee is hired, a reorganization is announced, or a new procedure is implemented, computer learning is required."[1]

Training and support professionals can partner with the line manager, the end user, and the systems developer in designing and delivering effective learning strategies. Everyone has much to gain when these stakeholders work together. The manager, who is responsible for work performance, sees work done smoothly. The end user feels a sense of accomplishment. The systems developer finds acceptance for the system. Even technical deficiencies can sometimes be overcome if users understand how a system works and how it can help them work more effectively.

Despite the importance of training, however, EUIS training often is given a low priority; resources formally committed to training are often less than 2 percent of total IS resources.[2] This finding is contrasted with recommendations that at least

20 percent of the project budget go toward training. Other experts in EUIS recommend that investment in training should match dollar for dollar the investment in technology. In short, the key to ensuring that new technologies are used effectively is recognizing the value of training and providing resources so that training can be done right. Even the most technically advanced system may fail if workers do not know how to use it.

In some organizations, turf wars exist between the IS department and the training department regarding who is responsible for end-user training. IS professionals report that trainers are not technical enough; trainers believe that "techies" do not have the interpersonal communications skills or instructional design skills they need. Regardless of who is responsible for training, it is clear that cooperation between the two departments is in the organization's best interest.[3] Because online help and Help Desks are almost always part of an information systems department, not the human resources/training department, these learning options and their management are discussed in detail in the next chapter.

This chapter expands on the human side of systems implementation. It offers theoretical foundations and practical approaches to initial training and continual support for systems users, which typically involves human resource/training professionals. As used in this text, end-user training and support is a teaching/learning process whereby individuals acquire technology knowledge, skills, and abilities that enable them to perform their jobs more effectively. While *training* implies a learning experience that has a beginning and an end, *support* implies ongoing learning that empowers end users to use systems creatively and effectively. This chapter is organized into four sections around an action research approach to training: assessment, design, implementation, and evaluation. This action research approach, termed the *training cycle* here (see Figure 6-1), tells us that training solutions are best determined by those who have something to gain from the successful implementation of a new system—managers, end users, and systems analysts. Because the cycle data from one training effort become assessment data for the next, this cyclical approach supports effective, efficient training and organizational learning. Every system is different. What is important is that training and support are based on a clear assessment of performance requirements, are properly designed, are effectively implemented, and are evaluated for results.

Figure 6-1
The training cycle

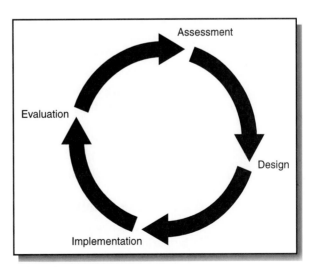

All training projects begin with research, whether the research is termed a needs analysis, needs assessment, or performance analysis. The goal is to determine what must be learned, who needs to learn, how that learning can best take place, and how best to use resources. A training program that is initiated as part of the implementation of a new system is an implementation strategy, and care should be taken that the training program results in the *right* users learning the *right* skills in the *right* way for the *right* tasks in the *right* priority order.[4]

To ensure that everything is done *right*, it is important to assess the organization, the task, and the individual. Typically, formal investigations are best done in conjunction with the firm's organizational development or training department. Such professionals offer skills and an understanding of needs assessment methodology as well as the organization, the individual end user, and how the task fits into the end user's overall job. Not all training programs demand intensive, formal analysis. However, in designing any training program, the designer makes judgements on the knowledge, skills, and abilities (KSAs) of the target learning population. Therefore, it is important to know why such analyses are useful as well as research strategies that may be applied to determine the KSAs.

6.2.1   Organizational Analysis

Individual trainees are expected to acquire KSAs in one environment (training) and then use their new KSAs in another environment, back on the job. If what is learned in a training program cannot be used on the job, the training program is almost always considered a failure. Sometimes, when top management or supervisors are not part of the needs analysis process, training programs teach techniques or attitudes that are contrary to the way work is done. The way work is done is termed *organizational culture,* and a current evaluation of the morale of an organization is its climate. Specific questions to determine the organizational culture and climate include:

Is everyone committed to the training program?
Has everyone been involved in determining the training program's goals?
Will trainees be rewarded for their new skills?
How supportive is management in terms of providing corporate resources,
    including time for employees to learn?
Will trainees have an opportunity to *use* their new skills at their jobs?

Like individuals, organizations go through stages of development. Typically, the further along an organization is in adapting information systems to the way they do business, the larger their investment in training is.[5] In other words, the more entrenched an organization is in information systems, the more valuable they consider training to be. Thus, gaining support and commitment for training programs in organizations that have developed applications and infrastructures is easier than gaining that support in less technologically based organizations.

6.2.2   Task Analysis

A task analysis begins with task descriptions. Beginning with a summary of tasks to be performed, an expert in doing the task could be interviewed or an analyst could observe the expert doing the job. The task descriptions should follow some simple guidelines: Each description should be a complete sentence that includes a functional verb that describes the primary job operation. The description should include what the worker does, how the worker is to do it, for whom, and the reasons for the work. This listing can be used to prioritize the tasks and identify those tasks that training can address. For example, a task description could read:

> Using PLAN software, the project manager develops and installs a planning matrix on the Intranet making the matrix accessible to the entire project team; the matrix keeps team members aware of progress and reminds them of their next steps and how all roles interrelate in the overall project plan.

Additionally, understanding how software is actually used by people can help the training designer. For example, researchers watched experienced users navigate a spreadsheet package, identified the most commonly used commands, and then designed a training program around those 27 commands.[6] Alternately, after watching an expert do the same tasks with a wider variety of commands, an assessor could discover additional, useful commands that could be part of an advanced users' learning program.

6.2.3   Individual Analysis

While the organizational and task analysis provide a picture of the task and the environmental setting, it does not paint a picture of the individual end user. Questions that need to be addressed here include the user's aptitude, previous experience using technologies, and motivation to learn. The right users are as important to systems success as the right system is. The question, in a nutshell, is What do prospective users need to know before they can be trained successfully? Moreover, an assessment of user perceptions of the value and utility of a new system is a key factor for willingness to learn and initial acceptance.

6.2.4   Needs Analysis Tools

In selecting appropriate tools, the question to ask first is what questions need to be answered, and then determine who has the answers. In short, data gathered from a needs assessment come from individuals or secondary sources that can provide answers to questions such as:

- How are current systems being used?
- Who could benefit from training?
- What are users' current and desired levels of expertise on a given system or application?
- Which systems require additional training support?
- Which applications need to be taught?
- Which skills and features need to be taught for a particular application?
- What level of training is needed?
- How much time could employees have to train?
- What tasks must employees be able to perform when training is completed?

The most frequently used techniques to find answers to these questions are observations, interviews, focus groups, and questionnaires. Figure 6-2 is a summary of their advantages and disadvantages with regard to training needs analysis. Time, money, and usable objective data are important variables to consider in choosing an

Techniques	Advantages	Disadvantages
Observation	Firsthand view of situation	Time consuming
Personal interviews	Interviewees carefully chosen	May require a large interviewing staff
Telephone interviews	Less expensive than personal interview. Can be monitored and evaluated. 80% to 90% of those called usually agree to discuss	Not everyone is good at telephone interviews; subtle body language is missing
Focus groups	Offer fairly reliable access to ideas and attitudes of a work group	May be difficult to schedule; require strong group leader
Questionnaires	Can reach a large audience at a limited cost; recipient can complete one at his/her leisure; offer anonymity to respondent; do not need a large staff to administer	Difficult to design; non-responses can diminish cost savings; possible bias; long turnaround; not sure the right person completes; requires statistical treatment

Figure 6-2
Advantages and disadvantages of various investigation techniques for training assessment and evaluation

assessment technique. For example, if a large, geographically dispersed group must be contacted, a questionnaire might be the most effective approach. Well-designed questionnaires also result in objective numerical data. However, if users must be trained on a system immediately, observations may be adequate. Also, consider that while the time and costs involved with conducting one-on-one interviews and focus groups are high, qualitative data—while subjective—is considered rich and can provide more in-depth analysis of an issue.

Figure 6-3 is a template for a value-added needs assessment interview, adapted from a strategy outlined by Meyer and Boone.[7] Note the emphasis on work tasks in this illustration.

Other guidelines for conducting needs assessments include using a variety of different needs assessment techniques when possible, and the selecting method(s) that involve as many stakeholders as possible. No matter how assessment is done, however, the target population—the end users—should be key participants.

Of all the steps in the training process, needs assessment is the most frequently overlooked—and the most important. The remainder of the process—design, delivery, and evaluation—is worthless if the right skills are not taught to the right people for the right tasks in the right way, and presented in the right priority order.

6.3 Designing Successful Programs

The importance of careful needs analysis, especially for first-time users of computer systems, cannot be overemphasized. The mistake that training program designers frequently make is to cram everything about operating a system into a

Opening: Put your interviewee at ease. Have a conversation opener ready; for example, "Congratulations on being the company's salesperson of the year! I read about your success in our newsletter."

State the problem: For example, "I'm from the training [or information systems] department. We're doing an audit of our technology training options, and I'm here to see if we are offering workshops in areas you need. You've been selected because we know you have a reputation of being a whiz at computing and we want your advice."

Explain data collection and analysis procedures: For example, "May I record this interview? I'll be transcribing your responses and will keep those transcriptions anonymous. I'll be writing a report, and will send you a copy."

Explain how long you anticipate the interview to be: For example, "This interview session should take around 10 minutes. I'm going to ask you about your work, what computer tools you use, how the tools help you, and what you might want to learn more about."

Divide your questions into useful categories as shown:

BACKGROUND

What is your job title?
What are your job responsibilities?
How will you (or your boss) know if you are successful?
Describe your most important tasks/projects/goals.

TOOLS

What computer tools do you currently use?
What tasks/activities do you use them for?
How would you describe your skill in using the tools?

BEHAVIORAL IMPACTS

What do the tools do?
What would you do differently if the tools disappeared tomorrow?

BENEFITS AND EVALUATION

What are the benefits to you?

FUTURE

What are you doing now that you believe technology could assist?
Why aren't you using those tools?
How would you prefer to learn to use the tools?

Figure 6-3
Template for a value-added needs assessment

training program at the time of implementation and then walk away, believing that users are prepared to use the system effectively. Unfortunately, this type of training is often more a demonstration of system capabilities than skill development. This approach might be appropriate for experienced computer users who are learning a new system or software package, but it is not effective for most users. More often than not, such an approach leaves users overwhelmed, discouraged, and ill-prepared to begin using the system. The likely result is that they will return to their jobs not knowing where to begin.

To design an effective training program, one must know not only what people need to learn but also how they learn. To be an effective trainer, one must master the subject being taught and also know appropriate methods of delivering that knowledge and know-how to the trainee.

A careful needs analysis ensures that training is done for the right things. The following sections provide an overview of how the EUIS analyst or planner can ensure that training is done the right way. Selected principles of adult learning are offered as a means of identifying assumptions that the trainer has about the learning population. After the theoretical foundations, this section describes individual and group learning and support strategies. Individual strategies include simple communications pieces, hands-on training, CDs, and Web-based Training. Group strategies include a computer fair, newsletters, and professional organizations. This section concludes with an overview of the use of technology to deliver training.

6.3.1 Principles of Adult Learning

Andragogy and *pedagogy* refer to the study of teaching. *Andra* comes from the Greek word *andr,* which means "man, not boy." *Peda* comes from the Greek word *paid,* which means "child." Both words use the Greek suffix *agogus,* which means "leading."

As a theory, pedagogy originated with early monks who recorded common characteristics among children learning basic skills. Only in the middle of the twentieth century did instructors realize that their assumptions about learning did not fit the adults they were teaching. Andragogy, which originated in Europe, was introduced as a teaching theory in the United States in the 1960s by Malcolm S. Knowles. Andragogy is learner-directed learning experiences; pedagogy is teacher-directed experiences. Knowles emphasized that the two assumptions can coexist. The task to be learned and the individual's learning style dictate whether a pedagogical or andragogical approach should be used in the design and delivery of a training program. For example, how would you prefer to learn each of the following?

- to use a new desktop publishing system
- to be oriented to a new job
- to understand French history
- to improve your writing
- to understand the technical aspects of Intranets

Your preferred learning style related to each of these learning tasks reflects a particular educational background and experience level. To improve desktop publishing skills, you may need to learn how to use the mouse in a hands-on workshop, or you may need to learn printing terms from a textbook, or you may want to learn elements of graphic design through a lecture on the topic. A new job could entail classroom-based informational training on corporate policies and benefits, job shadowing, and personal coaching. If you are a novice French history buff, you may learn best by the lecture method; however, if you are a graduate of a liberal arts program in French history, you may need to tour the French countryside to get the historical perspective that is desired. Likewise, to improve your writing skills, you may need a refresher course in grammar; or you could read Strunk and White's *Elements of Style;* or you may need an intensive, hands-on workshop. Learning the technical points of Intranets could entail hands-on, problem-based workshops or reading technical manuals. The point of this discussion is that andragogy and pedagogy are approaches that help you consider the individual learner's needs in guiding learning experiences, no matter how old the learner is (see Spotlight: Why It's Easier For Kids).

WHY IT'S EASIER FOR KIDS

Documenting the problems adults have in learning to use computers has become a mini industry. There are so many bizarre stories that one begins to think that many of them are part of the Net culture of creating hoaxes. You may have heard a few yourself. The Help Desk that reported that someone thought the mouse was a foot pedal and couldn't get it to work. The secretary who was asked to copy a disk and came back with a photocopy. The man, confronted with the computer message "press any key to continue," couldn't find the "any" key on the keyboard. Another "hit" the keyboard so hard he broke it. When asked by a support line if she had Windows, one woman apparently replied, "No, we have air conditioning." One person was said to be found deleting files on a disk using white-out. Another, when instructed to "insert the disk and close the door," inserted the disk and then closed her office door. There are hundreds of stories.

Source: Reprinted with permission from *Growing Up Digital: The Rise of the Net Generation* by Don Tapscott. Copyright © 1998 by McGraw-Hill Companies.

Following are some basic premises from what we know about how adults learn. These premises are applied to teaching/learning computer applications.

For Adults, Learning Is Not Its Own Reward. Adults are not motivated by gold stars or good report cards; they want a learning outcome that they can put to use. Because human behavior is directed toward goals, trainees learn best when they have a specific use for the knowledge or skill being taught.

Therefore, EUIS training strategists should remember that their trainees (adults) prefer practical, hands-on training sessions over general, theory-oriented classes. The best way to motivate individuals to learn a spreadsheet software package, for example, is to show them how they can apply it. Otherwise, trainees will probably learn very little.

Adult Learning Is Integrative. Adults bring a wide variety of knowledge and experiences to the learning situation. They learn best when they are able to integrate new ideas with what they already know. Moreover, if the information conflicts with what they know or value, learning is more difficult. Elliott Masie refers to an adult's information storehouse of knowledge as a hard disk and says that the reason adults have difficulty learning to use systems is that "most hard disks get write protected in one's early twenties."[8] Therefore, training strategies should build on what the trainee already knows.

For example, when teaching desktop publishing skills to administrative support personnel, the trainer could use word processing and printing terms to describe the desktop publishing software functionality. In a desktop publishing workshop for managers, however, the trainer could emphasize the advantages of desktop publishing over traditional typesetting. The trainee's previous experience with software programs also influences the training methods that should be employed. In general, the more proficient trainees are with *any* applications package, the easier it will be for them to learn another software package.

In addition, value adjustments must be considered. Because EUIS change how work is processed, the trainee should know *why* the technology is used, as well as how to use it. In this case, *value adjustment* means understanding why work that has been done a specific way in the past will no longer be performed that way. Trainees will accept change more readily when they know why the change is taking place.

Trainees typically want more control over their learning experiences. Instructors should consult with trainees about curriculum content as well as evaluation strategies. Including trainees in these deliberations gives learners an opportunity to contribute to course content, instructional strategies, and learning goals that fit their own learning needs and styles.

Practice Must Be Meaningful. Repetition for repetition's sake does not produce a substantial learning effect. However, if repetition has meaningful results, learning can take place. This principle is borrowed from the work of E. L. Thorndike, an early leader in developing learning theory, who was opposed to meaningless drill.

Therefore, rather than have learners work on textbook or Computer-based Training drills, the trainer should have them "practice" on actual work in the learning environment. A similar suggestion is that trainees apply what has been learned "back at the desk" as an assignment or, in the language of training, as prework for the next learning session.

A related premise is that the older the trainees are, the slower they perform some psychomotor tasks. Older learners compensate for this by being more exact; they make fewer trial-and-error ventures and fewer errors. Therefore, trainees should be given every opportunity to proceed at their own pace. In many instances, self-paced learning materials, such as Web-based Training, can support self-paced learning. Some organizations, such as Apple Computer, give their employees a computer to take home, enabling learning to take place in the privacy of the home rather than in the office or classroom.

6.3.2 Individual Learning and Support Strategies

Individual learning and support strategies are specific ways that training can support a systems implementation within an organization. As part of an implementation plan, training on a given system can include one or any number of these strategies.

Innovators and early adopters (see Chapter 13, Innovation and Strategic Planning) find technology fascinating, and if they have sufficient time they will pick up class notes and computer manuals and learn on their own. Most people, however, will feel pressured to catch up on work that accumulated while they were in class for several days. They may try to use the system, flounder, and then return to doing their work in the usual manner, with the good intention of learning to use it as soon as they catch up on their work and can spare the time. By the time they return to the system, they will have forgotten 80 percent to 90 percent of what they learned in class. They may make excuses for not using it and, unless compelled by a superior, probably will use it only minimally or not at all.

A single training experience, a one-shot answer to a user's learning needs, is seldom enough to ensure system success. Individual learning and support strategies are presented here as part of a continuum of activities that address the training needs of a given population. Note from Figure 6-4 that training's role in implementation includes a variety of strategies that the trainer will adopt to the needs at hand. The continuum has simple awareness pieces (brochures and promotional pieces) at the bottom and seminars (implying high-level applications) at the top. The degree of implementation may be measured by Lewin's Unfreezing—Moving—Refreezing phases. (See Chapter 11, Organizational Change.) Unfreezing strategies attempt to get the targeted user group thinking about new ways to do work. Moving strategies are instructional approaches designed to ensure that the end user is able to apply the system to job tasks. Refreezing strategies are support strategies designed to ensure that the new system becomes the way work is done. Each of these strategies is discussed in the following section.

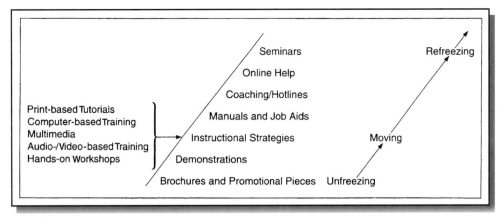

Figure 6-4
Training as part of an implementation and learning support system

6.3.2.1 Brochures and Promotional Pieces

The most basic implementation strategy is designed to instill awareness of the new EUIS and create motivation to use them. Brochures and promotional pieces that outline the capabilities of the target system should overview the system and explain how the system will help the end user do the job. The key premise is that awareness can defray user concerns about how the new system will impact an individual's job. Brochures and promotional pieces are unfreezing strategies, as they allow the end user to anticipate the system and be convinced of its value *before* being is expected to use it.

6.3.2.2 Demonstrations

Demonstrations involve an experienced user showing a prospective user how to use the new technology, typically on a one-time-only basis. The following example illustrates the use of demonstration for training:

> Professor Quinn is suggesting to her research class that they learn to use a bibliographic management tool, ProCite. She begins her demonstration by talking about how she used to do library research with 3 x 5 index cards and a recipe box. She then shows the class a ProCite database she uses in her own work and quickly generates the end product—a perfect bibliography in APA style. She shows how easy it is to produce that same bibliography in AMA style, one of a dozen other styles. The class is amazed. She then adds items to the database, by adding the class textbook and a journal article to the list. Opening up her Word Program, she drafts two short paragraphs of a research paper. When she needs to cite references from the database, she goes to the Word tool menu and opens "ProCite," and then clicks "insert citation." With three different references inserted, she generates a bibliography within Word. Learners see how the text changes and the bibliography is generated automatically. Professor Quinn listens to questions and then repeats the demo, encouraging her class to use the system on the library's notebook computers as they do their research project.

When a demonstrator is training individuals who have had experience with the software, such as in the Professor Quinn example, learning new features or new ways to use familiar features may not be a problem. In other words, when the technology is neither novel nor complex, a simple demonstration may suffice. A demonstration may be inadequate if it is hurried or if the trainee cannot keep up with it. In the earlier example, if learners were not competent already in using Word, the demonstration might not have been enough. Although end users ultimately will need to refer to the manual, help guide, or other instructional medium, they will have been motivated to want to learn the system, which is an important aspect of any training effort.

6.3.2.3 *Instructional Strategies*

The trainer who needs to provide end users with guided help in learning a system has a number of options. A specific strategy is selected depending on the performance objectives, the learning preference of the trainee, the trainee's current expertise, time and money available for training, and how critical it is that the system be up and running by a specific date. Following is an overview of ways to move or deliver instruction. The pros and cons of print-based tutorials; Computer-based Training; multimedia, audio- and video-based training; Web-based Training; and hands-on workshops are detailed.

End users can be categorized as procedural or navigational learners. Procedural learners prefer to learn step by step. Navigational learners, on the other hand, prefer to learn by doing—exploring, making errors (which they learn from!) and asking for help at the specific time they need it. The instructional strategies that follow support learning preferences of either or both types of learners.

6.3.2.3.1 Print-Based Tutorials Manuals for off-the-shelf software sometimes include tutorials, or written descriptions and exercises designed to help the user learn how to use the software. These self-paced, linear tutorials can be used in initial training efforts by procedural learners. Understanding directions and tasks may be difficult for the novice, however, as manuals typically assume that the learner has a base of knowledge and technical vocabulary. Thus, as a training tool, print-based tutorials are of value primarily to experienced computer users who want to learn new software programs. The following example illustrates the use of print-based tutorials as a training tool:

> The EUIS task force has determined that corporate and divisional offices should use an updated package, Spreadsheet V. Currently, all employees use either Spreadsheet III or Superspread IV. Because all prospective trainees are proficient with an earlier version of the spreadsheet package, users will be expected to learn Spreadsheet V on their own, using the tutorial that is part of the new version's manual.

6.3.2.3.2 Computer-Based Training Computer-based Training (CBT) refers to a variety of techniques that use the computer as a training medium. *InformationWeek* reported results from a survey that found that the second-most-popular computer training method was the learner's own PC. The most popular method remained the hands-on workshop. Although the least-used training method was Web-based Training, Web-based Training is also the newest and fastest growing instructional method.[9] This section will overview a number of CBT options, with the caveat that learning should be the driving force for choosing an instructional medium. Technology for its own sake is to be avoided. "In short, don't let the flashy means of tech-delivered training blind you to the end: delivering learning."[10] Various terms have been associated with different types of Computer-based Training. Beginning with

Programmed Instruction (PI) in the early 1950s, and cumulating today with Web-based Training, the use of technology to deliver instruction has been revolutionary.

Programmed Instruction (PI). PI originated with B. F. Skinner in the early 1950s. A behaviorist, Skinner theorized that for effective learning, students must be reinforced constantly. At that time, media for such experiences were either books or teaching machines. The book or teaching machine took the student, step by step, through learning activities (similar in many ways to print-based tutorials, mentioned previously). When students completed an exercise, they turned to the next page or frame and immediately knew whether or not their answer was correct. When the answer was incorrect, the correct answer was explained or the student was directed to review and then attempt to answer the question again. These early teaching machines, such as PLATO (Control Data Corporation) and AIS (McDonnell Douglas Corporation), required customized terminals and software.

Computer-assisted Instruction (CAI). CAI expanded on PI principles but with an important difference; CAI did not require special hardware. The first CAI programs ran on mainframe computers. Today, CAI programs run on all types of hardware and are delivered by all types of media from disks to CDs to the Internet. Systems design projects often have CAI programs developed simultaneously with system design so that the training program is ready when the system is completed. Likewise, software vendors sometimes supply a learning disk, CD, or Web site link with their software. This tutorial, or CAI, offers various degrees of interaction between the trainee and the computer. Using the tutorial, the individual completes a series of lessons that include directions and practice in using the software. CAI often includes companion paper-based exercises and instructions.

Computer-Managed Instruction (CMI). CMI systems, on the other hand, typically combine instructional modules with other classroom management tasks such as enrollment management and other record keeping tasks. CMI systems can be used for testing, instruction, and/or maintaining student transcripts. They can generate, administer, and score tests. Many CMI programs have built-in pretests and posttests.

An example of CMI is Pathlore's Registrar system, which includes a wide range of reporting options including chargeback reports, cost performance reviews, and cost performance reports. Figure 6-5 illustrates a sample individual transcript report. Note that the report provides information regarding not only where Artie Alvares, Ramesh Baheri, Gale Black, and Jane Davis are in the training program, but also their total number of contact hours.

6.3.2.3.3 Interactive Multimedia Systems *Multimedia*-based, interactive learning systems combine the capabilities of many media. The interactive computer feature of these media enables self-paced and self-directed instruction. Because of the sensory input of graphics, animation, sound, and video, multimedia systems match many learners' preferred learning style. Of the two options discussed here, the interactive video tape is no longer a mainstream technology training tool. Learning and reference materials that are CD-based, however, are very popular.

6.3.2.3.4 Interactive Video Interactive video combines the capabilities of video with computer-assisted instruction and comes in two formats: laser disk (digital) and videotape (analog). When first introduced, interactive video was revolutionary. For the first time, multimedia was available to enhance Computer-based Instruction. Moreover, rather than having to go through the same set of experiences as everyone else, learners could pick and choose learning modules that fit their needs and skill levels. A major limitation to this technology was the need for special disks and dedicated disk players.

ALL EMPLOYEES WITH LESS THAN 40 HOURS TRAINING
(This report does not include people who have not taken any training.)
11/28/1999

Alvares, Artie

COURSE CODE	CLASS NAME	START DATE	STATUS	CONTACT HOURS
EXC100	Introduction to Microsoft Excel	10/11/1999	E	8.00
ADM160	Customer Billing Procedures	7/16/1999	E	8.00
ADM101	PC Computing	10/30/1998	F	8.00
MGT109	Time Management	8/27/1999	E	8.00
VID300	Stress Management Video	1/1/1999	F	1.00
			Total Hours	**33.00**

Baheri, Ramesh

COURSE CODE	CLASS NAME	START DATE	STATUS	CONTACT HOURS
ADM160	Customer Billing Procedures	7/16/1999	E	8.00
ADM220	Word Processing Fundamentals	7/9/1999	M	8.00
CLN100	CPR Training	10/11/1999	E	8.00
MGT109	Time Management	8/27/1999	E	8.00
VID300	Stress Management Video	1/1/1999	F	1.00
			Total Hours	**33.00**

Black, Gale

COURSE CODE	CLASS NAME	START DATE	STATUS	CONTACT HOURS
ADM160	Customer Billing Procedures	7/16/1999	E	8.00
ADM170	The Basics of Cost Accounting	9/2/1999	C	0
CLN100	CPR Training	8/4/1998	F	8.00
			Total Hours	**34.00**

Davis, Jane

COURSE CODE	CLASS NAME	START DATE	STATUS	CONTACT HOURS
MGT110	Management Leadership Seminar	9/27/1999	E	7.00
ADM220	Word Processing Fundamentals	7/9/1999	E	8.00
ADM101	PC Computing	10/30/1998	F	8.00
MGT109	Time Management	8/27/1999	E	8.00
			Total Hours	**31.00**

E = Enrolled	F = Finished
C = Canceled	M = Mastered

Figure 6-5
Pathlore transcript report. Reproduced with permission.

CD-based Training. The versatility, costs, and widespread availability of CDs as a delivery format have made interactive video disk technology old hat. PCs almost always include a CD player, and CD products include all the advantages of interactive video with none of the drawbacks, most notably the need for special equipment. CDs can hold incredible amounts of data from a wide variety of media, including text, numbers, audio, video, animation, and graphics. As an instructional delivery medium, CDs can include traditional Programmed Instruction (PI) and

Computer-assisted Instruction (CAI) tutorials. However, it is the CD's ability to store vast amounts of data that support multimedia enhancements—audio, video, animation, and graphics—that make CDs so versatile and useful for delivering instruction. The CD is merely the delivery technology.

Instructional CDs almost always add animation, video, and sound to the text-based CAI. Authoring software (discussed earlier) enables an instructional designer to incorporate computer graphics, animation, digitized video, still images, and sound into learning programs. Generally, these programs allow information to be imported in various forms from various sources. This information is structured into instructional units, and interactivity is added. Multimedia programs also are used to create presentations.

Learning materials based on CDs sometimes emphasize the multimedia entertainment aspects of training. Such courses appeal to end users whose learning style is visual. These courses utilize "books plus" meaning text with enhancements such as short videos or data sets that help the learner more quickly understand or apply the printed material.[11] CDs are found everywhere today, and some are loaded on local area networks and Intranets. Most, however, are stand-alone products that are simply "presented to end users, from car mechanics to astronauts, with no instruction in how to use them."[12] For effective use of CDs as an instructional material, users need training in search strategies and how to navigate the material. Simply having a disk does not mean that the user will intuitively know how to use it. Some companies provide video-tapes or audiotapes to demonstrate how to use and navigate an instructional CD.

Figure 6-6 is a listing of CD-based training options for learning Microsoft Office applications. Most are narrated and include screen shots, an index, and a glossary. Programs such as the NETg Inc.'s offering may include an assessment system, quizzes, and simulations.

6.3.2.3.5 Web-Based Training and Support Web-based Training (WBT) and support involves learners using the World Wide Web to access learning materials, connect to a wide range of supplementary resources, and have direct communication with their fellow learners as well as the instructor. Other terms that describe this technology are Web-based Learning (WBL), Internet-based Learning (IBT), or E-Learning. WBT is increasingly the distance learning medium of choice. In fact, WBT vendors such as SmartForce predict that in the near future, 80 percent of all corporate education will be delivered via the Internet. While this prediction is lofty, WBT has a distinct advantage over CD-based learning as instructional and informational programs can be easily updated and even more easily distributed. When materials are Web-based, the learner can access them whenever he or she has access to the Internet. Moreover, WBT tools are designed to support self-paced instruction as well as live interaction with an instructor and other learners.

Figure 6-6 PC productivity CDs

Microsoft Excell 2000 Fundamentals	Catapult Inc.	pbt.com
Discover Word 2000	DiscoverWare Inc.	discoverware.com
Excel 2000	Individual Software, Inc.	individualsoftware.com
Word 2000 Level 1	InfoSource Inc.	infosourcenet.com
Microsoft Office 2000 Step by Step Interface	Microsoft Press	mspress.microsoft.com
Microsoft Word 2000 Fundamentals	NETg Inc.	netg.com

WBT products, which are typically instructor-facilitated, can support registration, discussion boards, chat rooms, multipoint audio and video, whiteboards, class assignments, interactive quizzes, and even course development. Internet streaming—both audio and video—allows learners to replay educational lectures on demand. A total distance learning solution can integrate other products that support data and/or video transmissions. Software components can include an instructor client, a student client, and a server. Several popular products were listed in Chapter 4 (see Figure 4-12), along with their vendor.

Additionally, training vendors are packaging content along with Internet delivery tools. A corporate training department might choose, for example, to purchase an entire learning solution related to acquiring Microsoft Certification (see Figure 6-8) from any number of vendors, including SmartForce (*www.smartforce.com*). Other WBT providers, such as click2learn.com (http://click2learn.com), include training on their authoring products via their Websites and Cyberstate University (cyberstate-university.com) even has an electronic student union. Moreover, entire WBT learning solutions are available from many traditional universities, including New York University, Columbia University, and Stanford University, which have created for-profit entities that sell complete learning solutions to corporations and educational institutions alike. Most WBT content vendors also provide products via CD-ROM, as well as through the Internet.

An organizing tool for WBT is the portal. Learning portals are Web sites that offer trainees or organizations a "consolidated access to learning and training resources. Portals can range from a simple page filled with hyperlinks to a sophisticated virtual classroom and learning center."[13] Learning portals can be related to learning resources on a given topic or customized to a given user. Companies, universities (see the following Spotlight), communities, and training consultancies are developing portals. Masie explained that learning portals are hitting the marketplace as a response to e-commerce and appeal to those who like the idea of a single portal for all-world learning.

Although WBT advantages are obvious, limitations may include the need for streaming players, which are platform specific and must be downloaded, although most are available free. Additionally, most support either Windows or Macintosh.

SPOTLIGHT ON SOLUTIONS → Technology, People, Structure, Processes

NEW YORK UNIVERSITY INTRODUCES NYUHome

NYUHome is a portal—a door to many web-based services and tools. Using Netscape or Internet Explorer, you will be able to access your e-mail, Albert account [registration and transcript service], web forums, classes, research tools and more, bringing together all your Internet needs in one web page. Your NYUHome page is customizable, and can be adapted by you to fit your needs and interests. Different services and information, such as reference searches or a schedule of campus events, are provided through channels, and you can choose which channels you want to display on your page.

NYUHome will provide greatly enhanced e-mail, with ten times the current quota for e-mail and a built-in web-based e-mail client. This new service lets you access your e-mail from anywhere in the world with web access. Because your messages are stored on the server, you can work on e-mail from an office workstation, a home computer, a laptop in a hotel room or a public terminal, without having to transfer files between computers. In fact, all of NYUHome is designed for global access. You can go Home no matter where you are.

Source: Marilyn McMillan, NYU Chief Information Officer, e-mail to the NYU community on April 20, 2000.

However, most organizations are platform specific and can overcome these limitations easily, allowing learners to have several senses engaged in the learning process through the Web.

6.3.2.3.6 Advantages and Disadvantages of Computer-Based Training   In short, Computer-based Training programs can include media at many levels of interactivity that incorporate text, audio, and video. CBT systems conform well to several principles of adult learning. For example, CBT ensures that trainees are able to proceed through the lesson at their own pace. Training is time-independent; trainees need not adhere to a rigid time frame. Training is done independently of an instructor; the student guides the lesson. Although computer-based media vary in interactivity, the learner always is active in the learning process. Moreover, such training is fiscally sound as training can be done just in time.

The list of drawbacks to CBT typically begins with its development expense, which is followed closely by its perceived lack of personal touch. Such costs involve the author (the person who codes screen layouts, interactivity, test questions, etc.), the content expert (the expert in the subject matter to be taught), and the instructional design expert (the person who understands learning theory and how it is applied to the skills and concepts being taught).

Costs to consider with the development of an interactive, multimedia CBT program include the authoring system; the course designer; the script writer (the person who writes the audio and video sections of the program); and the film/video producer, actors, and actresses (individuals who produce and perform in the production). In addition, if the delivery is by CD, the CD must be pressed (this includes costs associated with producing the disk itself); otherwise, the time and expense involved with streaming technologies must be considered. Web-based distribution decreases this latter cost significantly. Recent cost figures for developing CBT range from $150/hour to $500/hour, depending on the quantity and quality of the medium.

Although CBT development expenses can be high, they are often cost justified by showing per-person or marginal costs. Per-person costs spread the expense of production over the number of trainees expected to benefit from the training. Marginal costs are the expenses of adding a trainee—in other words, the expense, once the disk is produced, to train yet another person. Other disadvantages include the necessity that the trainee often operate more than one piece of equipment and the scarcity of well-written, job-applicable, off-the-shelf programs. However, with the advent of the Web as a delivery medium, instructional systems can be updated and distributed easily. Just-in-time availability of learning makes the Web a delivery option of choice. Figure 6-7 summarizes advantages and disadvantages of various types of Computer-based Training.

6.3.2.3.7 Audio- and Videotape-Based Training   Today in many bookstores, audiotapes and videotapes sit on shelves alongside the books. While such media are not in contention to replace books, they are alternative forms for information dissemination. Audiotapes and videotapes sometimes supplement paper-based training manuals. Some trainees consider such media more personal than a book; others explain that audio or visual cues illustrate or explain things in a manner that a book cannot. Whatever the reason, the use of such media for training is growing. The following example illustrates the use of audio- and video-based training delivery:

> Company RST has just installed workstations on the desks of its mid-level managers. Although the managers have been using personal computers for some time now, they are suddenly introduced to a wide range of new

Approach	Commonly Used When	Advantages	Disadvantages
Computer-assisted Instruction	Content is stable; Actual situations need to be simulated	Portable learning materials	Development time and costs high
Computer-managed Instruction	Recording of learner performance is important	Provides learners with assessment and recordkeeping	Protecting test banks; Must be linked to other learning resources
Interactive multimedia	Large numbers of dispersed learners exist to offset high development costs; Content is stable	Appeals to multiple senses; Portable learning materials	Long development time; High expense; User must be motivated and trained to use
Web-based Training	Audience is large and dispersed; Content needs continuous updating	Universal language; Easy, affordable distribution; Content easily updated; Affordable technology	Need for technological infrastructure bandwidth and cabling; Ensuring learners do their own work

Figure 6-7
Advantages and disadvantages of computer-based training approaches

applications, including database management. The organization has in stock a number of VCRs, and its approach to training is to lend a VCR and training video to any manager who requests it for a period of one week.

Audio and video add a human element to self-paced training. Video goes a step beyond audio in providing visual information—demonstrations and examples that aid the learning process. In addition, such media enable trainees to learn at their own pace and convenience. Besides the problem of ensuring high-quality audio and video learning packages, other problems include maintaining the trainee's interest. Also, quality training programs are expensive to produce and buy. Costs to produce an in-house, application-specific video, for example, may range from $5,000 to $100,000. Prices for ready-made videos typically begin at $100.

6.3.2.3.8 Hands-On Workshops   Workshops are training sessions in which a facilitator guides the trainees to use technology. In a workshop situation, trainees learn and use skills through hands-on exercises, in which they also can learn from each other. The following example illustrates the use of workshops to deliver training:

The organization has subscribed to the DIALOG database for years. Despite its known benefits, however, few people seem to be using it. Roger Deveau, training director, invites managers and professionals to attend a 2-hour workshop to review principles of data retrieval and share ideas on how the system could be used in the organization. Roger uses exercises to review how Dialog works, and the group then proceeds at its own pace, with Roger offering one-on-one help and participants helping each other when appropriate.

Advantages to using a workshop approach to training are that learners get hands-on training using software features with immediate practice and application on (hopefully) examples similar to their own needs. The best workshops give learners a chance to bring at least one of their own applications to work on.

6.3.2.4 Manuals and Job Aids

Beginning the "refreeze" stage, where using the system becomes automatic with the way work is done, are manuals and job aids. These tools serve as references or reminders for completing tasks.

Manuals, which also are referred to as *system documentation,* are a written description of how a system operates and are a vital component of any system. Because a reference manual is comprehensive, individuals may need to know something about a system before they can even understand how to use the index. This is because programmers often are more concerned with what the program can do than in being able to explain how to use it. On the other hand, experienced users often can use a manual to teach themselves on a need-to-know basis.

Although manuals are valuable references for experienced users, they are seldom good learning tools for the novice. Well-written documentation does exist for some programs, but manuals rarely are recommended for initial training. Only if the manual is accompanied by an interactive tutorial and a motivated learner are manuals effective for training novices. However, used appropriately, manuals provide backup that allows experienced users to troubleshoot their own problems.

For specifics on how to complete a given task, job aids are useful. Job aids can be simple procedure lists or templates to which a user can refer easily. The operative word is *easily.* Rather than having to check indexes and read the manual materials, these simple aids provide a summary of functions and procedures. Even the most experienced user of Word or Access, for example, can find a list of frequently performed functions reassuring.

6.3.2.5 Coaching

Coaching, one-on-one training, is effective but a costly method of training delivery. Its effectiveness stems from direct interaction between trainee and trainer, so concerns and problems are addressed immediately. The trainee does not have to spend time reading manuals or trying extensive trial-and-error approaches. It is often difficult to justify monopolizing the time of a trainer with one person when, in a classroom situation, a trainer can teach 10 to 15 people. However, coaching may be the best approach in selected situations, such as for executives and specialists whose time is limited and expensive, for highly specialized applications or skills, and for resolving problems.

Coaching has long been recognized as the most effective way for adults to learn. It entails direct and immediate interaction between trainer and trainee. In such a situation, trainees get personalized feedback throughout the learning experience, and they proceed at their own rate of learning. The following example illustrates the use of coaching to deliver training:

> When Edward Thomas began his new job as manager of the loan department at City National Bank, he needed to learn how to use the bank's customer databases. Because the databases were online and available for verifying customer records, they would be an asset for him. Ed's supervisor spent an afternoon with him going over access codes, key words, and what to do when problems arose. Ed's intensive training enabled him to learn the system easily and quickly.

6.3.2.6 Seminars

"Lecture only if you must."[14] This advice is offered frequently by people interested in training results. Lecture is a traditional classroom approach to learning and usually involves an individual trainer giving information to a group of trainees. The trainees typically listen and take notes in an effort to understand and remember the

COLLEGE KIDS COACH BUSY BANKERS

Tech trainers at investment firm Morgan Stanley Dean Witter are using part-time college students to bring coaching straight to end users' desktops.

That's because when the trainers held past classes, no investment bankers came. "They don't like to leave their desks. They don't really find training that important. They think it's very important that if a customer calls, they're available," says Shannon Lally, who works in the user technology training group within MSDW's information technology training department.

The coaches circulate though the I-banking department answering questions and teaching end users how to use applications, which are mostly MSDW proprietary software. The young semi-trainers also help end users connect up with Help Desk staffers who can answer more complicated questions and fix hardware and software breakdowns.

Since it began in 1995, the program has grown to cover eight departments in addition to I-banking. "It became really popular," says Lally. She says that when a coach arrives at an employee's desk, the employee frequently has a handful of sticky notes with questions.

The training department has brought 19 coaches on board. Lally and her colleagues recruit the students from placement offices at New York City colleges and universities—many are MBA students. In addition to the on-the-spot coaching, they build Web pages, create handouts and quick reference cards, and even teach some classes.

Lally says the program has spared the training department the cost of hiring some professional trainers. And the appeal of the coaching program is pretty universal, Lally says. "Whenever I tell people about it, they always say, 'I wish I had a coach, too.'"

information. The following example illustrates the use of seminar as a method of training delivery:

> Company DEF, with a network of personal computers in place, trained its supervisory people on new software designed to report performance appraisals. The new system could tabulate scores and help the supervisor identify recurring problems or trends. It also could plot an employee's progress from quarter to quarter. Because the system needed to be operable within two weeks and because the supervisors were centrally located at the organization's headquarters, the seminar, combined with demonstration, was deemed the most appropriate mode of training delivery.

The term *seminar* is used here to describe learning experiences that may include a minilecture, but are small enough to include opportunities for trainees to interact with the lecturer and with each other. The advantages of the seminar are that such a learning experience is easy to establish, trainees are familiar with the lecture method, and it is an effective way to disseminate information to groups of people quickly. Seminars are effective when the seminar designer provides ample opportunity for trainee interaction. Research has shown that when individuals leave a traditional lecture, they retain only 25 percent of the material to which they were exposed. Seminars are most effective when they are combined with other strategies such as a demonstration or hands-on training.

6.3.3 Group Learning and Support Strategies

In addition to training for new systems and identified business needs, organizations may offer various other educational programs to promote and support the effective use of computers in the workplace. Some of the most commonly used are discussed in this section.

6.3.3.1 Computer Fair or Expo

"The [insert the name of your state, e.g., Indiana] State Fair is an opportunity for [insert the nickname that describes people in your state, e.g., Hoosiers] to display their latest developments—agricultural, industrial, technological—to the rest of [insert the name of your state again]." This is also the purpose of a computer fair.

Such an event may be similar to a state fair or national conference, such as the annual Federal Office Systems Expo (FOSE) in Washington, D.C.; the annual INFO show in New York City; or the semiannual COMDEX Show (Fall, Las Vegas; Spring, Atlanta). At these events, vendors display their latest hardware and software developments. These events also feature talks by leaders in information systems planning and management. Topics typically include developing standards, implementation techniques, training, and industry forecasts. Workshops for users are often included. These events provide an opportunity for information sharing and learning.

Likewise, a computer fair held in an organization can be a forum for information sharing and learning. On a less grandiose scale, a company-based fair can provide an opportunity for EUIS to display hardware and software that are available to end users. In addition, a seminar, presentation, or even roundtable discussion can increase user acceptance of new technologies. Such forums also provide an opportunity for users to communicate individual needs and concerns to planners.

6.3.3.2 Advisory Council

An advisory council is a select committee that offers advice to the EUIS analyst or task force regarding technology and information-related concerns. An advisory council typically is created after the fact. With the new technology in place, a council may monitor the implementation of the current project and perhaps help the systems analyst develop new products or identify training requirements. Like any advisory council, it is composed of individuals at the upper levels and in user departments who have a vested interest in the success of the project. Success of the council rests, in large part, upon its membership and the ability of the EUIS analyst to listen and respond to its suggestions.

6.3.3.3 Newsletters

Newsletters and internal newspapers (often called house organs) are part of the organizational culture of most large companies. Newsletters typically are written and disseminated by a human resources department and offer updates on company policies, news about business performance and company events, and personal notes about employees (promotions, transfers, marriages, etc.).

The EUIS analyst can use such newsletters to disseminate information about plans, new products, an upcoming fair, users' groups (discussed later), and so on. As an alternative, many EUIS groups write and disseminate their own newsletters. Either way, a newsletter can be an effective way to reach everyone in the organization with news of technology plans, new products, training programs, and success stories in which end-user computing has been well accepted.

6.3.3.4 Internal Consultants

Internal consultants are full-time employees of the organization. An internal consultant is available to company employees on an ongoing basis to aid with information processing needs. Consultants perform a variety of roles. They may provide technical expertise to analysts, provide planning expertise to managers, or fulfill other high-level roles. They may aid end users in applying information technologies to their jobs or departments. The internal consultant offers individualized support that is often extremely important to implementation. The individual may work within the EUIS department or be a member of the information center staff.

6.3.3.5 Information Center

The information center is a focal point for supporting the use of computers by non-technical personnel. The center is a place where users can go for help in learning new programs or developing new applications. An information center usually includes a Help Desk for quick response to questions or problems (see chapter 7). The information center can provide the tutoring and expertise users need in applying new computer technologies on the job. Employees who know where to get additional training and help in using technologies are less resistant than employees who feel left on their own.

6.3.3.6 User Groups

User groups are informal groups of users of computers or other technologies who meet to exchange expertise, experiences, and problems. Members usually are highly motivated and skilled individuals who want to share and learn techniques related to technology. User groups were first formed by users and supported by vendors of software products. IBM, Wang, and Goal Systems (CBT software and online reference) all supported very active user groups, including national conferences with many hundreds of users. As an organizational learning strategy, it supports users sharing—and learning—with each other.

Many cities have metropolitan users' groups, and organizations may sponsor members. What is becoming more prevalent, however, is that organizations sponsor user groups within the organization. Often over brown bag lunches, users discuss successes and problems. User groups are extremely motivational in fostering not just more use of new technologies, but more creative uses.

6.3.3.7 Professional Organizations

Professional organizations such as the American Society for Training and Development (ASTD), the Association of Information Technology Professionals (AITP), and the Organizational Systems Research Association (OSRA) provide a source for information systems professionals to learn about new developments in information technologies and what is happening nationwide and in their communities. Such networks enable individuals to participate in seminars, presentations, and conferences on topics related to effective technology application. This networking—meeting others with similar concerns, problems, and new ideas—offers many benefits, such as learning how another organization handled a particular situation. A more complete list of information processing professional organizations appears in Appendix 1.

6.4   IMPLEMENTING SUCCESSFUL PROGRAMS

No training method will work unless the learner is convinced that the skill to be learned is useful to him or her back on the job. To this end, it is important that a learner's preferred learning strategy be supported as much as possible. An effective training initiative will match the right content to the right learners—those that have a need to know—and in the right way. Moreover, effectively learning to apply technology typically calls for more than one approach to learning. And when live instruction is the solution, just as important as targeting the right learning audience is finding the right instructor(s) for the learning program.

6.4.1 Checklist for Choosing Instructional Strategies

The trainer must choose from a variety of methods and media for meeting training needs. Likewise, delivery includes a variety of strategies. Answers to the following questions can be used to develop criteria for appropriate instructional strategies:

How many people must be trained? Where are they located?
What is the current level of trainee expertise?
How complex is the learning?
How soon do people need to be trained?
What methodologies have been successful in the past?
What facilities are available?
Are training materials available or must they be developed?

6.4.2 Selecting Training Participants

Selecting the right training participants occurs in the assessment stage. Perhaps the most important rule is that the trainees selected for the learning activity should have a need to know; in other words, they should be able to apply the skills they are going to learn directly to their jobs.

Another consideration is how workers should be grouped for the training. It is not always practical to group people solely on their need to know. Other considerations are the current skill levels of trainees, their organizational levels, and the skill levels required (performance objectives). For example, putting novice and advanced spreadsheet software users together to learn a newly adopted version of the software is not recommended.

Grouping individuals with different learning objectives also poses problems. Some individuals may need a thorough working knowledge of all software features, while others may need just a general overview of capabilities and applications. Also, when managers and subordinates are grouped together for the same learning activity, an even split of managers and subordinates is suggested.

6.4.3 Selecting Training Instructors

EUIS workshops and seminars, as well as support materials, may be developed and/or delivered by the technology vendor or a vendor's agent, by an outside consultant or firm, or by an internal trainer.

6.4.3.1 The Technology Vendor as Trainer

Most EUIS equipment and software vendors include training in their customer support offerings. Vendor training can range from a demonstration of how to use a printer to a five-day seminar on Intranets. Training often is included in the vendor's proposal to sell and install the new system. It is expected that the vendor has the most expertise in using its products and a vested interest in ensuring that the equipment is used effectively.

When a large system is new, a vendor often provides complimentary basic training for one or two people at no charge. Courses for additional persons or for advanced skills are then made available on a fee basis. Although courses are sometimes offered at the customer's site, many courses are available only at the vendor's facility. IBM, for example, offers a multitude of seminars. IBM's courses are offered at various instructional levels, from novice to highly technical. A fee is charged for some IBM courses, others are free.

Some vendors have developed training courses and materials that can be purchased by the customer for in-house trainers. In effect, a vendor may offer purchasers a course to train the trainer. In addition, vendors often offer Web-based tutorials, reference manuals, or other learning aids for their products.

Most hardware and software vendors, such as Dell, Gateway, IBM, Microsoft, WordPerfect, and Intuit, have customer hot lines. Using a toll-free number, purchasers can call for online, expert assistance. The use of such hot lines is not intended for training; rather, it offers support for problem resolution. In addition, vendors often establish user groups.

However suited vendor training may be to learning specifics of a system, it does not always meet organizational or individual needs. The type or amount of training available may not be appropriate for the particular individual or group. This lack of control over content and delivery options may not result in the desired learning outcomes.

A relatively recent development are certification exams that certify that individuals have a specific skill set. These routes can be categorized as software, hardware, or networking, and are described in Figure 6-8.

6.4.3.2 The Outside Consultant as Trainer

An outside consultant usually is used when an organization does not have the expertise or resources (time, staff, materials) to develop a training program for an identified need. When an organization chooses an outside consultant to conduct the training, they commonly select a trainer who was involved in the initial needs assessment. At other times, the assessment was done internally, and a consultant is hired to develop a program to address the identified training needs.

When choosing an outside training consultant, the planner should check the reputation of the consultant, ensure that the consultant knows what outcomes are expected, and continually follow up with the consultant. Because the training planner is accountable for the learning experience, continuous evaluation of the classes being conducted is advised.

An example of a training vendor (not a technology vendor) that offers a variety of training and support services is the Masie Center. Described as an international think tank focused on learning and technology, the Center (http://www.masie.com) offers public and customized seminars. Additionally, the Center cohosts TechLearn, an annual conference that brings together leaders in the field to discuss new technologies and learning issues. A compendium of materials from their meetings is available on CD, as well as through the Internet. Their Web site also includes links to other resources such as news releases and recent articles and books.

6.4.3.3 The Outside Educational Institution as Trainer

Many organizations offer tuition reimbursement programs to employees who take job-related courses or attend seminars outside the organization. In such cases, the training planner has virtually no control over course content. However, institutions generally publish performance objectives and content outlines, which the training planner can use to select courses or seminars that fit the overall training strategy for learning new systems or applications.

The major disadvantage of courses provided by outside institutions is that they are general in nature, and trainees must sift through the information to select what

SOFTWARE

Many certification exams are available for applications software packages (spreadsheets, database management systems, word processing, and presentation graphics). The Microsoft Office User Specialist (MOUS) certifications cover popular applications. For most applications, more than one certification (core and expert) is available. In addition, operating system software certification, e.g., Windows 2000, involves operating system basics and various levels of server technology.

HARDWARE

More than 120,000 professionals hold the A+™ Certification, which assesses desktop computer service and repair technology skills. The exam is developed and administered by the Computing Technology Industry Association (CompTIA), an association representing over 7,500 hardware and software firms. While the certification is designed for hardware technicians, it is considered valuable for anyone who will support computer end users.

NETWORKING

Microsoft Corporation, Novell Corporation, and CompTIA offer certifications that deal with computer network technologies. Network+™, a product- and vendor-neutral certification, is the most recent certification examination to be developed by CompTIA. Novell and Microsoft certifications require expertise in vendor-specific networking software/hardware solutions

The following sources provide excellent information about certification. Specific URLs for the Web sites may change from time to time, so conducting a Web search may be necessary to locate Internet resources.

www.certification.com. This site, sponsored by about.com reviews publications, offers current news, and presents dozens of vendors, training providers, salary surveys, and general information about computer certification

www.certifiedcomputerpro.com. Primarily links to certification-related sites, this site contains links to news groups. Its Certification Program Counts section lists the number of people certified in each program.

www.gocertify.com. An EarthWeb site, this resource organizes information by certification vendor and by topic. Its Reading Room links articles and white papers related to certification.

www.comptia.org. This is the site of the Computing Technology Industry Association, the organization that develops A+ hardware and A+ networking certification examinations.

Source: Ray, Charles M. and McCoy, Randy. (2000), "Why Certification in Information Systems," *Information Technology, Learning, and Performance Journal.* (18)1, 1–3. Reprinted with permission.

Figure 6-8
Software, hardware, and networking certification routes

applies specifically to their job environments. Trainees also must take the initiative to acquire practice on the job and apply the skills they have learned.

On the other hand, when trainees go outside the organization for training, they have opportunities to exchange ideas with others. This aspect persuades organizations to sponsor employee participation in organizations such as the American Society for Training and Development (ASTD), the Association of Information Technology Professionals (AITP), or the Organizational Systems Research Association (OSRA).

6.4.3.4 The Internal Trainer

Internal trainers may work full time at training or be practitioners who have part-time training responsibilities. Trainers often develop expertise in certain areas of instruction (e.g., word processing, database management, graphics) and plan and conduct all courses in their specialty. Many large organizations have extensive internal training programs to meet business, technical, and office computing needs.

An internal training staff assures the organization of good, consistent training. Most importantly, it provides efficient training because programs can be tailored to specific business needs or project objectives. In addition, large organizations can provide internal training at a low cost per trainee. However, trainers may become too narrow; they may determine that their expertise is always needed, or (like some teachers) they may become too rigid in their plans.

Advantages and disadvantages as well as costs must be considered by any training manager. For example, for special requirements or small organizations, it may be less expensive to hire a $1,200-a-day expert to conduct the training than to pay an internal trainer to learn the content, then plan and deliver the course.

6.4.4 The Training Plan

Plan the work and work the plan. Planning the training experience entails defining the performance objectives and knowing what needs to be taught and to whom. The complexity of the material or skill to be learned and the abilities of the trainers are taken into account as the designer puts together an instructional program and follows it through to completion. The designer also should ensure that the training program is given adequate time and priority.

A training plan may be simple or complex depending on the requirements. A plan to develop proficiency with a single software program in one department may be fairly straightforward. A training plan to support a large reengineering project could be very comprehensive. It could easily involve dozens of training requirements for hundreds of users at all levels of the organization, geographically dispersed, over an extended period of time with a budget in the millions of dollars.

Technology is often underused because practitioners do not know how to use it to the fullest, and this means training and on-going support strategies are considered. Dissatisfied users often complain that insufficient time is spent in classroom training, course content is complex, and training manuals are difficult to understand. Users also report a need for training that is more practical than theoretical and for training that focuses on how they could *use* the system.[15] Follow-up training sessions, users' groups, and a newsletter for sharing ideas should always be part of the plan.

6.5 EVALUATING TRAINING PROGRAMS

Evaluation is the fourth stage in the training cycle, yet is a continuous process. Although evaluation is time consuming and can be costly, its role in ensuring that the right things are done at the right time with the right learners in the right priority order is invaluable. Planning evaluation strategies should take place prior to the design stage, as evaluation criteria will be benchmarks for determining whether or not program goals were met. The overall goal of evaluation is not to label a training effort as good or bad; rather, its goal is to determine what went right and what went wrong, and learn from those experiences.

Despite knowing the value of evaluations, training evaluation is not always done. Reasons abound. Deadline pressures, projects that are considered too big or too small to bother with, and an attitude that it's always been done it this way are given as reasons (excuses). Training evaluation, however, is important and should be done at least from time to time. The first step is to determine what should be evaluated, or the evaluation criteria.

Criteria are measures of success that can be used to determine whether or not the objectives of the training program were met. Donald Kirkpatrick, the guru of training evaluation strategies, has identified four domains, which are categories of similar ideas or thoughts, that can help planners determine what they intend to evaluate. These are reaction, learning, job behavior, and organizational results.[16] A fifth domain, process, is also an important consideration (see Figure 6-9).

Reaction refers to the learner's perception of the value and appropriateness of the training efforts, including course design, the instructor's performance, and whether or not the learning activities met their expectations. Adult learners are resources to effective training design as well as its target; their feedback can be invaluable to training designers. The most common strategy to obtain reaction data is an end-of-the-program survey, often referred to as a smile sheet, because instructors sometimes use such a survey to get feedback on how well they (the instructor) did, and feedback usually makes them smile.

Evaluation strategies to assess *learning* include tests, demonstrations, role plays, portfolios, or other performance outcomes. Learning is the overall objective of any training effort. Although tests are much more common in academic settings than organizational settings, test data can help the designer or instructor determine where the program's strengths or limitations are. Testing in an organizational setting is almost never used to assign grades. Increasingly, performance-based activities are used to assess whether or not learning occurred.

Job behavior refers to a category of evaluation techniques designed to determine whether or not the skills learned in the training activities were applied back on the job. One way to make this determination is to survey learners or their managers two weeks, two months, or even a year after the training effort to determine their perceived usefulness of the training. As with all evaluation data, it is important that those who are asked to evaluate job behavior know that data will be used to evaluate the training program, not their job performance.

The most difficult evaluation domain to evaluate is *organizational results*. The primary question asked here is how training efforts match the larger goals of the organization. The goal is to link any improved learner performance to soft (improved morale) or hard dollar outcomes (increased sales, lower error rates).

Training Process, the evaluation techniques that describe the training cycle itself, extends Kirkpatrick's domain list[17] and is added here as a fifth domain. Data from these techniques are used to assess or audit the training department. Because a learning organization has a goal to learn from its successes as well as its failures,

Figure 6-9
Five domains of training evaluation criteria

- Reaction
- Learning
- Job behavior
- Organizational results
- Training process

documenting which training efforts work and which do not work in a given organization is useful to training professionals. Because training can be delivered in more than one way, can we determine what the *best* way is?

In developing evaluation strategies, it is useful to keep in mind who is interested in the results of the training assessment—top management, supervisors, systems developers, or the training director. Top management may want data that justify the costs of training (organizational domain). They may want to know whether trainees were able to apply what they learned to their jobs (job behavior domain) and to what degree performance was improved (job behavior domain). The systems developer will want to know if the system was easy to use (learning); evaluation data could be used to redesign screens or keystroke sequences. The supervisor will want to know if the user is able to perform a specific task (learning). The training director will want to know if training was done the best way possible and whether trainees considered the training experience valuable (process domain). The trainer may want to know whether trainees were pleased with the specific delivery of the workshop (reaction). Figure 6-10 illustrates several reaction evaluation forms—midpoint reaction, workshop rating, and courseware evaluation.

6.6 SUMMARY

Technology is useless unless it is used, and using it requires training. Training for EUIS encompasses learning needed skills, understanding why the technology is used, and most importantly discovering how to apply it on the job. Training for EUIS will increase in importance as users are trained and retrained to use new technologies, as the use of desktop computers grows, and as the number of knowledge workers employed in offices continues to increase. Moreover, employment trends show that skill requirements will continue to change.

This chapter took an action research approach to training programs—assessment, design, implementation, and evaluation. Organizational, task, and individual assessment helps the training program designer understand exactly what the

Figure 6-10
Typical training evaluation forms

> **TRAINING PARTICIPANT REACTION FORM**
> —Midpoint Evaluation—
>
> At this point in the training program, you understand the purposes and procedures of your classroom experiences. Please take a few moments now to share your reactions with me. I will use the information from these forms to make the remaining sessions as valuable to you as possible. Complete the following sentences:
> 1. To date, the topics I have valued most in this program are
> 2. To date, the topic(s) I have valued least in this program are
> 3. The method of instruction I prefer is
> 4. The method of instruction I least prefer is
> 5. The next time the instructor teaches this material, I suggest
> 6. The instructor should emphasize the following in the next sessions
> 7. I suggest we discontinue doing
> 8. Overall, this program has been

```
WORKSHOP RATING SHEET

Participant # _____

Rate each of the following on a five-point scale:
1 = Disagree strongly
2 = Disagree
3 = Neutral
4 = Agree
5 = Agree strongly

1. _____  Presentations were well organized.
           Comments:

2. _____  Trainer used appropriate visual aids and used them well.
           Comments:

3. _____  Trainer chose appropriate methodology for instruction.
           Comments:

4. _____  Trainer knew the subject matter.
           Comments:

5. _____  Entire course design was appropriate for skills/concepts.
           Comments:

6. _____  Trainer's overall presentation style was good.
           Comments:

Topics/activities most valuable:


Topics/activities least valuable:
```

Figure 6-10
(*continued*)

training program is to accomplish, who the target audience is, and how results of training will be applied on the job. Assessment is considered a critical stage. Identifying what needs to be learned by whom should be determined up front. To conduct a needs analysis, the training program developer can use interviews, questionnaires, observations, or focus groups. The purpose of such inquiries is to determine whether training could result in improved performance.

Basic to designing effective training programs is knowledge about how adults learn. Although the terms *pedagogy* and *andragogy* have roots that are related to the age of the learner, the terms refer to strategies for specific learning needs based on the experience of the learner. Pedagogy means teacher-directed learning experiences that are structured, making the instructor responsible for learning results. Andragogy, on the other hand, is learner-directed training and requires the learner to be responsible for learning. Adult learners tend to prefer hands-on learning that they can apply to their work immediately. They tend to be self-directed and prefer to work at their own pace. Generally, they like to have control over their learning environment.

With knowledge of who needs to learn what, the next step is to identify specific learning strategies. This chapter examined training and support as part of an

---

COURSEWARE EVALUATION FORM

Following is a list of courseware used in this session. Please rate each item as to its overall quality as well as the overall impact you believe it had on your comprehension.

Quality scale:

N/A	throw away!	poorly done	neutral	nicely done	superb!
0	1	2	3	4	5

Comprehension scale:

N/A	confused me!	of no help	neutral	of some help	of great help
0	1	2	3	4	5

Book   Quality: _____   Comprehension: _____
   Comments:

Handouts   Quality: _____   Comprehension: _____
   Comments:

PowerPoint slides   Quality: _____   Comprehension: _____
   Comments:

Videotape   Quality: _____   Comprehension: _____
   Comments:

Peer tutoring   Quality: _____   Comprehension: _____
   Comments:

Figure 6-10
(*continued*)

implementation and learning support system. Thus, the overall goal of training and support activities is to ensure that the target population is ready to learn (motivation or "unfreezing"), uses appropriate methods to learn (instructional strategies or "moving"), and that use of the new skills meshes with the way work is done and becomes the accepted way of doing tasks (ongoing support, or "refreezing").

Specific strategies to ensure that learners are motivated to learn, really do learn, and apply what they learn back on the job were classified here as supporting individual or group learning. Individual learning and support strategies include brochures and promotional pieces, demonstrations, tutorials (print-, CD-, or Web-based Training) and hands-on workshops. Web-based Training, because of the ease and low cost for delivering training, is a fast-growing option. Ongoing individual support activities include manuals and job aids, coaching, and seminars. Group learning and support strategies include computer fairs, advisory councils, newsletters, user groups, and professional organizations.

Experts agree that the choice of instructional strategy depends upon the complexity of the skill and knowledge to be learned, the current expertise of the learner, how many people need to be trained on a system, the time frame for learning, and individual learning styles. With answers to these questions, the training designer can choose one or a variety of methods for doing the training.

Evaluation answers the question, "Did the training program do what it was expected to do?" Evaluation reports need to address the concerns of who has requested them. Top management, supervisors, the systems developer, the training director, and the trainer may all want an evaluation of a training effort. Evaluation, the final stage of the action research model, employs the same techniques as the needs assessment.

In short, the key to successful systems implementation is to see that end users are trained and supported. Training is continuous, not a one-shot, ad hoc effort. As organizations become more and more reliant on technologies, they are investing more and more company resources in seeing that workers can use the technology. EUIS experts recommend that dollar investment in training and support match dollar for dollar the investment in technology. Training should be done for the right things and for the right people in the right way in the right priority order. Training should be allotted adequate time and resources. Systems training is continuous (it never ends!). The next chapter, "Support and Help Desk Management," overviews those learning and support services that are typically part of an Information Systems Department in large organizations.

KEY TERms

- Computer-based Training (CBT)
- Individual analysis
- Interactive multimedia systems
- Organizational analysis
- Organizational culture
- Task analysis
- Training needs assessment
- Web-based Training (WBT)

DISCUSSION QUESTIONS

1. Discuss the role of training in implementing EUIS.
2. Distinguish between andragogy and pedagogy.
3. What is the purpose of assessment? Why is assessment the most critical step in designing training programs? What are some of the key questions to be asked when assessing training requirements for a new EUIS installation?
4. Draw a picture of the person who will be sitting down at the computer to use your training package. Include facial details and the work area. What does this picture tell you about instructional design needs?
5. List learning and support strategies commonly used to ensure a successful systems implementation. Which strategies are used at the (1) unfreezing stage, (2) moving stage, and (3) refreezing stage? Which strategies are aimed at an individual learner? Which are aimed at learners in groups?
6. What circumstances lead organizations to develop training programs themselves, rely on the system developer, or hire external consultants to provide training? Give an appropriate training situation for each alternative.
7. What is the purpose of training evaluation? Why is it important? Using the five domains of training evaluation discussed here, discuss how one would go about determining what to evaluate, as well as who would be interested in the results.

APPLICATION EXERCISES

1. Select a microcomputer software program, such as a bibliographic management, spreadsheet, or presentation graphics package. Conduct a needs analysis among your classmates and design a training program to teach the package to them, including a means for evaluation. Conduct a training session to teach the first part of your program, demonstrating the software to the class, and have the class evaluate the presentation.

2. Visit the Web site of Blackboard, Inc. (www.blackboard.com). At the time of this writing, they offer a free, 30-day trial shell of their distance learning software, Download the shell and use it to support the course you developed in exercise 1.

3. Investigate the training program for EUIS provided through the computer center (or other facility) on your campus. Interview the director or an instructor in the center. What courses are offered? How are the courses taught? How was the appropriate content for courses determined? Evaluate the center's training offerings in light of what you learned in this chapter.

4. Talk with someone you know who works in an office to find out about the training programs offered in his or her organization for EUIS. If possible, obtain samples of course offerings, internal newsletters, or other information about the program. Has your interviewee participated in any of the computer training programs? How does he or she evaluate the experience? Summarize your findings in a report or organize them for presentation to your classmates. Compare your findings with the findings of other students.

5. Obtain tutorial software programs for popular PC packages. Try them out and evaluate their effectiveness in helping first-time users learn to use the software programs.

SUGGESTED READINGS

Masie, Elliot. *The Computer Training Handbook.* 2nd ed. (Minneapolis: Lakewood Books, 1995).

Merriam, Sharan B., and Rosemary S. Caffarella. *Learning in Adulthood.* (San Francisco: Jossey-Bass, 1998).

O'Connor, Bridget N., Michael Bronner, and Chester Delaney. *Training for Organizations.* 2nd ed. (Cincinnati: South-Western Educational Publishing Company, 2001).

Parry, Scott B. *Evaluating the Impact of Training.* (Alexandria, Va.: American Society for Training and Development, 1997).

Schank, Roger. *Virtual Learning.* (New York: McGraw-Hill, 1997).

Tapscott, Don. *Growing Up Digital: The Rise of the Net Generation.* (New York: McGraw-Hill, 1998).

ENDNOTES

1. Elliot Masie, *The Computer Training Handbook,* 2nd ed. (Minneapolis: Lakewood Books, 1995), 20.
2. Ibid.
3. Bob Filipczak, "The Tug of War over Computer Training," *Training* 6 (June 1997): 35–40.
4. Bridget N. O'Connor, Michael Bronner, and Chester Delaney, *Training for Organizations,* 2nd ed. (Cincinnati: South-Western Educational Publishing Company, 2001).
5. L. E. Raho, J. A. Belcher, and K. D. Fielder, "Assimilating New Technology into the Organization: An Assessment of McFarlan and McKenney's Model," *MIS Quarterly* 11 (1987): 47–57.
6. H. Albert Napier, Richard R. Bastell, David M. Lane, and Norman S. Guadagno, "Knowledge of Command Usage in a Spreadsheet Program: Impact on User Interface Design and Training." No date.
7. N. Deane Meyer and Mary Boone, *The Information Edge* (Toronto: Gage Publishing Co., 1989).
8. Masie op. cit., 34.
9. Marianne Kolsabuk McGee, "Save on Training," *InformationWeek* 688 (June 22, 1998): 141–146.
10. Online Learning News, (Lakewood: Bill Communication, Oct. 19, 1999).

11. Marilyn MacKellar, and Franki Elliott, "The Importance of Training CD-ROM End Users," *Computers in Libraries,* 2 (February 1999), 63–66.
12. Ibid.
13. Elliott Masie, "Special Report: Learning Portal Watching Guide," *TechLearn* (Monday, October 18, 1999).
14. Julius Eitington, *The Winning Trainer* (Houston, Tex.: Gulf Publishing Co., 1989), 297.
15. Barbara Braverman, Thomas J. Castle, and Barbara McKee, "Implementing OA: A Case Study of Techno-stress." In *A Compendium of Materials from the Fifth Annual Office Systems Research Association Conference* New York City. (Cleveland: Office Systems Research Association, 1986), 313–325.
16. Donald L. Kirkpatrick. *Evaluating Training Programs: The Four Levels.* (San Francisco: Berrett-Koehler Publishers, 1996).
17. Bridget N. O'Connor, Michael Bronner, and Chester Delaney, *Training For Organizations*, 2nd ed. (Cincinnati: South-Western Educational Publishing Company, 2001).

Chapter 7

Support and Help Desk Management

Learning Objectives

Upon completing this chapter, you should be able to:

➤ Differentiate indexed online help systems from context-specific help and wizards.

➤ Match Computer-Telephony Integration (CTI), Interactive Voice Response (IVR), and Web-enabled support to how each can support Help Desk service goals.

- Give examples of ways in which customer support software can be used in the Help Desk environment.
- Suggest ways a Help Desk agent can help callers explain their problems.
- List personal and professional characteristics of an effective Help Desk agent.
- Identify professional organizations devoted to training and supporting Help Desk professionals.
- Explain the value of evaluating Help Desk operations.
- List pros and cons of outsourcing Help Desk operations.
- Describe the Help Desk of the future.

7.1 INTRODUCTION

Information Systems Departments are responsible for ensuring that end users use the technologies designed to support their work effectively and efficiently. Well-planned and implemented training programs (as discussed in chapter 6) are vital strategies to ensure use and acceptance of information technologies. However, even the best of training program designers cannot anticipate the issues and problems that individual users will experience in their day-to-day work. One thing we know about systems is that they sometimes do not work exactly as expected, and system glitches and operator errors are commonplace. One thing we know about formal training is that its designers can't anticipate every application or problem a user may have. Therefore, ongoing support—or just-in-time learning—and trouble-shooting is the focus of this chapter.

Just-in-time learning (JITL) is the training approach that makes context-sensitive learning material available exactly when a worker needs to learn something specific.[1] This chapter explores two ways to deliver this JITL learning: mediated, (*performance support*) and live (*Help Desk*). Performance support tools include CBT-based course modules as well as online help and reference, hypertext, computer-based training, multimedia, databases, and expert systems. Performance support can also encompass printed materials, video, classroom training, or other more traditional materials. Like knowledge management, which describes efforts to capture an organization's collective experience and make it accessible to everyone, performance support's objective is to provide information or assistance at the time the user needs it, rather than to teach some broader set of skills and knowledge for future use. Sometimes one needs information, not learning. Alternatively, when a user gets immediate help from a person in real time via the telephone or asynchronously via the Web, these live professionals are called *agents*, analysts, or support engineers. They work in an environment called the Help Desk.

This chapter gives an overview of the considerations that go into developing and managing online help and Help Desk support systems. These support functions are vital as systems become more complex. Most large organizations use 30 to 50 different applications and types of hardware.[2] In any such environment, problems will occur; it is the goal of the IS Department to ensure that troubles disappear. The chapter concludes with a look at the Help Desk of the future.

Performance support is an application of technology that provides direct links to performance. The most effective learning happens when training is embedded in the work that needs to be done. Noted consultant Gloria Gery pioneered this area by emphasizing what technology *could* do for training, rather than what was being done with it through her books, *Making CBT Happen* (1987) and *Electronic Performance Support Systems* (1991), both from Weingarten Publications in Boston. This section will use performance support to encompass online help, hypertext, databases, and expert systems. Peformance support is used much as a library—but with the added computer capabilities that ease communication, retrieval, examination, and manipulation of data.

7.2.1   Online Help

The goal of *online help* is to help users help themselves. Users are increasingly self-directed and independent learners. Most users prefer to figure out a problem on their own if they can do it quickly. Nearly everyone's first choice for assistance would be a tutor who shows up just at the right time to immediately help solve the problem. Because that is a costly and unrealistic solution, most individuals use the online help function when they believe it will provide help.

Help functions have evolved from being solely indexed lists to *wizards* that guide and sometimes demonstrate the task in question. Indexed lists linked with instructions on how to do tasks are useful only when users know the exact name of the feature they want to use. *Contextual help* addresses the "I don't know what to call my problem" issue. Word's Mr. Paperclip, for example, appears automatically when it senses the user is floundering in an application. PowerPoint's wizard goes a step further in providing advice about structuring presentations, as well as how to use the system technically. Companies also design their own customized help systems for proprietary in-house developed applications.

7.2.2   Expert Systems

When knowledge is rule-based, rules can be automated. An *expert system* is a computer program that incorporates the knowledge of an expert or group of experts on a particular subject and enables a user to systematically ask questions related to

SPOTLIGHT ON SOLUTIONS → Technology, People, Structure, Processes

Eli Lily's Scientific Performance Improvement Network (SPIN) is based on Lotus Notes and includes threaded discussions, a directory of subject-matter experts who can be contacted, links to databases, and entire, online courses. SPIN is an example of performance support that is designed to impart existing knowledge, as well as create new knowledge through human interaction.

JCPenney's performance support system of help, reference, and just-in-time training is integrated with their network of transaction processing systems that support their retail stores. Each of Penney's 1,200 plus stores formerly relied on more than 100 reference manuals that had to be updated regularly. Online help and reference was built into existing systems and all new applications include help and training capabilities built right into the design. At JCPenney, hardcopy documentation is disappearing.

that knowledge. It mimics human reasoning by using facts, rules, and inferences, which respond to non-linear thinking and problem solving skills. Expert systems development requires that a computer programmer, known as a knowledge engineer, work closely with a subject-matter expert (or domain expert) to ascertain the facts, identify the rules, and then develop an effective user interface.

7.2.3 Databases

While expert systems support structured information, most knowledge is less structured and takes the form of wisdom, experience, and stories rather than rules. Knowledge systems have been developed on groupware products such as Lotus Notes. Help Desk agents (discussed later in this chapter) often use *databases* of user problems and solutions as a means of tracking problems and sharing solutions among each other as well as with callers. The goal of such databases is not simply to create a warehouse of information but to keep track of the wide variety of wisdom, experience, and stories that comprise information. A side benefit is that such systems can reduce the need for paper documents and books, which can be hard to search and catalog. A database of frequently asked questions or well-described technical procedures can actually prevent calls to the Help Desk. Knowledge databases can be accessed through the corporate network or Intranet. When the company itself is the product vendor, it often offers such help facilities on its Internet site for its customers.

7.2.4 Hypermedia

Hypermedia is a way of accessing text as well as graphics, video, and audio information. The term *hyper* means over or above. One way to describe hypermedia is that it is software that sits over the application software. This provides navigation functionality that is independent of the sequential flow of the text. Employing hypermedia commands allows users to take multiple, alternative routes through information, depending on their particular needs. Hypermedia functionality is part of most CD-ROMs. And hypertext is the tool that allows users to surf the Web. This flexibility provides a wide variety of opportunities to meet the needs of audiences who have varying expertise and diverse strategies for using diverse sources and reference materials.

7.3   HELP DESK MANAGEMENT

Help! I was working on a file and it just disappeared!
Help! When I print text, it comes out as hieroglyphics!
Help! I think my computer just crashed!
Help! I need to create a table for a report due 5 minutes ago!
Help! I dropped my notebook computer and can't get it going again!

According to the Gartner Group, an organization with 2,500 desktops will pay support personnel costs ranging from $660,000 to almost $6,000,000 a year.[3] Support personnel are responsible for any number of different support tasks, including answering questions such as those listed previously, installing and maintaining computers and networks at the desktop level, and providing suggestions about which are the best products. The individual calling for support expects an agent to solve problems and solve them quickly.

This section begins with a discussion of the technologies available to support Help Desk agents as they respond quickly and effectively to clients' questions. It continues with an overview of management issues, including how to hire, train, and motivate the Help Desk agent. Help Desk evaluation strategies are reviewed, and because the Help Desk is becoming a specialty of its own, a discussion of the pros and cons of outsourcing also will be offered. The importance of communicating or selling Help Desk services to clients is discussed, as well.

7.3.1 Help Desk Technologies

Traditionally, a Help Desk agent's responsibility is to respond to a user's question in real time over the telephone. The user describes the issue or problem, and the agent responds. Perhaps the biggest challenge to a Help Desk with many users is handling the large infusion of calls that are received daily, often with users calling at the same time (peak times) or with the same problems. Increasingly, too, users are needing support 7/24 (seven days a week, 24 hours a day). To respond to these issues, a wide range of technology options exists, ranging from call center technology to Computer-Telephony Integration to Web-enabled support.

Help Desk management chooses the most appropriate tool for its clients (users), and at the same time must ensure that its agents know the systems they are supporting and have the interpersonal and communications skills to share what they know with their clients.

7.3.1.1 Call Center Technology
A relatively simple technology that begins to address the high volume of calls is call center technology. In its easiest-to-understand form, call center technology routes calls in a round-robin fashion to the help center's agents. However, Computer-Telephony Integration (CTI), Interactive Voice Response (IVR), and the Web are changing the basic definition of a call center. Some call centers are now being called contact centers because they also are fielding faxes, e-mail, and Web site hits.[4]

7.3.1.2 Computer-Telephony Integration
Computer-Telephony Integration (CTI) takes call center technology and goes one step further. As its name implies, computer support is bundled with the telephone system. With CTI, the client still calls the center, and as the client is describing his or her problems, the system automatically gives the agent the caller's history. This history includes how previous problems were handled and a list of the equipment owned by the user, as well as system configuration details. Having all this information at the time of the call can speed up response time greatly.

7.3.1.3 Interactive Voice Response
Interactive Voice Response (IVR) networks are telephone-based menu systems that allow the user to interface with other technologies to get information to perform a specific function. The caller uses the telephone keypad to navigate through options, listening to announcements and having the ability to be transferred to a live person, leave voice mail, and/or send and receive faxes. Additionally, the IVR can interface with call center technology to allow users to report problems, make requests, or check on a request status.[5]

For example, should the organization be experiencing a common problem or issue, the caller could expect to hear something like "Press (or say) 1 to learn the extent of the network downtime" or "Press (or say) 2 to learn about software upgrades." In situations where a considerable wait time is anticipated, the system could prompt the caller to "Press (or say) 3 to leave a message for an agent to get back to you." Lucent Technologies and Unisys, well-known voice technology vendors, are working with Help Desk vendors such as Remedy to change their touch-tone responses to natural language. Pushing the envelope even further, products such as Lucent's Intuity Conversant voice response system provides local language speech recognition and dial pulse recognition.

7.3.1.4 Web-Enabled Support

Web-enabled support has the dual goals of decreasing the number of Help Desk telephone calls and at the same time giving users a broader range of problem-solving possibilities. Introducing Web-enabled support is an attempt to change the established culture of picking up a phone to call somebody.[6] Several options exist that take advantage of the ubiquitous Web, whether it be Intranet or Internet based. In the most basic model, a Web site could be the repository for searchable help information. Help Desks keep records of the problems users encounter, and users may find a "frequently asked questions" list or a searchable, indexed database a useful tool. Another simple option would be to have an e-mail address to which users could address questions and expect a quick reply via that same medium.

Users who can explain exactly what the problem is can use an indexed database effectively or follow the directions of a help wizard. However, many users encountering problems do not have the vocabulary or technical know-how to describe their problem. In such situations, desktop conferencing systems (described in more detail in chapter 4) can be an invaluable real-time tool. Desktop conferencing or screen sharing systems can allow the Help Desk agent to:

- see and operate what is on the user's desktop, taking over keyboard and mouse controls.
- type information into dialogue boxes.
- install new programs.
- open configuration files.
- transfer or retrieve a file.
- use the screen to demonstrate new products.

Another option would be for a user to get online with an agent via desktop conferencing software such as Microsoft's Net Meeting. In yet another model, the user could initiate an instant messaging or chat session with an agent. When a Help Desk supports these Web-based services, it usually also supports faxes and e-mail messages. In such blended calls, agents respond to users using the most appropriate tool available. The key here is that users should have choices. Online help and Web-enabled support are useful as learning tools only if they support the users' preferred information retrieving strategy.

In addition to desktop conferencing systems, another category of Web-based support, called "e-support," services exists. Figure 7-1 lists Web-enabled *customer support software* that supports companies' abilities to manage all points of contact with their customers. According to International Data Corp in Framingham, Massachusetts, the e-support market is around $10.4 billion.[7]

SmartDesk Service	Computer Associates International, Inc. (*www.cmi.com*)
HP Front Office	Hewlett-Packard Co. (*www.hp.com*)
LANDesk Management Suite	Intel Corp. (*www.intel.com*)
eCRM	Primus Communications Corp. (*www.primus.com*)
Motive Solo	Motive Communications, Inc. (*www.motive.com*)
Ezdesktop.com	Perpetual Systems (*www.perpetual.com*)

Figure 7-1
Customer support software

Primus eSupport software, for example, describes its customer relationship management product, eCRM:

> eCRM is Customer Relationship Management for eBusinesses. Primus® eCRM software enables companies to effectively manage all points of contact with their customers by providing self-service and assisted service through a single integrated system. With Primus software, customers have fast access to the information they need through multiple channels—web, e-mail, chat, voice—and businesses share valuable customer knowledge across the enterprise, leveraging the value of their customer interactions to grow their customer relationships.
>
> *Source:* Reproduced with permission from Primus. *http://eServer.primus.com.*

Another product, EZDesktop, is software that troubleshoots technical problems.

Here's how Perpetual Systems describes its product:

> Why EZDesktop? If you're supporting users' PCs, you know the kind of chaos application conflicts can cause. We even know of one major financial institution that has one full-time employee on every floor of every facility just to deal with application conflict resolution. EZDesktop doesn't deal with one problem at a time, nor with just one PC at a time. It looks at the whole PC to determine—and apply—the most effective combination of application configurations for an individual user, group of users, even multiple groups of users—all with different needs.
>
> Here's how it works: First, an agent on each client PC builds a snapshot of the applications on that PC, comparing each to a knowledge base of golden configurations. Perpetual hosts this database server, so there's no lengthy setup—and we do all the maintenance. (If your security policies require it, the server may be hosted inside your firewall.) This comparison lets you pinpoint the cause of application conflict on a PC, so you can apply appropriate new golden configurations from the definition server to resolve it. And because EZDesktop lets you preview any changes to a PC or group of PCs, you can use it to discover in advance what conflicts will result when you roll out that new application or OS upgrade. You can even use it to handle the entire deployment process. EZDesktop is the solution to application conflict resolution: web-delivered technology that gets you out of the business of visiting every

PC on the network to fix software conflicts and back where you belong. Using your hard-won skills on strategic priorities to keep your company at the cutting edge.

Source: Reproduced with permission from Perpetual Systems. *http://www.perpetual.com/productinfo.html.*

7.3.2 Problem Management

The Help Desk agent's phone rings.

Agent: Hello.
Client: I've just lost my file.
Agent: What application are you using?
Client: Word processing.
Agent: Can you describe what you were doing when the problem occurred?
Client: I was just typing along and presto, the system froze.
Agent: And then what did you do?
Client: Well, I hit control, alternate, and delete and started over.
Agent: And what happened when you went back into word processing?
Client: Nothing, but my file is gone.
Agent: Open your temp file.
Client opens temp file.
Client: Great! Here it is. Thanks!
Agent: You're welcome.

Such is the gist of an incredibly lengthy discourse that frustrates both the caller and the Help Desk agent. What strategies exist to help the Help Desk agent respond in a more timely manner? What management techniques and communications skills can support a more efficient, effective problem/solution exchange?

Management techniques begin with the establishment of clearly defined procedures for handling calls. Once routed to the agent, the agent's first task is that of logging the call and categorizing it within broad domains. With a clear understanding of the caller's concerns, agents can handle the inquires themselves or route the caller to someone who can help. Caller logs are important records from the standpoint of documenting the number and type of calls received as well as documenting frequently asked questions and the development of a database of issues, problems, and how they were resolved.

The key to problem resolution is that the caller receives useful, timely information—that the problem is resolved! The success of the Help Desk is related directly to the skills with which a caller can explain the problem being encountered and the skill with which a Help Desk agent can solve and communicate that solution to the user. Tools such as screen sharing software discussed earlier can support this communications process. Perhaps the best trainer, however, is experience. With positive experiences in encounters with Help Desk agents, clients become more adept at problem description. Consider the following dialogue as a counter to the opening passage in this section:

The Help Desk agent's phone rings.
Agent: Hello, Help Desk. How can I help you?
Client: I was writing my monthly report when my system froze. I rebooted the system, but it seems the file is lost.
Agent: Not to worry. Open your temp file.

Client opens the temp file.
Client: Presto! Here it is! Thanks!
Agent: You're welcome!

7.3.3 Hiring and Supporting the Help Desk Agent

"'*Frustrated user syndrome*' is an affliction that is spreading with the increase of computer-based functions in corporations. It triggers instantaneous phone calls to the department at the smallest technical problem. The first symptom is an irritable voice."[8]

The Help Desk agent is the voice at the other end of the telephone that assesses, coaches, and guides callers to answer technical questions and solve a wide variety of hardware and software problems. A key job requirement is technical knowledge. At least equally important to that requirement, however, is a variety of communications skills and problem-solving strategies. A Help Desk agent often must coax callers into giving needed descriptions of their problems and then must be able to provide support in the form of well-considered, easily understood directions. When the Help Desk agent cannot do this, the previously cited frustrated user syndrome can occur, and such a caller is the agent's (and the organization's) worst nightmare. It takes special people to be successful in a Help Desk position. Noel Bruton, author of *How to Manage the I.T. Help Desk* (Butterworth–Heinemann, 1997), summarized these qualities as patience, assertiveness, thoroughness, enthusiasm, responsibility, technical knowledge, empathy, communications skills, and the ability to work well under pressure.[9] Bruton contends that technical skills are best developed by education and experimentation. To develop interpersonal skills in someone who doesn't already have some, he suggests, is much more difficult. He recommends hiring personable people and teaching them to be technicians over hiring technicians and teaching them to be personable. Figure 7-2 offers some suggestions on how to handle problem users.

Hiring and then supporting Help Desk agents is important to the success of the Help Desk operations. The most useful training and support activities center around staff team building and the development of ways to avoid stress and burnout.

Figure 7-2
How to handle problem users

- Begin by displaying empathy to their problem.
- Practice active listening—repeat key words; paraphrase the caller.
- Don't take user frustrations personally.
- When the caller has trouble articulating the problem, suggest nontechnical terms that might be useful.
- Take users through each step of problem resolution; do not always assume they know basics.
- If you cannot solve the problem, pass the caller to someone who can; however, remain responsible to the caller.
- Avoid emotional trigger phrases such as "we can't," "we don't," and "you don't understand."
- End by being empathetic to their problem.

Team building is vital because Help Desk agents learn with and from their colleagues. When agents cannot handle a particular issue, they should be able to refer the caller to someone who can (and perhaps learn in the process). When individual agents believe that the work load is even and everyone has something to share with others, morale is high.

However, Help Desk agents, like any professional staff, need continuous training. Technical skills and interpersonal skills are in need of continual upgrading or renewal. Technical skills must be strong, and agents must be trained in a timely manner to deal with software and hardware upgrades, networks, and new systems. Additionally, ongoing interpersonal training can help develop the customer service skills and attitudes that ensure that Help Desk operations are smooth. Training can be formal programs and/or weekly staff meetings where agents have an opportunity to vent their frustrations and share their successes with others in the group in an environment where they learn from each other.

One key suggestion to ensuring Help Desk agents' job satisfaction is to have them work as a team to develop their working schedules. Another is to ensure that they have job variety and are not tied to their chairs interacting with clients for long periods at a time. Special projects or opportunities for advanced training could be interspersed throughout their day.

Another increasingly important support tool is the professional association. Encouraging Help Desk agents to join professional groups of like-minded professionals from other companies and industries establishes their professional roles and at the same time gives them yet another outlet to learn, network, and share information. Figure 7-3 is a listing of Help Desk professional associations that offer any number of information sharing and support services including newsletters, training, and conferences. For example, Help Desk 2000 educates Help Desk professionals in the best practices of operating a Help Desk and results in the certification of Help Desk professional managers, technicians, and instructors.

7.3.4   Evaluating the Help Desk

Evaluation strategies for evaluating the Help Desk mirror those of evaluating any training and support effort. As described in the previous chapter, the domains of training evaluation are reaction, learning, job behavior, and organizational re-

Figure 7-3
Help Desk professional
associations

Help Desk Institute
5475 Tech Center Drive, Suite 210
Colorado Springs, CO 80919
800-248-5667 U.S., 719-268-0174 Worldwide
Fax: 719-268-0184

Help Desk Professionals Association (*www.hdpa.org*)
PMB 426
14241 NE Woodinville-Duvall Road
Woodinville, WA 98072-8564
Telephone: (425) 398-9292
FAX: (425) 398-9494

Helpdesk 2000 (*www.helpdesk2000.org*)
(decentralized; check Web site for mail addresses)

EQUAL PARTS CARE AND CURE: THAT'S THE RECIPE FOR THE MODEL HELP DESK STAFF AT SHELL SERVICES

As the main point of contact between IS and the rest of a company's workforce, organizations have tried to build desks that not only answer technology questions but show a positive face to the user as well. The essential ingredients are a diverse staff with a proper mix of customer service skills and diagnostic abilities.

At Shell Services International, the independent IS arm of Shell Oil Co., the desk's success depends on the personal touch. "Remembering details about customers' lives, what kinds of issues they were having with their computers, knowing what's going on in their businesses, calling them after it's over to check up—those are just a few of the ways we stay in touch with our customers," says Reesa Thorne, Shell Services' manager of customer and infrastructure technology services for Europe and Africa.

Thorne keeps her staff on the lookout for all kinds of problems, "both those that have already happened and those that might happen soon," she says. For example, the Help Desk recently received three calls from one building on the same day, all different problems, but all coming from the same floor. That was enough of an anomaly that one of the staffers suspected there might be a wiring problem. The help desk was not only able to respond to the calls, but it also fixed the wiring problem before it caused a real disaster.

Thorne attributes her staff's powers of deduction in part to its diversity. The group includes the expected techies, but it also has a number of people with backgrounds in such areas as theology and zoology. By employing different people with different problem solving methods, Thorne says, the Help Desk can act as more of a strategic resource.

—R. Greenberg

Source: R. Greenberg, "Equal Parts Care and Cure," *CIO*, May 15, 1998, p. 46.

sults.[10] With the overall goal of getting evaluative feedback on the impact of the Help Desk on one or all of these levels, a variety of evaluation options exists. These options range from focus groups, to structured interviews of individuals in key departments, to attempts to tie the workings of the Help Desk directly to the overall success of the Information Systems Department.

Perhaps the simplest and most frequently used method of obtaining feedback is a client satisfaction (reaction level) survey. Carefully written to ensure that the right questions are being asked and that they are aimed at the right survey audience, results from a client satisfaction survey could help the Help Desk agents identify their strengths, as well as areas in which they may need further training or development. Survey findings also could point out issues that are beyond the control of agents (e.g., a delayed system rollout) and are management issues, not agent performance problems.

7.3.5 Pros and Cons of Outsourcing

User support is a "must have" in an ever-changing, complex information technology environment. The question is not whether Help Desks are needed; it's how best to staff them and manage their operation. With information technology, it seems the more you know, the more you want to know, and the more technology that is on your desk, the more you will be challenged to use it in innovative ways. The extent to which clients can learn to learn on their own and use their preferred learning strategies is, likewise, an important consideration in choosing and supporting the wide range of Help Desk tools that are available. The overall goal is to ensure that the Help Desk contributes to the organization's competitive advantage through improved worker productivity. Therefore, the decision to keep the Help Desk in-house or to outsource it should be tied to this consideration.

PROS	CONS
• Staffing and supporting Help Desk agents is in the hands of professionals. • Reduced physical facilities costs when vendor is located outside the organization. • Help Desk databases can include problem resolution strategies from a variety of organizations. • Help Desk data are professionally managed.	• Complaints that outsourcers' failure to learn their clients' business prevents them from answering users' questions. • Contracts must be designed and managed carefully. • Vendor must learn the corporate culture. • Day-to-day operations are outside organizational control.

Figure 7-4
Pros and cons of outsourcing the Help Desk

Perhaps the biggest challenge to staffing the Help Desk is that the Help Desk operator often is viewed as an entry-level employee. Moreover, as discussed earlier, technical and interpersonal skills training must be developed, and Help Desk personnel at this point often do not have a definitive career route.[11] Organizations can choose to address these issues or opt for outside management of their services.

According to International Data Corporation (IDC), the market for Help Desk outsourcing is more than $3 billion worldwide.[12] Many organizations, IDC reports, cite the complexity and costs of managing a Help Desk and the complexity of client/server software as being reasons to turn to outsourcing. Figure 7-4 lists the pros and cons of outsourcing the Help Desk, and Figure 7-5 lists considerations for choosing the right outsourcing firm.

Another issue to consider is whether or not an externally run Help Desk should be located off premises or on site. Advantages of on site include being closer to the clients being served and a greater understanding of the firm's culture. However, when the vendor is on site, the organization does not see any reduced costs related to physical facilities. Moreover, off-site vendors typically are required to offer more feedback on their services (called *metrics*) than they might if they were on site. Such metrics include:

• average time until a call is answered by a live person.

• average time for problem resolution.

Figure 7-5
Considerations for choosing the right outsourcing firm

• Vendors should specialize in a variety of systems.
• Vendors may offer a wide range of training options.
• Vendors should be able to respond to geographically dispersed users.
• Vendors should have a proven record of quick response time.
• Vendors should be willing to be compensated on a sliding scale, contingent on its ability to perform against definite response metrics, throughout the duration of the contract.

- the number of callers who hang up before a call is answered.

- customer satisfaction.

While the number of firms that are outsourcing Help Desk operations is increasing, many organizations are finding that the time required to manage these vendors and difficulty in responding to clients who are finding the services unuseful are troublesome. To this end, contracts should be complete and precise. Vendors need to know the customer's equipment and technical infrastructure, as well as the number of calls the current Help Desk takes, in order to develop appropriate bids. Organizations need to ensure that key metrics (such as those described earlier) are reported frequently and include service-level definitions.[13]

SPOTLIGHT ON SOLUTIONS → Technology, People, Structure, Processes

NEW BREEDS OF TECH SUPPORT

No computer comes worry free. Despite all the advances in computers, software, and networks, our wired universe, sadly, often becomes tangled. And since the pace of business has revved up to Internet speed, random crashes and network traffic jams are becoming more taxing than ever. Of course, if your budget has room for a full-time tech-support team, kinks like these are mere headaches. Pop an Advil and call the help desk. But what about the smaller and solo businesses that can't afford to devote precious resources to computer support?

One option is performance support. You have to know what type of support you need and what sort of turnaround time is sufficient. Do you need live chat, or will e-mail be fast enough? Will remote diagnostics serve your purposes, or do you require onsite support as well? With all the options available, including Net marketplaces, interactive tech advisors, knowledge bases, Web-based problem-tracking software, and remote-diagnostic tools, you should have no problem finding a solution that meets your needs.

Many e-support companies targeting small businesses offer a blend of these services. Net marketplace NoWonder (*www.nowonder.com*), for instance, puts you in touch with thousands of support providers in more than 100 countries. These providers participate in a reverse-auction bidding process. You submit a problem and select a service option, either a spot transaction or a long-term contract, from numerous providers. Solutions can range from figuring out why a printer won't print to providing ongoing support for an upgrade from Windows NT 4.0 to Windows 2000. Support options include live help, e-mailed solutions (turnaround time is usually 24 hours), and links to self-help. Desktop sharing, which gives a technician access to a user's system, can enhance the process.

But what if you need more? A growing band of support warriors including CenterBeam and Everdream are providing affordable and timely help. By providing standard sets of PCs, software, and networking products—and, in some cases, by requiring lengthy subscriptions—these new businesses can keep their costs so low that even soloists and two- and three-employee companies can have full-service tech support at their beck and call. Some of these technology soldiers configure, install, and regularly monitor individual companies' systems in an effort to spot problems before they turn into crises. Just call it Fortune 500 service for mom-and-pop shops.

While this type of support is relatively new, and there are not many national providers of this type of support, their popularity is growing. Competition is expected to increase and bring lower prices and better-quality service, which is good news for small companies that until now were unable to afford the kinds of services that their larger counterparts benefited from having.

Source: Adapted from Anne Marie Borrego, "It's Midnight. Do You Know Where Your Tech Support Is?," *Inc.*, March 15, 2000; Dennis Schaal, "E-Support Goes Live—Online Support for Small Businesses is Moving into the Real-time Realm," *Computer Shopper*, June 2000.

7.4 THE HELP DESK OF THE FUTURE

The overall goal of the Help Desk is to make users more successful, not just satisfied.[14]

Call centers and Help Desks continually compile data describing organizational operations. These sites contain large amounts of data, information, and knowledge. Data, information, and knowledge lie along a continuum. Data are individual incidents and facts, information is what is made of data, and knowledge is what someone does with the information. In discussing the Help Desk of the future, central is the role of an integrated service desk's contribution to developing knowledge and a means of distributing that knowledge to the organization as a whole.

The term that describes this compilation of data is *data warehouse*. Organizations striving to become learning organizations collect bits and pieces of data and store them for future use. What's missing is the organization of these disparate data. While information systems professionals are adept at developing ways to plan for storage, access, and networking, they need to understand what the content should be. An integrated service desk, which can ensure that users get one-stop shopping for all their information needs, can increase an organization's ability to learn. The best of these desks make employees, customers, vendors, and even competitors sources of knowledge.[15]

The Help Desk or integrated service desk of the future will rely on the technologies discussed previously in this chapter. Emerging technologies—including intelligent tutoring systems, neutral networks, fuzzy logic, and expert systems—are expected to organize information into knowledge systems that are comprehensive data sources and that are accessed easily. The integrated services desk is, in other words, providing the content and a means of accessing it for the entire learning organization.

7.5 SUMMARY

Online help and Help Desks are user-support mechanisms that have a goal of ensuring that learners are successful in using their information technologies. To this end, this chapter began with an overview of the role of online systems and went into detail describing the mission of the Help Desk and strategies for managing its operation.

Online help—whether it be indexed lists of functions, contextual help, or a wizard—is a component of a comprehensive performance support system (PSS), discussed in chapter 6. PSSs are typically developed in tandem with system development, which means they are rolled out for use at the same time the system is ready. Online help is a just-in-time learning resource that is usually the user's first stop for assistance. However, when online help isn't useful and the user needs a real person to address the problem, the Help Desk is called.

Help Desks, increasingly referred to as integrated services desks, are staffed by Help Desk agents who tutor users through their technical problems. Most large Help Desks are supported by call center technologies that help route callers to available agents (call routing); that bundle computer support with the call (Computer-Telephony Integration); that allow users to use voice commands rather than keypad or pulse commands (Interactive Voice Response); and that allow users to use their Web browser to access central databases or communicate directly with Help Desk agents (Web-enabled response). Key to selecting and supporting these technologies is to give the user a wide variety of choices for accessing Help Desk agents for timely resolution of their problems.

Frustrated user syndrome describes the ailment of callers who are having trouble explaining their problems or understanding the Help Desk agent's directions for problem resolution. Because people skills are so vital to success in this position, it is recommended that Help Desks hire individuals with interpersonal skills and then train them on the technical solutions. Help Desk professional organizations are increasingly popular locations for individuals to network with others in their field and share and learn from each other's experiences.

The outsourcing of Help Desk operations is an option that relieves the organization of problems related to hiring and supporting Help Desk personnel and at the same time may provide more timely problem resolution. On the other hand, an outsourced Help Desk operation may not know the business and may not perform as effectively as anticipated. Suggestions for managing this complex relationship include having detailed contracts that mandate frequent performance data (metrics) and continual communications between the organization and the vendor.

The Help Desk of the future, the integrated services desk, is in a position to use an organization's data repository. Data, information, and knowledge are continuums on which a learning organization relies. By determining what is useful and not useful data and/or information, as well as who has the data and/or information, the integrated services desk is in a position to be a focal point for knowledge management.

KEY TERMS

- Computer-Telephony Integration
- Contextual help
- Customer support software
- Expert Systems
- Frustrated user syndrome

- Help Desk
- Help Desk agent
- Hypermedia
- Interactive Voice Response
- Metrics

- Online help
- Performance support
- Web-enabled support
- Wizards

DISCUSSION QUESTIONS

1. What is the Help Desk? Who usually is responsible for its operations? What role does it play in providing user support?
2. What is a call center? Differentiate among call routers, Computer-Telephony Integration, and Interactive Voice Response.
3. Under what circumstances might a user prefer to contact a Help Desk agent via the Web? What Web-based tools might be used to establish this connection?
4. Describe the consummate Help Desk agent. What professional and personal qualities should this person possess?
5. Under what circumstances might an organization consider outsourcing its Help Desk operations? What are pros and cons of this management strategy?
6. Discuss the role of the Help Desk in light of its role as a keeper and manager of information.

APPLICATION EXERCISES

1. Assume your organization is interviewing a Help Desk vendor. Create a list of the questions you would ask.

2. Using the Internet, identify two Help Desk vendors. Compare the offerings of the vendors on criteria including their scope of services and past performance metrics.

3. Visit the Web sites of the three Help Desk professional associations identified in this chapter (Help Desk Institute, Help Desk Professionals Association, and Helpdesk 2000). What services do they have in common? What services are unique to each organization?

SUGGESTED READINGS

Bruton, Noel. *How to Manage the I. T. Help Desk.* (Woburn, MA: Butterworth-Heinemann, 1997).

Czegel, Barbara. *Running an Effective Help Desk*, 2d ed. (New York: John Wiley & Sons, Inc., 1998).

ITG Trainers Forum: An Essay Letter for the I/S Training Profession. Free publication to the I/S training commu-nity. E-mail: *Info@ITG-Web.com. http://www.ITG-Web.com.*

Microsoft Sourcebook for the Help Desk. (Redmond, WA: Microsoft Press, 1997).

ENDNOTES

1. Bridget N. O'Connor, Michael Bronner, and Chester Delaney. *Training for Organizations,* 2d ed. (Cincinnati, OH: South-Western Educational Publishing Company, 2001).

2. Stannie Holt, "Help Desks Must Help Themselves," *InfoWorld* 21 (1999): 67.

3. Tamara Gignac, "Are You Being Served?" *Computer Dealer News* 15 (1999): 29–30.

4. Ken Fauerbach, "High-Volume Call Centers at NYU," *Connect: Information Technology at NYU* 10 (1999): 35–37.

5. Barbara Czegel, *Running an Effective Help Desk.* (New York: John Wiley & Sons, Inc., 1998).

6. Gignac, op. cit.

7. Deni Connor, "Dell Adopts Online Support; Compaq Soon to Follow," *Network World* 16 (1999).

8. J. L. O'Brien, "People Skills More Useful Than Technical Expertise," *Computing Canada* 225 (1999): 25–26.

9. Noel Bruton, *How to Manage the I.T. Help Desk.* (Woburn, MA: Butterworth-Heinemann, 1997).

10. Donald L. Kirkpatrick, *Evaluating Training Programs: The Four Levels* (San Fransciso: Berrett-Koehler Publishers, 1996).

11. Madeline Locke, "Outsourcing Your Help Desk for Efficiency and Cost Reduction," *Call Center Solutions* 17 (1999): 102–110.

12. Ibid.

13. Julia King, "Users Discover Dark Side of Help Desk Outsourcing," *Computerworld* 33 (1999): 24.

14. Søren R. Kirchner, "Focus On: Database Integration and Management for Call Centers," *Call Center Solutions* 16 (1997): 22–24+.

15. Ibid.

Case Study   Sarah's Experience

When Sarah took over the Help Desk, it was in a sorry state. She had come into Support from Development, where she had been a project manager. (Sarah is philosophical about this—with all this shrink-wrapped software, who needs projects anymore?) Out of six Support staff, she had Mick, a supervisor who resented her coming in, believing the job should have been his; Ron, whose hypochondriac absenteeism verged on the legendary; Susan, who had already handed her notice in and was there in body if perhaps not in spirit; Sam, rather older than the others, a hardware spe-cialist who had designed his own job; and Tim and Jean, two of the most knowledgeable, overworked computer wizzkids she had ever come across whose desks looked like the aftermath of a hurricane.

She was not sure if she had been put there to change things or to stop her from having to be made redundant. Her boss did not seem to know what he wanted, except an easier time from his peers, whose numerous and highly vocal complaints about Support were beginning to turn into threats. Sarah knew that 'created job' or not, she had to achieve something. Her first attitude had been along the lines of 'they put me here against my will, this is their problem, not mine.' After a long soul-search, and it must be said, no sympathy for that attitude from her husband, she decided the only thing to do was make the best of it. Like the theme-park employees who clean up behind the tourists, she would do it with a smile, because the smile would be her ticket to something better.

The first thing she did was tell Mick she would achieve nothing without him, and she asked him to write a brief list of the things he would have done had the job gone his way. She called Ron at home (he was off sick at the time) to introduce herself and start her strategy for him. She needed Ron back, she said, because a little bird told her he might have some useful pointers for her. As well as getting him thinking, this told Ron she was not considering his prolonged absences, at least for now, so he did not have to be so much on his guard. She asked Susan to meet her for lunch, a long way off site, where they could talk freely—after all, Susan had nothing to lose by giving her frank criticisms that other employees might prefer to keep to themselves. The conversations with Sam, Tim, and Jean were cursory; Sam was giving nothing away, preferring to protect the niche he had carved for himself. Tim and Jean were too busy; their heads too full of detail and their perspectives too short to be of any long-term use. She knew that in practice these conversations would provide information she could use in the long term. The reason she held them before doing anything else was to get the staff on her side. It could have been disastrous if she had come in and started changing her people's working lives without consulting them.

Two weeks before taking over the job, she had started to ask around, to get impressions of the Help Desk's image in the company as a whole. She did not emphasize that she was moving to the Help Desk—that might cause her interviewees to complain rather than inform. By the time she got to her new desk, she knew what she had to do. She realized there must be more success than failure in Support, or it would have been reorganized out of existence by now. What she had to do was find that success and focus attention on it. Then she had to pick the Help Desk's dirtiest linen and wash it in public. For both of these tactics, the key was going to be communication.

She spent a couple of days watching the way the department worked, identifying its main services and taking measurements of its output. With what she found, she created an alternative picture of success, which the company knew too little about. She took that picture straight to her boss, so he had a more positive view of the Support Department with which to defend himself against his critics. It would give her boss a reason to get on her side, and to get others on it too. She also fed the results of this back to the Support staff. The effect on morale and productivity was nothing short of dramatic. By the time Ron got back from his latest illness, the place was humming—and Sarah was ready for him with a nice juicy project for him to get his teeth into. Ron was going to improve the department newsletter—the communications medium she needed. He had to get out a four-pager in less than a week. He complained, but he made it. The department did not miss him from the support effort, and now Sarah had something she could measure him on.

The main complaint of the users had been about the reliability of response to their queries. It had shown up in a number of ways: Some thought that from a response point of view, reporting a problem was akin to tossing it into the Grand Canyon; others simply complained about not knowing when or how a problem would be dealt with. When Sarah looked at the way problems were handled, she found that 80 percent of the queries were ultimately dealt with by the highly overworked Tim and Jean. She gave Mick the job of watching every incoming query to see that there was at least a response to it within an hour, and if not, to ask the technician why not. She left it to Mick to figure out, as he did, that he would have to start to take more control of Sam too, as just watching Tim and Jean quite rightly showed they could not do it all themselves.

The result was a turnover in the department's performance and their image within around three weeks. Over the longer term, Sarah began to implement the ideas she had heard in her earlier conversations with her staff and the users. The Support staff were all the more willing now to accept these incoming changes; they recognized the ideas as their own, with a bit of managerial improvement here and there, and they had clear evidence that Sarah could deliver the goods. Late that summer, on a Florida beach, Sarah congratulated herself on a job well done and holiday well deserved.

Source: Reprinted with permission of Butterworth-Heinemann Publishers, a division of Reed Educational & Professional Publishing Ltd.

CASE STUDY QUESTIONS

1. Summarize the problems Sarah faced in her new position. Are these technical problems or management problems?

2. Before moving to the Help Desk, Sarah interviewed users to discover what they thought worked well and what didn't—why was this a useful tactic?

3. What specific strategies did Sarah use to develop the Help Desk team of agents?
4. What metrics did Sarah use to analyze Help Desk operation? Can you think of others that might have been useful?

5. What advice do you offer Sarah for ensuring the continued harmony of the Help Agent team?

Chapter 8

Management Issues

Learning Objectives

Upon completing this chapter, you should be able to:

➤ Identify critical factors for managing and supporting end-user information systems.

➤ Discuss major policy issues for the management of desktop hardware and software.

➤ Describe steps managers and users can take to provide adequate security for personal computers and data.

➤ Explain why backup of computer data is important and how data can be protected.

➤ Plan strategies for protecting computers from viruses.

➤ Identify legal issues related to software and data.

➤ Discuss ways managers can ensure the accuracy and reliability of user-developed systems.

➤ Explain the role of auditing in protecting computer resources.

8.1   INTRODUCTION

Developing and managing end-user information systems (EUIS) have become high priorities for managers. Issues that were previously of concern only to managers of technical data processing departments have become general concerns in the workplace.

In today's workplace, procedures that monitored and controlled information processing in the paper-based office are no longer adequate. Likewise, control procedures used in technical data processing centers may not be practical in a decentralized office. New techniques for controlling and monitoring information processing are being developed and implemented. The solutions will vary from one situation to another, but guidelines can help.

Managers and end users alike must know about the opportunities, risks, and issues related to the effective, efficient, and safe use of desktop computers. Otherwise, they may not recognize problems until after disaster strikes. When new technologies are introduced, it takes time to understand the wide range of issues that effective use entails. These issues, related to hardware and software maintenance and management, are discussed in this chapter, and fall into five major areas:

1. *Policy issues.* What policies should managers establish, and how should these policies be communicated? How do managers integrate information systems policies into an organization's overall policy? What auditing procedures should be established to ensure compliance with corporate policies?

2. *Physical security of hardware and software.* How do managers protect computers and disks from theft and physical damage?

3. *Data security and confidentiality.* What safeguards should be taken to protect data that are stored on disks and hard disks? How can organizations protect information from unauthorized access or use?

4. *Accuracy and reliability of information.* How can managers be sure that data developed with spreadsheets, databases, and other user programs are accurate and reliable? What kind of documentation is needed, and who develops it and keeps it up to date?

5. *Legal issues.* What risks and liabilities are an organization and its managers exposed to in connection with EUIS? For example, who is liable when employees make unauthorized copies of software?

This chapter also discusses a variety of resources, products, and services that can be used in dealing with these issues. Discussion points include auditing procedures, data-protection and encryption products, hardware security products, and others. The most viable techniques, however, are practical guidelines and good management practices.

8.2   POLICY ISSUES

Policies established by top management are a first step toward showing employees that computer-related risks are an important corporate concern. Senior management is often too busy running the business to address these risks until a serious problem arises. Even organizations that have established security and disaster-recovery plans for their centralized computing operations may overlook the risks and issues of managing desktop computers.

Policies for EUIS vary among organizations according to their corporate cultures. Many managers have sign off authority for purchases of up to perhaps $2,000, which is enough for a complete desktop or notebook computer system. Moreover, few off-the-shelf applications packages cost more than $500. Therefore, managers and analysts generally want to stimulate creative use of EUIS, and at the same time ensure compatibility, security, and cost effectiveness. Specific goals include:

- Avoiding incompatible hardware and software
- Minimizing duplication of effort
- Avoiding unnecessary spending
- Coordinating EUIS with corporate information systems activities
- Coordinating EUIS with corporate strategy
- Providing adequate protection for corporate resources
- Simplifying technical support requirements[1]

The manager who wants to address these goals needs a corporate policy. The key steps for establishing a policy for EUIS include the following:

1. *Develop acquisition guidelines.* Centralize buying as much as possible; large transactions can save money and secure better maintenance terms.

2. *Take inventory.* Sudden costs must be known and evaluated before any *de facto* standards are set; the installed base will affect policy decisions and future acquisitions.

3. *Develop hardware and software standards.* Standards will facilitate the sharing of resources and the porting of development work (transferring an application developed on one computer to another).

4. *Establish return-on-investment (ROI) standards and schedules.* Some enterprises require this type of cost/benefit analysis, and return-on-investment analysis (sometimes referred to as *payback*) will assist decision makers in evaluating and justifying hardware and software investments (see chapter 9).

5. *Establish maintenance, housekeeping, and security standards and schedules.* Computers and data must be maintained, and standards must be developed that describe proper hardware and software care. Care can include how to secure the machine physically, as well as data backup schedules.

6. *Develop legal guidelines for hardware and software use.* Large sums of money may be at risk if legal issues are ignored. Novice users may be unaware of copyright restrictions on some software, and corporations have been sued for violations of these laws. These issues have become even more complex with Internet use.

7. *Establish periodic policy reviews.* Technology changes so quickly that a solution defined today may not be cost effective tomorrow.

Management can be proactive in *avoiding* problems. Preventive measures can include a written policy statement that identifies all computer and information resources as significant assets. The intent of an information policy should be to encourage care and concern by making employees accountable for unauthorized acts involving computer and information resources. The policy statement should clearly state the company's position on unauthorized copying of software and should be distributed to all employees who have access to information resources. Figure 8-1 presents a typical policy statement on the use of corporate information resources.

Organizations can help establish personal accountability by having employees sign *confidentiality covenants.* By signing such a document, employees agree not to disclose any proprietary information or to misuse corporate computer resources to which they have access. These covenants acknowledge that failure to comply with company information policies will result in disciplinary actions.

8.2.1 Acquisition Guidelines

Managers try to balance needs for encouraging innovative application of technology against wasteful spending, duplication of effort, or incompatible equipment. Many managers have sufficient budget control to purchase hardware and software and may be tempted to circumvent corporate procurement procedures. If the equipment meets the department's needs and the purchase can be cost justified, why not?

One reason "why not" is that such ad hoc equipment purchases may be incompatible with other corporate hardware, thereby limiting future options. Regardless of whether an organization maintains strict or flexible controls, managers should be aware of the issues relating to hardware and software acquisition. Vendors often portray personal computing to end users as effortless and immensely beneficial; they understate the risks, pitfalls, and problems. Shortcomings of products are not usually evident until the novice gains experience. Users often learn the

Computer Software Resources

Growing numbers of company employees and associates use computer software resources in connection with their jobs. Such resources are crucial company assets that make our tasks easier and enable us to perform our jobs with greater accuracy and efficiency. Many employees are not aware of the legal duties that accompany the use of computer software, however. Often, people do not realize that unauthorized copying or disclosure of software has a costly impact.

When software has been developed here at the company, unauthorized taking or copying of that software diminishes the value of a company asset. When software is used under license from an outside supply firm, improper duplication or disclosure deprives that firm of revenue, ultimately raising costs for the customer community. More importantly, whether software resources are developed in-house or licensed from a vendor, unauthorized copying or disclosure is illegal.

Consequently, the Company has issued the following Policy Statement on Computer Software Resources. It is the responsibility of every employee and associate who uses or has access to software resources to adhere strictly to this policy.

Policy Statement on Computer Software Resources

The computer software resources are assets of the company that are vital to our operation. Such resources may be exclusive company property or may be proprietary products used under contractual license from program supply firms. Either way, software is a valuable commodity that the owner is entitled to protect. Consequently, whether using software owned exclusively by the company or software licensed from program supply firms, it is the responsibility of every employee and associate to prevent destruction, misuse, or misappropriation of such resources.

This policy has two components. First, the unauthorized copying or reproduction of any software program, program documentation, or related material is strictly prohibited. This policy also prohibits using any program, program documentation, or related material, or any copy thereof, for personal purposes or making such materials available to anyone outside the company.

Reproducing computer software without authorization may constitute an improper taking of a company asset or may violate the terms of a license agreement into which the company has entered. The money paid for proprietary products generally represents a license fee for the use of one copy. It does not represent an authorization to make unlimited copies. More importantly, unauthorized duplication of software violates U.S. Copyright Law. Civil damages can be as much as $50,000, and copyright infringement can qualify as a federal misdemeanor punishable by up to $10,000 in fines or up to one year's imprisonment. Consequently, this policy must be followed strictly. Second, employees and associates must make every effort to maintain and protect the integrity of confidential data contained in software programs, program documentation, and related materials. Employees and associates must not disclose these data and must take reasonable precautions to see that they are not left in the open or haphazardly discarded.

Computer software resources may constitute confidential material or trade secrets entitled to legal protection. Software license agreements often require the company to treat software resources as confidential. The unauthorized disclosure of software materials could thus create legal liability. Therefore, this policy also must be strictly regarded.

Violation of the above policy may result in disciplinary action, including termination, where appropriate. Employees or associates with questions concerning the policy should contact the head of the Computer Security and Contract Administration Department.

Source: Courtesy of Massachusetts Mutual Life Insurance Company.

Figure 8-1
A typical policy statement on the use of corporate information resources

limitations of hardware or software too late, when they discover that if they had only bought another product, it would be able to do what they wanted.

Also, unmonitored acquisition procedures can mean higher costs because organizations usually can negotiate volume discount purchase agreements. Managers should recognize the many trade-offs in computer products in terms of price, performance, and features. Selecting appropriate hardware and software can be time consuming and fraught with problems. The immense diversity of products means that novices may select incompatible hardware or software. Incompatibility can lead to costly mistakes that preclude the transfer of data between systems or greatly increase the complexity of supporting, aiding, or training users. In-house technical resources may not support nonstandard hardware and unique software, thus forcing the department to go outside for more expensive services.

Another reason that technology should not be purchased ad hoc is that options may be overlooked that limit or increase the equipment's use for applications other than the one for which it originally was justified. Managers can seek the advice of knowledgeable EUIS analysts when considering the purchase of computer devices for their departments. Experienced analysts, whether in-house or outside consultants, can save managers valuable time, money, and frustration. Moreover, they often can cite considerations or opportunities not apparent to managers who have limited experience with the technology.

8.2.2   EUIS Standards

Standards, though often looked upon as restrictive, offer benefits for both IS professionals and end users. Most large enterprises have standards that cover many aspects of their operations, including EUIS. Generally, standards are recorded in formal standards and procedures manuals, but even informal, handwritten notes about company procedures could be considered standards.

Standards provide consistency, save resources, reduce errors and problems, and, as already pointed out, provide greater compatibility among EUIS hardware and software. Most importantly, standards significantly affect productivity. Software user interface standards, for example, provide greater consistency in the way applications work, which in turn makes them easier to learn and use because they are more predictable and users can benefit from previous experience with other software.

To the user, this means that standards are an important requirement for building systems that are well thought out. Standards establish a performance baseline. End users, managers, and EUIS professionals should be familiar with their firm's standards and ensure that they are followed.

8.3   PHYSICAL SECURITY OF HARDWARE AND SOFTWARE

Physical security involves avoiding potential threats and deterring anyone with intentions to steal or tamper with equipment or information. Managers are responsible for protecting valuable equipment and files. What should I do when two computers turn up missing on Monday morning? How did the spreadsheet software and manual disappear? Where is the department notebook computer that has our competitive analysis worksheets?

A list of all computer hardware and software and their serial numbers should be kept in a safe location, and physical inventories should be made regularly. A signed authorization should be required for all hardware and software that is taken into and out of the office building. Devices should be insured adequately.

8.3.1 Avoiding Damage

Appropriate work space should be set aside to safeguard equipment. Analysts should assess possible environmental hazards such as heat from direct sunlight or rain from windows that might be left open. Proper electrical outlets and wiring should be provided. Cables and wiring should not be exposed where employees may trip over them or accidentally snag them, bringing everything crashing to the floor. Spilled liquids are a major cause of damage, and beverages and other liquids should be kept away from hardware and software. Liquids can leak into electrical circuits or damage disks. Smoking should not be allowed near computers and stored disks because smoke can deposit on sensitive drive heads, shortening their useful life and increasing the danger of losing data.

Routine computer inventories and maintenance could be assigned to one individual whose job it is to keep track of all desktop computers in the area, or this task could be assigned to various individuals for different types of peripherals. In addition, computer hardware and software need to be protected from static electricity during dry, winter months. Humidifiers, carpets that resist static buildup, and antistatic sprays and mats are resources that managers can consider.

8.3.2 Protecting against Viruses

While computer bugs are software glitches that are accidentally in the program code and cause computer malfunctions, viruses are malicious attempts to annoy a user or cause irreparable harm to data, programs, or operating systems. Both *bug* and *virus* are terms from the biological sciences. In 1945, Grace Hopper coined the term *bug* when she reported finding a moth in an early computer. Viruses, sometimes referred to as malware, "can't be killed by Lysol" and are capable of causing computer users and information systems managers much dismay when they attack their systems.[2]

This discussion of viruses (not bugs!) classifies recent strains of viruses as either Trojan horses or Worms, and includes a discussion of virus inoculation (antivirus) software and suggestions for how to keep desktop systems from getting virus infections.

8.3.2.1 Trojan Horses and Worms

Initially, *viruses* infected files or disks on a single computer. Increasingly, their more powerful (destructive) offshoots, Trojan horses and worms, are spreading havoc among computers in a corporate network or on the Internet.

Trojan horses (sometimes referred to as Trojans) are true to their Greek reference. Greek soldiers hid inside a wooden horse and then launched a surprise attack on the city of Troy. In the computer sense, Trojans are viruses masquerading as something else, such as an attachment from a friend, an attachment that offers you a free product, or simply an e-mail message that says "urgent!" Once opened, Trojan horses can wipe out the entire contents of documents, spreadsheets, and databases that are created by certain programs. At the time of this writing, Microsoft programs, particularly Outlook, Word, and Excel, are the most frequent targets.[3]

Other targets have included service providers such as AOL, where a Trojan horse created havoc in stealing users' passwords.

Worms, on the other hand, don't attach themselves to other programs. Instead, they duplicate themselves continually until your hard disk or your entire network's disk space is filled. Worms can paralyze computer operations.

Although antivirus software is useful as a cure, it isn't useful until someone has detected the virus and a cure is established. It is estimated that more than 10,000 virus types exist, and the number is increasing daily. [4] Therefore, antivirus software is a must for any user who shares data or programs with others. The current leading antivirus software providers are Symantec, producer of Norton Anti-Virus (*www.symantec.com*), and McAfee VirusScan (*www.mcafee.com*) software. Both companies provide (for a fee) downloadable updates, and their Web sites serve as central command sites for information and cures for recently uncovered viruses, Trojans, and worms. Once installed, these antivirus programs can be set up to be updated automatically and scan e-mail attachments and other documents upon arrival at the user's system.

8.3.2.2 Procedures to Prevent Virus Damage

It is a good idea to have procedures in place to minimize the risk of damage and productivity loss from viruses. Following a few basic rules and procedures will go a long way in avoiding problems:

- Install antivirus software and keep it updated.

- Avoid using freeware or shareware acquired from friends or bulletin boards on business computers.

- If you receive a lot of e-mail, put a number of blank entries in your e-mail address folder. Some e-mail-related viruses read your address book and send messages to those at the top of your list.

- Scan all disks or CDs that are new, unfamiliar, or brought in from outside the firm *prior* to using them.

- Back up all computer files on a regular basis.

8.3.3 Protecting Software (Backup)

"There are only two kinds of computer users: Those who have lost data, and those who will."

—Bob Levitus, *The Houston Chronicle*

What happens when your computer gets hit by a virus? What if you accidentally hit the delete key and wipe out your contact list? What if you make an error in entering your spreadsheet formulas? What happens when the new network administrator mistakenly deletes the directory containing all the department's form letters? Data stored on the computer must be protected from modification, destruction, and disclosure. Data are also vulnerable to accidental loss and erasure. To safeguard data, backup systems are required.

Backup refers to duplicate copies of electronically stored data. In computer centers, data are routinely backed up, and two or more copies of all data files are maintained in different locations. Copies of critical information often are stored in specially constructed vaults at a site separate from the computer center. These procedures serve much the same purpose as records management departments.

EUIS have greatly increased the volumes of data that are stored electronically within departments instead of in carefully managed data or records centers. Today, managers must take responsibility for establishing procedures to protect data files created and stored in their departments. Common sense is that copies should be maintained of all work stored electronically. Following are some useful guidelines:

1. Clearly assign accountability for backup. If a network is used, a system administrator can be assigned to perform backup each night. Individuals should be held accountable for backing up their own personal files. Responsibility for the backup of all departmental files, however, should be specifically assigned.
2. Store backup disks and tapes in a secured location, not at random in individual desks. Consider off-site storage.
3. Clearly label and date backup disks and tapes.
4. Maintain at least two backup copies of critical data. If a problem occurs during the backup process and both the original and the backup are damaged, a second backup copy would still be available. When multiple backup copies are maintained, they usually are updated on alternate days. For example, on Day 1, Backup Copy A is updated; on Day 2, Backup Copy B is updated; on Day 3, backup is made to Copy A again; on Day 4, to Copy B; and so on.

Because electronic storage is reliable, it is easy to become complacent about electronically stored data. In the absence of strict procedures, people tend to become careless about maintaining up-to-date copies of their work. When problems occur, however, as they invariably do, reconstructing lost information can be time consuming and expensive. Figure 8-2 presents strategies for safeguarding data through better backup procedures.

Fortunately, today a variety of tools are available to help make regular backup procedures easier and faster. In addition, other media such as magnetic tape can be used to ensure continual backup. At the simplest end, inexpensive software and zip drives can help you back up files. For Windows programs, for example, there's Microsoft Backup and Iomega software and hardware. However, for complex or critical file backup, special purpose hardware and software often are required. In other cases, a small organization may want to store its data through the Internet or even completely outsource its information systems operations through a value-added reseller (VAR). Here's a discussion of each option.

8.3.3.1 Backup Hardware and Software
In the hardware arena, the most popular choice for backup is zip drives or tape backup systems. A zip or internal tape drive may be adequate for many users.

Figure 8-2
Tactics for achieving better backup

1. All new computers should include a tape or zip drive for backup purposes.
2. Policies should indicate clearly what types of data and programs need (a) no backup, (b) secure on-site backup; or (c) on-site and off-site backup.
3. Every user should attend comprehensive training programs on backup procedures.
4. The Data Security Office (or an assigned group under another name) should be readily available to consult on questions about whether and how to make and store backup for desktop applications.
5. Supervisors should be required to perform periodic audits on backup activities. The data security officer should perform regular checks on the supervisors' audit records.

OnStream, Inc.	ADR	onstream.com
NovaStor	NovaBackup	novastor.com
Veritas Software	Backup Exec	veritas.com
Highware	Personal Backup	highware.com
Dantz	Retrospect	dantz.com

Figure 8-3
Desktop tape backup systems vendors, sample product lines, and URLs

However, when computer users want to backup their 12-, 18-, or 36-gigabyte hard drive or when files are scattered, special hardware and software are needed.

Figure 8-3 lists backup software that may fit the needs of desktop computer users. Even the inexpensive, low-end systems typically offer features such as automatic backup. OnStream, Inc., for example, offers a tape that holds the space of about 10,000 floppy disks for less than $40. On the other hand, feature-rich, high-speed systems can cost more than $1,000.[5] Dantz's Retrospect, instead of providing full backup, takes snapshots of a disk drive as needed and can restore in a single pass.[6] Veritas Software even offers online training to its customers. Keep in mind that tape capacity is growing; at the time of this writing, storage capacities of backup systems range from 30 to 70 gigabytes. "Tape drives are like kids' sneakers—if you don't wear them out, you outgrow them. And constantly replacing tape drives quickly becomes prohibitively expensive."[7] Fortunately, most of these systems are designed to grow with the user.

8.3.3.2 Internet-Based Backup Options
Another data backup/storage option is through the Internet. For a monthly fee, organizations such as those listed in Figure 8-4 will encrypt your data, give you data transfer software, and keep your files off site in a secure location. Speed of transfer can be an issue, however, to anyone using POTS (plain old telephone service) lines to transfer data; high-speed lines are recommended.

8.3.3.3 Value-Added Resellers (VAR)
Virtual office services were described in chapter 4 as Level 1 groupware, Internet-based services that were either free when bundled with other software products or leased for a monthly fee. VARs such as CenterBeam have taken this concept one giant step further, offering virtually (no pun intended) all needed hardware, software, Internet access, backup, security, support and service components in a single package for a monthly fee.[8] In essence, this means that an organization can outsource its entire information systems department, leaving complex issues of backup and

Figure 8-4
Internet backup data suppliers

safeguardinteractive.com
blackjack.com

security to other professionals. Such relatively inexpensive services are useful for organizations that want to avoid the costs associated with software and hardware and supporting IT personnel.

8.3.4 Developing Naming Conventions

Users and managers may need to work together to establish standards for naming data files and storing shared data. When left to the whim of individual users, it may be difficult or impossible for someone else to locate files. At the very least, hours of valuable time can be wasted finding the correct files or directories. The importance of a systematic approach to naming and storing information becomes even more apparent when departmental networks are used. All employees who create, research, and request information must talk the same language, or considerable time and effort can be wasted locating information.

8.3.5 Managing Networks

Networks introduce even greater risks and challenges for business managers. In one sense, protecting a network from equipment failure, power outages, natural disasters, or other problems is no different from protecting the mainframe. Even a straightforward approach of backing up the network's servers once a week or once a month, with incremental backups scheduled on a daily basis, can be time consuming and costly. A backup unit can cost as much or more than the file server itself.

As networks expand from small workgroups run from single servers to Intranets, Extranets, and Internet linkages, adequate protection becomes more complex. With so much more data, enough downtime may not be available in a day to copy an entire disk drive image for each server on the network to tape each night. Network administrators will need better hardware and backup software technologies to help them cope with large networks.

At the same time that network management issues are being addressed, analysts must address a number of other issues, such as the following: Should responsibility for backup be handled by a centralized IS resource, or should it be the responsibility of each department? Should there be only one backup service provider on the network? If multiple providers are used, on what will the division of labor be based? Should selected enclaves of users be allowed to back up their own servers? How about their own workstations? Should workstation backup be included in the network-based backup service? If there are multiple backup providers, should they all be required to use the same backup hardware and software? How much of the data needs to be backed up and where is it located? Where should backups be stored? Is off-site storage of backup data necessary? What type of hardware and software should be used? All too often, these issues and others are not addressed until after a disaster occurs. The EUIS analyst may find it a challenge to persuade management of the importance of well-managed backup and to enforce disciplined procedures.

8.4 DATA SECURITY AND CONFIDENTIALITY

Data security and the confidentiality of data in computers and data banks are continuing concerns. EUIS increase these concerns because they provide wider access to data and to devices for manipulating them and easily transmitting them. Desktop computers are linked to other company computers, and, through the Internet, to the world.

EUIS present several distinct security problems. The first is protecting programs and data from unauthorized access from inside as well as outside the organization. Insiders who gain access to specific information or inadvertently damage files are perceived to be a greater threat than outside hackers. The second security issue is the problem of protecting stored or archival information. A third issue is related to safe and appropriate use of internal and external communications—e-mail.

End users may be less informed than computer professionals about the requirements of confidentiality for client and employee data. Control of databases often is separated from responsibility for their integrity and reliability. The same level of control usually is not built into desktop computer applications as is built into central systems. Yet stored information may be used and updated by novices unfamiliar with many of the software features. Moreover, the Internet enables work to be done away from the office—at home, in airplanes, in hotels, or in client offices—which increases the risk of loss, damage, or theft.

It is extremely difficult to safeguard programs and data. Data can be copied or destroyed easily, and with Internet connections, the potential for abuse has increased. Theft or misuse of sensitive data has always been a threat, even before computers. Before networks, however, it was more difficult to conceal large piles of paper or large computer tapes. It took time to hand copy, type, or even photocopy pages of information. Today, individuals can copy a wealth of information onto disks or through the Internet. Moreover, one can easily steal data by copying it and leave the original data intact.

Intranets are internal networks that typically have firewalls to protect their internal operations from outsiders. *Firewalls* provide a barrier for employees to transfer data out and better protect information and internal communications from those outside the organization. To improve communications and data flow between an organization and its partners, suppliers, or clients, organizations increasingly are using Extranets. An *Extranet* is a Web-based platform that controls data exchange with specified parties, viewable through a Web browser. This minimizes software requirements[9] and allows authorized users access to the data they need to do their work.

Managers must assess the company's exposure carefully. They must identify what it is they need to protect and the possible risks. They must determine how much time and expense are warranted and establish appropriate measures. The resources invested may depend on factors such as the number of users, types of applications, corporate culture, and whether the network is connected to other networks, an Intranet, Extranet, or the Internet. For example, an Intranet that supports an important transaction processing application, critical databases, or confi-

Figure 8-5
Tactics for better protection of sensitive computer data

1. Establish a clear, organizational policy on what types of data are considered sensitive. Ensure that every sensitive data set has a designated custodian to bear responsibility for its safekeeping.
2. Establish a policy that no sensitive information may be stored in a file, either temporarily or permanently, on a hard disk when that computer also is connected to the Internet.
3. Ensure that a locked area or cabinet is available for all backup data containing sensitive information. Access should be possible only for the data custodian.
4. Encourage the use of encryption for sensitive data files.

This message is for the named person's use only. It may contain confidential, proprietary, or legally privileged information. No confidentiality or privilege is waived or lost by any mistransmission. If you receive this message in error, please immediately delete it and all copies of it from your system, destroy any hard copies of it, and notify the sender. You must not, directly or indirectly, use, disclose, distribute, print, or copy any part of this message if you are not the intended recipient. (Company Name) and each of its subsidiaries reserve the right to monitor all e-mail communications through its networks. Any views expressed in this message are those of the individual sender, except where the message states otherwise and the sender is authorized to state them to be the views of any such entity.

Figure 8-6
E-mail disclosure statement

dential legal documents would warrant a firewall. Suggested tactics for protecting sensitive computer data are presented in Figure 8-5.

Additionally, in networked, global organizations, e-mail policies are being revised constantly to protect communications for corporate confidentiality, as well as to protect the organization from legal misuse of data. Figure 8-6 is a sample disclosure statement that could appear at the bottom of users' e-mail messages.

8.5   INFORMATION ACCURACY AND RELIABILITY (INTEGRITY)

What does a manager do when the individual who developed a program that is used regularly is promoted to another department or leaves the company? Who is responsible when a monthly report is inaccurate because a formula was altered inadvertently? Whose figures does the executive accept when department managers show up at a meeting with three different versions of divisional sales results? These are just some of the questions and issues related to the accuracy and reliability of computer information.

Problems arise in part because of the complexities of computer programs and the difficulties involved when one person tries to figure out the logic of a program developed by someone else. These problems can be reduced significantly when computer programs are documented adequately.

8.5.1   Preparing Documentation

Documentation is a detailed, written explanation of how a computer program works. It details the programming logic, variables, formulas, processed data (and where it comes from), and any other items pertinent to the creation and use of the program. Documentation usually is contained within a program and also in supplementary reference documents (referred to as *run books*). Database and CASE tools provide support in the form of data dictionaries and other tools to help manage the onerous task of documentation.

If a spreadsheet or a program is used by someone other than the individual who created it or is intended for departmental information (rather than individual calculations), thorough documentation is essential. Without documentation, it is extremely time consuming for anyone other than the program originator to modify or correct it. Documentation also serves as a tool for verifying the correctness of a program or reconstructing it if disks containing the program are destroyed or damaged. A good technique for documenting spreadsheet programs is to print out all the formulas used to create the program. Most spreadsheet programs provide this option.

8.5.2 Ensuring the Accuracy of Computer Programs

Professional programmers are well aware that many errors and problems can creep into computer programs, and they realize that errors are difficult to detect. The structured design and programming methods used by technical departments are designed to minimize risks. Managers also need to be aware of potential problems and see that programs developed by their staff are tested and verified adequately.

In the rush of everyday business, it is easy for users to overlook the importance of extensive testing and verification. Managers and users must be aware of the risks and learn appropriate procedures. The Association of Computer Users recommends that before any program is put into full use, it be run concurrently with the existing manual system, if one exists. Good programming helps a user discover errors. Accounting programs with audit trails or database management systems that will reject letter input where there should be numbers (and vice versa) help keep input errors to a minimum. For number-crunching applications, users could calculate the number of entries and batch totals before data are entered in the computer. These item counts and totals can be used to verify the accuracy of the data and determine whether errors were made as the data were keyboarded into the program. Applications packages themselves can help managers and users verify and document the accuracy of spreadsheets. Excel, or example, includes an auditing function on its Tool menu. Most users, however, are unaware of its existence.

Managers could cross train personnel to do each other's jobs to prevent an operation from coming to a stop when an employee is sick or on vacation. Job rotation can help keep skill levels up, as well as provide employees with opportunities to review each other's work. Dividing responsibility for various phases of computer operation increases the chance that one user will detect another's errors.

Managers can insist on careful testing and validation of all calculations performed on the computer. An error in a single formula or a mistyped figure easily can produce inaccurate results in computer spreadsheets—just as they do in manual calculations. Actions that a manager can take to establish controls include the following:

1. *Establish controls to verify the accuracy and integrity of spreadsheets.* Examples include independent reviews, walk-throughs, and parallel runs. (A walk-through checks the program logic by manually doing each step in the program in the programmed sequence.) The accuracy of spreadsheets can be verified by comparing results against the same calculation done manually. Old manual reports can be used for test data, or duplicate calculations can be performed.
2. *Carefully document all spreadsheets.* Documentation could include data prepared, programs used, department of origin, and other relevant information. It also is recommended that employees print out and verify the accuracy of all formulas used in the spreadsheet.
3. *Remind individuals that they are accountable for their work.* "The computer made a mistake" is not an acceptable excuse.

1. All customized programs should be validated and certified for accuracy.
2. All corporate databases, wherever they are stored, should have user-accessible date and time fields to indicate the last time the database was modified.
3. All EUIS output should be marked clearly with date and time of production. If the report draws upon any external database, the report should note that database's date and time stamp.
4. All analytical data reports done on desktop computers should have independent validations of data input and embedded formulas. Analytical models are to be checked for conceptual accuracy as well as clerical accuracy. The checkers should initial the reports and note the date and time.
5. As a matter of policy, no corporate decisions shall be made on the basis of any desktop computer-based data unless they meet all the conditions set above.

Figure 8-7
Tactics for improving the integrity of computer data

For additional recommendations on improving the integrity of computer data, see Figure 8-7.

8.5.3 Developing Guidelines for Information Systems Security

Major threats to information system security are shown in Figure 8-8. The types of security threats are listed in the left column, and the two right columns differentiate between intentional acts of malice and human error or naturally caused accidents.

Disasters and vandalism (Items 1 and 2 in Figure 8-8) that damage equipment or software are risks to microcomputers just as they are to large systems. Items 3 through 6 in Figure 8-8 represent cases where information is compromised either by unsystematic error or total loss. The key to solving these problems is the maintenance of adequate backups. Items 7 and 8 represent situations in which systematic error is entered into data through incompetence or criminal intent. The controls

Figure 8-8
Threats to information system security

THREATS TO INFORMATION SYSTEM SECURITY		
	HUMAN ERROR AND NATURAL ACCIDENT	ACTS OF MALICIOUS INTENT
Physical resource damage	1. Disasters	2. Vandalism
Random information modification	3. Mistakes	4. Pranks and nuisances
Destruction of information	5. Erasure	6. Sabotage
Systematic information modification	7. Incompetence	8. Fraud and embezzlement
Disclosure of confidential information	9. Exposure	10. Data theft

against these threats are primarily quality-assurance checks, audits, division of responsibility, and the like. Items 9 and 10 represent threats of disclosure of sensitive information. Controls involve taking care to secure information behind physical and logical locks.[10]

8.6 LEGAL ISSUES

Who is responsible when Marc damages a company's notebook computer in an accident while he is transporting it home? Courteney decides to market a software program she developed at home on the company's computer. She uses the program on her job, but developed it primarily on her own time at home. Preston claims that a fire in his home was started by a short circuit in his company's desktop computer, which he brought home from work. Bob's four-year-old son destroyed the program disk for the database package that the department just purchased for $500. Bob brought it home to finish a project that was due the next day. Clearly, EUIS have raised a number of legal issues and concerns for business managers.

8.6.1 Defining Corporate Versus Personal Data or Programs

An important measure that organizations can take is to establish clear policies on the ownership of programs or data created on company time or equipment and to require employees to sign covenants before being assigned to development projects or authorized to borrow equipment. Whether strict measures are warranted depends, of course, on how sensitive or important information is to the company.

8.6.2 Preventing Unauthorized Copying of Software

Software *copyrights* limit the rights of purchasers to copy or modify software programs. Making multiple copies of software to distribute in an office is a clear violation of most copyright agreements, and violation of these agreements subjects the organization to liability suits from software vendors.

The right to copyright software was established by the Software Act of 1980, which modified the federal Copyright Act. When software programmers (or others) obtain a copyright, they retain the exclusive right to reproduce or modify their software. Thus, others are prohibited from copying or modifying. A copyright grants five exclusive rights:

1. The exclusive right to make copies.
2. The exclusive right to distribute copies to the public.
3. The exclusive right to prepare derivative works.
4. The exclusive right to perform the work in public. (This applies mainly to plays, dances, and so on, but also could apply to software.)
5. The exclusive right to display the work in public (such as showing a film).

Software often is sold under licensing agreements that may be more or less stringent than the copyright laws. It is common to see a warning on a package of program disks that the purchaser read all terms and conditions carefully *before* opening the package, because opening the package constitutes acceptance of such

PUBLIC SECURITY

Imagine if hackers broke into your local health department's computer system and discovered sensitive information in your medical history. What if they compromised the 911 system or tinkered with your property tax assessments? The consequences of such security breaches are almost unthinkable—and that's exactly why government agencies *have* to think about them.

In October 1998, R. A. Vernon of the City of New York's Department of Investigation became the city's first chief information security officer, heading up its new security organization: Citywide Information Security, Architecture, Formulation and Enforcement (CISAFE), a unit of the Department of Investigation. CISAFE has been given the task of overseeing and coordinating security in all city agencies—more than 60 in all—covering everything from Intranets and Extranets to networks, desktop security and communications.

"Our goal is to make the City of New York a star location by creating the right security model, deploying the right technology and keeping it on the cutting edge," Vernon declares.

The City of New York—which has more than 350,000 employees and more than 100,000 computer systems—is moving toward an e-government model. For instance, it is enabling drivers to pay parking tickets and allowing property owners to check their property tax assessments over the Internet. At the same time, it is taking steps to employ the latest technologies to keep these systems secure.

Deploying updated security standards and tools is key to this effort. "We're working on guidelines," Vernon reports. "The agencies already have controls in place, and CISAFE is studying them so it can leverage the existing efforts and expertise of the city agencies to identify best practices."

Implementing standards based on these best practices will provide consistency across city agencies. "Consistency will give the city the ability to leverage its intellectual capital," Vernon explains. "If all agencies use the approved standards and tools, an individual agency can look to another for assistance when it encounters a problem. What they're trying to protect may differ from agency to agency, but standards are standards, and the controls are similar."

Once implemented, standards must be kept current. "Standards have to change rapidly or you risk exposure," Vernon explains. "It's a constant battle. As security breaches are identified or new technologies are introduced, the right measures and technologies must be deployed. After all, security is only as good as the latest technology. Our job is to stay one step ahead of the hackers."

Vernon plans to work closely with the city agencies to see that they adhere to similar security procedures. He wants to ensure, for example, that firewalls and routers throughout the city are current and configured in a similar manner, that servers aren't accessible without proper authorization and that applications are developed with proper security safeguards, such as virus protection.

Currently, many city agencies use Extranets, and data often moves beyond the confines of city agencies to the state government and even the federal government. Thus, CISAFE is doing a formal assessment of the connections and controls in place. "We need to work with the state to make sure data passes in a secure way," Vernon emphasizes.

Technologies such as public key infrastructure (PKI) will also play a role. "In the future, we'd like to take advantage of PKI, which offers a set of security tools the agencies can use as they develop applications," he reports. "It will provide a single point at which everyone, including external users, must sign in."

All security technologies, he adds, depend on users to make them effective. "Security is a people issue, not an IT issue," he says. "Everyone needs to be aware of it, and education is the key. If you explain to employees why security is important and sell them on the concept, they become your foot soldiers."—*Eileen McCooey and S. D.*

Source: Reprinted from an article by Sam Dickey, with permission from *Beyond Computing* magazine, January/February 2000, © Copyright IBM Corporation. All rights reserved. For more articles on information security go to *www.beyondcomputing.com*.

terms and conditions. Often these agreements stipulate (among other conditions) that use of the program is restricted to one machine and often one user. The purchaser may be requested to provide the serial number of the machine when returning the software registration form (which is required for ongoing support from the manufacturer). It is not yet clear to what extent these licensing agreements are valid and under what circumstances they will stand up in a court of law. Some states have passed, or are considering, laws to make such agreements valid.

Many users object to copyright restrictions or licensing agreements on the grounds that they encumber legitimate uses of software. For example, some agreements specify no copying, which leaves it unclear whether making a copy of a software program on a hard disk violates the copyright. Even if the first copy is legal, what about copies created during routine backup of the hard disk? For example, wording, such as "Although you are encouraged to make a backup copy of the Software for your own use, you are not allowed to make unlimited copies," still leaves the issue of multiple backup copies ambiguous. Some software manufacturers prevent the user from copying the program diskette more than once. Thus, if the hard disk fails, the user would not be able to recopy the programs onto a hard disk a second time. These restrictions also may interfere with regular backup of the hard disk. Corporations and other large software purchasers have been pressuring manufacturers for site-licensing (discussed later in this chapter) and other agreements that would better meet their needs. EUIS analysts and managers should monitor these legal issues and keep them in mind when negotiating with software vendors.

Managers can take several steps to help control unauthorized copying of software. First, the organization can establish a clear policy forbidding unauthorized copying of software. The policy can establish penalties for infractions and should be published and disseminated to all employees. Second, employees can be educated regarding the rules and restrictions for copying software. Users can be reminded of the ethics of unauthorized copying and the corporation's exposure to legal action.

Some companies make software available on their network server through contractual arrangements with vendors that allow it to be used on any desktop computer connected to the server. Such agreements reduce the use of application programs on hard disks, which are copied easily.

Figure 8-9
Summary of software contract terms

- Specify all sales claims and promises in writing.
- Establish the time frame within which these claims should be carried out.
- Clarify the performance of the system or services the vendor will provide.
- Specify the price of the product or service.
- Specify how payment should be made.
- Describe the kind of product or service provided.
- State any provisions that allow the purchaser to reject the product or service if it fails to perform to standard.
- Identify the forum that has jurisdiction in the event of litigation.
- Spell out any penalty or cancellation clauses, and when they come into play.
- Clarify responsibility for installation and maintenance of the equipment and for training in-house personnel.

8.6.3 Developing Hardware and Software Contracts

When managers have the autonomy to sign hardware or software purchase contracts, they should be aware of possible pitfalls or problems. A well-drawn contract should specify the rights, duties, and obligations of the seller and purchaser. Managers should check with their legal departments before signing computer hardware or software contracts. Figure 8-9 lists terms that contracts should include:[11]

Some vendors offer *site-licensing* arrangements that can help organizations reduce their exposure to illegal copying. Site-licensing arrangements also can reduce the order, reorder, and program-upgrade headaches that come with buying volume copies of software. Two categories of site-licensing arrangements often are offered by vendors:

1. *Full site-licensing agreements,* which allow users to duplicate the program disk and documentation in-house.
2. *Volume-purchasing agreements,* which offer pricing discounts based on the number of copies ordered.

Site-licensing agreements may offer additional benefits, such as technical support, newsletters, or training. Some plans incorporate clauses that limit an organization's liability for unauthorized copies to the retail price of the copies duplicated.

8.6.4 Preventing Unauthorized Access to Programs and Data

Passwords are like underwear. Change yours often . . .
Don't share yours with a friend.

> — University of Michigan Guidelines

A first-line defense against unauthorized users gaining access to computer systems is the use of passwords. A password is a group of characters that a user must enter into a system to gain access to programs or data. Although computer hackers typically have little trouble getting beyond this first-line defense, passwords that are updated frequently and regularly can better ensure that the system is used only by those who are cleared to use it. Without passwords, for example, an employee could tamper with the department budget, perhaps adding some fictitious expenses and then collecting the money later. Tips for creating passwords are offered in Figure 8-10.[12]

An emerging problem is how to remember all the passwords one has for various systems. We now have to develop and maintain passwords for work-based computing,

Figure 8-10
Tips for creating passwords

- Avoid personal information and common words.
- Use at least six characters, and mix uppercase and lowercase.
- Combine numbers and symbols.
- Put in a spelling mistake on purpose.
- Take a phrase and use only the first letters (e.g., "To be or not to be" would be TBONTB).
- Translate your password into a foreign language.

as well as home-based computing. A given user could have a password for an AOL account, a mutual fund, an e-mail account, and so on; it is not uncommon for a user to have more than 25 different passwords. Suggestions abound for dealing with password overload: You could use the same password for multiple applications; however, this is a security risk. You could keep all your passwords together in a single file, with a password for access (yet another security risk). High-tech remedies currently being used include smart cards and biometric devices that rely on fingerprints or retina scans.[13]

8.7 RESOURCES, PRODUCTS, AND SERVICES

A variety of resources, products, and services is available to help monitor hardware and software. Managers must assess the risks and determine how much effort and expense should be spent to provide adequate protection. The answer to the question of "which product to buy" depends on how much protection is needed. Managers also must assess how much convenience and accessibility they want to trade for protection and security.

8.7.1 Auditing Procedures for EUIS

The auditing department is an important ally in helping managers establish control procedures to ensure the proper use of information systems. Auditors can help a manager in several ways:

- Designing control systems and procedures for managing information flow.
- Stipulating specific requirements for documentation, control, and systems access.
- Developing audit trails that document personal responsibility for actions taken.
- Reviewing procedures for meeting requirements and ensuring that they are met.

One argument is that security and audit procedures should be concentrated on applications rather than hardware or systems software. The question should not be How do I protect a PC? or What security do I need on a LAN? Instead, managers and auditors should focus on requirements for specific applications.[14] The following directions and questions would be more appropriate: Describe the applications. What is the nature and value of the information? Who is involved in the process? Where does the information come from and where does it go? At what point in the process can I attest to its integrity?[15] Organizations must make a clear statement about the importance of information security and auditing controls.

8.7.2 Hardware and Data Security

Several products and services that address desktop computer and peripherals security needs are available. This section provides a sampling of some of the types of products that offer solutions. A comprehensive discussion is not intended.

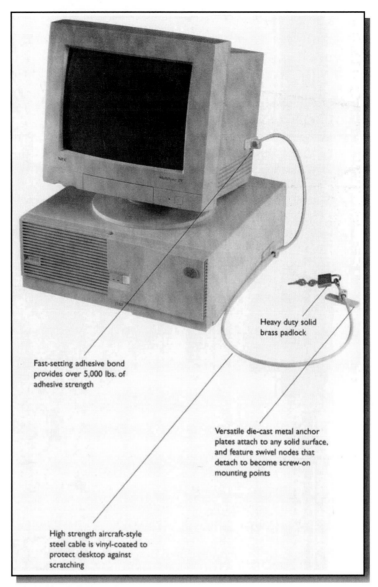

Heavy duty solid brass padlock

Fast-setting adhesive bond provides over 5,000 lbs. of adhesive strength

Versatile die-cast metal anchor plates attach to any solid surface, and feature swivel nodes that detach to become screw-on mounting points

High strength aircraft-style steel cable is vinyl-coated to protect desktop against scratching

Figure 8-11
Computer security devices
a. Cable security

Source: With permission from Christopher Meyer, AnchorPad Products, Cypress, CA.

8.7.2.1 *Hardware Security Systems*

Many devices are available to secure computers to work surfaces or lock them so as to control access. AnchorPad International markets a myriad of such security products, and samples are pictured in Figure 8-11. Devices can be as simple as cables, adhesive bond, and padlocks (Figure 8-11a) or more elaborate entrapment systems that encase the computer system (Figure 8-11b). Another device protects tower computers from theft, tampering, vandalism, and damage by suspending the tower beneath the desktop, freeing space on top of the desk and at the same time keeping the tower off the floor (Figure 8-11c).

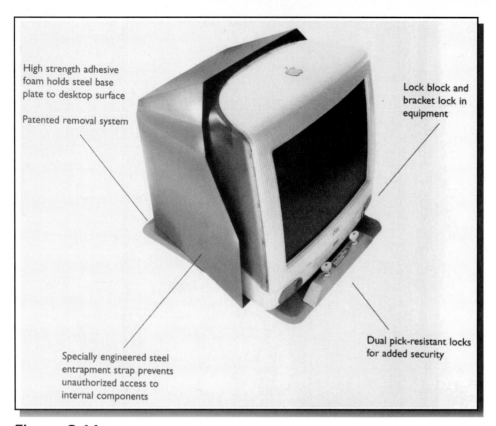

High strength adhesive
foam holds steel base
plate to desktop surface

Patented removal system

Lock block and
bracket lock in
equipment

Specially engineered steel
entrapment strap prevents
unauthorized access to
internal components

Dual pick-resistant locks
for added security

Figure 8-11
b. Entrapment security

Source: With permission from Christopher Meyer, AnchorPad Products, Cypress, CA.

The importance of security is underscored with the Computer Security Institute estimate that half of U.S. companies have notebook computers stolen every year.[16] To counter this danger, security devices for notebook computers allow users to lock their notebook down in virtually any location (Figure 8-11d); another is an anchoring plate that can be used at a workstation (8-11e).

Another type of security system is aimed at the operability of a computer. It comes on a circuit board and is plugged into one of the computer's expansion slots. Users must provide their correct identification code and password. Although board-based products provide tight control, these products may work with only certain models of computers.

Some software-based products control access to the hard disk but do not prevent users from working with disks, unless the computer has no disk drive. While some of these products are designed only for specific models, other products work with almost any operating system. They are virtually hardware-independent, and some offer data encryption.

8.7.2.2 Data Encryption

The products just described are designed primarily to prevent access to devices or data. Data encryption goes a step farther by making information unintelligible even

16-gauge steel enclosure bolts directly to underside/side of desk frame

Simple hardware required for installation included

Access to components is blocked by front and rear 16-gauge steel bars

Bars are each 2 3/4" wide and can be placed directly in front of drives to block access

Front bar features two sturdy cam locks

Figure 8-11
c. Covert under desk tower security system

Source: With permission from Christopher Meyer, AnchorPad Products, Cypress, CA.

if it is accessed. *Data encryption* uses a mathematical algorithm to scramble data. Two types of data encryption are the public-key type and the Data Encryption Standard (DES). DES, developed in the early 1970s by IBM and adopted by the National Bureau of Standards in 1976, combines two operations called substitution (replacing information) and transposition (scrambling information). These two operations transform plaintext or cleartext into ciphertext. The person who deciphers the encrypted text uses the same key that encrypted the data to reverse the substitution and transposition process. The algorithm for DES encryption has 64 bits, 56 of which are active bits, and 8 are used to detect errors in transmission. Public-key encryption

Figure 8-11
d. The sentry

Source: With permission from Christopher Meyer, AnchorPad Products, Cypress, CA.

works with two keys for each user: a public encryption key and a private decryption key. The user keeps the private key to decrypt messages sent by anyone who has a public encryption key. The two keys are linked mathematically, but it is not feasible in terms of time and energy to figure out from the public key what the private key is. DES-based encryption is the most widely used, although many experts favor the public-key method and predict increased use.

Although most of us associate data encryption with government secrets and spy novels, complex systems increasingly are being used to safeguard corporate data and secure sensitive information such as credit card numbers in e-commerce transactions. For desktop users, products such as Norton Secret Stuff (Asymetrix),

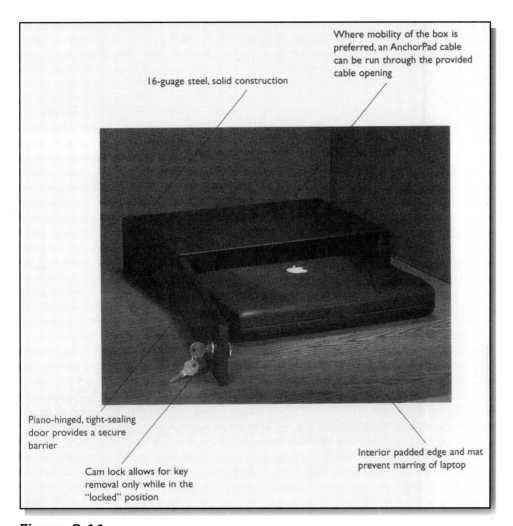

16-guage steel, solid construction

Where mobility of the box is preferred, an AnchorPad cable can be run through the provided cable opening

Piano-hinged, tight-sealing door provides a secure barrier

Cam lock allows for key removal only while in the "locked" position

Interior padded edge and mat prevent marring of laptop

Figure 8-11
e. Notebook cable security

Source: With permission from Christopher Meyer, AnchorPad Products, Cypress, CA.

a simple encryption program that keeps e-mail messages private, works well but can be time consuming.

8.8 SUMMARY

Responsibility for managing safe and legal computer use falls directly on business managers. Often, in their enthusiasm for new-found opportunities, managers and users have overlooked risks and responsibilities. Unless they are informed about the issues related to managing EUIS, they may not recognize potential problems until disaster strikes.

Policies established by senior managers are an important first step toward showing employees that computer-related risks are a legitimate corporate concern.

Policies can foster an attitude of care and concern by making employees accountable for unauthorized acts involving computer and information resources. Policy statements should be distributed to all employees and should state clearly the company's positions regarding protection of information resources.

Acquisition guidelines must be established to avoid incompatible hardware and software, duplication of effort, and unnecessary spending. Equipment must be protected against damage, loss, or theft. Regular backup procedures are required to safeguard electronically stored data against accidental loss. Standard procedures for naming and storing files save time and effort. Managers also need to protect sensitive data against unauthorized access, tampering, or copying.

Viruses are malicious codes transferred to computer files (usually through the network) to destroy data or annoy users. Trojan horses attach themselves to specific application files, disrupting their operations. Worms attack data files by multiplying to the point where systems are shut down. All users are wise to use antivirus software to protect their valuable programs and data.

Without strict procedures in technical data processing departments, errors in end-user-developed programs may go unnoticed. A dangerous tendency is to accept detailed computer analyses without adequate verification. Managers must establish procedures to ensure that data produced and stored on departmental computers are accurate and reliable.

Among the legal issues raised by EUIS are ownership of employee-developed programs, prosecution from infringement of copyright laws, purchase and licensing arrangements, and responsibility for damage to hardware and software. Policies and guidelines are needed to minimize risks.

Several resources and services are available to help provide controls for managing technology in the workplace. Auditors help assess risks and exposures, as well as recommend procedures to protect corporate resources and comply with corporate policies. Various products, such as locks, log-on programs, encryption programs, and security access controls, help secure hardware and software resources against unauthorized use.

Managers and employees need adequate guidelines and technical support to translate business needs into computer solutions. A long learning curve is involved as nontechnical personnel gain experience in applying new computer tools. Managers must be aware of both the opportunities and the related risks of managing EUIS resources.

KEY TERMS

- Backup
- Copyright
- Data encryption

- Documentation
- Site license agreement
- Trojan horse

- Virus
- Volume-purchase agreement
- Worm

DISCUSSION QUESTIONS

1. What is the purpose of policy statements? Who writes them? Who follows them? Why are they important to the EUIS analyst?
2. Summarize the issue of data security in today's office environment.
3. What is meant by the term *backup?* Why are backup practices often ignored by computer users? What solutions to the problem exist?
4. Why is documentation considered a data reliability issue?
5. What options are available to the manager who wants to audit computer operations?

Part III   End-User Information Systems: Implementation and Support

6. Identify legal issues related to computer software about which managers should be aware.
7. List steps a manager can take to help control unauthorized copying of software.
8. What is a computer virus? How do Trojan horses differ from worms?
9. Describe three devices that secure desktop computers from theft and two that secure notebook computers from theft.

APPLICATION EXERCISES

1. Compose a policy statement that addresses legal concerns related to computer operations.
2. Visit the Web sites of security device makers. How do their products differ in terms of functionality and price?
3. Assume you are a manager who has hired a college student for a summer job. The job entails using an Intranet-based database. Role-play the computer orientation you will give the student, including backup policies and virus protection procedures.

SUGGESTED READINGS

Fites, Philip; Peter Johnston; and Martin Kratz. *The Computer Virus Crisis.* (Upland, PA: Diane Publishing Company, 1999).

Kane, Pamela. *PC Security and Virus Protection Handbook: The Ongoing War Against Information Sabatoge.* (Upland, PA: Diane Publishing Company, 1999).

Spar, Debora and Jennifer Burns. *Network Associates: Securing the Web.* Harvard Business School Case Study 799087: May 10, 1999.

Tipton, Harold F., ed. *Handbook of Information Security Management.* (Boca Raton, FL: CRC Press, Inc., 1999).

ENDNOTES

1. Ken Michielsen, "A PC Policy Primer: A Few Basic Rules Lend Direction to MIS Departments Supporting Micros," *IBM Innovation* (1986): 4–5.
2. Mark Rowh, "Cy-Ber-Speak," *Office Systems* 16 (1999): 12.
3. Michael Gips, "Tracking Trojans," *Security Management* 43 (1999): 18.
4. Bruce Schneier, "The Trojan Horse War," *Communications of the ACM* 42 (1999): 128.
5. Todd Coopee, "Ecrix VXA-1 Launches New Tape Technology," *InfoWorld* 21 (1999): 48–50.
6. Joseph F. Kovar, "Storage Vendors Invade Networld + Interop," *Computer Reseller News* (1999):129–130.
7. Coopee, op. cit. pp. 48–50.
8. Kelly Carroll, "A Whole New Provider," *Telephony* 237 (1999): 48.
9. Michael Mendoza, "Opening Up with Extranets," *Computer-Aided Engineering* 19 (2000): 20–26.
10. Joel S. Zimmerman, "PC Security: So What's New?" *Datamation* (1985).
11. August Bequai, "A Management Guide to a Good Computer Contract," *The Office* (1986): 23.
12. Gene Graber, "People Feeling Overwhelmed by Having to Recall So Many," *Denver Post,* January 10, 2000.
13. Ibid.
14. Harry B. DiMaio, "Who's Guarding Your PC?" *Words* (1985): 24.
15. Ibid.
16. "Hedging Hardware Heists: Quick Fix Lockdowns," *Security* 36 (1999): 89–90.

Part IV

Workplace Performance: The Impact of Information Technology on Individuals, Groups, and Organizations

The previous sections described applications of technology to specific business needs and issues related to implementing technology and ensuring its effective use. Part IV turns to the impact of information technology (IT) on work performance and explores organizational and behavioral issues related to the introduction of new technologies. Translating the capabilities of technology into tangible and intangible operating benefits can be examined on many levels: individual tasks and jobs, departmental operations, business processes, organizational structure and culture, and quality of work life. Technology is an important productivity tool, but it is not the only factor or perhaps even the most important factor in improving performance in the workplace. How individuals in the organization effectively *use* technology and the managerial support they have for their activities are important.

Part IV presents considerations for effectively using end-user information systems to achieve organizational goals. It emphasizes the need to evaluate technologies on the basis of their potential for changing the way people work—not simply as a means of automating the tasks they are currently performing. Improving performance is viewed as a process of creating efficient, effective work environments. Integrating technology into the jobs of end users is viewed as a process of managing innovation and change, not simply managing technology.

Chapter 9, "Assessing the Value of Information Technology," asks what performance is and how it can be measured. The definition of *productivity* is examined with regard to its applicability to knowledge workers. Then, current techniques for determining IT benefits and costs are described. These techniques are useful to planners who must cost-justify expenditures. Because of large investments in hardware, software, maintenance, and user training, cost justification is increasingly important in making purchasing decisions. The chapter concludes with an overview of concepts related to Enterprise-wide Information Management.

Chapter 10, "Human Factors: Software, Hardware, and Workplace Design," addresses the interface of people with their work tools and environment. Three key areas are covered: software design issues, hardware design issues, and workplace design considerations. This chapter provides an overview of current research on what is known about these areas, emphasizing the need for ease of use, safety, comfort, and overall well-being of the end user. These issues and considerations can affect performance.

Chapter 11, "Organizational Change," presents theoretical foundations and strategies for introducing new technologies into an organization. The introduction of innovations often requires organizational and work modifications to achieve the intended results. Technology implementers play major roles as change agents and leaders. The chapter takes the stance that implementing organizational changes is a learning process that must be planned and managed carefully.

Chapter 12, "Business Process and Job (Re)Design," examines the relationships among information technology, business process, job design, and performance. When implementing IT, EUIS planners need to consider potential changes at the organizational, work group, and individual levels. This chapter focuses on the transformational nature of IT and effective approaches for (re)designing business processes and jobs. Job design methods that improve performance are described under the premise that it is *people* who are productive, not systems.

Case Study   How Ford Motor Company Is Embracing Technological Change

This case focuses on how Ford Motor Company is reinventing its information technology (IT) structure, the strategies used to develop this structure, and the ways technologies are changing how Ford does business.

Introduction

Ford Motor Company is a nearly 100-year-old corporation that is one of the "Big Three" in the automobile industry. Ford is given credit for the invention and implementation of the modern assembly line for producing mass quantities of goods. Now Ford is leading the way car manufacturers are reinventing the industry with information technology and digital networks.

The Facts and Numbers

Ford's headquarters are in Dearborn, Michigan. It has alliances and independently owned dealerships all over the world. The CEO is 52-year-old Jacques Nasser. In 1998, Ford has $144.4 billion in revenues and $22.1 million of net income. Several layers of management and workers account for most of its 350,000 employees.

Ford's IT Strategy

Ford was four times as profitable in 1998 as any of its big competitors based in the United States, Japan, and Germany. The company has accelerated dramatically the pace of its business, cutting everything from vehicle-development time to the speed at which it deploys new software applications. Ford, however, was not satisfied to rest on its past performances.

CEO Jacques Nasser plans to transform the company from a maker of cars to "a consumer company that offers automotive products and services." What isn't known is how, exactly, Ford intends to make sure its IT function is contributing to the change. Nasser says he recognizes the pivotal role IT must play in Ford's transformation: "You must integrate IT into the texture of the business." A closer look at Ford's IT operations shows that Nasser and company offer specific strategies for business-technology integration.

Try to imagine focusing a company of 350,000 employees worldwide on a common goal, and it's hard to keep from comparing the challenge to the old saying about herding cats. For Ford, a four-stage business strategy model has been the answer. The model's stages describe the company's mission, strategy, processes, and infrastructure; that basic model then is reiterated and mirrored, with the appropriate level of detail, at each level of the company. Proceeding downward, each level provides a bit more detail and how-to for achieving the goal or stage above it. For example, the IS and process-leadership group has its own version to mirror the corporate model, and subgroups within the IS organization have their own mirror models, as well. The technical services group, which is the part of the IS organization that provides computing infrastructure such as networks, data center services, global server support, application support, Help Desk, and technology R&D for the entire company, carries the mission statement, "To deliver the best-in-class, highest-quality, lowest-cost technology infrastructure utility, providing the foundation for the company to achieve its business goals and encouraging the creation of new and innovative ways of doing business." George Surdu, director for technical services, says the mission statement reflects again Ford's newly embedded customer focus—the references to quality and cost mean his group must offer levels of service and price them to be competitive with outside providers.

Until recently, Ford had no centralized IT group. Instead, each functional arm or geographical unit of the company developed its own systems as it saw fit. One element of the Ford 2000 vision was to act like a truly global company rather than a company with disjointed units in many countries. The result of Ford's old structure was incompatible systems, which slowed the task of sharing information; that, in turn, slowed the velocity of decision making. So, beginning in 1994, Ford took the first steps toward consolidating its systems groups into a central organization—a plan that culminated in Bernard Mathaisel's arrival in 1996 as Ford's first CIO and executive director of process leadership.

Centralizing IT caused major changes at Ford. For example, the company now has an enterprise technology architecture and a process for identifying which technologies fit in, which need to be replaced, and so on. These standards are adhered to by the business globally. If it isn't in the standards, that technology doesn't get rolled out, although there is a process for identifying exceptional needs. Essentially, all the company's desktop systems are provided by one supplier—Dell Computer Corporation—and Ford uses two standard configurations for those desktops. The benefits are lower hardware costs, lower support costs, and easier software rollouts because of simplified testing requirements.

"Indeed," says James Yost, Ford's newly anointed CIO and head of process leadership, "a lot of our commonization of systems couldn't have been done before the current centralized organization was put in place."

At the same time, though, Ford is careful not to let the desire for standardization squelch the need for different applications around the globe. "They are very careful to leave alone those things they should," says former CIO Mathaisel. Although the U.S. units operate on standardized financial and manufacturing software, for example, Ford groups working in emerging markets such as China tend to run their operations on smaller ERP packages to give them a simpler, consolidated look at their regional business.

Additionally, on February 3, 2000, Ford Motor Company announced that all 350,000 of its employees will be receiving their own home personal computers and Internet access to link to other Ford workers all over the world. The $300 million price tag was peanuts for Ford. The decision was based not on altruism but on a realization that a connected workforce is a more productive workforce. The idea is to open up the flow of information and smash the geographic fiefdoms that traditionally have slowed decision making.

One of the biggest challenges for ongoing business–IT alignment at Ford is that the business is a moving target. The "consumer company" is in many ways still a better description of where Ford is headed than where it stands now. Ford's answer to keeping IT on top of the changes is a group responsible for both IT and process leadership. The group documents corporate processes and acts in a consulting role to help facilitate reengineering.

The group has identified five key areas of its business for focused reengineering efforts: design to delivery, order to delivery, services, manufacturing, and product design. That isn't an exhaustive list of everything the company does, and the more areas the company can target, the faster it can change. However, initiatives of such large scope—like designing a new car or all the steps that turn an order into a delivered vehicle—take several years to design and implement.

A dedicated team is examining and documenting each area. IT–process staff work together with operational personnel to document first the existing processes in a given area. Then they ask a lot of why and what-if questions, functioning in a sort of advisory–consulting role. Lower-level improvements—those of smaller scope than the big five reengineering areas—that can be addressed more quickly are handled as "focused improvement opportunities" that might take a year, or as even smaller increments called "rapids" or "just do its" that might be implemented in a day. Again, the cascading approach allows for thoughtful management at all levels of the enterprise. The little changes don't have to wait for the huge initiatives to be completed, and yet the big-picture processes, where payback for the company is greatest, receive the attention they merit. As the reengineering teams identify process changes or best practices, they use the company's intranet to catalog and inform similar business units in other places. Ford has identified and replicated more than 2,700 practices or processes and claims a value of nearly $600 million delivered from best practice replication since August 1996. Another measure of the company's streamlined processes: Ford is the most efficient auto manufacturer in North America, requiring 35 hours to build a vehicle, compared with 44-plus hours for its U.S. competitors.

One driving IT change at Ford is its ConsumerConnect strategy. A group of individuals assembled to change the way consumers purchase vehicles. To help plot the strategy, in 1999 Nasser hired a young executive from General Electric, Brian Kelley, to oversee Ford's push into the new era. Kelley began bringing in other nonauto executives, blending them into teams with younger Ford executives. Some older Ford executives, meanwhile, quietly retired. Creating a younger management team seems to have been part of Nasser's strategy. "Now, we're in the age group with people in the Internet era," he says. "We talk the same language." The new team sees themselves as a kind of Alpha squad, here to lead change and help make the cultural difference required to bring Ford into the twenty-first century.

Traditionally, when customers wanted to buy a car, they looked in the newspaper, went to the dealer, haggled over the price, and then left with a car they may or may not have wanted. Customers now can log on to *www.ford.com* and design their own car. The site allows customers to choose a model and add options as desired. When they are finished, an estimated bill is calculated. The site also allows customers to examine different financing scenarios by changing rates and down payments. Once customers have chosen "their" car and financing, they can then input their zip code and find the nearest dealer. The problem is the dealer may have other plans for the car the customer likes.

This is where ConsumerConnect improves the process. Ford's goal within two years is to allow individuals to build their own car on the Web, provide them with financing opportunities, and deliver the car to them. The benefits are that customers get the car they want and Ford doesn't build in-

ventory that may take days and millions of dollars to move. Although this sounds great, what about the dealer? The Internet is making some dealerships uneasy. Some have gone as far as successfully lobbying state lawmakers to keep new Internet cars out of their state. However, carmakers are fighting back with innovative partnerships and are providing dealerships with incentives to sell and distribute Internet cars.

To accomplish technological changes, Ford formed several alliances. Oracle is doing the heavy lifting on the software and databases needed to swap information and conduct transactions seamlessly. Cisco, which signed on as a partner on February 9, 2000, will provide much-needed networking expertise. Microsoft Corporation's CarPoint, an auto sales and information Web site, will help Ford develop a build-to-order service. Internet service provider UUNet, PC maker Hewlett-Packard, and middleman PeoplePC signed on to put Ford's sprawling workforce online, starting in April of 2000.

Other tech partners are helping Ford get closer to its customers. Online powerhouses Yahoo! and Priceline.com, along with Denver-based call-center wizard TeleTech, will design systems that deliver highly personalized warranty, loan, repair, and customized services based on more detailed knowledge of driver lifestyles and buying habits. "It could give us a bird's-eye view of what consumers want out of a car before we build it," says Ford design chief J. Mays.

Meanwhile, ConsumerConnect and Ford's Visteon auto-parts unit are teaming up to wire future Fords for e-mail and news, voice-recognition systems, and satellite phone services that will, says Kelley, "turn the family car into a Web portal on four wheels." The payoff: a whole array of new services in a marketplace where basic car prices are declining. Better yet, Web services and phones can be sold on a subscription basis, generating monthly fees that keep cash flowing into Ford's coffers for the life of the car.

Reinventing IT structure is a huge task, but one that Ford has embraced head-on. The change will meet with some resistance, and the cost is huge. However, Nasser remains determined. The risk of not embracing the change could be much more costly.

Sources: Adapted from Holstein, William J., "The Dot Com within Ford," *U.S. News & World Report* (February 7, 2000); Holstein, William J., "Let Them Have PCs," *U.S. News & World Report* (February 14, 2000); Kerwin, Kathleen, Marcia Stepanek, and David Welch, "At Ford, E-Commerce Is Job 1," *Business Week* (February 28, 2000); Slater, Derek, "Alignment Check," *CIO* (November 15, 1999). *www.ford.com.*

CASE STUDY QUESTIONS

1. Ford has operations all over the world, and they claim to have two standard configurations for desktop computers. What are some of the considerations (e.g., software, hardware, languages) in configuring the desktops across multiple countries?

2. Ford has created a centralized IT group. How might the group gather information from users of the technology to know their needs?

3. All employees of Ford are given a personal computer and Internet access for $5 per month. As IT manager in charge of implementing this program, address the following questions.

   Should employees be required to accept the computers?

   What software applications should Ford distribute with the computers?

   Should Ford provide training for the computers? If so, how might the training be delivered?

   Should other family members be allowed to use the computer?

   Should Ford enforce any restrictions on the use of the computers?

   How might Ford deal with separation of employment issues?

4. Ford's goal is to have consumers design, finance, and eventually purchase autos online. Who do you think will be the primary users of this new way of purchasing vehicles? Will dealerships be eliminated, or how might dealerships still play a role in the purchasing of a new car?

5. Visit the Ford Web site at *www.ford.com.* Use the sight to design a vehicle, choose financing options, and find a dealer. After your visit, list the benefits to the customer and to Ford. Also, give your suggestion about things you would add to the Web site to benefit the customers and/or Ford.

Chapter 9

Assessing the Value of Information Technology

Learning Objectives

Upon completing this chapter, you should be able to:

➤ Define the terms *productivity* and *performance.*

➤ Explain why information worker productivity is difficult to measure.

➤ Discuss ways that information technology can contribute to performance.

➤ Understand the importance of linking information technology to corporate strategy.

➤ Point out how factors such as managerial leadership, previous experience with information technology, and user satisfaction can impact performance.

➤ Differentiate between direct and indirect performance measures.

➤ List and discuss specific approaches to determining the benefits of information technology.

➤ Use benefit analysis techniques to calculate the benefits of information technologies.

➤ Use accepted quantitative techniques to calculate the costs of technologies.

➤ Given a specific situation, develop a plan to cost-justify EUIS computing expenditures.

➤ Summarize the key concepts of Information Economics.

9.1 INTRODUCTION

Productivity is a fascinating concept. Debate continues on its definition and on the validity of its measures. Debate continues as to whether or not descriptions of productivity that were developed in factories can be used in the office workplace. Likewise, the relationship between knowledge worker productivity and investment in information technology (IT) is elusive and difficult to determine.

Productivity generally is seen as a means of increasing the bottom line profit of organizations. Organizations make enormous investments in both people and tools. Stephen Roach, an economist with Morgan Stanley Dean Witter, does not believe that investment in technology can be credited with the 5 percent growth in worker productivity achieved in the second half of 1999. He says workers are simply working harder, not better:

> Courtesy of laptops, cell phones, home fax machines and other appliances, knowledge workers are now online in cars, planes, trains, and homes, virtually tethered to their offices. The "24/7" culture of nearly round-the-clock work is endemic to the wired economy.[1]

Roach also attributes the productivity increase to cost-cutting measures such as downsizing and outsourcing.

Not everyone agrees with Roach's analysis. Erik Brynjolfsson (MIT) and Lorin M. Hitt (The Wharton School) say traditional productivity measures are not useful because they look at the overall economy rather than individual companies.[2] Others attribute the explosion in productivity to e-commerce. Others say workers are working better, not just harder.

This chapter will look at the issue of knowledge worker productivity, suggesting that performance is a more usable concept than productivity when examining the impact that technology has on work and workers. The need for hard numbers is to justify purchasing technology—to reduce expenses or create a better output—not to measure productivity, per se.

In this Information Age, more and more attention is being paid to using limited resources efficiently and effectively. Trends toward downsizing (decreasing the number of middle managers) and outsourcing (using outside firms to provide services) attest to this *need*. Organizations are expecting managers to take wider responsibilities. Departments are finding that outside service providers can be more cost effective than internal service providers. Individuals know that to survive (and thrive) in such climates, new work methods may be required. A theme throughout this text is that technology offers an opportunity for enhancing worker performance.

Moreover, technology is viewed here as an important resource that must be managed like any other resource. IT professionals typically view technology investment planning in terms of the costs of hardware, software, and maintenance required. A manager looks at the impact of IT on productivity gains, cost savings, required training, and effectiveness. CEOs are increasingly concerned that they have evidence that IT expenditures will affect the bottom line. However, no one method will provide all this evidence. Decisions to upgrade from one application software suite to another might require a simple cost-benefit analysis. A more complex system might require more sophisticated metrics.[3] Yet in other cases, when it is important just to get the new project going, formal analysis is not done.

The chapter's practical aspect is to help managers ask the right questions when trying to cost-justify IT expenditures. Assuming that improved performance is the goal, the cost-justification challenge is to measure the improvement and then translate that benefit into dollars. First, the definition of *productivity* is offered and contrasted with a definition of *performance*. Then, specific measurement techniques related to assigning dollar values to information technology's benefits and costs are offered. These techniques are useful to the manager or planner who must justify IT expenditures. The chapter concludes with an overview of Information Economics (iEcon), an approach to measure the relative value of IT projects and prioritize them.

9.2 PRODUCTIVITY AND PERFORMANCE

The formula for productivity, borrowed from factories and industry, is simple:

Productivity = Output/Input

The application of this formula requires an ability to identify and measure inputs and outputs. This is a simple mathematical exercise when applied to factory work. For example, 50 workers each earn $10 an hour and work 4 hours. They use raw materials worth $500. They produce 200 widgets, with a profit margin of $60. Their productivity can be computed as follows:

Output = $(200 \times 60) = 12{,}000$
Input = $(50 \times 10 \times 4) = 2{,}000 + (500) = 2{,}500$
Productivity = $12{,}000/2{,}500 = 4.8$

In this case, a planner would show an increase in productivity by demonstrating that workers produced *more* widgets with the same input or produced the same number of widgets with *less* input.

The productivity formula is much more difficult to apply to knowledge work. What is the output of the manager or professional? Is it determined by the number of meetings held, the number of phone calls completed, or the number of reports produced? Is support staff's output the number of letters typed, the number of phone calls handled, or the number of travel plans completed? What are the input resources? Supplies? Time?

The impact of IT on performance, not productivity, is the emphasis in this chapter. Following is a discussion of three key questions related to the relationship of IT and end-user productivity: (1) Does IT contribute to organizational performance? (2) What key issues or variables are related to information worker performance? and (3) Can performance be measured?

9.2.1 Does Information Technology Contribute to Organizational Performance?

IT produces profit by improving the company's performance in areas that drive profit.[4]
—Robert Benson, Principal of the Beta Group

The issue that most end users and managers consider today is not whether investment *should* be made in IT, but how *much* investment should be made. Researchers have attempted to investigate the impact that information technology has had on the *organization.* Not surprisingly, research findings are mixed. For example, Cron and Sobol found that extensive information technology users were either high or low performers. Harris and Katz found that high performers spent considerably more on information technology than their counterparts. Bender, however, found that information technology was associated with weaker performance.[5]

The premise here is that IT has the potential to increase performance in more ways than simply enabling work to be done faster and/or more easily. IT can support better communications, more informed decisions, and worker creativity. For example, communication technology such as groupware can add synergy to team projects. Decision support systems can help managers make more informed decisions. Hypertext can augment human reasoning, allowing the user to make connections among ideas that were not known before. Project management systems can serve to keep projects on track. Examples of such benefits from IT are discussed throughout this text.

9.2.2 What Are the Organizational and Individual Variables Related to the Impact of IT on Worker Performance That Must Be Understood?

Perhaps the most important factor related to IT success is the need for top management commitment and the tying of technology expenditures to identified goals. In discussing strategic planning in the next part of this text, reference will be made to the need for Information Economics. Discussed in detail later in this chapter, the thrust of Information Economics is that information technology must be tied to organizational goals. In other words, technology plans must be linked to strategic plans. At the individual level, technology must be linked to helping the individual work not only faster but also in a way that will increase creativity. Such an approach can provide strong evidence for investment in IT.

Other variables that could have a direct bearing on performance are the organization's experiences with technology and the individual's skill level in using technology. Organizations have not all implemented IT at the same time or infused technology into jobs at the same rate. End users are individuals and therefore do not have consistent skills in using IT. Not surprisingly, organizational experiences with IT and end-user skill levels often are related. Organizations in which users have been using IT for decades typically have workers who are advanced users. Organizations that are just beginning to introduce computing for individuals may be expected to have more novice users. Moreover, organizations in which technology is a long-term investment, not a one-shot deal, have better results.

In addition, it is important to keep in mind that each individual end user has had experiences using IT that enforce either negative or positive perceptions toward its value. Unsuccessful experiences using technology once or twice may translate to technology aversion. On the other hand, successful experiences using technology often breed more successful experiences and the desire to learn more. Technology use and its learning curve are additive; the more one uses IT, the easier it is to use. The more skilled one is in an application, the more likely it is to be used to address specific goals creatively.

9.2.3   Why Measure Performance?

Measuring performance is a difficult and important task. More than 80 percent of the 150 IS executives at U.S. companies reported that they are required to demonstrate the value of IS expenditures.[6] Sometimes it seems to be intuitive that benefits will accrue from getting users data that will enhance their decision-making abilities or ensure that they don't miss opportunities.[7] Thus, the challenge for IT planners and managers is not only how to measure performance, but also how to assign a dollar value to any improvement.

Such numbers (dollar values) are important because individuals who decide whether to buy information technologies often must cost-justify the expenditure to upper management. Cost justification is a way of saying that by purchasing such-and-such technology, we will increase performance by X amount, and that translates into a savings of $X.

The crux of the problem of assigning dollars to performance improvement is how to apply hard-dollar figures to soft-dollar savings. *Hard-dollar* figures are actual values of benefit gains in dollars and cents. IT's worth, however, is frequently measured in *soft-dollar* savings, which implies an intangible value. An intangible value could be the better decision made with an expert system, better customer service, or the impact that an ergonomically designed workstation had on the comfort of the user.

Early efforts in office automation often focused on clerical personnel. It soon became apparent, however, that all knowledge workers do a considerable amount of information handling and analysis. Planners realized that IT's biggest payoff was likely to come from improving the performance of the manager, not the secretary. Improving the performance of a $100,000-a-year manager will have more impact than improving the performance of a $30,000-a-year secretary. Although the logic for this approach makes sense, the task is difficult; managerial performance is even less tangible than secretarial performance.

The value of all these measures is in their application to provide justification for IT expenditures. In selecting a technique to describe the relationship between IT and benefits, the planner must conform to the corporate culture, its cash flow, and acceptable accounting techniques. Again, most organizations require that IT expenditures over a certain dollar amount be cost justified. Managers and IT planners consider such figures useful, especially in the following areas:

- Preparing a budget and developing long-term IT plans.
- Ensuring that IT fits into the organization's long-term business objectives.
- Developing a contract for organizational commitment of long-range expenditures.
- Prioritizing IT projects.
- Evaluating IT projects (prepared after implementation).

This chapter began by discussing problems inherent in identifying and measuring the impact that IT can have on the bottom line of an organization. IT may impact information worker performance and sales volumes. The task of correlating any IT investment with worker performance is a science, as well as an art. With this in mind, following is a discussion of techniques for tying IT expenditures to benefits. Then, quantitative techniques related to developing meaningful cost figures are offered. This chapter concludes with an overview of Information Economics (iEcon), a method for prioritizing investments in IT.

9.3 BENEFIT ANALYSIS TECHNIQUES

Many techniques used to determine the benefits and costs of IT are related to historical factory and office performance measures. From Frederick Taylor came the development of standards based on the "best" way to do something. Using this approach, stopwatches were used to determine the best way to complete a task. In the early days of word processing, when rows and rows of typists keyed documents, worker output was actually measured line by line.

In assessing the value of information technology, such as cost savings, or value-added approaches, planners often use some of the same techniques used in establishing standards. This results in many of the same problems, particularly unreliability. A benefit figure is considered reliable if the figures are the same when the process or approach is repeated. Because of the "human element," however, reliability among benefit figures is difficult to achieve.

Therefore, in developing cost-justification figures, the planner must choose a method applicable to the situation. When traditional methods do not work, the planner must be innovative and develop an original strategy. There is no right or wrong approach, just an *appropriate* approach.

Marilyn Parker and Robert Benson developed a taxonomy for techniques to develop benefit figures for information technology expenditures. Stemming from their work on Information Economics (iEcon), discussed later in this chapter, the taxonomy offers three types of applications within which a specific technique can be placed: substitutive, complementary, and innovative.[8] *Substitutive* applications of information technology substitute technology power for people power. *Complementary* applications focus on increasing worker effectiveness. *Innovative* applications are those that are used to maintain or gain a competitive advantage. Based on the work of Parker and Benson, Figure 9-1 uses this taxonomy to categorize cost-justification techniques that will be discussed in this section.

Substitutive cost justification measures rely on traditional return on investment approaches. When IT's benefits can be tied to a particular product or product line, and measures can show specific cost savings or cost displacements, substitute techniques can be used. Examples of end-user computing applications where *substitutive* techniques are appropriate include teleconferencing (for travel) and electronic mail (for mail). A second, perhaps more creative, approach is to look for intangible values that technology adds to work and translate that value into dollars. This second approach, *complementary* techniques, includes hedonic wage models or benefit acceleration approaches. Application examples here include the use of spreadsheets, graphics, and database applications, as well as professional use of word processing. The third approach, *innovative* applications, encompasses those that are designed to maintain or gain a competitive edge. E-commerce is a good example of a category of innovative applications. Another approach is simply to explain that technology adds to the *quality of work life* or is simply the *cost of doing business*. Following is an overview of specific techniques.

9.3.1 Substitutive Techniques

The theory behind substitute techniques is simple: The cost of IT is charged against the benefits obtained from the technology. Such return-on-investment (ROI) measures are based on the premise that one can measure the "before technology" costs and compare them with the "after technology" costs. Two strategies are used in this category: cost savings and cost displacement.

Figure 9-1
Techniques for cost justification

Type of Application	Technique
Substitutive	Cost savings
Teleconferencing	Cost displacement
Electronic mail	
Secretarial word processing	
Complementary	
Spreadsheets	Hedonic Wage Model
Graphics packages	Applications Transfer Team
Query packages	Benefit acceleration
Innovative	
Direct customer order entry	Value added
Home banking	Innovation risk analysis
Other	Quality of work life
	Cost of doing business

9.3.1.1 Cost Savings

Using a cost savings approach, the planner would be able to explain that the information technology will enable a worker to do the same task at less expense. For example, suppose managers in New York City and Louisville need to meet. If the managers meet by videoconferencing rather than face-to-face, travel expenses are eliminated. The planner can justify the projected costs of the videoconference by comparing its cost with the projected travel expenses:

TRAVEL COSTS	
Business class airfare for two executives	$1,500
Ground transportation	200
Hotel accommodations (two nights) in New York City	1,200
Food expenses	500
Total	*$3,400*
VIDEOCONFERENCING COSTS	
Hardware purchases	300
Transmission time	40
Total	*$340*

This cost comparison shows that the audio conference would be much less expensive than the travel ($340 as compared to $3,400). A creative planner could even put a dollar amount on the time that the executives who are traveling would be away from their desks and not doing other productive work for the organization. Although this approach is simplistic, it can be effective in developing a cost justification argument.

9.3.1.2 Cost Displacement

Historically, office technology was justified in terms of cost displacement or cost avoidance. Using a $20,000 word processor, a typist could do the work of three typists, thus reducing personnel costs by two workers. In the 1960s and 1970s, office automation *was* word processing. Most planners justified the expense by decreases in the number of secretaries. If secretaries were paid $20,000 per year (including fringe benefits), the purchase of a word processor would displace personnel expenses of $40,000.

Interestingly enough, as the number of secretaries was reduced, much of the clerical work of proofing, copying, and "goforing" was inadvertently offloaded onto managers and professionals, who were paid two or three times as much as the secretaries. Thus, cost displacement strategies must be applied cautiously to avoid achieving savings in one area at the expense of another. Performance is increased only by improving the effectiveness of the entire system.

9.3.2 Complementary Techniques

Complementary techniques discussed here are Hedonic Wage Model analysis, IBM's Applications Transfer Team approach, and the benefit acceleration model.

9.3.2.1 Hedonic Wage Model

Sassone and Schwartz's Hedonic Wage Model is a two-part procedure that first measures work and then applies dollar values to that work.[9] This procedure requires the planner to first identify employee classifications (manager, administrator, senior professional, junior professional, technician, and secretary). An average (or actual) hourly wage is determined for the employee. In addition, specific tasks are assigned certain values for certain classifications. Then, individuals in these positions are asked to use a work log to detail their activities. As shown in Figure 9-2, activities are classified according to the value of the activity, and then are applied to the wages received for the activity. This procedure can serve as a pretest, describing "work" before technology, and as a posttest to describe "work" after the new technology is implemented.

9.3.2.2 Applications Transfer Team

IBM's *Applications Transfer Team* method is based on identifying shadow functions. To help potential customers identify the type and amount of technology desirable, IBM planners help their customers estimate the time they spend on specific tasks such as writing, reading, looking for files, or answering the telephone. Gains are measured by calculating the time saved by performing these tasks more efficiently.

For example, a strong case could be made for voice mail as a means to eliminate unscheduled meetings and taking messages from calls. A $90,000 executive who works 40 hours each week, 50 weeks each year, would earn $1,800 per week, $360 per day, or $45.00 per hour. Two hours saved each week ($90) for 50 weeks equals a savings of $4,500 for this employee alone.

9.3.2.3 Benefit Acceleration Model

Benefit acceleration model analysis has its roots in economics rather than in business finance. Parker and Benson explained that it is appropriate to use when the effects of IT can be linked to specific outcome measures through increased revenues or decreased costs.[10] For example, an information center can be cost justified by explaining that a center could help the organization achieve its financial objectives faster or better than by traditional means. This is *not* the same argument that an information center would help keep operating costs or labor costs low, as in cost savings approaches.

Figure 9-2
Hedonic Wage Model

	EXAMPLE BENEFIT CALCULATION FOR MANAGERS			
WORK CATEGORY	IMPLICIT VALUE (HOURLY)	INITIAL HOURS*	FINAL HOURS**	VALUE
Management	$83.99	600	700	$8,399.00
Specialist professional	$65.11	320	400	$5,208.80
Routine professional	$48.75	260	300	$1,950.00
Administrative	$41.15	320	300	($823.00)
Clerical	$20.90	140	100	($836.00)
Nonproductive	0.00	360	200	$0.00
TOTALS		2,000	2,000	$13,898.80

*Pre-System
**Estimated Post-System

Source: Sassone and Schwartz.

9.3.3 Innovative Techniques

Two innovative techniques are discussed here. The first technique is value added. The second approach is innovation risk analysis. While the value-added technique could be described as complementary, because it includes an emphasis on doing work creatively, it is considered innovative.

9.3.3.1 Value-Added Techniques

Value-added techniques put a dollar figure on the value of work done by information technology by making one or more of the following determinations:

1. Determining the activities that were done by the information technology that could not have been done if the technology had not been available.
2. Determining how much more work was done as a result of the information technology.
3. Determining how much the quality of output increased as a result of using new information technology. (For example, were better or more timely decisions made because information was more accurate or more quickly compiled?)

In *The Information Edge,* N. Dean Meyer and Mary Boone offered more than 50 cases in which IT measurably enhanced profits. For example:

- a spreadsheet made $76 million for a chemical company
- electronic mail got a product to market two months early, with a ROI of 1,000 percent
- a $600 search of public information data banks made a material difference in an $18 million lawsuit[11]

Meyer and Boone offer creative methods to perform cost justification and IT performance auditing. In short, the method is for the planner to work with the user to determine the impact of IT on behavior, the benefit of that impact, and the value of that benefit to the organization's overall strategy.

9.3.3.2 Innovation Risk Analysis

Innovation risk analysis is used to evaluate information technologies and choose alternatives. Important considerations related to innovation risk analysis are identifying the cost of being the first to have a technology and the value of (any) competitive advantage the technology may offer. Also considered in the analysis are the costs involved should the technology application fail.[12]

9.3.4 Other Approaches

Two old techniques that are used increasingly in justifying information technology expenditures are *quality of work life (QWL)* and *the cost of doing business* techniques.

9.3.4.1 Quality of Work Life Approaches

IT's value also can be determined by assessing the quality of work life. Are workers who are using technology able to do routine activities with ease, thus freeing them for more creative, more rewarding activities? If so, information technology has made a contribution to their quality of work life (QWL).

To develop a measure of QWL, Figure 9-3, Productivity/Job Satisfaction Survey, is offered. This survey was used by a major vendor to determine if (and how) IT affected the worker's perceived performance and job satisfaction. While the problem remains of how to put a dollar figure on QWL, such data are valuable

Performance/Satisfaction Survey

Following is a list of work situations that may impact your productivity. Pick the eight that are most important to you. Rank them from 8 (most important) to 1 (least important). Write rankings to the left of items in the "P" column.

Then, pick the eight items you feel are most important to your personal on-the-job satisfaction. Rank them from 8 (most important) to 1 (least important). Write these rankings in the "S" column.

Indicate the degree to which you experience each situation as an impact of using the new product ordering system. Larger numbers indicate more effect. Judge the degree of effect independently from the importance you attach to each item.

			EFFECT OF TECHNOLOGY				
P	S	WORK SITUATION	HIGH				Low
____	____	Faster reaction to problems/opportunities	4	3	2	1	0
____	____	Improved quality of work	4	3	2	1	0
____	____	Increased control over operations	4	3	2	1	0
____	____	Decrease in time needed to do work	4	3	2	1	0
____	____	Better personal organization	4	3	2	1	0
____	____	Reduced interruptions	4	3	2	1	0
____	____	Reduced time spent on clerical tasks	4	3	2	1	0
____	____	More creativity	4	3	2	1	0
____	____	Reduced mistakes	4	3	2	1	0
____	____	Clearer communications	4	3	2	1	0
____	____	More rapid communications	4	3	2	1	0
____	____	Increase in accuracy of data	4	3	2	1	0
____	____	Increase in amount of data	4	3	2	1	0
____	____	Improved access to needed data	4	3	2	1	0
____	____	Reduced waiting for information	4	3	2	1	0
____	____	Data in more understandable form	4	3	2	1	0
____	____	Improved decision making	4	3	2	1	0
____	____	Better planning	4	3	2	1	0
____	____	Timely completion of work	4	3	2	1	0
____	____	Additional work undertaken	4	3	2	1	0
____	____	Less overtime	4	3	2	1	0
____	____	Less waiting for work	4	3	2	1	0
____	____	More job satisfaction	4	3	2	1	0
____	____	Increased motivation to work	4	3	2	1	0
____	____	Cost reduction	4	3	2	1	0
____	____	Other _____	4	3	2	1	0
____	____	Other _____	4	3	2	1	0

Figure 9-3
Productivity/job satisfaction survey

1. How much time do you use the new system per day?
2. Compared to the way you used to do your work, does using the system save you time on an average day? Yes No Sometimes

   If you answered "yes" or "sometimes,"

   2a. How does the system save you time?

   2b. What do you do with the time saved?

   2c. Are there any negative effects of using the new system? What are they?

	High				Low
3. Rate your overall degree of satisfaction with the system.	4	3	2	1	0
4. Rate your skill level in using the system.	4	3	2	1	0

Please check your job classification:

____ Secretary/Clerical
____ Professional
____ Manager
____ Supervisor
____ Director, VP, GM
____ Other

Please add any comments on the back of this sheet. Thank you!

Figure 9-3
(continued)

because factors that contribute to performance are often the same as those that contribute to job satisfaction.

Other measures may require using historical data to determine that turnover rates have changed since the technology was introduced. Despite its difficulty, another measure may be to document that *better* employees were attracted to the organization because of the technology. Of interest, employers who hire people directly from business schools are finding that a state-of-the-art PC connected to the Internet is the prospective employee's expectation and is part of the hiring agreement.

9.3.4.2 The Cost of Doing Business

This third and final argument for persuading managers to invest in IT is simple: The organization cannot go on without it! Sometimes danger exists in bureaucracies where every purchase is suspect and must be justified. Creativity and performance may be stifled when long delays occur between identifying a technological solution for a problem and implementing the technology. In some cases, the task to be done cannot be done without technology. In other cases, the technology improves customer service. Perhaps the most convincing of arguments is that use of the technology gives the organization a competitive edge.

These arguments have been discussed in previous chapters and may be the route that IT justification will take in the future. As business school graduates who negotiate for a computer as part of their hiring contract know, IT is often just the way that work should be done. IT can be related to performance via better customer service. Good service results in repeat customers, which equals more sales, which equals more profit. The third situation, where IT gives the organization a larger share of the market because marketing was innovative or orders were processed and shipped more quickly, is of undescribable value.

THE COST OF DOING BUSINESS

- Tom Hall, manager of electronic commerce for Michelin North America, said an immediate, monetary return-on-investment (ROI) was not among the chief goals of an initiative to provide electronic-commerce links between Michelin and the 1,000-plus dealers who sell the company's tires throughout North America. The primary objective, Hall said, was improving relationships between Michelin and its dealers, something the company believed it had to do in order to keep those dealers as long-term customers. The project was launched after a customer service study revealed that the dealers thought Michelin had excellent products and a knowledgeable sales force, but the company was difficult to do business with and was particularly slow at responding to dealer problems.

- Shawn Carson echoed that sentiment in speaking about the implementation of a front-office customer interaction application at Computational Systems (CSI), an $80 million-a-year manufacturer of reliability analysis equipment based in Knoxville, Tennessee, where he is director of customer services. The new system provides a smooth flow of information throughout the organization, which has eliminated what Carson described as a recurring problem of CSI salespeople visiting customer sites and "being blindsided" with questions about unresolved problems that had been reported to customer service. In addition to making customer visits more pleasant, Carson said the new system allows salespeople to spend more time with customers by automatically performing administrative tasks such as producing

mailing lists. It also has helped CSI get a better return on its marketing dollars by identifying which promotions generate the most sales. Overall, Carson says, the system has helped boost sales by roughly 10 percent through more efficient customer management.

- An insurance company wanted to invest in a decision support system to help claims assessment using a workflow package. The investment would cost $2 million, and using certain benefits and the net present value calculations, they were able to say that the project would lose $250,000. But they then identified uncertain benefits, often called intangibles, which added up to $3 million. One intangible was faster training for new claims assessors. Another would be a more consistent face to their customers. A third would be capturing the knowledge of what makes good claims and building it back into the system. Now this last was a very uncertain benefit but a very attractive one. The IT invest board said this system met their business maxims. They realized they would lose $250,000 on tangible benefits, but they could get back $3 million on intangibles. And they asked themselves whether they were prepared to pay the $250,000 they would lose on the project for the chance of getting those intangibles. That's how you make the decision. This company recognized that the knowledge management piece was very risky, and they wanted to do a pilot on it. They decided to double the amount of money for project management of this very risky project. That's good practice. And that's how companies manage an IT portfolio.

Source: Sidney Hill, "More Than a Number," *Manufacturing Systems* 16 (1998): 10–11. Reprinted with permission.

Source: Copyright © 1998 COMPUTERWORLD, Inc. Reprinted with permission of *Computerworld Magazine.*

9.4   COST ANALYSIS TECHNIQUES

Important to consider in a discussion of cost justification techniques is that the cost of technology is falling rapidly. Many line managers have budgetary approval for items that are, say, less than $3,000. Much hardware and software costs less than this figure, and line managers approve such expenditures routinely. This ability to cut through the red tape of the capital expenditure process in an organization is considered desirable by departments (although sometimes not so desirable by any centralized information technology group). The point here is that although quantifying inputs and outputs is not always necessary, determining prospective *value* to the end user remains important.

Titman argued that costs are top-heavy when inputs have large overheads that are then allocated directly to labor costs.[13] The emphasis in this section is on costing, which involves putting dollars on the price of technology. While accepted accounting techniques exist for this process, keep in mind their strengths and limitations when attempting to measure the costs of information technology.

IT planners have been innovative in estimating the cost benefits of technology. Likewise, they continue to be innovative in using tactics borrowed from accounting practices to develop realistic technology costs. Accounting techniques can be used to develop more realistic cost figures or to expense the technology over time. Selected techniques discussed in this section include: (1) salvage value; (2) depreciation; (3) payback period; (4) total-life averaging, (5) return on investment; (6) net present value; and (7) purchasing versus leasing/renting.

9.4.1 Salvage Value

Salvage value, or the value of the equipment being replaced, often is overlooked when cost figures are developed. For example, if the information technology planner can trade in or sell existing equipment, the value of the existing equipment can decrease the cost of the new equipment. If a microcomputer that costs $5,000 is assumed to have a useful life of 3 years (3 years is the norm), but it is anticipated that it may be sold at the end of that period for $1,500, the cost may be lowered to $3,500. The expected salvage value of this microcomputer is $1,500. This approach is used to reduce the initial cost figure.

9.4.2 Depreciation

The accounting concept of depreciation spreads the cost of equipment over its expected life span. *Depreciation* may be likened to rent expense; in other words, the cost of equipment is expensed over a period equal to how long it is expected to be operational. Two depreciation approaches are *straight line* and *sum-of-the-year's digits.*

The straight-line depreciation method decreases the cost of technology by spreading its costs evenly across its useful life. It also may assume that the technology has a salvage value. For example, assume that a $25,000 system has an expected 5-year life span and a $5,000 salvage value. A straight-line formula for this situation, using a straight-line approach, is illustrated in Figure 9-4. Using this method, the planner may find that the $4,000-a-year figure may be more useful than the one-time but much larger $25,000 figure.

Figure 9-4
An example of the straight-line method for computing yearly depreciation

Original cost of equipment − Estimated disposal value ÷ Years of useful life = Depreciation

Example: A $25,000 piece of equipment with a salvage value of $5,000 and an expected life of 5 years can be "expensed" as $25,000 − $5,000 ÷ 5 = $4,000 yearly depreciation expense.

Because the value of technology often declines rapidly in its initial years, an alternative depreciation technique is sum-of-the-year's digits. The assumption is that the organization will get the most value from the system the first year it is in operation, and its value will fall and then totally diminish in remaining years. No salvage value is assumed. Figure 9-5 shows how the same $25,000 expenditure described in the straight-line example could be "expensed" by the sum-of-the-year's-digits method.

While using a sum-of-the-year's-digits approach results in first-year expenses that are larger than the straight-line approach, its use is appropriate to IT expenditures because only rarely do systems have identifiable resale value. A planner attempting to cost-justify technology would need to determine if a lower or higher first-year cost figure would be realistic and convince decision makers of the viability of the purchase.

Both of these depreciation techniques are acceptable accounting practices. The planner must choose. The choice of one of these (or another) depreciation methods may depend on the organization's accounting policies and/or government regulations.

9.4.3 Payback Period

Calculating a *payback* (or payout) *period* is a commonly used technique in business. It is favored because of its straightforward calculation and ease of interpretation. However, it may not always give a realistic picture. Intangible costs may be ignored, for example, or the enterprise may not realize the full benefits of a new system until several years into implementation. Payback period does not take into consideration factors other than cost, such as the risks involved in implementing a project. Nor does it provide a basis for comparing alternative projects.

Related to cost displacement, the payback period shows how long it will take an investment to pay for itself, or break even. This technique involves the following steps:

1. Calculate projected system development costs.
2. Calculate expected annual operating costs with new system.
3. Calculate annual operating costs of current system.
4. Subtract operating costs of new system from costs of current system to calculate projected annual operating cost savings.
5. Divide the projected system development costs by the projected annual operating cost savings to calculate the payback period (in years).

Figure 9-5
An example of the sum-of-the-year's-digits method for computing depreciation

- $1 + 2 + 3 + 4 + 5 = 15$
  The depreciation figures, then, could read as follows:
- Year 1 $(5/15 \times 20,000) = \$6,600$
- Year 2 $(4/15 \times 20,000) = \$5,400$
- Year 3 $(3/15 \times 20,000) = \$4,000$
- Year 4 $(2/15 \times 20,000) = \$2,600$
- Year 5 $(1/15 \times 20,000) = \$1,400$
- Total $\qquad \$20,000$

Yearly cost of traditional seminars	=	$250,000	
Yearly cost of teleconference seminars	=	100,000	
Yearly operating cost savings	=	150,000	
Cost of videoconferencing system	=	450,000	
Payback period = 450,000/150,000	=	3 years	

Figure 9-6
An example of the payback period method for computing technology cost figures

Assume that the yearly cost of updating a sales force on new products via traditional seminars is $250,000. If a videoconferencing system could do the task at an annual operating cost of $100,000, but with an initial cost of $450,000, the planner would calculate the payback period by dividing the initial development cost of $450,000 by the projected annual operating cost savings of $150,000. Thus, the payback period would be 3 years. This formula is depicted in Figure 9-6.

The example in Figure 9-6 is simple for illustrative purposes. In reality, the analyst may find that implementation costs are spread over more than 1 year and that operating costs will vary over the payback period. The calculation then might be broken out year by year over several years. The example in Figure 9-7 shows a possible calculation for a project with initial development costs of $100,000 and an anticipated system life of 5 years. Note that the break-even point would occur just prior to year 4.

The payback analysis for a 5-year period involves the following steps:

1. Estimate net operating cost for period.
2. Estimate expected benefits for period.
3. Calculate cumulative costs and cumulative benefits.
4. Compare cumulative costs to cumulative benefits. The year in which the cumulative benefits match or exceed the cumulative costs is the break-even point for the installation.

Does the example in Figure 9-7 indicate a good or bad investment? The answer depends on the payback expectations of the project sponsor. If the guideline were 5 years, the project could be considered a desirable investment. If the payback

Figure 9-7
Payback analysis for 5-year period with an initial investment of $100,000

YEAR	0	1	2	3	4
Development cost	100,000				
Operating cost		5,000	5,000	6,000	7,000
Cumulative cost	100,000	105,000	110,00	116,000	123,000
Expected benefits		30,000	35,000	55,000	70,000
Cumulative benefits		30,000	65,000	120,000	190,000

(break even 4 years)

criteria for projects were 2 years, however, then the project probably would not be considered a good investment.

9.4.4 Total Life Average Method

Every capital cost brings with it revenue costs that last for the rest of the item's life. The corollary to this rule is that these extra costs are never less than one expects them to be.[14]

The *total life average method* for justifying IT expenditures is related to the cost savings strategy discussed earlier in this chapter. Total life averaging involves summing all expenses related to purchasing and operating a piece of equipment. For example, the cost of a new software package might include its retail price, the anticipated costs of upgrades, transferring data using the current package to the new package, and end-user training. That comprehensive cost figure then is divided by the estimated life of the equipment.

For larger expenditures, such as a companywide voice mail system, the total could include all costs, including interest (if the money is to be borrowed), opportunity costs (loss of income if the money had been invested elsewhere), and salvage value, as well as all operating costs.

The planner may find this approach useful when comparing two different systems or when justifying new technology because the existing technology has expensive maintenance or supply costs. The example in Figure 9-8 illustrates that maintaining the existing copier is less cost effective than replacing it.

9.4.5 Return on Investment (ROI)

ROI compares the projected lifetime benefits, or savings, of alternative solutions based on a percentage rate that represents the expected return on the cost of implementing a new system. The solution offering the highest return on investment is the best alternative. However, a project sponsor may have guidelines governing an acceptable ROI for all investments. In this case, minimum acceptable ROI becomes the platform for comparison, and none or all of the alternative solutions may be accepted or rejected.

The formula to calculate this rate of return is the projected lifetime benefits minus the projected lifetime costs divided by the projected lifetime costs. The formula is shown in Figure 9-9. Using the example for the payback analysis in Figure 9-7, the ROI would be calculated as follows:

$$\text{ROI} = \frac{190,000 - 123,000}{123,000} = \frac{67,000}{123,000} = 54\%$$

Figure 9-8
An example for the total life average method for computing cost figures

EXISTING COPIER		NEW COPIER	
Monthly maintenance fee	$120	Monthly maintenance fee	$50
Monthly supplies and toner	$200	Monthly supplies and toner	$100
Monthly depreciation costs	$100	Monthly depreciation costs	$200
Monthly down hours	20	Monthly down hours	0

Formula:

$$ROI = \frac{\text{Projected Lifetime Benefits} - \text{Projected Lifetime Costs}}{\text{Projected Lifetime Costs}}$$

$$ROI = \frac{190{,}000 - 123{,}000}{123{,}000} = \frac{67{,}000}{123{,}000} = 54\%$$

Figure 9-9
Return on investment analysis (ROI) method for determining technology benefits

If this calculated percentage is compared to the ROI for alternative projects, the alternative with the highest ROI would be the best investment.

ROI has its drawbacks, however. The rate of return is an average rating. The actual ROI may vary over the lifetime of a system. This method also does not consider the time factor (the fact that the ROI in earlier years may be less than in later years or vice versa.

9.4.6 Net Present Value (NPV)

Net present value (NPV) takes into consideration the time value of money and allows the analyst to compare alternatives that have different costs, benefits, and discount rates. For this reason, it is often the preferred justification method among managers with strong business finance expertise.

SPOTLIGHT ON SOLUTIONS → Technology, People, Structure, Processes

ROI CALCULATION EXAMPLES

- Assume that a remote campus generates performance calls to the Help Desk that cost $10,000/month (20 calls/day × 20 business days × $25/call). An upgraded network connection will cost $8,000 per month ($72,000 capital/36 months plus $6,000 recurring monthly costs). The return is $2,000 on an expense of $8,000, so the ROI is 25 percent.

- A daily production order is sent every morning to a factory management system that must have all the orders to calculate the detailed work flow. Each order takes 5 seconds to transfer. On normal days, this system works just fine, but on some days network congestion adds 10 seconds to each order. Because there are typically 1,000 units, this translates to a 2.8-hour delay of production. It costs the company $10,000 per hour to operate the

factory, so each incident costs nearly $30,000. When such incidents climb to about one per month, an upgrade that costs $20,000 per month would be considered a good investment, because it will generate a 50 percent ROI.

- A shipping firm has to get its ships containing highly perishable food through the Panama Canal on a regularly scheduled basis. The ship's manifests, which detail everything being carried, must be presented to Canal authorities just as the ship approaches the Canal. If the manifest is incomplete, the ship is sent to the end of the line, which means a 5-day delay. If this were to happen even once, it would be catastrophic for the company, so it was easy to justify a faster system that could deliver the manifest as the ship left the last port-of-call before the Canal.

Source: Peter Sevcik, "Customers Need Performance-Based Network ROI Analysis," *Business Communications Review* 29 (1999): 12–14.

NPV takes into account the fact that some of the costs and all benefits of a new system will be accrued in the future. Therefore, when doing a cost–benefit analysis, projected dollar values should be brought back to *present value dollars*. NPV is calculated by determining the costs and benefits for each year of a new system's projected lifetime. The costs and benefits are adjusted based on a present value factor. The adjusted costs and benefits are then compared. The formula for calculating NPV is:

$$\frac{1}{PV_n} = (1 + i)^n$$

where PV is the present value of $1.00, n equals number of years from now, and i equals discount rate.

Therefore, the present value of a dollar 2 years from now with a discount rate of 12 percent is:

$$PV_2 = \frac{1}{(1 + 0.12)^2}$$

For example, suppose a proposed system was projected to realize a benefit of $40,000 in 2 years and the current ROI is running 10 percent. It would take an investment of $33,056 today to give us the $40,000 estimated benefit 2 years from now. The NPV of the estimated benefit is, therefore, $33,056. See Figure 9-10 for the calculation of NPV for the same example used for the payback analysis in Figure 9-7.

9.4.7 Purchasing Versus Leasing or Renting

Purchasing is buying equipment outright. *Leasing* is a contractual agreement to use a piece of equipment for a given amount of time. *Renting* is buying the use of it for an unspecified time. Sometimes, it makes good business sense to lease or rent equipment rather than to purchase it outright. In addition to decreasing immediate, out-of-pocket expenses, leasing or renting puts responsibility for upkeep and repairs on the manufacturer or dealer. It also protects the consumer against product obsolescence; when a newer or better model comes on the market, it is easier to

Figure 9-10
Net present value: a project with initial development costs of $100,000 and an expected life of 5 years

YEAR	0	1	2	3	4
Development costs	$100,000	0	0	0	0
Operating costs		$ 5,000	$ 5,000	$ 6,000	$ 7,000
Discount rate at 12%	1.000	0.893	0.797	0.712	0.636
Present value	100,000	4,465	3,985	4,272	4,452
Total costs					$ 17,174
Benefits	0	30,000	35,000	55,000	70,000
Discount rate at 12%		0.893	0.797	0.712	0.636
Present value		26,790	27,895	39,160	44,520
Total benefits					$138,365
NET PRESENT VALUE					**$121,191**

upgrade. Renting or leasing spreads the cost of equipment over its useful life to the organization; it is unnecessary to develop life estimates. Perhaps most important, renting or leasing is usually a fully deductible operating expense.

Deciding whether to purchase, lease, or rent information technology hardware requires the planner to assess pros and cons of ownership. Advantages of ownership must be weighed against the advantages of renting or leasing.

9.5   INFORMATION ECONOMICS

A comprehensive methodology for valuing and comparing investments in information systems, *Information Economics (iEcon),* takes a much broader approach than traditional ROI or cost-benefit analysis. Although typically used within large systems projects, iEcon can be used as a method to compare EUIS projects among themselves or against other information technology projects.

iEcon suggests that an expanded definition of *value* is needed to measure the relative worth of individual information technology projects and their impact on the business. This definition of value encompasses both *hard* and *soft* benefits and costs. Taken together, these hard and soft measurements give a better picture of exactly how information technology projects will affect the business. The *hard* costs are those project elements that are quantifiable. In addition to normal return on investment calculations, Information Economics uses several advanced techniques to compute the hidden economic benefits and costs of a project. The *soft* component of value includes the intangible benefits and costs of a project. Although these intangible elements are not convertible to dollar figures, they are often critical in determining a project's value to the enterprise. Some of these criteria include:[15]

Strategic Match	The relative benefits derived from supporting the business strategy.
Competitive Advantage	The relative advantage in the marketplace gained from applying IT.
Technical Uncertainty	The relative risk involved in undertaking projects using unproven technology.
Strategic IT	The relative benefit derived by having a project that will allow other projects to occur.
Enterprise CSFs	The relative benefit derived when the project achieves a critical success factor (CSF) bearing on enterprise performance.

A problem facing information systems professionals and line managers is whether a particular information systems project should be done, and from among the many projects that could be done, which project(s) should be given priority. iEcon's assessment strategy helps decision makers link information technology to business goals. The actual implementation of an Information Economics-based analysis involves top management from both the business and information systems (technology) units. These top managers identify financial concerns and organizational goals. The information systems specialists and middle managers select criteria from among those listed above and analyze each criterion as to how it contributes to the organization's goals. The dual goal of this process is to tie the value of IS projects to the enterprise goals, and then help managers and IS specialists prioritize projects.

The essential process for information systems professionals and managers can be summarized as follows:

1. In addition to determining return on investment figures (discussed earlier in this chapter), determine which *value* criteria are appropriate (strategic match, competitive advantage, technical uncertainty, strategic architecture, and/or enterprise CSFs).
2. Using a scale of 1 to 5, assess the relative advantage of each criterion. "Five" would represent the highest possible benefit to an organization; "zero" would have no impact.
3. Rank the projects. Criteria can be weighted; for example, when finances are tight, the strategic advantage criterion may be worth twice the value of strategic IT architecture.

Figure 9-11 depicts these essential concepts in action. Assume decision makers need to determine which of three projects will provide the most value to their organization, and therefore should be given the highest priority. The specific projects (e.g., electronic mail, a document management system, and an electronic meeting system) are listed in the first column. Managers and information systems professionals assess the relative value of each specific project to their organization on each of the identified criteria. The *relative values* of the project, based on ROI and the established criteria are then assessed on a 1 to 5 scale (5 = high benefit; 3 = medium benefit; 1 = low benefit). These values are listed under the heading "Values" and summed for each project. The composite scores are the basis for the initial rank ordering. In this example, e-mail and electronic meeting systems tie for first place.

While these projects appear to be the most opportune projects to begin based on an initial ranking, iEcon suggests that the contribution of each project in terms

Figure 9-11
Information Economics: essential concepts applied

	VALUES				
PROJECT	ROI	SM	CA	IT	RANK
E-mail	4	3	3	5	(15)1
Electronic meeting sys.	5	4	5	1	(15)1
Document mgt.	1	5	3	5	(14)3

Strategic Investment Profile

	VALUES				
PROJECT	ROI (0.40)	SM (0.30)	CA (0.10)	IT (0.20)	RANK ($1)
E-mail	4×0.4=1.6	3×0.3=0.9	3×0.1=0.3	5×0.2=1	(3.8)2
Elec. meet. sys.	5×0.4=2.0	4×0.3=1.2	5×0.1=0.5	1×0.2=0.2	(3.9)1
Doc. mgt.	1×0.4=0.4	5×0.3=1.5	3=0.1=0.3	5=0.2=1	(3.2)3

ROI = Return on investment
SM = Strategic match
CA = Competitive advantage
IT = Strategic I/T architecture

of the organization's overall investment strategy also should be examined. To do this, a weighting can be spread so that the assigned criteria get different scores. One way to do this is to assume you have $1 to spread across the various projects. How would you allocate that dollar? In Figure 9-11, under *Strategic Investment Profile*, the value of each criterion as compared to other criteria is shown. ROI was given a value of $0.40; strategic match, $0.30; competitive advantage, $0.10; and strategic information technology infrastructure, $0.20. These respective weights multiplied against the earlier ratings result in a different priority listing. Because top management sets the investment strategy of the business, investment in the electronic meeting system is a better match at this point than the other projects.

9.6   SUMMARY

Knowledge worker productivity is difficult to measure because input and output figures are difficult to establish. Even when numbers can be applied, the productivity formula ($P = O/I$) does not consider quality or effectiveness of output. Likewise, input figures are difficult to establish. Therefore, performance measures were offered as a more useful measure.

Assuming that performance can be measured or rated, the challenge is to assess its dollar value. Such figures are often the basis for selling top management on the desirability or need for new technology. Although it appears that business is evolving to the point where technology is simply the cost of doing business, planners often need cost-justification figures to help them prepare budgets that include IT in the long-range plans of the organization and ensure commitment for long-range expenditures. Cost justification figures also are used as a basis for prioritizing IT projects and for evaluating results following implementation.

Parker and Benson's taxonomy of benefit calculations was used as a framework for a discussion of quantitative techniques to put hard dollars on benefits gained through the use of information technologies. *Substitute* techniques included cost savings and cost displacement. *Complementary* applications included the Hedonic Wage Model, Applications Transfer Team, and benefit acceleration. *Innovative* techniques were valued added and innovation risk analysis. Other approaches included QWL and the cost of doing business. It should be stressed that several of these techniques commonly are combined. Choosing an appropriate technique requires careful analysis of the situation, including the organization's history, needs, cash flow, and standard accounting procedures and policies.

Technology costs also must be quantified. Accounting techniques can help the planner develop meaningful cost calculations. Such techniques include but are not limited to salvage value, depreciation, total-life averaging, return on investment, net present value, and purchasing versus leasing/renting.

The chapter included a discussion of Information Economics, a method of measuring value and prioritizing projects by measuring hard and soft IT benefits. Benefits used to determine IT's value to the enterprise include those derived from IT's relation to strategic match, gains from competitive advantage, the risk of technical uncertainty, support of a strategic IT architecture, and the achievement of enterprise critical success factors.

In short, measuring worker performance and analyzing costs and benefits of IT is an inexact process, but because of the considerable expense in hardware, software, maintenance, and user training, IT cost justification is a requirement in most organizations today. The strategies outlined here overview some accepted approaches. Determining the best cost justification approach depends on many factors, including the strategic value of the technology, the overall impact of the technology, and the costs involved.

KEY TERMS

- Cost displacement
- Depreciation
- Effectiveness
- Efficiency
- Hard dollar
- Information Economics
- Leasing

- Net present value
- Payback period
- Performance
- Productivity
- Quality of worklife (QWL)
- Renting
- Return on investment (ROI)

- Salvage value
- Shadow functions
- Soft dollar
- Standard
- Total-life-average method
- Value added

DISCUSSION QUESTIONS

1. What is productivity? Why is it so difficult to measure the productivity of knowledge workers?
2. What is performance? Why is performance often used as a substitute for productivity?
3. To justify the purchases of the following technologies, what approach might the information technology planner take? Defend your answers.
   a. An Intranet
   b. A color laser printer/fax/copy machine
   c. An electronic meeting management system
   d. A project management system
   e. A value-added reseller (VAR) to manage data backup and security
   f. An upgrade from Office 2000 to Office 20XX
   g. A move to e-commerce
4. Assume that you, the EUIS planner, have determined that your organization could benefit from a $100,000 group support system. Of the accounting techniques described in this chapter, which would you use to calculate cost savings? Using this $100,000 figure, show how you would use the technique. You will need to develop your own figures for other variables required in this exercise.
5. Summarize, in your own words, the concepts behind Information Economics (iEcon) as a planning methodology.
6. If performance measures and IT costs and benefits are so difficult to determine, why is it done? Does the process offer any benefits to IT planners? Discuss.

APPLICATION EXERCISES

1. Interview an accounting professor for his or her views on what's appropriate for cost-justifying IT expenditures. What techniques does the professor offer that expand on those in this text?
2. Write a report comparing Japanese with American views of workers' productivity.

3. As a class project, each student should interview a person who recently has begun using a new information technology. How pleased is the person with the new technology? Does he or she view it as a performance enhancer? If so, in what way? Compare the results of your interview with what your classmates found. Are answers consistent? Why or why not? Is the length of time a person has been using the technology important in the response?

SUGGESTED READINGS

Lucas, Henry C. *Information Technology and the Productivity Paradox.* (Oxford: Oxford University Press, 1999).

Meyer, N. Dean, and Mary Boone. *The Information Edge: Measuring Profits from Office Automation Tools,* 2d ed. (Toronto: Gage Educational Publishing Company, 1989).

Weill, Peter, and Marianne Broadbent. *Leveraging the New Infrastructure: How Market Leaders Capitalize on Information Technology.* (Cambridge: Harvard Business School Press, 1998).

ENDNOTES

1. Stephen S. Roach, "Working Better or Just Harder?" *The New York Times,* February 14, 2000, p. A21.
2. Jenny C. McCune, "The Productivity Paradox," *Management Review* 87 (1998): 38–40.
3. Bob Violino, "ROI in the Real World," *Information Week* 679 (1998): 60.
4. Wendy Leavitt, "Technology and Profit: Crunching More Than the Numbers," *Fleet Owner* 93 (1998): 51–55.
5. Peter Weill, and Margrethe H. Olson, "Managing Investment in Information Technology: Mini Case Examples and Implications," *MIS Quarterly* 13 (1999): 3–7.
6. Violino, op. cit.
7. Ibid.
8. Marilyn Parker, and Robert J. Benson, "Enterprise Information Economics: Latest Concepts," *Journal of Information Systems Management* 6 (1989): 10.
9. Peter G. Sassone, and A. Perry Schwartz, "Cost Justifying OA," *Datamation* (1986): 83–88.
10. Parker, and Benson op. cit.
11. N. Dean Meyer, and Mary E. Boone, *The Information Edge.* (Toronto: Gage Publishing Company, 1989).
12. Parker, and Benson op. cit.
13. Lionel Titman, *The Effective Office.* (London: Cassell Educational Limited, 1990).
14. Ibid.
15. Marilyn Parker, Robert J. Benson, and H. Edgar Trainor. *Information Economics: Linking Information Technology to Business Performance.* (Upper Saddle River, NJ: Prentice Hall, 1988).

Human Factors: Software, Hardware, and Workplace Design

Learning Objectives

Upon completing this chapter, you should be able to:

➤ Identify characteristics of well-designed EUIS software.

➤ Differentiate among command, menu, icon, natural speech, and pen and speech recognition-based software interfaces.

➤ Discuss principles of good interface design and screen layout.

➤ Explain the objectives of usability analysis and how they contribute to good interface design.

➤ Define terms that describe characteristics of computer monitors: *glare, flicker, bezel,* and *character quality.*

➤ List six terms that describe the ergonomics of keyboard operation.

➤ Explain how mouse manufacturers are incorporating ergonomic design into their products.

➤ Describe the application of AMCO-PACT in designing office spaces.

➤ Discuss the relationship between lighting and worker productivity.

➤ Offer at least three solutions to alleviating noise in the work environment.

➤ Discuss the relationship between workstation design and worker productivity.

➤ Suggest how individuals can improve their posture when using a computer.

➤ Explain the impact of reach and viewing distances on workstation design.

➤ Give several examples of territoriality in the workplace.

➤ Explain why socialization patterns must be considered in workplace design.

➤ Explain the relationship of productivity to personal space, backs and sides, eye contact, privacy, and status.

10.1 INTRODUCTION

Human factors engineering, or simply *human factors,* is the application of information about physical and psychological characteristics of human beings to the design of devices and systems for human use.[1] It is also commonly referred to as *ergonomics,* which is based on the Greek words *ergon,* which means "work," and *nomos,* which means "natural laws." Regardless of terminology, everyone knows

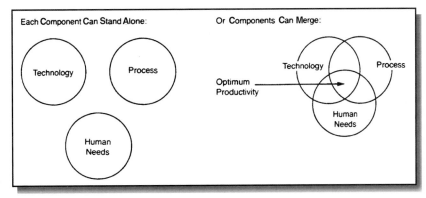

Figure 10-1
A systems approach to productivity

that improving the way people interact with their work environment and technology is important.

Human factors, or ergonomics, can be applied to all types of work. As a science, it began during World War II in the design of airplane cockpits. Pilots needed to have the most frequently used instruments within easy reach or sight and to have easily adjustable controls. Applications of ergonomic principles have spread to the automobile, the factory floor, the automatic teller machine, and now the anytime/anyplace office. Ergonomic principles apply to any situation in which individuals and technology interface.

Initially, the study of office ergonomics was centered primarily on hardware and workspace design, drawing upon the sciences of anatomy, physiology, and psychology. Increasingly, however, ergonomic principles are applied to software interface design. Human factors issues surfaced in the office environment as workers expressed concern about safety and comfort. Business has a stake here, too: increased productivity. Most importantly, good human factors design provides a productive environment that minimizes distractions and allows employees to focus on their tasks. It also can contribute to reducing absenteeism and medical insurance costs. Attention to ergonomic issues demonstrates the organization's concern about workers' health and safety.

Ergonomic principles can be organized around a conceptual systems model of productivity. Figure 10-1 depicts the areas of technology, procedures, and human needs as distinct circles, each of which can stand alone as a factor that either increases or impedes productivity. For any task, an optimum technology exists. However, when a technology is imposed without regard for procedures and/or human needs, it is not used to its optimum potential.

The discussion of ergonomic principles related to EUIS is divided into three main parts: software design, hardware design, and workplace design. Each part includes a discussion of managerial implications related to integrating ergonomic principles into the workplace.

10.2 SOFTWARE DESIGN

The trade press has popularized the term *user friendly* to describe the ease with which an individual learns and uses a particular software product. Vendors, likewise, are often guilty of overselling their products as being user friendly. While everyone has a working definition of what the term means, the problem is that everyone has a different definition.

Perhaps more descriptive terms to describe the underlying meaning of this concept are *user addictive* or *user seductive*. These terms may mean "the more you learn about the software program, the more you want to use it" and "the more you use it, the more *creatively* you use it." Any software program that meets these criteria is, indeed, user addictive or seductive. This notion gets more to the heart of the issue, which is the usability of software.

The means through which users interact with a software program are referred to as the *user interface*. The user interface handles all input and output. Effective user interface design is based on well-established principles of human factors. These principles include making the interface visual, consistent, user-driven, forgiving, transparent, and flexible (modeless). Ease of use and ease of learning are two different factors. A software program that is optimized for ease of learning may, in fact, contain many features that are slow or distracting to an experienced user. This section categorizes the types of interfaces and outlines principles related to interface design and screen layout. EUIS specialists can apply an understanding of human factors to help the computer programmer design better interfaces or to help the end user make better choices from off-the-shelf software.

10.2.1 Types of Software Interfaces

The basic types of software interfaces are command, menu, and icon-based (direct manipulation). A fourth is natural language (human language) interface. Two increasingly popular and useful interfaces are pen-based interfaces and speech recognition technology. Fundamental differences and distinct trade-offs exist among them. These interfaces are not mutually exclusive, however, as multiple options are sometimes provided in the same program.

10.2.1.1 Command-Based Interfaces

Today, few if any end-user information systems are command based. A *command interface* requires users to type *commands* (directions) that are typically shorthand instructions. For example, under the DOS operating system, users typed *dir* (directory) at the command line (DOS prompt) to obtain a listing of files on a disk. A mainframe text editor of that era may have required that the user type ":p" for a paragraph command. Many individuals who are expert in using such *command-based* systems have a background in computer science.

Although well-designed command interfaces can be fast and flexible, they are generally more complex than menus. They are harder to learn because the user must memorize large numbers of commands that must be recalled precisely. Effective error handling and help systems are important. In addition to the need to memorize specific commands, another interface problem with command-based systems is that the end user may not know the limits of the system. What can the system do? What questions can I ask of the database? For example, users of early versions of MS DOS, when faced with the "A>" prompt, had to know what options existed and what specific command to use to get the desired response.

10.2.1.2 Menu-Based Interfaces

Menu-based interfaces allow the end user to choose possible commands by using a menu or series of menus. As the user selects words and phrases, the menu changes, building on logical completions to the inquiry. Such a system prohibits the user from asking questions the system cannot understand or does not know. A well-designed menu interface can be easy to learn and requires little training. A menu interface also eliminates the need for the user to be a good typist or speller.

In menu-based interfaces, the program is largely in control of the execution sequence. The user only needs to recognize (as opposed to recall) the options that are needed. Menu interfaces are basically hierarchical in design. Thus, they can be slow and have limited flexibility. Speed problems can be minimized by allowing type-ahead and command options for menu choices. Flexibility can be increased by providing options such as drop-down menus and by supporting a range of input devices and techniques for menu selection.

10.2.1.3 Icon-Based Interfaces

Icon-based, or direct manipulation, *interfaces,* also known as *graphical user interfaces* or *GUI* (pronounced goo-ey), are fundamentally different from command and menu-based systems. With both command and menu-based interfaces, the user first selects the operation (action) and then selects the object (name, document, form, etc.). With a direct manipulation system, the user selects the object first and then selects one or more actions. Thus, command and menu interfaces are operation oriented, while icon-based interfaces are object oriented. Today, icon-based interfaces are the norm and human factors experts consider them much more natural or intuitive to use because the *object-action sequence* more closely parallels the way people work in a paper-based world. Generally, for example, individuals pick up a document or file folder and then decide what actions they will take on them.

Well-designed icon-based interfaces offer the speed and flexibility of commands, while relying on intuition and recognition memory to make learning and using the system easier. Direct manipulation reduces the complexity of the user interface and simplifies it by reducing the levels of action hierarchies. The visual approach also supports user exploration and user control because only actions applicable to selected objects are available to users. Users can view all available actions and perform them in the desired order. Icons are generally easy to interpret and can overcome ambiguities of natural language. People also respond more quickly to icons than to text. Apple Computer Company's computer line is renowned for its easy-to-use, icon-based system, although icon-based design was first introduced by Xerox Corporation. Today, nearly all desktop applications use icons in conjunction with drop-down menus.

10.2.1.4 Natural Language Interfaces

An ideal system would be able to understand its user's commands in normal, everyday language instead of responding only to well-defined commands or computer syntax. Considerable research has been invested in trying to develop such systems, referred to as *natural language systems.* Efforts to program a computer to respond to natural language commands involve several complex problems.

1. As the example in Figure 10-2 illustrates, the meaning of human speech often depends on its context.[2]
2. A very real problem is that questions are frequently hidden within questions; for example, "What time is the flight to Memphis?" (Is there a flight to Memphis?)
3. Human speech is often incomplete. For example, consider the statement, "What is the Dow Jones average?" Is the person asking the question seeking a definition of the term or a specific figure?

Figure 10-2
Defining the word *hand*

Source: Reprinted with permission of Professor Roger Schank and Northwestern University.

4. Human speech often requires interpretation. For example, consider the statement, "Give me some recent inventory figures." How many is "some"? What is considered "recent"? What specific figures are being requested?

To handle such problems, natural-language interfaces require tremendous "overhead" in both computer speed and storage capacity. Therefore, analysts must evaluate whether the flexibility of a natural-language interface is worth its cost in computer resources.

10.2.1.5 Pen-Based Interfaces

An interface that is considered an enabling technology for small, personal digital assistants (PDAs), such as the Palm Pilot, is the *pen-based interface.* PDAs are used by managers and professionals who are on the run because a pen can substitute for a heavy keyboard, allowing the user to fit the device into a pocket.

Pen-based interfaces serve two major roles in applications: that of data input and that of data manipulation. When used for data input, pens can be used to create documents that are stored in the user's own handwriting as images, or they can translate handwriting or printing to digital form. When used for data manipulation, a pen interface with its own intelligence can distinguish between a circle, a zero, and the letter o. The potential of the pen interface is just beginning to be tapped.

10.2.1.6 Speech Recognition Technology

Two main categories of *speech recognition technology* exist. In the first category, keyboard, the user can speak to the computer rather than key input commands or text. In the second category, keypad, the user speaks to the computer through a telephone, accessing, for example, voice mail or navigating a telephone system's menus.[3] Systems can be speaker-dependent, whereby users train the system to recognize their voice, or speaker-independent, where the system is designed to recognize any voice.

Keypad applications have limited vocabularies and are usually speaker independent. An example of a keypad application could be an organization's call center, where callers can be quickly and easily routed to the right agent without human intervention. Keyboard applications that go beyond simple commands, on the other hand, tend to be speaker dependent because they handle large vocabularies. Dragon System's NaturallySpeaking Preferred is an example of software designed to support voice commands and speaker-dependent data entry. Dragon

Part IV   Workplace Performance: The Impact of Information Technology

Systems, Inc. indicates that its users can speak URLs and can launch applications and drop-down menu commands by voice in virtually any Windows application. Additionally, the system supports dictation up to 160 words per minute, with words transcribed immediately into software application packages, e-mail, and chat rooms.

It has been estimated that approximately 30 percent of users use speech recognition technology for some aspect of their work.[4] The conventional keyboard has been called a primitive data entry device by proponents of speech recognition technology. As systems become more sophisticated and thus user seductive, they inevitably will gain acceptance. A caveat is that today's speech technology is not yet like Hal from the movie *2001*, as much time and effort must be invested to learn to use the system.[5]

10.2.2   User Interface Design

Effective user interface design is critical in the end-user information systems environment, where software is merely a tool to get business tasks done. Software's use should be transparent to users; that is, the interface should not distract the user's attention from business tasks. Like picking up a pencil, working with software should feel natural and not require special concentration. Unfortunately, the significance of this point easily gets lost among IT professionals whose job *is* technology. Learning and using technology in the IT environment is a legitimate objective in its own right. In contrast, for most business personnel, IT is just another means of getting their business tasks accomplished, and, given a choice, they usually will elect the easiest, fastest means, which may be familiar manual methods rather than complex software packages.

Effective user interface design is based on two basic human factor principles:

- To learn a software program, users develop a conceptual model of the interface.
- A software program should allow users to control the dialogue.

Interfaces that follow these design principles are easier to learn and to use. Techniques for applying these two principles are discussed briefly in the next two sections. Designing effective interfaces requires understanding the intended users' perspectives, and knowing, in depth, how the software's intended users think about the tasks that the software will be designed to perform. Creating prototype designs and conducting usability tests are essential techniques for creating highly usable interface designs, as well as for evaluating commercially available systems. Applying design principles frequently involves trade-offs between usability and technical efficiency, between consistency and flexibility, and between optimum design and cost and time limitations. These types of trade-offs most be evaluated based on project priorities and knowledge of the user environment.

10.2.2.1   *Improving User Understanding*

Several techniques are important to developing and reinforcing the user's conceptual model of the interface. These include using metaphors, avoiding modes, ensuring consistency, making the user interface user-driven, and making the interface transparent.

Using Metaphors   A metaphor, or analogy, relates two otherwise unrelated things. Writers use metaphors to help readers create a conceptual image, or model, of the subject. The same principle applies to software. When metaphors are familiar and real-world based, users can transfer previous knowledge of their environment to the application interface. To work effectively, the metaphor must meet the expectations users have because of their real-world experience. Examples of metaphors are forms fill-in and icons such as erasers to delete information or paintbrushes to color objects.

Avoiding Modes   Modes refer to control sequences that govern computer actions. Most people who have used computers are familiar with modes like command mode, input mode, or edit mode. Within edit mode may be found delete mode, modify mode, insert mode, append mode, or others. The problem with modes is that the same user actions have different results in different situations. It's easy for users to lose track of the mode they are in and become confused. Modes also force users to complete what they are doing before they can do something else. Modes interfere with users' ability to use their conceptual model of how the application should work. It is not always possible to design a modeless application; however, the most effective interfaces make the uses of modes the exception and limit their scope.

Ensuring Consistency   Making the user interface consistent is important to reinforcing the users' conceptual model of software. Software is much easier to learn and use when actions work consistently within a single software program as well as across software applications, and even across different software and hardware platforms. Consistency is important on all levels including:

- Presentation—what users see; how components and objects are depicted on the screen.
- Interaction—how users interact with components.
- Process sequence—how users and the computer communicate with each other.
- Actions—how similar actions are implemented in the same way.

Making the Interface User-Driven   Effective design should support the user's work environment and goals. A task analysis can reveal not only what users want to do and how they want to do it, but also factors such as the amount of variability in processing sequences, exception conditions, problems, and interfaces with other systems or manual procedures.

Making the Interface Transparent   A good user interface does not bother users with mechanics. Users view computers as tools for completing tasks, as a car is a tool for getting from one place to another. Users should not have to know how an application works to complete a task, as they should not have to know how a car engine works to get from one place to another. A highly usable interface is simple and natural to the user, effectively shielding the user from the technical complexities of making it all work.

10.2.2.2   Allowing Users to Control the Dialogue

Users want to be and should be in control of the dialogue. Few tasks have a single optimum way that they are performed under all circumstances. Moreover, any two people seldom perform the same task exactly alike. Putting users in control of the dialogue requires a design approach that is fundamentally different than traditional approaches.

Users are in control when they are able to switch from one activity to another, change their minds easily, and stop activities they no longer want to continue. Users should be able to cancel or suspend any time-consuming activity without causing disastrous results. Techniques that put users in control include making the interface forgiving, making the interface visual, and providing feedback.

Making the Interface Forgiving User actions should be able to be reversed easily. When users are in control, they should be able to explore without fear of causing an irreversible mistake. Because learn-by-exploring environments involve trial and error, users should be able to back up, or undo, their previous action. Actions that are destructive should always be confirmed before being completed. Mistakes should not cause serious or irreversible results.

Making the Interface Visual A visual interface allows users to see, rather than have to recall, how to proceed. The presentation of components and the user interaction with the components should be visual. Whenever possible, the dialogue should present users with a list of items (objects or actions) from which they can choose instead of making them remember valid choices.

Providing Feedback The dialogue should provide feedback for user interactions whenever possible. Users should never perform an action without receiving visual feedback, audible feedback, or both. For example, color, emphasis, and other presentation techniques show users which choices they can select, when a choice has been selected, and when a requested action has been completed.

10.2.3 Screen Layout

A well-designed data entry screen (form), such as a database input screen, would allow an end user to input data into a system with a minimal number of keystrokes or spoken words, no redundancy, and little ambiguity. Screen design principles are related to paper-based forms design. To ensure good screen design, the EUIS manager would want to:

1. Review tasks and task sequences.
2. Diagram the dialogue.
3. Recheck the data required.
4. Work with the programmer to develop a prototype (sample) screen.
5. Require that many different users test the prototype to discover problems with its use before the final version goes into production.

10.2.4 Performance Support Systems (Learning Aids)

In their individual definition of what constitutes *user friendly,* many end users list performance support systems. When using software programs, users inevitably come across situations where they do not know what to do. Sometimes error messages are not meaningful (e.g., what does "Error 19" mean?). Users frequently find software manuals, even when well written, to be of limited value. This may be due, at least in part, to the fact that these manuals generally contain everything that anyone would ever need to know about a software package. Because new users have limited experience on which to discriminate or even formulate their questions, it is often difficult to locate the applicable sections of the manual. Recent advances in providing *embedded training, help facilities, online reference, hypertext,* and other *performance support systems* aids address this issue. (See Chapter 7.)

Because programmers have a technical perspective rather than a user perspective, many early computer programs did not include well-written descriptions of the system and directions on how the end user could accomplish specific tasks.

Because the programmer knew the system so well, the assumption that others could use it equally easily was a common misconception. Manuals effectively documented how things were supposed to work but omitted the exceptions, what can go wrong, and what to do about it. Increasingly, large software development projects separate the responsibility for documentation writing from the program writing by hiring a technical writer to work *with* the programmer. In such cases, the documentation is likely to be easier for the end user to understand.

When the documentation is part of the software program, it is considered a help facility. On-screen help facilities offer instructions to users when they are having the problem. Some systems will have a specific function key that will list help options alphabetically, requiring the user to specify the type of help needed. Other *context-sensitive* help facilities assume that the user needs help at the point where help is requested. Such systems then automatically take the user to information that relates to the task in progress.

The value of many early help facilities was limited by how easy it was for the end user to put a label on the problem, then determine how the topic was classified and where it was located. Advances in online help and reference options, such as Microsoft Office's Mr. Paperclip, guide or show the user how to complete a task. An ideal help system should not force the user to figure out where to look or under what topic the author classified information. The user should need only to indicate what the problem or question is, and the computer, using indexing and search capabilities, should find the information. Programmers and managers increasingly are treating the development of performance support aids as part of the system development process. In other words, they are being developed when the system is developed and integrated with system operation. Performance support systems were discussed in more detail in Chapter 7, Performance Support and Help Desk Management.

10.3   HARDWARE DESIGN

Figure 10-3 is a picture of Ralph carelessly violating several important guidelines for using computers. What is wrong in this picture? List the problems before you read the descriptions of the five major problems. This pretest is designed to introduce you to some ergonomic principles.

Computer hardware manufacturers have been interested in ergonomic principles for decades. IBM, AT&T, and Xerox, for example, have developed large research divisions to integrate ergonomic features into their products. Identifying the need for health and safety standards, the Human Factors Society has developed guidelines in the United States. Europe, however, is the front-runner in acknowledging the need for standards and enforcing them. In particular, the Scandinavian countries and Germany are known for stringent guidelines and strict enforcement.

It makes good sense for hardware purchasers to be aware of what constitutes well-designed equipment. As a potential user or purchaser, it is important to be aware of ergonomic factors relevant to equipment selection. Manufacturers continually are updating and revising their products based on what is known about ergonomics. This discussion on computer hardware is limited to three peripherals: the monitor, the keyboard, and the mouse. Typically, the purchaser of a Dell computer, for example, buys a Dell monitor, keyboard, and mouse when purchasing a new system. However, these computer peripherals all have distinguishing charac-

How many things are wrong in this picture?

Here's an exercise you might want to try out on some of your IC's users (or the IC staff, for that matter). Take a good look at the photo of "Ralph" who is working at his PC. Can you tell what's wrong in this photograph? An IBM press release listed these possible problems.

The card table supporting the PC probably isn't steady enough to prevent harmful movement or vibration. Use a sturdy desk or table—or better yet—a desk designed specifically for computer equipment.

The radiator generates heat that could damage the equipment. Make sure the work space is well ventilated and away from direct heat sources.

The open window will ventilate the room, but it also allows dust, heat, and humidity to damage the internal components of the computer. Keep the PC away from open windows and sunlight.

Ashes from a cigarette or from the kind of stogie that Ralph smokes can interfere with the read/write heads in the disk drive. If you must smoke, blow it away from the unit and place your ashtray away from the computer.

Drinks spill. The keyboard might be damaged if Ralph's coffee cup falls off of the monitor. Crumbs from his donuts can have a similar effect on the machine's internal components.

Those are IBM's suggestions. Given that IBM is a hardware vendor, it's not suprising that its hints concern the health and happiness of the hardware. Here in the office, we think we've located a few things Ralph could do for his own comfort and peace of mind.

Ralph's chair doesn't look as though it was designed for style or comfort. He might be more comfortable (and more productive) in a different chair. This may sound like a minor point, but little things make a difference.

The light hanging from the ceiling probably creates glare on the screen. Use low-intensity light or provide rear or side lighting out of the line of sight.

Figure 10-3
What is wrong with this picture?

Source: Reprinted by permission by International Business Machines Corporation.

Chapter 10 Human Factors: Software, Hardware, and Workplace Design 327

teristics and the consumer has many choices, even within a given manufacturer's product line. The intent of this section on hardware design is to share some basic principles of ergonomics that can help inform this decision.

10.3.1 The Monitor

Conventional computer monitors are known as CRT monitors. CRT stands for cathode-ray tube, the technology that gives them their bulk.[6] CRTs are not only bulky, they are frequently associated with user discomfort and safety issues. Discomfort issues center on a hard-to-read screen that can be worsened by glare. Computer vision syndrome is the term given to a variety of eye-related problems related to intensive computer work. Because users continually focus and refocus their eyes, moving from the display to other work materials or the office environment, eye stress can result. Of note, computer users blink only 4 to 6 times a minute, compared to the required 22 blinks per minute to keep eyes moistened. Reduced blinking can result in dry eye, which can trigger a headache.[7] Additionally, CRTs emit miniscule amounts of radiation (much like a hair dryer) and have been linked to other health concerns.

The upcoming generation of monitors, known as LCDs (liquid crystal displays) or flat-panel displays, have sharp resolution and high durability. LCDs are comprised of gas plasma, and because they weigh very little and are durable, have been used in notebook computers for years. As their prices fall, they quickly may replace their TV-like predecessors. Figure 10-4 offers illustrations of desktop-sized LCD panels from Sharp Electronics and Sceptre Technologies. Specific monitor at-

Figure 10-4a
LCD monitors. Sharp's LC-20VM2C LCD AVC monitor

Source: Reprinted with permission of Don Meyer, Sharp Electronic Corp. Mahwah, NJ.

Figure 10-4b
LCD monitors. Sceptre's super slim LCD monitor

Source: Reprinted with permission of Edwin Pizarro, Sceptre Technologies, City of Industry, CA.

tributes to be covered in this discussion of monitor characteristics are size, glare and reflection, bezel, character resolution, flicker, contrast, color, and radiation.

Size   The size of the screen is perhaps the first feature to be considered. The screen must be large enough for the user to distinguish characters easily. Most CRT displays used today are at least 17-inch screens (measured diagonally). For desktop publishing, users typically choose screens that are 19 inches and can hold one entire page, or 24 inches and can hold two complete pages. LCD screens, on the other hand, have no wasted border space. Therefore, a 15-inch LCD screen can be equivalent to a 17-inch CRT monitor. Some operating systems allow users to add a second monitor card, allowing two monitors to be used at the same time. This is a useful option for the busy, multi-tasking user.[8] *Footprint* is another term used to describe the size of the *entire* monitor, not just the screen. Footprint is described in square inches. If limited desktop space is a problem, footprint is an important variable. CRTs can have rather large footprints—18 inches or more—compared to the 2 inches to 4 inches of an LCD panel. Moreover, LCD panels can be suspended from the ceiling or hung like a picture.

Glare and Reflection   Perhaps the factor most critical to user comfort, and perhaps safety, is the ability to see the screen clearly and without strain. *Glare* is light that comes through the monitor. Glare often can be reduced by adjusting screen contrast. *Reflection* is light from the environment deflected off the screen. Both glare and reflection can be problems for the user. However, just as the causes are different for each problem, so are the solutions.

Those who have sat with their back to a sunny window while using a monitor have probably experienced reflection, not glare. Monitor surfaces reflect light from the sun, as well as light from the immediate environment. Reflection causes discomfort and can result in eyestrain. To determine the source of reflection, one could position a mirror in front of the monitor. The source reflected in the mirror may be a white copier across the aisle or, as one operator was surprised to discover, the white shirt he was wearing!

Polarized screens allow less diffused light (glare) to penetrate from a CRT; however, such screens do little to reduce reflection. Polarized screens tend to reduce *contrast* (discussed later in this chapter), which increases readability problems. Research remains unclear as to the effectiveness of glare-reducing devices. Much of the benefit of polarized screens is ascribed to the positive attitude workers develop when they see that their employer is trying to make the workplace more comfortable.

Reflection can be reduced in many cases by simply closing the blinds or adjusting the lighting so that no *direct* light hits the screen. In other cases, repositioning the monitor so that light originates behind or perpendicular to the screen works well. When such solutions are not possible, swivel devices, hoods, and special glasses may be used. Figure 10-5 depicts two styles of glasses—products from UVEX—that are credited with minimizing eye fatigue. Some monitors come with antiglare coatings. Many products are available that serve as low-cost solutions to the reflection problem.

Because they are based on completely different technologies, LCD screens tend to be brighter, but the viewing angles are more limited. "The screen might look great head on, but when you lean back or stand up, parts of it may look washed-out or even completely unreadable."[9]

Figure 10-5
UVEX PCvision eyewear: Uvex Surfer and Uvex Webmaster

Source: With permission by Anne Chambers, UVEX, Smithfield, RI.

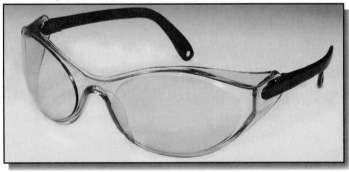

Bezel Webster's dictionary defines *bezel* as (among other definitions) "the slanting faces of a cut jewel." Bezel describes the tendency for the CRT to be clearer in the middle than at its margins. Like a well-cut jewel, the screen is brightest in the middle. For ease and comfort of viewing, VDT characters must be straight and even. "Pincushioning" occurs when a character in the middle of the screen appears higher than characters closer to the margins. Today's high-resolution CRT monitors have virtually eliminated bezel as an issue, and because LCD technology operates so differently, bezel is not a factor to consider in LCD purchases.

Character Resolution and Flicker What is resolution? How is it measured? For years, the sole measure of *character resolution* or display clarity was the number of pixels on the screen. A *pixel* is a dot of momentarily glowing phosphor. Monitors are made up of thousands of pixels. Although the number of pixels is important, the size of the pixel and the number of dots in the character cell also must be considered. As the pixel grid increases in size, the need for a faster, more powerful deflection, or refresh rate, also increases. The image on CRTs, like the image on televisions, is the result of electron charges sweeping by a dot of phosphor on the screen, causing the dot to glow momentarily. The dot must be recharged for the image to remain on the screen. When the dot fades before it is recharged, a *flicker* results. Most images are recharged at high rates (about 65 times per second or more), and this frequency, or *refresh rate,* keeps users from noticing the flicker. No evidence exists to prove that flicker affects productivity, but flicker can be an annoyance. Flicker-free to one person may not be flicker-free to another. The better one's eyesight is, the more annoying one will find flicker to be.

The sharpness of a CRT display depends not only the number or pixels and their size, but also on the refresh rate. Every pixel in an LCD panel, on the other hand, is wired separately and can be turned on or off independently, eliminating flicker. The 20-inch Sharp Electronics LCD panel pictured in Figure 10-4 offers flicker-free, 920,000-dot image reproduction.

To address flicker in CRTs, some displays employ interlaced scanning. Interlacing works by dividing the screen into odd- and even-numbered lines. The eye integrates, or interlaces, the screen. The result, however, is that no sharp images are seen. If the user sees a ghosting afterimage, it is the result of interlacing. High-resolution screens often are described as noninterlaced and provide clear, stable characters.

Contrast *Contrast* is the difference in luminance between a character and its background. On most monitors, contrast can be controlled. The premise is that a screen with high contrast is easy to read because the characters are distinguishable. Most monitors have a control knob by which the user can regulate contrast.

Color Red, green, and blue (RGB) displays can create 256 colors and several thousand variations of these colors by blending shades of red, green, and blue. The number of colors that can be used effectively is related to the application. Some graphics applications require a minimum of 256 colors but may work more vibrantly with 65,536 colors or up to 16.7 million colors. Color can add to the user's understanding and enjoyment of the charts or figures on the screen. For alphanumeric screens, experts recommend using no more than four colors on the screen at one time, with a maximum of eight colors for the total system. This is because most people cannot discriminate among more than eight colors at one time. Color must be used judiciously or it can interfere with the user's understanding of information.

Experts concur that the preference of the user is the key to screen color selection. Notable exceptions are saturated blue on a dark background (this combination tends to hinder character resolution), saturated red and blue or red and green (this can cause chromostereopsis), and red (some people have difficulty seeing the color red).

Radiation   Radiation is everywhere. It is found in nature, with the sun as the most obvious illustration. It also is found in power lines and industry. It also is found in X-ray machines in medical offices. In our homes, televisions and hair dryers emit radiation. Radiation also is found in our offices—office technologies, including the CRT, emit radiation. The electron gun that forms the characters on a CRT creates a pulse, which is a regular pattern of electromagnetic wave forms (EMFs). Although the level of the radiation emitted by displays falls below levels set by the government, many people are concerned that these levels are not strict enough. Similar concerns were raised in the 1960s about radiation from color TV sets. Whether the level of radiation is sufficient to pose health hazards has been the subject of considerable debate. End users are asking questions related to the impact of CRT radiation on fertility, pregnancy, and cancer. The safest user is an informed user, and staying up to date on research findings is recommended.

At the time of this writing, LCD panels are significantly more expensive than CRT monitors; however, LCD prices are falling. Figure 10-6 summarizes the comparison of CRT monitors and LCD panels.

10.3.2   The Keyboard

Assessing the user's individual keyboard needs and evaluating products on the market is the emphasis of this section. Health and safety issues related to the keyboard (and often its appropriate placement) include stiff shoulders, back pain, sore

Figure 10-6
Comparison of CRT monitors and LCD panels

FEATURE	CRT MONITOR	LCD PANEL
Size of Display	18" or more deep 17" to 19" measured diagonally	2" to 4" deep No wasted space; a 15" LCD is the equivalent of a 17" CRT
Weight	+/− 40 pounds	Up to 13 pounds
Power Consumption	130 watts	25 watts
Resolution and Flicker	Limited problems	No flicker
Glare and reflection	Glare, yes. Reflection handled by adjusting location of screen	Glare, no. Reflection handled by adjusting location of screen
Durability	Limited durability	Very durable
Bezel	No problem on high-resolution monitors	No problem
Contrast	Controlled by user	Controlled by user
Color	Can be bright and clear	Bright and clear
Radiation	Probably not significant	Probably not significant

necks, tendonitis, pinched nerves, and carpal tunnel syndrome. *Repetitive stress injuries* (RSI) or *repetitive motion injuries* (RMI) are catch-all terms often used to describe these ailments. Topics described here in examining ergonomic principles related to keyboard design are: (1) key pressure, (2) auditory feedback, (3) layout, (4) profile, and (5) finish and shape.

Key Pressure   The energy required to depress a key is called *key pressure.* Anyone who has used a manual typewriter remembers the relatively large amount of energy required. Electric typewriters reduced that problem. The electronic keyboard has all but eliminated it. How much pressure is best for a keyboard depends upon the operator. Typically, the more efficient the operator, the lighter the touch. Moreover, many keyboards can be sensitized so that only minimum pressure is required for keyboard operations.

Additionally, University of California researchers have demonstrated that a keyboard with springs underneath each key that change the force or feel of the key switches was effective in decreasing hand paresthesia—numbness, tingling, and burning in the hand—experienced by frequent computer users.[10] Through a series of focus groups, Key Tronic Corporation, a manufacturer of keyboards, learned that users found that keyboards that allowed them to use less force with their third and fourth fingers were more comfortable. A product they subsequently developed, ErgoForce, requires 35 grams of force on the keys controlled by those two fingers rather than the standard 55 grams of force.[11]

Auditory Feedback   "Click" is the sound one hears and equates with knowing that the character has been entered. Research has shown that users need an aural stimulus when keyboarding, and the click serves as reinforcement. Many keyboards enable the user to control the volume of the click by a special button or an option provided by the software.

Layout   A keyboard's layout impacts how easy the keyboard is to use. For example, alphanumeric and/or special-function keys that are used frequently should be within easy reach. Any function key that results in major changes should be in a position where it will not be struck accidentally. Most keyboards are designed for right-handed users. When a 10-key pad is part of the keyboard, for example, it usually appears on the right-hand side, although left-hand keyboards are available. Another option that left-handed users can benefit from is a detachable 10-key pad that can be moved for efficient keying. A movable keyboard enables the operator to place it at an angle or whatever location is most comfortable. Cordless keyboards also provide greater user flexibility.

Manufacturers of ergonomically designed keyboards suggest that the location of the keys and the positioning of the hands can keep muscle problems, including *carpal tunnel syndrome,* at bay. The carpal tunnel consists of those tendons and nerves that connect the arms to the hands and are depicted in Figure 10-7. Carpal tunnel syndrome results from excessive keying in particular positions.[12] To address carpal tunnel syndrome, manufacturers of keyboards have redesigned the conventional keyboard. Goldtouch, for example, has an "advanced ergonomic system" consisting of a hinged keyboard, a mouse, a mousepad, two wrist rests, and a separate numeric keypad; this system is depicted in Figure 10-8. Research conducted at Cornell University found that a split keyboard provided user flexibility, and when used in conjunction with appropriate positioning of the chair and the

Figure 10-7
Hand and arm muscles

Source: Courtesy of Animax.

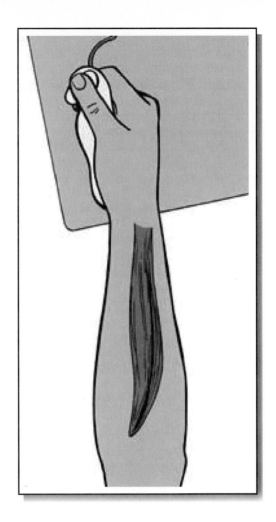

keyboard, results were positive. (The complete study can be found online at *www.typesafe.com.*)

The standard typewriter layout is termed *QWERTY* for the first six letters of the top row of alphabet keys (see Figure 10-9a). The QWERTY keyboard was designed to separate keys in the mechanical type basket, and their awkward placement served the purpose of reducing the number of key clashes.

The QWERTY layout has been challenged as a standard by the Dvorak or *American Simplified Keyboard* (ASK), shown in Figure 10-9b. In the ASK, the most frequently used keys are located in the home row. Although controversial, the ASK layout has been demonstrated to be more efficient than the QWERTY layout. ASK users have recorded speeds of up to 162 words per minute on 60-minute tests. In speed tests, the user of the ASK almost always outperforms the QWERTY user. Because QWERTY users are reluctant to change, the use of ASK has been hampered. With computer keyboards, however, ASK can challenge QWERTY because simple programming can change a traditional keyboard into an ASK keyboard and back again. This enables the same keyboard to be used by both a QWERTY and an ASK typist.

The keyboard layout of function and hot keys also can differ from manufacturer to manufacturer. Figure 10-10, Microsoft's Natural Keyboard Pro, is an

Part IV   Workplace Performance: The Impact of Information Technology

Figure 10-7
(continued)

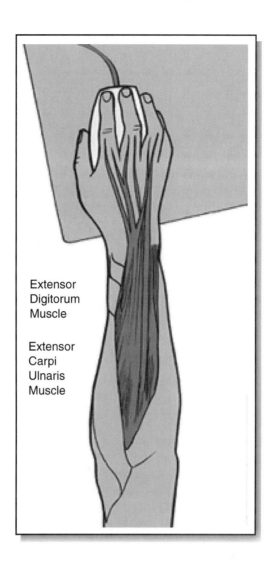

Extensor
Digitorum
Muscle

Extensor
Carpi
Ulnaris
Muscle

Figure 10-8
Goldtouch ergonomic keyboard

Source: Courtesy of Goldtouch.

Chapter 10   Human Factors: Software, Hardware, and Workplace Design

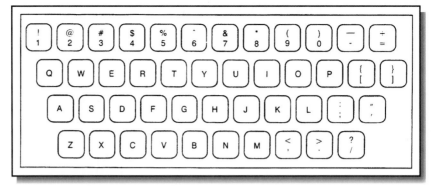

Figure 10-9a
The QWERTY keyboard

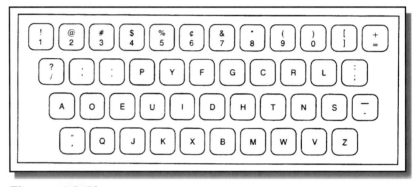

Figure 10-9b
The Dvorak or American Simplified Keyboard (ASK)

Figure 10-10
Microsoft's Natural Keyboard Pro

Source: Courtesy Microsoft Corporation.

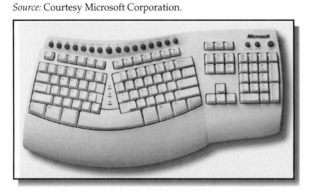

example of a new order of keyboard that offers hot keys, which provide one-touch access allowing users, for example, to launch a browser and surf the Web directly from the keyboard. Multimedia hot keys on this keyboard model include mute, volume down, volume up, play/pause, and so forth, giving the user the power to control music CDs and PC audio and video. An e-mail hot key allows users to check their messages with a single stroke. Users also can customize their own hot keys.

Profile *Profile* refers to the thickness or height of the keyboard. Early typewriter keyboards had a stair-step profile. In other words, rows of keys were arranged in a manner that required touch typists to move their fingers from the centered home row up or down to other rows. Most of today's keyboards are flat. However, some split keyboards can be arranged vertically so that the palms face each other. In one study of the vertical keyboard's effectiveness, typing speeds dropped about 10 percent and accuracy dropped by 2 percent.[13] Experts typically do not recommend one profile over another. The best profile is the profile the user prefers.

Finish and Shape The key itself offers tactile feedback. The operator should feel when the key is accepted. Tactile responses are considered more reliable and timely than audible feedback; therefore, the finish and shape of keys are important factors.

Keys typically are struck at an angle; for this reason, they generally have a matte finish and a bowl shape. The matte finish offers a nonslick surface for the operator and less keyboard glare. Keys are often dish shaped to allow the fingertips to rest in the dish. On many keyboards, the shape is more profound in the home row keys than on other rows. This gives the user more tactile feedback—confirming without looking that one's fingers are on the home row. In addition, some keyboards have grooves on the *f* and *j* keys (for index fingers on the QWERTY layout) or bumps on the *d* and *k* keys; such measures provide even stronger tactile feedback.

10.3.3 The Mouse

Some workplace injuries have been connected to the mouse. This point-and-click peripheral is used in conjunction with GUI interfaces and is a standard part of any computer system. Ideally, a mouse is close to the user's dominant hand on a platform that is conducive to movement. The conventional mouse has two buttons: a left button that controls the cursor's location on the screen and is clicked on icons or menu options to start commands, and a right button whose functions are shortcuts to features related to the application being used. Another mouse type has a little wheel that helps users quickly scroll up and down.

A notebook computer version of a mouse can be simply a button in the middle of the keyboard that can be pushed to the desired location and special thumb-operated bars pushed to start the command. Other notebook mouse devices are touch pads, allowing the user to manipulate the cursor's location with fingertips. Yet another device allows the user to manipulate the mouse as a foot pedal. A new generation of mouse-type devices is evolving; some are cordless and some are vertical. Figure 10-11 pictures several products in this new generation. Note how each attempts to make its use easier, more flexible, and safer.

Advances in computer interfaces and computer hardware peripherals have made the computer more accessible to the handicapped. Any number of innovative products exist that can accommodate disabled individuals who would otherwise be barred from participating in the workplace or school. The Application Spotlight on page 340 offers three real-life scenarios.

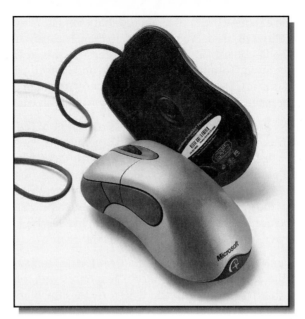

Figure 10-11a
A new generation of mouse
Microsoft IntelliMouse Explorer

Source: Courtesy Microsoft Corporation.

Figure 10-11b
Logitech cordless
MouseMan wheel

Source: Courtesy Logitech Inc.

Figure 10-11c
The Whale mouse

Source: Courtesy Human-scale Corporation.

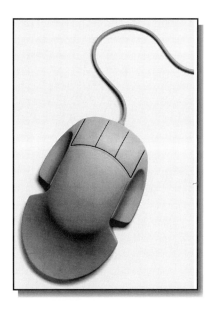

Figure 10-11d
The Anir vertical mouse

Source: Courtesy Animax.

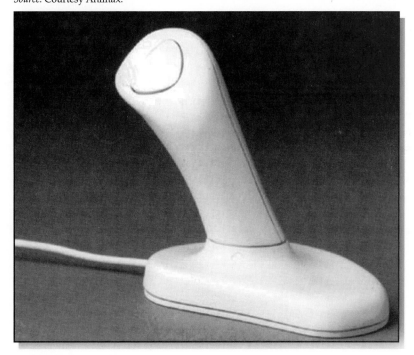

HANDICAP: BLINDNESS

Keyboard Alternatives & Vision Solutions (*www.keyalt.com*) specializes in ergonomic resources and product guides. Joe Smith (pseudonym), one of their staff members, is blind; he has been blind since birth. His job requires that he access a Windows-based computer database to look up client information and then make outbound calls. He enters notes and follow-up instructions into the database. To perform his job, Joe has a number of special tools including "screen-reading" software, which allows him to hear the details that a sighted user would view on the screen. He also is equipped with keyboard hotkeys that are programmed to read his menu choices aloud. The software also can read aloud the text of documents that he is writing or Web sites that he is viewing.

Joe uses a custom telephone headset that allows him to hear what his computer is saying with one ear, while listening to the phone conversation with the other ear. His caller never knows that he is simultaneously listening to his computer.

To further accommodate his needs, Joe has a Braille notetaker that interfaces with the computer. He types notes in Braille and then sends them to his computer. His Braille notetaker also has a Braille display; this allows him to read menu choices or text that appears on his computer screen simply by reading (feeling) the Braille display. As he moves up and down the screen, or through menu choices, his Braille display changes to reflect that text.

HANDICAP: CEREBRAL PALSY

Mark Jones (pseudonym) has cerebral palsy. The condition causes his hands to tremble, often causing him to depress the wrong key on the keyboard. To compensate for this problem, he would have to bend over and carefully study the keyboard, then look up at the monitor to confirm that he had hit (typed) the correct key. This made typing a painstaking effort. His vision also is challenged, making it hard for him to find his place or to refocus constantly from keyboard to screen and back again. To accommodate the tremor in his hands, he uses a keyboard tray positioned at a more correct height. Moreover, the keyboard has wrist/palm support. Another solution for Mark was a copy of Large Print Windows with Speech (LPW-S), a magnification software application that allows him to magnify and/or hear text as it is typed or to listen to text in a review mode. Mark did not need the magnification element of the software, and there are other software applications designed to read only keystrokes and text (without the magnification), but he chose LPW-S because of its simplicity and ease of use. LPW-S software allows Mark to maintain his focus on the keyboard. To confirm that he has hit the correct key, he merely has to listen as he types. He reports that he is working faster, more efficiently, and more comfortably.

HANDICAP: QUADRIPLEGIC

Jack Williams (pseudonym) is a quadriplegic who works for a bank. To enable him to work with the computer, he uses a variety of interfaces. Using one approach, he simply uses a mouthstick, which is a stick designed to be held by his mouth, so that he can type text and control his computer. To be somewhat more efficient, Jack also uses voice dictation software. Why does he take advantage of the primitive mouthstick? Because over the years, prior to his getting voice dictation, he learned to become skilled and fast in using it. He still finds that some basic tasks are accomplished faster by simply depressing a couple of keys with the mouthstick.

Some other simple devices that we take for granted make Jack's work possible. For example, he uses a speakerphone to communicate with his clients. He also has a custom table with an electric lazy Susan that allows him to take advantage of the work surface of his desk.

Source: Reprinted with permission of John Simkovitz JD, of Keyboard Alternatives & Vision Solutions, Inc. Santa Rosa, CA. All rights reserved.

Knowledge work traditionally has involved information creation, storage, retrieval, and dissemination. Although the nature of knowledge work has not changed, the tools used to do that work have changed dramatically, and with those changes have come fundamental changes in the design and features of the workplace.

The traditional office was paper based, with filing cabinets, writing desks, lighting, and even chairs conducive to paper processing. The traditional office had row upon row of clerical workers, with higher-status managers and supervisors in enclosed offices around a large, central office area. Often described as a bullpen, this arrangement worked well for the paper-processing operations of the day. Because the paper documents were often transferred from one worker to another, such an arrangement was effective. Facilities management had a simple job of purchasing standard desks and lighting and tended to avoid concerns of noise pollution and aesthetics.

The process of entering, processing, and distributing information electronically makes new demands on the environment. For example, desks that are the proper height for writing are not the proper height for a keyboard. Lighting that was appropriate for row upon row of desks does not fit the needs of an individual using a computer. Additional electric, telephone, and cable lines are required. In addition, the noise of printers, copiers, and keyboards (and increasingly voice input) has put new acoustical demands on the workplace. Today's office must accommodate a wide range of new tasks and tools.

Management needs to take a new role in ensuring worker health, safety, and productivity. Technology impacts the layout of entire offices as well as individual work space design. Space planning is important; most organizations place as many people as they can in work areas. The computer is putting some new limits and restrictions on just what (and whom!) can be moved where. The end user's private space, likewise, has new needs and restrictions. This section discusses ergonomic considerations related to office layout and individual work spaces.

10.4.1 Office Layout

Office layout is both a science and an art. When implementing systems, EUIS specialists may need to address issues of office layout or obtain the assistance of work space design experts in their institution. Despite specific guidelines, the planner must do more than follow the principles of layout. The tools, the work, and the individual worker must be considered. To better explain the relationship among technology-driven, work-driven, and people-driven design, the AMCO-PACT Model of Office Layout is discussed. This segment also includes an overview of environmental impacts related to office and work space design.

10.4.1.1 The AMCO-PACT Model of Office Layout

Effective office layout centers around the need for the effective use of space. Design considerations can be described through George Terry's *AMCO-PACT model of office layout* (see Figure 10-12). The manager can use AMCO-PACT to better ensure that space design addresses individual worker needs and supports work procedures and work tools. AMCO identifies physical aspects related to ideal space utilization. PACT identifies practical limitations to the ideal. Following is a discussion of each aspect and limitation.

Figure 10-12
The AMCO/PACT model
of office layout

Source: Reprinted with permission of Richard Irwin, Dow Jones-Irwin, Inc. New York, NY.

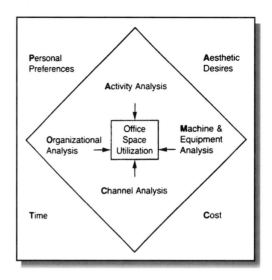

A = Activity analysis

Activity analysis is the means of examining just what work is being done in the office. What specific tasks are being done? Who works with whom? How much room is needed to do a specific task? What problems currently exist? Figure 10-13 shows an office designed to support a professional worker in a variety of different tasks. The reader should note the wide variety of seating and work surfaces in this workstation.

In addition, activities specific to using information technologies must be supported. Specialized activities have unique space and location needs, such as the need for training rooms, small and large conference rooms, copying and printing rooms, and teleconferencing rooms. Rooms for each activity must be given special design consideration.

M = Machine inventory

Machine inventory is the process of determining which equipment/technologies are used to perform office tasks, as well as those expected to be used in the future. How many machines are being used? What are they? How large are they? What is the type/size/shape/number of technologies to be added to the workplace?

Figure 10-13
An office designed with a wide variety of seating and work surfaces to support a professional worker in performing diverse tasks

Source: Courtesy of The Image Bank.

C = Channel analysis

Channel analysis is the process of accounting for power, communications, and ventilation needs. Most new construction takes these into consideration; older buildings, however, may present challenges. Planners agree that it is easier to design a new office building than to redesign a building to accommodate new technology. Where are the electrical channels, cable lines, telephone lines, and conduits? What will be needed to accommodate new technologies?

O = Organizational analysis

Organizational analysis is determining the size and nature of the workforce. How many people need to be housed in a given facility? What is their work level—how many clerical workers, managers, supervisors, and vice presidents are there? Who needs to communicate with whom? What are the identified work groups?

In many respects, AMCO describes the *ideal* space allocation, but office layouts often must be designed under less-than-ideal conditions. The second half of the model, PACT, outlines the restrictors, or concerns that can undermine or preclude the best space allocation plan. The letters in PACT refer to the following aspects of office layout:

P = Personal preference

Personal preference relates to the need to consider individual needs and desires. Who likes to work with whom? Who cannot work with whom? Who smokes? Is anyone handicapped? What do people want or need to do their work properly?

A = Aesthetics

Aesthetics refers to the sense of beauty and harmony. With regard to space allocation, what is the most pleasing way to group workers? Where can partitions be placed so that they are not perceived to be obstacles? Can a sense of design be maintained?

C = Cost

Cost is often referred to as the universal regulator. What will the design cost? The ideal design is not possible if funds for its construction are not available.

T = Time

Time refers to how long the design will remain in effect. Is the building rented on a short-term lease? Will the organization be in these headquarters indefinitely? Obviously, the more permanent the time factor is, the more care and cost should go into space allocation.

In short, an effective office layout would facilitate human interaction, proper use of technology, and work processes. People need to be close to those with whom they work and the tools they use to do their job. The layout should help, not hinder, the work process. AMCO/PACT is useful for asking the right questions.

10.4.1.2 Environmental Impacts

A good office layout supports not only the work that is being done, but also supports human interaction with the work environment. Workers are affected by lighting, sound, air quality, and even colors and textures. Following is a discussion of these environmental impacts.

Lighting Lighting can affect productivity directly. In laboratory experiments, employee speed and quality of output increase as lighting is improved. Two organizations that are focused on the lighting question are the Illuminating Engineering Society of North America (IES) and the American National Standards Institute (ANSI). ANSI and the Human Factors Society (HFS) have produced one of the first standards for lighting—the *American National Standard for Human Factors Engineering at Visual Display Terminal Workstations.*[14]

The visual environment is important not only to worker productivity, but also to worker health and safety. It is perhaps in lighting that the needs of the workplace have changed most dramatically. The problem is compounded when lighting must support a variety of tasks. Tasks such as writing or sorting require a high level of lighting. The same light that supports these tasks, however, can impede visual clarity on the monitor. The general rule is that enough light must be available to do the task at hand, and it must contribute to the task being done, not hinder it. Also important to keep in mind is that older workers often need good lighting and respond quickly to lighting improvements.

Technical terms that describe lighting include *candela* (cd), a measure of light intensity; *lumen* (lm), a measure of light radiation; *lux* (lx), a measure of the illumination that is actually seen; and *reflection factor* (p), the measure of the capacity to reflect light. These measures are important. The addition of a computer to a work environment dramatically changes lighting requirements. To avoid glare and strain in a stress-producing environment, experts recommend the following:

- Provide low ambient (general) lighting and increase task-ambient (task-specific) lighting.
- Provide ambient lighting that originates from areas other than the ceiling.
- Build lighting into the workstation.

The lighting system shown in Figure 10-14 incorporates all of these recommendations. Note that the ambient light originates from the top of this workstation and beams upward, reflecting the light down to the user from the ceiling. The intense, controllable task lighting is built directly into the workstation panels.

Sound   Just as the visual environment has changed with information technologies, so has the acoustical environment. Office workers and designers should know the terms that are used to measure sound.

For example, the articulation index (AI) is the acoustical level at which people can work without being distracted by outside conversation. AI ranks speech intelligibility from 0.0 to 1.0. At an AI of 0.0, one cannot understand anything a person is saying in a normal voice; at 1.0, everything anyone says in a normal voice is intelligible. Bolt, Beranek & Newman, a Boston-based consulting firm, reported that an AI level over 0.5 means that the noise level in the office is "out of control." In such a situation, everyone would be able to hear everyone else's conversations.

The decibel (dB) is a measure of the loudness or intensity of a sound. The following are the decibel ratings of some common sounds:

- The human voice, 50 to 60 dBs; when shouting, 80 to 90 dBs
- Laser printer, no measurable noise
- Two electronic typewriters, 68 to 73 dBs
- Large, quiet office, 46 to 52 dBs
- Copying machine, 55 to 70 dBs

Figure 10-14
Task and ambient lighting within a workstation

Source: Reprinted with permission of Louise King, Steelcase, Inc.

Acoustic control is necessary in an office. According to (the National Institute of Occupational Health and Safety), continuous exposure to high noise levels can damage the ear. Characteristics of sound include absence, frequency, adaptation, and variety.

A total absence of sound can be as disturbing as too much sound. *Frequency,* as used here, refers to the regularity of sound: Consider a constantly humming printer as opposed to a printer with many starts and stops. *Adaptation* refers to the ability to adapt to new sounds. *Variety* means that throughout the day, different pitches, tones, and decibels are needed.

Solutions to the problem of noise are not easy to implement. Nevertheless, noise reduction techniques fall into three broad categories.

1. *Sound-absorbing materials.* Add sound-absorbing materials (such as cloth) to wall partitions. Absorb the sound of footsteps with carpeting; it can absorb

10 to 30 percent of the sound that hits it. Ceiling boards or tiles of soft, absorbent materials can be used to improve the AI index.

2. *Sound-masking systems.* Students living in a dormitory, rather than complain about the noise their neighbors are making, often resort to the "fan technique." They turn on a fan that makes a humming noise, and the fan's noise masks the disturbing sound. The same principle can be applied in the office. "White sound," a gentle humming, is used in many buildings to mask unwanted sound. Music is another sound masker. The productivity of routine clerical workers typically goes up when music is piped into an office. The impact of music on other workers depends upon the work and the individual. For routine work, music can *increase* worker productivity.

3. *Office layout.* Wall partitions block sound, and heights of 5 feet are effective noise reducers. Another sound-reducing practice is to isolate noisy equipment from work areas.

Air Quality　A computer can generate about the same amount of heat as a person. Therefore, as the number of computers rises, so does the demand on an organization's existing cooling and electrical systems. The comfort and safety of an environment are dependent upon temperature, air movement, and cleanliness. Facilities managers refer to systems that determine air quality as HVAC (heating, ventilation, and air conditioning).

Office temperatures, if not regulated by legislation (ordinances in some cities limit temperatures to 68 degrees Fahrenheit in the winter and 78 degrees Fahrenheit in the summer), are regulated by personal preference. In one office at any given time, a number of individuals will be either too hot or too cold. (This phenomenon has a lot to do with body weight.) No specific temperatures are recommended for computer use, but the American Society of Heating and Ventilating Engineers recommends a temperature of 74 to 78 degrees Fahrenheit in the summer and winter, with a humidity level of 40 to 50 percent in the summer and 30 to 40 percent in the winter.

An important but often overlooked air circulation problem is static electricity buildup. Static electricity is a discomfort, and it can erase data. Data that seemed to have disappeared in thin air may actually have been erased by static electricity.

Colors and Textures　Colors and textures add aesthetic appeal to an office and can boost worker morale. The appearance of an office is known to affect workers' emotions, senses, and thought processes. Colors also affect perceptions of temperature; for example, blue is regarded as a cooling temperature, pink as a warming temperature. Colors can create an atmosphere that is either conducive or not conducive to work. Office colors should fit the type of work being done, as well as the location of the office:

> Vivid colors may work in a creative magazine office, but at a law firm, where analysis and deep thought is prevalent, soft tones might be better. Another important factor in determining appropriate colors for an office or workspace is location. The calming sense of a blue office may work in sunny Phoenix, Arizona, but not in rainy Seattle, Washington.[15]

Other advice is to avoid stark contrasts in colors. The wall behind the computer and any peripherals should not be in stark contrast to the computer screen. If the user's eyes continually move from a dark screen to a bright window or document holder, for example, they are constantly opening and closing. The result could be computer vision syndrome, which may include sore eyes and a headache. This is why most computers and their peripherals are gray or beige.[16]

The relationship between color and lighting has been researched extensively. Generally, softer colors reflect more light, and darker colors absorb more light. Walls or partitions covered by soft-color materials add light, as well as sound absorption.

10.4.2 Workstation Design

The designer of a *workstation,* defined here as an individual's work area, applies all office design considerations on a micro level after examining what work is being done. A work analysis will show the major work activities. Once a workstation is classified as paper, computer, or telephone driven, the planner begins to work, taking into account anthropometric, social, and psychological concerns.

10.4.2.1 Work Analysis

Offices should be designed to support the work that people do, providing easy access to the tools they use and resulting in a safe, pleasing environment. In beginning the analysis, the primary question is to determine what the worker does. For example, does the worker spend most of the day on the computer, on the telephone, or meeting with clients? First and foremost, workspace needs to support the work that is done.

Additionally, factors of user satisfaction and ergonomics need to be considered. Personal satisfaction includes the ability to concentrate and have conversational privacy. Ergonomic considerations include the appropriateness and comfort of the chair, appropriate lighting, and the elimination of unsightly and potentially dangerous wiring. Moreover, as in all issues related to user satisfaction, it is advisable to offer options for personal preferences whenever possible regarding as many factors as possible—storage space, lighting, chair, colors, and the like.

10.4.2.2 Anthropometric Concerns

Anthropometrics measures the size and proportions of the human body. Applied to workstation design, anthropometrics is used to evaluate body movement. Examples include posture, reach, and viewing distances.

10.4.2.2.1 Posture Musculoskeletal disorders account for many worker compensation claims. Unfortunately, because data regarding age and occupation of these workers are not available, it is difficult to estimate the impact of computer use on musculoskeletal disorders. However, it is known that computer users are more likely than other workers to complain of neck pains; stiffness; cramps; and numbness in the back, neck, shoulder, arms, and hands.

Research studies into why computer users have more musculoskeletal complaints than other workers have taken the following variables into account: age; existing disorders; and visual problems including nearsightedness, presbyopia, and whether or not individuals wore bifocals while using the computer. Studies also have examined the way a worker interacts with the environment—the keyboard (hand), chair (body), and screen (eyes)—as well as the repetitiveness of the task, length of time spent at tasks, and physical constraints.

Significantly, research that found musculoskeletal disorders among computer users also indicated that the screen was viewed from an unsuitable angle, the keyboard was too low or too high for proper keying, the chair and desk were unsuitable or of incorrect height, or the work area did not allow sufficient movement.

Computer users also have expressed concerns related to frequent visual and musculoskeletal strains and discomfort, including eye fatigue; irritation; blurred vision; and pain or stiffness in the neck, shoulders, back, arms, wrists, and hands.

NIOSH has pointed out that these effects are most prominent among computer users who engage in repetitive or intense work with little opportunity for variation, or those who spend long, uninterrupted periods at the computer. According to NIOSH, user complaints often are related to glare, poor illumination, and poorly designed workstations.

Experts concur that good posture contributes to worker well-being. While no best posture exists, good working posture is natural and relaxed as the computer user changes positions throughout the day. The following recommendations can help alleviate musculoskeletal disorders.

1. Use detachable, movable keyboards and adjust table heights for their use. Adjustable keyboard drawers can be a useful desk addition.
2. Never bend your neck more than 20 degrees. When entering information from hard copy, use a copy stand that is eye level with the monitor or directly in front of you.
3. Keep the monitor at a viewing distance of 24 to 30 inches.
4. Keep upper arms at a 90-degree angle to your forearms.
5. Keep a 105-degree angle between your trunk and thighs; use a chair that tilts slightly forward and supports your back. An ideal chair will have adjustable height controls and a high backrest. A great chair would have five wheels to

Figure 10-15
Herman Miller's Aeron chair

Source: Reprinted with permission of Herman Miller, Zeeland, MI.

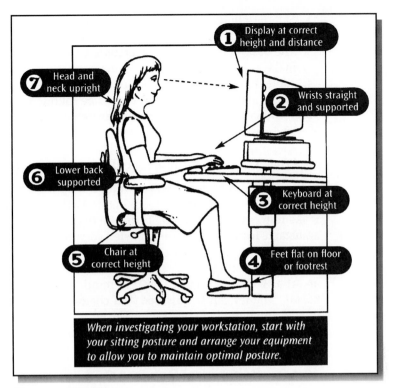

Figure 10-16
Ways to make your workstation more comfortable

Source: NYU Benefits Newsletter. With permission of Anita Perr, New York University, New York, NY.

allow movement. Chairs should be padded and covered with an absorbent fabric. See Figure 10-15, for an example of an ergonomically designed chair.

6. Position thighs parallel to the floor when feet are flat on the floor. If your feet do not reach the floor, use a footrest.

These and other proper seating guidelines for using computers are illustrated in Figure 10-16.

10.4.2.2.2 Reach and Viewing Distances   An efficient workstation provides effortless access to needed tools so that a seated worker can reach all tools without excessive stretching or getting up. For example, an administrative assistant should be able to get letters and envelopes from a printer without having to stand. A manager who uses a personal computer frequently should have it within arm's reach.

Workplaces often are designed with use of the computer as the primary task. However, this is not always the case. For example, a manager may use a computer only minutes a day. In that case, having the computer in the prime work area would not be the best arrangement. Again, a primary reason for task analysis is to determine what major activities should be accommodated in the workstation.

Desks need to be not only the appropriate size for the task but also the appropriate height. A desk that is right for writing is not the same height as a desk for keyboarding. Desks should have a matte finish, rather than a shiny one, to avoid monitor reflection. Experts recommend the following guidelines for selecting the height of desks and tables.

1. Standard height is 30 inches for writing and 26 inches for keyboarding.
2. The height should provide sufficient legroom.
3. The desk or table should be adjustable, and adjustments should be easy to make.
4. Table legs should be located so that the user's knees are not immobilized.
5. Edges and corners of tables should be rounded.
6. Terminal tables should be a size and shape appropriate for the computer, the keyboard, and the mouse. Likewise, printer tables should be of a size and shape appropriate for printing.
7. When necessary, furniture should accommodate special wiring needs.

Ergonomically designed furniture can address many of the problems related to workstation ergonomics. Keep in mind, however, that ergonomic furniture can make things worse.[17] "Ergo" furniture typically requires many adjustments. This adjustable furniture must be adjusted correctly to the individual user. Any design effort that includes the introduction of new furniture also should include end-user training. Adjusting tables, chairs, screen viewing distances, and computer cables is an art as well as a science. Keep in mind, too, that *ergonomic furniture may not be needed*.[18] Tables can be lowered and chairs swapped among users. Desks can be moved and blinds can be drawn. The most expensive ergo furniture used improperly may not be as effective as existing furnishings used correctly.

10.4.3 Behavioral Concerns

The AMCO-PACT model points out that the design of workstations cannot ignore the needs of the individual worker. The workplace is people driven, not machine driven. In designing workstations, the planner must be aware of some basic principles of human behavior: territoriality, personal space, backs and sides, eye contact, privacy, status, and socialization.[19]

10.4.3.1 Territoriality

The tendency to make our mark on a space is known as *territoriality*. Even in lecture classes where seats are not assigned, students typically choose the same seat for each class meeting. Likewise, in exercise classes, participants tend to take the same place in the room. When someone else is in the seat or position normally taken, the individual who has been displaced may feel a bit unsettled.

Territoriality also can be applied to the office. Workers need a place to call their own, and an office or a desk is theirs—at least until the end of the day or shift. Workstations need to include space for and security of individual belongings such as coats, umbrellas, and briefcases. Workers also like to place their own memorabilia around their work area—pictures, flowers, calendars—things that designate "Michael's desk." In designing an office, the planner would do well to arrange for such ownership. In fact, regulations that restrict the type or amount of personal artifacts at a workplace always meet with resistance.

10.4.3.2 Personal Space

Personal space depends upon many factors, including occupation, ethnic background, sex, and age. For some overgeneralizations, a blue-collar worker is often much more comfortable than a bank president on a crowded bus. A salesperson is typically outgoing and will stand closer to a client than individuals in other occupations. Younger people require less space. Personal space has been divided into zones as follows:

TAKE AN ERGONOMIC BREAK

If you spend many hours at your desk and at a computer, try these exercises at least every few hours.

- Alternate closing your eyes tightly and opening them at least 10 times.

- Alternate spreading your fingers and making a fist; hold each position for about 10 seconds.

- With fingers spread, place your hands together with fingertips under your chin. Then slowly lower your hands and your fingers will peel apart.

Reverse the process and repeat several times.

- Turn your head as far as it will go and hold it for 10 seconds. Repeat in the opposite direction.

- Tilt your head to the left and hold the position for 10 seconds. Repeat in the opposite direction.

- Rotate shoulders (like a shrug) first in one direction and then in the other. Place hands on hips, feet about a shoulder width apart. Slowly push hips forward and lean shoulders slightly back. Maintain that stretch for 10 seconds.[20]

Source: Copyright © December 1999 by the American Institute of Certified Public Accountants, Inc. Reprinted with permission. Opinions of the authors are their own and do not necessarily reflect policies of the AICPA.

Zone 1: Intimate distance (up to 18 inches apart). Zone 1 is reserved for people we want to be close to: friends, family members, spouses, and children.

Zone 2: Personal Distance (18 inches to 4 feet away). Zone 2 is within an arm's reach and is reserved for friends.

Zone 3: Social distance (4 to 12 feet away). Social distance is the zone in which much business is conducted. A desk is typically 3 to 4 feet wide, and the addition of a chair on either side increases this space. Zone 3 distances are enough to be considered formal.

Zone 4: Public distance (12 to 25 feet or more). Individuals attempting to communicate in Zone 4 must raise their voices and, depending upon obstacles, may not be able to see each other. If one wishes, one can avoid individuals who are in Zone 4.

What do these zones have to do with workstation design? From an evaluation of zones, it may be concluded that one needs a work space large enough to ensure that one's personal space is respected. Designers should avoid overcrowding; too many workers in a given area either force people to become temporarily friendly or deny them needed space.

10.4.3.3   *Backs and Sides*

The most desirable location in any building is the corner room, where a person is protected from interference from two sides and is able to minimize contact. Restaurant goers typically gravitate to a corner window. If a corner window is not available, they will choose a window seat. Only when the restaurant is full will they select a center table, and then they will most likely choose the table farthest from other diners.

What can be learned from "backs and sides"? The most desirable offices are in the corner of the building and along the outside walls. Desks in a landscaped building are often positioned so that the worker's back is to the hallway, which most people find unpleasant. Designers should consider workers' needs to be "flanked" on at least two sides and have their backs protected. Figure 10-17 illustrates these principles. Note the location of the desk in each of the three offices in the picture.

Figure 10-17
Desk positions in office design

Source: Courtesy of Herman Miller, Inc.

10.4.3.4 Eye Contact

Another overgeneralization is that New Yorkers dislike looking strangers in the eye and that people in the Southwest distrust anyone who does *not* look them in the eye! At any point where eye contact is possible, some sort of barrier needs to be developed if that contact is not necessary or desirable. This is why workers with desks facing each other have difficulty working. This is why partitions that are less than 5 feet high are often unacceptable. Many people require visual privacy. Depending upon the task being done, efforts should be made to ensure that such privacy is provided.

10.4.3.5 Status

A status symbol is a possession regarded as a sign of rank. Following is a partial list of office status symbols:

- A large office has more status than a small one.
- A leather chair has more status than a cloth one; a chair with five casters and an armrest has more status than a three-wheeled chair with no arms.
- An office with a window has more status than an office without one.
- Dark woods imply more status than light woods or metals.
- Enclosed offices have more status than open offices.

The planner often takes workers' status into account when furnishing offices. Many large organizations have developed standards that apply to various levels of workers. In other words, workers at each level are assigned a specific size of office, a specific type of chair, and a specific size and kind of desk. Such policies allow planners to address status concerns more uniformly. Within the guidelines established by policies, planners frequently allow individuals to pick and choose among furnishings and office layouts. Such options, they explain, enable each workstation to reflect the needs of individual workers.

Planners traditionally have taken workers' status into account when designing building space layouts. For example, it is not unusual to have senior managers grouped together in a status location, removed, often by several floors, from their subordinates. However, as management styles change, so does the thinking about who needs to be near whom and why. Increasingly, functional managers must talk to each other and executives must work more closely with work teams, rather than in isolation. To this end, newer office layout concepts remove barriers and support increased worker interaction. Figure 10-18a depicts how one organization added col-

Figure 10-18a
Individual spaces with collaborative work areas

Source: Courtesy of Steelcase.

laborative work space to individual spaces, and Figure 10-18b shows a combination of mobile tables, screens, and carts for a highly flexible group work environment.

10.4.3.6 *Socialization*
When redesigning the office to take advantage of new systems and to support new management styles, care must be taken to assure that workers can communicate easily. With greater frequency, managers are supporting the creation of coffee rooms

Figure 10-18b
Group work space

Source: Courtesy of Steelcase.

and break rooms. These rooms can include white boards or computers that visitors can use for note taking into consideration and idea sketching. The premise is that serendipitous conversation can lead to new ideas. Taking the need for human interaction and supporting that interaction rather than barring it is considered good business sense.

When new systems are planned and designed, care should be taken not to disrupt workers' social interactions. Systems have failed because desks were stationed in areas or at angles that eliminated or discouraged worker interaction. The socialization needs of workers must be considered.

10.5 SUMMARY

Concern about productivity as well as the health, safety, and comfort of workers in the office workplace has led to increased interest in human factors. This information about physical and psychological characteristics is applied to the design of devices and systems for human use. The term *human factors* generally is used synonymously with the term *ergonomics,* which is the study of the natural laws of work. Ideally, office workers should be in an environment that fosters good work habits, combining design and usability principles that balance systems components of technology, procedures, and human needs. This chapter offered an overview of ergonomic principles related to software design, hardware design, and workplace design.

Human factors principles that help define user friendly software were discussed within three categories: user interfaces, screen layout, and performance support (learning aids). Command-, menu-, icon-, natural language-, pen-, and speech recognition technology-based interface systems were described. Issues were discussed relating to effective interface design that centered on the need to provide users with a conceptual understanding of the interface and the ability to control the dialogue with the system. Guidelines for screen layouts that support data entry and software usability were outlined. Performance support was discussed, including paper-based documentation, help facilities, and online reference.

Hardware design issues centered on the need for comfortable and safe monitors and keyboards. Health problems categorized as repetitive stress syndrome (RSI) or repetitive motion syndrome (RMI), including eye fatigue and strain, carpal tunnel syndrome, musculoskeletal disorders, fatigue, and stress, often are attributed to the monitor and the design of keyboards and workstations. Conventional CRT monitors were compared to newer, yet much more expensive counterparts— LCD panels. In comparing monitors, the purchaser should consider such characteristics as resolution, size, glare, and reflection. Likewise, the purchaser has options with regard to keyboards. Keystroke pressure, tactile and auditory feedback, keyboard layout and profile, and key finish and shape all affect user productivity. Mouse technology, likewise, is evolving. The mouse comes in numerous sizes and shapes; the best mouse is the one that the user finds most comfortable.

The workplace has changed dramatically as a result of information technology. Traditional principles of office layout and design are no longer applicable, or not as applicable as they once were. AMCO-PACT, a framework for office design, helps the planner balance the ideal with real-life restrictions.

In addition to layout, environmental impacts such as lighting, sound, air quality, and color have an impact on worker productivity, health, and morale. Bright colors, for example, are typically cafeteria colors, not workplace colors. Optimum lighting for computer use is not the same as lighting for other tasks, such as writing or sorting. Noise can make conversation or concentration difficult. The computer adds as much heat to a room as the body heat from a worker, which impacts a location's HVAC requirements. Color schemes also impact productivity and worker morale.

Finally, the workstation, an individual's work area, must be examined from a technical and a human perspective. It is known, for example, that a good chair promotes good posture, that the proper table height can relieve musculoskeletal disorders, and that a flexible keyboard allows individuals to adjust their sitting positions, which is especially important for individuals who must sit at a desk for hours on end. People behave in predictable patterns. Issues of territoriality, personal space, backs and sides, status, and the need for socialization have an impact on workstation design that supports productivity.

In short, worker health and comfort impact productivity. Software, hardware, and work space design can be addressed through human factors. Applications of ergonomic principles—those already known and those still being developed—can result in a positive outcome for the organization and the individual.

KEY TERMS

- American Simplified Keyboard
- AMCO-PACT
- Anthropometrics
- Articulation index
- Bezel
- Bit-mapped
- Candela
- Carpal tunnel syndrome
- Character resolution
- Command-based interface
- Context-sensitive help
- Contrast
- Decibel

- Documentation
- Ergonomics
- Flicker
- Glare
- Graphical user interface (GUI)
- Help facilities
- Human factors
- Icon-based interface
- Lumen
- Lux
- Matrix density
- Menu-based interface

- Natural language interface
- Pen-based interface
- Pixel
- QWERTY keyboard
- Radiation
- Reflection
- Refresh rate
- Resolution
- Speech recognition technology
- Territoriality
- User friendly
- User interface

DISCUSSION QUESTIONS

1. What are human factors? What is ergonomics? What is the relationship between ergonomics and workplace performance?
2. At some time, every software user has had a problem that better software ergonomics could have addressed. Offer examples from your own experiences.
3. Compare and contrast the six types of software interfaces discussed in this chapter. In which situations is each interface most useful/desirable?
4. What steps can be taken to ensure that users understand how an interface operates?
5. The computer monitor frequently is accused of causing eyestrain and fatigue. Why? What are some solutions?
6. You have shopped for a new PC and have limited your choice to models offered by two vendors. The major difference in the hardware configuration, it appears, is the keyboard. Compile the list of criteria you would use in comparing keyboards.

7. Differentiate between glare and reflection. Offer solutions for each problem.
8. Discuss the social and psychological considerations important to workstation design. Have you seen evidence of these considerations? Describe your experiences.
9. Many states and cities are passing legislation and statutes regulating the office environment. Discuss the pros and cons of such laws.

APPLICATION EXERCISES

1. Examine the work space of an individual who works with a computer and then interview the individual to determine what they do and the person's major concerns with the workplace. Redesign the work area so that it is more ergonomic. Prepare both a minimalist ($300) and an ultimate (money-is-no-problem) solution. (Note: For a collection of ergonomic solutions, you might want to visit the Web site of Keyboard Alternatives and Vision Solutions, Inc. at *www.keyalt.com.*)
2. Visit a showroom where LCDs are displayed and compare them. Then write a short report, using the vocabulary in this chapter, describing and comparing them.
3. Compare the user interface of several popular software packages. Why do some packages on the market today include several options for the user?
4. Use the Internet and your library to prepare a report on U.S. legislation relative to computer safety.

SUGGESTED READINGS

Grandjean, Etienne. *Ergonomic Design for Organizational Effectiveness.* (Boca Raton, FL: CRC Press, Inc., 1998).

MacLeod, Dan F. *The Office Ergonomics Tool Kit with Power-Point Disc* (Book + Disk). (Boca Raton, FL: Lewis Publishers, 1998).

O'Neill, Michael. *Ergonomic Design for Organizational Effectiveness.* (Boca Raton, FL: CRC Press, Inc., 1998).

Salvendy, Gavriel. *Handbook of Human Factors and Ergonomics.* (New York: John Wiley & Sons, Inc., 1997).

USEFUL WEBSITES

Keyboard Alternatives & Vision Solutions Ergonomic Resource Catalog. http://222.keyalt.com. (Note: Perspectives on workstation design and ergonomic tools are included in this comprehensive catalog of products.)

The Occupational Safety and Health Administration of the U.S. Department of Labor. *www.osha.gov.* The site

includes information on events sponsored by the administration and news releases regarding ergonomic studies and legislation.

www.usernomics.com is a portal for locating information on human factors and ergonomics.

ENDNOTES

1. Encyclopedia Britannica, s.v. "Human Factors Engineering."
2. Roger C. Schank and Peter G. Childers, The Cognitive Computer, (Reading, MA: Addison-Wesley, 1984).
3. Kimberly Patch and Eric Smalley, "Speech Recognition Makes Some Noise," Infoworld 20 (1998), 69-74.
4. Ibid.
5. Jon Simkovitz, Solutions for Humans: Ergonomics Research Catalog (Santa Rosa, CA: Keyboard Alternatives and Vision Solutions, Inc., 2000).
6. Henry Norr, "Thin Is In for Monitors / Sleek Flat Panel Displays Replacing Clunky Terminals," San Francisco Chronicle (15 September 1998), D3.
7. Anne Chambers, "Computer Vision Syndrome: Relief Is in Sight," Occupational Hazards 61 (1999), 179-183.
8. Cheryl Currid, "Using Two Monitors Changes View from the Driver's Seat,"Houston Chronicle (23 July 1999), sec.working@home, 3.
9. Simkovitz, op. cit.

10. "Keyboard Design Is Effective in Decreasing User Pain," IIE Solutions 31, (1999), 14.
11. John Barnes, "Ergonomic Keyboards Make Typing Easier," Computer Dealer News 15 (1999), 29.
12. Peter Wayner, "Vertical Typing Easy On the Wrists," The New York Times (16 December 1999), G12.
13. "Keyboard Design Is Effective."
14. Human Factors Society, American National Standards for Human Factors Engineering of Visual Display Terminal Workstations (ANSI/HFS 100-1900) (1988).
15. Justin T. Scott, "Ergonomics Economics," Office Systems 16 (1999), 39-43.
16. Ibid.
17. Ronald M Baecker and William A. S Buxton, Reading in Human-Computer Interaction: A Multidisciplinary Approach (Los Altos, CA: Morgan Kaufmann Publishers, 1987).
18. Ibid.
19. Elaine Cohen and Aaron Cohen, Planning the Electronic Office (New York: McGraw-Hill, 1983).
20. Stanley Zarowin, "The Perfect Office," Journal of Accountancy 188 (1999), 24-29.

Chapter 11

Organizational Change

Learning Objectives

Upon completing this chapter, you should be able to:

➤ Discuss the relationship between technology and change.

➤ Explain the technology implementer's role as a change agent.

➤ Discuss the characteristics of effective change leaders.

➤ Identify effective strategies for organizational change.

➤ List and discuss important considerations in implementing technological changes.

- Use Lewin's force field analysis to identify forces pushing for and resisting technology.
- Identify major causes of resistance to change in an organization and explain how a manager or EUIS analyst can avoid them.
- Diagnose pressures for and resistance to a planned technological change.
- Discuss the importance of top management support and employee participation in ensuring the success of information technologies.

11.1 INTRODUCTION

> For all the dollars spent by American companies on research and development, there often remains a persistent and troubling gap between the inherent value of the technology they develop and their ability to put it to work effectively. At a time of fierce global competition, the distance between technical promise and genuine achievement is a matter of especially grave concern.[1]
>
> Dorothy Leonard-Barton and William A. Kraus

Implementing information systems (IS) for individuals and for work groups is as much about changing the behavior of end users as it is about the technology itself. Whether technology is used as a catalyst for innovation or to replace existing equipment, successful implementation requires changes in skills, work procedures, business processes, jobs, and even organizational structure. Enterprises cannot effectively implement technologies such as the Internet, Intranets, extranets, group support systems, and knowledge management without drastically changing the way business operates. It takes new business models and new ways of working.

Many important considerations for successful implementation are behavioral rather than technological. End-user computing is, first and foremost, about changing the way people work. Workers must change their behavior to use new technologies effectively, and changes in behavior are not automatic. Thus, it is not sufficient for EUIS analysts to be technical experts; they also must be effective agents of change. Managing the change process is even more important for EUIS analysts than for technical systems analysts who implement transaction processing systems (TPS) or other enterprise systems where workers sometimes have little choice but to use them. With end-user information systems, however, acceptance is largely up to the individual worker.

This chapter summarizes important considerations for managing innovation and change, with an emphasis on implementing information technology at the desktop. First, a brief overview of the need for planned change and the resultant role of the implementer—the analyst or manager—is offered. Then, models from behavioral science that describe the dynamics of change are discussed—in particular Leavitt's systems approach and Lewin's force field analysis. Next, reasons why people resist change and how technology implementers can overcome that resistance are outlined. The chapter ends with practical suggestions for managing the change process.

The introduction of new information technologies implies organizational change. Although the need for change and innovation in organizations is widely recognized, the savvy required to implement organizational change effectively is not.

Change occurs continually in organizations. Many of these changes are unplanned; they occur at random or spontaneously. Unplanned changes may be disruptive, such as a strike, or beneficial, such as a machine breakdown that leads to a good idea for new procedures. Such unplanned changes constantly take place in personnel, work methods, routine office procedures, the locations of desks or machines, and many other day-to-day activities. Many of these changes seem small when taken individually, but in total they add up to much of the improvement and progress of the organization.

Changes on a much larger scale, which were the exception prior to the 1960s, now occur more and more frequently. In *Megatrends 2000,* Naisbitt and Aburdene explained that "in the decade of the 1990's we are moving from managing control to leadership of accelerated change."[2] Whereas in the past change was viewed as an evolutionary process, today change often verges on the revolutionary. Change strategies must be planned.

Planned organizational change, which is the intentional attempt by an enterprise to alter the status quo, refers to a set of activities designed to alter the behavior or job tasks of individuals, groups, or the entire organization. Planned changes may be reactive or proactive. Changes include major technological changes as well as sweeping organizational changes that affect many divisions and levels at once.

Planned change has a technical and a social aspect. The technical aspect of change refers to modification of physical routines. The social aspect refers to the way those affected by change think it will alter their relationships in the organization. Research indicates that the social aspects of change play a greater role than the technical aspects in determining the extent to which changes are accepted or rejected.

Because of the complex interrelationships between variables, it is easy for even the most carefully conceived plans to produce unanticipated consequences. Some changes are implemented smoothly while others raise havoc. Resistance is as likely to arise for small changes as for large ones. To dismiss resistance with the cliche that "people resist change" is shortsighted. The key to managing change is understanding its dynamics and the true nature of resistance.

Whether change is a threat or an opportunity depends upon how one views it at the time. Managing organizational change involves understanding the variables and their interdependencies; creating a climate for learning; recognizing new power distributions; and handling complexity, ambiguity, and uncertainty. These and other important aspects of change are discussed in ensuing sections.

11.2.1   Successful and Unsuccessful Change

What is successful change? How do we know when change is successful or unsuccessful?

Planned organizational changes seldom fail completely, but on the other hand, few succeed entirely. Most changes take longer and cost more than expected. Change sometimes exacts a heavy toll on employee morale and managerial time and emotion. Sometimes plans are abandoned because of strong employee resistance

SOFTWARE AS SOCIALWARE

How do we manage change? Let's face it, we don't, says Thomas H. Davenport, professor and director of the Information Management Program at the University of Texas at Austin. There might be a bit of training, a few interviews, at best a checklist of organizational change issues. However, it's not taken seriously. It's nobody's job to deal with these issues, and for decades now we have allowed project managers and systems analysts to say, "It's not my fault; the system did what it was supposed to do." As a result, most systems don't succeed in delivering the intended business value. A recent study suggests that 90 percent of business-critical systems projects fail. I suspect that the success rate for groupware projects is even lower. Take Notes, for example. In talking informally with numerous organizations, I have yet to find one that believes that Notes transformed how groups worked.

What would we do if we were to get serious about changing the information behaviors of individuals and groups? Like most things in life, this won't happen until somebody is supposed to do it. The responsibility must be assigned for making change happen or at least for making it more likely. Also, like most things, this idea isn't brand new; it goes back to the "sociotechnical" approach in the 1950s.

One alternative is that organizational change could be added to the responsibilities of systems developers. However, systems development is a pretty tough business these days, even without forcing developers to be responsible for social and behavioral engineering. Can we really expect a programmer to learn organizational change readiness diagnosis at the same time we expect mastery of object orientation, client/server, and Java?

No, I think we need specialists in this field. We could call them social systems analysts (SSA). They would have to be able to communicate with technologists, but they would have to be changemeisters first and foremost. On large systems, plenty of activities could keep an SSA busy full-time; smaller systems could benefit from a fraction of a social analyst's time. The widespread use of SSAs on systems projects also could be a way to institutionalize reengineering or at least process improvement.

TASKS FOR THE SOCIAL SYSTEMS ANALYST

- Shadow managers and workers to determine actual information needs and likely usage of planning systems.
- Participate in system design to fit the system to the organizational structure, culture, and behavior.
- Facilitate user participation in the design activity in order to improve the system and acquire user buy-in.
- Assess current work processes and create new ones.
- Plan the implementation and rollout, including education and training.
- Observe the new system in use and make changes

Source: Adapted from Thomas H. Davenport, "Think Tank: Software as Socialware," *CIO* (March 1, 1996): 24–26.

or because the managers feel unprepared or unable to implement the changes successfully.

Whether or not a change may be judged successful depends on how well it accomplishes the major objectives. Planned organizational change requires changes in employee behaviors. An organization cannot implement technological changes unless its members learn to use the technology and behave differently in their relationships to one another and to their jobs.

For example, when an automated calendaring and messaging system was introduced in an insurance office, the manager advocated that the 4 project managers, 12 analysts, and secretary use it for scheduling and communicating. The implementer demonstrated the system features for everyone. The manager, implementer, and a few others were enthusiastic; the rest went along and started using the system. After a few weeks, use of the system began to decline, however, and the manager took no action. A few weeks later, when the manager and implementer returned from vacation, the system had fallen into complete disuse. One worker had even deinstalled the software from his PC.

Ultimately, organizations either prosper or fail because of their employees' behaviors—the things their employees do or fail to do. To succeed, changes must be supported by those affected by them. People must be motivated to make the change happen and achieve the intended objectives. The most elegant technological system may fail to improve productivity, whereas a less-than-ideal system may perform beyond expectations with supportive users.

11.2.2 Technology Brings Change

Information systems and digital networks are shaking up the workplace. The changes cross traditional boundaries and upset traditional ways of thinking. The impact of the digital revolution extends far beyond the way people perform tasks; it affects how people organize and communicate. The following example of an office without secretaries is a case in point.

At the six-year-old Software Publication Corporation in California, no one, not even the president, relies on support staff to screen calls, arrange schedules, or type memos. All 115 employees have a personal computer and printer on their desks. A voice mail system handles all telephone messages and an electronic mail system delivers interoffice correspondence.[3]

Organizations must learn to deal with the impact of digital networks on work and management. Peter F. Drucker, a noted management authority, was quoted as follows in the *Wall Street Journal:*

Both factory automation and office automation require changes in job design, in the organization and flow of work and in organizational relationships. . . . To be effective, office automation requires fairly radical changes in work flow, job design, job relations, and staff. . . . The shift to knowledge work as the center of gravity of the workforce will altogether force us to rethink the traditional organizational structure.[4]

Many organizations that have achieved less-than-anticipated performance benefits from technology are looking beyond technology for solutions. Movements such as reengineering, business process redesign, and total quality management have emerged to improve the design of jobs and tasks, the organization of work itself, and the general approach to planning and implementing technological change.[5] Historically, technology always has brought change. More precisely, technology always has been a means through which people have been able to implement change. Organizations must learn to coordinate technology, business processes, organizational structure, and business planning to manage change. The EUIS analyst must assume a major burden of responsibility for change, along with managers.

11.2.3 The Technology Implementer as Change Agent

A *change agent* is an individual or team responsible for designing and introducing a change—usually new technologies in the case of EUIS analysts. The change agent plays an important role as a champion who promotes and shepherds new ideas into action. A change agent must translate the vision of how things could or should be into step-by-step plans for achieving the envisioned goals.

The change agent may be an outsider, such as a consultant, or someone from within the organization with an outsider's perspective, such as a new manager, an employee with ideas, a training or organizational development specialist, or a systems analyst. It is often difficult for someone who is familiar with existing operations (an insider) to break out of the bounds of an organization's culture, politics, and traditions. To change, an organization usually relies on someone with a fresh perspective—someone with a vision of how things could be.

As change agents, analysts must work closely with others in the organization. Seldom are analysts in a position to make all the decisions or command all the resources to implement new systems. Neither analysts nor managers are likely to have direct control over all the organizational dimensions that are important to successful implementation of a new system. Some organizational dimensions are subject to more direct managerial control and change than others. EUIS analysts, however, must understand why changes do or do not occur in the desired directions.

When new systems do not meet expectations, failures seldom can be attributed to technical inadequacies. Failures generally result when EUIS analysts neglect to consider the impact of new systems on people and the organization. Thus, it is important for the analyst to understand the role of a change agent and the change process. The systems analyst who understands the dynamics of change can be a powerful catalyst for helping managers achieve technological changes.

11.2.4 Important Considerations in Technological Change

Several considerations affect the success of technological change, including the following.

1. *The ability of employees to conceptualize change.* Some people find it difficult to conceptualize—or envision—change on an organizational or even a departmental level. If the planned change is complex or difficult to comprehend, the problem will be even more acute. When people have a problem conceptualizing change, they tend to become preoccupied with methods and means rather than ends.
2. *Employees' readiness for change.* An individual's readiness for change has to do with preparedness to entertain differences, ambiguity, and uncertainty. Employees must be ready intellectually and emotionally.
3. *Employees' capacity for change.* Some individuals have a higher tolerance for change and uncertainty than others.
4. *Individual differences among users.* Individual differences in learning styles will determine to some extent the effectiveness of information about a change. The three basic learning styles are cognitive, behavioral, and affective. Individuals are not necessarily limited to just one learning style, but there are combinations that each prefers. The individual with a cognitive learning style responds to a logical presentation—what changes are planned, how, and why—but might become frustrated with experiential exercises to create readiness for change (behavioral). For an affective learner, an exercise where participants brainstorm how they anticipate a target group will feel about a planned change may be especially helpful.
5. *Environmental uncertainty and complexity.* When the environment is stable and predictable, people are reluctant to change. When it becomes uncertain and confusing, however, people accept change more readily as they strive to stabilize the situation. If uncertainty and complexity become too great though, learning can be impeded.

6. *Change itself.* Change is always more difficult than it appears. The greater the number of people and departments that are involved, the more complex and harder it will be to implement the change.

7. *Organizational structure.* Organizational structure and corporate culture affect the introduction of new ideas. Structure defines jobs, lines of authority, responsibility, and accountability and controls the flow of information. *Spotlight on Solutions:* Structural Cybernetics gives some examples of the relationship between organizational structure and corporate culture. Understanding the impact that culture has on decision making and adversity (or propensity) to change can help the implementer plan strategies that will better ensure adoption of a new technology. For example, the emphasis on hierarchy or authority in organizations with traditional structure encourages employees to take minimal risk in changing the status quo. However, within a more participative culture, users are much more likely to assume the risk if the technology's value (or value added) can be demonstrated.

8. *The distribution of power.* Novel ideas and uses of resources can upset the power relationships in an organization. People may perceive changes as a threat to their power and influence. Power in most organizations is achieved by access to vital information or resources, and the politically astute manager often controls others by manipulating this access. Even when new ideas are in the organization's best interest, they may never be implemented if they threaten the existing power structure. The power of the initiator of change in relation to the power of individuals who are affected by the change will influence the type of strategies that will be effective.

9. *The experience of the change agent.* The amount of time and effort required to introduce changes depends on the knowledge and experience of the change

SPOTLIGHT ON SOLUTIONS → Technology, People, Structure, Processes

---

STRUCTURAL CYBERNETICS

N. Dean Meyer and Associates (Ridgefield, Connecticut) has researched the impact of corporate culture on change strategies. Following are Meyer's definitions and findings.[6]

Traditional Culture: Vertical structure (top-down decision making). Large organizational groupings (usually departments) structured around functions. Communications are up and down. The central staff is powerful. Decisions are made high in the organization. *Reluctant to recognize the need for change.* Changes are made slowly. There is active resistance to change.

Consensus-Driven Culture: Wide rather than vertical (tall) structure. Decisions are made by consensus of middle managers. Staff groups are large but do not carry as much authority as line management does. A matrix organization is common.

Innovations are assigned to task forces or committees. New ideas can get lost in the bureaucracy. Risk taking is limited to senior management and committees.

Profit-Center Culture: Cluster structure—small, autonomous modules with clearly stated goals. Small central staff. If the innovation is not related to business goals, they reject it, even if the return on investment is good. *Overall, favorable toward innovations*—payoffs of success are high. Payoffs could include profits and/or promotions.

Futurist Culture: Small, flat, and fluid structure. Characterized by a charismatic executive and organized around a mission or new idea. Decision making is made at the lowest possible level. *Positive toward innovations, but few are implemented successfully; employees have their own pet projects.* These are leading edge, creative organizations.

Source: Copyright 1996, NDMA Inc. Reproduced by permission.

agent. In some instances, the change agent may be the expert who orchestrates the change. Under other circumstances, the change agent assumes the role of adviser who directs the efforts of the experts responsible for implementing the change.

10. *The risks involved.* The greater the threat is to organizational performance and survival if the situation is not changed, the greater the pressure will be to make changes arbitrarily and quickly. The more people that are involved in a change effort, the longer the implementation will take.

11. *Required resources.* The implementation of most changes requires budget dollars and staff resources. Even though an enterprise wants to implement change, plans may have to be compromised, postponed, or scrapped because of insufficient resources. For example, four departments may submit automation proposals for budget approval, but executives may approve funding for only two, or they may approve all four at a level below the estimated costs, forcing cuts in plans.

These are only some of the considerations that may affect the success or failure of technological changes. Clearly, some rationale for understanding the dynamics of change in organizations is needed to develop strategies for effective implementation.

11.3 MODELING THE DYNAMICS OF CHANGE

Analysts often have difficulty understanding situations that involve change. Anticipating how individuals may react to a new knowledge management system, for example, is difficult. Theorists offer various explanations that can help analysts visualize how a proposed system might impact a group of employees and what steps need to be taken to gain their support. This section begins with Leavitt's systems model for change and then presents two theories proposed by sociologist Kurt Lewin for analyzing the dynamics of change. These two models serve as the basis for EUIS Project Management introduced in chapter 14.

11.3.1 Leavitt's Systems Model of Change

The systems model of change, sometimes referred to as the "Leavitt Diamond," identifies four interacting variables that must be considered when planning change in an organization: people, structure, process (tasks), and technology.[7] Although this text focuses on technological change, any of the four variables may serve as the primary focus for change efforts.

As illustrated in Figure 11-1, these four variables are highly interdependent. By knowing that changes in technology will result in changes in structure, process, and people, the implementer may be able to counter resistance or other problems that could jeopardize the anticipated benefits. Leavitt's systems model of change provides a framework for understanding these interrelationships. Each of these variables, as related to technology implementation, is discussed here.

Technological variables refer to the tools and methods used to accomplish work and solve problems. The systems implementer is interested primarily in applying computer and networking technologies for processing work and distributing information. What technology should be selected and how should it be used? Other

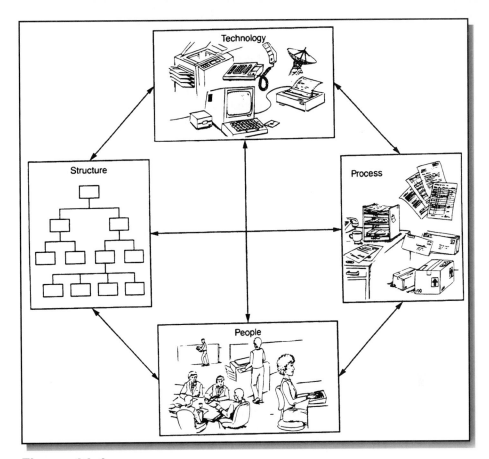

Figure 11-1
A systems model of change: The interrelationship of variables

Source: James March, Stanford University. School of Education, Palo Alto (used with permission).

variables are related to the technology itself. How easy is it to use and how does it support work processes?

Structural variables refer to the system of responsibility, authority, and communication within an organization. These variables determine how work units are organized, how groups relate to each other, and who reports to whom. Structure also determines how decisions are made, how leadership is characterized, and how communications are handled. Each organization has its own structure, which reflects its management style, corporate culture, and power relationships. New technology may alter role responsibilities, reporting relationships, span of control, hierarchical levels, and decision-making authority. Experience demonstrates, for example, that when electronic mail and message systems are introduced, communication patterns change.

Process (task) variables relate to the business processes that are performed in the work unit. Are the tasks simple or complex, repetitive or varied, standardized or unique? Some tasks (such as stuffing envelopes) are highly standardized, simple, and repetitive. Other tasks (such as designing a new mailer envelope) are creative and complex. The way that tasks are combined into business processes determines how independent, interdependent, or dependent relations among departments are in an organization. Business processes directly affect the efficiency and effectiveness with which business results are achieved.

Strategies for changing process variables focus on jobs performed by workers. When new technologies are introduced, the nature of tasks usually changes. Thus, in practice, it is difficult to make technological changes without also making task changes that affect job design. Some tasks may be eliminated, new ones added, others modified, and responsibilities shifted. Strategies for redesigning white-collar jobs are discussed in detail in chapter 12, "Business Process and Job (Re)Design."

People variables refer to competencies, values, attitudes, skills, performance, and motivations that individuals bring to their jobs. People are an organization's most valuable resource for accomplishing business goals, as well as the major force pressing for or resisting changes. New technologies may affect the number of people and kinds of competencies needed to perform the work of the unit, reward systems, working relationships with peers and supervisors, and job satisfaction. Changes also may upset the way individuals meet personal and professional needs. Valued employees suddenly may feel inadequate when skills and experience acquired through years of dependable service are rendered obsolete by new technologies.

Analyzing the dynamics of planned technological change efforts can become complex because of the large number of variables involved. Building on the systems model of change, noted social psychologist Kurt Lewin developed methods to conceptualize change. His widely applied theories of force field analysis and change stages can be useful for technology implementers.

11.3.2   Lewin's Force Field Analysis

According to Kurt Lewin, any problem situation can be understood better by using this metaphor: *a sea of forces in motion.* Some forces are negative; some are positive. These forces are in constant motion, and their pressures and counterpressures produce a situation of stability at any one point in time. *Force field analysis* envisions change as a dynamic process rather than as an event. The existing situation can be considered a state of equilibrium, resulting from a balance of these forces pushing against each other. According to Lewin, organizations are pressured by various internal and external forces.

Driving forces encourage change, growth, and development, whereas *restraining forces* resist change and encourage stability and the status quo. The framework of the model in Figure 11-2 shows the organization in terms of a force field analysis of the four variables (people, structure, process, and technology) of the systems model of change.[8]

Figure 11-2
Force field analysis

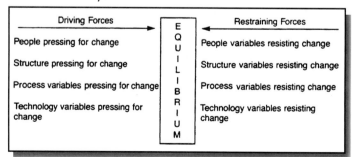

Part IV   Workplace Performance: The Impact of Information Technology

To illustrate Lewin's force field analysis model, we will consider an example of implementing an Intranet into an accounting department. A force field analysis of an accounting department is shown in Figure 11-3.

The change agent can use *force field analysis* to help identify the relevant positive and negative forces related to the introduction of the new technology. By identifying relevant factors, change agents can understand which factors they can influence and which they cannot. To implement a new technology, the change agent must modify the equilibrium of forces by increasing pressures for change, reducing resistance to change, or altering the direction of a force (turn a resistance into a pressure for change).

The natural tendency is to increase the pressures for change. However, it is often preferable to reduce the restraining forces rather than increase the driving forces. This is because increasing driving forces without decreasing the restraining forces can stimulate new forces resisting change or create excessive stress—like blowing up a balloon until it pops. In other words, implementers must be sensitive to the pressures for and against change and how they interact. Otherwise, unanticipated problems or outcomes may result when implementing a project, or employees may revert to former practices as soon as driving pressures are relaxed. *The most effective way to make technological changes is to identify possible forces of resistance and reduce or eliminate as many as possible.* After an action plan has been formulated, the implementer is ready to proceed.

11.3.3 Lewin's Three Phases of Change

Implementing planned organizational changes is essentially a learning process through which people modify their behaviors. An important part of Lewin's theory suggests a three-step process for guiding and managing change: unfreezing, changing, and refreezing. These phases represent a learning curve similar to the one depicted in Figure 11-4.

Unfreezing is the process of building support for change and creating readiness for learning. It involves creating an awareness of the need to change, challenging previous beliefs or practices, removing barriers to change, and emphasizing the benefits of change. *Changing,* the second phase, is the period when learning occurs

Figure 11-3
Force field analysis of an accounting department

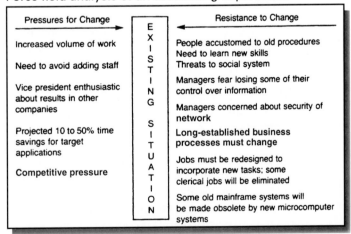

Source: Organizational Development: Values, Process and Technology p.211, 1972. Reprinted with permission of the McGraw-Hill Companies.

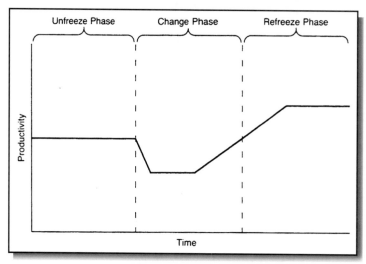

Figure 11-4
The learning curve for introducing information technologies

and attitudes are changed. It involves the search for new information or learning new skills. It moves people toward new behavior patterns. This is the phase in which individuals acquire the skills to use new systems, adopt new procedures, and change work flows and working relationships to meet goals. *Refreezing* consolidates new behaviors after they have been tried and confirmed. The refreezing phase ends when new business processes have been fully established and new behaviors are integrated into the organizational norms.

Building on the previous force field analysis of an accounting office introducing an Intranet (Figure 11-3), following is an example of how resistance and pressures were addressed with an understanding of Lewin's three phases of change.

Unfreeze phase. To introduce the project to the accounting staff, the manager discusses the difficulties of meeting monthly and year-end deadlines for filing reports and the amount of overtime required to get the job done. No additional staff positions are approved for the current year, and everyone agrees that working overtime has become a burden. The manager talks about some ideas for restructuring the department work flow that she has learned from peers at professional meetings and read about in accounting journals. She encourages other staff to share what they have heard or read, pro and con. She summarizes some of the potential benefits to the department from the Intranet, then proposes that the department work with an analyst to identify applications and alternative solutions. She invites the staff's ideas and suggestions during the process.

Change phase. After discussing the project with the manager, the analyst arranges demonstrations of solutions implemented by other companies. The analyst explains that the demonstrations are intended to start people thinking about possible applications in their own areas. The analyst works with the department to identify required reports, the major steps in their preparation, where their data come from, and where they should be sent when completed. Working closely with the manager and staff, he develops work flow diagrams. During the 2-month analysis, several staff members make suggestions, work groups discuss the ideas and make recommendations, and several suggestions, including one to consolidate two work teams and eliminate some intermediary reports, are included in the final recommendation. The project is implemented according to plan. The department starts by focusing on six initial solutions; staff attend training classes and then begin to set up the less complicated reports. The manager brings in temporary help to free staff time for learning and applying their new skills. Proposed changes are implemented in phases as staff acquire more skills, ending with the consolidation of the two work teams.

Refreeze phase. Staff are encouraged to develop their PC skills and are given release time to attend advanced training sessions. Six additional solutions are implemented. Some suggestions are revised as they are implemented, and one suggestion is scrapped. Several new ideas evolve. At year end, all reports are produced on time, with only 20 percent of the overtime required the previous year.

11.4   UNDERSTANDING RESISTANCE TO CHANGE

Before analysts can develop a plan for implementing a project, it is essential that they understand the sources and reasons for resistance to change. An organization's objective for implementing changes is generally to become more effective or to reduce costs. The individuals affected by the changes, however, often view change from another perspective: how the changes will impact their individual jobs.

Resistance may manifest itself subtly, as indifference, excuses, complaints about related matters, absenteeism, or tardiness. Often, resistance is more overt, such as reduction in output, outright complaints and objections, resignations or transfers, chronic quarrels, hostility, work slowdowns, or strikes.

The successful change agent needs to recognize these symptoms and determine why individuals are resisting. Following is a list of reasons why individuals sometimes resist planned changes. The list is followed by approaches planners can use to overcome resistance. When legitimate concerns that underlie worker resistance are understood, planners can address the concerns directly to build confidence in the technology and gain worker support.

11.4.1   Reasons for Resistance to Technological Innovations

People resist new systems because of poor system design, because it interferes with the way they work, or because of their own internal factors. Chapter 10, "Human Factors: Software, Hardware, and Workplace Design," discussed the need for well-designed systems; systems that are not user friendly typically are not well accepted. Systems that fail typically do not fail for technical reasons. Ten of the most important concerns related to how a system becomes part of work and how individuals react to the system are addressed here.

Social Uncertainty. Often, employees do not resist technological change as much as the social changes that it brings. People need to interact with others at work. When changes disrupt social patterns or isolate employees, employees resist. For example, when one company upgraded clerical workstations with new, ergonomically designed furniture that doubled the work space and provided privacy and features that almost matched those of professional workers, some clerical employees complained. Space design personnel were dismayed. The nature of the complaints revealed that the clerical employees were accustomed to sitting in clustered work groups, which allowed them to chat as they worked. The chatter broke up the monotony of their routine. The new furniture incorporated high, soundproof panels that isolated the employees physically and visually. The boredom of their tasks soon got on their nerves.

New technologies can disrupt close working relationships, such as that between a secretary and a manager. Technology also might decrease workers' autonomy. For example, when changes in work procedures require close supervision or training to master new skills, highly proficient workers, who normally require little direct supervision, may react negatively to their loss of independence, even if it is only temporary.

Limited Perspectives. Once people develop a mindset, they tend to respond to ideas and suggestions within that framework. They selectively attend to and retain information that reinforces their attitudes and ignore or downplay information that, if perceived, would be incongruent with their perceptions and behavior. For example, managers enrolled in executive training programs may be exposed to various approaches for redesigning jobs to capitalize on digital networks to empower workers and facilitate work group collaboration. Although they may adeptly discuss such approaches in class, in their minds they may screen out approaches that are inconsistent with their own management styles, which may be directive rather than collaborative. They may dismiss such approaches as good ideas for some other department but not applicable to their own.

Lack of Understanding. Workers are likely to resist change when they do not understand its purpose. Workers—especially those on the lower levels of the organization, who are least involved in planning changes—often do not receive the details of the project, why changes are necessary, and what the objectives are. Worse yet, they may receive much of the detail through rumors, which tend to distort facts. Under these circumstances, it is likely that distrust will build. This distrust, sometimes labeled *fear of technology* or *resistance to change,* can be avoided if users are meaningfully involved, if rumors are settled early, if training is provided throughout the project (not simply tacked on at the end), and if credibility is built by project leaders.

Threats to Power and Influence. When individuals perceive that new technologies or procedures may reduce their power or influence, they are likely to resist their implementation. As Web-based technologies are used to improve access to information, for instance, individuals who formerly served in gatekeeper roles may resist the perceived loss in power and influence.

Resistance to Technical Personnel. Most technical specialists are outsiders as far as the organization is concerned. Specialists may have certain blind spots and faulty attitudes because of preoccupation with the technical aspects of new ideas. Change agents must demonstrate that theirs is a facilitative role, rather than purely technical. If the change agent builds credibility, it becomes possible to work cooperatively to achieve mutually agreed-upon goals and resolve problems.

Perception That Costs Outweigh Benefits. Employees will accept change more readily when benefits clearly offset the costs of change. In the eyes of users, costs are measured not in dollars but in terms of the time and effort required to learn new systems, the pressures of initial loss in productivity, frustrations in working out the glitches of a new system, and many other concerns discussed in this section. Cost savings and productivity increases are benefits to management, but what are the benefits to the employees? Will they receive a raise? Recognition? Grade-level increase? Increased responsibility? Better opportunity for advancement? Improved working environment? Do they see the potential benefits?

For example, in a series of studies on the failure of electronic calendaring, Jonathan Grudin found that one reason calendaring was not successful was the disparity between those who benefited from the tool and those who had to do additional work to support it. Not only did users (managers) not want to learn how to use the system, they found that its benefits did not offset the time and effort involved in actually scheduling their own calendars. Users reported that secretaries could perform the same task more quickly and with less work required by the manager.[9]

Fear of Failure or Inadequacy. Workers frequently have spent years developing their business competencies. When new systems threaten to make these competencies obsolete, workers are likely to resist. Rather than welcome the opportunity to learn new skills, they may fear that they will be unable to cope. Suddenly, the skills that have provided job security are no longer sufficient. Instead, workers are faced with the need to learn new skills and procedures and to establish new working relationships.

Moreover, many workers still find computers intimidating and frustrating. Until recently, these magical machines have been protected behind the locked doors of computer centers and attended by technical wizards. When workers suddenly are confronted with computers on their desktops and their jobs depend on using them, they may wonder if they are capable of learning to use them, or fear they will cause disaster if they push the wrong button. Many people feel inadequate when faced with simple technologies, let alone a computer. From the perspective of the intimidated worker, the computer creates problems rather than solving them.

Loss of Control. Sometimes people perceive computers as devices that control their behavior rather than as machines that they control. Thus, computers are seen as a threat to their autonomy. When correspondence is sent via electronic mail or when voice messages are stored centrally, users sometimes perceive that their work is being monitored. This idea that Big Brother is watching may give workers a sense of powerlessness. In extreme cases, they sometimes develop pathological symptoms such as anxiety, depression, or even violence.

Feelings of Insecurity. People often become anxious when faced with a new situation, whether the change is seen as good or bad. Anxiety stems from unknown factors that may require new responses. Rules, policies, and procedures frequently become habits, and people rely on them for guidance and protection. These habits provide a feeling of security. Habits also promote productivity when they allow workers to attend to routine chores without having to think about them or make decisions about what or how to do things. Change not only disrupts the security of work habits but may temporarily reduce productivity, as well.

Threat of Economic Loss. Any change that threatens to eliminate jobs or decrease work hours usually meets with resistance. Even promises to provide retraining may not reduce the concern. Changes that affect career ladders and promotional opportunities may likewise meet with resistance.

11.4.2   Overcoming Resistance to Change

With potential resistance to planned changes identified, the change agent can plan appropriate strategies to reduce or avoid resistance. People are key. Individuals react differently to change. Determining which strategy or combination of strategies is most appropriate depends on the type of change, the time involved, situational factors, type of resistance anticipated, and sources of resistance. The strategies that change agents select for implementing changes also may depend somewhat on their management styles. The following strategies can be used to overcome resistance to change:[10]

Education and Communication. Employees should be informed about changes before they are introduced. Education can reduce resistance by helping people understand the need for and the logic of a change. Education can involve one-on-one discussions, presentations to groups, and memos or reports. Videotapes or broadcast voice mail messages also can be effective. Education and communication are especially appropriate when resistance is based on inadequate or inaccurate information. It is important for employees to be well-informed when their help is needed to implement changes. An effective educational program requires time and effort. If the change agent and resisters do not have a good working relationship, it is unlikely that resisters will believe what they hear. When new skills must be learned, adequate training and support are important. Education should start early and continue throughout a project. Implementers should not tack on education at the end of the project.

Participation and Involvement. When people are involved in designing and implementing changes, they are more likely to feel committed to making the changes work. Participation can generate new ideas and alternatives not considered by designers. Participation has its limitations, however. If the process is not managed carefully, employees may feel resentful when all their ideas cannot be implemented. Participation does not lend itself to problems that require quick solutions.

Facilitation and Support. Managers or change agents can help reduce resistance by being supportive. They can listen to concerns, provide emotional support, give employees time off after a demanding period, and provide training in new skills. Facilitation and support are especially helpful for overcoming fear and anxiety. It is all too easy for managers to overlook these causes of resistance or to dismiss them as silly or irrelevant.

Negotiation and Agreement. Another way to reduce resistance may be incentives to employees for compliance with the change. For example, management might give employees higher wage rates in return for work procedure changes. Negotiation is especially appropriate when it is clear that one group is going to lose out because of a change. Negotiations usually are required when new technologies create changes in work procedures for union workers.

Manipulation and Co-Optation. In some cases, especially if changes are urgent or other methods have not worked, change agents may resort to manipulation or co-optation. They may control selectively who gets information, present only information that is favorable to a change, or create a false sense of urgency. Another technique is giving an individual a favorable role in design and implementation to gain his or her influence (co-optation). The problem is that managers or change agents risk their credibility when they resort to manipulating people.

Explicit and Implicit Coercion. Finally, if managers have sufficient power, they may resort to forcing people to accept change by threatening them with discharge, poor promotional opportunities, or transfers. Coercion is risky because people resent forced change. Moreover, as soon as coercive pressures are decreased, individuals likely will revert to their former methods or behaviors. If changes must be made quickly, however, a manager may in some cases have little choice but to use coercion. In addition, if changes are going to be unpopular regardless of how they are implemented, an arbitrary decision may be appropriate.

Each of these six strategies for overcoming resistance to change may be especially effective or ineffective in particular situations. Advantages and drawbacks of each strategy in various situations are summarized in Figure 11-5.

Figure 11-5
Advantages and drawbacks of methods for overcoming resistance to change

APPROACH	COMMONLY USED IN SITUATIONS	ADVANTAGES	DRAWBACKS
Education + communication	Where there is a lack of information or inaccurate information and analysis.	Once persuaded, people often will help with the implementation of the change.	Can be time-consuming if lots of people are involved.
Participation + involvement	Where the initiators do not have all the information they need to design the change, and where others have considerable power to resist.	People who participate will be committed to implementing change, and any relevant information they have will be integrated into the change plan.	Can be time-consuming if participators design an inappropriate change.
Facilitation + support	Where people are resisting because of adjustment problems.	No other approach works as well with adjustment problems.	Can be time-consuming, expensive, and still fail.
Negotiation + agreement	Where someone or some group will clearly lose out in a change, and where that group has considerable power to resist.	Sometimes it is a relatively easy way to avoid major resistance.	Can be too expensive in many cases if it alerts others to negotiate for compliance.
Manipulation + co-optation	Where other tactics will not work or are too expensive.	It can be a relatively quick and inexpensive solution to resistance problems.	Can lead to future problems if people feel manipulated.
Explicit + implicit coercion	Where speed is essential and the change initiators possess considerable power.	It is speedy and can overcome any kind of resistance.	Can be risky if it leaves people mad at the initiators.

Source: "Choosing Strategies for change" by John P. Kotter and Leonard A. Schlesinger. March/April *Harvard Business Review,* 1979.

People are vital to the success of information systems projects. Poorly conceived projects that have the support of staff can succeed. By the same token, well-conceived projects that are resisted by employees can, and often do, fail. People can sabotage a project even while overtly seeming to cooperate. The following sections discuss several important considerations for understanding resisters and managing the human dimensions of the change process. Specific strategies for managing the project implementation are detailed in chapter 16.

11.5.1   Ensuring Participation

Participation is frequently recommended as the solution for overcoming resistance to change. Participation is more than asking for opinions or inviting users to take part in discussions. It is a feeling that people's opinions are respected because the people themselves are respected. Participation encourages open, two-way communication and is an effective way to address specific concerns or causes of resistance. Most importantly, participation generally leads to sound solutions with commitment to their success.

In reality, however, participation is not always practical, and pseudoparticipation can be counterproductive. It is important to avoid pseudoparticipation as a guise for collaborative problem solving. True participation requires collaboration and empowerment. Management must be prepared to accept and implement recommended solutions. Therefore, it is critical that senior managers clearly define at the outset the parameters within which participants make decisions and implement solutions.

11.5.2   Providing Incentives

Project leaders must provide incentives that encourage individuals to use new systems and implement new business processes. When incentives are not addressed explicitly, current practices and corporate culture may inadvertently provide disincentives that undermine change efforts by continuing to reward the status quo.

One of the most frequently overlooked areas that must be addressed is the reward system. Corporate cultures provide formal (promotion and compensation programs) and informal (peer recognition, management support, mentoring, and "the way things are done around here") reward structures. Managers must examine carefully these reward structures and make necessary adjustments to align them with planned business results. Otherwise, reward structures will continue to reinforce existing practices and processes despite stated objectives and directives for change.

The change agent can work with peer leaders to ensure their acceptance of new technologies. By identifying and nurturing work-group leaders who demonstrate a capacity to handle change and are adept at learning the technology, the implementer may be able to ensure and/or speed up the technology assimilation process. However, peer leaders who selfishly guard their new-found skills or have little patience for teaching others can be obstacles.

Another incentive is adding mastery of technology as a criterion for job and career advancement. Creative and skilled use of information technologies should be included in formal performance evaluations to ensure that employee efforts are recognized and rewarded.

Yet another incentive could be a measurement and reward system to encourage change. Measurement incentives, however, must be implemented with caution. It is important to avoid creating undue pressure or making people feel that they are constantly under electronic surveillance. Measurement systems that enable employees to monitor their own progress can be effective, especially when directly aligned with benchmarks and goals.

11.5.3 Gaining Management Support

Management support is critical to the acceptance of change. Managers must convey their support through actions as well as words. Subordinates can read between the lines if support is limited to verbal approval rather than changed expectations, actions, and recognition from managers. Many managers underestimate not only the variety of ways people react to change but also the ways they personally can influence individuals and groups during change. By the use of symbolic actions that endorse or promote new technologies or behaviors, for example, managers can make a powerful statement to demonstrate their support for change. Managers also can be effective at staff meetings when change is being discussed by shifting attention from schedules, technical details, work assignments, and so forth to address underlying issues and questions related to resistance and receptiveness to change.

11.5.4 Monitoring Results

The most difficult step in the change process is monitoring results. Because change is complex and comprehensive, it is difficult to isolate specific causes and effects. When changes take place over a period of time, other events also might influence results. Moreover, the process of collecting information about results can bias the findings. Some of the difficulties of measuring results of technological change were discussed in chapter 9.

To measure results, a change project must have clear objectives. Benchmarks with agreed-upon measures must be established at the start of the project. It is not necessary to measure everything. In fact, the simpler things are, the better. It is best to select three or four measures related to critical success factors, core business processes, or customer value. The more directly measures provide feedback on performance, the better they are. It is important that everyone agrees or recognizes the measures as important indicators of success.

Monitoring results is an important element of the refreezing phase of change. It provides information about the costs and benefits of a change, and it offers opportunities to make modifications. Evaluation provides valuable feedback for making adjustments in the systems, methods, work flow, or intervention strategies. Neglecting evaluation (the refreezing phase) can result in changes that are abandoned or incompletely implemented. It is important, therefore, to have ways of verifying that changes have accomplished the intended results.

11.6   SUMMARY

The introduction of new technologies always brings change, and implementing organizational change is a learning process. Managing this process effectively is a critical part of implementing technology for individuals and for work groups.

Some of the variables that affect change include the ability of employees to conceptualize change, readiness for change, individual differences, environmental uncertainty and complexity, the number of people involved, the formal structure, distribution of power, knowledge related to change, and the stakes involved.

Leavitt's systems model of change and Lewin's force field analysis theory can help EUIS analysts understand the forces that affect change in an organization. To be successful, technology implementers must use strategies that create readiness for change (unfreezing); implement the needed modifications in process, structure, people, and technology (changing); and provide reinforcement, support, and modifications as necessary to institutionalize changes (refreezing). Improper refreezing results in changes that are abandoned or incompletely implemented.

Resistance is a frequent by-product of change and may be indicative of problems with the change itself, the change strategy, or the implementation procedures used by the change agent. Sources of resistance often are related more to social issues or the methods of implementing changes than to technical aspects of the change. Sources of resistance include social uncertainty, lack of understanding, resistance to technical personnel, lack of confidence in the project, fear of failure, loss of control, feelings of insecurity, fear of the unknown, or economic reasons.

Change agents commonly employ a number of strategies to avoid or reduce resistance, depending on its source. Strategies include education, participation, facilitation, negotiation, manipulation, and, as a last resort, coercion.

By effectively managing the change process, the implementer can avoid unforeseen problems or consequences when new individual and work group technologies are introduced and can help ensure that technology is used efficiently and effectively.

KEY TERMS

- Change agent
- Driving forces
- Force field analysis
- People variables
- Planned organizational change
- Process (task) variables
- Restraining forces
- Structure variables
- Technology variables

DISCUSSION QUESTIONS

1. Why must the EUIS analyst be a change agent?
2. What impact is the growth of digital networks and Web-based technologies—the Internet, Intranets, extranets—having on the need for change in organizations?
3. "The more things change, the more they stay the same." Discuss this statement in light of the information in this chapter.
4. What differentiates successful from unsuccessful changes? What advice would you offer an analyst in planning for organizational change?
5. Describe the three phases of Lewin's change process. Give an example of this process.
6. List barriers to successful change. Then discuss why it is important for an analyst to be aware of these barriers before beginning a systems implementation.
7. Assume your university is implementing a Web-based registration and grade reporting system. Using Lewin's force field analysis approach, identify pressures and resisters for the system.

8. What incentives might the EUIS analyst use to ensure that workers accept (use) a new information technology? Are there instances when incentives are not useful? Explain.

APPLICATION EXERCISES

1. Locate case studies of successful information technology implementation on the Internet or in journals or trade publications such as *The MIS Quarterly; The Information Technology, Training, and Performance Journal; Knowledge Management Magazine; BusinessWeek; Fortune;* or *CIO.* Using Lewin's phase theory, explain how each system was implemented (unfreeze, change, refreeze).

2. Interview an information systems analyst or consultant to obtain examples of two successful and two unsuccessful (or less successful) technology implementations. Identify factors that led to successful or less-than-successful implementation.

SUGGESTED READINGS

Kanter, Rosabeth Moss. *The Change Masters.* (New York: Simon and Schuster, 1983).

Kotter, John P. *A Force for Change: How Leadership Differs From Management.* (New York: The Free Press, division of Macmillan Publishing, 1990).

Lawrence, Paul R., "How to Deal with Resistance to Change," *Harvard Business Review* (January–February 1969): 4–13.

Meyer, N. Dean. *RoadMap: How to Understand, Diagnose, and Fix Your Organization.* (Ridgefield, Conn: N. Dean Meyer and Associates Inc., 1997).

Meyer, N. Dean. *Structural Cybernetics: An Overview.* (Ridgefield, Conn: N. Dean Meyer and Associates Inc., 1995).

Miles, Robert H. *Leading Corporate Transformation: The Blueprint for Business Renewal.* (San Francisco: Jossey-Bass Publishers, 1997).

ENDNOTES

1. Leonard-Barton, Dorothy, and William A. Kraus, "Implementing New Technology," *Harvard Business Review* (November-December 1985): 102.

2. Naisbitt, John, and Patricia Aburdene. *Megatrends 2000.* (New York: William Morrow and Company, 1990), 239.

3. Rodgers, Louise, and Roxane Farmanfarmaian, "Technology Shakes Up the Organization (for Better or Worse)," *Working Woman* (November 1986): 100.

4. "Goodbye to the Old Personnel Department," *Wall Street Journal,* 22 May 1986, 30.

5. Burch, John L., "Ergonomics of Management Will Inherit the Energy of VDT Health and Safety Movement," *Report and Catalogue* (Summer 1986): 3.

6. Meyer, N. Dean, and Associates. *GamePlan,* Microcomputer-Based Simulation and Guidebook and *Structural Cybernetics: An Overview.* (Ridgefield, Conn.: N. Dean Meyer and Associates Inc., 1992, 1995).

7. Leavitt, H. "Applied Organizational Change in Industry: A Structural, Technological, and Humanistic Approach," in *Handbook of Organizations.* Edited by J. March. (Chicago: Rand-McNally, 1965), 1144–1170.

8. Lewin, Kurt, "Quasi-Stationary Social Equilibria and the Problems of Permanent Change," in *Organizational Development: Values, Process, and Technology.* Edited by N. Margulies and A. P. Raia (New York: McGraw-Hill, 1972), 65–72.

9. Grudin, Jonathan, "Why CSCW Applications Fail: Problems in the Design and Evaluation of Organizational Interfaces," *Proceedings of the Conference on Computer-Supported Cooperative Work* (New York: The Association for Computing Machinery 1988): 85–93.

10. Kotter, John P., and Leonard A. Schlesinger, "Choosing Strategies for Change," *Harvard Business Review* (March-April, 1979): 109–112.

Case Study   ASPs—Applications on the Web

An application service provider (ASP) is a type of computer business that offers outsourcing with an Internet twist. An ASP hosts software applications, which its customers access over the Web instead of running them on their own computers. ASPs aim to save their customers the costs and hassle of owning and managing technology by renting to them whatever software they need, rather than wrestling with a new upgrade.

In the early years of business computing, outsourcing was known as time-sharing. Expensive and complex mainframe computers were beyond the reach of all but the largest corporations. Consequently, many businesses shared the processor time of an off-site mainframe that was managed by a third party. This time-sharing, or bureau, service typically rented the mainframe for relatively easy-to-manage tasks, such as payroll processing or receivables billing. Mainframes were used mostly for number-intensive data processing rather than for managing complete applications. When affordable minicomputers and personal computers arrived on the scene, demand for time-sharing dropped, and many processing tasks were brought in-house.

ASPs range from simple, free e-mail services to complex custom applications. Here's how it works. The application (for example, a word processor) resides on the ASP's Web site. Customers sign up for an account with the ASP and receive a user name and password. Whenever customers need to use the word processor, they access it from the ASP's site through a Web browser, enter their user name and password, and type away, saving documents either to the ASP's server or the PC's hard drive. Depending on the terms of the customer's account, they are billed either a flat fee or on a per-use basis (some new entrants to the ASP market, such as ThinkFree, offer free Web-based applications). Although they're not currently available, Microsoft and Corel are planning online versions of their popular shrink-wrapped suites.

Right now the window for entry in this business is incredibly wide open. Many different kinds of companies are jumping into the ASP industry, including computer hardware and software makers (such as Sun and Microsoft), network service providers (AT&T and Qwest), Internet service providers (UUNet), and newly minted start-ups.

Lost amid the hype is the fact that the ASP sector, with $933 million in revenues last year, is still minuscule compared with the $74 billion software-application market. It is estimated that less than 1 percent of companies are renting their software through ASPs, though that number is projected to grow exponentially as the market swells to $11.3 billion by 2003. What follows is a selection of the variety of ways start-ups are joining the ASP gold rush.

ASP Outsourcing Benefits and Drawbacks

Outsourcing something like an enterprise resource planning (ERP) application to an ASP has many benefits that apply to any type and size of business. The ASP maintains the hardware server "farms" (large facilities of servers) required to host complex applications efficiently and removes the need for companies to buy, maintain, and upgrade in-house hardware. The ASP can make sure that the latest versions of applications are available to enterprisewide users without the need for costly, site-by-site, in-house upgrades. Using an ASP-based ERP system also means that the only client software required on the user's desktop is a Web browser, which eliminates the need to manage client software on a desk-by-desk basis. These three benefits alone could reduce the IS staff needed to manage an in-house ERP system by one or more full-time positions.

IS cost reductions are not the only reason why ASP outsourcing is attractive: ASP customers can sign up new users or work groups for an application at almost a moment's notice without the need for complex infrastructure and implementation resourcing planning. New users can access the application without expensive upgrades to the local technology environment. This means that businesses can get new applications, such as sales force automation or customer relationship management software, up and running faster; can bring on more users or users from remote offices more quickly; and can adapt more easily to merger and acquisition activity. Small businesses and geographically dispersed multinationals alike can capitalize on the benefits of ASPs. The basic pricing model of an outsourced ASP application, which usually includes an initial setup fee plus a monthly rental fee per user, simplifies cash flow management. The fees don't change from month to month because such variables as cost peaks due to upgrades are factored into the cost. Small businesses can afford big-ticket applications that would be too costly to buy outright and implement. In addition, ASP clients don't need to worry about the operating system, database or application user-license fees, and compliance because the ASP bundles all the license fees within the single monthly fee.

However, the ASP outsourcing model has some clear drawbacks. Switching from an internally managed and accessed local or wide area network (LAN or WAN) to the publicly managed and accessible Internet means that access to outsourced applications may be subject to influences beyond your control. For example, heavy Internet traffic may slow application response times, and malicious hackers could get hold of accounting, employee, or customer data. Furthermore, not every application available today has a complete or thoroughly field-tested Web interface—something that could restrict its availability to users. Also, a complex system such as an ERP suite requires considerable time to configure to a company's specific business needs, and integrating an ASP-managed ERP system with complementary in-house systems, such as a customer relationship management system, could prove challenging. Using an ASP doesn't make sense for companies that need to have a packaged application modified extensively for their specific needs. The objective of an ASP is to have every customer using the same code base, not to manage dozens of different customized versions. Because ASPs are in their infancy, service options and expectations are in a state of flux, so prospective users must make sure the ASP offers a clear and comprehensive service-level agreement (SLA).

Who Will Rent?

Actual and projected amounts expected to be spent on ASPs (in millions)

Employees	1999	2000	2001	2002	2003
0 to 99	$316	$649	$1,233	$2,257	$3,850
100 to 999	562	1,188	2,304	4,090	6,623
1,000 to 4,999	44	100	203	370	605
5,000 or More	11	27	63	128	233
Total	$933	$1964	$3,803	$6,845	$11,311

ASPs are new and have yet to be thoroughly tested. Over the next few years, their fate will be decided based upon performance and costs. Some applications will be more suitable than others and will catch on faster. There's a good chance that some combination of ASPs and traditional desktop applications will be adopted.

Case Study Project

You are the IS systems manager for a company that produces heavy-duty machine parts for several corporations including John Deere and Caterpillar. The entire workforce consists of approximately 600 employees. The company has three factories. The factories are located in Louisville, Kentucky; St. Louis, Missouri; and Paris, Tennessee. The Louisville site is the largest site and also maintains the corporate offices. The Louisville site has a staff of approximately 50 users of word processing and spreadsheet software. The St. Louis and Paris, Tennessee, offices have approximately 25 users each who also need these applications. Each user currently has a copy of these applications on his or her desktop. There are varying versions and sites licenses associated with these products. It is predicted that in the near future (1 year), the number of users will increase 20 percent among all sites because of the CEO's desire to expand the company.

As the EUIS systems manager, you have been assigned to put together a committee to make recommendations to the CEO on how best to meet your organization's word processing and spreadsheet needs. The CEO was wondering if ASPs could be an alternative. The CEO realizes that an upgrade in hardware may be necessary but insists that only about one-third of current desktop computers can be replaced each year for the next 3 years.

Make a recommendation to your CEO. Look at different alternatives for software upgrades, such as LANS, Intranet desktop installation, and ASPs. Be sure to consider locations, costs, hardware, software, and present technology in making your recommendation. Would your recommendations change if all operations were located in St. Louis instead of being geographically dispersed?

Source: Adapted from Bianchi, Alessandra, "Upstarts—ASPs Are Coming ASAP," *Inc. Magazine* (April 2000) 61. McKie, Stewart, "Outsourcing with ASPs in the Internet Age," *Business Finance* (November 1999) 67. Ward, Lewis, "How ASPs Can Accelerate Your E-Business," *e-Business Advisor* (March 2000) 20–24.

CASE STUDY ASSIGNMENT

Free ASP applications are available at *www.thinkfree.com*. Visit the site and try the applications from different desktops. Express your opinions and the likelihood that you would use the application.

Chapter 12

Business Process and Job (Re)Design

Learning Objectives

Upon completing this chapter, you should be able to:

➤ Recognize how end-user computing introduces change at the organizational, work group, and individual levels throughout the organization.

➤ Explain why business process redesign is a critical competence for contemporary organizations.

➤ Describe the four basic phases of business process redesign methodology.

➤ Explain the difference between command-and-control management and empowerment.

➤ Describe how to establish boundaries to create empowerment while maintaining appropriate managerial control.

➤ Discuss the need for job (re)design.

➤ Differentiate between task analysis and job analysis.

➤ Identify various approaches to business process and job redesign.

➤ Explain the major characteristics of jobs that motivate workers.

➤ Identify core job dimensions to be considered when designing jobs.

➤ Choose appropriate techniques for redesigning jobs.

➤ Evaluate the way organizations are using technology to redesign jobs.

12.1 INTRODUCTION

As indicated in the previous chapter, implementing end-user information systems (EUIS) is as much about new ways of working as it is about information technology. The unprecedented pressure for change in organizations is being driven by more than technology. Many of the basic principles and assumptions underlying how enterprises organize and operate are changing as well. These changes have a powerful influence on the interrelationship of all four variables of the Systems Change Model: structure, people, process, and technology. Some of the most significant of these shifts are highlighted briefly.

1. *Structure.* One of the most far-reaching changes is a shift from a segmented, functional orientation in thinking about organizational structure to a process-driven, integrated orientation. This shift puts greater focus on satisfying customer needs and requirements, and meeting them at all points in the process of delivering products and services. It challenges industrial era rules regarding organization hierarchy and command-and-control management.

2. *People—both workers and customers.* Individual performance based on stable, defined responsibilities is shifting to a team performance model with greater flexibility to meet the requirements of the organization. Instead of being based on loyalty and obedience in exchange for long-term security, the psychological work contract has shifted to performance-based results in exchange for long-term employability and opportunity. Compensation models have shifted from security and predictability to risk-based models based on individual, team, and organizational performance. Workers in empowered environments have greater responsibility and control within defined boundaries.

   The increasing sophistication of customers, along with other competitive marketplace forces, have simultaneously raised the performance bar not just for today's products and services but in the realization that when a company is standing still, it risks being overtaken and left in the dust. The driving force of the organization shifts from an internal growth and profit-centered focus to an external customer satisfaction focus.

3. *Process.* The orientation for organizing work in the information economy has shifted from an internal focus on tasks and functions to an external focus on core business processes that deliver value for customers. The process view transcends traditional functions and departments and shifts the focus to the work that is actually done and the manner in which this work is performed. It profoundly alters the thinking about how to organize work and how to manage the workforce.

4. *Technology.* Advances in information technology have fundamentally altered established management models. With digital networks that provide instant access to information and knowledge at all levels of the enterprise, some of the traditional middle management roles of gathering, disseminating, and controlling information are no longer needed. The implication of data converted to information, to knowledge, and then to wisdom is just beginning to be realized.

Throughout this text, we emphasize that using information technology effectively involves more than implementing hardware and software. Job design and business process restructuring are key components of EUIS project management. Opportunities for business process and job redesign are assessed in the initial stages of EUIS projects. Depending upon the size, scope, and strategic importance of a project, EUIS analysts may need to address the issue of job and work group design, either alone or in conjunction with broader business process restructuring efforts. Redesigning business processes and jobs is extremely challenging. Major endeavors are not for the fainthearted. The endeavor must be approached in a systematic, structured way. It is important to understand the fundamental principles of business process and job design, as well as the technology.

This chapter considers the impact of technology on the design of business processes and knowledge work. It focuses on new opportunities to create work environments that meet organizational and individual needs in line with changing work values. The chapter begins with a discussion of the larger picture of business process redesign (i.e., reengineering). The discussion then turns to work groups and individual jobs. Several approaches to job and work group design are presented. The chapter concludes with a discussion of methods that take advantage of technology to design motivating and productive work environments.

12.2 BUSINESS PROCESSES, WORK GROUPS, AND JOBS

Technology is both an enabler and a constraint on business process, work group, and job design. System limitations can restrict greatly an enterprise's flexibility to innovate and change business processes. Indeed, many new approaches to managing business process and work tasks depend on the availability of advanced information networks. A long legacy of industrial era thinking about how to design jobs and organize work also acts as a constraint in efforts to change business processes. Work rules, especially when stipulated by union contracts, reward systems, corporate cultures, and other factors, can pose significant challenges.

Information technology affects business processes, work groups, and jobs. It's a long way from simply understanding the value of IT to realizing it on the bottom line. As important as IT is, its value in improving performance depends on aligning all four of the change variables. "My view is that technology is only a support—an enabler—for changing practices," says James Yost, Ford Motor Company's CIO and Head of Process Leadership. "You must integrate IT into the texture of the business."[1] Thus, Ford Motor Company has married IT and process leadership. Their IT group is divided into three service areas: process and technology (process documentation and change leadership plus translation of process into IT requirements), solutions delivery (application development and deployment), and technical services (IT infrastructure).

Technology always forces changes in job responsibilities, task content, and human interactions. It often brings change in organizational structure and culture, as well. Studies in the United States and Europe have shown that when organizations ignore people issues, new systems result in poorer job designs. Poor job design threatens the well-being and performance of knowledge workers. Thoughtful design, on the other hand, can enhance both productivity and quality of work life. Thus, to achieve the full benefits of technology, analysts must address the issues of job design, as well as systems design and business process design.

When analysts and decision makers design systems and select equipment, they need to consider how their choices will alter the tasks people perform. Decision makers mistakenly assume that selecting the right technology is the most important part of improving productivity. Considerable evidence to the contrary suggests that technology often affects productivity less than good job design does.

Although job design is an important issue in systems design, traditional analysts often consider job design outside their responsibility, or they assume that employees will apply technology intuitively. When job design is not part of the project scope, analysts frequently design jobs unknowingly. Consequently, changes may be haphazard and ignore worker motivation and job satisfaction. Even when attention is given to human factors, analysts often concentrate on such technical aspects as ease of use, lighting, and furniture, and ignore the role of workers. Implementers also need to look carefully at the characteristics of the jobs being changed or created when technology is introduced. They should know the elements of job and systems designs that meet personal, social, and technical objectives.

Many of the problems with the use of technology lie in the way systems analysts typically design and cost justify new technology. Using the cost savings approach described in chapter 9, analysts often justify equipment costs by projecting reduced operating costs. In the past, reducing operating costs usually meant cutting salary expenses by designing systems that minimize the need for skills. In the process, analysts often ignored worker motivation and job satisfaction. Resultant jobs usually were narrowly defined, and production goals and controls were set by supervisors with little or no participation by employees.

This narrow approach to job design limits opportunities for users to benefit from the full capabilities of new systems. For example, in one case, although analysts acknowledged the importance of worker satisfaction and motivation and expected workers to be capable and skilled, the system they developed was appropriate for only low-level, repetitive jobs. Not only did the narrow approach miss the point, it also created a climate that led to low morale and increased turnover. Thus, it is important when redesigning business processes or implementing information technologies to consider job design, as well.

Neglecting to address behavioral issues such as job design is at the root of many information system and reengineering failures. Assumptions about work performance, productivity, and worker behavior often implicitly affect decisions about systems design. This has led to misguided attempts to improve performance through downsizing rather than sound principles of business process and job design.

12.3   Business Process Redesign (BPR)

Much has been written in recent years about *business process redesign* (BPR), or *reengineering*. Reengineering guru Michael Hammer defines reengineering as the "fundamental rethinking and radical redesign of business processes to achieve dramatic improvement in critical, contemporary measures of performance, such as cost, quality, service, and speed."[2] The primary distinctions between reengineering and other work improvement methods are the emphasis on fundamental rethinking of work design rather than incremental improvement, and the focus on business processes rather than functions and work tasks.

Although often viewed somewhat negatively because of its association with widespread downsizing, reengineering has become a widely accepted methodology for business change. The need for BPR is greater than ever. Thousands of enterprises around the world are faced with the daunting task of shifting from stable, command-and-control hierarchical structures to more fleet, flexible, flatter organizational structures that fully utilize the capabilities of a diverse workforce in order to compete in the fast-paced, global marketplace of the twenty-first century. Harold S. Resnick, a Boston management consultant, characterizes the challenge in this way: "Steering the ship of our organizations has shifted from dealing with periods of turbulence amid relatively calm seas to continuous, relentless whitewater rafting."[3]

BPR can be approached at different levels. At the enterprise level, BPR generally focuses on reengineering an entire organization or a department or division within that organization. Changes of this magnitude may take several years to design and implement fully. At the business process level, reengineering efforts are generally smaller in scope, requiring a set of solutions that are less broad and can be addressed much more quickly. Business process redesign can be simple or complex, encompassing an entire core business process or limited to specific subprocesses. BPR may occur at the divisional, unit, work-group, and job levels. Because improvement opportunities usually are driven or enabled by information technologies, EUIS analysts and project managers may be called upon to lead or contribute to such efforts.

BPR challenges the core purposes or assumptions underlying a business process. It requires a willingness to undergo critical self-analysis and to be open to change of the broadest and deepest kind. To succeed at BPR, enterprises must be prepared to sustain the discipline required of a rigorous process.

Before undertaking BPR efforts, enterprises must have defined their core business processes. This step is key because it helps focus management attention on the important areas where work gets done and how that work relates to creating value for the customer. Once identified, core business processes can be further broken down, if desired, into smaller components that can be more suitable for redesign.

A *core business process* can be defined as "a collection of activities that takes one or more kinds of input and creates an output that is of value to the customer."[4] One approach to identifying core business processes is to identify their beginning and their end. For example, the sales process could be called the "prospect to order process," the manufacturing process might be called the "order to delivery process," and the customer service process might be called the "customer delivery to repurchase process." Most companies have between 5 and 10 core business processes that essentially define the business. Some enterprises find it difficult to identify core business processes because they tend to think in terms of departments and functions instead of in terms of what work must be done and the manner in which is it performed. Various techniques, such as mapping and tree diagramming, can help enterprises identify and define their core business processes.

Various reengineering methodologies have emerged, many of them proprietary to specific consulting firms. In general, BPR follows a highly structured methodology based on four basic phases involving diagnosis, (re)design, implementation, and institutionalization. Some methodologies also include a strategic planning phase—where core business processes are defined as described in the preceding paragraph—at the beginning as part of the reengineering methodology. The four basic phases are described briefly in the sections that follow.

12.3.1 Diagnosis

The diagnosis phase involves a series of structured steps intended to create a shared vision for the business process redesign, compare this desired state to current operations, and determine how to move the organization from the current state to the desired state. The following steps are involved in the diagnosis phase.

1. Once the core business process or subprocess to be redesigned is identified, the first step is to craft a shared vision for the reengineered process. The vision establishes clear goals for the new process in line with the business strategy and serves to focus the efforts of all stakeholders. At the heart of the vision must be a true understanding of customer needs. To move the enter-

prise forward, the redesign vision must radically challenge thinking about how the work is done, alter the assumptions underlying the current process, and set realistic but challenging performance targets. A meaningful vision defines specific characteristics and measurable objectives for the redesigned process. Creating a BPR vision is a balance among inspiration, innovation, and measurable targets. The clearer and more specific the vision is, the more likely the enterprise is to achieve the radical redesign required for organizational repositioning.

2. The vision is then tested against high-level, external benchmarks of the process. Unless the results of current industry leaders are examined, it will be difficult to determine whether the goals are realistic or might be set too low or too high. For example, if the BPR vision is to reduce the average time required to fulfill a customer order from 10 days to 3 days, is that a good goal? If the industry leader currently takes 6 days, perhaps it is unrealistic. On the other hand, if the industry leader does it in 2 days, the goal may not be good enough. Benchmarking should not be limited to current industry leaders, however. It should be extended to any environment in which a similar process is deployed. The best innovations often originate from applying successful practices in one industry or discipline to an entirely different field.

3. The next step is to define critical success factors (CSFs) that must be accomplished in order for the newly designed process to be successful for the enterprise. The CSFs may address technical performance, customer satisfaction, cycle time, technical quality, marketplace forces, or other such factors. Measures generally are defined in terms of customer value, costs, return on investment, time, quality, or quantity.

4. The next step is gaining agreement on the scope of the business process. It is important to define the boundaries within which the business process redesign must achieve its results. Boundary conditions may be established for products or services to be included, markets, customers, costs, physical space, technology, personnel, or other internal or external requirements.

5. Describing the current process. This step is intended to ensure that the reengineering team fully understands the current process before redesigning it. Usually the process will be diagrammed on a flowchart and then verified by users. The analysis should identify inputs, outputs, and measures of all major steps of the current process. All stakeholders must be clearly identified, including owners, users, and customers of the process.

6. Then, the current process is subjected to detailed internal and external benchmarking. Internal benchmarking involves a careful analysis to establish baseline performance measures. External benchmarking involves a detailed and thorough investigation of other enterprises to identify best practices. It is important to look not only at what results are achieved but also how they are achieved. Suppliers and customers are good sources of information regarding possible benchmarks.

7. Compare current performance with desired performance (vision). Gap analysis involves comparing performance on current benchmarks with the target benchmarks and assessing envisioned performance for the new process to identify strengths and weaknesses. Attention must be paid not just to what is done but specifically how it is done. If the envisioned process were implemented, what would it look like in terms of how work is performed, as well as outputs? This analysis identifies the key areas that must be addressed in the new process design phase.

8. The final diagnosis step is root cause analysis to determine why the current process fails to meet the desired vision and strategic goals. During root cause analysis, constraints and enablers are identified. This analysis provides a starting point for the redesign effort, which should seek to remove constraints and strengthen or maintain the enablers.

12.3.2 (Re)Design

The second phase of BPR is designing the new process, which includes flowcharting the new process and addressing the people, structure, and technology requirements. The design phase is completed in steps and tested to evaluate how well the newly designed process will achieve the vision and benchmarks. Steps in (re)design are initial process redesign, process walkthrough, prototype, pilot test, and final process design.

1. *Initial process redesign.* Process redesign addresses all four organizational variables: technology, process, people, and structure. This step seeks to create a true breakthrough design concept. Technology plays an especially critical role in this step as an enabler for process innovation. This is the phase in which the true distinction between reengineering and other incremental improvement approaches is realized. The objective is to invent a new approach based on new ways of thinking about the desired vision and outputs rather than merely refining the old process. Reengineering guru Michael Hammer calls it the breakthrough design concept. This step produces a new flowchart of how the process should work to meet its critical success factors, achieve desired benchmarks, and fulfill the process vision.

2. *Process walkthrough.* After the new process has been created (i.e., reengineered), it must be reviewed in detail with all key stakeholders and analyzed to determine whether it truly is capable of working as intended. Will the process fulfill the needs of all key stakeholders including users, interim customers, and suppliers? Is the enterprise capable of implementing and sustaining the required changes? If not, can it secure the required resources and at what cost?

3. *Prototype.* Based on feedback from the process walkthroughs, adjustments are made to the original design. Then, a prototype is developed and tested under simulated conditions to determine whether it meets performance expectations. Additional refinements are made as necessary until the process achieves performance expectations based on established benchmarks.

4. *Pilot testing.* The process now is ready to be tested in a live, controlled environment. Generally, it is desirable to select as favorable a setting as possible. Strong commitment of participants to the success of the endeavor is important because glitches and many questions still remain, which may require some perseverance and ingenuity to resolve. The pilot test identifies problems and additional changes, assesses the robustness of the new process under use, and provides initial measures of results against established benchmarks.

5. *Final process design.* The results of the prototype testing are analyzed and evaluated to modify the process and create the final integration of the new process. Formal approvals are then sought from process owners, a steering committee, user groups, suppliers, customers, and any other stakeholders. Once approved, the reengineering effort is ready to move ahead with full implementation.

12.3.3 Implementation

Implementation also is conducted in stages. The first step is to convert the pilot developed during design into steady state use. Implementation then continues in stages until all remaining parts of the newly designed business process are fully operational and the results have been measured against established benchmarks.

1. *Implementation plan.* The implementation plan defines the who, what, when, where, and how of implementation. The plan must address issues such as budget, timing, required resources, training of personnel, structural adjustments, and communication of changes to all stakeholders. Documentation, reference materials, training programs, and other tools may need to be developed. How will the implementation be phased, and most importantly, how will operations be transitioned from existing practice to the new process with minimal disruption? The plan must be approved by the process owner and steering committee.

2. *Initial field implementation.* Implementation generally is completed in phases to minimize disruption. Core business processes, by definition, are central components of the business. Making major changes can be somewhat like trying to change the tire on a car while it's speeding down the highway at 60 mph. Generally, the initial field implementation will require considerable resources and attention. The scope and length of the initial implementation depends on circumstances. Often, the timing for successive implementations may not be finalized until the initial implementation is fully operational and the new process consistently is meeting the vision, critical success factors, and defined measures. If problems occur or the process fails to perform as anticipated, further implementation may be delayed while the new process undergoes further redesign, based on the initial experience.

   It is especially important during this initial implementation to validate the benefits of the newly designed process. This is the point where it is important to remember that different is not necessarily better, and it is critical to demonstrate that the reengineered approach does in fact produce significantly better results. Any supporting infrastructure required to support full implementation of the reengineered process also must be implemented at this point.

3. *Phased rollout.* Once the initial implementation is stabilized and operating as envisioned, the next phases of implementation proceed. Implementation may be phased by region, by customer groups, by product groups, by plant, or using other approaches that make sense for the particular enterprise. As the implementation proceeds, the implementation team usually strives to refine the implementation process itself, as well as the reengineered design. The implementation team learns to anticipate potential problems and to avoid or minimize them. Each new phase generally benefits from the lessons learned in the prior implementations. As the success of early implementations is established and results are verified, concerns and resistance among user groups in the later installations often begin to dissipate.

12.3.4 Institutionalization

Once the reengineered business process is implemented and fully operational, the final stage is alignment with other business processes. This stage must be monitored regularly as an ongoing part of normal business operations based on the established benchmarks. This final step would include a transition to the enterprise's ongoing, continuous improvement process.

In addition to the focus on redesigning the business process, successful reengineering efforts also must address issues of job and work group design. This is a requirement not only for reengineering but for almost any technology implementation. The impact on jobs must be assessed with an eye to using technology as an enabler for improving work, encouraging innovation, and supporting high performance levels.

12.4 THE NATURE OF JOBS AND NEED FOR JOB DESIGN

The term *job design* means "the formal and informal specification of tasks that are performed by employees, including expected interpersonal relationships and task interdependence. Ideally, the needs and goals of both employees and the organization are taken into account in job design or redesign."[5] The term *job design* suggests a systematic process for determining the content of a job. It implies that the content, interdependencies, and personal relationships of a job are thought out carefully to accomplish organizational goals. In fact, not all jobs are the result of job design. Jobs often evolve haphazardly. All too frequently, work is divided based upon the skills and preferences of available staff rather than logical design principles. Every time a manager assigns work or gives instructions, job design occurs. Likewise, when analysts design information systems, jobs are affected. Consciously or unconsciously, many factors influence the design of jobs.

A *job* generally is defined organizationally. A formal description legitimizes the position and defines the tasks, responsibility, authority, accountability, role in the organization, and pay scale for the person in each job. Past practice has been to define jobs in terms of a set of specific tasks: preparing budgets, typing correspondence, writing computer programs, conducting meetings, writing reports, supervising employees, appraising performance, hiring staff, analyzing financial trends, evaluating market data, teaching job skills, or forecasting sales. The tasks that make up a job may change over time, and the group of tasks that constitute a job may be designed purposefully or may have evolved through trial and error. In the Information Age, the trend is to define jobs, especially for knowledge workers, in terms of results and the parameters within which those results are to be achieved. This approach provides greater empowerment and flexibility in how results are achieved.

Associated with a job are certain responsibilities, authority, accountability, and roles. *Responsibility* defines the obligation to carry out assigned tasks or to achieve agreed-upon results. Whereas the tasks define the what of a job, responsibility spells out the where, when, and how. *Authority* refers to the rights or power granted to the jobholder to carry out assigned tasks and responsibilities. Authority may range from a clerk's right to requisition office supplies to a supervisor's right to hire, train, evaluate, and dismiss staff to an executive's right to approve multimillion-dollar budgets and projects. *Accountability* refers to a personal liability to perform a job according to predetermined standards or requirements. Jobholders are accountable to their immediate superiors, as well as to others who are affected by their behavior. For example, corporate attorneys are accountable not only for performing the tasks assigned by their supervisors, but for performing all work according to professional legal standards.

A job's role within the organization refers to how or where a job fits into the work flow, the interdependencies among tasks and jobs, relationships with others, and the perceived status or prestige that a job has in comparison to other jobs inside or outside the organization. For most individuals, a job provides more than a livelihood; people identify with their jobs and derive gratification from them. The job defines a role within the business process and the social structure; it is the point of articulation between the individual, the technology, and the organization. Thus, it is not sufficient to talk about how information technologies affect business process. Technology affects jobs as well: the set of tasks, the responsibility, the authority, the role in the organization, and the self-perception of the employees.

To capitalize fully on information technology, people must be motivated to do high-quality work. Motivation is an internal psychological state, which is affected directly by the design of the job itself. The full benefits of technology cannot be realized without the support of the people who use the systems. A new computer system, even if it has the capacity to double output, may yield only a slight increase in productivity if people do not understand it, fear its impact, or see no benefit for themselves. Thus, it is important when redesigning business processes or implementing information technology to consider job design, as well.

12.5 APPROACHES TO JOB DESIGN

Prevailing practice in many enterprises still is based on the simplification and standardization of scientifically engineered jobs. Approaches to job design that attempt to break out of this mold include job enlargement, job rotation, job enrichment, job characteristics approaches, sociotechnical approaches, quality of work life programs, and, most recently, empowerment of individuals and self-managed work groups. Each of these is discussed in this section.

12.5.1 Job Enlargement and Job Rotation

A *job enlargement* approach to job design expands jobs to include a variety of similar tasks. On a production line, this might mean that a worker performs several assembly steps instead of just one. In an office, a typist might sort mail, order supplies, and file documents rather than type all day.

A *job rotation* approach, on the other hand, moves workers from one job to another rather than changing the tasks that make up the jobs. Job rotation often is used to train workers so that they are exposed to a variety of jobs. This results in greater scheduling flexibility and back-up coverage for absent employees. Job rotation also upgrades the skills and promotability of workers.

Job enlargement and rotation approaches expand jobs horizontally, not vertically. That is, these techniques do not necessarily provide workers with more control over their environment. The approaches assume that workers want more diversification in their jobs and will welcome the opportunity to do more or different kinds of tasks.

Although the techniques of job enlargement and rotation can be useful, results are mixed. Some workers appreciate the increased variety, but others perceive changes as just more boring tasks. New tasks may interfere with the daydreaming or chitchat in which workers engage to cope with boring jobs. Sometimes management views job enlargement or rotation as a way of getting more work out of fewer workers, and workers may understand and resent this.

12.5.2   Job Enrichment

As an approach to job design, job enlargement and job enrichment are based on the theory that employees are motivated by factors that meet psychological needs for achievement, self-fulfillment, recognition, responsibility, advancement, or challenge. Whereas job enlargement approaches expand jobs horizontally, *job enrichment* refers to vertical expansion, including a planning or control task (or both) in a job that previously included only operating tasks. The objective is to give workers control over their jobs from beginning to end, or at least over a segment, so that they experience their tasks as a more meaningful whole. Job enrichment frequently encompasses both horizontal and vertical expansion.

Job enrichment approaches are associated closely with Herzberg's *two-factor theory of motivation.* Herzberg argued that job content contributes significantly to worker motivation and job satisfaction. He identified workers' motivation and satisfaction by asking accountants and engineers to cite times when they felt exceptionally good or exceptionally bad about their jobs. Factors that were the source of good feelings he called satisfiers or *motivators,* and factors that were the source of bad feelings he called *dissatisfiers.* The motivators that produced the most long-lasting, positive attitudes included the following:

- The work itself
- Responsibility in the job
- Opportunities for achievement in the job
- Advancement (for a job well done)

The major dissatisfiers included the following:

- Company policy and administration
- Supervision
- Salary
- Interpersonal relations
- Working conditions

Herzberg said that only motivators are related to the design of the job and can influence a worker's motivation and satisfaction directly. Dissatisfiers played only a hygiene role. This means that organizational efforts to improve supervision, salaries, or working conditions can keep employees from being unhappy but could not make employees feel positive about their work and hence make them want to work harder. When management and unions address only hygiene factors, they are not addressing motivation or job satisfaction. One set of factors can reinforce another but cannot be addressed at the exclusion or expense of the other.[6]

12.5.3   Job Characteristics Approach

In the mid 1960s, Turner and Lawrence made a significant contribution to job design methodology. These researchers identified six task dimensions: variety, autonomy, required social interaction, opportunities for social interaction, required knowledge and skill, and responsibility. The dimensions are known collectively as requisite task attributes.[7]

Other studies followed. The view that has had the most impact on job-design research was suggested in 1975 by Hackman and Oldham, whose theory and measuring instrument, the Job Descriptive Index, is derived from earlier research, as well as from their own studies. Hackman and Oldham identified five core job dimensions that influence motivation and satisfaction: skill variety, task identity, task significance, autonomy, and feedback.[8]

1. *Skill variety* is the degree to which a job includes different activities that require a number of different skills and talents.
2. *Task identity* is the degree to which a job requires completion of a whole and identifiable piece of work; that is, doing it from beginning to end with a visible outcome. For example, it is more meaningful to an office employee to handle all orders, billings, and inquiries from a designated group of customers than to type invoices all day long.
3. *Task significance* is the degree to which the job has substantial impact on other people within the organization or in the world at large. Employees who type labels for medicines and drugs are likely to perceive their jobs as more significant than workers who type labels for file folders, even though the skill levels may be comparable.
4. *Autonomy* is the degree to which the job provides freedom, independence, and discretion to the individual in scheduling the work and in determining the procedures. In highly autonomous jobs, the quality and quantity of work depend on an individual's initiative and efforts instead of on regulations, quotas, and supervision. By building more autonomy into jobs, large organizations can address one of their greatest weaknesses: lack of accountability. A common example in clerical operations is the requirement that the manager sign every document that goes out of the department. Why not allow the individual who does the major part of the work to sign the documents, thereby assuming responsibility for their accuracy?
5. *Job feedback* is the degree to which required activities provide workers with direct, clear information about the effectiveness of their performance. It is much more effective if workers obtain direct feedback than if their supervisor evaluates results for them. As an example, clerical operations are especially inclined to use too many checkers (such as proofreaders) rather than having employees verify the accuracy of their own work.

Job characteristic theory is a major underpinning for the work redesign methods and work effectiveness model presented later in this chapter. Job characteristics theory, however, focuses primarily on jobs that are done independently by individuals working more or less alone. Sociotechnical systems, discussed next, are an alternative conceptual approach that deals specifically with properties of work systems that emphasize the use of groups in performing work.

12.5.4 Sociotechnical (Systems) Approach

Eric Trist used the term *sociotechnical system* to describe his observation that people (a social system) interacted with tools and techniques (a technical system) by choice, not chance. These choices, he said, are dictated by economic, technical, and human values. According to Trist, "information technologies, especially those concerned with PCs and digital networks, give immense scope for solving many current problems—if the right value choices can be made."[9]

A sociotechnical approach (also referred to as sociotechnical systems approach or just systems approach) to job design balances the social needs of workers with technological requirements. Technical systems influence the characteristics of the social (or people) system through the allocation of work roles and the relationships among tasks that are dictated by the technology. The performance of the organization is believed to be a function of the interface of the social and technical systems.

Sociotechnical approaches advocate changing the focus of work design from adapting people to technology to adapting technology to people. The objective is to design jobs that optimize relationships among technology, people, and the needs of the organization. Unlike the previous approaches, which emphasized designing jobs for individuals, sociotechnical approaches focus on designing tasks for work groups. By participating in the group's decisions, workers attain a sense of personal worth and achievement from the group and the relationships within it. The motivational value of these relationships is important because social needs outweigh achievement needs for 60 percent of the workforce. One of the major contributions of the sociotechnical approach to the theory and practice of work design is the idea of the autonomous work group. Autonomous, or self-managing, work groups have recently become an increasingly popular organizational innovation. They are discussed further in the section on empowerment.

Frederick Emery expanded on the ideas of sociotechnical systems, introducing the concept of open systems thinking. Emery said that it is not enough to know how the technology works. Nor is it enough to know how people work. In an open system, the current situation must be understood. In other words, everything counts. "The most useful way to understand technology *and* people within a system is to understand their relationship to the larger whole they serve."[10] Equifinality, a systems concept also described in chapter 14, says that there is more than one best way to solve a problem. This is a simple concept but one that markedly changes how management thinks about problem solving.[11]

12.5.5 Quality of Work Life (QWL) Programs

Quality of work life may be defined as the degree to which workers can satisfy their personal needs through their work. Quality of work life affects the health, well-being, job satisfaction, and productivity of employees. QWL programs emerged in the 1970s as a means of involving workers in problem-solving groups to make jobs more satisfying and productive. These programs are an effective way to implement workplace innovations and measure outcomes.

The QWL movement, which is based on the sociotechnical concept of work design, grew out of European experiments with semiautonomous work teams in manufacturing plants. In the manufacturing sector, QWL programs were spurred by declining productivity in the United States and increased global competition.

QWL programs are not necessarily related to technology, although the framework and methods are appropriate for implementing technology-related work changes. The characteristics of QWL programs are summarized in Figure 12-1.

A systems approach to the relationship between information technology and quality of work life reveals a number of patterns. Figure 12-2 shows the framework used by the U.S. Office of Technology Assessment to analyze these relationships. The core relationships are among the organization, technology, and individual. The arrows indicate patterns of association, not necessarily causal relationships.

- Achieving sustained commitment from management to an open, nondefensive style of operation that sincerely encourages employees to speak up regarding problems or opportunities. (A related element is providing practical means for members of the workforce to participate in refining and implementing promising suggestions.)
- Establishing a work environment that encourages continuous learning, training, and active interest regarding both the job and the product or service to which the job contributes. (Such an environment enables an employee to use and develop personal skills and knowledge, which in turn affects involvement, self-esteem, and the challenge obtained from the work itself.)
- Making the job itself more challenging by structuring it so that an individual (or work team) can self-manage and feel responsible for a significant, identifiable output if that kind of responsibility is desired.
- Providing opportunities for continued growth; that is, opportunities to advance in organizational or career terms.
- Training supervisors to function effectively in a less directive, more collaborative style.
- Breaking down the traditional status barriers between management and production or support personnel. Achieving an atmosphere of open communication and trust between management and the workforce.
- Providing not only feedback about results achieved and recognition for good results but also financial incentives, such as shared cost savings, where feasible.
- Selecting personnel who can be motivated, under appropriate conditions, to genuinely care about striving for excellence in task performance.
- Evaluating and analyzing results, including failures, leading to revised efforts toward improvement.

Figure 12-1
Characteristics of QWL programs

Source: U.S. Congress, Office of Technology Assessment, *The Automation of America's Offices* (Washington, D.C.: Government Printing Office, 1985), p. 12.

12.5.6 Empowerment

The concept of *empowerment* emerged during the 1980s. The objective of empowerment is to push responsibility down the organizational hierarchy to the level where the work is done. The basic philosophy is that within their scope of authority,

Figure 12-2
Office characteristics that contribute to an individual's quality of work life

Source: U.S. Congress, Office of Technology Assessment, *The Automation of America's Offices* (Washington, D.C.: Government Printing Office, 1985), p. 126.

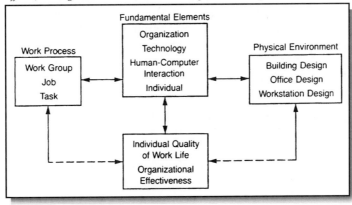

workers should be empowered to make the decisions necessary to accomplish their assigned tasks effectively. In practice, it puts the responsibility on the employee to identify impediments to getting tasks done and to take action to work with others to resolve those issues. It also allows employees to seek and implement ideas for improving the way work is done.

Unfortunately, the concept of empowerment is used and misunderstood with great frequency. Many enterprises have failed to implement it effectively because it flies in the face of a deeply entrenched command-and-control management approach. Much of the misunderstanding derives from differences in interpretation of its root word: *power*. Power in the classical sense has to do with the ability to impose a position on others or on the circumstances. Position power carries with it the authority (as described earlier) to commit resources, hire and fire workers, and make other decisions. When individuals or teams are told that they are empowered, they often respond from this classical interpretation of power. They want to know: How much budget do we have? What is our signature authority? Can we require or direct others about what to do? This interpretation is not what is meant by empowerment; it is delegation of formal authority in the classical sense.

Empowerment relates to a broader concept of power as the ability to influence others and cause them, or persuade them, to make decisions, select courses of action, or change behaviors. It has to do with credibility and fact-based decision making. Empowerment defined in this context creates a high degree of freedom of action, latitude to take risks, and opportunities to be innovative within the agreed-upon performance objectives, project results, or mission. Empowerment applies to the design of individual jobs and to self-managing work groups.

Self-managing work groups may be defined as "intact (if small) social systems whose members have the authority to handle internal processes as they see fit in order to generate a specific group product, service, or decision."[12] These groups also may be referred to as autonomous or self-regulating work groups. Self-managing work groups include temporary task forces set up to solve specific problems; permanent and cross-functional teams, such as decision-making committees and many kinds of management teams; and permanent production teams.

Self-managing work groups can be differentiated from more common types of coacting groups by three main characteristics. People in coacting groups may report to the same supervisor and work closely with one another, but they have individually defined tasks. Even when coacting groups have to coordinate their work closely, individuals are considered the basic performing unit of the organization. The three characteristics that distinguish self-managing groups are:[13]

- They are real groups. The group, even if small or temporary, must constitute an identifiable social system that is recognized as a group by members and nonmembers. At a minimum, its members must have differentiated roles with interdependent relationships.
- They are work groups. The group must have a significant piece of work to do that results in a product, service, or decision that is measurable or tangible. If a group does not generate productive output, it is not considered a work group.
- They are self-managing groups. Group members must have the authority to manage the work and interpersonal processes required to carry out their tasks. If management retains control over who does what and when it gets done, then a group is self-managed only in name.

The conditions required for high team effectiveness are different from those needed for optimal individual work effectiveness. For individuals, the emphasis is on the person-job relationship, whereas for groups, analysts must consider person-job, person-group, and group-job relationships, as well as interrelationships among these components.[14] Thus, designing work for groups never should be viewed as merely creating a team version of a good individual job design. One of the most important choices to be made in structuring a work system is the choice between individual and group designs.

In his book about BPR, Harold S. Resnick talks about the concept of shared responsibility.[15] In a traditional context, responsibilities are largely an individual matter. When individuals are assigned a responsibility, they are personally accountable for generating the results expected for the defined area. Typically, responsibilities are defined, measurable, tied to accountability, and form the basis for recognition and reward systems.

From a business process perspective, however, few tasks are accomplished individually. Business processes generally span multiple individuals and groups. The traditional view of individual responsibility tends to work reasonably well when work is going well. The tendency, however, is for individuals to optimize their own performance and to protect their personal areas of responsibility, assigning the blame or fault to others when problems arise. No one seems to own the entire scope of the work.

As enterprises transition to a process orientation and recognize the interdependence of work and the necessity for teams to work together, individual responsibility paradoxically becomes a limitation, as well as an asset. The concept of shared responsibility is intended to build full team interdependence and collective effort. Individuals have a shared responsibility for the success of the entire enterprise, process, team, or work product of which they are a part. This means that the failure of any individual member of the team represents the failure of the entire team. Resnick indicates that shared responsibility often creates initial anxiety and concerns. Each individual now realizes that the performance of others directly affects personal performance. When fully developed in a team environment, he hastens to add, shared responsibility is not only comfortable for all the team members, it is essential to the creation of high performance teams. Resnick cautions, however, that in order to implement the concept, the reward and recognition systems of the organization must be brought into alignment. Shared responsibilities require team-based reward and recognition systems in addition to individual-based performance systems. (See the Bailey and Bailey Spotlight in chapter 4.) It also leads to the demand for some risk-based compensation systems.

12.5.7 Perspectives on Job Design Approaches

Declining U.S. productivity in the late 1970s focused attention on the success of Japanese participative management. In his best-selling book *Theory Z*, William Ouchi challenged the traditional American premise that specialization increases productivity. Ouchi compared the productivity of U.S. firms practicing American-style scientific management to the productivity of U.S. firms practicing Japanese-style participative management. His findings demonstrated that Japanese-style management, with a low degree of specialization, achieved higher productivity than American-style management with a high degree of specialization. Moreover, Japanese management led to higher-quality output. According to Ouchi, American managers believe that quality is achieved through testing and control. Japanese managers, on the other hand, believe that quality comes from inviting workers to refine product design and manufacturing processes continually. Ouchi concluded that Japanese-style management was more effective than American-style management.

Futurist Alvin Toffler terms the current environment the Information Age or the third wave, with agricultural and industrial waves preceding it. In *Productive Workplaces*, Marvin Weisbord marries open sociotechnical (systems) thinking to team effectiveness and labels the result *third wave managing/consulting*. He maintains that in the Information Age, teamwork is essential to system success. In his view, this means that everyone needs to be involved with improving the whole system. Weisbord (Figure 12-3) shows the evolution of scientific management (Taylorism), to participative management (group problem solving), to systems thinking, to third wave managing/consulting.

Weisbord suggests three powerful levers that can be used to turn workplace anxiety into energy: purposes, relationships, and structures. Purposes (missions) are the business that the company is in—the future on which everyone's work security and meaning are attached. Relationships are connections with coworkers that contribute to feeling whole. Relationships require cooperation across lines of hierarchy, function, class, race, and gender. Structure refers to who gets to do what. Structure affects self-esteem, dignity, and learning.[16] Third wave managing and consulting levers are those practices that support the business purpose, allow for relationship building, identify roles, and assure individual accountability.

Despite decades of experience with alternative techniques, *command-and-control management* still prevails in most American enterprises. It is a major premise of this text, however, that enterprises that cling to these industrial era management

Figure 12-3
A brief history of management practices

Source: Weisbord, Marvin. *Productive Workplaces.* (San Francisco, Jossey-Bass/John Wiley & Sons, 1988), 254.

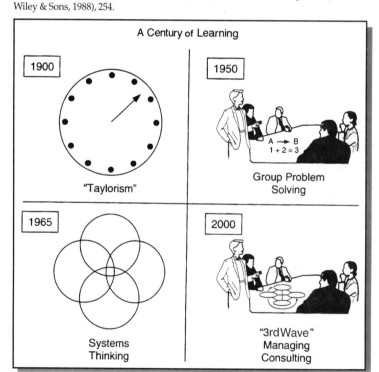

Part IV   Workplace Performance: The Impact of Information Technology

practices will be at a distinct competitive disadvantage in the Information Age. Enterprises cannot achieve significant benefit from EUIS technologies unless they are prepared to change the way work is done. Effective EUIS implementation requires that workers are involved in setting goals and standards, solving problems, and making decisions related to their work. In other words, EUIS technologies are driving job redesign efforts.

The concepts described in this section underlie much of the practice of job design and organizational change. Job characteristics and sociotechnical theories are the basis for intervention strategies used by enterprises to move from authoritarian forms of management to participative, or empowerment, styles. The following section offers more specifics on the impact of information technology on business process and job design.

12.6 THE RELATIONSHIP BETWEEN TECHNOLOGY, BUSINESS PROCESS, AND JOB DESIGN

The impact of technology on business processes and jobs goes beyond changes in tasks. IT changes jobs in several ways. The key point is that the best results with IT are achieved when these factors are considered as part of the project rather than being addressed at the end as an afterthought.

1. Procedures for completing tasks may change. When tasks are taken over by an automated system, jobs (or portions of jobs) may be eliminated. Workers must be retrained to do the new jobs, reassigned, or let go.
2. When jobs are modified due to the addition or deletion of tasks, boundaries between jobs may change as tasks are transferred from one job to another. Sometimes, but not always, these changes are accompanied by changes in job titles, descriptions, or compensation.
3. Automation creates new tasks that are required to support the system or that are related to new products or services. Existing jobs may be redesigned to incorporate these new tasks, or new jobs may be created. For example, a position of administrator may be created to operate a newly installed local area network, assign passwords, perform daily backup, troubleshoot problems, and so forth.
4. Technology may lead to the creation of new tasks not previously possible, practical, or cost effective. New capabilities may create opportunities for new products or services—a positive impact of technology.

To understand the effects of technology on jobs, business process, and organizational structure, consider the following four results related to the introduction of PCs with word processing and spreadsheet software in the office of a manager and secretary.

First, the way some tasks are accomplished may change; new skills will be needed and old ones eliminated. If the manager decides to use the PC to author documents, creating them will require different skills than writing them in longhand did. Previously important skills, such as the manager's dictation and the secretary's shorthand and transcription skills, may be used only rarely.

Second, the process that governs the interactions of author, secretary, and other people to produce documents may change. The secretary now may do only the final formatting and printing of documents. Documents that are filed electronically are no longer sent to records management or physically filed in one department. If these PCs are connected to a network, the potential for change is extended significantly. For example, if the manager uses e-mail for intercompany correspondence, the secretary and mail services may be left out of the process entirely. Moreover, e-mail gives many people in the enterprise direct access they never had before. The manager also has more direct information about what is going on in the enterprise. The power structure, in essence, is being changed—and therein is often the source of resistance.

At some points, technology allows for choice rather than mandating change. For example, a PC may be given just to the secretary. The manager still might continue to dictate documents that the secretary will transcribe and edit using word processing software. In this case, the computer becomes a substitute for the typewriter. The relationship between manager and secretary, and the flow of work, might change minimally with only the secretary needing new skills. Another alternative is to sever the relationship completely; the secretary might be reclassified as an administrative assistant. All managers schedule their own meetings and compose correspondence with the aid of word processing, electronic mail, and calendaring software. One administrative assistant can support an entire department.

Third, new technology may introduce new steps and new tasks. For example, use of a PC introduces the need to make backup copies, to design and use an electronic filing system, and to manage disk space or diskette storage. New technology also introduces the need for training. Decisions about these tasks—whether they will be handled by all users, by secretaries, by a systems administrator, or by some combination—will affect the work process.

Fourth, the availability of the technology will enable the manager and secretary to do new tasks that were not practical before. For example, if the secretary converts the old card file of clients to a PC database, it becomes practical to send personalized letters to hundreds of clients using the merge printing feature of word processing. The manager, using a spreadsheet, forecasts sales under different economic scenarios and tracks them against actual results.

Thus, with even this simple example one can see how changes at the level of the task, job, business process, and organizational structure could take place as a result of new technology.[17]

12.6.1 Computer-Mediated Work

Two characteristics of computer work are that the machine makes work more abstract and that the machine alters the worker's relationship to the task. The new relationship sometimes is referred to as *computer mediated,* which means that a person accomplishes a task through the information system rather than through direct contact with objects.[18]

Workers experience tasks as more concrete when the tasks involve manipulation of objects, as in pottery making or carpentry. Manipulation itself is a form of feedback; the object feels right. Machines remove workers as a direct source of energy, but workers still have contact with the objects of their labor. With computers, however, workers get only indirect feedback through the symbols on the screen. "Very often, from the point of view of the worker, the object of the task seems to have disappeared 'behind the screen' and into the information system."[19]

Thus, computers have made information processing more abstract. From the perspective of the knowledge worker, when information is in physical forms that can be touched and manipulated—such as cards, letters, reports, and invoices—it appears to be more concrete. When information is processed on the computer, however, many of these objects disappear. The knowledge worker is confronted with intangible information, which is manipulated in invisible ways inside the computer.

12.6.1.1 Coping with Computer Logic

The computer easily handles quantitative data, but qualitative judgments are difficult to program. Consequently, when computer systems are designed, qualitative aspects are either quantified or lost. A programmer defines correctness of data in terms of formal computer logic. Frequently, formal correctness can become more important than the relevance of the information. Judgment is replaced by computer logic, and errors become difficult to detect and correct.

Computers have become easier to use, but they still require codes and procedural commands. Although today's graphical user interfaces (GUIs) have made using computers much more intuitive, it is difficult for most people to learn to think in a way that parallels computer logic. It requires thinking and performing steps in the precise order dictated by the logical sequence built into the software.

The difference between how most people go about finding information in a file folder or reference book in contrast to a computer database illustrates the point. When physically searching for information, most people rely on intuitive aids. They recall that it was in a red volume, it was near the back, the page was torn, or it was on the second shelf. If searchers recall terminology inaccurately or misspell a term, they probably will find what they are looking for anyway. These memory aids are not available in computer databases; only names are used, and they are defined precisely by computer logic. Searchers must use the right key words in the right relationship, or the results will be faulty. GUIs have reduced these problems somewhat. New technologies such as intelligent agents (for example, Microsoft's "Mr. Paper Clip" in MSWord), Web bots that assist with self-service, and other artificial language techniques such as natural language interfaces hold additional promise.

One consequence of computer-mediated work is that it becomes more difficult to exercise judgment over it. This is true for both routine clerical jobs and complex knowledge work. The comments of a bank auditor illustrate this point.

> The job of auditing is very different now. More imagination is required. I am receiving data online. I don't go to the branches if I don't want to. I don't see any books. What do I audit in this situation? I always have to be thinking about what is in the system. I may be auditing, but it doesn't feel like it.[20]

The computer also has introduced new complexity in data. The auditor can compare branches according to selected criteria and search out new relationships in the data. To do this, however, the auditor must develop a theory of the auditing process. A conceptual framework is needed to guide the auditor through the mass of available information. Theoretical insight and imagination are the new keys to effectiveness. By creating a medium where imagination is more important than experience-based judgment, information technology challenges old procedures. In this auditing process, for example, planners are not automating the old, but inventing the new. Consequently, the traditional training of auditors—and others—must shift to provide a stronger theoretical or conceptual foundation.

12.6.1.2 Worker Frustration

Another consequence of computer-mediated work is that it can induce feelings of frustration and loss of control. "Computer mediation of simple jobs can create tasks that are routine and unchallenging, while demanding focused attention and abstract comprehension."[21] People who are action oriented, rather than abstract thinkers, may find computer-mediated work frustrating and stressful. Those who shift from conventional procedures to computer-mediated work feel this stress most acutely. It is impossible, however, to forecast how people will adapt to the abstraction of work over the long term.

12.6.1.3 Altered Social Structure

Computer-mediated work alters the social structure of an organization. The workstation itself can become the individual's primary focus of interaction. "This focus can lead people to feel isolated in an impersonal situation."[22] The importance of communities in the workplace has been widely recognized. Jobs that isolate people at computer workstations can lead to social problems.

12.6.2 De-Skilling Versus Enhancing Jobs

Perceptions differ over whether technology is de-skilling or enhancing office jobs. The term *de-skilling* means "using the computer to direct, control, and pace work so that the required level of skill is reduced and knowledge, judgment, and decision making are minimized." The term *enhancing* means "expanding the scope and level of responsibility by using technology to reduce routine, repetitive tasks and provide access to information and resources."

Many organizations that process large amounts of standardized data have elected to use technology to de-skill tasks, enabling lower-paid employees with minimum skills to process more data in a given amount of time. Sorting rules, decision trees, and analytical processes also can be built into computer processes and software packages as a means to de-skill professional tasks. This approach can create factory-like offices, which often reduce job interest and satisfaction and increase stress. Many of these jobs have been shifted offshore or overseas to third world countries because American workers are no longer willing to work under these conditions.

On the other hand, technology can enhance jobs by relieving people of routine, repetitive tasks. Simple tasks can be integrated into fewer, broader jobs so that the worker has a better sense of the purpose and outcome of the work. Information systems also can give a worker access to knowledge that previously could be obtained only through advanced education. This allows a clerical worker to take over interesting tasks that previously were considered the work of the professional. For example, clerks can use computerized databases to search for information that formerly only a lawyer, doctor, scientist, or Ph.D. in archaeology would have known about. Some organizations are using information technology deliberately to upgrade and enhance work at all levels. Flatter organizational structures and reduced costs of management may result.

In *The Age of the Smart Machine*, Harvard Business School professor Shoshana Zuboff differentiated between "automating" and "infomating" jobs. Zuboff explained that in jobs that are automated, the human body is replaced with a technology that allows the same processes to be performed with more continuity and control. In jobs that have been infomated, however, technology generates information about the underlying productive and administrative process through which an organization accomplishes its work.[23] Whether the introduction of information technologies results in work that has been automated or infomated rests, in part, upon appropriate job design.

12.6.3 Changes in Organizational Structure and Communications

When the work process changes, the organizational structure, which defines the relationships among jobs, also can change. Changes may result in revisions in the formal organization chart or simply may alter communication patterns or power relationships among groups or departments. Changes in organizational structure may take place immediately as part of the planned system changes, or may evolve over time as the enterprise gains familiarity with the technology and its capabilities.

Many changes in organizational structure and communication patterns can be attributed to technology. For instance, adoption of a centralized computer system created a tendency for enterprises to centralize control. On the other hand, the acquisition of PCs at the departmental level has led to decentralization of decision making. End-user computing has put new power in the hands of local departments because one source of power is information. E-mail has opened new avenues of communication that bypass former information gatekeepers. The Internet has significantly expanded the impact, providing wide availability of extensive information to which access previously was fairly limited. Senior managers have immediate, direct access to data formerly filtered to them in summary reports. Knowledge workers literally have the Library of Congress at their fingertips. Information can be consolidated in centralized databases and knowledge management systems while access and processing can be decentralized any place in the country or the world.

Observers have noted interesting changes in the boundaries between clerical and professional and between clerical and managerial positions. Some researchers have referred to this redistribution of labor as the clericalization of professional work and the professionalization of clerical work.[24] The most prominent trend is the shift of keyboarding tasks when professionals and managers acquire PCs. Individuals who would never have typed in the past now use word processing to author documents and send e-mail, and the time that clerical workers used to spend keyboarding original documents subsequently decreases. Sometimes secretaries are bypassed completely, or their involvement may be limited to revising, formatting, and printing. All of these effects of information technology are not inevitable. Changes in functions and shifts in power can be attributed as much to the characteristics of the organization and its management strategy as to the characteristics of the technology.

12.6.4 Technology as an Enabler for Job and Work Group Design

Efforts to improve organizational performance through the application of information technology must not overlook the key role of people in making technology pay off. According to a special report on the response of management to the human factors of automation:

> American managers are finally learning what the Japanese discovered years ago: The solution to fading competitive ability, sluggish productivity growth, and poor quality cannot be found in the mythical black box

of a miraculous technology. To realize the full potential of automation, leading-edge companies are integrating workers and technology in *sociotechnical* systems that revolutionize the way work is organized and managed. . . . This is an immensely important trend, one that is producing a new model of job design and work relations that will shape the workplace well into the twenty-first century.[25]

Because analysts seldom addressed job design issues, most early systems were implemented in ways that maintained old, functional lines of organization, often compounding weaknesses. Anticipated productivity improvements never were realized because technology created new bottlenecks in the old work flows. In some of the worst cases, disgruntled workers resisted the technology or failed to use it effectively because of inadequate training. Today, progressive enterprises are applying the concepts of BPR, turning technological changes into opportunities to rethink old forms of work organization in light of current and future objectives. Technology can be a catalyst for restructuring on both individual and work group levels in addition to an enterprise level. Decision makers should determine which level is most appropriate prior to embarking on redesign projects. Even EUIS projects that are small in scope should offer opportunities to rethink the way work is organized.

Instead of attempting to optimize each task and function separately, analysts can use electronic integration to optimize a whole procedure. For example, they might focus on improving customer service or marketing. Electronic integration is possible because the technology allows the integration of information from many sources and the distribution of information to many locations.[26] Electronic integration can be used to design jobs that give workers a variety of tasks and, at the same time, allow them to understand how the job contributes to the department or enterprise. This gives workers greater autonomy and responsibility, and it contributes to job satisfaction and productivity.

For example, an international letter of credit at one bank required 23 steps, performed by 14 workers, and generated forms and copies stored in several locations. When customers called, they had a difficult time finding the worker with the right information to answer their questions. Moreover, if the customer wanted to change something, the process had to start again. The bank revised the process so that one worker, with the aid of a PC and a client database, now performs all the necessary steps in processing letters of credit for a particular set of clients. The database contains all information related to the accounts. The service worker is the single contact between the customer and the bank for corrections or inquiries. Thus, a task that previously took 14 people more than 3 days now is completed by one person in a single day with the aid of powerful information systems.

The capabilities of an integrated client service system at a major insurance company (Figure 12-4) provide another example. With PCs on their desks, client service representatives have word processing, spreadsheet, and administrative systems at their fingertips. In addition, they have direct access to the company's database of policyholder information. They can answer telephone inquiries, send written replies, check policyholder information (such as loan balances or current cash value of policies), make policy changes (such as address or beneficiary changes), issue special statements, and much more. Most importantly, electronic integration has changed the focus of the job from processing

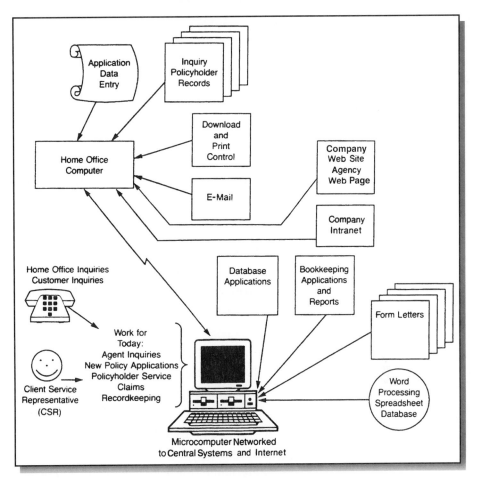

Figure 12-4
An integrated client service system at a major insurance company

Source: Courtesy of Roy W. Walters and Associates, Inc.

paperwork to serving clients, or, in other words, from efficient paperwork to effective client service.

Electronic integration also can be used to design work groups. Some insurance companies have restructured work groups that formerly were organized by function into self-managed teams that service a specific market. For example, one company combined the expertise of raters, underwriters, and clerical workers on a single team and assigned them responsibility for specific product lines. Organizing workers in teams, rather than isolating them in functional groups, allows greater understanding of the production process and empowers workers to remove impediments and make changes required to improve results.

When designing solutions, analysts should remember that job design influences productivity more than technology does. Without a well-thought-out design, chances are that new systems will reinforce functional organization rather than invent integrated ones. In fact, analysts often strive to tailor new technology to the existing organization to avoid disrupting the work environment. When job design is overlooked, however, important opportunities to make technology pay off may be missed.

When people find their jobs motivating, they feel good about themselves and the work they do. They do not have to be cajoled or forced to perform their work; they strive to do their jobs well because they find good performance rewarding and satisfying. They are excited about their work rather than motivated solely by external (hygiene) factors such as compliments from the boss or a paycheck.

In *Work Redesign,* Hackman and Oldham describe a methodology for designing jobs that people are motivated to perform effectively and find rewarding and satisfying. Their approach is based on a combination of behavioral and sociotechnical systems that emphasizes the importance of individual differences and the need to analyze the requirements of each organization. They focus on the actual work that people perform, and they emphasize important distinctions between designing work for individuals and designing work for groups.

12.7.1   Characteristics of Motivating Jobs

Hackman and Oldham suggest that jobs that people find motivating have three characteristics:

- Workers experience their work as meaningful.
- Workers have responsibility for the results of their work.
- Workers have knowledge of the actual results of their work.[27]

Other measures that relate to job design—although they are not, strictly speaking, characteristics of the job—include the following:

- Growth satisfaction, or the degree to which the employee believes the job provides opportunities for personal growth and development.
- Growth need, or the strength of the employee's desire for growth and personal development.

These characteristics of motivating jobs relate directly to the five core job characteristics described previously under "Job Characteristics Approach." As illustrated in the work effectiveness model in Figure 12-5, the absence or presence of the five core job dimensions directly affect the extent to which workers experience the critical psychological states that are characteristic of motivating jobs. In other words, these characteristics lead to high internal motivation. Skill variety, task identity, and task significance contribute to experienced meaningfulness of the work. Autonomy contributes to experienced responsibility, and feedback from the job contributes to knowledge of results. Growth satisfaction and growth need (desired personal and work outcomes) indicate how an employee will respond to a job with high motivating potential. The next section discusses implementing concepts, or strategies, for designing jobs that encompass the five core job characteristics.

12.7.2   Designing Jobs for Individuals

When redesigning jobs for individuals, analysts should focus on job dimensions that encourage employees to work hard and perform well because they want to rather than out of fear or in response to close supervision. Hackman and Oldham recommend the following five strategies for redesigning work. As illustrated in

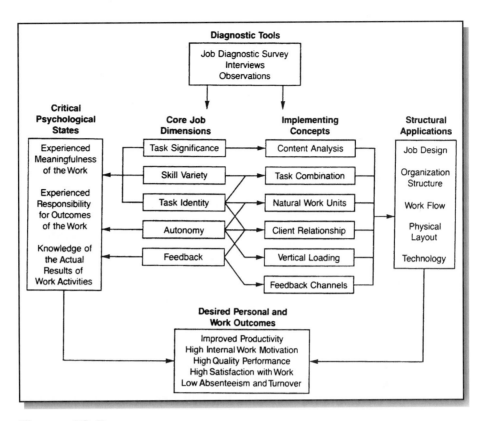

Figure 12-5
The work effectiveness model

Source: Courtesy of Roy W. Walters and Associates, Inc.

Figure 12-5, each of these strategies directly addresses one or more of the five core job dimensions:[28]

1. *Task combination.* Task combination puts fragmented job tasks into new job modules, combining all the tasks required for a given piece of work. Information systems can reduce many repetitive tasks, making combination more practical than it was with manual systems. A complete job module increases skill variety and task identity and generates challenge and responsibility for the worker. At times, task combination may be constrained for organizational or technical reasons. For example, enterprises may want to keep internal auditing separate from other processing.

2. *Forming natural work units.* Forming natural work units, in conjunction with task combination, provides further opportunities for task identity and significance. A natural work unit refers to grouping tasks in a logical or inherently meaningful way. Natural work units are organized according to groups of customers, types of transactions, geographical distribution, or any other arrangement that makes good sense to those performing the work. For example, a customer service representative might handle all contact with clients in the Chicago area rather than handling work randomly as it comes into the department.

3. *Establishing client relationships.* When natural work units are formed around specific groups of clients, it may be possible to put the employee in direct contact with the clients and give them continuing responsibility for

managing relationships with them. Clients may be customers of a firm, other individuals or departments within an enterprise, or other publics of the enterprise. An effective client relationship provides direct contact between client and employee, clearly establishes criteria for evaluating the quality of the product or service, and provides a regular channel for relaying feedback directly to the worker.

Enabling employees to establish direct relationships with clients can improve jobs in three core dimensions. Feedback increases when workers get direct praise or criticism from persons who receive the work. Skill variety increases because establishing client relationships requires interpersonal skills in addition to task-specific skills. Autonomy also increases because individuals have personal responsibility for managing their relationships with clients.

4. *Vertically loading jobs.* Vertical loading pushes down responsibility and authority formerly assigned at a higher level, thus giving employees more control over their jobs. Vertical loading can be accomplished in many ways. Controls can be removed to give employees more discretion in planning, scheduling, and checking their work. The job can be broadened by adding more difficult tasks. Workers might consult with others in the organization rather than immediately calling the supervisor, give technical advice, author their own reports, interview job candidates, or perform other appropriate tasks. Jobs also can be vertically loaded by granting new authority, such as discretion to set one's own goals to accomplish a specific short-term objective.

5. *Establishing feedback channels.* Feedback channels should give workers direct, immediate, and regular information about how well they are performing their jobs. It is generally more effective for employees to learn about their performance directly, by doing the job, than to rely on a supervisor as their main source of feedback. Direct job feedback is usually more immediate and private, and it increases the employee's sense of control over the job. In most instances, establishing feedback channels involves removing barriers or blocks that insulate employees from information about their performance. Establishing direct client relationships (discussed previously) is one of the most effective feedback channels. Other examples include returning documents to the same word processing operator for revisions and corrections rather than to random individuals or moving quality control close to the workers.

Although the implementing concepts are mutually reinforcing, each can be a separate action strategy. Other possibilities also exist for redesigning jobs. The five areas outlined by Hackman and Oldham, however, address some of the most common problems associated with job design. They are intended as guidelines for generating ideas about how jobs might be improved rather than as hard and fast rules. In order to work, these principles must be implemented in a supportive organization. Work redesign efforts must have the support of all stakeholders or the intended results will be diminished, if not thwarted.

12.7.3 Designing Self-Managing Work Groups

Although the same principles apply, designing work for work groups is more complex than designing work for individuals. In addition to the five core job characteristics, two additional characteristics must be addressed: task-required interdependence and opportunities for social interaction.

Designing work for work groups requires addressing issues of motivating individuals and group dynamics, as well. The focus is on the overall task of the group

MANAGING CHANGE: HIGH TOUCH ESSENTIAL TO HIGH TECH SUCCESS

Do human resource specialists have a role in information systems (IS) implementation? Recent studies indicate that they should.

Despite remarkable advances in information technology (IT), many computer-based IS still fall short of performance expectations. A growing share of these implementation failures are due to nontechnical factors.

The role of IT in industry and commerce has rapidly risen during the past half century. IT now represents about half of all capital investment on a global basis while much of the workforce in the developed world relies on telecommunications and computer-based IS. Unfortunately, IS success can be elusive. An effective IS will improve performance, but IT applications that are poorly planned, developed, or implemented can retard individual and/or group performance. Many organizations have become internally stressed or competitively disadvantaged after deploying a major new IS.

IT is of little benefit by itself. Technology is certainly introduced to foster economic efficiencies, but if it is not also designed to increase human resource effectiveness, it will be a disaster. IT can help people to do a better job, but only if they are willing to use the technology and if they become effective users. Unfortunately, many IT applications are misused, underutilized, or abandoned. Even a good technical system may be sabotaged if it is perceived to interfere with an established social network. Thus, a good understanding of the intended end-users, their tasks, and the interdependencies between the two is a likely prerequisite for IS success.

The unique characteristics of each organization must be considered when determining whether, where, and to what extent IT should be applied. After a decision is made to develop a specific IT application, the issue of how to effectively implement the resulting IS must be addressed. The operating performance of an IS will be impaired if it does not fit with the needs and expectations of intended users, the natural patterns of work and communication, and the goals of relevant business processes. Elegant technical solutions are of little value unless they can be effectively implemented where they are needed. This inevitably involves the resolution of social and organizational issues. Thus, clear allocations of responsibility and the inclusion of appropriate expertise are both likely to improve the prospects for IS success. With the recent evolution towards end-user computing and the propensity for downsized and outsourced IS, the dynamics of the partnerships between management and technical specialists have changed. Much of the responsibility for IS has been passed on to line managers and user groups. They are now using IT as a resource in their business activities. This transfer of IT management responsibilities raises both the ability and duty of assorted specialists to contribute during the IS adoption process. As IT usage increases, and the disparities in computing skill levels grow, the need for end-user support will increase.

The rigid linear approach to IS development, whereby implementation follows design, has been supplanted by greater iteration. As a result, early and sustained user participation should be encouraged, but specialist support, from both technical and human factors experts, can also contribute to IS success. Time and resource constraints may preclude an ideal IS outcome. However, it is important that stakeholders with conflicting interests and perspectives as well as differential levels of political power have the opportunity to participate in the IS adoption process. The geographic reach of modern IT applications can make it difficult to involve all end-users and appropriate specialists. Face-to-face participation may be infeasible, but advances in telecommunications do favor the use of electronic meetings to discuss both technical and human factor issues and achieve a consensus on how they will be addressed. Goals can be identified for both the IS and the associated change program. These goals will help to guide the development and implementation effort. The satisfaction of users, the perceived quality of information outputs, and key dimensions of organizational performance, such as productivity, may be used to measure IS success.

One solution, according to recent studies, is a proactive level of HR involvement during the IS adoption process. By acting as agents of change, HR specialists can help both end users and IT specialists adjust to their new roles. User satisfaction can be promoted by creating an IS that supports rather than disrupts effective work and communication patterns, and explaining how the new system is to benefit individual users and the organization.

HR specialists can help to match the technology to the users, plan for the associated organization change, and deliver programs to smooth the transition process. They have traditionally been slow to introduce or effectively use information technology and their involvement in IS adoption processes across the organization has also remained modest. However, a change in this situation appears to be justified because of the positive link studies have found between HR specialist involvement and IS outcomes. Information systems should not be considered only in terms of money, technology, and business processes, but also in terms of how they affect attitudes and behaviors. The effective management of human resources is critical if the potential benefits from an IT investment are to be realized. Business improvements ultimately depend on people working smarter and more effectively. Those with human factors expertise can enhance both their own stature and improve key dimensions of organizational performance by contributing to the IS adoption process.

Source: Maris G. Martinsons and Patrick K.C. Chong, "The Influence of Human Factors and Specialist Involvement on Information Systems Success," *Human Relations* 52 (January 1999): 123(3).

rather than on tasks of members. Up to this point, the discussion has centered on redesigning work for individuals.

12.7.3.1 Criteria for Group Effectiveness

Effectiveness means doing the right things. A group is effective when it does the right things and efficient if it does them right. When designing systems and work to take advantage of new information technology, the analyst and organizational development specialist need to understand what makes a group effective. Systems and job design should support group effectiveness, as well as efficiency. The three criteria of group effectiveness identified by Hackman and Oldham include the following:[29]

1. The work of the group meets or exceeds organizational standards of quantity and quality. If the work of the group is not acceptable to those who receive and use it (e.g., reports are inaccurate or untimely), the group cannot be considered effective.

2. The group experience contributes to meeting the personal needs of members. Sometimes groups develop patterns of interpersonal behavior that are destructive to the well-being of members. If most members find that their experiences in the group frustrate their needs and block them from achieving personal goals, it would be hard to argue that the group is a successful social unit.

3. The social process in carrying out the work maintains or enhances the capability of members to work together on subsequent tasks. Some groups operate in ways that destroy their integrity; that is, the group burns out in the process of performing the task. Even if the product is acceptable, a group cannot be considered successful if it generates so much divisiveness and conflict that members are unwilling or unable to work together on future occasions.

Hackman and Oldham also identified three intermediate criteria of team effectiveness:[30]

1. The level of effort that group members bring to bear on the task.
2. The amount of knowledge and skill that group members apply to the task.
3. The appropriateness of the task performance strategies used by the group in doing its work.

12.7.3.2 Composition of Work Groups

An additional consideration in designing work for groups is the composition of the group. Hackman and Oldham recommended the following characteristics for a work group:[31]

1. The group should include members who have high levels of task-relevant expertise.
2. The group should be large enough to do the work but not much larger.
3. Group members should have at least a moderate level of interpersonal skills in addition to their task-relevant skills.
4. The group membership should strike a balance between homogeneity and heterogeneity.

Implementing and managing work groups is far more complex than designing jobs for individuals. The tasks of self-managing work groups generally have a much greater impact than individual jobs do on the organizational structure and management climate. Supporting and sustaining work groups without the commitment of top management is highly improbable. Some tasks are so large or complex, however, that they can be accomplished only by groups. Nevertheless, if given a choice, the systems analyst should use individual rather than group strategies unless the latter are significantly superior and the management climate is highly supportive.

12.7.4 Analyzing Opportunities for Work Redesign

Before undertaking any job design or redesign project, the analyst must assess the situation and ask such questions as the following.

- Is there a need or opportunity for job design?
- Is job redesign feasible for the unit?
- Which aspects of the job can benefit from improvement and which are fine as they are?
- How receptive will employees be to change, and how will changes fit with their needs and skills?
- How will changes fit with the rest of the organization?
- What opportunities for innovation are offered by the new technology?
- How should the affected employees be involved in the process?
- Are individual job redesign strategies appropriate, or is the task large or complex enough to require group strategies?

Resources, tools, and methods that analysts can use to answer these questions include consultants, organizational mission statements, work flow analysis, observations and interviews, survey instruments, and physical layout. When jobs are designed in conjunction with technological change, it is also important to keep in mind that innovations that are not initially apparent may emerge as workers gain experience with the technology.

12.7.4.1 Consultants

Consultants and organizational development specialists can be an excellent resource for the EUIS analyst. Consultants can offer objectivity, an outside perspective, and methods and assessment tools for diagnosing job redesign opportunities and developing solutions. Job redesign efforts often are tied to broader business process restructuring projects. (More information about working with consultants is provided in later chapters.)

12.7.4.2 Mission Statement of the Work Unit

A mission statement defines the purpose of the organization or work unit. If such a statement does not exist, the analyst should ask the manager of the unit to write one. The objective is to state the single reason why the organization exists. A well-designed organizational structure should establish one main purpose for each unit, and secondary goals should be related directly to this primary purpose. Armed with a clear statement of a work unit's mission, the analyst can then determine the extent to which current procedures support that mission and whether the organizational structure is consistent with the mission.

12.7.4.3 Work Flow Analysis

Before redesigning a job, the analyst should determine precisely what tasks are being done in the work unit and what purposes they serve. It is helpful to draw work flow diagrams similar to the ones in Figure 12-6. (Details on how to draw a flowchart are provided in later chapters.)

Figure 12-6
Work flow diagrams of a clerical operation

Source: Courtesy of Roy W. Walters and Associates, Inc.

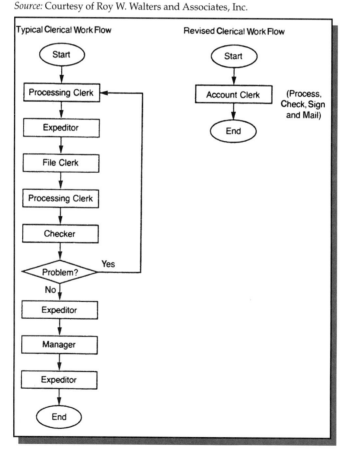

Roy W. Walters and Associates, Inc., a consulting firm that specializes in job design, suggests that questions such as those that follow be used in analyzing work flow diagrams. How does each employee get the work, and where does it go next? How do separate tasks relate to one another? Are all current tasks necessary? Can any tasks be eliminated? For example, are reports prepared that are not used? Could reports be prepared less frequently? Is all the information in the reports needed, or would a more concise report serve just as well—or perhaps better? Should any tasks be added? Should additional information be included or current information be replaced?

12.7.4.4 Observations and Interviews

The analyst's observations of the work unit and knowledge of the new technology to be implemented are key to understanding the opportunities for job redesign. The analyst should also solicit the observations of knowledgeable senior managers about the unit's operation. Individuals familiar with similar operations in other enterprises also can provide valuable insights. Also, the employees serving in the work unit are a key source of information and can provide valuable insights into work procedures, problems, receptivity to change, and ideas for improving the work.

Analysts should not overlook the clients of the work unit as a valuable source of information. Clients may include other departments or individuals within the enterprise who receive output from the unit, as well as consumers of the enterprise's products or services. It is important to determine how the client defines a superior service or product.

To gather information, the analyst can use either formal or informal interview techniques. Keep in mind, however, that interviewers should spend 80 percent of their time listening. (Interview techniques are summarized in a later chapter.) Data from interviews and observations can provide information about the unit's mission, detailed work procedures, efficiencies and inefficiencies of the work flow, who makes decisions about work, who evaluates work, and how the unit relates to other organizational units. The analyst should be sure to assess the perceptions, attitudes, and feelings of employees about their jobs and the organization.

12.7.4.5 Survey Instruments

The analyst can develop or purchase survey instruments to obtain detailed information about the jobs that are candidates for redesign and the skills, needs, and motivations of the employees who staff the positions. One such instrument, the Job Diagnostic Survey (JDS), was developed by Hackman and Oldham to gauge the degree to which each core job dimension exists in a given job.[32] The JDS asks objective questions to measure the core job dimensions and subjective questions to measure employee attitudes related to job satisfaction, motivation, and personal growth. The JDS is used to collect information from job incumbents. A separate instrument, the Job Rating Form (JRF), would be used to collect data describing a job from others in the organization besides the jobholder.

12.7.4.6 Physical Layout

The physical layout should support the work flow. When jobs are redesigned and work flow is changed, the physical layout also may need to be redesigned (see chapter 10).

When work was redesigned in the field offices of a large insurance company, creating the new position of client service representative, the physical layout of the office was redesigned, as well. Each client service representative was assigned a new workstation that was designed ergonomically to provide room for a PC, printer, client files, reference materials, personal items, and work area. The workstation area was designed in a U shape to facilitate the work flow and provide convenient access to necessary materials. Sound-absorbing panels created privacy, reduced disruptions, and housed electrical cables and wiring.

The end result was a more productive work environment. Having all essential information at their fingertips contributed to client service representatives' achievement of objectives such as being able to respond to 90 percent of client inquiries immediately, eliminating the need for callbacks after information was gathered.

12.8 TECHNOLOGY, BUSINESS PROCESS, AND JOB DESIGN IN PERSPECTIVE

The major goal of BPR and job design programs is to improve performance in meeting customers' needs and carrying out the organizational mission. When BPR and job design principles are coupled with technological innovations, enterprises have new opportunities to rethink the way products and services are produced and delivered.

> Using technology to create routine jobs that can be easily performed with minimum training constrains the capabilities of both technology and people. The greatest potential of information technology in the long run derives from the computer's capacity to enhance human capabilities. Just as humankind has historically used the lever to amplify the physical strength of the body, we can now use the computer to extend the thinking and creative power of the mind. . . . Those organizations that learn to use technology to unleash and capitalize on people's creative potential will have a tremendous competitive advantage.[33]

By this point, a reader may feel overwhelmed by the number of factors that affect the way work is organized and managed. This is precisely why organizations do not undertake these projects more often. Theories can serve only as aids in planning design strategies; no blueprints detail how changes should be implemented. The use of technology as an enabler to redesign processes and jobs is largely uncharted territory. It takes skilled, knowledgeable analysts, working with organizational development specialists and department management, to implement effective job design or business process changes. EUIS analysts must be sensitive to the ways that technology affects organizations, business processes, and people and be prepared to deal with them.

12.9 SUMMARY

Business process and job (re)design play a vital role in making technology pay off. To achieve the full benefits of information technology, project managers must address organizational issues, as well as technical ones. Implementing end-user solutions is as much about new ways of working as it is about technology. This chapter discusses the effect of technology on the design of business processes and knowledge work.

Technology is both an enabler and a constraint on business process, work group, and job design. BPR and job design can be approached at different levels.

At the enterprise level, BPR generally focuses on reengineering an entire organization or a department or division within the organization. At the business process level, reengineering efforts are smaller in scope and can occur at the unit, work group, and job levels. Because improvement efforts usually are driven or enabled by information technologies, EUIS project managers and analysts may be called upon to lead or contribute to such efforts.

BPR challenges the core business processes or assumptions underlying a business process. Before undertaking BPR efforts, enterprises must define their core business processes. Various reengineering methods have emerged, many of them proprietary to specific consulting firms. In general, BPR follows a highly structured methodology with four phases involving diagnosis, design, implementation, and institutionalization.

Technology has affected knowledge work in a number of ways. Technology takes over some tasks completely, replacing jobs in whole or in part. Jobs are modified when automation eliminates, adds, or shifts tasks. Technology also creates new jobs when new tasks are required to support systems or are generated by new opportunities. Computers make work more abstract and alter the worker's relationship to tasks. In some instances, jobs have been de-skilled, while in others they have been enhanced. When the business process changes, the organization's structure, which defines the relationships among jobs, also can change.

The influence of scientific management is still prevalent in most enterprises today, as their production line methods and functional organizations show. All that is beginning to change as enterprises begin to understand the dynamics (i.e., new paradigms) of competing in a twenty-first century, networked global marketplace. The Ford Motor Company Case at the end of part IV provides a good example. The chapter describes several work redesign concepts based primarily on behavioral and sociotechnical systems approaches.

The purpose of a job design program is to organize work and assign responsibility for completing tasks in ways that create jobs that motivate and empower employees to achieve organizational objectives. Major characteristics of motivating jobs are autonomy, skill variety, task identity, task significance, and feedback from the job itself. Five strategies for designing individual jobs are combining tasks, forming natural work groups, establishing client relationships, vertically loading jobs, and establishing feedback channels.

Designing effective work groups is more complex than designing individual jobs. Additional characteristics that must be addressed include task-required interdependencies and social interaction. Self-managing work groups include temporary task forces, permanent cross-functional teams such as decision-making committees and many types of management teams, and production teams. By far the most difficult to design are self-managing production teams.

Technology is a catalyst for redesign programs that provide new opportunities for helping people work more productively and creatively. Redesigning work is a complex process, but the payoff for those who succeed can be extremely high.

KEY TERMS

- Accountability
- Authority
- Business process redesign (or reengineering)
- Command and control management
- Computer-mediated work
- Core business process
- De-skilling
- Empowerment
- Enhancing
- Job
- Job design
- Job enlargement
- Job enrichment
- Job rotation

- Quality of work life (QWL)
- Responsibility

- Self-managing work groups
- Sociotechnical systems

- Third wave management
- Two-factor theory of motivation

DISCUSSION QUESTIONS

1. Define *business process redesign*. What is the relationship between information technology and business process redesign?
2. Define *job redesign*. Discuss the importance of job redesign in the Information Age.
3. List and describe the four phases of BPR methodology.
4. Differentiate *task analysis* from *job analysis*.
5. Trace the development of approaches to job redesign from scientific management to third wave management.
6. Technology changes the very nature of work. Discuss. Offer examples of how PCs and digital networks have changed the way work is done.
7. Define *empowerment*. How does the concept of empowerment differ from delegation of authority in the industrial era command-and-control management model?
8. Hackman and Oldham have done pioneering work in job redesign, offering basic strategies for implementing work design. For each of these strategies, explain how a marketing manager's job could be redesigned.
9. How do jobs typically get designed? How should they be designed? Who should be involved?
10. Define *self-managing work groups*. How do they differ from coacting groups? In addition to the five core job characteristics, what factors must be taken into consideration when designing work for self-managed work groups?

APPLICATION EXERCISES

1. Ask a secretary or administrative assistant with 5 to 10 years experience how PCs have changed job requirements and practices. Compare your answers with those of your classmates. How do the responses compare?
2. Interview a manager or other knowledge worker who has recently begun using a PC or the Internet. What software are they using and for what purposes? Ask for a summary of how the job has changed as a result of information technology. Integrate the answers with your comments. How do your findings compare with those of your classmates?
3. Find two or three recent articles about business process redesign (reengineering) and job redesign efforts in different types of enterprises. Identify key characteristics that contributed to the success of the restructuring efforts described in these articles. As a class, compare the characteristics found in different articles. What role did technology play in these redesign efforts?

SUGGESTED READINGS

Champy, James. *Reengineering Management: The Mandate for New Leadership.* (New York: HarperBusiness, A division of HarperCollinsPublishers, 1995).

Davenport, Thomas H. *Process Innovation: Reengineering Work through Information Technology.* (Boston: Harvard Business School Press, 1993).

Evan, Philip, and Thomas S. Wurster. *Blown to Bits: How the New Economics of Information Transforms Strategy.* (Boston: Harvard Business School Press, 2000).

Hackman, J. Richard, and Greg R. Oldham. *Work Redesign* (Reading, MA: Addison-Wesley, 1980).

Hammer, Michael. *Beyond Reengineering: How the Process-Centered Organization Is Changing Our Work and Our Lives.*

Hammer, Michael, and James Champy. *Reengineering the Corporation: A Manifesto for Business Revolution.*

(New York: HarperBusiness, A division of Harper-Collins Publishers, 1993).

Ouchi, William. *Theory Z: How American Business Can Meet the Japanese Challenge.* (Reading, MA: Addison-Wesley, 1981).

Weisbord, Marvin R. *Productive Workplaces: Organizing and Managing for Dignity, Meaning, and Community.* (San Francisco: Jossey-Bass/John Wiley & Sons, 1988).

Zuboff, Shoshana. *In the Age of the Smart Machine: The Future of Work and Power.* (New York: Basic Books, 1988).

Useful Websites

- Business Processes Reengineering Learning Center–BPR.

  http://www.prosci.com/bpraccess.htm

  The BPR Learning Center for Business Process Re-engineering provides a number of resources online including best practices, online tutorial, white papers, and more.

- Process management and improvement.

  http://www.dtic.dla.mil/c31/bprcd/3003s2.htm

  A Department of Defense (DoD) document that helps explain the differences among various approaches to process management, such as business process reengineering, business process redesign, and others. Links are provided to other material from the government's extensive Electronic College of Process Innovation.

- Business process reengineering and innovation.

  http://www.brint.com/BPR.htm (@BRINT—A Business Researcher's Interests)

  The Business Process Reengineering (BPR) section of @BRINT includes links to BPR articles and papers, books, periodicals, bibliographies, and tools, as well as other resources and related topics.

- WARIA Web Sites (Workflow and Reengineering International Association).

  http://www.waria.com/@5sites.html

  This site provides links to publications, associations, research organizations, and government bodies concerned with work flow and related topics.

- Process management glossary.

  http://www.carras.com/glossary.html

  This site defines basic terms and concepts used in process management. Developed by Jim Carras, a Texas-based business process management consultant, the site includes information about activity-based costing, integrated definition language (IDEF), cause-and-effect diagrams, knowledge-based processes, and more.

Endnotes

1. Derek Slater, "Profile: Ford Motor Company, Alignment Check," CIO 1 (November 15, 1999), 66.
2. Michael Hammer and James Champy, Reengineering the Corporation: A Manifesto for Business Revolution, (New York: Harper Business, A Division of Harper-Collins Publishers, 1993), 32.
3. Harold S. Resnich, Business Process Reengineering: An Executive Resource for Implementation (Boston: Work systems Associates, Inc., 1994).
4. Hammer and Champy, op. cit., 35.
5. Don Hellriegel, John W. Slocum, and Richard W. Woodard, Organizational Behavior, 4th ed. (St. Paul, MN: West Publishing Co., 1986), 362.
6. Frederick Herzberg, Mernard Mauser, and Barbara Block Snyderman, The Motivation to Work, 2nd ed. (New York: John Wiley & Sons, 1967), 113-119.
7. A. N. Turner and R. Lawrence, Industrial Jobs and the Worker (Boston: Harvard Graduate School of Business Administration, 1965).
8. J. R. Hackman and G. R. Oldham, Work Redesign, (Reading, MA: Addison-Wesley, 1980), 77-80.
9. Eric Trist, The Evolution of Socio-Technical Systems: A Conceptual Framework and an Action Research Program, Occasional paper no. 2 (Ontario: Ontario Quality of Working Life Center, June 1981), 16.
10. Marvin R. Weisbord, Productive Workplaces, (San Francisco: Jossey-Bass/John Wiley & Sons, 1988), 159.
11. Ibid., 130.
12. Hackman and Oldham, op. cit., 164.
13. Ibid., 165.
14. Ibid., 67.
15. Resnick, op. cit., 55.

16. Weisbord, op. cit., 259.

17. Example adapted from U. S. Congress, Office of Technology Assessment, The Automation of America's Offices (Washington, DC: Government Printing Office, 1985), 97.

18. Shoshana Zuboff, "New Worlds of Computer-Mediated Work," Harvard Business Review 82513 (September-October 1982), 142.

19. Joan Greenbaum, Cydney Pullman, and Sharon Szymanski, "Effects of Office Automation on the Public Sector Workforce: A Case Study," in U. S. Congress, op. cit., 103.

20. Zuboff, op. cit., 145.

21. Ibid.

22. Ibid.

23. Zuboff, Shoshana, In the Age of the Smart Machine: The Future of Work and Power (New York: Basic Books, 1988), 9-10.

24. U. S. Congress, op. cit., 101.

25. John Hoerr, Michael A. Pollock, and David E. Whiteside, "Special Report: Management Discovers the Human Side of Automation," Business Week (September 29, 1986), 70.

26. U. S. Congress, op. cit., 101.

27. Hackman and Oldham, op. cit., 72-73.

28. Ibid., 135-142.

29. Ibid., 168-169.

30. Ibid., 170.

31. Ibid., 174-177.

32. A copy of the JDS, with instructions and scoring information, is available in Hackman and Oldham, op. cit.

33. Elizabeth A. Regan, "Behavioral and Organizational Issues of Office Automation Technology" (Ph.D. dissertation, University of Connecticut, 1982), abstract in Dissertation Abstracts International 830 9253 (1982), 167.

Case Study   The Reengineering of Camera World

Some e-commerce companies believe Internet shoppers are too demanding and impatient. Are shoppers' expectations really out of line? When they place an order with a traditional brick-and mortar mail order house for two-day delivery, they receive the package in two days. The satisfying experience builds customer trust and loyalty in a company and brand. One company that has integrated their fulfillment into their e-commerce business is Camera World Company.

In the 20,000-square-foot warehouse behind the front office, 15 workers scurry down long concrete aisles, clutching sales orders fresh off the network printer. To the casual observer, these warehouse folk seem to have X-ray eyes. Quickly scanning the metal racks loaded with thousands of indistinguishable-looking boxes of equipment, they have an uncanny ability to tell a box holding a $10,000 lens from a virtually identical package bearing a $1,000 one. When they locate the box they're after, they place it in a plastic tub; a bar-code check at the packing station ensures that the order is complete. There, a young man nodding to rock music on a boom box pours Styrofoam peanuts into labeled cardboard shipping boxes and then seals the goods with a deft pull and twist of tape.

Camera World's order-fulfillment and delivery systems have stood the company in good stead. During the 1999 holiday season, many of the company's stalwart 300,000 customers came back and spent an average of $600 a pop. Thanks largely to the explosion of interest in digital cameras, sales soared from $80 million in 1998 to more than $115 million in 1999.

In December 1999, the company's Web site handled an average of 25,000 unique users each day, and Web sales rose by 245 percent over the previous year's figure for the month. (At the same time, mail-order business shot up 67 percent, and sales at the company's downtown Portland, Oregon, store were up 22 percent.) Some 90 percent of Web and mail-order shipments left the warehouse within 24 hours. Return rates for Web sales hovered around 4 percent, paralleling the rate of returns from the store and the mail-order business. "We maintained heavy inventories to ship on time, and it all worked pretty well," says Camera World's new CEO, Terry Strom. "But one thing's for sure: the Internet is raising the standard of performance for any retailer."

No kidding. The 1999 Christmas season, during which shoppers spent an estimated $6 billion online, saw many a Web site disappointing customers. According to a November 1999 report by the New York City Internet research firm Jupiter Communications, 46 percent of business-to-consumer Web sites took five or more days to respond to a query, never responded, or failed to post an e-mail address on the site for customers' inquiries.

"An awful lot of Web sites don't realize that customer service should be a priority," says Jupiter analyst Cormac Foster. "They focus on customer acquisition but don't spend time on the unsexy stuff, like customer-support infrastructure. Infrastructure doesn't get you headlines, but if you don't have a staff of people to take care of business behind the firewall, you won't get much." Case in point: Toys "R" Us, whose online subsidiary ToysRUs.com (announced with great fanfare in June 1998) found itself suffocating under the rush of online holiday traffic and was unable to fulfill orders on time. The company's back-end infrastructure was built to send truckloads of products to hundreds of stores—not to ship single orders to millions of consumers.

Don't call Camera World a "click-and-mortar" or an old-fashioned retailer with a Johnny-come-lately Web site. Rather, call it a dot-com with lots of back-end "not-com" experience. Camera World has long known that the boring stuff—attention to the fine details of customer service, simple and solid fulfillment processes, and trusted supplier relationships—is what really matters. Unless a company masters those three areas well before putting up a Web site, no amount of bells and whistles or transactional and design prowess online will make the Web component of the business successful.

Camera World already was known for excellent customer service, but with e-commerce different goals were spelled out. For starters, the company's Web pages would have to be transformed from simple brochureware into a true transaction site. Its back-end systems would have to be married to whatever happened on the Web. The company itself would have to move into a larger, better-organized space, with a warehouse that would allow orders to be shipped within 24 hours as opposed to the 5 days required by the mail-order business. To speed everything up, they had to cut out obstacles. They needed to staff up, to fix the bugs in the computer systems, and to upgrade the telephone systems for more lines. They also started streamlining processes.

Today Camera World's site, which costs roughly $10,000 a month to maintain, handles at least 15,000 unique visitors and 400 transactions a day. It's now a full-fledged community for shutterbugs. It keeps visitors interested with increasingly snazzy features—3-D images of featured products, an online auction area, forums, online chats with celebrated photographers, a selection "wizard" that helps customers choose the right camera by assessing their expertise and frequency of use, and so on.

Customers also can get quick answers to their e-mailed questions. Professional photographers respond to them by e-mail or phone—and customers even receive a notice via e-mail showing them where their question is in the queue. For those who eschew telephone handsets, an Internet-telephony feature lets customers whose computers are equipped with a sound card and a microphone connect over the Internet to talk with the sales and support staff.

When a customer orders a camera through the Web site, the transaction is zapped from the servers to the order-fulfillment database via a dedicated, high-speed T1 line. A software interface between the Web site and the database reads the order and translates it into the order-entry system. Sales reps, customer-support personnel, and shippers and other warehouse workers can review the order by tapping into Camera World's database from PCs.

Every few hours, warehouse personnel print a batch of 50 or so orders. Rush orders are printed on red paper; white paper signifies a standard UPS ground order. After workers locate the correct products and place them in a plastic tub along with the paper orders, they cart them to the shipping station, where the bar-code checking occurs. If the bar code doesn't match the order, a computer screen at the station notes the mismatch. If the match is correct, the inventory database records the product model number; when inventory reaches a low enough level, Camera World reorders. Once the product is packaged for shipping, it's loaded onto a waiting UPS van, which departs at the end of the day. Meanwhile, an e-mail message is sent to the customer, noting the time the package is scheduled to ship. Using a confirmation number supplied by the company, the customer can check the Web site to track the order. The customer tracks the package through the UPS link that is on the Camera World Business2Business Web page.

Most of Camera World's customers are not aware of these systems and do not really care about the specifics. They are just extremely satisfied with the customer service and have shown their loyalty when making purchases. Camera World realized earlier on that they had to provide the same excellent service they had provided for years with the traditional infrastructure.

Sources: Fryer, Bronwyn, "When Something Clicks," *Inc.* (March 15, 2000): *http://www.inc.com/articles/details/ 0,, ART17848,00.html* accessed on 12/26/00; Rigney, Patrick, "Eliminate Fulfillment Problems," *e-Business Advisor* (March 2000), 28–30; Holstein, William J., "Rewiring the 'Old Economy'," *U.S. News and World Report* (April 10, 2000), 38–40.

CASE STUDY QUESTIONS

1. Camera World reengineered itself from a brick-and-mortar shipping store to a full-fledged business-to-customer and business-to-business Web site. Customers always had been Camera World's top priority. How did the Web site change customer relationships?

2. Many retailers maintain a Web presence. Camera World decided they wanted a fully transactional Web site. What back-end system changes were necessary? Consider changes to design, hardware, software, and so forth.

3. In the near future, a greater percentage of camera suppliers will sell their products via the Web. What are some changes that Camera World could make to enhance their fulfillment process?

4. Visit Camera World's Web site (*www.cameraworld. com*) and Kodak's Web site (*www.kodak.com*). Browse the two sites and note their similarities and differences. Do the sites serve different customers? In your opinion, which site is more customer friendly? Why?

Part V

End-User Information Systems Project Management

Project management is a critical skill in today's marketplace—especially for IS professionals. Although many basic principles apply, methods for effective project management vary considerably from operational to general management. In a fast-paced digital economy where change has become a way of life, the ability to bring together a project team to accomplish a specific task on time, within budget is critical.

Part V discusses concepts, methodologies, and tools a project manager can employ in assessing business needs, designing new systems to improve business processes, implementing new systems, determining if the systems are operating as intended, and institutionalizing change. Part V begins with a chapter on strategic planning for EUIS systems. To be truly successful, EUIS projects must be tied to organizational directions and goals. The three subsequent chapters describe EUIS project management, its foundations, and specific stages.

Chapter 13, "Innovation and Strategic Planning," explains why strategic planning is important to achieving effective use of desktop computing and end-user information systems. Technology is viewed as a catalyst, or enabler, for productivity improvement and business process redesign. Consideration is given to how organizations foster innovative use of technology—and most importantly, how it can enhance people's performance. Characteristics of innovations, innovative people, and innovative organizations are discussed. The chapter includes guidelines for developing strategic plans for end-user information systems.

Chapter 14, "EUIS Project Management: Foundations and Overview," begins with a discussion of theory and frameworks relative to EUIS project management. This theory and framework serves as the basis for the EUIS project methodology. The chapter concludes with an overview of the eight-step project management method, which is explained in more detail in chapters 15 and 16. This project management model provides a unique framework for marrying information systems development with business process redesign.

Chapter 15, "EUIS Project Management: Assessment and Design," explains the first five steps of the EUIS project methodology. It describes techniques for defining the project scope, planning a project, assessing requirements, describing the proposed solution in detail, and selecting or developing the EUIS solution. It defines the specific deliverables—or results—that would be produced from each project step. Attention is paid throughout in aligning these steps with business process and change management activities.

Chapter 16, "EUIS Project Management: Implementation, Monitoring, and Aligning Business Process" discusses specific strategies for the last three steps of the EUIS project methodology, implementing the solution, evaluating results, and realigning business processes to institutionalize results. Implementation must be a carefully managed process that addresses all aspects of putting a system into operation: site preparation, equipment installation, business restructuring, conversion of procedures, training, technical support, and problem resolution. Evaluation is defined as measuring results against specified business objectives. Techniques appropriate for evaluating the effectiveness of new systems are discussed. Institutionalizing results is the final, and often neglected, step in systems implementation. To truly capture the benefits of new technology, this final step must do more than simply correct problems; it must realign business processes and incorporate the insights from new learning. Strategies are discussed for institutionalizing the linkages between technology and business restructuring.

Case Study Restructuring for Growth and Excellence

As part of its long-term strategy for excellence, Insurance and Financial Management (IFM), MassMutual Life Insurance Company's largest strategic business unit (SBU), examined its position in the financial industry with the objective of strengthening its general agency distribution system. The comprehensive strategic planning process, facilitated by outside consultants, examined the company's core competencies, product/market matrix, basis of competing, performance measures, mission, values, and operating principles. As a result, IFM senior management decided to implement a broad series of changes in its distribution system, involving major business restructuring, technology, and cultural change. This case describes how the implementation of one of these projects was managed.

The MassMutual IFM sales distribution system is comprised of 90 sales offices, called agencies. The managers, called General Agents, who head up these sales offices (agencies), are essentially sole proprietors under contract with the MassMutual. Thus they enjoy a fair degree of autonomy in their operations. In the past, the company had taken a fairly hands-off approach to managing these sales agencies. While this approach encouraged individual entrepreneurship, it essentially left each sales agency on its own reinventing the wheel. In an increasingly complex financial services industry, this approach limited the ability of these sales agencies to grow and achieve higher levels of success. The restructuring program was designed to provide a more standardized 'MassMutual' way to doing business that provided a better foundation for agency growth and success while allowing the home office to focus resources on improving its operations in key support areas.

Described here are the steps the company took to create conditions conducive to change and implement their 'Agency Models for Success' project.

Models for success: shared visions/mutual decisions. The 'Agency Models for Success' are based on a shared vision for excellence and growth of the MassMutual sales agency distribution system. Based on the best practices of successful general agencies throughout the insurance industry, 10 models, addressing key areas of agency operations, were shaped through a two-year strategic review process involving agency and home office staff working together in the spirit of interdependence and partnership.

The models focused on three strategic areas of agency operations: getting, keeping, and building field force; getting, keeping, and building clients; and agency management. The resulting models were:

- Business enterprise
- Frontline management
- Recruiting and selection
- Agency marketing
- Building and retaining agents
- Technology
- Strategic business planning
- New business
- Investment services

The models addressed 5 basic questions. What is recommended? Why is it important to me? How will it achieve better results than the way in which I am now doing it? How do I implement it? And what resources are available to help me implement it?

In addition, the program defined a vision for the sales agency of the future. Three different size agencies were detailed, looking at factors such as organizational structure, management and support staff, services, operating costs, budgeting, and marketing, among others. This shared vision was communicated through various events and media, including major sales conferences, special brochures, manuals, letters, executive summaries, and company newspapers, to name a few. Various strategies were used to reinforce the vision constantly and consistently.

The consulting process—a mirror. The models incorporated significant management, operational, and cultural changes for both the field and the home office. Implementation of the models required first obtaining the buy-in of the General Agent (sales agency manager) to the program. The home office then worked with each sales agency in analyzing current operations, identifying high leverage opportunities for growth, establishing goals, developing action plans, executing these programs, and monitoring results.

Implementing this program required working closely with representatives of the General Agents Association to create a five-step consulting process. After piloting the program in four sales agencies, the company organized four Agency Model Consulting Teams. Each team was headed by a regional second vice president plus three other knowledgeable consultants. One member of that team was a technology specialist.

General Agents interested in using the best practices to grow their agencies to new levels of success could request a visit from an Agency Models Consulting Team. The four

member teams spent two and a half days with the General Agent and his or her staff to help assess how the sales agency was doing and how current operations compared with the 'Agency Models for Success'.

The consultants conduct a day or more of intense interviewing with a minimum of 16 people in each sales agency. These include both agency staff and agents. The results are compiled and 'mirrored' back to the agency staff as a snapshot of reality as seen by the consulting team.

Impacting the future. The 'mirroring' process, because it is non-judgmental, is a powerful technique in helping the agency management staff identify opportunities for improving their performance. Following the 'mirror' presentation, the consultants work with the management team to identify high leverage opportunities for growth and what the agency wants to do about them. The consulting team works with the agency management team to help clarify needed actions to achieve the objectives they set. The outcome of this session is a 'win/win' partnership agreement with formal action plans and a commitment to work together to achieve results.

Some of the critical success factors of this approach are: vision and strategic alignment; managing the process; business/technical partnership; training and supporting innovative procedures; and sustaining long-term commitment.

Vision and strategic alignment. In order to support the changes being implemented in the distribution system, the company needed to realign internal operations. Five teams were assigned to formulate plans for reengineering IFM home office operations in the following key areas: marketing, building and retaining field force, recruiting and selection, agency management, and client building.

The six-month effort was guided by outside consultants. Each team included a mix of business and systems people, headed by a vice president as team captain. The entire project was managed by a senior vice president with oversight provided by a senior management steering committee. The reengineering recommendations of the five teams were integrated into a single proposal that was presented to the IFM committee for approval. Implementation was closely coordinated with the implementation of the Agency Models in the field.

Managing the process—roles and responsibilities. Implementation of Agency Models is essentially a bottom-up process working directly with each sales agency and involving staff and agents in implementing changes. The key roles and responsibilities for managing the implementation process are:

- The project sponsor, who is the senior vice president in charge of the Field and Sales Development division.

- Home office line managers. Responsibility for results resides with operational areas, reporting to the sponsor.
- General Agents and their management teams.
- Two change agents who coordinate the project and report directly to the project sponsor. Responsibilities of the change agents include: managing the process (change management), 'inventing' and piloting the implementation process, working with all stakeholders, sustaining long-term commitment, administering the program, planning intervention and implementation strategies, working to incorporate changes into standard home office operating procedures.

Business/technical partnership. Both the Agency Models and the home office reengineering efforts were driven by business requirements; technology is viewed as the enabler. Technology specialists were actively involved throughout the strategic planning process. They played a key role by helping business managers understand the opportunities that technologies provided to improve business operations. Many of the reengineering recommendations were also supported by technology recommendations. A separate technology model was developed expressly to support the other nine models. Thus, the business requirements were the driver for the technology strategy.

Train and support innovative procedures. To support implementation, the company published Agency Models manuals, offered workshops and seminars, and provided other resources to encourage sales agencies to adopt those best practices that could help them improve performance levels. In addition to their regional field offices and other home office resources, the company contracted with a former General Agent and field development vice president as coaches to assist agencies.

Sustaining long-term commitment. Some of the main strategies used to sustain long-term commitment include: intervention strategies, keeping the vision alive, reinforcing behaviors, strengthening the buy-in of stakeholders, communication with key stakeholders, publishing success stories, coaching, and institutionalizing results. An important focus was on working with the senior field development vice presidents and other important stakeholders to align home office operations with all the changes being implemented in the field. The Agency Models program is an ongoing effort for the long term.

Results and Progress

This program is viewed as a long-term investment in building production capability. Examples of early progress in agencies included implementation of new programs such as marketing, improved recruiting systems, restructuring and strengthening of frontline management staff, clarification of roles, and improved accountability for results. General Agents have been particularly enthusiastic about the consulting process, which is the backbone of the implementation approach. The cooperation and frankness during interviews and the level of commitment and follow-through on action plans are indicative of the success of this approach.

Summary

Implementating restructuring projects (major organizational change) is a constant challenge. When the going gets rough, as it inevitably does, there are always skeptics waiting in the wings to insist that new processes are not working and the solution is to go back to the old tried and true.

Critical to success was keeping people focused on the vision and creating successes along the way that reinforce needed behavior changes. Managing the implementation of this restructuring project was a constant balancing act: balancing the interests of all major stakeholders, change activities and operations, training and production time, orderly change versus chaos.

Implementation of Agency Models is viewed by the company more as a process than a destination. Ultimately, one of the goals is to create a learning organization that will continue to evolve and reach higher levels of success. Implementation is not viewed simply as a finite set of tasks to be completed by a certain date. The objective was to create a framework for continuous improvement. For example, consulting teams bring back ideas and success stories that can improve upon the original models. General Agents have initiated networking to support each other in implementing the Models. General Agents were encouraged to take a broader view of the general agency distribution system, seeing their success as ultimately linked to the success of the entire system.

'Learning organizations,' writes Peter Senge in *The Fifth Discipline* (Doubleday Currency, New York, 1990), 'are organizations where people continually expand their capacity to create the results they truly desire, where new and expansive patterns of thinking are nurtured, where collective aspiration is set free, and where people are continually learning how to grow together.'

CASE STUDY QUESTIONS

1. What was the business strategy for this project? How did the business strategy shape the approach to implementation?

2. The project used a best practices approach to implementing change. Do you think this was an appropriate strategy? Why or why not?

3. Why did the company select a consulting model rather than a training model to implement technology and business changes? How important was the buy-in and involvement of all key stakeholders in the implementation process? How important was creating a shared vision for change? Why?

4. What were the major roles and responsibilities involved in managing the project and the implementation process? Who had ultimate responsibility for project results in the home office? In the field?

5. The case does not tell us a lot about the specific technology solutions that were involved in this reengineering effort. It does stress however, that technology was viewed as the enabler for change rather than a driver for change. Based on the information you learned in Chapter 3 about sales force automation, why do you think the company took this aproach? What are some technology tools that might have been implemented as part of this project?

Chapter 13

Innovation and Strategic Planning

Learning Objectives

Upon completing this chapter, you should be able to:

➤ Define strategic planning and explain why it is important to achieving effective end-user information systems.

➤ Define characteristics of innovations, innovative people, and innovative organizations.

➤ Understand the relationships between technology and innovation.

➤ Discuss the use of technology to deliver products and services.

➤ Explain how technology can be used to restructure business processes.

➤ Give examples of how industries have used technology to gain a competitive advantage.

➤ Explain the role of R&D in developing technical solutions to problems.

➤ Offer guidelines for developing an EUIS strategic plan.

13.1   INTRODUCTION

There is nothing more difficult to plan, more doubtful of success, nor more dangerous to manage than the creation of a new system. For the initiator has the enmity of all who would profit by the preservation of the old institutions and merely lukewarm defenders in those who would gain by the new ones. The hesitation of the latter arises in part . . . from the general skepticism of mankind, which does not really believe in an innovation until experience proves its value.

—Niccolo Machiavelli, 1513[1]

The concept of planning strategically for information technologies and linking use of technology to strategic business planning emerged in the 1980s. Until recently, however, such planning has focused primarily on an enterprise level for large-scale systems. The idea of planning strategically for EUIS has much credence, primarily because information technology users have much to offer in visioning the technological direction of the organization. In fact, evidence exists that end users are, indeed, included in decisions to adopt, use, and manage technologies.[2] Strategic planning for EUIS, which generally occurs on the business unit level, implies innovation, and it implies linking that innovation directly to business goals and missions.

Innovation is a two-edged sword; it is both applauded and feared. Although organizations acknowledge the value of new ideas, corporate cultures (in actuality) seldom foster and reward innovation. Technologies (innovations) bring opportunities as well as threats. Information technologies can help improve the way organizations and their employees at all levels perform work and provide products and services. However, information technology also poses threats to the status quo and the quality of work life. To take advantage of technology's opportunities and avoid its threats, planners and end users must integrate carefully their use of technology with business operations and goals. Capitalizing on new opportunities requires foresight, careful planning, and good leadership.

The purpose of this chapter is to explain how innovations in the form of information technology fit into the strategic plan of an enterprise. In many cases, technology is the driving force for organizational directions. The chapter begins by explaining why planning is important to achieving widespread benefits from EUIS. Then, characteristics of innovations, innovators, and innovative organizations are discussed. Two models that describe how technological innovations are infused and assimilated by enterprises are presented. Strategies for restructuring work processes are discussed in the next two sections. The chapter concludes with an overview of strategic planning for end-user information systems.

In reading this chapter, the reader should keep in mind that innovation theory borrows from ideas discussed in previous chapters regarding worker performance, job design, and change management. This chapter should be read with a view to seeing how the need for improved organizational, work group, and individual performance affects planning for EUIS technologies.

13.2   EFFECTIVE USE OF EUIS MUST BE PLANNED AND MANAGED

Although every EUIS pioneer can recount examples of innovative applications, there are just as many tales of technologies collecting dust. Analysts would be shortsighted indeed to assume that plugging in the right equipment is sufficient. That is precisely what happens in most enterprises, however. Typically, analysts assess the business needs, recommend an equipment configuration, and, if the project is approved, install the system, arrange initial training, and then walk away.

Department managers are often mystified when new equipment is not used as anticipated. After all, the systems analyst identified a long list of appropriate applications, and staff members attended classes. A flurry of excitement followed the first few applications. Months later, however, everything seemed to have reverted to business as usual. Where does the department manager turn for help?

Innovative use of technology must be nurtured and managed. Skilled analysts can provide leadership through the stages of technological innovation. To succeed, analysts must work with end users to understand how technology can contribute to improving operations and meeting business goals, but even more importantly, they must work to empower entrepreneurial workers to use new tools that allow them to apply their knowledge and creativity to create new value.

However, not all impacts of technology are beneficial. *Undesirable* consequences include routine, boring jobs; social isolation; shifting work bottlenecks rather than eliminating them; high absenteeism and turnover; excessive monitoring of work; and stressful work environments. Such outcomes may be related to inexperience with the technology, inadequate planning, or lack of foresight. Negative outcomes can be expected when management focuses on short-term benefits or is insensitive to employee welfare. Whatever the reason, managers and analysts should not overlook the personal and organizational impact of new systems. In the long term, ignoring these issues lowers the quality of work life and productivity, as well.

We no longer have a choice as to whether or not to use technology; the question is how best to use it, as technology is an important resource to be managed and leveraged, just like the traditional resources of labor, materials, and capital. We've seen an explosion in the number of uses for information technology in the past few years. Many economists are crediting productivity growth and GDP as a result of improvements in information technology.[3] These results may be tempered, according to Roger W. Ferguson, Jr., a member of the Board of Governors of the Federal Reserve System, depending upon:

- the rate of investment in new equipment that embodies the new technology.
- the rate at which the labor force is able to acquire needed skills.
- the fundamental potential of the technology itself.[4]

Moreover, the networked organization does more with technology than reengineer business processes or make a shift from hierarchical to team-based structures. Technology requires a radical rethinking of the nature and function of organizations, and their relationships to each other.[5]

No good idea succeeds on its own merit. Technology in and of itself is not sufficient: It *must* be coupled with changes in the way work is done, and these changes go far beyond the task level. Systemic changes are difficult to achieve, as reflected by the quotation at the beginning of this chapter, and few prescriptions for success are available. Managers or analysts can start, however, by looking more closely at the process of technological innovation.

13.3   ADOPTION, INFUSION, AND ASSIMILATION OF TECHNOLOGY

To apply technology innovatively, EUIS specialists must understand how it is used and assimilated into the work environment. Research shows that individuals or enterprises typically progress through a number of phases as they adopt, use, and assimilate new technologies. Various models have been developed by researchers to describe this process. Although these models vary somewhat in their description of the various stages, they all basically suggest an evolutionary process similar to that depicted in Figure 13-1, whereby an enterprise adopts an innovation (technology) and gradually learns to use (infusion) and assimilate it.

Progression through the stages of technological innovation is not automatic for many reasons. Enterprises may need to adapt their internal structures in ways that encourage employees to change the way they work. Work procedures and standards may be changed, work flow patterns altered, reporting relationships changed, jobs redesigned, and performance criteria revised. Executives may need to make changes in the enterprise's culture: its business philosophy; management style; departmental relationships; and relationships with its partners, suppliers, and especially its customers. Changes of this magnitude are easy to talk about but difficult to accomplish. As discussed in chapter 11, "Organizational Change," changing people's behavior is a complex and slow process, and may require the intervention of a skilled change agent.

Figure 13-1
Basic innovation model

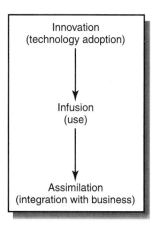

Employees who embrace technology and quickly fly on their own are the exception rather than the rule. Thus, placing a computer on an employee's desktop does *not* automatically lead to improvements and innovations. To use technology creatively, individuals must reach a "critical mass" of know-how and experience. Without appropriate training, support, and guidance, this critical mass may never be achieved amid the pressures of everyday work. Until individuals understand the potential opportunities and benefits, they have little incentive to expend the time and effort required to learn to use and apply the technology. Moreover, these efforts must be supported by an environment that fosters initiative and rewards innovation. Otherwise, the efforts of even the most innovative employees can be thwarted easily.

A planning team can bring together the technical resources, business expertise, and management decision making essential for innovative application of technology. This implies not only that analysts must work closely with decision makers, but that executives should become more knowledgeable about technology. To recognize new opportunities, executives do not necessarily have to know how the technology works. However, executives do need to understand how technology can address business problems.

13.4 INNOVATIONS, INNOVATORS, AND INNOVATIVE ENTERPRISES

As a basis for understanding innovativeness, this section presents characteristics associated with innovations, innovators, and innovative enterprises. As we discuss planning for EUIS, some important questions guide the discussion:

- What are the characteristics of the technology innovation that lead to productivity gains?
- What are the characteristics of the users that spur them on to achieve productivity gains?
- What are the characteristics of companies that achieve substantial productivity gains?

This section presents some useful descriptive models of technology infusion and assimilation.

13.4.1 Characteristics of Innovations

In *Diffusion of Innovation,* Everett Rogers defined an *innovation* as *a new idea, practice, or object that is perceived as new by an individual.*[6] According to Rogers, characteristics of both the innovation and the adopter influence the *infusion* (use) of technology. Comparing two innovations, blue jeans (quick adoption) and the metric system (slow adoption), Rogers explained that their differing rates of adoption are dependent upon each innovation's (1) relative advantage; (2) compatibility; (3) complexity; (4) trialability; and (5) observability.

Rogers defines *relative advantage* as the degree to which the innovation is perceived as better than the idea it supersedes. *Compatibility* is the degree to which it is perceived as being consistent with existing values and past experiences. *Complexity* is the degree to which an innovation is considered difficult to use and understand. *Trialability* is the degree to which it may be experimented with on a trial basis. *Observability* is the degree to which the results of an innovation are visible to others.[7] Comparing these characteristics for blue jeans and the metric system, it is easy to see why nearly everyone wears blue jeans but few have completely adopted the metric system (in the United States).

Blue jeans are more rugged than most other pants (relative advantage), can be worn with most anything (compatibility), are simple to care for (not complex), inexpensive—until designer jeans came along at least (trialable), and nice looking (observable). The metric system, by comparison, basically replaces an incompatible system with which people are already familiar (little relative advantage), requires study and practice to use (complex), requires a major conversion effort to implement (not trialable), and does not physically change objects—just how they are measured (not observable).

Using these characteristics to describe information technologies, it is easy to see why electronic mail was slow to catch on. Yet, once a critical mass had the technology, its usage skyrocketed. Initially, facsimile was preferred as its speed far exceeded that of the fastest overnight delivery service (relative advantage). Facsimile, unlike e-mail, is paper-based (compatibility), and its basic features are as easy to use as a telephone (less complexity). It was integrated slowly into the workplace (trialability), and outputs were tangible to others (observability). Electronic mail, on the other hand, had slower adoption curves. While e-mail offers relative advantages over fax and overnight delivery services, it has many characteristics that do not resemble traditional communications (compatibility). For example, users who traditionally relied on secretarial support for letter writing and distribution found the responsibility shifted to themselves with e-mail. In addition, many early e-mail systems had complicated user interfaces (more complex). Moreover, use of e-mail requires the cooperation of others; recipients of messages are needed (trialability and observability).

However, once e-mail systems became easy to use, were integrated into a variety of other groupware products, and the relative advantage over other communication media was demonstrated, vast numbers began using the technology. In short, the greater any technology can score on these five characteristics—relative advantage, compatibility, trialability, observability, and (less) complexity—the faster its adoption will be.

13.4.2 Characteristics of the User Population

When implementing innovations, planners must take into consideration characteristics of the user population. Everett Rogers classified the general population with regard to its acceptance of innovations (here, technology).[8] The pattern of acceptance described here helps explain why new technologies may generate an initial enthusiastic response but never achieve the intended productivity benefits. Note that only the first group of users and possibly the second are apt to adopt innovations in the absence of specific strategies to promote use and modify business processes. These groups can be plotted on a bell curve, as shown in Figure 13-2.

Innovators are risk takers. They try new technologies just because the technology exists. They are always the first to try something new. Innovators typically have hoards of software catalogs and love gadgets. Innovators make up 2.5 percent of the population. This is the group that enthusiastically embraces new technology and sees the possibilities right away.

Early adopters wait until innovators have proven the technology useful, but once the usefulness is shown, are quick to implement the technology. Early adopters make up 13.5 percent of the population.

The *early majority* wait until the technology has been established useful by 16 percent of their peers. They are not quick to implement the technology but can be reasoned with once proof of the technology's value is well documented in the enterprise. The early majority makes up 34 percent of the population.

The *late majority* are real skeptics. They will use the technology only when it is well accepted by others and only after much trepidation. The late majority makes up 34 percent of the population.

Laggards will use new technologies only when their resistance (screaming and kicking!) get them nowhere. They can be described as set in their ways and will change only under duress. Laggards make up 16 percent of the population.

13.4.3 Characteristics of Innovative Enterprises

Technology adoption has been described in relation to characteristics of both the technology itself and its users. Likewise, enterprises can be described as having characteristics that foster innovativeness. Innovation in enterprises has been defined as "the creation or adoption of new products, services, processes, or procedures. The capacity to innovate is central to the ability of an enterprise to adapt to changes in its environment."[9] In the *Harvard Business Review*, Quinn identified the

Figure 13-2
The innovativeness of the user population

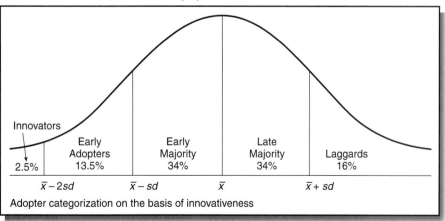

Adopter categorization on the basis of innovativeness

Source: Reprinted with the permission of The Free Press, a division of Simon & Schuster, Inc., from *Diffusion of Innovations*, 3/e by Everett M. Rogers. Copyright © 1962, 1971, 1983 by The Free Press.

following characteristics of small and large innovative enterprises in the United States and other countries.[10]

1. *Innovation requires flexible management.* Managers need to think carefully about how innovation fits into their strategies and to structure technology, skills, resources, and organizational commitments accordingly.

2. *Innovation is an incremental process.* Quinn's research revealed that "few, if any, major innovations resulted from highly structured planning systems." Rather, "major innovations are best managed as incremental, goal-oriented, interactive learning processes." (The OTA Model for Technology Innovation described later is such an incremental process.) Think about this incremental process in relation to the characteristics of users described in the preceding section. Gaining the acceptance of each group of users successively requires additional effort.

3. *Successful managers of innovation attack a problem from several angles simultaneously.* Innovative managers often encourage multiple efforts to address opportunities until more information becomes available. "Not knowing precisely where the solution will occur, wise managers establish the widest feasible network for finding and assessing alternative solutions. They keep many options open until one of them seems sure to win . . . incrementalism helps deal with psychological, political, and motivational factors that are crucial to success. By keeping goals broad at first, a manager avoids creating undue opposition to new ideas."

4. *Effective managers of innovation allow for chaos within guidelines.* In other words, managers avoid elaborate planning or control systems and manage by "setting goals, selecting key people, and establishing a few critical limits and decision points for intervention." Choosing among competing projects can be difficult, and the decision is often intuitive rather than scientific. Innovative companies also find special ways to reward innovators.

5. *Management practices in innovative companies reflect the realities of the innovation process itself.* "Innovation tends to be individually motivated, opportunistic, customer responsive, tumultuous, nonlinear, and interactive in its development." Innovative companies strive to keep their plans flexible and freeze them only when they become essential for strategic purposes, such as timing.

Managers must balance the need for continuity and stability with the needs for fostering creativity and nurturing innovation. This is a tough job. Technologies have characteristics that make them more or less likely to be adopted. People have characteristics that influence their attitudes toward adopting new technologies. Enterprises have practices that influence innovation. Few managers can afford to make many mistakes. Moving too aggressively can mean making costly mistakes or causing chaos; moving too slowly, on the other hand, can lead to obsolescence.

13.5 THE INFUSION OF TECHNOLOGY: DESCRIPTIVE MODELS

This section presents two models which describe technology's infusion in enterprises: the OTA Model of Technological Change and Day's Five Stages of Office Systems Evolution. These two models are complementary and provide a useful

Part V   End-User Information Systems Project Management

framework for the planner by clarifying interrelationships among people, process, and technology.

13.5.1 OTA Model of Technological Change

At the request of the U.S. Senate Committee on Labor and Human Resources and the House Committee on Education and Labor, the U.S. Office of Technology Assessment (OTA) studied the consequences of the rapid growth in the use of information and communication technologies in offices. In conducting this study, OTA used Joseph Coates's simple conceptual model. Depicted in Figure 13-3, the model provides a useful conceptualization of the process through which enterprises use and assimilate new technologies.[11]

According to the OTA model, when enterprises adopt new technology, three kinds of effects are likely: *substitution, adaptation,* and *transformation.*

Substitution   Initially, direct substitution effects are seen at both the process and organizational levels. New technology replaces an older technology, human labor, or both. Word processing, spreadsheets, and databases replace the typewriter, bookkeeping ledgers, and payroll systems. E-mail augments telephone systems. E-commerce affects advertising, order entry, customer relations . . . everything! These changes have effects on productivity, the size of the workforce, job content,

Figure 13-3
The OTA model of technological change

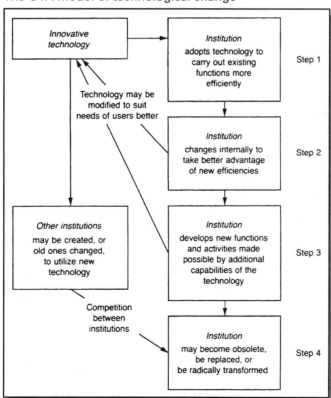

Source: United States Congress, Office of Technology Assessment. *The Automation of America's Offices.* (Washington, D.C.: Government Print Office, 1985) p. 10.

workers' skills, and other variables. These effects are perceived as good or bad depending on one's perspective and interests.

When technology is seen as substitution, institutional structures, culture, operating procedures, and management expectations still reflect the old work flow and business process. Tension may result because the characteristics of the new technology and/or the requirements for its use are different than what existed before the new technology was implemented. Until this tension is resolved, the full benefits of the substitution are not realized, and productivity may even fall. Many enterprises see technology as a new way of doing the same things.

Adaptation   Gradually, the institution, deliberately or unconsciously, by plan or by trial and error, begins to adapt to new ways of doing things. This stage may include, for example, formal reorganizations, shifts in power relationships, adjustments in responsibilities, or changes in the way workers are recruited and compensated. Two kinds of problems, however, may arise in this stage. If significant changes are made quickly and arbitrarily, they may meet resistance from those who lose power or are uncomfortable with changes in the status quo—especially when people do not understand the reasons for the changes or have not participated in the decisions. On the other hand, if adaptations are not planned, those affected may undergo a long period of frustration and inefficiency before they discover what changes are necessary.

Transformations   The third kind of effect, transformation, is possible because new technologies have entirely new capabilities that the enterprise may use to develop new activities, products, or services. For example, e-commerce not only offers a more efficient way to do business, but also expands the potential for new business and relationships with customers, suppliers, and partners. Thus, new, potentially more effective activities replace the old.

Some enterprises, as soon as they are computerized, begin to offer new services. This round of effects may bring about the restructuring of an industry or a mix of industries. Some financial institutions, for example, have used new information systems to overcome legal boundaries between banks, insurance companies, brokers, and other elements of the industry. Likewise, higher education is using new technologies to provide a broader range of educational services.

Enterprises that fail to adopt new technology, even when it becomes the norm among competitors, risk eventual obsolescence and failure. For example, any mail order business that is not on the Web is in serious trouble.

The feedback loop in OTA's Model of Technological Change is important. Ongoing development of technology is shaped by the market and the demands of users. New businesses emerge that specialize in innovative use of the technology or in helping other firms use it.

13.5.2   Day's Five Stages of Office Systems Evolution

An early yet still useful model that depicts the evolution of technology was developed by L. H. Day of the Diebold Office Automation Group. Day's Five Stages of Office Systems Evolution focuses on how an enterprise moves from isolated tools to integrated systems. Like the OTA Model of Technological Change, Day's model characterizes the assimilation as an evolutionary process.[12] This model may be even more relevant today than originally because of the current thrust to downsize enterprises and place technology at the desktop.

1. *Conception.* In the conception stage, individual tools, like word processing or spreadsheets, are judged to be inadequate. The need to support knowledge workers directly with integrated tools is recognized.
2. *Initiation.* Planners look beyond cost-displacement applications and implement the first value-added pilot. Studies are initiated and requirements for a pilot are determined. Implementation begins.
3. *Contagion.* Integrated pilots are implemented (and evaluated) to improve the work of professional, multifunction clerical, managerial, and executive personnel.
4. *Consolidation.* Full operational systems are implemented to consolidate many developments in the contagion stage.
5. *Creative evolution.* Integrated systems are developed that are inherent in the plans to improve services, meet objectives, expand markets, and revise the mission of the enterprise.

Notice shifts in the progression through Day's stages. The first shift is from using new technologies as a replacement for old technologies or people to using new technologies for changing the way work is done. The next shift is from isolated applications to integrated systems. Then, the emphasis changes from applications for clerical workers to an emphasis on managers and knowledge workers. Finally, technology efforts shift away from individual tasks to focus on the objectives and mission of the enterprise. Understanding this pattern can help the planner determine where the enterprise currently is and predict action plans that need to be put into place to move the enterprise forward.

13.6 USING TECHNOLOGY TO REDESIGN BUSINESS PROCESSES AND GAIN COMPETITIVE ADVANTAGE

When left to chance, adoption, infusion, and assimilation of technology can be painstakingly slow. However, when planned, the process can be managed and accelerated. Through planning, enterprises can use EUIS to meet two major goals: improve performance and give the organization a competitive advantage. Organizations can gain competitive advantage by creating innovative products and services and creating new delivery systems in the marketplace.

13.6.1 Using Technology as a Catalyst for Improving Performance

The ultimate image of the workplace of the future still may be hazy, but the trends are clear. The most significant productivity improvements have been achieved by using technology to change the way people work and the way business is conducted. Successful companies are adopting innovative work practices that get the most out of technology.

Information technology can improve employee performance by streamlining information processing, which improves accuracy and timeliness and eliminates unnecessary duplication of effort. By focusing on the more effective flow and use of information, planners can work to allow users access to the *right information at the right time*. This approach requires that technology be adapted to people (not people to technology), so that it increases the effort focused on business goals and reduces the effort required for supplementary chores. Perhaps the most important performance enhancer is to support applications that begin with the individual user, empowering individuals and teams to do their work more efficiently and effectively.

> It is becoming evident that advanced computer technology calls for radical change in traditional practices. New technologies are being used as a catalyst to institute major changes in the way jobs are designed and enterprises are managed. . . . The old idea that a manager's main function is to control workers is replaced with the concept that a manager should encourage employees to use initiative.[13]

Because productivity increases do not result just from the speed of computer processing, the pertinent questions become the following. How can the analyst and/or manager facilitate innovation and shorten the learning curve? What are some of the successful techniques used by innovators? How can business processes be restructured? How can technology help empower individuals and work teams?

13.6.1.1 *Replacing Old Procedures*

For systems to become productive, technology-supported procedures must *replace* manual procedures, not continue them. Manual procedures must be eliminated when new ones have been learned. In practice, replacing the old with the new is not as simple as it may appear. For example, employees who are not yet confident of their computer abilities may cling to old, manual procedures to verify computer output or as a backup just in case something goes wrong with the computer. Employees may receive inadequate training, resist the intrusion from outside, or have insufficient motivation to change ingrained habits and practices.

E-business, for example, is changing the way office supplies are routinely ordered. Superstores are offering online purchasing of their products, and in many cases, buyers are developing systems that allow users to shop directly online with the store, skipping central purchasing departments. Such streamlining of activities replaces cumbersome purchasing orders, and more just-in-time ordering of supplies is cost effective.

13.6.1.2 *Eliminating Work and Combining Tasks*

Whenever possible, work procedures should be scrutinized *before* technology is implemented. Usually, this means looking at the overall work flow in an organizational unit instead of just individual tasks. Analysts should look for opportunities to simplify or eliminate work. This is a departure from the typical approach of identifying applications and recommending hardware and software based on existing tasks.

Japan's experience with high-technology robots illustrates the dilemma. In retrospect, some Japanese manufacturers discovered that in some cases they had programmed the inefficiencies of former technologies into their robots. They overlooked opportunities to streamline old procedures before automating them. For example, a different assembly sequence might be called for, or a robot might be able to perform two or three tasks simultaneously that would need to be done one at a time if they were performed manually. Manufacturers are not alone. In the early days of office computing, the then-president of Xerox reported an inverse relationship between the dollars invested in technology and organizational productivity. He explained this relationship by saying these organizations were simply doing the wrong things faster!

Moreover, with the aid of technology, one individual may be able to handle a job from start to finish that formerly had been broken down into several steps performed by different people. Such task combination can reduce duplication of effort and improve coordination. For example, Monsanto redesigned previously separate jobs into *vendor account representative* positions, giving employees responsibility for all ordering and servicing for a specific group of customers. Many tasks in transferring work from one department to another and checking work in between departments were eliminated. Most importantly, the vendor account representatives took pride in servicing *their* customers. (Redesigning jobs and work flow was discussed in detail in chapter 12, "Business Process and Job (Re)Design.")

Many business processes that are performed sequentially can be restructured with technology to be performed concurrently, called parallel processing. Sequential processes often evolved due to a need to pass paper files of information from one individual or department to another. Online information, however, can be viewed simultaneously by many users in multiple locations. New groupware applications, for example, can make information available simultaneously to multiple work groups and help manage workflow (see chapter 4).

13.6.1.3   Finding Synergy between Technology and People

The most innovative improvements result from the synergy of linking people skills and technology. Analysts should devote time to analyzing the overall purpose of the work, as well as specific tasks and procedures that are to be performed. All too often, jobs are created by default, rather than by design, when new technologies are brought into the workplace. People need to be part of the design, not tangential to it. The ultimate objective should be a synergistic relationship between people and technology that will attract capable employees and encourage them to achieve their fullest potential and process information in the most efficient and cost-effective manner.

13.6.1.4   Changing Job Roles

Analysts should not limit technological solutions within existing job roles. For example, a tax accountant's use of tax preparation software *may* allow the accountant to do more tax returns or spend more time on analysis than on calculations. The result of the technology is that either a larger number of tax returns can be completed or more thoughtful tax returns can be completed. To the extent that more thoughtful tax returns equates to improvements such as reduced errors or increased savings to tax filers, it could translate into higher revenues than just doing more returns would.

Another example is professional and managerial use of word processing and electronic mail, which requires changes in secretarial roles. With decreased time spent on keying and rekeying text, secretaries' jobs could be expanded both horizontally (job enlargement) and vertically (job enrichment). Moreover, many professionals have found that replacing the pad and pencil with technology improves their writing and saves them time, as well.

13.6.1.5   Integrating Functions

Some opportunities require that enterprises integrate functions typically managed as separate entities. For example, groupware-based project management systems cross traditional lines that separated word processing, forms design, graphic services, and records management. (See chapter 4.) In her classic book *The Change Masters*, Rosabeth Moss Kanter referred to segmentation as *"the great inhibitor of creativity."*[14] She pointed out that in a segmented enterprise, units work in isolation. Little lateral communication occurs, relationships are restrictive, and members are indifferent to the efforts and achievements of other units. Innovative enterprises, however, can seize the opportunities afforded by computer technologies to integrate functions, thus reducing the limitations of excessive segmentation and opening the door to more creative efforts.

13.6.1.6 Making Systems Analysis More Innovative

The high level of structure characteristic of traditional systems analysis does not lend itself to creativity and innovation. Structured analysis can be unduly restrictive, especially with respect to the definition of problems and conceptualization of solutions. Systems analysis methods emphasize technically correct systems rather than usefulness of systems. Systems analysts must be encouraged to develop innovative systems, the result of analyzing a large number of alternatives. New development methods are helping the systems analysis process be more innovative.

Systems analysts generally rely on the user to explain how work is accomplished. These analysts seldom have the insight needed, because of limited business experience, to suggest new business processes. Conversely, users' inexperience with the technology limits their ability to envision how the technology could help solve problems. What is needed is an analyst with both perspectives. These emerging roles for systems analysts are vital to the innovative application of computer technologies to end users. Some firms provide opportunities for system analysts to take rotation assignments into business units to gain business experience.

13.6.1.7 Translating Problems into Opportunities

The way a problem is defined determines, to a great extent, the alternative solutions. For example, if the problem of a clerical operation is defined as escalating costs, the solutions usually focus on ways to reduce costs by using automation to eliminate jobs. If the problem were redefined as lagging revenue, the new definition suggests considerations for generating additional revenue to offset rising costs. Alternatives may call for investing additional dollars to train service personnel to better support marketing operations.

For example, a major life and health insurer was alarmed at the escalating costs of policyholder services. Services were provided by administrative departments in each of the company's independent agencies throughout the United States. The original task force identified the problem as excessive cost and recommended reducing operating costs by consolidating service in regional units or centralizing it at company headquarters. When results of the pilot test of regional service units were reviewed, executives recognized that they were missing opportunities. They had focused on cost reduction at the expense of quality service. The problem was redefined, and the new objectives called for more personal, responsive service in concert with the company's marketing strategies. To accomplish that objective, the company formulated a strategy to use technology in ways that would improve service and reduce paperwork.

The ultimate solution turned a problem into an opportunity by changing the job focus from paperwork processing to customer service. The company invested $10 million to ergonomically redesign offices; put a microcomputer (connected to mainframe insurance systems) on every desk; and restructure procedures, work flow, and employees' jobs. The *payback* was achieved in the long term by avoiding staff additions as the workload increased, attracting better-qualified agents to sell products, and improving the level of customer satisfaction.

13.6.2 Using Technology to Gain Competitive Advantage

The idea of information as a competitive weapon emerged from a growing awareness of the volume of information in today's computer systems and its value as a corporate resource. Alarmed by declining productivity and increasing global competition, many corporations seem to have picked up on the idea. Some experts are quick to point out, however, that an enterprise's strategic information system, if it is truly strategic, will be adopted quickly by competitors. "The iron law of market competition prescribes that those who do not imitate superior solutions are driven out of business."[15]

End-user computing has been credited with providing the biggest boost to the idea of technology as a competitive weapon. As long as corporate computers were locked away in data processing shops, which had months or years of backlogged requests for programming, managers rarely took advantage of electronically stored information. In the early 1980s, as managers began to manipulate data on microcomputers, they demanded more and better information. Progressive companies developed ways to give managers access to sources such as external databases that provide intelligence on competitors, markets, and inventory management systems. Putting computer power in the hands of the workforce (and helping employees learn to use it) has become a catalyst for innovative applications of technology. The best ideas often come from those in close contact with the enterprise's tasks, products, and customers or even from the customers themselves. Such innovations are thus part of the culture of the firm.

Major success stories about technology as a competitive weapon, such as those about American Hospital Supply, General Electric, and American Airlines, have been well publicized in the business press. American Hospital Supply gave computer terminals to purchasing agents at hospitals, offering them direct information about products and prices as well as direct order capability. Hospital purchasing agents quickly adopted the system, as it made just-in-time inventory possible. General Electric generated a wealth of information that helped improve old products and develop new ones by creating a toll-free hotline for customer complaints and questions. American Airlines' SABRE system, a highly successful computerized reservation system, was built to address the internal problem of monitoring the inventory of available seats and attributing passenger names to booked seats.[16] However, because of the system's ability to track individual users, American Airlines came up with the now universal Frequent Flyer program. American Airlines had the advantage for a while, but its competitors also were able to offer such services quickly.

Translating information into innovative products and services is not easy. Two approaches can be taken to help end users translate problems and opportunities into innovative solutions. The first approach is to allow and encourage people to combine and apply their tools and techniques to existing problems. The other is to smash established routines intentionally.[17] The best environment is one in which end users can experiment and learn from their experiences with information technology.[18] Two specific suggestions are offered in this discussion—to nurture innovation and to support research and development.

TOSHIBA: CHANGES COME FROM INSIDE AND OUT

Perhaps the greatest difference between E-transformation and previous trends like reengineering is this: It changes your customers' culture and business processes as well as your own. So you better make sure they're ready.

About 2 years ago, Toshiba America Information Systems Inc. launched FYI, an Extranet for 350 North American dealers of its copiers, fax machines, and network printers. At that time, Amazon.com wasn't the household name it is today, and many dealer employees were essentially being asked to go online for the first time. "The key was making the first steps be very valuable to the customer," says Lisa Richard, Toshiba's VP of strategic planning. For that reason, Toshiba gave its dealers discounts and access to information they never had before, such as their own sales profitability down to the machine level. Says Richard, "The biggest mistake that companies make with new online systems is saying to customers, 'Here it is, come and get it.'"

Toshiba has continued to enhance FYI. It now includes a data warehouse, built with an Oracle database and Toshiba mapping tools, that lets dealers see their 2-year sales histories by month and product model. The company recently added to the system its national accounts business, by which Toshiba sells its products directly to large companies, and local dealers provide support. Later this fall, Toshiba will launch an online service for its dealers' 2,000 service reps called Service Information System, which will feature an Oracle8i database of CAD drawings, product schematics, and video clips.

"In the beginning, we had to help our customers change and feel comfortable about it," Richard says. "Now their expectation levels are very high, and we can barely keep up."

Richard is the first to admit that transformation doesn't come easily. "It wasn't just the customers—our own internal thought processes had to change, too," she says. "There's always an inherent desire to stay with what's in place and keep costs down. You have to be willing to chink away at that."

13.6.2.1 Nurturing Innovation

Innovation and creativity must be nurtured actively. Successful strategic systems are *not* a natural evolution from existing systems and a tradition of investing heavily in reengineering business processes. A direct correlation exists between a strategic system's success and top management's support for its end users' creative application of information systems.

In a discussion of what he calls *third-era computing,* John F. Rockart, Director of the Center for Information Systems Research at the Massachusetts Institute of Technology, stated that new-product marketing opportunities are

> usually spotted by people on the firing line—people close to both markets and products and who have a working feel for the new information technology. Consequently, companies that do the best job of managing their end-user computing resources also have the best chance of becoming the marketing leaders of tomorrow. . . . Indeed, the long-term value of end-user computing is accelerated learning on the part of end users. They learn more about the limits and opportunities of the technology. More important, they discover *innovative* approaches to tasks that can actually transform the nature of the job being done.[19]

In Rockart's view, the important distinction between computing in the first two eras and in the third era is the role of end users. During the first two eras (batch systems and online transaction processing), information processing remained under the control of data processing professionals. In the third era, computers have moved out of the realm of specialists "into the hands of end users—whoever and wherever they may be."[20] Rockart saw no end in sight as the growth rate of end-user computing is at least five times that of conventional systems. The major EUIS growth areas initially were word processing, business programs (such as accounting and sales analysis), electronic spreadsheet analysis, groupware, desktop publishing, presentation and business graphics, and writing new programs. Today, growth tends to focus on creative applications of Internet and Intranet technologies, improving and speeding processes and communications.

Rockart was ahead of his time. Even in the mid-1980s, he was describing the seamless web of computing services that are only beginning to take shape today. "Just as a society needs its highways, bridges, railroads, and airports to survive, so a company needs its 'seamless web' of computing systems."[21] This third-era computing requires the involvement of senior managers in ways that the first and second eras never did. The significance of this growth "is that computing systems are rapidly becoming a part of the corporate infrastructure, requiring senior management involvement."[22]

Strategic use of information implies a direct tie between business strategy and information systems. Thus, it strikes at the heart of the way enterprises do business. In their enthusiasm to use information as a strategic tool, many companies make the mistake of moving ahead without thoroughly researching and analyzing how the enterprise works. Consequently, they underestimate the structural changes needed to implement innovations. "In fact, the greatest drawback in managing information as a strategic tool may be the changes it often imposes on the way a company conducts its business and how its employees do their jobs."[23]

Strategically successful corporations understand the structure of their industry. They recognize the activities that can have the greatest impact on strategic success. They use innovative and creative thinking to search for and use information for competitive advantage. In addition, strategically important systems seem to develop best in an environment of broad communication and widespread understanding of corporate strategy. Strategic systems also seem to develop best in environments that facilitate and encourage the use of information technology by functional employees throughout the organization.[24]

In summary, using information as a strategic tool is a complex challenge. Decision makers must understand the critical factors that affect the success of their business and how technology can impact those factors. They also must support organizational change and job redesign, and encourage and reward innovation at all levels of the enterprise.

13.6.2.2 Supporting Research and Development

Although the emphasis in this text has been on designing information systems in response to identified needs, the preceding discussion on strategic applications points out a need to experiment and take chances. Enterprises provide for such experimentation—or research and development (R&D)—in a number of ways. They may develop prototype applications, conduct pilot studies to evaluate alternative solutions to a problem, or fund technology R&D groups.

In short, managers must not be too efficient in resource allocation; they must encourage creativity in R&D. Rapidly developing technology surpasses our understanding of how to use it. The tendency to use new technologies as substitutes for the old usually produces short-term benefits at the expense of long-term opportunities.

Large enterprises that have the resources at their disposal often have internal R&D teams to experiment with the application of technologies. Some companies call these teams Advanced Technology Groups (ATGs). The flowchart in Figure 13-4

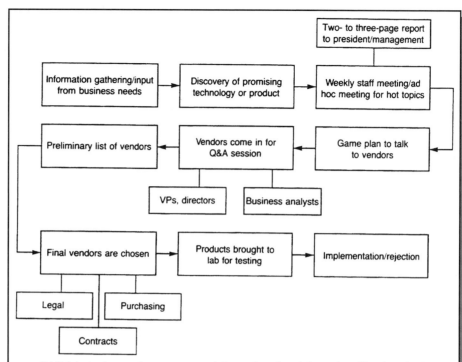

Fidelity's technology services group responds to users' needs and also explores blue sky technology by gathering information from research organizations such as the Gartner Group, reading periodicals like *InformationWEEK,* and attending conferences on topics such as communications and artificial intelligence (AI).

If an engineer comes across an interesting technology or a vendor's idea for a new product, it can be discussed at a weekly staff meeting. If it's a hot item, the engineer can call for an ad hoc meeting.

At the meeting, engineers decide if the new technology or product can support the strategic goals and specific objectives of the company. They outline a plan for detailed research—talk to the vendor, attend conferences, read the industry press, check with the Gartner Group.

Engineers also can submit a two- to three-page report to Michael Simmons, president of Fidelity, and to managers and end users where appropriate, explaining the planned use of the technology. Several reports at several stages may be necessary to get final go-ahead.

If the research finds the technology promising, the group develops a game plan to talk to vendors. The vendors visit Fidelity, where they submit to a Q&A session with engineers. They may be joined by business analysts from the systems group, who act as a conduit, carrying information from the technical specialists to the business end users and vice versa. Business analysts, who are organized as a task force, also evaluate the financial soundness of vendors, determining, for example, whether new vendors, who are historically poorly funded, have the resources to remain in business for a year or two. No commitments are made at this stage.

During the selection-of-vendors process, which Fidelity calls "qualifying," other corporate people become involved. Directors and VPs attend to evaluate contract options—lease vs. purchase, for example—and financial and technical soundness of vendors. Purchasing managers and contract people then follow through after the initial meeting.

Fidelity whittles down the list of vendors for further discussion and more specifics. These meetings are often governed by nondisclosure rules that protect everyone involved. At this stage, the legal department becomes involved. If Fidelity plans to enter into a joint venture, which means swapping sensitive material with a vendor, the firm wants legal protection. Counsel also helps the purchasing managers, laying out the basis for a contract—whether it's a joint venture, custom-build, or straight purchase agreement.

Finally, the technology services group evaluates the products in an isolation lab, poking and prodding to see if they will stand up to requirements and vendors' claims. If they do, final purchase or lease agreements are signed and implementation can begin. If they don't, the product can be rejected. For ATGs, there's room for failure; not every project comes to fruition.

Figure 13-4
Boston Fidelity Investments' route to new technology

Source: Copyright © 1987 by CMP Media Inc., 600 Community Drive, Manhassett, NY 11030, USA. Reprint from *InformationWeek* with permission.

shows how one such group, the Technology Services group at Boston Fidelity Investments, operates. Boston Fidelity Investments responds to user needs and also explores "blue-sky" technologies. These groups often work closely with vendors, signing nondisclosure statements, testing new products before they are released for general sale. The company gets a product better suited to its needs, and vendors benefit from careful market testing of their products before release. Some of the products that ATG groups are looking at include artificial intelligence, supercomputing, voice recognition, data-entry alternatives, wireless networks, thin clients, application service providers (ASPs), intelligent agents, and multimedia, such as video streaming and Web casting. These R&D teams also serve as in-house technical resources for EUIS systems analysts who develop solutions to business problems.

Many companies view research and development groups as a luxury. However, even those without formal research groups often encourage their analysts to experiment with new technologies. Such experiments usually are tied more directly to identified user needs than are R&D projects.

13.7   STRATEGIC PLANNING FOR EUIS

Information technology has become integral to business at every level. That means that any technology implementation—whether at the desktop, in the work group, or on the enterprise level—must be tied to the achievement of business goals and objectives; i.e. must take a strategic view. Whether implementing desktop productivity tools, local area networks, knowledge management, or any other technology, experience clearly shows that just putting technology in place, does not necessarily mean that it will be used well. Technology should never be implemented without a clear business purpose in mind. To get results, it is important to have a clear sense of purpose and direction and a purposeful plan for making it happen. As the Cheshire Cat said to Alice in Wonderland, if you don't know where you're going, any road will do.

Strategic planning for EUIS is tied to line of business (or business unit) planning. This section explains what strategic planning is, why it is important, and who should do it. The discussion then provides an overview of the strategic planning process and explains how a strategic EUIS plan is put into action.

13.7.1   What Is Strategic Planning for EUIS?

Strategic planning is a process of defining business goals and objectives. It determines what an enterprise should do. In other words, it establishes direction. IT strategy should always relate directly to an enterprise's business goals, or business strategy.

Strategic planning can be long term or short term and should not be confused with tactical planning or needs assessment. Tactical planning helps the enterprise do what the strategic plans say they should do. Tactical planning answers the question "how are we going to do this?" Thus, it is usually highly procedural, providing step-by-step details. The needs assessment, which is also an important part of implementing systems, looks at particular users or applications and establishes how the technologies can be applied. Both tactical planning and needs assessment should be guided by the enterprise's strategic plan.

Strategic planning for EUIS is the process of linking specific technology directions to organizational goals. In Figure 13-5, Pieter Ribbers, a professor at Tilburg

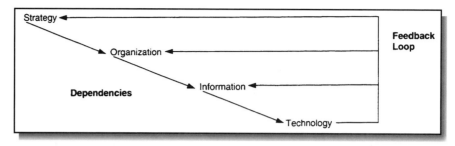

Figure 13-5
Technology as an enabler: The relationship among strategy, organization, information, and technology

Source: Pieter R. Ribbers, Keynote Address at the Office Systems Research Conference, San Antonio, Texas, March 1992.

University, Netherlands, offers helpful perspectives on the relationship of EUIS to an enterprise's strategic plan.[25] Figure 13-5 shows the relationship among strategy, organization (structure), information, and technology. The diagonal arrows indicate the dependencies: Strategy dictates the appropriate organizational structure, which in turn dictates required information, which ultimately dictates the appropriate technology. Technology is described as an enabler. The feedback loop shows how technology, in turn, influences the other three variables.

For most businesses, a new competitive agenda has emerged. Providing high levels of quality and service are necessary but not sufficient conditions to remain in business. The strategic imperative for the business of the near future will be time and efficiency. Enterprises will be differentiated by their ability to compress time required for product design, manufacturing, delivery, and service. The most common stumbling block to achieving these goals is the organization of the information work that supports the enterprise. Therefore, time and efficiency are the performance measures that determine the way information work should be organized and structured. Transform first, then automate is the message. Redesigning information work is for that reason a matter of process restructuring, and technology is an integral part of that. Management must be able to react more quickly to business cycle demands, which, in turn, mandates that workers and business processes be flexible.[26] Such improvements are possible with EUIS technologies, but only with careful planning linked to business strategies.

13.7.2 Why Is Strategic Planning Important?

Strategic planning for information technologies requires that leaders understand the industry, environment, line of business, and operations. A strategic plan allows for "the manager to act with some confidence through an interactive, ongoing process of reading the business environment and assessing stakeholder expectations."[27] A big divide no longer exists between the business and the technology domain. Figure 13-6 places the business and technology domains together, and offers an appreciation of strategic planning problems facing managers in both domains.[28]

As shown in Figure 13-6, planning within the business domain and the technology domain should be parallel. In fact, planning for each domain requires interaction with the management from the other domain. While companies differ in structure, management complexity, and organization, the planning activities that lead up to information economics can be similar.[29] Figure 13-6 emphasizes the interrelationship of technology to the business.

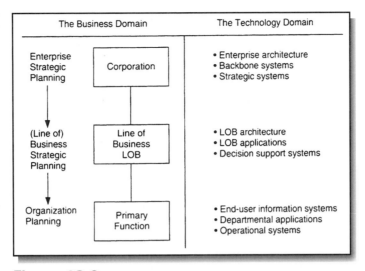

Figure 13-6
Planning for information technology: Where companies differ

Source: INFORMATION STRATEGY AND ECONOMICS by Parker/Trainor/Benson, © 1990. Reprinted by permission of Prentice-Hall, Inc., Upper Saddle River, NJ.

13.7.3 The Strategic Planning Process

The strategic planning process is intended to meet the following objectives:

1. Determine where the business unit or enterprise is with regard to a certain requirement.
2. Decide where the business unit should be at a certain date.
3. Develop strategies to achieve the desired result.

Strategic plans require making assumptions about future marketplace demands, which is always risky. To plan strategically for EUIS, managers also must predict where the technology is going. The fainthearted give up in despair, but wise business managers make their best estimates and remain flexible enough to correct the course en route. Dealing with Internet technologies makes the task even more challenging.

Important questions and considerations for beginning a strategic planning process are outlined in Figure 13-7. Here, the directions of the organization are detailed and decisions are made defining the scope of the planning process, as well as available dollars and other resources.

Once the directions are clear, the EUIS planners can use a structured strategic planning framework, such as the one outlined in Figure 13-8, as a blueprint for action. Although this framework originally was intended for strategic planning on an enterprise level, it is adapted here to serve as a guide to developing an EUIS strategic plan. Keep in mind that the focus of strategic planning for EUIS is generally on the level of business units. The method should be adjusted depending on the scope and complexity of the situation at hand.

1. *Understand business strategies.* Depending on the business, strategies may be explicit, implicit, or not fully developed. If they are not explicit, assumptions should be made for each major business unit and their reasonableness agreed

Questions	Considerations
Where are we?	Nature of business or organization Current state of development Position relative to other organizations
Where do we want to go?	Capabilities and opportunities Assumptions Issues Objectives
How will we get there?	Strategy and policy Political pressures Programs, projects, and procedures
When do we want to arrive?	Priorities Timing
Who will be responsible?	Senior-level generalist at the helm Organization
How much will it cost?	Budget Resources

Figure 13-7
The strategic planning process

to by the top management of those units. "If users are not well aligned with business strategy, IS can only help them go the wrong way faster."[30]

2. *Determine critical success factors (CSFs).* Critical success factors (CSF) are those things that an enterprise must do right to achieve its business goals. CSF planning methods require leaders to project themselves into the future and identify what would have happened if they were, indeed, to say that their enterprise had achieved the intended goals. This process requires that the leaders be able to explain the business goals to the analyst and what will need to have happened for success to have occurred. The analyst, in turn, can use these critical success factors as baseline goals for systems planning.

3. *Relate CSFs to information flows.* Each critical success factor defines a set of management information needs. These needs are invariably interrelated, and the content, timeliness, accuracy, and form of the information to be

Figure 13-8
EUIS strategic planning framework

1. Understand business strategies.
2. Determine critical success factors.
3. Relate CSFs to information flows.
4. Develop information technology assumptions.
5. Conceptualize information systems solutions.
6. Prioritize the solutions.
7. Determine resource requirements.
8. Understand the available resource base.
9. Time-phase the solutions.
10. Formulate an action plan.

consumed need to be interpreted. Allowance should be made for the variations in personal behavior and style that inevitably alter information consumption patterns over time. The likely sources (both external and internal) of the information should then be traced, and rudimentary flows from source to use established.

Departments and users have critical success factors just as enterprises do. The EUIS analyst would do well to help these groups identify their particular CSFs, and then integrate them with the larger IS strategic plan.

4. *Develop information technology assumptions.* Just as the formulation of a business strategy is based on environmental and economic assumptions, an IT strategy must be based on assumptions relating to the availability, price, and performance of hardware, software, networking, and related technologies. Most of the forecasts upon which these assumptions can be based are readily available from trade publications and technical consultants.

Increasingly, end users themselves come with a myriad of information and *misinformation* about technologies. Lured by the promises of vendors, end users sometimes understand the opportunities of technologies, but not the realities of their implementation. EUIS analysts should be prepared to explain technology alternatives and associated benefits and risks so that end users can make informed business decisions regarding technology options.

5. *Conceptualize information systems solutions.* Conceptualizing solutions involves matching the information flows and technology assumptions in steps 3 and 4 with an ordered list of potential applications. The selected solutions then must be assessed in terms of their architectural requirements. Architectural considerations relate to the physical compatability with enterprise architectures and networks, and the degree to which users have made direct control, and projected growth in usage. It is important at this stage that requirement opportunities for business process restructuring be understood and considered.

6. *Prioritize the solutions.* Systems solutions vary widely in terms of their importance in the attainment of business strategies, although those of lesser importance often are prerequisites for more important applications. This prioritization should be based on both quantitative and qualitative evaluation of how critical each potential solution would be to achievement of the business strategy it supports and, secondarily, on any building-block interrelationships among solutions. Information economics and other methods for assessing the value of information technology, described in chapter 7, are useful during this phase.

7. *Determine resource requirements.* Determining resource requirements involves sizing the potential solutions and their architecture. It also requires estimates of the number of people who will be needed to develop and operate the system and the cash outflow to fund development and operation. In addition to quantity, the needed competencies and skill sets should be determined.

EUIS projects vary in scope and, therefore, resource requirements. Increasingly, as end users themselves are coming up with innovative applications, they need to be aware of the opportunities and limitations of the overall system. Working with EUIS analysts, managers can judge whether or not solutions can be addressed within the current and planned systems architecture. Such discussions between EUIS analysts and line managers can help Information Systems Departments understand the information needs of the business and the individual user more completely.

8. *Understand the available resource base.* To stimulate fresh and incisive thinking about needs and solutions, the planning process intentionally has been structured up to this point to avoid the issues of technical, human resource, or funding availability. However, the pace of any practical plan has to recognize and strive to make maximum progress within availability constraints, and the purpose of this step is to identify these constraints. The scope of this assessment should include the quality as well as the raw capacity/quantity of the existing technical and human infrastructure within the enterprise.

9. *Time-phase the solutions.* The priority sequencing of solutions was largely determined in step 6. Now the solutions must be matched to the quality and capacity of development and operational resources available, plus those the enterprise can justify adding in the future. Many businesses undermine their strategic interests by taking an unnecessarily narrow view of their ability to fund and support beneficial systems projects. They often limit themselves by artificial year-to-year ceilings on computer and office equipment spending, rather than looking at the broader trade-offs from the perspective of cumulative return on investment and strategic management effectiveness.

10. *Formulate an action plan.* In the past, too many thickly documented systems plans have wound up gathering dust. This is usually due to the absence of any strategic relevance. Often, a plan's death has been preordained by the simplistic assumption that processes were adequate to support new systems solutions. Implementing decision support, for example, requires leaders to adopt a more structured approach to planning and decision making. These new techniques should be defined within the plan. For example, if managerial/professional performance is the rationale for new systems, the plan has to come to grips with the knotty issue of how to assess results at these levels. Furthermore, as new systems affect end-user involvement in the planning, development, and operational processes, fresh questions arise.

13.7.4 Who Should Do Strategic Planning?

The question of who should plan depends, in part, on the scope of the planning. Is the enterprise large or small? Will planning apply to the entire enterprise, a business unit, or one department? Is planning within the enterprise primarily centralized or decentralized? Strategic planning must be adapted by each enterprise to its own needs.

Strategic planning for EUIS is usually a responsibility of upper-level managers. In practice, however, planning for EUIS, if done at all, often is not done at top levels, nor is it strategic. Moreover, the limited planning that is done often focuses on the technology rather than achievement of business goals. Noted consultant N. Dean Meyer cautions that EUIS planning must do more than predict technologies. It also must forecast business needs, the broader business environment, the pace of organizational change, staff support requirements, and investment strategies. Thus, planning should not be done by staff groups alone.[31]

In many enterprises, strategic planning for information technology focuses on large IS applications, not EUIS. Strategic planning for EUIS tends to be a by-product of line-of-business strategic planning. Often, high-level technical staff, directly accountable to senior management, are responsible for relevant research and recommendations. Strategic planning, involving business process restructuring, is generally of a magnitude that can be authorized only at top levels. Often, it exceeds the scope of end-user systems and calls for integrating all information systems.

Systems integration is not easy. The ability of most businesses to assimilate and apply EUIS lags far behind the opportunities—a strategic void that can be critical. Senior executives often believe that they should receive more benefit from technology investment, but few are able to articulate how those benefits should be achieved. The process itself can appear bewildering to enterprises that do not have the staff or organization to pull key players together to develop a cohesive company strategy. In such cases, enterprises may hire a consulting firm to provide direction. External consultants can offer a broad exposure to similar problems in other enterprises and structured planning methodologies.

Ideally, a consulting firm provides an unbiased, outside perspective to balance the concerns of management. Involvement of both technical and business specialists is essential for planning a strong, practical approach to end-user information systems. To be effective, the consulting firm needs to work closely with the IT organization (who understand the potential of the technology) and the line managers (who know the business).

13.7.5   The Strategic Plan

A strategic plan for technology forms the basis for determining which applications should be addressed in what order. It should help executives answer several basic questions concerning information systems activities such as the following: Are there competitive opportunities in my industry that technology can help implement? Is the company spending its information systems budget effectively on the appropriate applications? Are the leadership and organization for EUIS appropriate for the role information now plays in the enterprise? What applications will produce the greatest business benefits? To develop a strategic plan for EUIS, planners must study the enterprise's long- and short-term business needs. Planners who develop an EUIS strategic plan should ensure that the plan:

1. *Supports business goals as defined in the corporate strategic plan.* In overall management planning, information systems are tools that can help an enterprise implement its business strategies. It is easy to lose sight of the role information systems play in the enterprise and to plan as if these systems were an end in themselves. Focusing on business objectives defined in the corporate strategy helps keep information systems planning in proper perspective.
2. *Responds to management concerns and changing business requirements.* A plan must be sufficiently flexible to take advantage of new opportunities or to address unexpected problems.
3. *Coordinates with overall information systems or information management planning.* Regardless of whether EUIS is part of a larger IS organization or has a separate reporting structure, plans and programs must be complementary and compatible. In an increasing number of enterprises, information systems leaders play a major role in strategic planning.

Once formulated, strategies are written in report format and submitted for management approval. Figure 13-9 illustrates the table of contents for a strategic plan. Generally, someone from the planning team makes a formal presentation to management, using slides or other appropriate presentation tools to help focus attention on key points. Clear explanations of objectives, business justification, recommendations, costs, and benefits are vital to gaining support. Top-management approval of the EUIS strategy is a key step in obtaining commitment to EUIS programs.

```
                    A Strategic Plan for
                  End-User Information Systems

                    Table of Contents                      Page
Introduction/Objectives                                      1
The Strategic Planning Process                               2
Industry and Competitive Advantage                           2
Current and Projected Environments                           3
    Current EUIS Environment                                 4
    Advantages and Risks of Current Capabilities             4
    Technology Alternatives/Futures                          5
View of the Future EUIS                                      6
Issues and Exposures                                         7
Recommended EUIS Strategy                                   11
Cost-Justification Figures                                  13
Three-Phase Implementation Plan                             16
Summary                                                     24
Appendix A: Detail of EUIS Strategy                         25
Appendix B: Detail of Issues/Exposures                     35
Appendix C: Detailed EUIS Technology Description           41
```

Figure 13-9
A strategic plan for EUIS

13.7.6   Putting the Strategic Plan into Action

Putting strategic planning into action requires mission statements, policies, programs, projects, and procedures. A *mission statement* is a clearly delineated statement of the major goals and objectives of the business unit. *Policy,* which is the strategy in written words, reflects guidelines developed by top management regarding major issues. The following is an example of a policy for the implementation of EUIS:

> *EUIS policy provides for the development of an information network that balances the needs of individual users and departments against the overall corporate needs and objectives. Within that framework, the information systems architecture will provide as much flexibility as possible.*

Programs put policies into effect. Programs refer to the series of efforts needed to follow through on the policies. *Projects,* the next level of activity, serve the objectives of programs. Several projects may be needed to implement one program. The most precise, measurable unit of activity is *procedures,* which are specific methods for accomplishing work activity. The following examples of this hierarchy are based on the EUIS policy described earlier.

Example of a Program:

- Develop a corporate Intranet that streamlines internal operations and improves responsiveness to customer needs.

Examples of Projects:

- Pilot test CourseInfo software to deliver training online.
- Develop a knowledge management system to support sales and customer service.

- Merge the mail- and telephone-order sales entry systems with the Internet-order entry system.
- Develop an office supplies ordering system.

Examples of Procedures:

- All microcomputer users who require access to warehoused data will submit a request form, authorized by the vice president of their division, to the Information Systems Department.
- All users needing access to the training software should develop their own four-digit codes and request a password from the systems manager.

In short, policies, programs, projects, and procedures are needed to support tactical plans. Tactical plans are linked directly to strategic plans of the larger IS and EUIS strategic plans. Subsequent chapters in part V offer foundations and a specific approach to develop EUIS projects. An EUIS project's ultimate success, however, often relies on its strategic value—how it supports changing information needs, organizational structures, and the enterprise's strategic plan. Only then will information technology transform the enterprise.

13.8 SUMMARY

EUIS strategic planning is part of an important process that aligns use of technology with business goals and objectives. Business needs should drive the selection of technology, but, at the same time, technology is an enabler that creates new opportunities for the business. The major opportunities offered by EUIS technologies are associated with their potential for transforming the way work is done. Thus, fostering innovation is an important aspect of strategic planning.

Although enterprises acknowledge the value of new ideas, corporate cultures do not always foster and reward innovation. Technologies, like new ideas, bring both threats and opportunities. Capitalizing on technology to improve performance and quality of worklife is complex and challenging. It requires foresight, careful planning, and good management.

Innovation is best characterized as a process whereby individuals or enterprises adopt, use, and assimilate new technologies. Rogers suggested five characteristics of innovations that influence adoption of new technologies: relative advantage, compatibility, complexity, trialability, and observability. Rogers also described people as to how receptive they are to innovation on a scale ranging from the very innovative to laggards. Quinn revealed the characteristics that innovative enterprises have in common: flexible management, attacking problems from several angles simultaneously, allowing for chaos within guidelines, and freezing plans only when necessary.

The infusion and assimilation of technology into the work environment is a change process. Two conceptual models of technological change were presented. The Office of Technology Assessment's (OTA) Model of Technological Change, developed by Joseph Coates, describes the process in three stages: substitution, adaptation, and transformation. L. H. Day of the Diebold Office Automation Group offers a five-stage model: conception, initiation, contagion, consolidation, and creative evolution. Left to chance, the adoption, infusion, and assimilation of technology can be haphazard and painstakingly slow. However, the process can be managed and accelerated through effective strategic planning directed at transforming business processes.

Transforming business processes requires innovative approaches to business needs. When technology is used innovatively, it offers new opportunities for managing information and empowering individuals and work groups. EUIS planners and analysts are challenged to design systems that capitalize on technology for productivity improvement and competitive advantage. Enterprises that succeed will reap benefits in improved products and services.

Without strategic planning, enterprises miss opportunities and often gain only immediate, short-term benefits. Strategic planning is a process of defining major business goals and objectives for an enterprise. It identifies actions required to move an enterprise from where it is to where management determines it should be. A strategic plan for EUIS should support the goals defined in the corporate unit strategic plans. Strategic plans are translated into action through policies, programs, projects, and procedures.

KEY TERMS

- Adaptation
- Assimilation
- Catalyst
- Compatibility
- Competitive advantage
- Complexity

- Infusion
- Innovation
- Laggard
- Mission statement
- Observability
- Policies

- Programs
- Procedures
- Relative advantage
- Strategic planning
- Synergy
- Trialability

DISCUSSION QUESTIONS

1. Define the term *innovation*. Why is it a "two-edged sword"?
2. Are you a technology innovator, a laggard, or somewhere in between? Can you describe colleagues, friends, and family in terms of these categories?
3. What is the relationship between technology and innovation?
4. What do the two models of technology infusion show about technology's assimilation in enterprises?
5. The text makes a number of suggestions about using technology as a catalyst for performance improvement. Why do you suppose these approaches are not used more widely?
6. List characteristics of companies that have used technology successfully as a competitive weapon. What do these characteristics suggest about their management style?
7. What is strategic planning? Why is strategic planning for EUIS important?
8. Who usually is responsible for strategic planning in an enterprise? Why would responsibility reside at that level?
9. How are strategic plans put into action in an enterprise?

APPLICATION EXERCISES

1. Working with a group of classmates, identify an office, small business, or other organizational unit with which you are familiar, and brainstorm ideas for using technology to improve performance or give it a competitive advantage. How would such changes alter the way products or services are provided? How would they improve productivity? How would they affect

employees' jobs? Which ideas do you think would be most profitable? Summarize your recommendations to share with the class.

2. Identify an EUIS application at your college or a local business that you feel is innovative. In what way is it innovative? Who thought of the idea? How was it implemented? What technology is involved? Were the changes implemented when the technology was installed or afterwards?

3. Using current literature such as *Business Week* or trade publications (see list at end of text for suggestions), give examples of how industries have used technology to gain competitive advantage. What was required to turn the idea into action?

SUGGESTED READINGS

Applegate, Lynda M., F. Warren McFarlan, and James L. McKenney. *Corporate Information Systems Management.* (Chicago: Irwin, 1996).

Gerrity, Thomas P., and John F. Rockart. "End-User Computing: Are You a Leader or a Laggard?" *Sloan Management Review* 27 (Summer, 1986): 25–31.

Kanter, Rosabeth Moss. *The Change Masters* (New York: Simon and Schuster, 1986). Upper Saddle River, NJ: Prentice Hall, 1989.

Lientz, Bennet P. *Strategic Systems Planning and Management.* (San Diego: Harcourt Brace Professional Publishing, 1999).

ENDNOTES

1. Niccolo Machiavelli, *The Prince.* (New York: Appleton-Century-Crofts, 1947).

2. Ray Hackney, John Kawalek, and Gurpreet and Dhillon, "Strategic Information Systems Planning: Perspectives on the Role of the 'End User' Revisited," *Journal of End-User Computing* 11 (1999): 3–12.

3. Jeff Zaleski, Charlotte Gediman, and Sarah Gold Abbott, "Growing Prosperity: Striving for Growth with Equity in the Twenty-First Century," *Publishers Weekly* 246 (Dec. 20, 1999): p. 68.

4. Roger W. Ferguson, "Is Information Technology the Key to Higher Productivity Growth in the United States and Abroad?" *Executive Speeches* 14 (1999–2000): 5–9.

5. Don Tapscott, "Strategy in the New Economy," *Strategy & Leadership* 25 (1977).

6. Everett M. Rogers, *Diffusion of Innovations,* 3rd ed. (New York: The Free Press, 1983).

7. Ibid.

8. Ibid.

9. Don Hellriegel, John W. Slocum, and Richard W. Woodward. *Organizational Behavior,* 4th ed. (St. Paul, MN: West Publishing Company, 1986).

10. James Brian Quinn, "Managing Innovation: Controlled Chaos," *Harvard Business Review* 63 (1985): 73–85.

11. Joseph T. Coates. "Aspects of Innovation: Public Policy Issues in Telecommunications Development," *Telecommunications Policy* (July 1987): 10.

12. L. H. Day, "Stages of Growth in Office Automation." Special Report, Diebold Office Automation Group (1979).

13. John Hoerr, Michael A. Pollock, and David E. Whiteside, "Management Discovers the Human Side of Automation," *Business Week* 2966, Industrial/Technology edition (Sept 29, 1986): 70–76.

14. Rosabeth Moss Kanter. *The Change Masters.* (New York: Simon and Schuster, 1986).

15. C. U. Ciborra, "From Thinking to Tinkering: The Grassroots of Strategic Information Systems," *Proceedings of the 12th International Conference on Information Systems* (1991).

16. M. D. Hopper, "Rattling SABRE—New Ways to Compete on Information," *Harvard Business Review* 68, no. 3 (1990): 118–25.

17. Ciborra, op. cit.

18. Ibid.

19. "End Users and Technology Combine to Extend the Range of Information." *IBM Information Processing* (1986).

20. Ibid.

21. Ibid.

22. Ibid.

23. Ibid.

24. Michael R. Vitale, "Strategic Systems Are No Fad, and MIS Must Lead the Way," *Information Week* (1986): 72.

25. Pieter Ribbers, "Strategic Vision, Globalization, and Office Systems." *Proceedings of the 11th Annual Office Systems Research Association Conference,* 1992.

26. Marilyn M. Parker, H. Edgar Trainor, and Robert J. Benson. *Information Strategy and Economics.* (Upper Saddle River, NJ: Prentice Hall, 1986).

27. Hackney, et al., op. cit.

28. Parker, et al., op. cit.
29. Ibid.
30. N. Dean Meyer and Mary Boone. *The Information Edge.* (Roseville, CA: Prima Publishing Company, 1985).
31. N. Dean Meyer, "Two Very Different Meanings to OA Strategies," *Office Automation Conference* (1985).

Chapter 14

EUIS Project Management: Foundations and Overview

Learning Objectives

Upon completing this chapter, you should be able to:

➤ Understand the role of conceptual approaches to systems analysis and design.

➤ Differentiate among the six conceptual approaches to systems investigation described in this chapter.

➤ List and define characteristics of systems.

➤ Define the term coordination and how coordination theory may be useful to a systems analyst or project manager.

➤ Describe the basics of action research and third wave management as problem-solving techniques.

➤ Define project management and explain its importance.

➤ Discuss the systems model of change as applied to EUIS project management.

➤ List the eight EUIS project management steps and identify deliverables for each step.

14.1   INTRODUCTION

Designing and implementing end-user information systems (EUIS) that support business process restructuring and facilitate knowledge work can be a formidable challenge to managers and information systems professionals. Part II of this text provided background on business value, human factors, business process and job design, and organizational change. Chapter 13 discussed how innovations (here, technologies) are adopted, infused, and assimilated by enterprises. Chapter 13 also advocated the use of strategic planning to link EUIS to the achievement of business goals and objectives. The next three chapters (14, 15, and 16) describe EUIS Project Management which is a systematic approach for analyzing business requirements and developing effective solutions that are in the form of projects.

Where does one begin EUIS investigations? How are projects planned and managed? Answers are not simple and differ markedly from enterprise to enterprise and situation to situation. Fortunately, however, conceptual models exist that can help guide the work of analysts and designers. Insights on processes and outcomes that others have collected have been compiled and can be adapted to the work at hand.

Kurt Lewin, the noted social psychologist (see chapter 9), said "Nothing is so useful as a good theory." A theory helps us explain and predict events that are of interest to us. Theories help explain why something happens or what will happen under given circumstances. Theories provide the foundation for the conceptual approaches to EUIS analysis and design that help the analyst understand the information needs of individuals, work groups, and the organization. These approaches also can be used as a framework for project teams to define problems and work toward effective solutions. Theory results in conceptual models that are useful in understanding business functions and work processes. Theory is a basis for determining how these functions and processes can be restructured to meet more effectively business goals and objectives. An attempt is made here to offer both traditional and evolving theory that explains how workplace problems are assessed and technological interventions are designed, implemented, and evaluated.

To suggest different perspectives from which an EUIS project can begin and then be evaluated, conceptual approaches to EUIS systems analysis are presented. Systems theory and coordination theory are examined. Systems theory is the basis for systems analysis and has applications for both technical and work (social) systems investigations. Coordination theory suggests that we look at how systems coordinate activities. Conceptual approaches to problem solving, action research, and third wave problem solving, introduced in earlier chapters, are expanded here with regard to their application to systems design. The chapter concludes with a summary and overview of the EUIS project management model, the framework this text will follow as it offers specific how-to's on EUIS enalysis, design, implementation, and evaluation.

14.2 EUIS PROJECTS AND PROJECT MANAGEMENT

EUIS assessment, design, implementation, and evaluation generally are done on a project basis. A *project* is an activity with defined goals and starting and stopping points. Projects may be limited in scope to the information needs of a single individual. More comprehensive projects may address the needs of a work group or an entire department (e.g., analyze the needs of the Law Division and implement an integrated system for document management). Large projects may involve multiple departments or offices.

14.2.1 Examples of EUIS Projects

Many EUIS projects are small and can be solved quickly by the analyst ad hoc. The planning method described in this text, however, supports projects that require planning and integration, and should be adapted for projects of varying sizes. Projects such as the following make up the majority of projects addressed by EUIS analysts:

- Developing a document management system to reduce paper files and speed retrieval.
- Providing productivity tools for specific work groups
- Networking microcomputers in regional offices with the home office.
- Providing the marketing research department with the ability to download data from data warehouses and perform statistical analyses.
- Designing and implementing a knowledge management system for the sales department.
- Providing training programs to support new technology or business process redesign.
- Analyzing work flow for the vice president of a regional service unit to recommend where time could be saved by using word processing, spreadsheets, database applications, and so forth.

- Installing a departmental local area network.
- Equipping a conference room with hardware and meeting management software, then training and supporting managers in using it effectively.
- Implementing an imaging and workflow management system to streamline processing of invoicing and collections.

14.2.2 Project Management Defined

Project management is a structured process for planning, directing, and monitoring tasks and resources required to achieve some business result. The final result sought in an EUIS project is a working business system incorporating some combination of people, technology, and business processes and structure. Project management involves the coordination of:

- activities or tasks.
- people with skills to perform the tasks.
- time schedules.
- budgets.
- intermediate results from completing tasks, referred to as deliverables or project milestones.
- review points to assure quality is achieved in the results.
- communication among all stakeholders.

The *project manager* is the person responsible for directing an EUIS project. Responsibilities of this role, usually assigned to a senior specialist, generally include planning the project, selecting the project team, assigning tasks, coordinating all project activities, keeping project deliverables on schedule, and communicating progress to senior management.

Effective project management is essential to the successful completion of complex projects. Even small projects benefit from at least informal project management. The larger and more complex the project is, the greater the importance is of structured project management.

14.3 CONCEPTUAL APPROACHES TO EUIS ANALYSIS

The conceptual approaches described here offer perspectives for either initiating, analyzing, or evaluating projects. The value of these approaches is in the structure they provide for helping groups of people focus on problems and work toward effective solutions. Several approaches that have proven useful for EUIS analysis are: (1) organizational communications, (2) functional, (3) information resource management (IRM), (4) decision support systems (DSS), (5) quality of work life (QWL),[1] and (6) management of computing resources (MCR).

These six approaches represent different perspectives that decision makers are concerned with in examining the information needs of departments, work groups, or individual worker. The ability to see problems from different perspectives is important to understanding the interests of various stakeholders in a process and is a cornerstone for innovation.

For example, a professional writer may expect EUIS to solve her grammar and communications problems. An accountant may want a system to address the firm's auditing practices. The data entry operator may be concerned that the interface of the new system is easy on the eyes. The chief information officer may want a system that takes advantage of the organization's existing database and existing hardware inventory. The chief executive officer may look at the project's value from a standpoint of how it helps in personal decision making tasks. Understanding the perspectives of all stakeholders is important for anyone who is planning EUIS. The issue is complex in that more often than not, perspectives overlap. The value of identifying perspectives is in establishing a frame of reference for the analyst, organizational development professional, managers, *and* the end users to understand that the same system can be planned for and evaluated in a number of different ways.

14.3.1 Organizational Communications Approach

Using an *organizational communications approach,* analysts examine how individuals and groups communicate. The logic is that if communication among workers is good, individuals are able to work well. The goal is to empower users by giving them communication tools. For example, analysts might want to focus the investigation on how communications patterns have emerged and how individuals and groups communicate. Technical solutions such as electronic mail, listservs, meeting management systems, or knowledge management could be considered as a way to support more frequent, more timely, and more efficient/effective organizational communications.

14.3.2 Functional Approach

As the term implies, when using a *functional approach,* the analyst and manager examine business functions such as accounting, finance, or human resources management. The emphasis is on *functions,* not tasks. A *task* is an activity that enables the *function* (job) to be done. EUIS should help the worker do a function better, not merely make a task easier.

For example, entering data into a spreadsheet is a task; accounting is a function. When accountants first began using spreadsheets, the task of inputting data into a budget was improved. Taking a functional approach, the accounting function, *not* the data entry task, would be examined to determine the types of support tools required to improve worker or department performance. This approach may identify opportunities for work process restructuring.

14.3.3 Information Resource Management Approach

Using an *information resource management* (IRM) *approach,* the analyst regards information as a resource of the organization to be managed much like any other resource—money, people, materials, facilities. By quantifying the value of the information resources of an organization, analysts can attempt to ascertain where and how this resource can be used effectively.

When an analyst considers information to be a resource, he or she looks for ways to enhance the use or value of that information. The example in chapter 13 of how analysts used existing databases to develop American Hospital Supply's ordering system and American Airlines' SABRE system are excellent examples of an information resource approach to systems analysis.

14.3.4 Decision Support Approach

Using a *decision support approach,* analysts examine work activities from the standpoint of quality decisions. The objective of any study to assess computing needs is to determine end users' needs for information that could aid them in their decision-making processes. Emphasis here is on the *quality* of decisions. Quality assessment can link the value of the system back to the organization's mission and critical success factors.

Thus, a decision support approach focuses attention on understanding the business and what information decision makers use to monitor and control business activity. What information is critical, where does it come from, and how is it used? What time frames are important? In some organizations, such as banks or brokerage houses, a delay of a day or even an hour can mean a difference worth thousands of dollars. When the objective is to use information systems to support decision making by providing access to critical information and allowing it to be manipulated, analyzed, and compared easily, the analyst is using a decision support approach.

14.3.5 Quality of Work Life Approach

The *quality of work life (QWL) approach* is based on sociotechnical theory. Using a QWL approach, the analyst looks at the nature of the work being done, worker motivation, and job design. Because EUIS alters the way people work, a QWL approach focuses on opportunities to improve workers' job satisfaction and productivity by providing meaningful jobs in a supportive work environment. The underlying assumption is that a productive, satisfied workforce is critical to meeting the enterprise's service and quality objectives.

The QWL approach promotes worker involvement and satisfaction. When employees feel that the organization is doing all it can to provide a healthy work environment and enable workers to make meaningful contributions to the organization's goals, they are typically more productive and have greater job satisfaction. When it is applied appropriately, EUIS has immense potential to improve QWL. Analysts who begin an EUIS project with workers' motivation and satisfaction as a rationale are using a QWL approach.

14.3.6 Management of Computing Resources Approach

The key goal of the *management of computing resources* (MCR) *approach* is the efficient use of existing technology. In many organizations, computers and communications tools are not used to an optimum level, and because of the dollar investment in the tools, decision makers may want to see how the tools *could be* used better. This is a cart-before-the-horse approach in that applications are an afterthought, not the driving force for the investment in technology. The objective is to do more with the same resources. Although this is not a recommended approach to begin an investigation, it is more common than managers and information systems professionals would like to believe. Outcomes from such an investigation begun this way may be useful, however. The MCR approach is often a means to justify application development. It is used easily in conjunction with other approaches.

Figure 14-1 summarizes these conceptual approaches to examining problems. Keep in mind that a given project may use several approaches at the same time.

Approach	Goal	Example Solution
Organizational communications	Improve individual and group communications	Meeting management software
Functional	Improve the way work is done	Order entry systems
Information resource management	Use the information we have more effectively	Training class registration systems
Decision support	Improve decision making	Project management systems
Quality of work life	Improve worker job satisfaction	Ergonomics training
Management of computing resources	Use the tools we have more effectively	Advanced presentation software training

Figure 14-1
Conceptual approaches to EUIS analysis summary

14.4 CONCEPTUAL APPROACHES FOR SYSTEMS DESIGN

Several theories/problem solving approaches are useful in understanding the systems analysis and design process. First is systems theory, which is borrowed from the physical and biological sciences. Second is coordination theory, which uses and extends ideas from computer science and behavior sciences. Third is action research, which is based on the work of Kurt Lewin. Fourth is third wave managing/consulting, which extends ideas from participative management and systems theory. Fifth is a systems model of change that identifies relevant variables to the systems analysis and design process. These approaches are useful because they promote understanding of both technical design (hardware and software) and the systems analysis process itself. Following is a more detailed overview of these selected foundations.

14.4.1 General Systems Theory

Examples of systems abound: the respiratory system, a car's exhaust system, a school system, a political system, an economic system, a computer system. Each system is made up of distinct, identifiable components, or parts. A change in any part has a direct effect on the operation of the system. In addition, one system can be a *subsystem* of another system or a *suprasystem* of another. Systems can be technical or social.

General systems theory can be used to understand how systems are interrelated and work together for a specific process. Borrowed from the sciences, systems theory is used to explain why things work and do not work. In the recent past, the use of mechanical science was a useful metaphor for understanding how computer systems operate: "There's a missing cog in the system." Today, metaphors tend to relate to the biological sciences: "The system has run down." Such metaphors are useful to the systems designer who needs to make sense of how to put together a system that relies on the operation of a variety of parts and how users interface with those parts.

As used in this text, a system is a set of separate but interrelated components (people, technology, and tasks) that process input (data in the form of voice, data, words, and graphics) into desired output to reach an identified objective. The following discussion of general systems theory will help clarify this definition.

14.4.1.1 Systems Characteristics

Systems—both technical and social—can be identified by their characteristics. In this section, selected systems characteristics are listed and defined, and the terms that describe them are then discussed in terms of their relationship to EUIS.

Open and closed systems   Systems are often described as either open or closed. These terms refer to whether or not the system is affected by activities outside its boundaries. If a system is open, it is greatly affected by occurrences that are not under its control; if a system is closed, it is *not* affected by occurrences outside itself. It is difficult, however, to imagine a *completely* closed system.

Inputs and outputs   Inputs and outputs are the energies that go into and come out of the system, respectively.

Throughput   Throughput is the process of transforming input into output.

Boundary   Boundary is the term for the area that separates one system from another. A system is bounded by everything controllable by the systems analyst and important to its operation.

Environment   A system's environment is anything outside the boundary that has an impact on the operation of the system but which the systems analyst cannot control.

Entropy   Entropy (pronounced *en-trō-pē*) is a tendency toward disorder. The more closed a system is, the more it is subject to entropy.

Interface   The interface is the point at which systems meet and interact, transferring the output of one system into the input of another.

Feedback   System output is measured against evaluation criteria, or standards. Information comparing what was produced or provided with what was expected to be produced or provided is fed back into the system as input.

Equifinality   The concept of equifinality means that equal paths to the same place exist. In other words, there is more than one way to solve a problem.

Knowing this vocabulary is basic to understanding how systems work. Although mechanical systems are designed to achieve coordination, EUIS systems are comprised of people, business processes, structure, and technologies. Using systems characteristics to define or explain how a system operates as an entity by itself or interfaces with other systems helps analysts and managers understand the system more fully.

Understanding the system is important because EUIS systems are often conceptual rather than physical things. Systems are created in the minds of people as a basis for thinking and talking about the things these systems represent. For example, any system or subsystem has a boundary, which is the border between the system being studied and other systems or the environment in which it exists. The boundaries, by choice, may include a certain part of an organization, specific functions, or a certain set of tasks or processes. Because systems are created by people's perceptions, project teams must be careful that all stakeholders are thinking and talking about the same things contained within the systems boundaries. Boundaries define the scope of the project—an important and sometimes complex first step.

14.4.1.2   Systems and Subsystems

An organization is made up of a number of subsystems, each with a specific purpose. As shown in Figure 14-2, organizational subsystems can be based on specific business functions, such as operations management, sales, finance, marketing, accounting, and the like. A useful way to describe business systems is to examine the way these subsystems work together to produce value for the organization.

14.4.1.3   Organizations as Systems

To understand better how to use systems terminology, Figure 14-3 shows a system input-processing-output model. An organization has a purpose, which adds value to inputs from the environment by processing them, and it offers the outputs, in the form of products and services, back to the environment. If the system is compensated for the value it adds, it will obtain more resources and will continue its existence. If not, it will use the information feedback loop to adapt and change, or it will cease to exist.

Figure 14-3 also identifies some of the entities in the environment that affect organizations. The environment is the source of inputs to an organizational system and the receiver of its outputs. For example, people are hired from the environment, and data, information, and raw materials are acquired from the environment. These inputs are used to generate products and services offered to the environment. Customers provide feedback regarding an organization's products

Figure 14-2
The organization and its subsystems

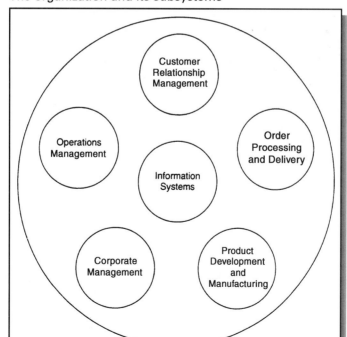

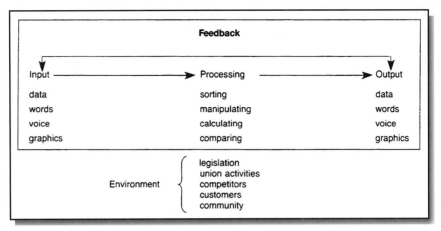

Figure 14-3
Systems in operation

and services. Other entities in its environment also may impact an organization's operations. Legislation and competition are often catalysts for organizational change. When an organization's competition introduces a new product, for example, the organization likely will respond.

As Figure 14-4 shows, a salesperson using an order entry system (see chapter 5) may send orders for products via purchasing orders, telephone calls, or online direct entry. Input data are put into the system via an OCR system, voice, keyboard, or other method. Processing is the manipulation of input (numbers or words). Manipulation of these data occurs, and orders are processed and invoiced. Outputs, the results of this processing, may be in the form of shipping orders, as well as data that are then used as input for other systems, such as credit checking, billing, or further correspondence.

14.4.1.4 Systems Analysis and Design

Open and closed systems do not always operate (process or throughput) as intended (entropy). The source of the problem may be within the system's boundary, environment, or interface. *Feedback,* sometimes referred to as *control,* is the means for identifying that something is amiss. Systems analysis is the process of determining whether intended output differs from what was expected, then identifying the cause of any problems and attempting to fix them. Systems analysis is not con-

Figure 14-4
An order entry system in operation

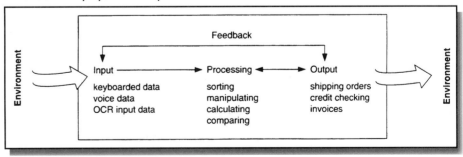

ducted by taking apart the entire system. Rather, systems are analyzed by examining discrepancies between expected outputs and actual outputs. More than one way to solve a problem exists (equifinality).

Metaphors related to the biological sciences also can offer aid in understanding the systems analysis and design process. For example, if one considers the human body as a system, the process by which a doctor diagnoses an illness (entropy) can be considered systems analysis. If one goes to the doctor with a headache, the doctor considers that headache as output. Rather than operate immediately (go into the system), the doctor asks questions about inputs and outputs (When did the headache begin? Does it occur frequently? What seems to trigger it?). Diagnosis may result in a prescription. If the prescription does not work, the individual returns to the doctor for more advice and another remedy is suggested; and so the process, which is a form of systems analysis, continues. Hopefully, the system (body) itself will not require an operation.

14.4.2   Coordination Theory

A useful theory to understanding how systems work together to perform their identified purpose is *coordination theory.* Thomas Malone and Kevin Crowston of the Massachusetts Institute of Technology have defined coordination theory as a body of principles about how actors (people or technology) perform independent activities that achieve goals; coordination is the act of working together.[2] Team sports such as basketball are examples of coordination. If one is trying to determine who does what, when, and under what circumstances, discussing work flow as a need to improve coordination can be useful. Moreover, as in basketball, there is always more than one best way to solve a problem. The team selects from a "catalog" of alternative ways (plays) to coordinate its strategies.[3]

Coordination theory's key tenet is that many of the most important uses of computers today and in the future do not involve just computing things (as in transaction and reporting systems), but rather involve coordinating players' (workers) activities. Therefore, understanding the costs, benefits, and other characteristics of different kinds of coordination is critical for understanding how information technology can help people organize their activities and work flow in new ways.

Coordination theory is a difficult concept to describe, but you know it when you see it. Coordination theory is perhaps best applied to examining the impact that information technologies have on organizational structures, to designing cooperative work tools, and to designing distributed and parallel processing computer systems. The emphasis is on coordinating activities rather than coordinating data. Evidence suggests that information technology leads to smaller firms, more delegation, and more widely shared ownership. Designers of cooperative work tools and parallel processing computer systems are using coordination theory as a basis for the design of systems; in such systems, sequencing and timing are important considerations.

14.4.3   Action Research

Action research (see Figure 14-5) is a practical approach for problem solving applicable to diverse needs. Basically, the approach involves all stakeholders, who have a lot to win or lose from introducing new technology, in solving the problem. Action research emphasizes the importance of feedback at all stages to refine

Figure 14-5
The action research
model

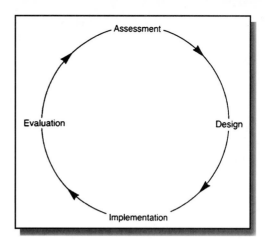

constantly the problem-solving process itself. Action research provides a practical framework for EUIS analysis and is made up of four stages:

Stage 1: Assessment—The investigation of the current state of the problem.
Stage 2: Design—The creation of an intervention targeted at modifying the existing state of the problem.
Stage 3: Implementation—The installation of the intervention designed in the second stage.
Stage 4: Evaluation—The assessment of whether or not the intervention has a positive impact on the problem.

Action research has twin goals—to solve the problem and to learn how to solve future ones. People who are involved with the identified problem or opportunity—people who work or live in the context in which the problem exists—are key to the problem-solving process. In other words, end users are more likely to modify their behavior (use/implement a new system) when they have participated in the problem analysis and solution development stages. During the fourth stage, EUIS analysts evaluate the problem-solving process in addition to the implemented solution so that the process of change within the organization can thereby be refined, as well. Users work together with the analyst to rethink their own work. While implementing a solution to one problem, the EUIS specialists help users learn to solve future problems for themselves; these are the dual goals of a successful EUIS project.

14.4.4 Third Wave Management

A recent model of interest to EUIS specialists is *third wave management.* A brief history of third wave management was offered in chapter 12. To recap, noted management consultant Marvin Weisbord extended open systems thinking and added teamwork to effectiveness. Teamwork, Weisbord suggested, is essential to system success. Weisbord's analysis is that problems are best solved when stakeholders examine the *whole* system, and not simply their own role or needs. Applied to EUIS, information systems problems and opportunities are not identified and addressed solely by experts in technical groups or by work groups solving their own localized problems. EUIS projects are best addressed by the participation of stakeholders who can see the big picture, as well as their individual roles in the work process.

Weisbord identified three powerful levers that can be used to turn workplace anxiety into energy: purposes, relationships, and structures. Purpose (mission) is the business that we are in—the future on which everyone's work security and meaning are attached. Relationships are connections with coworkers that let us feel whole. Relationships require cooperation across lines of hierarchy, function, class, race, and gender. Structure is who gets to do what. Structure affects self-esteem, dignity, and learning.[4] Third wave managing and consulting levers are those practices that support the business purpose, allow for relationship building, identify roles, and assure individual accountability.

14.4.5   A Systems Change Model for EUIS Projects

As suggested by the conceptual models just described, many valid perspectives exist from which planners might view business problems and assess opportunities. When planners attempt to use technology as the basis for redesigning business processes, it is often necessary to approach problems from many perspectives simultaneously. Moreover, EUIS development must take into account not only technical solutions, but also environmental design (hardware, software, and workplace design), business process design, job performance needs, and structure (open and whole systems). Managing this complex process effectively is one of the greatest challenges of EUIS. Because EUIS, by definition, mandate that *change* occurs in workers' behavior, the systems change model is used here to frame the interaction of the technical and social subsystems.

Figure 14-6 is a conceptual view of the variables that impact successful systems projects. Note that four key variables are found at the points of the systems model of change (sometimes known as the Leavitt diamond). The systems model of change, described in chapter 11, has as its premise that when an organization experiences a change in any of the four key variables—technology, tasks (business process), people (job performance), and structure (business goals/management)—there is a resultant change in each of the others. Visualize the diamond made of four plastic straws. When any of the straws is pushed, the shape of the diamond changes. Figure 14-6 also lists other intervening variables that affect the interrelationship among the four key variables. These intervening variables may be the cost/value of technology,

Figure 14-6
A systems model identifying variables related to successful EUIS projects

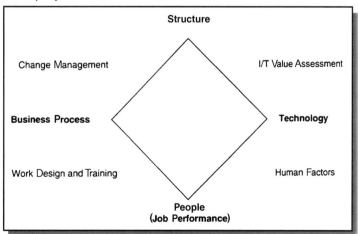

(chapter 9), human factors (chapter 10), change management (chapter 11), job redesign (chapter 12), and training and support (chapters 6 and 7).

Although Figure 14-6 offers a conceptual view of the variables related to successful EUIS projects, translating these concerns into action requires a specific approach. EUIS project management extends the traditional project management model to address the dimensions of job performance, business process redesign, and structure. This approach provides a framework for directly linking systems design to business restructuring.

The next section presents a framework for EUIS Project Management. The method adapts the steps of traditional Systems Development Life Cycles (SDLC) by incorporating the other dimensions that EUIS projects must address simultaneously. Thus, it incorporates design principles in line with action research and third wave problem solving. However, differences in the scope, requirements, design, and implementation mandate that the steps be adapted to the scope and needs of the project at hand.

14.5 EUIS Project Management (EPM)

EUIS Project Management (EPM) begins with defining the project scope and its objectives. The project is NOT considered truly complete until achievement of those objectives has been demonstrated. During the final step, the technology is incorporated into the way organizations operate. Using Lewin's term, the organization is *refrozen;* using the Coates Model of Technology Infusion, the organization is transformed. (See chapters 11 and 13 for a discussion of these models.)

EUIS project management method presented here uses Lewin's unfreeze–move–refreeze approach as an overall framework for its eight action steps. The scope of who solves the problem is expanded here to incorporate Weisbord's third wave management concept that all stakeholders should be part of the process. Specific steps include action addressing each of the four points of the Leavitt diamond—technology, task (work processes), people (job performance), and structure (organization/management).

The value of the EPM is its basis for project management. Each action step has specific tasks and *deliverables,* or outcomes, that represent important milestones and checkpoints. Deliverables document the work of each step in a format that can be handed off to others as input for subsequent steps. Following the steps helps keep the project on track and within budget. The project manager is accountable for planning and staffing the project, getting approvals from project sponsors, ensuring that all deliverables are completed on time, and following through to the completion of the project.

The method described in this text is the basis for translating the theoretical into the practical. Not all EUIS projects follow all the steps. *The usefulness of the EPM depends upon the scope of the project, as well as previous experiences in managing projects.* Even EUIS projects that are handled on an ad hoc or quick-fix basis benefit from following an abbreviated form of the method on an informal basis. When a project is larger, more people are involved, the project is more complex, the need for coordination is greater, and the structured EPM becomes more important to managing the project. Also, the more that is learned from previous use of specific tactics, the more one can adapt the steps to specific situations and organizations. Therefore, larger projects benefit more from the entire approach. In addition, the more EPM is used, the more it can be adapted to a given organizational environment.

14.5.1 EPM Action Steps

Following the process step by step helps keep the project focused (within its boundary) and on track. As anyone who has attempted to build a house knows, such project management is needed to keep various subcontractors on schedule. Each of the specific action steps, with its associated tasks and deliverables, is discussed in detail in the next two chapters of this text. Following is a brief overview of the steps.

1. Define Project Scope   As discussed in previous chapters, systems typically are built to satisfy a business objective. What is the system's goal? What is the scope (boundary) of the project? Who will pay for the project? Who are the major stakeholders? What are the expected results? When is the project to be completed? What is the budget? Answers to these questions identify the *scope* of the project. EUIS projects range from selecting the best notebook computer for an individual to designing an executive support system for the CEO of the organization or networking international offices. Obviously, the scope of the project determines the detail to which the other project steps are carried out.

Deliverables: Deliverables for step 1 include (1) a statement of project scope that identifies expected results, objectives, major stakeholders, and time frames; and (2) formal agreement of the project sponsor.

2. Plan the Project   The objective of the second step is to establish the project organization, assemble a project team, and develop a detailed work plan. An initial assessment is made during this phase as a basis for planning and estimating. Project planning is an iterative process. The project and plan depend upon the amount and accuracy of available information. As new information comes to light or as available information becomes more accurate, necessary changes in one step may cause the redesign and reworking of other phases of the project. Thus, the deliverables are evolving constantly until final project completion.

Deliverables: Important deliverables for step 2 include (1) a decision on a project method; (2) project team assignments; (3) definition of roles and responsibilities; (4) detailed work plan for the next step; and (5) a high-level work plan identifying major tasks and target dates for the entire project.

3. Assess Requirements   Sometimes the analyst can determine feasibility based on the statement from step 1. Often, however, a much more detailed analysis is needed to determine requirements and evaluate alternatives. Assume, for example, that the notebook computer mentioned in step 1 is for the entire sales force, not a single individual. Who would be impacted by this decision? How feasible would such a purchase be? How would the notebook improve performance? What software would be provided? Do the benefits outweigh the costs? Does the network fit in with the overall systems architecture of the organization?

Deliverables: The main deliverables for step 3 include (1) a series of models describing current jobs, business processes, organization structure, and existing systems; (2) a vision statement linking business goals and technology plans; (3) a statement of system requirements and possibly a design prototype; (4) a more refined comparison of expected benefits to expected costs; and (5) a detailed project proposal for sponsor approval.

4. Describe the Proposed Solution in Detail   Once the requirements study is approved by the project sponsors, the next step is to determine *exactly* how business processes can be streamlined and what the system is expected to do. Working with end users and managers, the project team develops detailed specifications for work process redesign and systems requirements.

Deliverables: Major deliverables for step 4 include (1) specifications for redesigning business processes, procedures, and jobs; and (2) systems specifications or a request for a proposal (RFP) that identifies systems requirements and other details, such as the needed implementation date.

5. Select or Develop Solution   If the system is bought off the shelf, a comparison among those systems that meet the systems requirements described in step 4 is made. If the solution is to be developed externally (e.g., by a consulting firm or vendor), a decision is made as to which option would result in the delivery of the right system at the right time for the right price. Internally developed solutions require that the programmers and analysts agree on specifications.

Deliverables: Important deliverables for step 5 include: (1) contracts with vendors or an agreement with a developer that details systems specifications; (2) developed or customized software and applications; (3) fully configured and tested hardware, software, or communications system ready for installation in the user environment; and (4) a detailed conversion and implementation plan that takes into account any physical changes (e.g., data conversion, wiring), as well as issues related to effective use (e.g., job design and training).

6. Implement the Solution   Implementation involves installing or putting into use all the previously planned components of the solution. Implementation may be done in phases if the project is large. For example, if the system replaces an existing system, files will need to be converted to the new system. In the case of document management systems, paper or electronic files must be set up on a server. Databases may need to be developed and populated, form letters automated using macro languages, mail merge procedures set up, and printers and software configured with appropriate fonts and drivers. Many other such requirements also must be implemented. Sometimes a trial or pilot test is scheduled. Implementation also includes job design, training, and work flow modifications. Ideally, however, these considerations were addressed continually within the previous five steps. At this stage, the focus should be on putting into use all previously planned systems, applications, procedures, and work flow.

Deliverables: The main deliverable for step 6 is an accepted working version of the new system, including redesigned jobs, business processes, and work flow, as needed.

7. Evaluate Results   Evaluation is ideally an ongoing process. The project team receives continual feedback (evaluation) from all those involved with the system assessment, design, and implementation process. This feedback should be monitored and, when necessary, the system corrected. In practice, however, projects have an end date and operations return to business as usual. Therefore, it is important in EUIS projects to allow sufficient time to evaluate results against planned business and system objectives and to identify additional actions needed to achieve them.

Deliverables: Important deliverables for step 7 include (1) progress reports or post-implementation benefit analyses that measure actual results against initial goals; and (2) specifications for remedial training; advanced training; additional applications; modifications or enhancements to systems; or further changes in business processes, procedures, and jobs.

8. Institutionalize New Business Processes In EUIS projects, performance goals and objectives seldom are reached simply by implementing new systems. In a dynamic business environment, it takes time and continual reinforcement to effect the alterations in work habits and patterns, business processes, management practices, and other variables needed to sustain significant changes that can be carried to the bottom line.

Deliverables: The deliverables for step 8 will vary. They may include (1) specific training programs; (2) new work procedures; (3) new applications; or (4) system enhancements.

14.5.2 The EPM Model

In summary, EUIS project management addresses improvement of individual job performance, business process design, and management control, as well as technology design. In other words, EUIS systems design takes a broad view that includes within the project scope people, structure, business processes, and technology and addresses all of these aspects. In Figure 14-7, this perspective is represented in a three-dimensional diagram that shows the eight steps of the EUIS project management method. The diagram depicts specific systems design tasks required to address the dimensions of job performance, business process, and structure at the same time as the technical system is developed. Note that the technology perspective cuts across the other three dimensions because technology is viewed as the catalyst or enabler for changes in the other three dimensions.

Strategies for completing each step are categorized as addressing job performance considerations, business process considerations, structure, and technology design. These steps in relationship to key design variables are summarized in Figure 14-7.

14.6 SUMMARY

This chapter provides an overview of theory related to concepts and frameworks for EUIS projects. Because of the expense, importance, and complexity of EUIS, danger exists in planning large-scale systems on an ad hoc basis. Systems implemented on an ad hoc basis may solve a particular problem, but the solution probably will not have considered the overall information needs of the organization, job performance, or business processes or addressed hardware compatibility issues.

The first part of this chapter outlined conceptual approaches to EUIS analysis and theoretical foundations of systems design. Six perspectives—organizational communication, functional approach, decision support, information resource management, quality of work life, and management of computing resources—were discussed. An analyst or manager needs to understand the variety of perspectives from which an EUIS project is viewed and evaluated by various stakeholders. Everyone involved in an EUIS may be examining a system's usefulness from a different perspective.

Then, general systems theory was examined. A *system* was defined as "a set of separate but interrelated components that process input into desired output." A system may be a subsystem of a larger suprasystem and may itself have subsystems.

Project Steps	People (Job Performance)	Business Process	Structure (Organization/Management)	TECHNOLOGY DESIGN
1. Define Project Scope **Establish clear understanding, or problems to be addressed, boundaries (scope) of the project, expected benefits, and resources required. Obtain project sponsorship (funding).**	Identify number of workers affected. Identify levels and types of jobs affected. Establish individual performance objectives.	Identify business departments affected. Identify and describe specific business functions and tasks affected. Identify high-level data subjects and information needs. Develop work process objectives.	Select business sponsor(s). Define business objectives. Identify expected benefits. Identify critical success factors (CSF). Identify all stakeholders (those who have most to win or lose by maintaining or changing current procedures, functions, organization). Assess project priority based on preliminary cost–benefit analysis. Establish target date.	Establish system objectives. Define system expected results. Define system expected benefits. Define system approach. Define preliminary approach. Obtain firm implementation agreement/implementation. Estimate development/implementation time. Estimate cost range.
2. Plan the Project **Establish project organization. Make initial assessment. Develop a detailed work plan and assemble project team.**	Establish approach for work process redesign.	Relate functions to current organizations. Relate functions to data subjects. Relate functions to information needs. Determine dependency among functions.	Establish project review board/steering committee. Define management control measures. Assemble project team. Assign roles and responsibilities. Develop initial project work plan with tasks, target dates, and responsibilities.	Establish project based on methodology objectives. Determine time, project scope, educate in the approach, educate in the approach and managers. Train and methods. Establish project team and process/method.
3. Assess Requirements **Understand and document the structure and purposes of the current system. Determine requirements for a new system. Evaluate alternative solutions and recommend the preferred solution.**	Identify knowledge, skills, and abilities of users. Collect current job descriptions. Determine current performance criteria/measures. Do a cost–benefit analysis for individual workers. Document what changes are needed and why.	Perform a task analysis. Document current work processes. Document current procedures and work flows. Identify major inputs and outputs for all affected work processes. Document what changes are needed and why. Develop business models.	Define mission of all functions/departments to be impacted. Assess impact on organization structure. Identify internal and external clients. Obtain organization charts of affected departments. Identify CSF for business. Develop more refined cost–benefit analysis. Develop vision statement linking business goals and technology plans. Assess organizational culture. Assess climate for change. Obtain sponsor approval to proceed to next phase.	Analyze current system (manual, mechanical automated technology). Determine interface requirem. need to interface system need to systems technology. Identify other systems technology with available. Assess project environ. As/convenient applic. environ capacity. Estimate alternative require/mature requirem. Study alternative. Study solutions prototype and solution a system tactics and design system achieving. Design system for achieving. Define alternatives/alternatives alternative. EUIS objectives.

Figure 14-7
EUIS project management model: Action steps and activities related to key design variables

Project Steps	People (Job Performance)	Business Process	Structure (Organization/Management)	TECHNOLOGY DESIGN
4. Design: Describe the System in Detail **Develop detailed specifications for the proposed project solution.**	Develop skills inventory. Define instructional strategies. Identify skills, knowledge, and information required for different positions. Analyze job design. Develop new job descriptions. Define team/group roles and responsibilities.	Identify tasks that can be streamlined, eliminated, or combined with automation. Document proposed new work processes design. Document proposed new work flows. Define business requirements for all applications to be automated. Define requirements for help systems. Develop performance benchmarks/measures.	Conduct client survey (to determine service/quality factors from client's perspective). Define quality. Define best practices. Develop proposed organization charts. Define requirements/ objectives for organizational restructuring. Set up model office, if needed.	Determine existing for requirement existing or system systems specifications of system Documents. Define system for proposal alternatives (for proposal request to be alternative request to be Develop/purchased. for systems/purchase contracted alternative Evaluate alternative, system product benchmark software. Conduct application, system testing.
5. Select or Develop Solution **Bring a working version of the system to a usable stage. Write and test all customized software, applications, procedures, documentation, and training materials.**	Develop training program. Develop cross-training plan. Develop documentation. Develop help systems. Develop CBT. Develop job aids.	Develop and document new procedures. Develop conversion plan. Create test cases and procedures. Develop training database, if needed.	Develop change management strategies. Develop new management measures. Define quality control measures and monitoring procedures. Create physical site plans. Create detailed implementation plan.	Select application, system Select communication. Software. Customize network/customized. Modify as software Modify as software software, construct menus. Constructions, menus. Applications or contracts. apfraceneeded and interfaces needed and Secure all hardware. Test all hardware and software.
6. Implement Solution **Implement all necessary steps to convert from existing operating environment to the new system.**	Train in software skills. Train in EUIS application development skills. Train in new job skills or cross train. Maintain business activity as training is conducted. Provide hot line and other support. Establish group procedures.	Install new procedures. Convert all work to new systems/procedures. Eliminate tasks/procedures replaced by new ones.	Implement model office activities. Make adjustments based on model office experience. Prepare facilities. Cut over to new systems or implement all planned installations. Implement new measurements. Implement change strategies. Install backup and security procedures.	Install pilot locations based Install pilot locations based Make adjustments and Make results and Install at all hardware locations on pilot hardware locations Install at all technical Resolve any technical software problems. Resolves problems.

Figure 14-7
(continued)

Project Steps	People (Job Performance)	Business process	Structure (Organization/Management)	TECHNOLOGY DESIGN
7. Evaluate Results **Determine if new system meets performance criteria, satisfies defined project objectives, and meets client expectations.** **Identify additional action (steps) to be taken.**	Identify any performance problems. Identify additional training needs, such as problems with tasks, and the use of system features. Identify where users are in the learning curve. Assess level of needed behavior changes.	Identify bottlenecks. Resolve problems with new processes. Respond to new ideas/new insights for additional improvements. Assess user problems, acceptance, applications.	Assess actual results against planned results. Assess client satisfaction with new system.	*Assess system performance.* *Assess problems.* *Troubleshoot problems or software.* *Troubleshoot hardware or software with hardware.*
8. Institutionalize New Business Processes **Provide reinforcement needed to sustain workplace changes.** **Capitalize on new learning and insight to improve results.**	Deliver remedial training. Deliver advanced training. Reinforce/reward desired new behaviors.	Modify work processes as needed. Implement additional/more advanced applications. Provide additional business training.	Refine business criteria and success measures. Develop new measures if appropriate. Reinforce organizational changes. Bring benefits to bottom line.	*Make any needed system modifications.* *Develop additional* *Develop enhancements.* *Acquire additional hardware/software.*

Figure 14-7
(*continued*)

Systems may be either open or closed, depending upon the degree they are impacted upon by events outside their boundaries. It is difficult to conceptualize a truly closed system because even the most closed system is affected by what happens in its environment. Systems have a tendency toward disorder; the more closed a system is, the more likely it is that entropy will result. Interface, the region between systems, is responsible for the transference of one system's output as the input for another system. Systems analysis is based on feedback—knowledge that the actual system output is or is not what was expected.

Coordination theory was overviewed. Researchers at Massachusetts Institute of Technology explained that coordination theory is a body of principles about how actors perform independent activities that achieve goals. Many of the most important uses of computers today are not just for computing things, but for coordinating activities. Understanding this coordination is important to studying the impact that technology has on the organizational structure, the design of cooperative work tools, and the design of distributed and parallel processing computer systems.

Weisbord's third wave consulting extends participative management (Lewin) and systems thinking (Emery and Trist) to incorporate a third aspect, the entire system and all its stakeholders. Weisbord, in an attempt to provide workers with more meaning and community in the workplace, and therefore with information technologies, explains that involvement by workers in all steps of the project is important, and that steps change dependent upon specific situations that also are changing constantly.

The EUIS Project Management Model marries these theoretical foundations with standard project management practices. The result is a systematic approach for addressing the development of IT solutions that meet the needs of individuals, work groups, and the organization. The EPM consists of eight separate steps, with each step requiring a deliverable or outcome to be used in the subsequent step. The steps are: (1) define project scope; (2) plan the project; (3) study project feasibility; (4) analyze project in detail; (5) select or develop solution; (6) convert and implement new solution; (7) evaluate results and modify; and (8) institutionalize results. The EPM may be viewed as an action research cycle as the outputs of one step become the inputs for the next step, and the evaluation stage of one project may lead to the assessment stage for another.

KEY TERMS

- Boundary
- Closed system
- Coordination theory
- Decision support approach
- Entropy
- Environment
- EUIS project management
- Feedback

- Functional approach
- Information resource management approach
- Interface
- Open system
- Organizational communication approach
- Project

- Quality of work life approach
- System/subsystem/suprasystem
- Systems analysis
- Systems theory
- Third wave management
- Throughput

DISCUSSION QUESTIONS

1. What is a theory? How does theory relate to practice?
2. A conceptual approach to EUIS analysis is simply a way of assessing the perspective from which different people in the organization view a project. Which of the following would be the primary perspective from which the

CEO, the CIO, the branch manager, the salesperson, and the claims adjustor would view a new claims management system?

   a. Organizational communications
   b. Functional
   c. Information resource management
   d. Decision support approach
   e. Quality of work life
   f. Management of computer resources

3. What is a system? Give an example of a system and describe it, using the systems components listed in this text.

4. Define *coordination*. Give examples of coordination that you see every day. How is coordination theory considered useful for systems design and project management?

5. Explain how the systems model of change can be used to show the relationship among technology, business processes, job performance, and structure goals. What other variables help explain successful systems?

6. How does the EUIS Project Management (EMM) compare with the traditional Systems Development Life Cycle (SDLC)?

7. How is the work of Lewin, Leavitt, and Weisbord the conceptual base for the EUIS Project Management Model?

8. List the eight steps of the EUIS Project Management Model. What are the deliverables for each step?

APPLICATION EXERCISES

1. Interview two systems analysts or project managers and ask what their jobs entail and how they go about their work. Which approach or approaches do they follow? Can each approach be labeled? Compare responses from your interviews with classmates' findings.

2. Put yourself in the role of a systems consultant. You've just been called in by a major company to manage an EUIS project. Make a list of the questions you will need for your first meeting.

SUGGESTED READINGS

Tapscott, Don, Alex Lowy, and David Ticoll. *Blueprint to the Digital Economy: Creating Wealth in the Era of E-Business.* (New York: McGraw-Hill, 1998).

Weisbord, Marvin R. *Productive Workplaces.* (San Francisco: Jossey-Bass, 1987).

ENDNOTES

1. Don Tapscott. *Office Automation: A User-Driven Approach.* (New York: Plenum Press, 1982): 66.
2. Thomas W. Malone and Kevin Crowston, *"Toward an Interdisciplinary Theory of Coordination,"* Technical Report CCS TR# 120 (Cambridge, MA: Massachusetts Institute of Technology, 1991).
3. Ibid.
4. Ibid., p. 259.

Chapter 15

EUIS Project Management: Assessment and Design

Learning Objectives

Upon completing this chapter, you should be able to:

➤ Identify appropriate person(s) to conduct an EUIS study.

➤ Define the scope of an EUIS project.

➤ Explain the role of a project sponsor.

➤ Explain the role of the project manager.

➤ Define project objectives in demonstrable, measurable terms.

➤ Choose appropriate means of gathering data for assessment.

➤ Prepare a flowchart to describe business processes.

➤ Design an interview guide, questionnaire, and observation guide.

➤ List the components of a project proposal.

➤ Understand the role of the request for proposal (RFP).

➤ Compare vendor responses to RFPs with a view to selecting appropriate hardware and/or software.

15.1 Introduction

The eight-step EUIS project management model described in part V provides a systematic process for analysis, design, and implementation of EUIS projects. Although this model parallels the standard systems development life cycle in many respects, it also differs in significant ways. These differences reflect a heavy emphasis on the organizational aspects of implementing information technologies and restructuring business processes. The EUIS model also reflects a much higher level of collaboration between end users and technical staff.

The applicability of the EUIS project management model depends on the nature and scope of the project. Moreover, business managers may be expecting quick, inexpensive solutions. EUIS analysts may be expected to meet tight deadlines rather than come up with ideal solutions. An 80 percent solution delivered within a week might be preferred to a 100 percent solution delivered in two to three months. In general, EUIS analysts and project leaders would be expected to be familiar with the spectrum of project methodologies and select the appropriate tools and methodologies for the project at hand.

This chapter describes the first five assessment and design steps of the EUIS project management model. These steps include:

Step 1   Define project scope
Step 2   Plan the project
Step 3   Assess project requirements
Step 4   Describe proposed solution in detail
Step 5   Select or develop project solution

The purpose and expected outcomes (deliverables) for each step are identified, followed by a discussion of specific tasks and methodologies that an analyst or project team might employ. It also includes guidelines for preparing the deliverables for each of these first five steps. The implementation and institutionalization phases will be covered in chapter 16.

15.2 Step One: Defining the Project Scope

Purpose: Establish clear understanding of problems or opportunities to be addressed, boundaries (scope) of the project, expected benefits, and resources required.

Deliverables:

- Project proposal that defines business objectives, expected benefits, the business units, jobs, tasks, business processes, procedures, and workflows that would be impacted; a description of how work is currently done; and EUIS objectives, required resources, and target dates.
- Statement of expected results for job and business process redesign.
- Preliminary cost-benefit analysis.
- Formal approval of the project sponsor.

The scope of an EUIS project may be as simple as selecting a single application software package for one individual or as complex as implementing a global network of LANs to provide desktop computing in 50 branch offices. Even selecting a software package can vary in complexity depending on the situation. If a large corporation already has established standard software packages, an EUIS analyst might only interview the client to confirm the need, order the software package, see that it is properly installed on the client's PC, and arrange for appropriate training. Without an established corporate standard, however, the analyst may have to do considerably more work in order to be confident that an appropriate package was selected. The analyst may be required to document and prioritize all needed functionality, establish performance criteria, and complete a detailed evaluation of alternative packages against those requirements.

Ideas or requests for projects may originate from various sources. They may be suggested by business personnel or managers seeking opportunities to improve operations, or they may be recommended by the systems organization in an effort to promote new technologies. Sometimes project requests are initiated because of requirements to implement new business strategies, enhance or replace existing systems, or to reengineer business processes. Project ideas also may be generated by empowered work teams, from annual planning and budgeting activities, or through operational changes.

Before projects can be undertaken, however, they must have a sponsor. A *sponsor* is a business leader or organizational unit willing to commit the time and resources required to complete the project. The sponsor plays a critical leadership role in gaining support for the project, communicating goals and objectives, and implementing business process changes.

The initial step of defining project scope usually will be assigned to a project leader, analyst, or possibly a team for large projects. Defining scope may not always be as evident as one expects. The scope depends not only on the business opportunities or problems that need to be addressed, but also on the available time and resources. A manager, for example, may want to implement a department LAN for 20 staff, but may need a solution in two weeks and with only a maximum of $15,000 to spend—a clearly unrealistic budget for the envisioned goal. Obviously, the project would need to be scaled back or implemented in phases as additional budget dollars become available.

In defining the scope of a project, the project leader identifies the extent of the investigation; in other words, the boundaries of the project. The information required includes business objectives; expected benefits; and the organizational units, jobs, tasks, business processes, and workflows that will be affected. It is often helpful to identify clearly what will NOT be included in the project as well, especially if time and resources are limited. It is also necessary to assess the way work is done currently. Based on this information, the project leader develops a preliminary definition of EUIS objectives, a list of resources needed to complete the project, target dates, and a preliminary estimate of project costs. A project sponsor also may require a preliminary cost-benefit analysis at this time. All this information is presented in a project proposal that includes an initial high-level plan for proceeding with the project.

The project proposal must be approved by both the project sponsor (business unit) and a senior manager in the IS or EUIS organization. Approval indicates concurrence with both the scope of the project as defined and a commitment for budget and resources. Sometimes, however, management may just grant approval to proceed to the next step, project planning, at which time approval must again be sought before proceeding further.

Large organizations with many projects generally have procedures for prioritizing projects prior to approval. The preliminary cost-benefit analysis is usually the basis for comparing projects. In some enterprises, EUIS projects compete for resources only against other EUIS projects, while in others they may compete against all IS projects.

15.2.1 Defining Business Objectives

The first step in defining the project scope is to identify the business objectives. A business objective is a clear statement of what the business unit must do or achieve—the end in mind. Business objectives should be stated in measurable terms so that they provide a basis for measuring success. They should contribute to the enterprise's bottom line by either increasing revenues or decreasing costs. Examples of business objectives are:

- Decrease the operating costs of the department by 15 percent.
- Increase the number of cases that the department can process by 25 percent without increasing staff.
- Handle 75 percent of all inquiries immediately while the customer is on the telephone, eliminating the need to call back later.
- Match or exceed industry averages on all key benchmarks.
- Reduce insurance claims processing errors to less than 1 percent and the average turnaround to 2 days by implementing a comprehensive knowledge management system that delivers all necessary product and financial information to the desktop.

Business objectives serve to focus project activities. Without a clear statement of business objectives, analysts can waste considerable time studying problems, analyzing business activities, and collecting data that may not be relevant to the sponsor's goals.

15.2.2 Defining Job and Business Process Objectives

In order to affect workplace performance, EUIS projects need to identify specific objectives for improving business processes and job performance. The goal is to streamline tasks and business processes *prior* to automating them. These objectives often are harder to define than the business objectives and require analysts and users to work closely together. The analyst's role is to help users understand the ways in which technology can support work changes. The business users, however, must make the ultimate decisions on how the technology will be implemented in the workplace. The most innovative ideas usually come from individuals or work groups close to the business who understand the technology well enough to have a vision for how it can help the business. Examples of job performance objectives are as follows:

- Estimator errors in calculating construction estimates should be reduced by 75 percent.
- The proposed online help system should reduce data input errors from an average of three per order to less than one in every three orders.
- Improve coordination among geographically dispersed work groups and reduce travel requirements by 50 percent.

- Reduce cycle time to 3 days for issuing a mortgage by making customer database and documents available online so that processing by different departments can be completed simultaneously instead of sequentially.

If objectives for improving job performance or business processes are not defined clearly, it is unlikely that installing hardware and software will result in significant cost savings. This is a seemingly obvious point that is easily overlooked.

15.2.3 Identifying the Impact on the Current System

An initial estimate should be made of the number of business functions, departments, jobs, tasks, business processes, and procedures that will be affected by an EUIS project. Because changing operations in one area often affects others, it is important in defining project scope to find out what other departments or units outside the sponsor's authority might be affected by the project.

15.2.4 Identifying Stakeholders

It also is important to identify all stakeholders, especially those who have the most to lose or gain by maintaining or changing current procedures, functions, or organizational structure. These individuals may not necessarily be the intended users of a proposed system. For example, the marketing department, though not directly affected, might be considered a stakeholder in an order processing department's project to change invoicing procedures. The marketing department might consider delays in invoicing clients as an extra edge in selling because it gives clients a few extra days to pay for shipments. Because of their regular contact with customers, sales personnel can be a good source of information about client preferences, concerns, or complaints with current practices. The marketing department also may be able to use additional customer data that will be collected to target marketing campaigns for new products more effectively.

Getting the buy-in of all stakeholders is usually critical to achieving project results. When stakeholders have an opportunity to voice their perspectives and interests, they are more likely to support the success of the project. Even more important, obtaining the viewpoint of stakeholders helps to ensure that important opportunities or problems are not overlooked. When stakeholders are excluded or overlooked, the likelihood for misunderstanding increases, and support for a project may be only lukewarm at best.

15.2.5 Clarifying and Communicating Project Goals

The statement of scope should clarify project goals and briefly describe the expected results. The primary reason an EUIS study is initiated is that a problem exists (e.g., telephone coverage is poor, customer service complaints have increased, decisions are taking too long, administrative costs are escalating faster than revenue) or an opportunity is identified (e.g., an improvement to customer service). The analyst's role is to determine exactly what the needs are and whether an EUIS solution is appropriate.

The description of expected results includes a logical description—an explanation of *what* the proposed new system will be expected to do. The analyst should avoid physical descriptions, or explanations of *how* it will be done, at this point.

As the expected results are defined, it may become evident that a solution will require interfacing multiple systems. This finding suggests that a combined IS/EUIS solution may be required. When analysts identify this potential, the project leader confers with management and gets additional IS analysts involved. A joint solution might significantly expand the scope of the project beyond that anticipated by the project sponsor. In such instances, the project sponsor may elect to pursue only the EUIS solution or to expand the project solution to encompass IS development. Project goals and expected results should be communicated so that everyone involved is working toward the same project goals, schedule, and budget.

15.2.6 Defining System Objectives

Based on the initial study, the analyst defines the objectives for the proposed EUIS system. These objectives document what the technical solution must do to meet the business needs. It identifies what is needed in an EUIS solution, including what the boundaries of the system will be, what input and output are needed, and or how business processes will be changed. The following example illustrates these objectives.

> The EUIS solution is to provide the six research team leaders with tools to plan and schedule project tasks and assign and track resources, including simultaneous assignment of one resource to multiple tasks. Team leaders need to have the tools available at their own desktop as well as be able to share project information and consolidate information for department-level reporting. Data about resources and time on tasks are input required for the existing internal charge-back system. Therefore, selected software should be compatible or should permit conversion of the data to the charge-back system.

15.2.7 Estimating Resources and Costs Needed

After the scope of the project is agreed upon by the project sponsor and project leader or analyst, an initial estimate is made of the resources and costs needed to complete the project. This estimate must take into consideration the skills and expertise needed to accomplish the project, both system resources and users. It also is essential to identify key people to be involved in the study.

Initial cost estimates include anticipated costs for hardware, software, and resources. Although it is too early in the project to identify specific solutions, the experienced analyst or project leader should have enough information about the problem, objectives, and expected results to identify one or more feasible alternatives that will be investigated in the next phase of the study. For example, if the purpose of a project is to implement a system to manage complex research projects, one alternative to be investigated might be a department LAN with six PCs, one for each research team leader, with project management software. This would be sufficient information to make an initial rough cost estimate.

Although it may be argued that these early cost estimates cannot possibly be accurate, the reality is that most project sponsors will demand at least a preliminary cost estimate before authorizing work to proceed. Early estimates may be used for budgeting or to prioritize projects competing for limited resources, based on cost-benefit analysis.

15.2.8 Preparing a Preliminary Cost-Benefit Analysis

Finally, estimated project benefits are compared to estimated project costs. This rough estimate is intended to help answer the basic question, "Is this project worth doing?" If the benefits appear to far outweigh the costs, the project is likely to be pursued.

If they are roughly proportionate, the project probably will be taken through the next step of investigation to develop more refined estimates. If the estimated costs far exceed the expected benefits or the sponsor's budget, the project proposal probably will recommend that the project not be pursued.

In large enterprises, Step 1 may be completed for many more projects than are ever approved or funded. After projects are approved, work may not begin until many months later. They may be held up for funding approval or until resources are available.

15.3   STEP TWO: PLANNING THE PROJECT

Purpose: Establish the project approach, make an initial assessment, assemble a project team, and develop a work plan.

Deliverables:

- Project team assignments.
- Definition of roles and responsibilities.
- Detailed workplan for Step 3 identifying all tasks, accountabilities, and target dates.
- High-level work plan for entire project indicating major tasks, deliverables, and target dates.

Based on the initial project study and definition of project scope, the project leader prepares a project plan that lists the major tasks and deliverables along with an estimated time schedule. The plan must be reviewed by all members involved in the project, including systems and business areas.

Project planning is an iterative process. The project and plan are dependent upon the amount and accuracy of known information. As new information comes to light, or as known information becomes more accurate, necessary changes in one phase of the project may cause the redesign and reworking of other phases of the project. Thus, the deliverables are evolving constantly until the final project is completed.

Although flexibility is desirable, project managers must guard against *scope creep.* Expanding the project beyond the originally agreed-upon scope generally will require increased cost and time. Although this may be appropriate, it should never be taken on without going back to the project sponsor for approval.

15.3.1   Assigning a Project Manager

The project leader or analyst who conducted the initial study for Step 1 may continue in that role, or a new project manager may be assigned when the project is scheduled to begin. The question of who should manage the project depends on the particular organization and the scope of the project. For small projects, a single EUIS analyst is typically the project leader, charged with planning and implementing the project. In many instances, others are called upon to assist in various phases of the project (e.g., other technical resources, a vendor, or an outside consultant). For large projects, however, an experienced project manager is assigned and charged with organizing a project team or task force.

15.3.2 Assembling an EUIS Project Team or Task Force

Organizations often begin large-scale projects by establishing a project team or task force. This project team works under the leadership of a project manager, perhaps in conjunction with an outside consultant or a designated vendor.

The difference between a project team and a task force is the way responsibilities are assigned. If participants are assigned full time to the project, being relieved of other responsibilities, it is considered a project team. If participants are assigned part time to the project while continuing regular job responsibilities, it is considered a task force. Task forces are used most often in organizations that do not have an EUIS department or when the project will impact a number of different departments or business units, all of whom need not be involved full time.

The project leader should choose individuals who represent the major users of the proposed new system and other major stakeholders. In selecting members of the task force, Larry Penwell, a former systems planning specialist for General Electric, recommends that the leader ask himself or herself the following questions:

- Who is pushing for the change?
- Who stands to lose from any change?
- Who are key organizational players?
- Who has power to designate dollars toward the project?

The individuals who are described by answers to these four questions are likely candidates for the task force. In addition, it is recommended that the task force be made up of representatives from as many types of jobs and departments as possible. Task force members should be interested in working on the project and have the time to devote to it. Because of the desirability of top-down support for a project, highly ranked individuals should be included. The project manager must assess the specific skills required to carry out the project and select individuals with the right expertise.

It should be kept in mind that the project manager does not always get to choose task force members. Sometimes senior executives appoint representatives from their areas with little or no consultation with the project manager. The project manager must take appropriate steps to build an effective working relationship among team members and ensure that the team has access to information and expertise needed to complete critical tasks.

Getting the right mix of individuals on the task force is important to the success of the project. This same team may have responsibility for implementation, and implementation (discussed in chapter 16) requires strong coordination and good communications skills. The task force itself is not a closed committee; members share the team's ideas with others in their organizations. This communication should be two way. Team members disseminate information and gather information, ideas, and issues from nonmembers to take back to the task force meetings. Task force members should be empowered to represent the views of their organizations and make decisions on their behalf.

Task force members may require training in tools or methodologies that will be used to carry out the project. The project manager plans appropriate training sessions to achieve the necessary knowledge base for the project team. The project team must clearly understand the process and be strongly committed to the success of the project.

15.3.3 The Vendor as Investigator

Most equipment manufacturers (vendors) have a staff for client consultation. Sometimes for a fee, sometimes for no fee (assuming the organization buys the vendor's line of equipment or software), a manufacturer will offer advice or even conduct the needs assessment. Typically, highly trained, experienced vendor analysts can help an organization identify tasks and functions where EUIS support can make the worker more efficient and effective.

With a thorough understanding of how to conduct a needs assessment, vendor representatives may be in a good position to assess the current situation and design a new system. An obvious outcome is that the needs assessment will result in a recommendation that the organization buy the vendor's goods. While not denying that the vendor may have a good solution, such an approach does negate the possibility of choosing another vendor's solution that may be equally desirable or less expensive. Vendor studies also tend to focus on problems for which the vendor has a solution and to ignore problems that their technology cannot solve. For example, a local area network vendor may not notice or attend to a phone system deficiency.

Despite such drawbacks, organizations with an extremely good opinion of a given vendor often choose to have its representatives conduct or assist in the needs assessment. Deciding to be a single-vendor organization has potential benefits in terms of discounts, service, and (hopefully) elimination of compatibility problems. Organizations with an approved vendor list may not have a choice but must select from a given vendor's solutions. In such situations, vendors are an appropriate choice for systems assessment.

15.3.4 The Outside Consultant as Investigator

An organization may determine that it needs outside, independent assistance in managing or executing a project. The organization may not have personnel with the required expertise or enough time to devote to the project or may simply want fresh views on how it operates. In such a case, the organization may choose among hundreds of consulting firms and individual consultants to aid in the project. Usually, consultant-aided projects are large in scope. Guidelines for selecting an outside consultant include the following:

- Choose the *right* consultant.
- Know what you want the consultant to do.
- Work closely with the consultant at all stages of the project.
- Make time available for people in your organization to work with the consultant.
- Ensure that the consultant follows up once the plan is in place.

The analyst or manager charged with working with the consultant must first choose the best person for the job. Picking up a directory of consultants and choosing one at random is risky. Choosing the right consultant may mean getting recommendations from others who have done similar projects, or perhaps using that directory but having the prospective consultant offer names and phone numbers of previous clients. Not to be overlooked is the need to select an individual or firm with whom the project leader can work. Business philosophy and working styles are two factors to consider, as the project leader and the consultant will be working closely together.

The next task is to ensure that the consultant has whatever is needed to conduct the assessment. Agreement on project scope, objectives, and expected outcomes are important. Ancillary to the investigation are office space for the consultant and clerical assistance. The wise organization will choose a consultant with a track record of success and will give that person (or firm) all the support needed to conduct the assessment.

Continuous monitoring, discussion, and feedback are desirable throughout the study. The adage that work expands to fit the time allotted can be applicable in the consultant–client relationship. Keeping communications channels open throughout the process is a part of good project management. The best consultant is involved with the project at all stages and monitors the project as it is implemented and then evaluated. Such follow-up on the part of the consultant shows professionalism and interest. Moreover, such a consultant is available to help change strategies or plans if necessary.

15.3.5 Managing the Project

With the decision to begin an EUIS investigation, the project manager, in conjunction with (perhaps) an outside consultant and/or task force, plans the project. Perhaps the most difficult question facing the task force is "How long will the project take?" Developing a realistic estimate of time for completing a project is essential to the planning. To develop a timetable, the task force must establish the activities for investigating the problem (e.g., if questionnaires are to be used, time is needed for development, distribution, and recording). With an overview of activities, the task force is in a position to estimate time needed to complete the project, as well as describe where the investigation should be at any given time.

Figure 15-1 is a hypothetical timetable (PERT chart) developed by a project team. Determining a timetable can rest heavily on team consensus, intuition, expert opinions,

Figure 15-1
Timetable for an EUIS project

TASK	TIME ALLOWED
Prepare formal study approach.	2 weeks
Obtain top-management approval.	1 week
Explain project to those who may be affected.	1 week
Develop assessment tools.	2 weeks
Validate assessment tools.	2 weeks
Train study teams.	1 week
Collect data.	3 weeks
Compile and analyze data.	3 weeks
Develop feasibility report.	2 weeks
Present feasibility report to top management.	1 week

and historical data (how long did such a project take the last time?). The amount of time required depends on the scope, complexity, and urgency of the project. Once these are developed, the project manager can chart the timetable on a Gantt charts such as the one in Figure 15-2, preferably using project management software.

Whereas the timetable in Figure 15-1 shows only length of time required to complete each task, the Gantt chart also shows start and end dates. It is evident on the Gantt chart that some activities can be done concurrently, but others are dependent upon the completion of prior tasks. A Gantt chart shows which activities overlap and which are serial. The Gantt chart can help the project manager (and team members) stay on schedule. As tasks are completed, the project manager can use the Gantt chart to compare the time the team expected each step in the project to take with the time it actually took.

The same project mapped out on project management software is shown in Figure 15-3. It shows the dependency among tasks. Project management software is available from several software vendors and was discussed in more detail in chapter 4, "Work Group Computing."

15.4   STEP THREE: ASSESSING PROJECT REQUIREMENTS

Purpose: Understand and document the structure and purpose of the current system. Determine requirements for a new system. Evaluate alternative solutions and recommend the preferred solution.

Figure 15-2
A Gantt chart for project management

Project Name		Jan					Feb				March				April				May
Phases	S/C*	2	9	16	23	30	6	13	20	27	6	13	20	27	3	10	17	24	1
Prepare formal study approach.	S																		
	C	✕	✕	✕															
Obtain top-management approval.	S																		
	C		✕																
Explain project to those affected.	S																		
	C			✕	✕	✕													
Develop assessment tools.	S																		
	C					✕	✕												
Validate assessment tools.	S																		
	C																		
Train study teams.	S																		
	C																		
Collect data.	S																		
	C																		
Compile and analyze data.	S																		
	C																		
Develop feasibility report.	S																		
	C																		
Present feasibility report to top management.	S																		
	C																		

*S = Scheduled; C = Completed

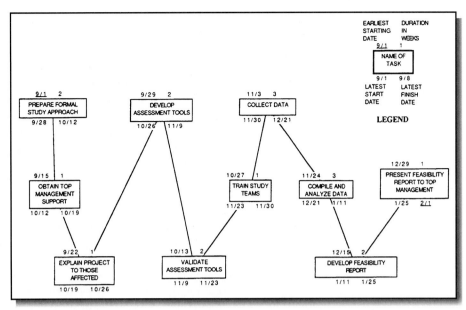

Figure 15-3
A timetable for an EUIS project using project management software

Source: Courtesy of Dr. Larry Penwell, Mary Washington University

Deliverables:

- A set of user-reviewed and accepted models of the current system, including tasks, business processes, procedures, job descriptions, work flows, and inputs and outputs.
- A requirements model for a new system.
- A comparison of alternative solutions.
- The proposed project solution.
- Possibly a prototype of the proposed solution.
- A more refined set of project costs and benefits.

15.4.1   Documenting the Current System

EUIS analysts must first understand the current system before proposing a new system. The depth to which the analysis should go depends on the project objectives. When the primary objective is streamlining an existing system, the analysis probably will need to be thorough with accurate documentation. When the primary objective is to redesign the business process, the analysis will focus on identifying critical requirements that must be addressed by a new system. A general understanding of the current business process may be adequate, but detailed documentation may not be necessary.

Analysts begin the requirements analysis by carefully documenting all existing systems within the agreed-upon project scope. It is especially critical to understand customer requirements and how the unit in question contributes to the enterprise mission. Where does it fit on the value chain, for example? In addition, analysts seek to understand the political, sociotechnical, and business environments.

This documentation process requires a great deal of planning and personal contact with business personnel. It is important for analysts to build a good working relationship and establish an atmosphere of trust and cooperation from the outset. The thoroughness and accuracy of information compiled will depend, in large part, upon the integrity of the working relationships among the project team and between team members and the user community. The ultimate acceptance and success of the project depends on this step. Neglecting this step would be comparable to a doctor prescribing a medical treatment without first examining the patient.

15.4.2   Reviewing Existing Documentation

Generally, analysts would begin by collecting and reviewing available written documentation. This information would include organization charts, job descriptions, task descriptions, procedure manuals, policies, mission statements, business objectives, budgets, reports, and any other written documentation. Analysts also would collect information about the business unit's clients, both internal and external.

This information provides a good background prior to conducting interviews and other investigation techniques. It provides an opportunity for analysts to begin building rapport and avoids wasting people's time asking for information that is available already.

15.4.3   Identifying and Gathering Information

After reviewing existing documentation, the analyst or task force plans appropriate strategies for gathering additional data required to describe the existing system. Complete information is needed about current technology, jobs and performance requirements, business processes, procedures, workflows, and business and organizational factors. Answers to the following questions are needed:

1. *Who* performs each procedure within the system? Why is this person doing the activity? Should someone else be doing it?
2. *What* is being done? Exactly what procedures are followed? Why are they used? (Often, procedures are followed for years and no one knows why.) Is the procedure needed at all?
3. *Where* is the work done? Why is it done in this location? Could it be done better somewhere else?
4. *When* is the procedure done? Is it done at an appropriate time? What are the delays in getting work done? Is this the best time?
5. *How* is the procedure performed? Could it be done in a more efficient manner? Would additional training or technology enable the procedure to be done better, more cheaply, or more efficiently?

Responses to these questions offer opportunities for job and business process redesign. In describing the current system, analysts look for opportunities to streamline processes and apply technology. Robert M. Curtice of Arthur D. Little, Inc. explains that principles of good redesign and the wise use of technology include:[1]

- Increasing the scope of individual jobs, and reducing the number of hand-offs required to complete tasks.
- Assigning tasks without regard to organizational boundaries.
- Moving control mechanisms to the beginning of the process, focusing on preventing rather than fixing problems.

- Eliminating bottlenecks, cross-checks, and nonvalue-added steps.
- Bringing information to work, not vice versa.
- Entering data once, at the source, and making it available on a shared basis when and where needed.
- Using systems so that those who make the rules don't have to be the ones to apply them.
- Effectively using global communications networks to short-circuit middle managers who buffer information flow.

Analysts use a variety of methods and techniques to gather information required for EUIS projects. Each system study is different, and analysts must select the most appropriate tools for the task at hand. It is important to know a variety of techniques and why and when to use them.

The techniques used to make an investigation more a science than a guessing game follow basic principles used in any scientific inquiry. Sources of data are described as either primary or secondary. *Primary data* reflects first-person accounts (eyewitnesses); secondary data are reports of those accounts. For example, a letter written by a president is a primary source document; an eyewitness report of an event is also a primary source document. When these documents are recorded by a reporter, however, the reporter's account becomes secondary data.

A primary source for data for most organizational studies is personal interviews. In addition, the analyst can choose from a variety of other research tools. Following is a discussion of various primary and secondary sources. These research techniques are offered as examples only; it is the analyst's job to determine which one(s) are appropriate in a given situation. In selecting a methodology, the analyst considers the scope of the problem, the potential impact on the organization, and the urgency of the problem. Data collected at this stage are used to document the current system and requirements for the new system.

15.4.3.1 Secondary Sources

Secondary data—data found in books, journals, files, and so on—may provide invaluable information about a specific problem. Any information that is not collected directly by the user is considered secondary.

The Internet is an excellent source of information on almost any topic, and the text companion Web site includes many useful references. Many Web sites, trade journals, and business magazines publish articles about technology solutions. Appendix 2 also contains a list of journals and magazines that may aid the analyst. For example, case studies or results of research projects in the *MIS Quarterly* or the *Information Technology, Learning and Performance Journal* can explain how a similar problem was solved in another organization or by someone else. Announcements and critiques of new products published in trade journals such as *PC World* or *InfoWorld* help identify new opportunities. Information exchange articles in publications such as *Knowledge Management Magazine, CIO* magazine, and others can provide the analyst with new ideas and contacts for learning how particular problems can be solved.

Large organizations often have technical libraries, which subscribe to various industry research services and may provide access to various online retrieval services. These sources can provide useful information and save time when researching technology alternatives. For example, industry research services regularly perform evaluations of PC software products and publish detailed comparisons of features and performance.

15.4.3.2 Interviews

Interviews are face-to-face meetings between an information giver and an information gatherer. The interview is the primary research method used in most companies. Key to success in using the method is knowing what information is needed and why. Interviews are most beneficial when they are planned carefully. Analysts should consult various sources, such as the project sponsor, to determine who is in the best position to provide needed information. It is also good practice to ask each interviewee if there is someone else with whom the analyst should talk. Analysts should plan in advance precisely what information they expect to obtain when talking with each interviewee.

Interviews can be *open* or *structured. Open interviews,* which are exploratory in nature, are used when analysts require a small number of interviewees to explain processes, offer opinions, or forecast needs. When many individuals are interviewed about the same topic or when specific data are needed, structured interviews are recommended. *Structured interviews* make use of preestablished questions that guide the interviewer.

A structured *interview guide* helps ensure that everyone is asked the same questions. The interview guide standardizes data collection and makes responses easier to compile and compare. A guide also improves the reliability of the investigation because it ensures that all respondents are asked questions in the same order and the same words.

To develop a reliable and valid interview guide takes skill and practice. Figure 15-4 offers some tips for developing an interview guide. Figure 15-5a presents a hypothetical situation for which an analyst constructed an interview guide. The interview guide that the analyst developed for this situation is shown in Figure 15-5b. Take a few moments to look at this example. Before examining the analyst's interview guide, formulate five questions that you think would be appropriate for this situation. Then compare your response to the example shown.

In solving problems, analysts frequently need to gather information from both managerial and support personnel. While a well-constructed interview guide is important, the skill of the interviewer is also important in collecting data. Interviewing skills are perfected with practice. It is important for the interviewer to remain as objective as possible. The tone in which a question is asked, for example, can lead the interviewee to respond a particular way. Also, when more than one interviewer is collecting data using the same interview guide, special training may be needed to establish the procedure and tone to be used in the interview.

Figure 15-4
Tips for developing an interview guide

1. Know the kind of data that are needed.
2. When appropriate, ask for "yes" and "no" responses.
3. Word questions so that they are easily understood.
4. Attempt to keep the interview guide short.
5. Always be prepared for explanations of answers.
6. A final question should always be an "open" question. For example, "What other information regarding this subject would you like to share?"

a. Situation: Users are having trouble locating documents and using files on the customer database. Inconsistent file names and incomplete data files are common. Information required to answer customer inquiries is not available. In order to answer customer inquiries, users generally must research questions and call the customer back.

b. Possible interview guide for situation described in 15-5a:

- Do you encounter any problems when looking for information needed to answer customer inquiries?
- If yes, can you give me examples of problems you have encountered? If no, are you aware of any problems encountered by others?
- Who is responsible for file updates? Why?
- How many times a day do you retrieve a file?
- Do you personally make changes in documents or files?
- Are you satisfied with the current system?
- Can you suggest ways that would make it easier to find information?
- Is there anything else that you feel is important to addressing this issue?

Figure 15-5
a. A hypothetical situation requiring development of an interview guide
b. The analyst's interview guide for a knowledge management system

Promptly after each interview, analysts should prepare a written summary of their findings. It is a good idea to take notes during the interview, but avoid too much time writing and not enough listening. Take down just enough information during the interview to assure accurate recall of details. Interviewers should, as a matter of courtesy, explain that they would like to take some notes and get the interviewees' agreement. Because interviewers must ask questions, record answers, and pay attention to the content of answers simultaneously, it may be advantageous for more than one project team member to attend each interview. In this way, the task can be divided. This process can be streamlined by putting the interview guide on a PC and using a laptop during the interview to capture information directly into a database. With a little practice, interviewers can become adept at capturing notes while conducting the interview.

15.4.3.3 Telephone Interviews

Telephone interviews, though conducted by phone, are designed to collect the same kinds of information as an in-person interview. Typically, telephone interviews are conducted when the interviewer and interviewee are at distant locations. Telephone interviews are appropriate for quick questions or when a survey needs to be completed rapidly. A drawback is that interviewees usually do not elaborate on telephone inquiries to the same degree that they might if the interview were conducted in person. An advantage is that those who are reluctant to give you a half-hour, face-to-face interview may be willing to give you the time on the phone, if they can be caught at a convenient time.

15.4.3.4 Questionnaires

A written or printed *questionnaire* is used when information is needed from a large sample of people or when time and expense do not permit personal interviews. Questionnaires can be completed by respondents at their leisure. Unlike a personal interview or telephone call, respondents can place the questionnaire in a to-do stack, and it can be lost or viewed as unimportant, so response rates for questionnaires tend to be low.

Guidelines for Effective Questionnaire Development

The analyst can use the following suggestions to ensure that (1) the questionnaire is well designed, (2) respondents fill it out honestly, and (3) it is returned promptly.

1. Have a strong opening paragraph or a cover letter with the questionnaire that explains the purpose of the survey. If appropriate, explain how the respondent can learn of the results. If appropriate, have an executive-level office endorse the project and author the cover letter.

2. Keep it short! The shorter the questionnaire, the more likely it is to be completed and returned. Rather than place it in a to-do pile, the recipient of a one-page questionnaire may fill it in on the spot.

3. Make the questionnaire as easy to complete as possible. When appropriate, ask dichotomous (two-choice) questions (yes/no, male/female, etc.) and offer checklists.
   Example:
   Static electricity can be a problem at my workstation. Yes   No

4. Word forced-choice questions so that they are easy to understand.
   Example:
   Which of the following projects should be started first?
   ____ An upgrade to the corporate e-mail system
   ____ Intranet Web site to connect field offices with the home office
   ____ An electronic indexing system for manual and desk files
   ____ Knowledge management system for the customer service department

5. Use ranking questions when preferences are solicited.
   Example: On a scale of 1 to 4, rank the following electronic mail features for their potential value to your work (1 = most potential; 4 = least potential):
   ____ Mailing list development
   ____ Message filtering capabilities
   ____ Message filing system
   ____ Spell checker

6. Intensity-scale questions and answers reflect the degree of positive or negative feeling.
   Example: Rate these proposals from 1 to 7 based on the following scale:

   1 = Something we absolutely should *not* do
   4 = Neutral
   7 = Absolutely necessary

   Install a voice message system   1 2 3 4 5 6 7
   Initiate a company-wide calendaring system 1 2 3 4 5 6 7
   Begin projects using desktop publishing   1 2 3 4 5 6 7

7. No matter how structured the questionnaire, it should end with an unstructured, open-ended question.
   Examples:
   What issues relative to improving the Help Desk has this survey failed to address?
   Do you have suggestions for ways in which computing could aid you in your job?
   What other services from the Help Desk would be helpful to you in performing your job?

Digital distribution and collection of surveys now offers a more effective alternative to paper-based questionnaires. Various survey software is available to create questionnaires and make them available over an Intranet, Extranet, or the Internet. Compilation of data can be automated and results immediately available for viewing and printing. Groupware, such as *Group Systems* by GroupSystems.com, allows administration of surveys over a network, over the Internet, or distributed on diskette. Results are calculated by the system and immediately available.

15.4.3.5   Observation

Observation is perhaps the oldest method of problem solving. Assessment by observation may be as simple as sitting down with an electronic mail user and identifying instances in which features could aid the process. Observation could be as complex as designing a schedule in which the investigator completes numerous random observations of workers and their activities. In formal, complex observation efforts, analysts may use time or document logs, or work sampling techniques.

Time or Document Logs. Logs are recordings (loggings) of work activities. Depending upon the activity examined, the log may be classified as *time* or *document*. For example, time logs are used in determining how much time an executive spends using a personal computer during the day. Time logs also may be a listing of the number of times a day a worker makes a phone call. Document logs typically are used to determine the number and type of documents a worker processes during a given period.

An analyst uses *work sampling* techniques in examining current system outputs with an eye to determining how they might be improved. For example, a review of the organization's house organs (newsletters) might result in a recommendation for a more powerful desktop publishing system. In an engineering consulting corporation, a review of contract proposals might result in a recommendation for new printers or new type fonts. Work sampling can be as easy as examining two newsletters or as involved as examining 20 proposals.

15.4.3.6   Summary of Information-Gathering Techniques

Analysts choose one or more techniques appropriate to the problem/opportunity being investigated. Knowing the kinds of information needed to make informed choices guides the task force in selecting appropriate methodology. Figure 15-6 charts the advantages and disadvantages of six primary data collection instruments.

15.4.4   Developing Models of the Current System

All collected information is then analyzed and used to develop a series of models that describe the current systems. Analysts have a variety of tools and techniques available. Many standard IS tools such as flowcharts, data flow diagrams, structure charts, and entity relationship diagrams also can be useful to document EUIS systems. Tools selected depend on the scope of the project.

Analysts will find that many of the processes and procedures in the desktop environment are much less structured than those for which traditional transaction processing systems have been developed. This is an especially challenging aspect of the job. It may be tempting to overlook or only casually document the many exceptions to standard procedures. This omission, however, can seriously affect user

Technique	When to Use It	Advantages	Disadvantages	Results
Flowchart	Process of doing work is taking too long or appears to be ineffective.	Provides graphic description of work.	May also need to interview key people to chart a process.	Identification of work delays, unnecessary storage, and transportation.
Interview Guide	Scope of problem is small. Opinions of key personnel are vital.	Requires top-level involvement. Quantitative results.	Time consuming. Skilled interviewers required. Interviewees not always available.	Identification of organization's needs. Applications. Areas needing more study.
Questionnaires	Scope of problem is large.	Less time consuming than interviews. Skilled interviewers not required. Quantitative results.	Paper intensive. Analysis is difficult. Limited accuracy. Writing good questions is difficult. Words are inexact.	Identification of department needs. Applications.
Observation Guide	Scope of problem limited to a given department or location.	Skilled interviewers not required. Quantitative results. Only way to collect some information.	Time consuming. Requires careful planning. Measures only overt acts.	Identification of individual and department needs. Applications.
Time or Document Log	Quantitative measures of work activities are required.	Skilled interviewers not required. Quantitative results.	Time consuming, disruptive, inaccurate. Follow-up interview often required.	Identification of quantity or type of work performed. Applications.
Work Sampling	Problem is identifiable as quality of output.	Skilled interviewers not required.	Subjective results. Time consuming.	Identification of department or unit needs. Applications.
Secondary sources	Interested in new technologies or new approaches to using technology.	Online sources are available and up to date.	May be time consuming.	Identification of new opportunities to use technology.

Figure 15-6
Advantages and disadvantages of seven techniques for gathering information

acceptance of new systems. These informal procedures can constitute a considerable proportion of the department work. The current system may handle 80 percent of the volume as routine, standard cases. However, the remaining 20 percent of the volume may require the majority of the time and attention of department personnel. Informal procedures tend to represent the work-arounds that people have devised to handle all the situations that aren't accommodated well by the current system. If analysts assume that the current system is truly representative of processing needs, the new system may carry forward many of the shortcomings of the old.

Analysts may need to analyze information flows, communication patterns, error patterns, problem logs, and other representative information in addition to work flows to get an accurate picture of the entire current system. They need to assess problems with the current system and identify what needs to be changed and why. Following is a discussion of tools that may be useful to describe systems. Note that these are the same tools that will be used later in the design stage of an EUIS project.

15.4.4.1 Representing Information about Systems

A variety of tools are available for documenting current operations, system specifications, and user needs. These tools provide systematic or structured methods for collecting and representing information about systems and operations. Data collection and analysis are time consuming and must be completed carefully. Analysts must avoid any temptation to rush the process or assume that they understand user needs. Both the ultimate business results and user acceptance depend to a large extent on how well everyone on the project team understands the business needs and how these needs can be met.

15.4.4.2 Equipment and Human Resources Inventory

A vital step in any comprehensive analysis is inventorying the organization's current technology and human resources. In large organizations, listing resources may not be an easy task. One department may have all IBM products; another may be using Gateway products; others may be using a collection of several vendors' products. An accurate inventory of current technologies is important to making future decisions, particularly where equipment compatibility and user preferences must be considered. The inventory list can be referred to in future phases of the study.

Large IS departments already may have this information and may have established long-range architecture strategies. If this is the case, EUIS analysts must see that proposed solutions fit with the corporate architecture. If the solution is outside the corporate IS architecture, the analyst must work with the appropriate IS personnel to justify the use of a new technology.

Human resources inventories are lists of job responsibilities and skills of employees who will be affected by the new system. It also is recommended that a list be kept of those individuals with technical skills because they will be invaluable when it comes to designing and implementing the new system.

15.4.4.3 Flowcharts

A *flowchart* is a graphic description of work activities. The flow of a work process is represented in sequence from the point of input through processing to final output. Flowcharts can be used to document work flow, system flow, document flows, or business process flows. While the technology and human resources inventories describe tangibles, the flowchart describes the process. The flowchart typically takes a standard form, using specific symbols that describe the activity being examined. Standard templates are available that conform to standards developed by the International Standards Organization (ISO).

To speed the flowcharting process, computer programs or preprinted forms may be used to describe work activities. Flowcharts sketch out how work is accomplished currently. With such a picture, the analyst can determine if work is being accomplished in the most efficient way. Figure 15-7 depicts a flowcharting template, and Figure 15-8 is an example of work that has been flowcharted with ISO symbols.

Other means of describing business processes also may be used. For example, narrative descriptions are sometimes used instead of symbols. Steps in the business process are described in narrative words or text that identify who, when, where, why, and how an activity is being performed.

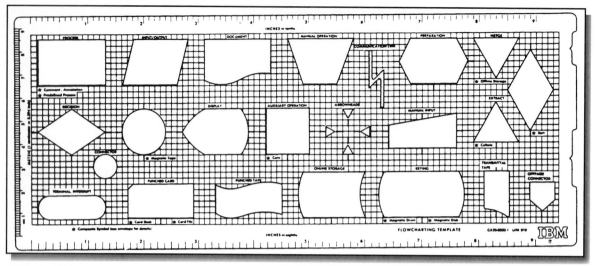

Figure 15-7
An IBM flowcharting template based on ISO standards

Source: Reprinted by permission by International Business Machines Corporation.

Figure 15-8
An example of business process that has been flowcharted
using ISO symbols

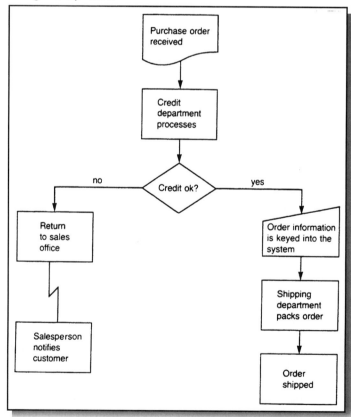

Part V   End-User Information Systems Project Management

15.4.4.4 Data Flow Diagrams (DFDs)

Data flow diagrams (DFDs) are network representations of existing or proposed systems. They form the cornerstone for structured systems analysis and design methodologies. The diagrams use four symbols to represent any system at any level of detail. The four entities, as illustrated in Figure 15-9, that must be represented are:

- **Data stores.** Depicted by an open-ended rectangle, data stores represent repositories for data that are not moving. For example, a data store may represent data in a file cabinet, computer file, database, desk drawer, reference book, or other locations.
- **Processes.** Processes, depicted by rectangles with rounded corners, represent transformations of incoming data flow(s) to outgoing data flow(s).
- **External entities.** Depicted as rectangles, external entities are sources or destinations outside the specified system boundary.
- **Data flows.** Data flows represent movement of data in the system. Arrows are used to represent the direction of flow and can connect external entities to processes, processes to processes, or processes to data stores.

DFDs represent systems graphically. They provide a means to describe, understand, and discuss the boundary of a system and its inputs, outputs, processes, and subprocesses. DFDs provide a logical representation, simply showing what a system does, rather than a physical description of how it is done. They are analogous to road maps, showing all possible paths. They do not show specific starting or stopping points, decision points, or timing of events. Processes are described at several levels of detail, beginning with a broad overview and progressing to more specific levels. Each level of detail is represented in a separate diagram, numbered

Figure 15-9
Data flow diagram (DFD) symbols

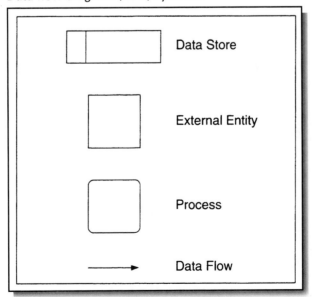

starting with zero. The definition of the highest (broadest) level of the system is called the *context-level diagram.* It represents the business view of the system that shows the system at the center with external entities providing data to and receiving data from the system.

The context level diagram is extremely useful for identifying the scope of a project. It contains, by definition, only one process. The concept is simple: Identify the output that is required and then the data needed to produce the output. In other words, by identifying both inputs and outputs, the context diagram helps analysts understand who is affected by the current system (key players or stakeholders) and how broad its impact is. Figures 15-10 and 15-11 depict a context-level diagram of a student registration system and an initial attempt at a level zero data flow diagram.

To develop the skill that is necessary to use this technique typically requires formal training and practice. Anyone familiar with the systems development life cycle methodology has a much more sophisticated understanding of these tools than can be addressed in this text. Keep in mind that the value of data flow diagrams is (1) to help determine the scope of a project, and (2) to describe graphically a working or proposed system.

Figure 15-10
Context-level diagram of a university admissions system

Source: Courtesy of Dr. Roger Deveau, University of Massachusetts, Dartmouth

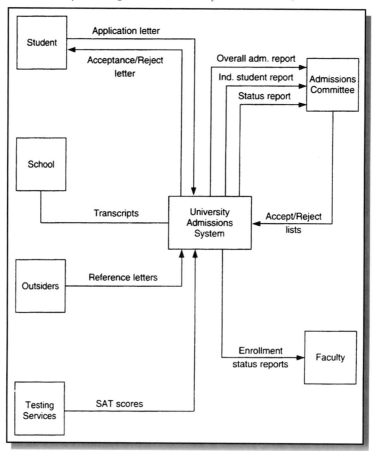

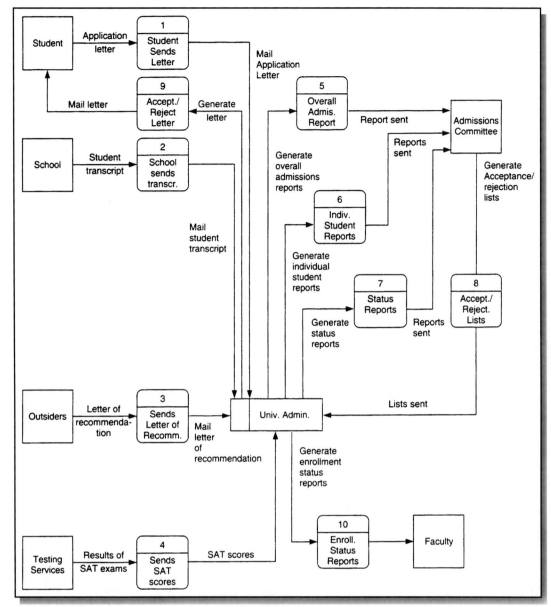

Figure 15-11
Level zero data flow diagram of university admissions system

Source: Courtesy of Dr. Roger Deveau, University of Massachusetts, Dartmouth

15.4.5 Reviewing Findings with Users

As models are developed, analysts review them with the users to verify that they are accurate. Reviews may be informal meetings between an analyst and user or may be formal meeting sessions with a group of users. Roles in formal review sessions include a moderator, recorder, presenter, and reviewers. A formal review is sometimes called a *walkthrough*, defined as a systematic, facilitated process for reviewing proposed models or system specifications to verify accuracy and obtain constructive feedback. A review ensures that the models accurately represent reality and capture all the necessary detail to design and implement the project successfully. Reviews should include persons who can contribute to a more meaningful end product in a constructive manner and should be conducted when analysts feel they have a reasonable draft of the model.

Generally, the analyst should expect that when users see the models, they will suggest additional details or find portions that are inaccurate or do not quite reflect the way the system really works. Variations and exceptions in processing routines are likely to come to light. It is not unusual for a model to go through several iterations before it captures the required detail and accuracy.

Care must be taken to ensure that review sessions are constructive and that feelings, egos, and pride are not offended. Conducting effective reviews requires good skills in group process. The moderator sets the tone for a review session and ensures that everyone understands and agrees to follow guidelines set for the review.

15.4.6 Identifying Alternatives

The results of data analysis are related to how the initial problem is defined. If a technology solution is appropriate, the analyst identifies appropriate technologies and systems. Here, two approaches are suggested: a technology grid and a prototype. A technology grid, such as the one developed by Robert Atkinson and depicted in

Figure 15-12
A technology grid helpful in matching tasks to technologies

Source: Courtesy of Robert A. Atkinson, Atkinson, Tremblay Associates.

Legend:
- ■ HIGH IMPACT
- ▨ MEDIUM IMPACT

Technology columns:
- A. AI/EXPERT SYSTEMS
- B. DECISION SUPPORT/EIS
- C. DESKTOP PUBLISHING
- D. END-USER QUERY LANGUAGE
- E. GRAPHICS SUPPORT
- F. HYPERMEDIA
- G. IMAGE I/O/FAX
- H. IMAGE OCR/ICR
- I. INFO STORAGE RETRIEVAL
- J. ELECTRONIC DATA INTERCHANGE
- K. INTEGRATED OA
- L. OPTICAL BAR SCANNER
- M. OPTICAL DISK STORAGE
- N. SMART/LASER CD
- O. SPECIAL PRINTERS
- P. VIDEOPHONE/CONFERENCE
- Q. VIDEOTEX
- R. VOICE RECOGNITION SYNTHESIS
- S. VOICE RESPONSE
- T. 4GL ACCESS
- U. IMAGE I/O DIGITAL
- V. LAPTOP
- W. POLICY HOLDER TERMINAL

Task rows:
- 1.0 PLAN AND CONTROL BUSINESS
- 2.0 WRITE BUSINESS
  - 2.1 RECEIVE CASE REFERRAL
  - 2.2 COMPLETE FIELD RISK ASSESSMENT
  - 2.3 REVIEW UNDERWRITING PACKAGE
  - 2.4 DEVELOP PROPOSAL/RENEWAL PKG.
  - 2.5 COMPLETE SALE
- 3.0 INSTALL POLICY
  - 3.1 DEVELOP PLAN DESCRIPTION
  - 3.2 DEVELOP RATES
  - 3.3 ENROLL GROUP
  - 3.4 COMPLETE INSTALL
- 4.0 ADMINISTER BENEFITS
  - 4.1 PROCESS REQUEST
  - 4.2 DELIVER SERVICES
  - 4.3 PERFORM CLAIMS ACCOUNTING
- 5.0 MANAGE CASE
  - 5.1 PERFORM CASE ACCOUNTING
  - 5.2 MANAGE CASE ACCOUNTS
  - 5.3 PERFORM CASE ADMINISTRATION
  - 5.4 PERFORM INDIVIDUAL MAINTENANCE

Figure 15-12, may be helpful in identifying alternative technology solutions to the problem.[2] Note that steps of a business process are written down the x axis. Technologies that may be effective in accomplishing the task are along the y axis. Technologies that could have a high or medium impact on work are indicated. Simple scanning of Figure 15-12 indicates those technologies that would offer the best payback.

Another useful tool for evaluating alternative solutions is *prototyping*. A prototype is a quick model that serves to verify understanding. It serves primarily to show users how a system will look and feel. A prototype quickly can assess whether the system the project team has in mind matches the users' expectations and needs.

As analysts attempt to match department and individual needs with technologies, they are continually reading, asking questions, listening, and trying to determine if the technology that is already in-house is good enough, or if something else is needed. If the solution requires an investment in new technology or is costly, compromises may need to be made. Other decisions are related to overall systems procurement—size (scope), capacity, and cost. Questions to consider include: Can the solution be installed in an acceptable time frame? Is it compatible with existing architecture? Are alternatives practical and reasonable? Is the required technology available? Is the expertise available to install, operate, and maintain the technology?

After identifying feasible alternatives, analysts begin to take a closer look to determine which solution is most workable and cost effective. The reader should keep in mind that those solutions that affect profitability—product development or delivery systems—or can be linked to organizational goals are the easiest to justify. The best solution is selected based on the established objectives and priorities. The selected solution is detailed in the project proposal along with an explanation of other alternatives considered and why they were rejected.

15.4.7 Determining Requirements for a New System

Once confident that the current system is understood, analysts begin to define the requirements for a new system. Analysts must assess factors such as requirements to interface with other systems, fit with the corporate architecture, and capacity requirements. Must a department database, for example, handle 200 client records, 2,000, or 2 million? How fast will it grow? How many new clients are likely to be added each year? How many people need to access the information and how often? Are they all in the same office area, department, building? All these details, or requirements, need to be documented as part of this step.

15.4.8 Redefining Project Scope

After business requirements have been modeled and verified with users, it may be necessary to redefine the project scope. The analyst should document and explain any variances from the original project scope and estimate the impact on project costs. This information should be presented to the project sponsor for approval. Analysts should never take for granted that additions or deletions can be made in the project scope because the analysis reveals that it is the logical thing to do or users ask for or support the changes. Remember that the project sponsor is responsible for funding the project and for the end result.

The boundaries of EUIS projects may remain fuzzy throughout the planning stages because of the nature of white-collar work. It is important to keep redefining the boundaries, however, to be sure that the work stays on focus and the project stays on schedule and within budget.

15.4.9 Preparing the Project Proposal

The *project proposal* documents the operational, financial, and technical feasibility of a proposed EUIS project. It describes alternatives considered and explains why the recommended solution was selected. The project proposal indicates the benefits to be derived from application of the technology to the identified needs/oportunities. (See chapter 9 for details on cost-benefit analysis.) The project proposal includes any data necessary for management to make an informed choice. An approved project proposal is, in essence, a contract between the design team and project sponsor. For this reason, details, including the proposed solution, estimated time frames, estimated cost figures, and an overall project plan, should be included. While the project proposal is usually not highly technical, it needs to provide adequate data to enable the decision maker to make one of three choices:

1. *Approve the project.* Approval means that decision makers understand and agreed with the proposed solution. In such a case, the analyst goes to the next step of development.
2. *Mandate further investigation.* Further investigation means that decision makers have questions that need to be addressed.
3. *Terminate the project.* Termination means that the proposed technology solution was not accepted. Projects may be terminated for many reasons. Sometimes projects are terminated because of environmental conditions that the analyst has no control over—cash flow, union activities, and the like. Sometimes the costs far exceed the sponsor's expectations, regardless of whether they are justified by the benefits.

An appropriate format for a project proposal is outlined in Figure 15-13. Note that the management summary provides an overview of the business objectives and proposed solution, the assumptions and constraints, a cost estimate and justification, and schedule. The detailed recommendation describes the business and operational problem or objectives, the project solution, implementation plan, and other alternatives considered.

15.5   STEP FOUR: DESCRIBING THE SOLUTION IN DETAIL

Purpose: Develop detailed specifications for the proposed project solution.
Deliverables:

- Specifications for proposed system, including hardware, system software, application software, networking, and any custom programming required.
- Request for proposal (if required).
- Documentation of proposed new business process design.
- Specifications for all major user solutions.
- Documentation of all tasks to be streamlined, eliminated, and combined with automation.

Management Summary (approximately 3 pages)

- Project Scope and Solution
  Describe the business or operational problems/objectives. Provide an overview of the solution clearly identifying business changes.
- Assumptions/Constraints
  Itemize all assumptions that, if not valid, might significantly alter the solution or make it completely infeasible. Identify constraints that force specific design directions.
- Estimates/Justification
  Summarize the major costs associated with developing and implementing the proposed solution, as well as the costs of ongoing production and support. Explain the benefits of the proposed solution.
- Schedule
  List the major deliverables with significant dates including critical decision points.

Detailed Recommendation (approximately 10 pages)

- Project Description
  Describe the business or operational problems/objectives. This background is intended to be helpful in establishing baseline quantification of the project.
- Project Solution
  Capabilities/benefits provided. Describe what will be provided in terms of business or operational capabilities and benefits. Business capabilities might include providing new customer services, establishing new products, and improving competitive monitoring. Operational capabilities might include streamlined work flow, faster response time, and reduced errors. Benefits may be computed in dollar or value-added terms and might include better service and improved marketability.
  Functionality. Detail the various processing functions as well as calculations and reports.
  Information needs. Include high-level models, including context diagram and data flow diagrams for the proposed project.
  Security impacts. Describe security requirements, highlighting additional/nonstandard capabilities.
  Training. Identify the training required by business and systems personnel to complete the development project. Estimate the number of users who will require training and identify what training will be required to ensure a smooth migration to the new system.
  Operational impact. Describe new or changed client work flows, business processes, and jobs.
  Technical requirements. Describe required hardware platforms and interdependencies with existing systems. Identify any special requirements for the project.
  Cost estimates for development, production, and maintenance. Describe all development costs for the detailed analysis through the implementation. Costs may include staff time (work month estimates for business and systems personnel), machine development costs (if mainframe), print, hardware, software, and training. Contrast these costs with the risks and costs of not implementing the solution.
- Implementation
  Client involvement. Identify who, what, where, when, and how much of client resources are needed.
  Detail schedule. Identify who, what, when, and how much time to allow for each task. Include coordination required with other systems. If the project is to be phased, estimate the timing of future phases and explain why phasing was recommended.
  Impact on other projects/systems. Provide any information concerning dependencies between this project and others. Be sure to consider issues related to the phase-out of the old system.
  Conversion/bridging requirements. Indicate detailed conversion requirements. This should cover the system and manual conversions required, the impact on resources, and timing.

Other Alternatives Considered (approximately 3 pages)

- Description of alternatives.
  Describe the nonrecommended alternatives considered.
  Reasons for rejection. For each alternative mentioned, identify the reasons for rejection. Reasons might include costs, lack of significant benefits, or maintenance difficulty.

Figure 15-13
Project proposal format

- Documentation of proposed new work flow.
- New job descriptions.
- Inventory of skills, knowledge, and information to be trained.
- Documentation of instructional strategies for training all user audiences.
- Documentation of change management strategies for systems implementation.
- Specifications for help, reference, or other performance support aids required to support the system.

There is always a tendency for people to resist systems, but, other things being equal, they are less likely to resist ones that are well designed.[3] Assuming that the project proposal is accepted by decision makers, the next step involves developing detailed specifications for the proposed solution. The goal at this point is to describe precisely what the system should be able to do and to provide all the details needed to configure and implement it. A system's specification details the logical and physical design for the proposed system. Whereas the objective of analysis is to "take things apart," the objective of design is to "put the pieces together into a workable solution."

15.5.1   Documenting (Designing) the Proposed Solution

The analysis of the current system and the identification of alternative solutions are the basis for describing the *proposed solution.* Using the same tools used in the initial investigation, analysts develop a model of the proposed system: flowcharts, narratives, data flow diagrams, and the like. In documenting the new system, analysts are proposing a combination of people and technology to meet the defined business requirements.

Analysts must be aware of constraints that may limit design alternatives. Resource constraints include factors such as budget, available resources, and time. Other constraints include established architectures, compatibility with installed hardware and software, make or buy policies, acceptable hardware and software vendors, and enterprise standards.

Analysts also must be aware that design is an iterative process. Design specifications are developed at different levels of detail. Ideally, they are developed from the top down. In reality, designers may have to work from the bottom up or from the middle out. The first draft of a design may have to be revised several times. Design reviews with users will result in additions, deletions, and changes. The design is finished when it is approved by the project sponsor.

Detailed specifications also should describe how the new system will increase the scope of individual jobs; eliminate bottlenecks; redesign business processes; allow simultaneous, distributed access; or implement other business objectives. A more complete list of these considerations was discussed earlier in this chapter. The goal is to show how the proposed solution improves upon the current system as well as the specific requirements of the solution. This description provides the basis for construction of the system or for preparing a request for proposal (RFP) if all or part of the solution will be purchased from a vendor.

15.5.2   Internal EUIS Development

If a portion of the system is to be developed internally, the systems specifications are given to the appropriate development group in the organization. EUIS projects generally make use of off-the-shelf software and hardware. However, EUIS development typically is used for projects such as the following.

- Development of Intranet Web sites.
- Development of knowledge management, reference, and help systems.
- Modification or custom development of specialized pieces such as menus.
- Development of end-user solutions with graphical user interface (GUI) tool sets.
- Development of user solutions such as spreadsheets or PC databases.
- Development of image and work flow solutions.
- Development of decision support systems.

The project leader is responsible for ensuring that the systems developers understand systems requirements. However, when outside vendors are used to develop and deliver the system, the analyst must be able to evaluate and compare the solutions that are proposed.

15.5.3 Preparing a Request for Proposal (RFP)

To shop for appropriate hardware and software solutions, analysts generally invite vendors to propose their solution for a problem. A *request for proposal* (RFP) may be sought for a complete solution or only specific parts. All relevant systems specifications are detailed in the RFP, as follows.

1. An RFP calls for vendors to address the identified needs with specific products and their costs.
2. An RFP provides an efficient way to send the same set of questions to multiple vendors and to analyze their replies in a consistent manner.
3. An RFP also can be used to help hold vendors to their answers by attaching their RFP responses to the contract when it is signed.
4. An RFP may be used when seeking vendors to outsource training documentation, development of online training, or other training and support services.

RFPs typically include the following.

- A description of the organization and objectives of the system(s) to be developed.
- Criteria for responses, including the conditions under which the procurement will be made, such as a firm fixed price or a cost plus incentive. Timetables for responses, as well as anticipated decision dates and target implementation dates, also are included.
- Descriptions of the solutions to be developed, including (if appropriate) data from the needs analysis stage. Descriptions also should include required functions and features, conversion requirements, and budgetary allotments.
- Request for description of the group or vendor's ability to respond, such as number of people available to work on the project, its financial viability, and (of course) price proposals.

- Identification of the process that will be used to evaluate the system once it is in operation.

15.5.4 Evaluating Vendor Responses to a Request for Proposal

An overgeneralization is that there are three kinds of vendors:

- *Aggressive*—takes part in the design and development process.
- *Passive*—takes the order, delivers, and presents an invoice.
- *Monopolistic*—is the sole provider of the service.

Large enterprises typically have procedures to follow in identifying vendors in any given procurement effort. Increasingly, end-user computing is a multi-vendor environment. Prices for services of these three types of vendors vary markedly. Enterprises that are not required by law or policy to put out RFPs often have agreements with specific vendors that result in lower prices (quantity discounts) or better service (service agreements). In such cases, evaluation of responses may be limited to determining that the vendor understands systems objectives and is prepared and able to develop the system. In other cases, comparisons need to be made.

Vendor selection is more than establishing that a specific vendor has a solution to the identified need at the lowest cost. To facilitate the vendor selection process, criteria should be listed, including functionality, service support, financial strength, contract terms and conditions, product reliability, maintainability, availability, research and development activities, and adherence to industry standards.

Figures 15-14 and 15-15 are forms that organizations use to evaluate vendors' responses to RFPs. These forms are used by the project team to evaluate the RFP responses. The forms are useful in selecting vendors because ratings can be quantified and compared. Weightings and grading scheme are established to score the vendor response to each question on the RFP, and a minimum score is identified for continued consideration. It is helpful to identify the "must haves" before the vendor replies are reviewed to speed the selection process.

Evaluation of the selected vendor's responses may take the form of pilot installations or benchmark testing. A *pilot installation* is a test application of the product in a given location. In this case, users confirm that the product is either acceptable or unacceptable. As an alternative, or in addition to a pilot installation, users may be asked to evaluate hands-on operation of various products. In such a case, users play an important role in product selection.

A benchmark test involves comparing prespecified performance with actual performance. It may be done by bringing in two or more alternative products and comparing features and performance. Benchmark testing usually is done under conditions as similar as possible to the final production environment.

Ascertaining that proposed hardware or software solutions address identified needs is the first step. Once that determination is made, comparison of vendor products should not be on a lowest-cost basis alone. Other considerations are ease of use, compatibility with chosen hardware, vendor training options and support, clarity of manuals, cost of licensing, and the personal preferences of users. The single most important criterion is fit with business tasks. How closely does the software support doing tasks the way the business operates or the business processes and job performance specifications call for them to be done?

VENDOR SELECTION RATING FORM
_____

Vendor _____

Name of Evaluator _____

Signature of Evaluator _____

Date of Evaluation _____

Please rate each vendor on the following criteria. The overall rating for each criterion should be between 5 (highest) and 1 (lowest). Brief comments also would be useful.

	RATING
1. Proposer's understanding of the scope and magnitude of the work to be accomplished, as evidenced by the proposal. Comments:	_____
2. Qualifications and experience of the Proposer's assigned personnel. Comments:	_____
3. Proposer's ability to provide the service and system features required. Comments:	_____
4. Quality of hardware/software configuration. Comments:	_____
5. Flexibility and longevity of proposed system. Comments:	_____
6. Ability of the Proposer to initiate and complete the project within the time frame specified in this RFP. Comments:	_____
7. Prior experience of the Proposer in providing systems of similar scope and complexity. Comments:	_____
8. Quality of technical support. Comments:	_____
9. Quality of training and maintenance programs. Comments:	_____
10. Total cost of the Proposed contract. Comments:	_____
11. Compliance with other terms, conditions , and provisions of the RFP. Comments:	_____
Overall Comments:	_____

Figure 15-14
A form for evaluating a vendor's response to an RFP

15.6   STEP FIVE: SELECTING OR DEVELOPING THE SOLUTION

Purpose: Bring a working version of the system to a usable stage. Write and test all customized software, applications, procedures, documentation, and training materials.

VENDOR COMPARISON FORM			
RANK THE THREE VENDORS 1 TO 3 ON EACH CRITERION; TIE SCORES ARE ALLOWED.			
	VENDOR A	VENDOR B	VENDOR C
Ease of operation	1	2	1
Compatibility with corp. architecture	1	1	1
Fit with business tasks	1	1	1
Special needs*	1	2	3
Technical requirements	1	1	1
Vendor support (reputation)	3	2	1
Experience with proposed system	1	3	2
Growth/adaptability	1	1	1
Cost (Rental)** (monthly)	($2,393)	($2,637)	($2,131)
	2	3	1
Total	12	16	12

*Special needs include high-quality print, proportional spacing, super and subscripts, and special characters.

**This is the rental price on the basic system with compared optional features. The final rental figure may vary somewhat depending on the final configuration of optional equipment selected.

Figure 15-15

A vendor comparison form. Nine key factors for comparing and selecting vendors.

Deliverables:

- Fully configured and tested model of system.
- Physical site plans.
- Conversion plan.
- Fully tested documentation, procedure manuals, training materials, and job aids.
- Test cases, procedures, and training databases.
- Quality control measures and monitoring procedures.
- Change management strategies.
- Evaluation criteria for assessing extent to which business objectives are achieved.
- Detailed implementation plan.

Assuming that the decision is made to begin development, the next step is to select or design the new system. This step entails analyzing outcomes of the assessment stage and applying work requirements to available technologies. Keeping in mind the problem to be solved, the goal is to determine the best way to design the new system.

The best way to design a system is based on the scope and strategic importance of the project. If the system is to be designed externally, the proposal should outline the development strategy. If the development is to be done internally, several options may be considered. The IS or EUIS department may build a new system from scratch, following the traditional systems development life cycle (SDLC) methodology. Alternatively, they might use a prototyping methodology. Users may develop their own systems with guidance from the EUIS department. Another option would be to purchase an off-the-shelf system and modify it to meet the goals identified in the assessment stage. The solution also may be some combination of these approaches. No one best way to develop a system exists; decisions are based on the scope of the project, available resources, costs, the technology to be implemented, and strategic importance to the firm.

15.6.1 Selecting Application Software

Selecting application software may be as simple as confirming that a user's request for a spreadsheet package is justified and securing a copy of the corporate standard package, or it may require a complex process of matching specific requirements to unknown alternatives in the marketplace.

Once identified, the information about alternatives must be reviewed, evaluated, and validated. Criteria for selecting among the alternatives include the following.

- Does the package do what the user needs? Are the specified tasks and business processes supported? If not, how will they be handled? Is the package designed to support only individual tasks or does it support work groups or facilitate work flow?

- Is the package compatible with existing or planned hardware, system software, and networks? How easy or difficult is it to install?

- Is the package easy to learn? How long will it take for a new user to get started? To develop proficiency? Are training or training materials available? Is the documentation effective?

- How flexible is the package? Can the software be modified or customized? Does it have potential to meet future needs? Does it provide for alternative ways of doing tasks or is it highly structured?

- How well does the software package perform? Does it meet requirements for throughput, response times, storage, and network traffic?

- How much does the package cost per user? Per network? Is a site license available? Can volume discounts be negotiated?

- How reliable is the vendor? Does your enterprise have experience with this vendor? Are they responsive? Do they have a good track record?

- What support is available from the vendor? Is a technical hotline available? Can they meet special requirements and make modifications if necessary? Is training available for users and technical support personnel?

Many factors must be considered when selecting application software. Analysts must be especially careful to verify vendor claims about what a package will or will not do. It is important to consider not only what the package will do but how it does it. Marketing brochures are long on wind and short on substance, and they should not be relied upon exclusively to measure what a product will do. Often, publicized features may fall far short of meeting expectations. Analysts should test software using actual examples of work that is processed in the business unit. It is highly recommended that users have an opportunity to test real work prior to making a final software selection.

15.6.2 Selecting Hardware, System Software, Networks

The specifications developed during Step 5 provide the basis for selecting hardware, system software, and networks. If an RFP was solicited from vendors, the responses will provide detailed information about alternatives under consideration.

Even if no acquisition is necessary, an estimate is needed of the additional demand on existing facilities. Are memory and hard disk capacities adequate to handle new software and solutions? Will new software be compatible with existing solutions? How will they be integrated? Who will add them to the menu? A host of issues needs to be addressed.

Application requirements should drive the selection of hardware, system software, and networks. In reality, however, when existing systems are already in place, it is usually unrealistic to consider total replacement unless the systems are out of date. Therefore, EUIS analysts often find selection of new hardware, system software, or networks constrained by the need to use or interface with existing systems.

EUIS analysts may need to have specifications reviewed by appropriate groups such as computer operations, technical support groups, and others with special technical skills. Selecting hardware, system software, and networks is a complex process of identifying all the requirements, assessing existing capabilities and constraints, evaluating alternatives, and choosing the best solution.

15.6.3   Securing Needed Contracts

Contracts are used to document the obligations and responsibilities of two or more parties. Contracts for software may take the form of purchase agreements, leases, license and maintenance agreements, service and consulting agreements, and evaluation and nondisclosure agreements. Large enterprises generally have special staff who negotiate vendor contracts, and analysts would be expected to work with them. In small firms, however, analysts may be responsible for negotiating the contract. In that case, analysts may want to have contracts reviewed by a legal advisor prior to signing.

The up-front financial consideration for a product is only part of the cost, and not necessarily the vendor's greatest source of profit. Maintenance and training fees easily can exceed initial cost over a four- or five-year period. Even after an evaluation, things can go wrong with software and hardware. That's why an acceptance period is important, even after entering an agreement to license or purchase a product. After an initial acceptance or burn-in period, the vendor's warranty usually begins. The warranty should include, at minimum, the vendor's services necessary to keep the product operating in accordance with the defined performance specifications at no additional charge.

Once the contract is signed, there is the matter of compliance. What happens if the product or the vendor fails to perform, or if the vendor goes bankrupt or is acquired by another company? What rights does the enterprise have to terminate an agreement, and can any part of the investment be recovered? All promises and agreements should be documented in writing. This is critical to avoid misunderstandings, as well as to protect the enterprise in the event of nonperformance.

15.6.4   Modifying/Customizing Software

Many excellent off-the-shelf software programs are available to address EUIS requirements. These programs include desktop publishing, presentation packages, groupware, spreadsheets, word processing, graphics, and database applications packages. Such applications are often bundled as suites of services. Networking tools include voice mail, e-mail, and LAN management applications. Industry-specific programs include university course registration programs, human resource systems, real estate management systems, and hundreds of others.

In some cases, off-the-shelf programs only have to be configured for the hardware environment. In other cases, the original package must be modified to fit a particular hardware system configuration or particular application. In such cases, the organization may (1) hire the person/firm who sold the program to modify it to defined requirements, or (2) buy the source code and do whatever is needed to make it work within the enterprise's computer environment.

15.6.5 Constructing Software Solutions, Menus, Interfaces

Even when all hardware and software are purchased, some customization is required. User solutions need to be developed by the project team, users need to be taught to construct them, or some combination needs to occur. Examples of needed solutions include department databases, spreadsheets, or macros to create form letters with variables that can be merged with customer databases. Sometimes menu systems are needed to integrate various solutions. Fonts may have to be installed and software configured with appropriate print drivers.

Development of user solutions is an area where project teams sometimes fail to pay adequate attention. The users must struggle on their own, with only introductory startup training. This problem is a major cause of poor use and failure to achieve the envisioned productivity gains. For example, a user learning word processing for the first time cannot realistically be expected to start with building sophisticated macros to automate document production. Instead, analysts might build this initial application. Then as users gain skill, someone with the interest and aptitude could be selected to learn more advanced features of the product to build additional solutions.

How much of the application development the project team does and how much is left to end users is a key question. The answer depends on the experience level of the user community. In any event, all these requirements must be identified in advance and responsibility assigned so that they do not surface as problems after installation.

15.6.6 Testing the System Solution

User solutions and systems should be tested thoroughly prior to implementation. This is equally as important for a single spreadsheet or merge document application as it is for a complex system. Testing verifies that an application or system produces accurate and reliable results and operates the way it is supposed to under conditions of both correct and incorrect input.

Systems that are not well tested in advance can cause considerable disruption and wasted time during implementation and can even result in significant financial loss if calculations are incorrect. The system test plan should include all the things the application or system must do. All the business activities and combinations of business activities should be tested. Basic functions or transactions will be obvious, such as checking whether the deduction and payment amounts are correct, when, for example, recording an invoice payment in a client database. However, it's important to test combinations, such as what happens when a partial payment is entered one day and another payment and a credit are recorded the next day. Are the payment totals correct? Was the credit correctly deducted from the remaining balance? What if the credit exceeds the remaining balance? Does the balance show an overpayment?

All the anticipated problems (business error conditions) and the responses when an end user does something incorrect (error messages) also should be tested.

For example, suppose a payment is recorded for a client who is not yet in the database. Does the system respond with an appropriate error message? Testing should be done under conditions as close as possible to actual business procedures using actual data. The test plan should include both the test cases and the expected outcomes against which the system output will be checked.

15.6.7 User-Developed Solutions

As organizations progress into the Information Age, everyone becomes a user, and users will eventually (if not now) have the skills to build their own systems. This is both the dream and the worst nightmare of Information Systems departments. As a dream, user-developed systems could help eliminate systems backlogs. User-developed systems are bound to be valuable to the user and address specific needs.

As a nightmare, user-developed systems can cause problems related to data reliability and security. It has been estimated that 80 percent of user-developed systems have flaws or bugs.[4] User-developed systems may not use the organization's computing resources efficiently. They may also result in output that cannot be used as input for the next step of a process; coordination of development efforts may be difficult.

15.6.8 Developing Training Programs

Training is such an important part of effective system use that it is discussed in a separate chapter (chapter 6). Training programs and materials are developed during Step 5 so that they will be ready and tested for the implementation phase. A frequent mistake in systems development is to wait until the end of the development phase when implementation is almost ready to begin before addressing training. Effective training programs take considerable time to develop. Remember, training specialists need time to learn a new system themselves before they can develop training materials or programs.

15.6.9 Developing Online Help, Reference, or Training

Online help, reference, and other performance support system (PSS) tools offer many cost-effective alternatives to traditional stand-up classroom training. However, sufficient lead time is required for planning and development.

Knowledge management and PSSs are much better suited than traditional classroom training to support jobs that are redesigned to provide broader job scope. PSSs provide information at the workers' fingertips to support complex, information-based jobs that have high learning requirements. They are an important adjunct with other EUIS systems to support business process restructuring. Online help, reference, and knowledge management generally are developed by users and go through the same project cycle as other system components. PSSs are most effective when they are integrated tightly with other systems and are readily available at the desktop to support job performance directly.

15.6.10 Developing and Documenting New Procedures

Any time new systems are introduced, work procedures usually need to be modified. Especially when business objectives include restructuring business processes, this step can involve significant planning and effort. Work procedure changes may affect just a few people or hundreds of people in multiple departments. As with user application or systems development, analyses completed during Steps 3 and 4 provide the basis for redesigning business processes and procedures during Step 5. The objective is to take advantage of new systems to simplify and streamline business processes. These concepts are discussed in more detail in chapter 12, "Business Process and Job (Re)Design."

New work flows and procedures need to be documented thoroughly to support training and job performance. Procedures explain precisely what has to be done and how it should be done. They may be more or less formal depending on the nature of the work. The more complex the tasks are and higher the level of coordination involved is, the more likely it is that formal procedures are required. Well-documented procedures ensure that employees know what is expected of them. In other words, procedures define expected performance and provide a road map for achieving it. Documentation may take many forms such as reference manuals, job aids, or electronic performance support systems, as discussed in the previous section.

15.6.11 Developing Change Management Strategies

Managing the change involved with implementing information systems is complex and should be specifically planned for during the detailed design phase. Explicit strategies are required during each phase of the project to effectively address requirements and issues. Change management cannot be treated simply as an add-on; it must be integrated throughout the project. Business process changes must be identified early and often are the starting place for projects. Change management "unfreezing" techniques, such as awareness meetings, pilot tests, and extensive communications with the user community, can be vital to the eventual use of a new system. Training programs should be designed and management issues, such as conversion plans and documenting new work procedures, must be addressed.

Because of the complexity related to change management, human factors, training, and performance support, these issues are addressed in separate chapters of this text. Keep in mind, however, that the requirements identified in chapters 6 ("Training End Users"), 7 ("Support and Help Desk Management"), 8 ("Management Issues"), 10 ("Human Factors"), and 11 ("Organizational Change"), are addressed throughout the EUIS project management. The EUIS Project Management Model in Chapter 14 shows the relationships between various activities and actions throughout the project. The Model provides a valuable timeline for addressing appropriate issues at each phase of a project.

15.6.12 Conversion Plans

A conversion plan spells out how the old system will be phased out and how the new system will be activated. Conversion plans will vary considerably depending upon factors such as risk, cost, training requirements, and the complexity of the system. A conversion plan is important because it is often necessary to maintain ongoing production levels while implementing new systems. Careful planning is needed to avoid losing information or other problems. When significant amounts of data have to be converted, temporary staff may have to be hired to handle the workload. The objective is to ensure a smooth transition from the old system to the new.

15.6.13 Physical Site Plans

Physical site planning (facilities planning) can be a complex process. Planners need to consider factors such as layout, lighting, power, wiring and cabling, security systems, and furniture. Analysts may require the advice of specialists such as building specialists, space designers, engineers, architects, ergonomists, or electrical technicians. Site planning is discussed in more detail in chapter 10, "Human Factors," and in chapter 16 under "Implementation."

15.6.14   Implementation Plan

The implementation plan is a written explanation of expected changes and exactly when and where the proposed changes will take place. The plan identifies all activities and tasks to be completed, specifies how long each activity/task will take, who is responsible, and the required completion date. In developing an implementation plan, the project leader must have detailed delivery information from the vendor, as well as tasks and responsibilities of individuals in the business unit. In addition, the Human Resource Inventory is useful. The implementation plan is customized to the specific project needs.

The project manager must meet with all individuals charged with implementing the new technology, getting their commitment to perform given activities in the required time frame. The implementation plan may be in narrative (written) form, charts (see Figures 15-2 and 15-3), or any other descriptive format. It should explain the structure for the entire implementation, eliminating any surprises for implementers or users. For large projects, implementation requires close coordination of many diverse activities. A project manager may find it necessary to meet on a daily basis with all key players to ensure that activities are coordinated and important details are not overlooked.

The plan also may be viewed as a public relations document. Outlining what is happening, why it is happening, when it will happen, and the impact the technology will have on everyone is vital to the communication process. The communication process, in turn, is integral to acceptance of change. It is especially important to remember that communication is a two-way process. Successful implementation mandates that the planners and those to be affected by new systems have an accurate picture of what is—and what will be—happening. Such communication can minimize *mis*information (rumors) and is a key tenet of successful implementation strategies.

In addition, the implementation plan serves as a buffer between plans for the change and the actual change. People need advance time to evaluate the impact of the technology and adjust to the idea. Providing this document well ahead of implementation is highly recommended.

Implementation, evaluation, and alignment of business processes are covered in the next chapter.

15.7   SUMMARY

This chapter describes the first five steps of EUIS project management:

1. Define the project scope.
2. Plan the project.
3. Assess project requirements.
4. Describe the proposed solution in detail.
5. Select or develop the project solution.

To initiate a project, a project sponsor must be willing to commit the resources required to complete the project. The project sponsor plays a critical leadership role in major change efforts. The first step is to clarify the problem and define the scope of the investigation. This step in project management includes identifying business objectives, system objectives, and business process and performance improvement objectives for the project. The analyst makes an initial estimate of project costs and benefits and prepares a high-level project plan and schedule. This information is summarized in a project proposal that is presented to the project sponsor for approval.

If the initial proposal is approved, the next step is to develop a detailed project plan. Decisions about who should lead an EUIS study depend on who in the enterprise is charged with responsibility for EUIS projects, and the size and scope of the project. An IS department might assign one or two analysts or, for large projects, management may appoint a project team or task force representing several departments to aid in the investigation. Sometimes an outside consultant or an equipment vendor may be used during an investigation.

The third step is a more detailed analysis of project requirements. This assessment begins by gathering information to document the current system in detail. The success of the project depends upon the value of the information obtained in the assessment stage, and good rapport with users is critical. Analysts start by collecting and reviewing existing documentation and then employ various assessment tools—interviews, questionnaires, observation guides, work sampling—to gather additional information.

The gathered information is analyzed and summarized using various models to represent the current system and alternative solutions. The results are described to the project sponsor or other senior managers in a project proposal that documents the current system, requirements for the new system, alternatives considered, and what the study team recommends. Included is a more refined cost-benefit analysis and sometimes a design prototype. The project sponsor will determine whether it is feasible to continue the project.

Once the project proposal is approved, the fourth step is to analyze the proposed solution in detail. Analysts detail system specifications, including specific recommendations as to categories of equipment, number of units, software, solutions, and requirements for modifying or developing software in-house. It is equally important at this point to develop detailed specifications for changes required in tasks, business processes, procedures, and job performance. If an outside vendor is to be used, the request for proposal (RFP) outlines the enterprise's requirements in detail and asks that vendors respond with a description of appropriate technologies, cost, and other considerations deemed important (such as training).

Evaluating the proposals, whether for hardware or software, requires the team to determine which vendors have addressed the identified need and then to rank the vendors as to suitability. At this point, checklists that compare vendor responses are useful tools.

The fifth step is to select or build the project solution. The objective is to bring a working version of the system to a usable stage. The project team must configure the system, and write and test all customized software, solutions, procedures, documentation, and training materials.

KEY TERMS

- Context-level diagram
- Data flow diagram (DFD)
- Flowchart
- Interview guide
- Pilot installation
- Primary data
- Project proposal
- Project scope
- Project sponsor
- Prototyping
- Questionnaire
- Request for proposal (RFP)

- Secondary data
- Time log

- Walkthrough

- Work sampling

DISCUSSION QUESTIONS

1. What is meant by defining the project scope? Why is this step important?
2. Who is the best person to conduct an EUIS analysis?
3. Given the following situations, how would you plan to collect data? Which instrument(s) would be most effective? Support your answer.
   a. A large New York City organization wants its geographically dispersed divisional vice presidents to be able to collaborate on complex projects without constantly travelling.
   b. A book company in the Midwest wants to update its sales force on new books and services.
   c. The claims department of an insurance company can't keep up with the number of telephone calls it receives each day.
   d. The costs of printing and distributing the *Employee Manual* are going up. What are the alternatives to having it published outside the company?
   e. Despite installation of a LAN in the Law Division with a PC on every desktop, most of the legal staff are continuing to process work as it has been done in the past.
   f. The customer service representatives in the life insurance division frequently do not have the information necessary to answer customer inquiries. They must take a message, research the information, and then call the client back. It often takes two to three days to respond to customer inquiries.
4. Assume you are assigned to write a questionnaire to determine your department's desktop publishing needs.
   a. Write one ranking question.
   b. Write one intensity-scale question.
   c. Write one open-ended question.
5. If you were to ask, "What electronic mail features would you use?" what answers might you receive? Rewrite the question to get the response you are looking for.
6. Getting company employees to agree to sit for an interview or complete a questionnaire is frequently difficult. List some ideas for getting them to participate in your investigation.
7. What is a project proposal? Who prepares it? Who reads it? What are its major subsections?
8. What is a request for proposal (RFP)? What are its major subsections?
9. How would you go about comparing the proposals you've received from five vendors?

APPLICATION EXERCISES

1. Using one of the examples in discussion question 3, draft an interview guide, questionnaire, or observation form that you might use in collecting the needed information.
2. Use flowchart symbols to trace the way grades are processed at your university, beginning with the student handing in the final exam. Then, model the

same process using a data flow diagram. Compare the advantages and disadvantages of each of these methods for documenting an existing system.

3. Select an actual EUIS problem and define the scope of a project required to solve it. Choose problems from your university, your job, or even your personal information processing requirements. Use a context diagram to model the scope of the system. Identify departments, users, and all stakeholders that would be involved in a solution. Define business objectives, system objectives, and business process and performance improvement objectives for the project.

SUGGESTED READINGS

Davenport, Thomas H. *Process Innovation: Reengineering Work through Information Technology* (Cambridge, MA: Harvard Business School Press, 1992).

Katzenbach, Jon. *Real Change Leaders: How You Can Create Growth and High Performance at Your Company.* (New York: Times Business, division of Random House Inc., 1995).

Pfeiffer, William S., and Keller, Charles H. *Proposal Writing: The Art of Friendly and Winning Persuasion.* (Upper Saddle River: Prentice Hall, 1999).

ENDNOTES

1. Curtice, Robert M., "Toward the Information-Based Organization: Redesigning Business Processes to Create a High-Performance Business," presentation to the 10th Annual EwIM Conference, St. Louis, MO, September 1991.
2. Atkinson, Robert A., "Integrated Information Management: Catalyst for Business Change," in the proceedings of *EwIM Ten: Realizing the Value of Information Technology* (September 4–6, 1991).
3. Markus, Lynne M., "Power, Politics, and MIS Implementation," in *Readings in Human-Computer Interaction* (Los Altos, CA: Morgan-Kaufmann Publishers, 1987) p. 69.
4. Ibid.

Case Study Rhône-Poulenc Rorer Commits to a Worldwide Desktop Standard

Like most large enterprises today, French pharmaceutical Rhône-Poulenc Rorer (RPR) is challenged to meet current business needs while also having sufficient flexibility to respond to future needs. A pharmaceutical subsidiary of life sciences company, Rhône-Poulenc S.A., (1998 sales of US$14.7 billion with 65,000 employees in 160 countries), RPR has 28,000 employees and 1998 revenues of US$6 billion. A pending merger with German pharmaceutical Hoechst Marion Roussel (HMR) will form Aventis, one of the world's largest life sciences corporations.

Knowing that today's IT decisions would impact their ability to respond to future business opportunities and help them to remain globally competitive, RPR needed to evaluate and quantify the financial benefits and costs of migrating to a worldwide desktop standard. The existing desktop platform consisted of various editions of Microsoft Office as well as other software products. The complexity and difficulties of exchanging information was expected to increase with the anticipated merger. The company was considering implementing Office 2000 as a worldwide desktop standard, but wanted to determine if the benefits would justify the costs and implementation challenges.

Like all organizations, RPR has both IT and business concerns. The complexity and speed of change in today's global marketplace identify universal problems and opportunities. In particular, after identifying the business drivers, RPR established three primary objectives in considering whether to implement Office 2000 as a worldwide desktop standard.

- **Information Exchange.** RPR is a worldwide company where global configuration and multinational support are vitally important. In addition, document collaboration to facilitate productivity with merger partner, Hoechst Marion Roussel, was critical. RPR wanted true multinational support with consistent world-wide file formats.

- **Knowledge Management.** RPR needed better communication tools along with tools that support richer analysis to help make better decision making.

- **Reduce Desktop Operating Costs.** One of RPR's priorities is to reduce IT management and administration costs for implementing and supporting desktop computing. They sought to reduce deployment and management complexities. They also wanted to reduce help desk support with better tools and more customized help.

With the increased power and functionality of the Office 2000 platform, it was not immediately clear what the costs would be to implement and support it and whether the company would achieve sufficient productivity benefits to justify it. Moreover, RPR wanted to look at the total

cost of ownership, not just the initial implementation costs. The company decided to bring in an outside vendor to conduct the cost-benefit analysis. The vendor selected was Giga Information Group. Using Giga Information Group's Total Economic Impact (TEI) methodology, RPR determined that upgrading to Microsoft ® Office 2000 would have extremely positive business benefits by reducing desktop operating costs and positively impacting both personal and organizational productivity. From a financial perspective comparing an upgrade from Office 97 to Office 2000, the TEI cash flow analysis estimated that RPR's Office 2000 investment over three years could achieve an internal rate of return ranging from 134% to 333%. In comparison to Office 97, Office 2000:

- Reduces desktop operating costs by 17%

- Offers a potential 16% to 25% improvement in productivity

Mr. Guillaume Prache, RPR's CFO, stated, "The TEI analysis illustrates that deploying Office 2000 will enable full compatibility with the PC's of our partner in the Aventis merger, while reducing costs and increasing business productivity compared to other options." The graph below illustrates RPR's estimated Internal Rate of Return (IRR) of upgrading to Office 2000:

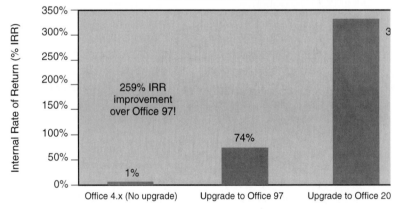

Office 2000: RPR Internal Rate of Return

*Note: 333% is the maximum IRR if Office 2000 is fully implemented (Office Server Extensions, OLAP, etc.) within one year of deployment. If it is not fully implemented until two years after deployment, the IRR is reduced to 210%. If no enterprise features are deployed, the IRR is reduced to approximately 134% due to the reduction in desktop operating costs.

Business benefits of IT investments are more than just showing that the investment reduces IT costs. IT must also show that the investment increases business productivity, or value for the entire organization. Giga's TEI methodology calculates this by estimating both increases in benefits

and reduction in costs, along with considering the investment's flexibility and risk. After being presented with the TEI analysis, RPR's chief financial officer, Mr. Guillaume Prache, made a strategic business decision to commit to Office 2000. He said, "The Giga TEI analysis is compelling because it quantifiably shows how deploying Office 2000 addresses both present and future organizational needs."

- **Reduces Desktop Operating Costs by 17%.** In RPR's environment, deploying Office 2000 is estimated to save 17% annually in desktop operating costs. Measurable savings are associated with new deployment tools and wizards, such as the Custom Installation and Office Profile Wizard, deploying a single worldwide executable with multilingual support, and other features that are focused on decreasing end-user support. End-user support, including help desk calls and peer-to-peer support, are projected to decrease due to self-repairing applications and the ability for RPR to customize the Office 2000 Help.

- **Potential to Increase Organizational Productivity between 16% and 25%.** While decreasing costs are important to all IT organizations, showing an increase in organizational productivity that results in greater organizational effectiveness is equally critical to achieving overall success. Increasing organizational productivity through Office 2000 enterprise features, like Web collaboration and information sharing or richer data analysis tools, is an optional benefit that is not available with previous versions of Office.

These potential gains in organizational productivity and document management are enabled by Web collaborative features such as Office Server Extensions, integrated NetMeeting, Web publishing with HTML, and rich analysis tools such as OLAP integration with Excel 2000. From a development perspective, Office 2000 has an integrated common development platform, Visual Basic® for Applications (VBA), which makes creating and deploying worldwide enterprise solutions more efficient.

The TEI analysis estimates these optional benefits to increase RPR's organizational productivity between 16% and 25%. The exact value of the producivity gains are determined when RPR decides to upgrade from Office 4.3 to either Office 97 or Office 2000 with those Office 2000 features implemented. If these features are implemented within the first year, RPR will realize the greatest business return—25% increase in business productivity. However, if RPR delays implementing these optional features until the second year, the additional organizational productivity gains will be approximately 16%. These featuers are treated like financial options: if they are never deployed during the Office 2000 lifecycle, they expire and will have no value.

Value Clearly Measured with Giga's TEI Methodology

TEI expands beyond traditional cost analysis to measure benefits, flexibility and risk, by assessing the overall financial impact of a specific technology. The TEI methodology, which for this analysis used RPR's data as inputs, quantifies the impacts of technology changes on all areas of an organization by measuring the estimated changes to the environment, not the absolute value of the technology.

A key benefit of the TEI methodology is that previously "intangible" benefits can be made tangible through a process of defining, benchmarking, and valuing these benefits based on real options modeling. The TEI analysis also shows why flexibility and risk are important to consider when conducting business benefit analyses. Giga's option valuation methods are based on widely accepted financial modeling techniques. For example, with Office 2000, the TEI calculations estimated that RPR's Internal Rate of Return could vary between 134% and 333% depending on which Office 2000 enterprise features, like Office Server Extensions, are utilized and when these features are implemented. Critical to RPR realizing these returns is the timing and execution of implementing these features.

The analysis demonstrated that there was greater economic value for RPR to deploy Office 2000 in one deployment cycle, rather than incrementally deploy each business unit and wait for the business unit to adopt the technology before deploying the subsequent business units.

When presented with the Office 2000 TEI analysis, Mr. Caryle Maranhao, RPR IS Global Project Manager for Office 2000, noted, "The TEI methodology is an effective way to create a comprehensive business case. Based on the TEI analysis, we are confident that Office 2000 will assist us in achieving our IT and business synergy goals." RPR believed that Office 2000 would meet their business needs today as well as position them to take advantage of future business opportunities.

Aligning People, Processes, and Technology

As part of the cost benefit analysis, RPR also clearly identified the stakeholders, their success metrics, and strategy for achieving success (see the following figure). This part of the analysis fundamentally aligns people, processes and a new technology in a way that meets overall business needs.

With the TEI analysis, the potential impact that a worldwide desktop platform could have on RPR's environment—both from a business and IT perspective—became quantifiably clear. The total potential benefit is estimated at a three-year minimum internal rate of return of 134%. This IRR could be as high as 333% depending upon

Aligning People, Processes, and Technology

Stakeholder	Success Factor	Key Performance Indicator	Office 2000 Benefit
Business Unit Manager	Research new drugs.	Time to get newly discovered compound to market.	Better data analysis tools.
End-users	Systems that are easier to use; focus on results and business process.	Reduce document collaboration time. Reduce amount of time spent in meetings.	Improved real-time team collaboration processes. Multi-language support. Improved document collaboration.
IT Staff	Increased user satisfaction and reduced support calls.	High user satisfaction. Less costly to deploy, administer and maintain.	Reduce end-user downtime and peer-to-peer support.

when various enterprise features are implemented. The TEI model clearly presented RPR with a complete business case for Office 2000. As a result, RPR made the decision to commit to Office 2000 as their worldwide desktop standard.

At the time that this case was written, selected business units had already begun their Office 2000 deployment. It was still too early, however, to evaluate the results.

CASE STUDY QUESTIONS

1. What were Rhone-Poulenc Rorer's main objectives for upgrading to a worldwide standard desktop?
2. What are the main people, technology, process, and organizational issues in this case?
3. What influence did the anticipated merger with German pharmaceutical Hoechst Marion Rous-sel play in the decision to adopt a worldwide desktop standard?
4. What information did the cost-benefit analysis provide and what were some of the implications for how RPR implements the worldwide desktop platform?

For more information via the World Wide Web, go to:

www.microsoft.com/office/enterprise/
www.gigaweb.com/

Source: © 1999 Microsoft Corporation. Used with permission. Accessed 10/29/00

http://www.microsoft.com/office/evaluation/studies.htm

EUIS Project Management: Implementing, Monitoring, and Aligning Business Processes

Learning Objectives

Upon completing this chapter, you should be able to:

➤ Describe the roles of implementing, evaluating, and institutionalizing new business processes in the EUIS project management model.

➤ List steps an organization could follow as a guide to implementing EUIS projects.

➤ Given a situation in which new technologies are planned, suggest strategies for their implementation.

➤ Identify major facility changes that must be considered in preparing a site for new technologies.

➤ List ten ways to conduct an EUIS evaluation and explain when they might be used.

➤ Develop an equipment feature analysis form, an interview guide, and an attitude questionnaire appropriate for EUIS evaluation.

➤ Explain the importance of the final step of the EUIS project management model: institutionalize business processes.

16.1   INTRODUCTION

Technology planners must remember that technology is useless unless it is used. The best-designed information system in the world will have value to the organization only if users are convinced of its value, are motivated to use it, and are adept in its use. Thus, the goals of the last three steps of the EUIS project management model go beyond the correct technical implementation of technology. These steps are intended to ensure that new technologies are used effectively at the desktop and are integrated into business processes. Significant cost savings are seldom achieved without specific strategies to tie use of technology to achievement of business objectives.

Chapter 15 explained Steps 1 through 5 of the EUIS project management model. This chapter presents the last three steps:

Step 6   Implement EUIS projects
Step 7   Evaluate results
Step 8   Institutionalize new business processes

It is difficult to put definite beginning and ending points on steps of the EUIS project cycle. Many of the tasks discussed here depend on deliverables produced during the assessment or design stages. Moreover, even if the tasks were not actually started, they were planned prior to the "Implementation" or "Evaluation" target date. Each step in the cycle is related to other steps. If the system does not address the right problem (assessment) or support the required business tasks (design), then efforts in implementation are doomed to fail.

The implementation step covers a broad range of activities required to convert from the existing operating environment to new systems and business processes. In EUIS projects, installation of hardware and software is often just the beginning of the implementation phase rather than the end. Unlike the traditional systems development life cycle, where implementation usually ends with initial training, end-user systems require ongoing training and support to promote infusion and assimilation of new end-user technologies. As pointed out in the discussion of innovation in chapter 13, the learning curve for users to master new software, apply it effectively to their jobs, and change ingrained behaviors is lengthy.

The evaluation step is critical in EUIS project management. In a sense, it is a continual process, and its outcomes are feedback to all of the other steps. Under the concept of continuous quality improvement, the result of an evaluation is often the input necessary to begin an entire investigative cycle again (see Figure 16-1). However, in terms of a project—which by definition has a definitive beginning and ending—it is important that EUIS projects have specific strategies for evaluating results in relation to project objectives and following through with necessary training, modifications, and business process changes required to achieve the intended results. This is the purpose of the last two project steps, evaluating and institutionalizing new business processes.

This chapter is divided into three main sections corresponding to the final three steps of EUIS project management. After an overview of the role and importance of an implementation plan, the first section discusses the tasks involved in implementing a new system. The second part of this chapter discusses specific ways to evaluate systems once they are in place. The third part discusses strategies for using evaluation feedback to align business processes.

Figure 16-1
The action research model

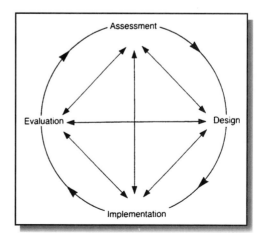

Purpose: Ensure that all technology is installed and operating properly. Ensure that new business processes and organizational changes are implemented as planned and that all employees are prepared properly to perform their jobs in the new environment.

Deliverables:

- Fully operational system.
- Applications installed to handle tasks and business processes.
- All users trained in initial skills required to operate new technology and use new applications.
- New procedures and work flows are operational.

The focus of systems implementation is threefold: job performance, business processes, and customer value/business results. People who will be using the system need to be eased into it, which means being aware of how the system will affect their jobs. It means more than users knowing how to use the system. It means restructuring job tasks, procedures, and business processes to use the new technology to best advantage. Some issues relate to hardware and software security. The technology itself mandates changes in the physical workplace. Technology may require special lighting, cooling, or ventilation. It needs a physical location and proper furniture to support it. These changes in work behavior and facilities can result in crisis if not managed properly. (See chapter 8, "Management Issues" and chapter 10, "Human Factors".)

Whenever technology is implemented, people's work and workplaces change. An implementation plan may be small (e.g., to install a spreadsheet package for a department manager) or large (e.g., to install PCs on every desk in the loan department). Even the simple project of installing a spreadsheet package, however, involves several considerations. The user must be trained to operate the software and be trained in developing proper spreadsheet applications. Department management must modify department operations to incorporate use of the new spreadsheets, ensure that applications are backed up regularly, and see that proper security is maintained. Managers also must identify and arrange training for a backup person to maintain the applications if the primary user is out or leaves the department.

The Spotlight, Palm Computers Help Emergency Room Physicians, provides a good example of a project involving significant changes in processes and individual behavior. Although the technology is critical to the solution, implementing the process and behavioral changes was the most challenging part of the project. Expanding on the success of the initial application poses ongoing challenges. Chapter 11 discussed concepts related to organizational change. This section is more pragmatic; it presents techniques that apply to introducing new technologies to users. Applying the concepts of Lewin's force-field analysis, the project team tries to reduce or eliminate forces that are counter to the change efforts and increase forces that are pushing for the change. In every enterprise, these forces are different, and the project team must select specific strategies to fit the situation at hand. A number of implementation strategies that have been used successfully by various enterprises are described in the sections that follow. These strategies work best in enterprises where:

1. The enterprise has a history of involving workers in making decisions that affect their jobs.

PALM COMPUTERS HELP EMERGENCY ROOM PHYSICIANS

Two patients enter the emergency room of St. Joseph's Hospital in Phoenix complaining of chest pain. The doctor who treats the first decides she's at high risk for a heart attack and requires ICU admission; the second doctor assesses his patient as low risk and keeps him for further observation before discharging. On the surface there's nothing unusual about this scene, which is played out in hospital emergency rooms every day. But at St. Joseph's there's a new twist: Palm computers help the doctors make better decisions, and that means both lives and money are saved.

This approach to diagnosing patients may be novel, but the problem it addresses is as old as emergency rooms themselves. With medical research constantly underway, it's impossible for every doctor to remember and access the results of every study. Taking outside information into account is particularly tricky in the area of heart attack assessment, which requires quick decision making.

As medical director of the ICU and other pulmonary and cardiac units at St. Joseph's, Dr. Philip Fracica was painfully aware of the abundance of medical literature that didn't always make it into doctors' hands. "Every physician's experience can be colored by the unique characteristics of the particular patients that they have cared for," he says. "But are those experiences truly representative of all patients?" When one of the hospital's monthly educational sessions introduced him to an objective scoring system for assessing heart attack risk, Fracica built a Web-based application so that doctors in the ER could access the system with a PC. The procedure was simple: After evaluating a patient, doctors would use the PC in the emergency department to answer a series of questions about the patient. The doctor could then incorporate the results of the studies into the diagnosis. "Some people have spent their lives studying this," says Fracica. "Now we can [use that information to] weed out patients that don't need admission to the hospital."

The remote application proved handy, but doctors still had to leave the patient's side, wasting critical seconds. So Dr. Fracica teamed up with AvantGo Inc., based in San Mateo, Calif., which specializes in delivering enterprise applications to handheld computers.

Now doctors can follow a link on the handheld's text-based browser to a Web page residing on St. Joseph's Web server, which in turn contains the risk assessment evaluation. The AvantGo software allows the Web page to transfer the information right on to the Palm computers—literally at the doctors' fingertips. The Web pages used in the application are then stored on the user's handheld, until doctors decide to delete them. This way, they can access the Web pages on subsequent occasions without having to download them again, which saves even more precious minutes.

Now when someone comes into the ER complaining of chest pain, the doctor performs the traditional assessment and examines the cardiogram. Then the Palm computer program takes him through a series of questions, which vary from patient to patient depending on the results of their cardiogram. At the end, the program delivers a percentage of heart attack risk, and the doctor can treat the patient accordingly. Avoiding unnecessary hospital admissions has benefits beyond the patient: It can help keep HMOs' bottom lines healthy.

All 14 of St. Joseph's emergency room physicians have been using the remote PC application for several months and have had access to the Palm application since June. And while it's difficult to quantify the value of lives saved, Fracicia believes that doctors are acting faster and making more informed decisions.

But it doesn't stop with chest pain. The software's flexibility means unlimited potential for targeting different illnesses. Fracica has introduced a similar program for treating pneumonia, though it had not been converted to a Web-based application at press time. But he stresses that these applications are meant to supplement, not supplant, doctors' judgment. Technology will never replace years of medical school, but it may just help make more study results common knowledge.

To Think About: How important was the support of the emergency room physicians to the success of this solution? What would be the incentives for physicians to participate? How significant do you think it is that the application was built by a physician (Dr. Philip Fracica, ICU Medical Director)? What does making the application available on handheld devices add to the process? Do you think that additional applications will be added as the spotlight suggests?

Source: Meg Mitchell, St. Joseph's Hospital's Heart Attack Risk Assessment. *CIO*, 12 (September 1, 1999): 72. Accessed on 10/31/00 at *http://www.cio.com/archive/090199 smart.html*.

2. EUIS is an identifiable function within the IS organization that supports business units in the enterprise.
3. EUIS is viewed as a continuous process rather than a one-shot remedy.

16.2.1 Managing Project Implementation

The *project implementation plan,* an important deliverable of Step 5, becomes the working project plan for Step 6. Like the work plans used throughout the project, it identifies all activities and tasks to be completed and should specify how long each activity/task will take, who is responsible for carrying it out, and target dates for completion. This detailed project implementation plan is an essential tool for coordinating tasks as well as communicating with everyone involved. It helps keep everyone on the same page.

The project manager, using the project plan as a guide, works with all individuals charged with implementing the new technology and gets their commitment to perform given activities in the required time frame. It is important that everyone involved understand what is expected of them, how to accomplish assigned tasks, and by what date tasks need to be complete. Managing and controlling implementation involves continually following up with everyone involved in the project, from vendor to committee members. As tasks are completed, the project plan is updated and, if necessary, modified. Meetings should determine that the project is on target and also identify any problems that may arise.

16.2.2 Staffing for the Implementation Step

As discussed in chapter 14, the EUIS project team brings together a mix of skills required to complete identified tasks and deliverables successfully. As the project progresses, the required skill mix and staffing levels may need to be adjusted. The implementation step is often a point at which such adjustments are necessary. In addition to planning the implementation process, the roles of project team members during implementation include the following.

- Coordinating dates, times, and places with systems vendors and users for specifics on delivery and use.
- Preparing the facilities.
- Preparing a conversion plan.
- Compiling test cases.
- Developing and testing end-user applications.
- Writing and disseminating status reports on the progress of implementation.
- Interfacing with the EUIS assessment task force (if the two groups are different).
- Writing new procedures or documentation.
- Implementing new business processes and work flows.
- Developing training materials.
- Developing computer-based training courses.
- Developing performance support systems or job aids.
- Training users to operate new software.
- Installing hardware and software.
- Customizing software, creating menu or other interfaces.

- Cross-training users in new job skills or business knowledge.
- Implementing change strategies.

The implementation team may appoint subcommittees with delegates from each department affected by the new system. Subcommittee members aid in coordinating plans and carrying out all necessary tasks in their own operational units. The implementation team also may call on other resources for completion of some tasks. For example, a facilities department may be responsible for ordering and installing new furniture and the network operations department may be responsible for installing the wiring for a local area network.

16.2.3 Selecting Pilot or Model Office Installations

Pilots or model office installations, which may sometimes be used as prototypes during the design stage, are also useful as a strategy when implementing large projects. A *pilot* or *model office* is a planned and managed installation of end-user computing support that serves as a model for providing the same support on a larger scale (e.g., multiple offices or the entire organization). Although the terms are often used interchangeably, a pilot generally is thought of as focusing mainly on installation of technology, while a model office suggests a broader scope that focuses on redesign of tasks, business processes, work flows, and jobs. The distinction in terms is unimportant as long as the objectives and plans for the pilot or model office are understood clearly by everyone involved.

As an implementation strategy, pilots are used as a trial run prior to full-scale implementation of a project. The results from the test can be useful for diagnosing learning problems and acceptance of the technology by its users. Such information can be valuable to the project manager or task force in determining appropriate implementation strategies. Sites for pilot or model office installations should be selected carefully. A well-planned pilot installation can play a key role in design and implementation. The following are some rules of thumb.

1. *Choose a site with high visibility.* The pilot installation is a trial run of the new system. Placing the new technology in a area where people see it, use it, and talk about it can help build acceptance: "Yes, we've been using the new knowledge management system for 6 months; it has increased the number of customer inquiries that we can resolve on the first call by 50 percent!" On the other hand, a high-visibility location also may have ramifications if a pilot goes poorly. The test site's success is dependent upon meeting technological standards and gaining users' acceptance.
2. *Choose a site with a high likelihood of success.* Selecting a locale where the installation has a high probability of success—where users are enthusiastic about the technology or where its success can be calculated by a large return on investment—is recommended. Find innovators—those who are willing and wanting to use the new system. Find high-payoff areas: "Desktop publishing saved the personnel department $200,000 the first quarter!"

Guidelines for choosing pilot applications likewise include selecting applications with a high potential for success. A pilot installation often will change the way people work, even if it is scheduled for a short period of time. Removing model office technology that appears not to be the best solution requires the same care as installing it. One planner whose pilot failed said, "Removing the pilot from the department was worse than curing people of a drug addiction! No one wanted to return to their former way of doing work, yet the system itself wasn't living up to expectations."

16.2.4 Preparing the Facilities

Critical to effective implementation is proper site preparation. Before a new system can be installed, the implementation team must ensure that facilities are appropriate for the new technologies. This step often involves deinstalling old equipment as well, for which adequate planning also may be required. The planner needs to ensure that the equipment is (1) installed correctly, (2) installed conveniently, and (3) installed to contribute to comfortable, safe employee use. Safety and correctness are discussed in chapter 10, "Human Factors," and security is discussed in chapter 8, but some key points are reviewed here.

16.2.4.1 Ensuring a Correct Installation

Correct installation requires that the equipment be put into place, keeping in mind power needs, space needs, and other conditions such as humidity and security. Installation may require physical alterations in buildings. In some instances, walls must be knocked down or put up. Air conditioning requirements must be evaluated. Also, wall configurations or high wall panels can impact airflow and ventilation.

Furniture and storage needs must be addressed. New furniture must be assembled and set up, wiring must be installed, and telephones have to be moved. Furniture must be placed conveniently, as well as near appropriate power and lighting sources. Supplies will need to be stored; the new copier will need paper and toner. Where will these supplies be? Where will computer supplies such as disks, printer paper, cartridges, backup disks, and other needed items be stored? How will old equipment be disposed?

As an example, a local area network installation requires cable wiring. The cables, in turn, must meet fire and safety regulations applicable to the building in which the LAN is installed. How far apart are desktop installations? In addition, a location must be determined for the server. Will access be restricted? To whom? Security issues (discussed in detail in chapter 8) also must be addressed. If, for example, portable PCs are part of the LAN installation, how will the organization address theft-protection concerns? In short, getting the physical site ready for installation requires careful preparation.

16.2.4.2 Ensuring a Convenient Installation

Convenient installation, though related to correct installation, has physical demands that are coupled with practical, usable designs. For example, the planner who intends to install shared laser printers throughout the organization needs to consider not only where they can be installed in keeping with their technological demands, but also where they can be installed *to meet the needs of users.* Laser printers placed in the middle of a busy office can be a source of aggravation for employees located near them—not only from added traffic, but also because the individual closest to them often is considered the resident expert on their operations. However, laser printers need to be located conveniently so that users can access them easily. Consideration needs to be given to factors such as who needs special forms and envelopes and how often they are used. Inconvenience is a disincentive to using new technology and often leads people to stay with familiar manual methods.

16.2.4.3 *Ensuring a Comfortable and Safe Installation*

Comfortable and safe installation mandates not only that the equipment be technologically aesthetic and properly installed, but also addresses ergonomic concerns (see chapter 10). Comfortable installation may require new or adapted furniture to ensure ease of use. The traditional desk was not designed to accommodate a personal computer. Health problems such as carpel tunnel syndrome can be avoided by following simple guidelines for correct placement of equipment. Is there room for the printer on the desk? Will windows or lights create glare on the screen? In other words, facility planning should be addressed prior to installation and should be completed before the equipment arrives.

16.2.5 Obtaining and Installing the System

The project manager should verify that all hardware, software, and required documentation have been ordered. It is also important to verify that special supplies such as cables, power-surge controls, wire management systems, and the like are ordered. Sometimes systems do not arrive with these necessary extras. Getting technicians to install the cable requires advance planning to ensure that cables and other supporting devices are in place when the system arrives. If part of the system, telephone service also must be arranged.

Installation includes setting up and testing all equipment. The amount of time required will vary, depending upon the complexity and scope of the system. All software must be installed and tested. Problems should be resolved and the stability of the system verified before it is used.

Systems arrival is another challenge. Who keeps inventory of goods that have arrived? Which box goes to which floor and to which workstation? What should be done with the refuse? Where should documentation be placed? What about employees who may not be at their desks on arrival day? Work goes on, but delivery of the technology can disrupt the entire business process. Without security measures in effect, how will the systems be secured?

16.2.6 Installing Security Measures

Security measures include protection of equipment and access to software. For example, will the server be in a locked room, or will it be accessible to everyone? Usually, the systems administrator has access to system and administration programs. Who else needs access? How will backup be handled? Who will provide support in the administrator's absence? The systems administrator needs the list of authorized users, along with the applications they will be authorized to use. Some users may have only "read" access, whereas others are authorized to both "read" and "write" to files and applications. *Read* means that one can access files but cannot make changes (*write*). These and other security considerations are discussed in chapter 8.

16.2.7 Developing Solutions

The project team will need to confirm requirements for new applications. Plans and schedules to design and implement applications must be established. Which applications must be ready for initial installation and which need to be phased in later? Does work need to be converted from manual systems or other computer systems? Who will do this work, and how? Is documentation available or does it need to be developed? Who will assist personnel with using or developing applications?

For example, it may be unrealistic to expect a user just learning a new database program to develop a complex database to manage customer inquiries. It would be more realistic for an analyst or experienced database user to develop this initial application for the department. The new user would learn basic database skills, learn to use the application, and gradually build database development skills starting with smaller applications. The user might then be expected to build additional applications later.

The task force (or an appointed committee) should arrange periodic meetings with users to review the implementation of new applications, get their ideas, and encourage "ownership" and acceptance of the application.

16.2.8 Delivering User Training

Perhaps the most important implementation strategy for new technologies is a strong training program. Study after study has shown that applications that a user understands and can apply with expertise to the job at hand are the applications that are used most. A manager, for example, who knows nothing of word processing is not likely to use word processing. Likewise, an administrative assistant who does not understand spreadsheets will not use spreadsheets. Although these two examples are simplistic, the point is clear: Effective, creative use of new technologies mandates user expertise.

When users seem reluctant to use technologies, it is generally because they feel insecure or uncomfortable with their use. Remember that users generally must maintain ongoing production during installation of new projects and may be working under tight schedules. They will be reluctant to use their newly acquired skills when they do not feel confident that they will be able to complete the work to meet deadlines. They would rather play it safe and do it the old way "just this time."

The planning team, the vendor, user departments, and even top management must decide on the right mix of training strategies: orientation seminars, product demonstrations, systems training, applications training, and so on. Because of its importance to the success of EUIS, training issues and strategies are described in chapter 6 and performance support and help desk management in chapter 7.

16.2.9 Establishing New Procedures

Work procedures should have been addressed during the design step. If not, they may need to be redesigned at the implementation step. The introduction of a new system does not automatically lead to acceptance of the system or improved work procedures. Left to chance, the tendency will be to adapt the technology to old ways of doing things.

The approach for establishing new procedures will depend on the extent to which work procedures must change. Whereas minor modifications may be handled with careful documentation and short training sessions, major transformations generally require considerable time and effort. During the transition phase, it is often necessary to run tandem activities; that is, work is done under both the old and the new systems concurrently. This allows for not only a comparison of systems but also for modifications. It also provides backup for the new system until all the bugs are worked out.

When major transformation is required, caution should be exercised to minimize the overload caused by too many new activities at the same time. It is important to avoid disruptions and inconvenience for clients during a transition period.

Balancing the demands for transforming work while avoiding chaos and disruption can be a major challenge. It can be rather like trying to change the tires on a car while racing down the highway at 65 miles per hour.

Other functional procedures include establishing who is to be responsible for the maintenance and repair of the system. Even tasks as seemingly straightforward as procedures for ordering supplies need to be addressed. Establishing departmental or unit responsibility for operation of the new system is important.

16.2.10 Managing the Change Process

Orchestrating significant organizational changes is a complex process. Chapter 11 discusses various strategies that are critical to success. When an EUIS project involves redesigning jobs and business processes, the implementation plan should include specific strategies to involve those affected, gain their commitment to the success of the project, and keep the words and music in synch. Line managers, not analysts, are ultimately responsible for the success of a project. Their commitment and cooperation is essential to the success of a change effort. Therefore, project sponsors should be involved in communicating business objectives and a vision for change, explaining precisely how implementation of the project will help achieve those goals and what is expected from those involved.

In summary, effective implementation of EUIS projects requires careful coordination of a broad range of activities to make the transition from an existing operating environment to a new system. Moreover, implementation usually needs to be accomplished while normal production is maintained.

16.3 STEP SEVEN: EVALUATING RESULTS

Purpose: Determine whether the results from implementation of the EUIS project match the established objectives. Identify problem areas and opportunities for additional improvement.

Deliverables:

- Inventory of performance problems.
- Inventory of additional training needs.
- Inventory of system problems.
- Inventory of bottlenecks, tasks, business processes, and work flows that need improvement.
- Measures of user acceptance, problems, and applications.
- Inventory of ideas and insights for additional improvements.
- Measures of actual results against planned results.

Evaluation is the seventh step of EUIS project management. After implementation is completed, it is important to determine how well new systems are working and to what extent project objectives have been met. The analyst or project team evaluates actual results against planned results in the domains of technology, job performance, business processes, and structure. Thus, the objectives established during Step 1, defining project scope, provide the basis for evaluation. This is why it is important to state objectives in quantifiable and measurable ways. The findings of the evaluation are used to make modifications in project implementation and to determine what additional action is needed to institutionalize new business processes.

Early planning for evaluation is important because the crux of evaluating information technologies is determining whether the technologies met their objectives. Why were the technologies installed? To improve the quality and quantity of written documents? To provide management with more information—or more timely information—on which to base decisions? To speed up order handling? Evaluation always involves knowing the original objective of the technology solution, as identified in the requirements assessment stage. That objective serves as a standard by which to say "Yes, the technology has met our expectations" or "No, the technology is not working out as we expected." Preestablished methodologies for evaluation also enable evaluators to be more objective.

Traditional systems evaluation usually takes the form of a post-audit review intended primarily to examine the effectiveness of the systems development process and to determine whether the system needs to be changed in any way. Although these are valid objectives for EUIS evaluation as well, they are not sufficient. With regard to EUIS, it is more important to determine how the technology is being used to improve performance and to what extent the project has achieved the planned business results. Chapter 9, "Assessing the Value of Information Technology," provided suggestions for developing performance measures.

This section addresses the following questions: Who should do the evaluation? When should it take place? What should be evaluated? How should it be done? In addition, some specific evaluation strategies are presented.

16.3.1   Who Should Do the Evaluation?

Whether planned or not, system evaluation is done by everyone who has contact with the system. The CEO who uses the new phone system, the vice president who reads the report that was published using desktop publishing, the administrative assistant who uses electronic calendaring to schedule appointments, the customer who receives an order—all are potential evaluators of the system. The overall responsibility of formal evaluation, however, rests with the project manager or task force that implemented the system. The project manager or team is charged with determining the evaluation strategy and carrying it out. Users may be one source for providing evaluation data.

16.3.2   When Should Evaluation Take Place?

In essence, informal evaluation of new technologies is taking place constantly. From the day the technology is introduced, its users are critiquing its value. Before project results are evaluated formally or users are rated on job performance using the new technologies, however, sufficient time should be allowed for learning. How long this period should be depends upon the complexity of the applications. A nonevaluative period allows users to be exploratory, to make mistakes, to correct them, and to gain experience using the technology.

Such a period is also important for gaining an understanding of the value of the technology. At first, work may be done more effectively with the old tools. Users need time to learn to use and appreciate the new technology, and the new technology needs time to become an accepted tool. Such a time period also allows for the Hawthorne effect, which is the tendency for people to perform better than normal when they are being observed. When inadequate time is allowed prior to evaluation, findings may be misleading because, without reinforcement, individuals tend to revert to their former behaviors once the newness of the system no longer motivates them to use it. In short, any new work tool or process should be given adequate time to have an impact on work before evaluation begins.

Although no exact time can be offered here, evaluation should be well planned. The project manager determines when evaluation should take place, depending upon the complexity of the technology and the rate at which users incorporate it into their business processes. Thus, a formal evaluation may take place any time after the technology becomes part of work.

16.3.3   What Should Be Evaluated?

The objectives established during Step 1, defining the project scope, provide the basis for evaluation. This is why it is important to state objectives in quantifiable and measurable ways. Thus, business measures are the best indicators of project success. Factors such as the following can be effective measures for evaluating business results.

- Number of customer complaints.
- Completion cycles for tasks.
- Numbers of errors.
- Response time.
- Number of hot line calls.
- Number of customers served.
- Reductions in expenses.
- Increases in revenues.
- Number of transactions handled.
- Average length of time to handle transactions.
- Reductions in questions or problems.
- Improvements in customer service.
- Additional tasks or outcomes achieved.

16.3.4   How Should Evaluation Be Done?

The evaluation process should facilitate understanding of what new technology has done for the individual, the organization, and the customer. Evaluation is both a science and an art. The evaluator must select the most appropriate data collection tool, design an instrument that follows accepted techniques, and determine what to do with the resulting data. A questionnaire designed with no view of what to do with the data that will result is pointless. Data collection techniques also must be administratively feasible, which means that while interviewing all users may be desirable, time and personnel constraints must be taken into account. The process of understanding and reporting primary data is a science/art that can be learned and is polished with every project.

Collecting and analyzing data can be streamlined with the use of group systems tools or by putting survey forms on the company Intranet.

The following strategies, which are offered strictly for illustration, have worked for various organizations. As explained earlier, any assessment tool described in Chapter 9 may be used for evaluation. The project director chooses from among these strategies, or even develops original strategies to determine whether the new system or technology is performing or being used as planned.

16.3.4.1 Feature Analysis

Feature analysis involves creating a list of the features of the new hardware or software that differentiate it from other technologies. Users can rate the features as mandatory, desirable, or optional. Specific features also might be rated based on frequency of use. The analyst can develop a composite score for the hardware or software by giving a numerical value to the ratings and adding up the columns. For example, the feature rating form in Figure 16-2 could be used to evaluate word processing software.

16.3.4.2 User Interviews

Interviews with users, which can provide information regarding the effectiveness of the technology, may be open or structured. Interviews are a means of finding out what is good and what is not so good about a system. Interviews help the project team determine how new technology is being used, where users are experiencing problems, and what additional action may be required. By discussing project results with users, team members gain new insights for enhancements or innovations.

16.3.4.3 Company Files

One benefit of well-planned EUIS projects is improved quality of work life (QWL). As discussed in chapter 10, EUIS has the potential to improve motivation and job satisfaction. A review of company records may provide the director with data regarding turnover rates, personnel evaluations (did individual or department productivity go up?), or even attendance. Improvement in any of these items may be attributed to the technology available to the worker.

16.3.4.4 Attitude Questionnaires

Rather than assess the technology itself, the evaluator may assess individuals' attitudes toward that technology. Although company files may provide hard data regarding the effect of the system on work, a questionnaire can offer information

Figure 16-2
A feature rating form for evaluating word processing software

	USE FREQUENTLY (10 POINTS)	USE MODERATELY (5 POINTS)	NEVER USE (0 POINTS)	TOTAL
Spell check				
Mail merge				
Footnote generator				
Headers				
Footers				
Table of contents				
Columns				
Pagination				
Total Value				

regarding attitude and worker acceptance of the technology. Again, to be effective, new technologies need to be used. If the individual who uses the technology feels it is of little value, chances are that it *is* of little value.

16.3.4.5 Communications Audit

A conceptual communications approach to EUIS analysis was described in chapter 14. EUIS projects sometimes are implemented to improve communications within an organization, and if measurements were collected during the assessment phase, a post-communications audit can determine whether the new technology facilitated more or better communications among employees. A communications audit is a form that shows who, when, and how many communications were made with others in the organization. Although a communications audit is a time-consuming endeavor, a project manager who can show that a system improved communications within a company has verified a valuable benefit of the system.

16.3.4.6 Work-Time Measurement

Work-time measurement simply compares the before-technology time involved in doing a task with the after-technology time for the same task. Time savings, as discussed in chapters 9 and 14, can show substantial cost savings (benefits) to the enterprise.

16.3.4.7 Cost Comparisons

An important measure that should be addressed in any evaluation report is a comparison of expected versus actual costs of the system. Such comparisons give little information about the effectiveness of a new system, but they can show that costs were reasonable or that a value is obtained when the operating costs of the current versus the previous system are compared. Figure 16-3 presents an example of a cost comparison report. Other methods for developing cost figures were discussed in chapter 9.

16.3.4.8 User Competency Testing

If individuals who are expected to use the system can use it to its fullest, chances are the system is a success. If it can be determined that users can use its features to their advantage—or have created even more ways to use it than originally outlined—the evaluator can assume a high degree of system success.

Figure 16-3
A typical cost comparison report

	COST SAVINGS SUMMARY		
	PROPOSED	ACTUAL	VARIANCE
Centralized Annual Operating Costs	$212,711	$227,122	+$14,411
Decentralized Annual Operating Costs	193,429	192,853	576
Annual Savings	$ 19,282	$ 34,269	$14,987
Development Costs	$ 12,320	$ 14,080	+$ 1,760
One-Time Equipment Costs	4,000	4,245	245
Total First-Year Development Costs	$ 16,320	$ 18,325	−$ 2,005
Payback	10.2 mos.	6.4 mos.	3.8 mos.

16.3.4.9 *Participant Observation*

Monitoring the use of new technologies is the final evaluation method to be discussed here. This technique requires selecting someone from the work environment and training that person to observe use of the technologies in question and record observations. A person who is part of a particular work environment is often in the best position to determine its effectiveness. Such an approach may conjure up images of spying; however, the purpose of the observer is to evaluate the technology, not necessarily the workers. This observer may be an outsider or a regular employee who simply fills out a technology-use observation form.

16.4 STEP EIGHT: INSTITUTIONALIZING NEW BUSINESS PROCESSES

The critical last step of *institutionalizing* new business processes is often overlooked. Yet this step is the key to making lasting changes and bringing productivity gains to the bottom line. In terms of Lewin's change theory, this is the refreezing stage in the change process.

Unfortunately, in practice, once the hardware and software are installed and some initial training is done, all too often the rest is left to chance. It has been the authors' experience that many of the important actions needed to assimilate new technologies into the organizational culture and sustain changes in job performance and business processes, in fact, are never addressed. There is a tendency in organizations for the project team to dissolve soon after implementation of the hardware and software solutions. The evaluation, if done at all, is done too early and is used primarily to justify the project. The work environment returns to "business as usual," and it is assumed that workers will assimilate and apply the new technologies automatically. This assumption more often than not proves incorrect. To achieve significant organizational changes, project teams need to work with business managers to plan and implement appropriate intervention strategies.

Assimilating new technologies involves a lengthy learning curve. Left to chance, the need for continued training and action often gets overshadowed by demands of the business. Many workers never progress beyond the most rudimentary use of the new systems, and some even slip back into old ways of doing things. The technology tends to get adapted to the old ways of doing things rather than taking advantage of the technology to modify work. As a result, opportunities to make significant improvements in business processes may be lost. It has been found that results of EUIS projects can be improved significantly when project plans include well-planned strategies to support continued learning and involve employees in continuous quality improvement.

16.4.1 Providing Remedial and Advanced Training

For a technology to transform an organization, users must be proficient in its use. Too often, training efforts are budgeted within a given project, but once the project is considered complete, training is considered complete, as well. This is not typically the case. For users to be able to use technology creatively to change the way they work, they must be highly skilled in its use. In chapter 6 and 7, specific strategies for institutionalizing technology's use are described in more detail. This remedial or advanced training is vital to system success.

16.4.2 Modifying or Enhancing Systems

As users gain experience with new technologies, they will gain new insights into how it might be used to make further improvements. Without specific strategies to continue to enhance new systems, these new ideas are often lost. EUIS projects should plan to capitalize on these new insights to further refine computer applications and business processes. The infusion and assimilation of technology is an iterative process, not a one-shot solution.

16.4.3 Meeting Job Performance Objectives

Meeting job performance objectives generally requires a sustained period of training. Most sophisticated software provides far more functionality and more potential applications than can possibly be absorbed by even the most astute employees during a one-shot training effort. Even employees who are motivated to continue learning on their own often find that business demands crowd out the time unless their managers make training and effective application of new technology a priority.

Without explicit programs to reinforce and build on new skills, individual efforts may not contribute significantly to overall department results. Managers must reinforce and reward desired new behaviors. Although this may seem obvious, in an environment of change, which often borders on managed chaos, it is not uncommon for people to be working at cross-purposes.

To achieve significant results, performance goals must be clearly defined and articulated to everyone in the organization. Employees must be committed to achieving those results and participating in the process. Feedback on results must be provided on an ongoing basis, and needed training and support must be available.

Significant job changes may have to be phased in over time because production must be maintained throughout the conversion. This may take a year or more for large-scale projects with significant job redesign.

16.4.4 Meeting Business Process Objectives

When new business processes are implemented, it takes time and effort to work out the kinks. Modifications and refinements will likely be needed. Seldom can one expect to get it perfect the first time. Unanticipated problems may crop up. New bottlenecks may be created. Often, these problems lead people to believe that the new methods are not working, and pressure mounts to go back to the old tried and true ways of doing the work. These threats should be of even more concern with professional and managerial staff because these individuals exercise more discretion over their work environment. Well-planned strategies are needed to involve staff in identifying problems early and implementing timely solutions. Moreover, some of the most innovative ideas emerge only after workers have gained experience with the technology. Significant opportunities may be missed in the absence of strategies for capturing them.

16.4.5 Meeting Business/Management Objectives

After the system is implemented, it may take several months to meet business objectives. Because of the learning curve, production can be expected to decrease during a period when new technologies and work procedures are introduced. Effective follow-up training, support, and advanced training can help to shorten the curve.

New measures of business effectiveness may be needed. If the expected business results are not achieved, it may not necessarily be due to shortcomings of the new system. It may be necessary for managers to reexamine related business practices, measures, and the reward structure. Sometimes the old reward structures have to be modified to reward different behaviors that are in line with new business practices. It may be necessary to refine business criteria and success measures.

If EUIS projects are expected to have a significant impact on operations and business results, achieving these goals must be managed as carefully as the design and implementation of the technology. This is the goal of this final step in EUIS project management.

16.5   WHY SOME SYSTEMS FAIL

Systems fail more often because of poor planning or lack of attention to organizational issues than because of hardware or software problems. Ensuring the success of EUIS projects may mean learning from the mistakes of others. The following is a list of reasons why some projects fail.[1] These mistakes are divided into organizational, people, implementation, and technological *barriers*. Barriers are factors that negatively affect the implementation and use of information systems. Note that these barriers to successful system adoption can occur at any phase of a project: assessment, design, implementation, or evaluation.

1. *Organizational barriers.* Top management or the EUIS planners:
    *   Based decisions on short-term goals/earnings.
    *   Failed to understand the potential for improved operations.
    *   Failed to understand productivity/cost benefits.
    *   Wanted benefits without costs.
2. *People barriers.* Users of the system:
    *   Resisted change.
    *   Wanted more control over selection of technologies or how they were to be used.
    *   Did not understand how information systems changed their jobs.
    *   Did not learn to use the technology adequately.
3. *Implementation barriers.* Implementers of the system:
    *   Were unsure of user requirements.
    *   Sought ultimate solutions.
    *   Lacked planning expertise.
    *   Did not understand the anxiety of employees toward change.
4. *Technological barriers.* The technology itself was:
    *   Too complex to learn to use.
    *   Incompatible with other technologies in the organization.
    *   Based on technology incompatible with existing technology.
    *   Wide open to security problems.
    *   Not given adequate or appropriate space in the office.

Identifying pitfalls related to management, users, implementers, and the technology itself can be of value to a project manager in avoiding potential problems or to an evaluator in diagnosing why things went wrong. For example, if a system is not being used, the reason may be any of these barriers. Identifying and correcting the problem (barrier) is of utmost importance to systems success.

This chapter explains tasks and deliverables for the last three steps of EUIS project management:

Step 6   Implementing EUIS projects
Step 7   Evaluating results
Step 8   Institutionalizing new business processes

Strategies relative to these steps were discussed as examples of techniques a project team could consider in carrying out plans for implementing and evaluating new technologies.

The implementation plan prepared in Step 5 (described in the preceding chapter) becomes the work plan for Step 6. This plan details the tasks needed to prepare the site, install hardware and software, convert applications, train personnel, and implement the planned changes in jobs and business processes. Large projects require considerable coordination, and effective communication is key. Communication reduces surprises, thereby contributing to user acceptance.

The project team responsible for analysis, design, and development may continue as the implementation team, or, more likely, some new resources may be assigned during the implementation phase. Pilot or model office installations allow users to test the technology; to prepare applications; or to test changes in job assignments, procedures, and business processes. The task force must manage and control the project and set goals and time frames.

Preparing the facility includes ensuring correct, convenient, and safe installation. The physical installation requires ensuring that the correct hardware and software arrive and are installed at the proper location. Installation also requires preplanning to see that cabling and electrical needs have been addressed. Security must be established and training provided.

Personnel must be trained in operating new technology, in using new applications, in performing new job tasks, in new business processes and procedures, and perhaps in new business knowledge, as well. All applications should be phased in gradually, allowing systems to become part of the work pattern. New procedures should be established and job descriptions updated.

The purpose of evaluation is to compare actual results against planned results. Thus, the performance, business process, management/structure, and technology objectives defined during Step 1 are the basis for evaluation during Step 7. Evaluation strategies should be well planned, well executed, objective, and verifiable and should provide information that will be useful to reinforce and institutionalize results. In addition, because the project team learns from errors, evaluation findings may mean that the next project has a higher likelihood of success. Keeping users involved at all stages also helps ensure system acceptance.

Equipment feature analysis forms allow an evaluator to determine the use (and desirability) of expensive or additional features of the new technology. Information in company files can tell the evaluator whether the technology has had an effect on employee performance and business results. Attitude questionnaires can determine what people think of their technologies; if the new system is highly regarded, chances are it is operating as expected (or better!). Work-time measures compare the before-and-after times for completing specific tasks. Cost comparisons contrast expected technology costs with actual technology costs. Although these figures do not necessarily indicate quality performance, they can show that the system is operating as planned.

The final step, institutionalizing new business processes, although often overlooked, is critical to achieving lasting changes and bringing productivity gains to the bottom line. Assimilating new technologies requires a lengthy learning curve. Left to chance, the need for continued training and action often gets overshadowed by demands of the business. Results of EUIS projects can be improved significantly when project plans include well-planned strategies to support continued learning and involve employees in continuous quality improvement.

KEY TERMS

- Barriers
- Evaluation

- Institutionalizing
- Model office

- Project implementation plan
- Pilot installation

DISCUSSION QUESTIONS

1. List the ten tasks offered as an approach for EUIS implementation. Why is the implementation step considered the key to a system's success?
2. Given the following implementation sites, develop a project management plan. Describe the resources needed to do the implementation and estimate a time frame for the site.
   a. A large community college has a new telephone system: new operating procedures, new telephone numbers, new handsets.
   b. A government office plans to install a local area network that will connect department heads on five floors.
   c. The corporate headquarters of a large manufacturing organization is offering laptops to all of its employees.
3. What is the role of evaluation in EUIS project management? What is the primary purpose of evaluation? When should it take place? What should be done with the results?
4. If you were charged with evaluating the systems identified in discussion question 2, what questions would you need to ask yourself before you developed an evaluation strategy and timetable?
5. What is the purpose of Step 8, institutionalizing business processes? What is meant by institutionalizing business processes? Why is this step often overlooked? Why is this step critical to achieving project results and bringing productivity gains to the bottom line?

APPLICATION EXERCISES

1. Interview at least three people who are using information technology at their workplace. How were they introduced to the technology?
2. Write an item for a company newsletter detailing the benefits of the knowledge management system that is scheduled for implementation in three months.
3. Prepare a written questionnaire for evaluating an organization's use of groupware tools. What will you be evaluating: the technology itself or acceptance and use of the tools?

Clements, Richard Barrett. *IS Manager's Guide to Implementing and Managing Internet Technology.* (Upper Saddle River, NJ: Prentice Hall, 1999).

Gordon, Gil E. *Work Transformation: Planning and Implementing the New Workplace.* (New York: HNB Publishing, 1998).

Katzenbach, Jon. *Real Change Leaders: How You Can Create Growth and High Performance at Your Company.* (New York: Times Business, division of Random House Inc., 1995).

ENDNOTE

1. Adapted from Alexia Martin, "The Human Connection: A Strategy for Making Automation Work," *Administrative Management* (February 1982): 33–35.

Case Study   Tranforming to an E-culture at Nabisco Inc.

Nabisco Inc., an international manufacturer of biscuits, snacks, and other premium food products, with global revenues of $8.27 billion, consists of three major companies: Nabisco Biscuit Company, Nabisco Foods Company, and Nabisco International. More than 50,000 employees meet the needs and individual tastes of consumers in more than 85 countries. Every day over 256,000 cookies per minute exit ovens as long as football fields. Products range from cookies and crackers to candies and gum to pet snacks and mustard. With such a varied product range, you can imagine the challenges in managing the existing IT infrastructure, while also transforming to an organization-wide e-culture.

The consumer food industry is going through significant changes. Health-conscious consumers are asking for higher quality at a lower price. Moreover, the Internet is making it possible for companies to form new channels for brand promotion, consumer shopping, and supply-chain management. Nabisco needed synergy and seamless integration among people, processes, and technology to respond to these changes and transition the company to an e-culture.

Transitioning Nabisco's IT organization into a global strategic partner for its business units was critical to meeting its business objectives of improved resource utilization, global IT consistency, and revolutionizing the organization into an e-culture. To meet these business goals, Nabisco's IT team proposed a global desktop standard of Microsoft Office 2000 running on the Microsoft Windows 2000 Professional operating system. "The Rapid Economic Justification (REJ) analysis provided the financial information to identify where we could save IT costs and how we could improve end-user productivity," said Orest R. Fiume, Vice President of Enterprise Technology at Nabisco, Inc. "The projected payback period of between 6 months and 1 year—depending upon when we implement specific technologies—exceeded our expectations, and gave us the critical information necessary to develop an effective business case."

Currently, Nabisco has a single desktop environment in the United States and Canada, with multiple desktop configurations in its international business units. Nabisco must support its diverse multicultural environment, yet leverage the desktop standard already in place. Nabisco's goal was a single worldwide desktop that could support employees in their local environments from a global data center and centralized IT organization.

The REJ analysis revealed that Nabisco could achieve a 1.7 percent increase in productivity (see the following Figure) among its international users due to a single, familiar, and powerful Windows Multilingual User Interface (MUI), which enables seamless language transition and is automatically deployed whenever Office 2000 is deployed. "Once we achieve global desktop standardization, Nabisco's IT team will manage one operating system worldwide, support one version of Office worldwide, and develop global applications to a single desktop image," Fiume noted. "There are huge benefits in standardizing on a single technology throughout the organization. Windows 2000 is a continuation of our strategy for a worldwide standard. That allows us to roll out applications faster, minimize training, and increase productivity. All this can be accomplished

Results of Nabisco's Rapid Economic Analysis (REJ)

CRITICAL SUCCESS FACTOR	PROJECTED BENEFIT	BUSINESS ENABLER
Improve resource utilization	+2.5 percent	Flexible platform
Global IT consistency	+1.7 percent	Global desktop standard
Transformation to e-culture	+1 percent	Collaboration and communications

with a single image and managed from a central location, resulting in tremendous savings of IT resources."

Doreen Wright, Chief Information Officer for Nabisco, said, "Narrowing the list of approved technologies by consolidating our business users on a single desktop image will enable us to attract, train, develop, and deploy our staff more effectively. This is the cornerstone for successful execution of IT programs, and by definition is mission critical for Nabisco."

"To be responsive in the Internet world, aligning business processes around Web technologies is not enough," said Wayne Shurts, Vice President of North American Order Management, Nabisco Biscuits Company. "We need to become as fast as an e-company where we think and act like a dot-com. We need a robust Web-enabled business desktop."

Nabisco wanted to use Internet technology to transition from push-style supply chain to pull-based supply chain. Rick Blasgen, VP of the supply chain in Nabisco's Sales and Integrated Logistics Company, said, "We have made great progress in the elimination of redundant data entry and multiple phone calls to confirm data integrity in most of our systems, however, we still need to improve our data reliability processes and increase information accessibility."

Nabisco also needed a more effective way of dealing with business acquisitions. "It is very critical that we create synergy, consolidation, and complete product introduction quickly and effectively to realize the potential benefits from acquisitions. Our geographically distributed and multidepartmental teams need to be highly productive," says Blasgen. A Web-enabled desktop productivity infrastructure can help Nabisco reduce the time and effort required for in-store brand promotion, reuse current best practices, and improve quality and timeliness of information flow during acquisitions.

The REJ analysis identified the following potential benefits enabled by Windows 2000 Professional and Office 2000 to Nabisco's emerging e-culture:

- Conservatively increase end-user productivity by 1 percent.

- Enable users to publish directly to the corporate intranet thereby minimizing the need for additional Webmasters.

- Provide the capability to perform instantaneous publishing and sharing of documents and data.

As part of the e-culture initiative, Nabisco wanted the workforce to be able to work anywhere, anytime, have time-sensitive information when they need it, and have flexibility when accessing the corporate network remotely. With laptops running Windows 2000, Nabisco will be able to improve the performance of applications used by a field organization that is currently "disconnected." The REJ analysis estimates that the combination of Windows 2000 Professional and Office 2000 can enable the sales and marketing organization to gain an additional one percent in productivity worldwide.

- Office 2000 provides native companion HTML file formats, Web publishing, in-line document discussions and collaboration, integrated NetMeeting® conferencing software, and similar file formats to Office 97 for Excel 2000, Word 2000, and PowerPoint 2000.

- Windows 2000 Professional offers offline file capabilities as well as integrated Web technologies, such as Extended Markup Language (XML), Personal Web Server, Windows Media™ player, advanced content indexing, and searching capabilities.

Nabisco is looking to drive the e-culture transformation to every employee. Dan Garlewicz, Senior Manager at Nabisco, noted, "The Windows 2000 desktop productivity platform allows us to develop and publish information on the company Intranet and the Internet in an easy and standardized way, thereby enabling a timely and consistent flow of information throughout the company. This has the potential to impact the bottom line by increased global sales."

Improved Resource Utilization

Nabisco needed an efficient, reliable desktop infrastructure that enabled real-time information and supported worldwide collaboration. Improving asset utilization involved directing user experience and IT functionality into areas where users spend the most time, such as the following:

- Reducing nonproductive time through increased availability and reliability of the desktop infrastructure (i.e., less downtime).

- Improving knowledge access and information sharing.

- Improving organizational productivity and decision making through real-time collaboration and real-time scheduling.

New features in Windows 2000 Professional reduce downtime, provide faster startup and shutdown, and improve performance and power management over Nabisco's current Windows NT® Workstation operating system environment. Microsoft Office 2000 provides customizable help, self-repairing applications, and install-on-demand features, all of which contribute to decreased user downtime, thereby enabling increased productivity.

"I am sure we are not alone in thinking that implementing the Active Directory™ service, IntelliMirror™ management technologies, and Group Policy using Windows 2000 server will improve IT efficiency and business productivity. It is fantastic that Windows 2000 Professional and Office 2000 can also enable a significant improvement in our effectiveness as individuals and as an organization," says Rich Burton, REJ project manager at Nabisco.

Single Platform for Streamlined Application Development

Nabisco recognized that a uniform platform for global application development could have a huge impact on business performance and use of IT resources. Robust custom business applications could provide cost savings as well as increased sales.

"We support a large number of applications that support our business processes and business units," said Bob Shannon, Manager, Client Technologies. "We spend a substantial amount of time installing and testing applications every time we deploy an application. Windows 2000 can reduce development and support requirements because we can use out-of-the-box functionality rather than writing these services ourselves."

The platform offers the scalable, secure Web services that Nabisco was looking for. Built-in development technologies, such as Extensible Markup Language (XML), COM+, component isolation, Windows Installer technology, and Windows Scripting Host (WSH) can improve the development processes and reliability.

Rich George, Manager of Application Development at Nabisco, said, "We would like to develop technologies to mine financial, frequent-shopper, sales, and marketing data, and apply tools to provide our business units with the latitude to retrieve meaningful information. The integrated data analysis in Microsoft Excel 2000, including OLAP (online analytical processing), and the ability to

reuse Office components on the Web and the desktop, can help us reduce time currently used for development, testing, and deployment."

The REJ analysis identified the following benefits for Nabisco application developers:

- Significantly improve overall development efficiency due to simplified and common application development platform.

- Eliminate up to 50 percent of integration testing that is currently necessary to ensure that applications can coexist.

- Complete selected reporting and data analysis projects as much as 30 percent sooner by leveraging development features in Office 2000 rather than creating them using other development tools.

- Reduce effort required for software deployment and hardware configuration by up to 25 percent.

Nabisco Plans Enterprise-wide Rollout of Microsoft Desktop Productivity Infrastructure

The REJ analysis identified the specific financial and business value available to Nabisco in utilizing Microsoft Windows 2000 Professional and Office 2000 to meet its business needs as it transforms to an e-culture-based organization.

Wright noted, "In an environment where cost management is critical, every drop of efficiency has impact. Establishing a global desktop standard is helping us increase IT efficiency and end-user effectiveness. The REJ study has demonstrated several areas of opportunity for improving business processes and user productivity. The combination of Windows 2000 Professional and Office 2000 has the potential to eliminate one hour per employee of non-productive time, resulting in a company-wide productivity improvement of 1 percent. The REJ study provided us with a framework to model the business value of IT decisions."

Since Nabisco is a global organization, global desktop consistency, IT asset consolidation, and ubiquitous communications are important aspects to help Nabisco further expand market share in international markets.

For more information via the World Wide Web, go to:
http://www.microsoft.com/windows2000/
http://www.microsoft.com/office/enterprise/
http://www.microsoft.com/technet/default.asp
http://www.nabisco.com/
http://www.gigaweb.com/
Source: Microsoft Corporation, accessed 10/29/00 at
www.microsoft.com/office, evaluation/studies.htm.

CASE STUDY QUESTIONS

1. What important people, technology, process, and organizational issues must Nabisco address in transforming to an e-culture?

2. How is adopting a global desktop standard helping Nabisco achieve its goal of transforming to an e-culture?

3. What are some of the major challenges Nabisco faces in successfully implementing the desired global desktop platform?

Appendix 1

EUIS-Related Organizations

American Management Association (AMA), 1601 Broadway, New York, NY 10019. *www.amanet.org.*

American National Standards Institute (ANSI), 11 West 42nd Street, New York, NY 10036. *www.ansi.org.*

American Productivity and Quality Center (APQC), 123 North Post Oak Lane, 3rd Floor, Houston, TX 77024. *www.apqc.org.*

American Society for Training and Development (ASTD), 1640 King Street, Box 1443, Alexandria, VA 22313. *www.astd.org.*

Association for Business Communication (ABC), English Building, 608 South Wright Street, University of Illinois, Urbana, IL 61801. *www.cohums.ohio-state.edu/english/organizations/abc.*

Association for Computing Machinery (ACM), 1515 Broadway, 17th Floor, New York, NY 10036. Special Interest Groups: Groupware (SIGGROUP); Computer Graphics and Interactive Techniques (SIGGRAPH); Computer-Human Interface (SIGCHI); Computers and Society (SIGCAS). *www.acm.org.*

Association for Educational Communications and Technology (AECT), 1800 N. Stonelake Dr., Suite 2, Bloomington, IN 47404. *www.acct.org.*

Association for Information and Image Management (AIIM), 1100 Wayne Avenue, Suite 1100, Silver Spring, MD 20910. *www.aiim.org.*

Association for Information Systems, P.O. Box 2712, Atlanta, GA 30301. *www.aisnet.org.*

Association for Women in Computing, 41 Sutter Street, Suite 1006, San Francisco, CA 94104. *www.awc-hq.org.*

Association of Information Technology Professionals (AITP), 315 South Northwest Highway, Suite 200, Park Ridge, IL 60068. *www.aitp.org.* (formerly DPMA).

Association of Records Managers and Administrators (ARMA), 4200 Somerset Drive, Suite 215, Prairie Village, KS 66208. *www.arma.org.*

Business Technology Association (BTA), 12411 Wornall Road, Kansas City, MO 64145. *www.bta.org.*

Canadian Information Processing Society (CIPS), 1 Yonge Street, Suite 2401, Toronto, ON M5V 1L5 Canada. *www.cips.ca.*

Computer Measurement Group, 414 Plaza Drive, Suite 209, Westmont, IL 60559. *www.cmg.org.*

Decision Sciences Institute (DSI), J. Mack Robinson College of Business, Georgia State University, Atlanta, GA 30303. *www.dsi.gsu.edu.*

Human Factors and Ergonomics Society, P.O. Box 1369, Santa Monica, CA 90406. *www.hfes.org.*

Information Resources Management Association, 1331 East Chocolate Avenue, Hershey, PA 17033. *www.hbg.psu.edu/faculty/m1k/irma.html.*

Information Technologies Industry Council (ITIC), 1250 Eye Street NW, Suite 300, Washington, DC 20005. *www.itic.org.*

Institute for Certification of Computer Professionals (ICCP), 2200 East Devon Avenue, Suite 247, Des Plaines, IL 60018. *www.iccp.org.*

International Federation for Information Processing (IFIP), IFIP Secretariat, Hofstrasse 3, A-2361, Laxenburg, Austria. *www.ifip.or.at.*

International Information Management Association, P.O. Box 648, Middletown, PA 17057, (717) 652–7794. *www.iima.org.*

International Society for Technology in Education (ISTE), 1787 Agate St., Eugene, OR 97403. *www.iste.org.*

Life Office Management Association (LOMA), 2300 Windy Ridge Parkway, Suite 600, Atlanta, GA 30339. *www.loma.org.*

Organizational Systems Research Association (OSRA), Morehead State University, UPO 2478 Department of Information Systems, Morehead, KY 40351–1689. *www.osra.org.*

Society for Information Management (SIM), 401 N. Michigan Ave., Chicago, IL 60611. *www.simnet.org.*

Appendix 2

EUIS-Related Publications

Andrew Seybold's Outlook, Andrew Seybold's Outlook Inc., P.O. Box 2460, Boulder Creek, CA 95006.

ARMA Records Management Quarterly, 4200 Somerset Drive, Suite 215, Prairie Village, KS 66208. *www.arma.org.*

Behavior and Information Technology. www.taylorandfrancis.com/JNLS/bit.htm.

Beyond Computing, IBM Magazines, 590 Madison Avenue, 8th Floor, New York, NY 10022. *www.beyondcomputing-mag.com.*

Business Week, McGraw-Hill, Inc., McGraw-Hill Building, 1221 Avenue of the Americas, New York, NY 10020. *www.businessweek.com.*

BYTE, BYTE Subscriptions, P.O. Box 590, Martinsville, NJ 08836. *www.byte.com.*

Communication Briefings, 1101 King Street, Suite 110, Alexandria, VA 22314. *www.briefings.com/cb.*

Communications of the ACM, ACM, 1515 Broadway, New York, NY, 17th Floor, 10036. *www.acm.org.*

Compute, P.O. Box 5406, Greensboro, NC 27403.

Computer4 Communication Decisions, Hayden Publishing Company, 10 Mulholland Drive, Hasbrouck Heights, NJ 07604.

Computer Industry Update, Industry-Market Reports, P.O. Box 681, Los Altos, CA 94023.

The Computer Instructor, 614 Santa Barbara Street, Santa Barbara, CA 93101.

Computer Telephony, P.O. Box 2049, Skokie, IL 60076. *www.computertelephony.com.*

Computers & Electronics, Ziff-Davis Publishing Company, One Park Avenue, New York, NY 10016.

Computing Newsletter, Center-for-Cybernetic Systems, P.O. Box 7345, Colorado Springs, CO 80933.

Datamation, McGraw-Hill Building, 1221 Avenue of the Americas, New York, NY 10020. *www.datamation. earthweb.com.*

Electronic Learning, Advanstar Communications, 201 Sandpointe Ave., Suite 600, Santa Ana, CA 92707.

e-Learning, 201 Sandpointe Ave., Suite 600, Santa Ana, CA 92707. *www.elearningmag.com.*

eWeek. www.zdnet.com/eweek.

The Industry Standard, P.O. Box 56527, Boulder, CO. *www.thestandard.com.*

Infoworld.com. www.infoworld.com.

Information Strategy: The Executive's Journal, Auerbach-Publications, 535 Fifth Avenue, Suite 806, New York, NY 10017.

Information Systems News, 333 East Shore Road, Manhasset, NY 11030.

Information Systems Research, The Institute for Operations Research and the Management Sciences, 901 Elkridge Landing Road, Suite 400, Linthicum, MD 21090.

Information Technology and People, MCB University Press Ltd., 60-62 Toller Lane, Bradford, W. Yorks, BD89BY, United Kingdom.

Information Technology, Learning, and Performance Journal, Organizational Systems Research Association, Morehead State University, 114 Combs Building, Morehead, KY 40351. *www.osra.org.*

Input, 1943 Landings Drive, Mountain View, CA 94043.

Inside Technology Training, Bill Communications Inc., 10 Presidents Landing, Medford, MA 02155. *www.ittrain.com.*

Interfaces, Institute for Operations Research & Management Sciences, 901 Elkridge Landing Road, Suite 400, Linthicum, MD 21090.

InternetWeek, 600 Community Drive, Manhasset, NY 11030. *www.internetwk.com.*

IT Focus, IEEE Service Dept., 445 Hoes Lane, Piscataway, NJ 08854–4150.

Journal of Business Communication, Association for Business Communication, Dept. of Speech, Baruch College, 17 Lexington Avenue, New York, NY 10010.

Journal of Education for Business, Heldref Publications, 1319 Eighteenth Street, NW, Washington, DC 20036. *www.heldref.org/html/jeb.html.*

Journal of Information & Image Management, Association for Information and Image Management, 1100 Wayne Avenue, Silver Springs, MD 20910. *www.aiim.org.*

Journal of Organizational Computing and Electronic Commerce, Lawrence Erlbaum Associates, Inc., 10 Industrial Avenue, Mahwah, NJ 07430.

Journal of Strategic Information Systems, Elsevier-Sciences, P.O. Box 211, Amsterdam, 1000 AE, Netherlands.

Management Technology, Institute of Management Sciences, P.O. Box 273, Pleasantville, NY 06850.

MIS Week, Fairchild Publications, P.O. Box 2036, Mahopac, NY 10541.

MIS Quarterly, Society for Information Management and Management Information Systems Research Center, 271 19th Avenue South, University of Minnesota, Minneapolis, MN 55455.

The Office, Office Publications, Inc., 1600 Summer Street, Stamford, CT 06905.

Office World News, Business Publications, 366 Ramtown Greenville Road, Howell, NJ 07731. *www.officeworldnews.com.*

PCWeek, Customer Service Dept., P.O. Box 10638, Riverton, NJ 08076.

PC World, PC World Communications, Inc., 501 Second Street, San Francisco, CA 94107. *wwwpcworld.com.*

Popular Computing, Audrey-Gruenberger, P.O. Box 272, Calabasas, CA 91302.

Publish, International Data Group, 501 Second Street, Suite 310, San Francisco, CA 94107.

T.H.E. Journal, The Journal L.L.C., 17501 17th Street, Suite 230, Tustin, CA 92780.

Telecommunications, Horizon House-Microwave, Inc., 610 Washington Street, Dedham, MA 02026. *www. telecomsmag.com.*

INDEX

Third wave managing/
	consulting, 400
3M, 47
Throughput, 466
Thurow, Lester, 44
Time, 343
Time logs, 499
Timeliness of information, 86
Tkach, Daniel, 164
To-do lists, 113–114
Toffler, Alvin, 8, 400
Toshiba, 444
Total life average method, 309
Tracking systems, 89
Traditional culture, 365
Trainers, 229–232
Training, 209
Training cycle, 209
Training end users, 207–209,
	536, 542
	evaluating training programs,
		232–234, 235–236
	needs, analyzing
		individual analysis, 211
		organizational analysis, 210
		task analysis, 210–211
		tools, 211–212
	successful programs, designing,
		212–213
		adult learning principles,
			214–216
		group learning and support
			strategies, 227–228
		individual learning and support
			strategies, 216–227
	successful programs, implement-
		ing, 228–232
Training needs assessment, 211
Training process, 233–234
**Transaction processing systems
	(TPS), 12**
Transformations, 438
Transparent interface, 324
Trialability, 434
Trist, Eric, 395–396
Trojan horses, 265–266
Tulgan, Bruce, 41–42
Turner, A. N., 394–395
**Two-factor theory of motiva-
	tion, 394**

U

Undesirable consequences, 431
Unfreezing, 369, 370

User addictive (seductive), 320
User-driven interface, 324
User friendly, 319
User groups, 228
User interface, 193–194, **320**
User interface design, 323–325
User interviews, 540
User population (innovators), char-
	acteristics of, 434–435
User understanding, improving,
	323–324
Utterback, James, 64–65

V

Value added, 302
Value-added resellers (VAR),
	268–269
Value-added techniques, 302
Variety, 345
Vendor as investigator, 490
Vendors, kinds of, 512
Vertically loading jobs, 410
Video, 127
Video-based training, 223–224
Videoconferencing, 180
Virtual communities, 60–61, 62
Virtual corporations, 60
Virtual Reality Modeling Language
	(VRML), 183–184
Virtual reality systems, 183
Virus, 265
	protecting against, 265–266
Vision, 389
Visual interface, 325
Visualization, 183–184
Voice mail systems, 116
Voice-recognition systems, 111
**Volume-purchasing agree-
	ments, 277**
Von Hippel, Eric, 64–65

W

Walkthrough, 390, **505**
**Web-based Training (WBT),
	221**–223
Web-enabled support, 246–248
Web publishing, 128–129
Web, seizing the, 65
Weber, Eric D., 62
Weisbord, Marvin, 400,
	470–471, 472
What if analysis, 90
Wireless communicators, 117

Wizards, 243
Work, EUIS impact on.
	See End-user information
		systems
Work analysis, 347
Work flow analysis, 414–415
Work group computing.
	See Group collaboration;
		Group technologies;
		Groupware
Work group support and business
	process, 21
Work groups, 386–387
	composition of, 413
Work groups without borders,
	53–54
Work Redesign, 408
Work redesign, opportunities for,
	413–416
Work sampling, 499
Work-time measurement, 541
Worker frustration, 404
Workflow analysis, 19
Workflow/process management sys-
	tems, 180
Workforce (people), 49
	diversity, 51
	flexible work hours, 53
	ownership and empowerment,
		51–52
	pay for performance, 52–53
	telecommuting, 53
	thinking work, shifting people
		into, 50–51
	work groups without borders,
		53–54
Working Knowledge, 46
*Working Knowledge: How Organiza-
	tions Manage What They
	Know*, 166
Workplace, changing, 41
	anytime, anyplace environ-
		ments, 42
	fast moving and flexible,
		45–46
	global digital economy (24/7),
		42, 44
	innovation, 47–48
	just-in-time, 46
	knowledge age learning organiza-
		tions, 48–49
	process oriented (versus func-
		tional), 47
	teamwork and collaboration,
		44–45